Encyclopedia of
Frontier
Literature

Encyclopedia of
Frontier
Literature

Mary Ellen Snodgrass

OXFORD
UNIVERSITY PRESS

OXFORD

UNIVERSITY PRESS

Oxford   New York
Athens Auckland Bangkok Bogotá Buenos Aires Calcutta
Cape Town Chennai Dar es Salaam Delhi Florence Hong Kong Istanbul
Karachi Kuala Lumpur Madrid Melbourne Mexico City Mumbai
Nairobi Paris São Paulo Singapore Taipei Tokyo Toronto Warsaw

and associated companies in
Berlin   Ibadan

Copyright © 1997 by Mary Ellen Snodgrass

First published in 1997 by ABC-CLIO, Inc.,
130 Cremona Drive, P.O. Box 1911, Santa Barbara, California 93116-1911

First issued as an Oxford University Press paperback, 1999

Published by Oxford University Press, Inc.,
198 Madison Avenue, New York, New York 10016

Library of Congress Cataloging-in-Publication Data
Snodgrass, Mary Ellen.
Encyclopedia of frontier literature / Mary Ellen Snodgrass.
p. cm.
Originally published: Santa Barbara, Calif. : ABC-CLIO, 1997.
Includes bibliographical references and index.
ISBN 0-19-513318-8 (pbk.)
1. American literature--Encyclopedias.   2. Frontier and pioneer
life in literature--Encyclopedias.   3. America--Literatures-
-Encyclopedias.   I. Title.
PS169.F7S65   1999
810.9'358--dc21   99-11766

1 3 5 7 9 10 8 6 4 2

Printed in the United States of America
on acid-free paper

For my father, Russell Robinson

I am here when the cities are gone.
I am here before the cities come.
I nourished the lonely men on horses.
I will keep the laughing men who ride iron.
I am dust of men.

    —Carl Sandburg
    from "Prairie" (*Cornhuskers*, 1918)

CONTENTS

PREFACE

The plan of the *Encyclopedia of Frontier Literature* is to present dominant themes, literary history, genres, writers, titles, and characters as a method of defining and exemplifying the vast trove of literature about the exploration and settlement of North America. For ease of use, I have put extensive textual commentary under author or style rather than title. Titles present a problem in the frontier canon. Overviews tend to refer to Teddy Roosevelt, Mary Hunter Austin, Laura Ingalls Wilder, Joaquin Miller, John Muir, or John James Audubon without naming individual works. In many critical works and frontier histories, commentary is so general that the authors fail to clarify which titles they have in mind. This lack of specificity is rampant in discussions of Louis L'Amour and Zane Grey, whom critics seem to think of as period legends without crediting individual works.

A second problem with titles from frontier literature is their length or highly forgettable wording, e.g., *Narrative of the Life of David Crockett of the State of Tennessee* by Davy Crockett and *Narrative of the Life of David Crockett of the State of Tennessee* by Thomas Chilton. Nonfiction titles, such as Annie Oakley's *The Story of My Life* and Samuel L. Metcalfe's *A Collection of Some of the Most Interesting Narratives of Indian Warfare in the West, Containing an Account of the Adventures of Daniel Boone, One of the First Settlers of Kentucky*, lack pizzazz. Translated titles are not always standardized, for example, Christopher Columbus's diaries and Richard Hakluyt's voyages. Some titles are like Francis Parkman's *The Oregon Trail*, which the publisher originally linked to the California gold rush. The title changed in the second printing and eventually shrank to its present length. In some cases—*Annie Get Your Gun, Pocahontas*, and "Rip Van Winkle"—there are several versions going by the same name.

In general, analysts treat frontier literature as a literary type rather than a canon of individual works. One of the weaknesses of criticism in this genre is the broad generalization: women's journals of the westward movement, captivity literature, or cowboy novels. Historians tend to refer to popular titles informally, as with Pat Garrett's *Life Story of Billy the Kid* or *The Authentic Life Story of Billy, the Kid*, by Pat F. Garrett. Other works get a general reference, notably, Nat Love's autobiography, Geronimo's autobiography, Black Hawk's autobiography, Belle Starr's biography, or Wesley Hardin's autobiography. The titles that stand free and clear are the obvious literary milestones: the works of Conrad Richter, Robert Service, Bret Harte, Mari Sandoz, Willa Cather, James Fenimore Cooper, Edna Ferber, O. E. Rölvaag, Johan Bojer, Jack Schaefer, and Mark Twain. It is beneficial to the reader and researcher that the best-known works—*Shane, The Ox-Bow Incident, The Virginian, Riders of the Purple Sage, The Sea of Grass, The Underdogs, Black Elk Speaks, When the Legends Die, Cimarron*—are too familiar to confuse with anything else.

In this work, entries appear alphabetically and provide pronunciations of difficult terms, textual commentary, historical background, literary analysis, and generous citations. Significant to the canon of frontier literature are extensive biographies of important contributors:

- Walter van Tilburg Clark's interest in vigilantism, as displayed in *The Ox-Bow Incident*.

- Johan Bojer's visit to America to study Norwegian-Americans, whom he depicts in *The Emigrants*

- Rudolfo Anaya's tribute to the *llanero* and the *curandera* in *Bless Me, Ultima*

- Marjorie Kinnan Rawlings's dramatization of regional themes, dialect, and lifestyle in *The Yearling*

- Charles Portis's re-creation of frontier justice on the border of Indian Territory in *True Grit*

Beneath each entry are cross-references, primary sources, and a bibliography offering additional commentary, for example, articles on the recurrent theme of Mormonism, on-line sources describing such historic figures as Davy Crockett and Annie Oakley, audiovisual materials such as Jean Shepherd reading the poetry of Robert Service and videos of Ken Burns's *The West*, and sources of frontier memoirs, songs, and outdoor drama.

As an adjunct to reading, lesson planning, research, or self-directed study of frontier themes or of individual genres, titles, and authors, this volume appends self-explanatory study aids:

- a chronology of focal works from frontier literature dating from 1532 to the present

- a list of major works from the frontier canon

- a list of authors of major works

- a chronology of cinema versions of major titles from the frontier canon, for example, the 1936 and 1992 versions of James Fenimore Cooper's *Last of the Mohicans*

- a listing of primary sources either in single issue or compendia, some of which feature maps, charts, and noteworthy drawings by Frederic Remington, John James Audubon, and George Catlin

- a bibliography of overviews, collections, compendia, commentary, and pivotal reference works, particularly Howard R. Lamar's *The Reader's Encyclopedia of the American West*, Kent Ladd Steckmesser's *The Western Hero in History and Legend*, and Carl Waldman's *Who Was Who in Native American History*

- a comprehensive index of genres, titles, authors, events, characters, themes, native tribes, and settings, e.g., myth, "Stickeen," Conrad Richter, Sun Dance, Wyatt Earp, genocide, Oto, and Sutter's Mill

Contrasting studies of major periods in the settlement of the West turn up surprisingly diverse depictions of familiar events, insights into literary careers, and an impetus to cross-cultural readings, as with George Armstrong Custer's *My Life on the Plains*, Thomas Berger's *Little Big Man*, Charles Windolph's *I Fought with Custer*, Elizabeth Custer's *Boots and Saddles*, Gen. Oliver Otis Howard's *Famous Indian Chiefs I Have Known*, Louis L'Amour's *Education of a Wandering Man*, and Mari Sandoz's *Battle of the Little Bighorn*. A casual perusal of the *Encyclopedia of Frontier Literature* offers the researcher, reader, writer, and teacher a compelling reason to sample several points of view and to contemplate the romance that still clings to the Old West.

ACKNOWLEDGMENTS

Charles Albi
Executive Director
Colorado Railroad Museum
Golden, Colorado

Gary Carey
writer and editor
Lincoln, Nebraska

Mike Coffey
Reference Librarian
Catawba County Library
Newton, North Carolina

Wayne Daniel
Reference Librarian
El Paso Public Library
El Paso, Texas

Avis Gachet
Wonderland Books
Granite Falls, North Carolina

Sallie M. Greenwood
Greenwood Research
Boulder, Colorado

Bruce Hanson
Southwest Collection
Denver Public Library
Denver, Colorado

Frances Hilton
Chapter One Books
Hickory, North Carolina

Jeanne Wakatsuki Houston
James Houston
writers
San Jose, California

Laura Kelleher
Reference Librarian
Elbert Ivey Memorial Library
Hickory, North Carolina

Burl McCuisten
Reference Librarian
Lenoir-Rhyne College
Hickory, North Carolina

Paul Nelson
Jackson Clinton Library
UNC Greensboro, North Carolina

Norwegian-American Historical
Association
St. Olaf College
Northfield, Minnesota

Dr. Lotsee Patterson
Oklahoma University
Norman, Oklahoma

ACKNOWLEDGMENTS

Reference Department
California State Library
Sacramento, California

Reference Library
Oregon Historical Society
Portland, Oregon

Lynne Bolick Reid
Catawba County Library
Newton, North Carolina

Wanda Rozzelle
Catawba County Library
Newton, North Carolina

Cindy Sears
Elbert Ivey Library
Hickory, North Carolina

Ed Volz, Editor
American Reference Books Annual
Englewood, Colorado

Jeanne Wells
rare book researcher
Powell's Books
Portland, Oregon

Special thanks to my secretary, Andrea Pittman, who makes A's in her ninth-grade classes while typing bibliographies, pulling reference books and files, replying to correspondence, restoring order, and bringing a spot of sunshine to the office each week.

INTRODUCTION

For four centuries following Europe's discovery of the New World, the frontier enlarged the world picture, offering intriguing possibilities, from homesteading in the Dakotas, fighting with the Buffalo Soldiers, and panning for gold in California to sailing to the Sandwich Islands. Many adventurers who broached the eastern shores of North America came in hope of a new start, a utopian dream of a more open and tolerant society than the homelands they left behind. Others journeyed west out of greed or ambition or the desire to aggrandize themselves by subduing native peoples and stealing their lands. Some pioneers brought a vital religious faith and literacy to educate preliterate Indian tribes and prepare them to read the Bible or the Book of Mormon. A composite of individual motives—curiosity, personal freedom, scientific advancement, conservation, escape—spools out like trails scored on the virgin land.

The creative response that grew out of myriad immigrations reflects the newcomers' experiences:

- Christopher Columbus's diary recounts the peculiarities of the Taino who welcomed him to the Caribbean.

- Willa Cather's *O Pioneers!* and *My Ántonia* convey the social interaction of neighbors newly arrived to the Midwest from numerous backgrounds, religions, lifestyles, and languages.

- Francis Parkman's chronicle *The Oregon Trail* pictures wagon trains filled with hearty travelers journeying to the Pacific Northwest.

- Mary Hunter Austin's *Children Sing in the Far West* captures the lyric grace of the Southwest desert and its indigenous peoples.

- Andy Adams's *Log of a Cowboy* recounts the herder's day-to-day labor.

- Mark Twain's *Roughing It* relates the hard, unpromising career of the prospector.

- Theodora Kroeber's *Ishi, Last of His Tribe* and *Ishi in Two Worlds* honor the adaptive skills of a Yahi survivor.

- Rosemary Benét and Stephen Vincent Benét's *Book of Americans* typifies in verse noted pioneer personalities.

- Grey Owl's *Men of the Last Frontier* and *Pilgrims of the Wild* warn that the scenic beauties of the Canadian wild lie at the mercy of developers.

This brief litany is a mere glance at the fertile imaginations of explorers, pioneers, hunters, settlers, mountaineers, miners, ranchers, farmers, herders, law officers, outlaws, teachers, writers, reporters, singers, and storytellers. A cornucopia of their literary output overflows with the rhythms and textures of frontier life:

- Joseph Glover Baldwin's humorous dialect commentary on the California gold rush

- Laura Esquivel's amorous recipes and family intrigues dating to the era of Pancho Villa

- Charles Eastman's childhood reminiscences of a traditional Sioux upbringing

- Black Elk's mystic out-of-body experiences that bring him oneness with the Great Spirit

- Sophie Trupin's reflections on growing up Jewish in the West

- Thomas Farnham's detailed journal of his transcontinental move to the Oregon Territory

- Isabella Bird's memorable adventures in the Rocky Mountains

- Zane Grey's spirited western romances, especially his masterpiece, *Riders of the Purple Sage*

The originality of classic frontier works stands out from the typical cowboy-and-Indian fare: the plains songbooks of John and Alan Lomax, ethnology in Dorothy Marie Johnson's short stories, Joseph Jefferson's autobiographical anecdotes of Western stage performances, Ruthanne Lum McCunn's biography of a Chinese woman enslaved in an Idaho mining camp, dogsledding adventures of Jack London, and the speeches of Dekanawidah and Satanta. Suited to the issues and impetus of the times, each contributes a strand to wilderness lore.

It is obvious from a cursory perusal that the frontier is too great a topic to fit on a single canvas. No outstanding moment or event explains why John Muir intoned prose hymns to the Sierra Nevadas, why Lauren Kessler lauded Asian-American entrepreneurs, or why Rebecca Burlend penned a warning to future homesteaders. The human drama that Merietta Wetherill observed among the Sioux in Chaco Canyon differs from the events that gnawed at Dee Brown's peace of mind or turned Carlos Fuentes to the romance of the Mexican Revolution. Eyewitness accounts by George Catlin, Mary Crow Dog, and Jack Reed bear little resemblance to fictional scenarios by Mariano Azuela, Hal Borland, and Jessamyn West. The giants of frontier literature—James Michener,

Mari Sandoz, Bret Harte, O. E. Rölvaag, Katherine Anne Porter, James Fenimore Cooper, Laura Ingalls Wilder, Henry Wadsworth Longfellow, Edna Ferber, Owen Wister, Jack Schaefer, Louis L'Amour, and Ambrose Bierce—belong on the same shelf with less familiar contributors—Paul Radin, Elinore Pruitt Stewart, Nat Love, Sarah Winnemucca, Cabeza de Vaca, Alida Young, and Richard Hakluyt.

Taken as a whole, frontier literature is as rich, varied, and satisfying as any branch of written and spoken art. Unique to the Western canon are several facets:

- a series of popular stage plays based on the lives of Pocahontas and Daniel Boone and on Washington Irving's fictional Rip Van Winkle

- a body of lore about and by the Mormons who followed Brigham Young to Utah and helped him build a religious stronghold in Salt Lake City

- oral autobiographies of Native Americans transcribed by white editors, including John G. Neihardt, Richard Erdoes, Joseph Epes Brown, Antoine LeClaire, S. M. Barrett, and Charles Brant

- outdoor dramas by Paul Green and Kermit Hunter, who initiated a national demand for historic spectacle, for instance, reenactments of the Lost Colony, Trail of Tears, lives of Daniel Boone and Sam Houston, and a staging of Harold Bell Wright's *The Shepherd of the Hills*

Of particular note is a wealth of reflection, description, and eyewitness accounts composed by ordinary people who wrote the minutiae of their lives in letters, journals, logbooks, reports, and diaries. It seems unlikely that Martha Ballard expected future generations to read her daily lists of home health care visits, herbal preparations, or midwifery or that wilderness correspondents sent letters from Fort Kearney for any but their families and friends to read. Chief Joseph would probably be amused and delighted that schoolchildren recite "I Will Fight No More Forever," and Fred Gipson might be surprised that feminists champion his young adult novel, *Old Yeller,* as a tribute to the pioneer housewife. In contrast, a long list of memoirists—James Sewid, Pat Garrett, Luther Standing Bear, O. M. Spencer, Susanna Moodie, Kit Carson, Sarah Royce, John Wesley Hardin, N. Scott Momaday, Jason Betzinez, William F. Cody, John James Audubon, Geronimo, Lula Parker Betenson, Thomas Harriot, Mary Canaga Rowland, Davy Crockett, Black Hawk, James Cook, Tom Horn, George Bird Grinnell, and Oliver Otis Howard—correctly anticipated that readers would be interested in their writings, which enliven the nonfiction branch of frontier lore.

Overall, frontier literature attains a valuable position in world literature for its depiction of the Zeitgeist—the spirit of the times that produced the American Fur Company, Pony Express, Homestead Act, Transcontinental Railroad, Santa Fe and Bozeman Trails, Fetterman Massacre, Texas Rangers, Pinkerton agents, Mormon handcarters, and Yukon mushers. Whether a part of a novel by Sylvia Lopez-Medina, Conrad Richter, Thomas Berger, Janice

Holt Giles, or Scott O'Dell; a segment of the verse of Adam Kidd or Joaquin Miller; a short story by Caroline Gordon or O. Henry; or a play by Hilda Mary Hooke or Dorothy and Herbert Fields, Western lore retains its appeal for the immediacy of its themes and the nostalgia of its vivid history. The perceptions of Larry McMurtry's *Lonesome Dove* and Michael Blake's *Dances with Wolves* continue the frontier tradition into the late twentieth century and beyond. As technology pushes the imagination toward a complex landscape in the stars, readers still return to the Old West to savor an earthly time of possibilities.

Encyclopedia of
Frontier
Literature

AFRICAN AMERICANS ON THE FRONTIER

The historical tendency of white Americans to ignore or discount the contributions of blacks, Indians, Asians, and Hispanics to the settlement of the West has obscured the role of African Americans on the frontier. One example of disdainful, patronizing treatment of blacks in the West occurred in the beginning of the twentieth century, when artist Frederic Remington was initiating a career in short fiction by publishing vignettes and tales of his adventures in the West in *Harper's Monthly* and *Cosmopolitan*. At his death in 1909 at the age of 48, he left a wealth of stories, which were collected in 1960 in *Frederic Remington's Own West*. Integral to these sketches and writings of the Southwest and Northern Plains are the standard motifs of law and order, whites against Indians, and the intriguing customs of natives, cavalrymen, and rodeo riders. An anomaly that captured his interest was a garrison of Buffalo Soldiers, the first all-black troop in Indian territory. While accompanying a detail on some hard riding on the plains, Remington discovers that black soldiers remain amused and uplifted on lengthy jaunts over dismal terrain while white riders become taciturn or too weary to talk. At an evening bivouac, Remington reconstructs black southern dialect in lines such as "Now I'se agoin' to scare de life outen you when I show down dis hand." (Remington 1994, 72) Remington's flaccid sketches allow drama to wind down without drawing any comparatives between the Buffalo Soldiers and either white officers or Pima visitors to the fort. Overall, his inclusion of black characters and idiosyncratic elements of their speech derives primarily from his interest in a freak scenario rather than an intention to preserve a segment of Western history.

Nonetheless, notable authors have preserved the contributions of three black frontiersmen—mountain man Jim Beckwourth, cowboy Bill Pickett, and homesteader Oscar Micheaux—all of whom thrived on the demands of the frontier. A detailed journal, *The Life of James Pierson Beckwourth, Mountaineer, Scout, Pioneer and Chief of the Crow Nation*, a hefty first-person narrative published by Thomas D. Bonner in 1856, recounts a protracted life story. The text was at first listed among the West's more colorful tall tales before corroboration proved the authenticity of the events. The son of Virginian Sir Jennings Beckwith and his mulatto slave, Beckwourth (who changed the spelling of his father's surname in adulthood to conform to the common pronunciation) gained his freedom around 1820, migrated down the Mississippi, and worked the levees of New Orleans. In 1824, he made his initial expedition into the Rocky Mountains with Colonel William H. Ashley, encountered trapper and explorer Jedediah Smith, and survived a first taste of the Indian wars. By fooling a Crow Chief into accepting him as a returned captive, Beckwourth lived as a tribe member until his mid-thirties, dressed in buckskin and moccasins, married a series of native wives, and was elected chief.

Overall, Beckwourth managed to be on the scene of some of the most historic moments of America's coming-of-age and has been charged with self-aggrandizement by notable experts, including historians Francis Parkman and Hiram Crittenden. Beckwourth associated with Jim Bridger and Kit Carson, fought in the Seminole Wars, and resettled in northern California during the gold rush of 1849, all the time earning a modest living as a trapper, muleteer, trader, guide, courier, prospector, rancher, innkeeper, interpreter, wagon master, and bartender. His eye for detail produced compelling accounts of scenes. Of Pawnee hunting methods along the Platte River, he describes the formation of a circular "buffalo surround" preparatory to slaughter:

> The chief then gives the order to charge, which is communicated along the ring with the speed of lightning; every man then rushes to the centre, and the work of destruction is begun. The unhappy victims, finding themselves hemmed in on every side, run this way and that in their mad efforts to escape. Finding all chance of escape impossible, and seeing their slaughtered fellows drop dead at their feet, they bellow with affright, and in the confusion that whelms them, lose all power of resistance. (Bonner 1972, 44)

After two or three hours, the surround concludes with praise from Pawnee women for a bountiful hunt and jeers for those tribesmen returning empty-handed. Beckwourth follows with details of flaying, dressing, and preserving meat, a job requiring several weeks' work to assure food for the winter.

Like Beckwourth's action-packed autobiography, the life story of cowboy Bill Pickett received only cursory attention until the publication of Colonel Bailey C. Hanes's biography, *Bill Pickett, Bulldogger* (1977). A protégé of Gordon W. "Pawnee Bill" Lillie, who ran the 101 Ranch Wild West Show in Ponca City, Oklahoma, Bill Pickett earned fame in the 1930s for introducing bulldogging, a rodeo slang term for longhorn wrestling. The height of his feat was the perfection of a nose-to-nose method of overpowering the animal: he leaped from his cow pony, grasped the steer by the horns or around the neck, then clamped his teeth on its upper lip. His longest recorded stint of bulldogging occurred in Mexico City when he maintained his bite for six minutes. The method had its practical application, but gained fame primarily as a bit of exotica to spice up rodeos, in which Pickett performed across the United States and in Europe, including before King George V and Queen Mary.

Hanes immortalizes Pickett with a flashback to an emigrant party from South Carolina who carried the cowboy's slave ancestors to Texas in 1854. The product of white, black, and Cherokee ancestry, Pickett, sometimes known as

A Tenth Cavalry trooper stationed in Arizona rides down a steep embankment in a drawing by Frederic Remington. Indians called such African Americans who served in the West "Buffalo Soldiers." The experiences of these soldiers as well as those of writers, such as mountainman Jim Beckwourth, South Dakota homesteader Oscar Micheaux, and cowboy Nat Love, enriched the Western literary tradition.

Will, worked in the Austin area as a ranch hand. According to a news clipping from a 1904 edition of the *Wyoming Tribune*, people thrill at seeing the cowboy

> attack a fiery, wild-eyed and powerful steer, dash under the broad breast of the great brute, turn and sink his strong ivory teeth into the upper lip of the animal and, throwing his shoulder against the neck of the steer, strain and twist until the animal, with its head drawn one way under the controlling influence of those merciless teeth and its body forced another, until the brute, under the strain of slowly bending neck, quivered, trembled and then sank to the ground, conquered by a trick. (Hanes 1989, 40–41)

The biography features additional citations from the press, photos, handbills, and memorabilia attesting to the star billing of Pickett, nicknamed the "Dusky Demon." After describing his fatal fall and the lethal kick of a gelding in 1932, Hanes concludes with a typical cowboy era verse eulogy, "Old Bill Is Dead."

More realistic in its view of ordinary settlers is the writing of Oscar Micheaux, novelist and pioneer black filmmaker. In his memoir, *The Conquest: The Story of a Negro Pioneer* (1913), he recounts his birth on a Cairo, Illinois, farm; working as a Pullman porter and stockyard laborer; saving $2,500 to buy land; and homesteading in Calais, South Dakota. Outside the influence of the Harlem Renaissance, he lived a different kind of achievement, wrought less through art than from self-determination, frugality, and labor. He downplays his position as the only black settler in town, but recalls that he received mail addressed, "Colored Man, Calais."

In a central chapter entitled "Where the Negro Fails," Micheaux declares that there are two types of blacks: pragmatic conservatives and "those who are narrow in their sympathies and short-sighted in their views." (Micheaux 1994, 142) To account for his self-actualization and wealth, he notes that "on the entire Little Crow reservation, less than eight hundred miles from Chicago, I was the only colored man engaged in agriculture, and moreover, from Megory to Omaha, a distance of three hundred miles." (ibid., 145) Micheaux studies the trainloads of emigrants from the Old Country and finds few blacks. He deduces that blacks lack the initiative to homestead. Newly introduced to luxuries, former slaves and children of slaves prefer the contentment of metropolitan areas to the labor-intensive life of a Dakota settler. (Bonner 1972; Hanes 1989; Lamar 1977; Low and Clift 1981; Micheaux 1994; Ploski and Williams 1989; Remington 1994)

See also Love, Nat.

ALASKA AND THE YUKON

A genuine North American frontier, Alaska and the Yukon are often excluded from histories of the westering era because they don't fit the paradigm of covered wagons, Indian wars, and the Transcontinental Railroad. The area was settled by Asians who crossed over the Bering Strait land bridge. The first Eu-

ropeans to visit were Danish and Russian fur traders, who explored the islands, interacted with the Aleut and Athapascan, and searched out new sources
of sea otters and fur seals. Visited by Spanish and French adventurers and the
British explorer Captain James Cook in the eighteenth century, Alaska did not
become an American passion until the nineteenth century, when it first sparked
entrepreneurial and literary interests. Subsequent bursts of immigrant enthusiasm have followed discoveries of gold and oil and the burgeoning fishing
and lumbering industries, both of which have provided writers with enticing
grist for stories, verse, novels, histories, biographies, and essays.

An early explorer, Jasper N. "Jap" Wyman, wrote of the exotic Alaskan
landscape near the end of the 1800s. In April 1898, he formed a fact-finding
expedition traveling from Illinois to Alaska for the Galesburg-Alaska Mining
and Developing Company. The resulting journal and 400-picture history of the
journey, edited by Aurlette Ingman under the title *Gold Dust*, remained unpublished until 1988. Retitled *Journey to the Koyukuk*, Wyman's reflections on Alaska
cover the entire Pacific leg of the journey: sailing from Seattle harbor and navi-
gating, dredging, and prospecting on the Yukon River. His gallery of photos
illustrates the all-male atmosphere and the purposeful attitude of expeditioners,
who intended to turn a profit on their investment.

It is not surprising that, in so difficult a voyage to a barren and undevel-
oped land, Wyman's daily entries tell of seasickness, rigorous labor, and hardship. The group's relaxations are simple and homegrown: the group clown, Eli
Juda, entertains with accordion renditions of "Yankee Doodle"; when winter
sets in, the men play checkers and cards. Encounters with the local Inuit and
tenting on the tundra precede arduous reconnoitering up the Koyukuk River,
which they begin on August 8. As a side note, Wyman narrates a half-hearted
one-man bear hunt. Heavily armed, he explores iron-hard trails for 15 miles
from camp and hides in a blind, but spots no animals. He admits, "I was like
the man hunting work and didn't want to find it. I was hunting bear, but in this
horrible dense place I didn't want to find them, for I was a little choicy about
where I wanted to meet them." (Wyman 1988, 41)

According to Wyman's conclusions, after 13 months of ice storms, caribou
meat, gastric illness, and loneliness, the 25 expeditioners leave Arctic City in
mid-May, when another wave of prospectors are idealistically pouring into the
country and pushing upland to the goldfields. The return trip takes the party
from St. Michael in the Brooks Range southwest to the Aleutian Islands and
east to Seattle. Letters that precede his return home comment on accidents,
drownings, and suicide and state his opinion of the Alaskan adventure: "I am
not afraid, but it is not pleasant, see?" (ibid., 124) The concise, detailed text
tells of disillusion and disappointment as other miners fail and a lucky few
strike it rich.

At the beginning of the twentieth century, Alaska found a literary champion in Californian Jack London, who spent only one winter in the far north
but centered much of his successful writing career on Alaska and the Yukon. In
his second published work, *The Son of the Wolf: Tales of the Far North* (1900), he
states the Klondike credo in the opening lines of "In a Far Country":

> When a man journeys into a far country, he must be prepared to forget many of the things he has learned, and to acquire such customs as are inherent with existence in the new land; he must abandon the old ideals and the old gods, and often times he must reverse the very codes by which his conduct has hitherto been shaped. (London 1992, 9)

More in admiration than fear, London's Klondiker parts company with the stiflingly civilized urbanism that was overtaking the Pacific Coast to reconnect with the frontier mystique that once imbued the West. London's wilderness narratives introduce readers to new horizons through place names like Yeddo, Akatan, Dyea, Moosehide Mountain, Skagway, and Kootenay. He peoples his Alaskan fiction with white, Eskimo, Indian, and French-Canadian characters called Sitka Charley, Poportuk, Merritt Sloper, and the Skookum Bench King and with animals of the wild such as the ptarmigan, snowshoe rabbit, elk, wolverine, Lip-lip the pup, Kiche the she-wolf, and an unforgettable sled dog named Buck, hero of his masterwork, *The Call of the Wild* (1903). Prodigious swarms of mosquitoes, hard paddling upstream, balancing stacks of pelts and grub, harnessing a moiling pack of sled dogs, tugging on the gee pole, and counting out the spoonfuls of coffee and sugar to last until the spring thaw tinge London's descriptions with the primordial challenge of the "white blank spaces on the map." (Labor and Reesman 1994, 31)

Appropriately, one of Western literature's most prolific and popular writers turned to Alaska later in the twentieth century. Louis L'Amour set *Sitka* (1957), an adventure saga, against the backdrop of icy straits and the Russian capital of Sitka. Borrowing on the land-centered approach of Jack London, L'Amour writes about the lure of untamed wilderness on protagonist Jean LaBarge and on sailors, trappers, and buccaneers. He concludes: "They were all the same, these men who went to the north country, they claimed to hate it, but they went back." (L'Amour 1983, 43) Drawn more to nature than to furs or gold, his outbackmen romance the wild currents and piercing cold. He salts his heavily plotted action story with the history of "Seward's Folly" and "Seward's Icebox" and notes with accurate hindsight that "Many of the arguments offered against Alaska were the same as those offered against the Louisiana Purchase." (ibid., 221)

Like L'Amour, another master of historical fiction, James Michener, worked his way across other frontier settings before arriving at Alaska. In 1988, he paralleled his honor of Hawaii, the fiftieth state, with a saga about Alaska, the forty-ninth. Sticking to his trademark one-word titles, he begins *Alaska* in prehistory and carries the story forward to cover the highlights of Russian exploration, the gold rush of 1896, and the latter-day burgeoning of the Alcan Highway, salmon industry, construction, and oil fields. He recaps the unpromising beginning of the territory and the orators who derided the purchase of a worthless "icebox" deserving no serious attention. He reports that

> America refused to give Alaska any form of government. It refused even to give it a proper name: in 1867 it was called the Military District of Alaska; in 1868, the Department of Alaska; in 1877, the Customs district of Alaska; and in 1884, simply the District of Alaska. (Michener 1988, 306)

The irony builds on repeated insults and claims that the territory will never achieve statehood and, even more certainly, will prove worthless.

Velma Wallis, a Native American author from Fort Yukon, Alaska, takes a different approach from Michener's wide-screen historical novel of young nation builders by selecting native characters and focusing on elderly females, the least likely to thrive in an Arctic setting. Recasting an Athapascan legend, she studies the abandonment of two aged women on the upper Yukon River in *Two Old Women: An Alaska Legend of Betrayal, Courage and Survival* (1993), winner of the Western States Book Award. The core of the story is the survival of rejected women, whose sacrifice to the wild is meant to save their tribe from starvation by redirecting food toward younger, more productive people. The graphic picture of their betrayal forms within the framework of tribal culture:

> The two women had not eaten for some time because The People had tried to conserve what little food they had. Now they realized why precious food had not been given to them. Why waste food on two who were to die? (Wallis 1993, 21)

Once the women prove to themselves and the tribe that they will not give in and die for the sake of tradition, the rest adopt their can-do spirit and welcome the two women once more. (Labor and Reesman 1994; L'Amour 1983; London, Jack 1992; London, Joan 1990; Lundquist 1987; Moore 1996; Morey 1965; O'Connor 1964; Perry 1981; Sinclair 1983; Snodgrass 1991, 1995b; Stone 1978; Tavernier-Courbin 1994; Wallis 1993; Wyman 1988)

See also The Call of the Wild; explorers of the frontier; Ferber, Edna; London, Jack; Service, Robert.

ANAYA, RUDOLFO

A skilled Chicano storyteller and weaver of mystic lore and myth, Rudolfo Alfonso Anaya has established himself as an authority on Hispanic Americana. He is the author of *Bless Me, Ultima* (1972), a classic novel that advanced him to a prime position among Mexican-American artists. In September 1996, Anaya was selected to speak knowledgeably about Latino history on *The West*, a Public Broadcasting Service television documentary series produced by Ken Burns. A native of Pastura near Santa Rosa, New Mexico, Anaya, a former guidance counselor in Albuquerque's public schools, centered *Bless Me, Ultima*, the first of nine novels about Hispanic Americans, in the desert land east of Albuquerque. In the book, he navigates the terrain of childhood through the thoughts and intuitions of six-year-old Antonio "Tony" Márez, an introspective boy coming of age on the rim of the *llano* or prairie in Guadalupe, near Tucumcari, New Mexico.

Set in the pastoral Indian and Spanish settlements of the Southwest in the postfrontier era, *Bless Me, Ultima* draws on early history, including the expeditions of the *conquistadores* and the eventual settlement of the land by farmers and stockmen, from whom the people of Las Pasturas draw their traditions:

> Always the talk turned to life on the llano. The first pioneers there were sheep-herders. Then they imported herds of cattle from Mexico and became vaque-ros. They became horsemen, caballeros, men whose daily life was wrapped up in the ritual of horsemanship. They were the first cowboys in a wild and desolate land which they took from the Indians. (Anaya 1972, 119)

From oral stories, Tony finds his place in the history of the land, which changed with the building of the railroad and the stringing of barbed wire. His memories are colored by the sad *corridos*, ballads of the bloodshed that accompanied the upheaval that pitted his Hispanic forefathers against white Texans. The end of the era places whites over Chicanos, who move west and become migrants.

Still vulnerable in a world of clashing males, Tony depends upon the humanity of his mother, Maria. She protects him from Gabriel, his hard-drinking father, who is a malcontented highway construction laborer and former *vaquero*. She informs her son that she comes from the Puerto de Luna valley, where Billy the Kid was known as *el Bilito*, a friend of Chicanos. The boy experiences harsh and, at times, violent interactions during World War II, when his three older brothers serve in the military. Maria reminds Gabriel that the Lunas were the first Mexican settlers of the area.

Gnawing at the heart of Anaya's fictional *llaneros* lies their ambivalence toward Tony's grandmother, Ultima, also called "la Grande," who is a traditional *curandera* or folk healer, herbalist, and midwife, whom vigilantes accuse of being a *bruja* or witch. Their spite derives from a slavish adherence to Catholicism, which, perhaps out of jealousy or fear, tends to polarize their attitude toward the strong, confident female healer as either a folk saint or demon. Young Tony tries to accommodate superstition, folklore, and church orthodoxy and ponders a posse's summary execution of Lupito, a war-crazed shooter. She realizes the turbulence in her grandson's spirit and gives him protective herbs to wear in a pouch around his neck. For good or ill, he finds Ultima's owl watching over him.

While learning the Hispanic past of the plains and establishing his place on the *llano*, Tony helps Ultima dig healing roots and collect herbs. He observes her forming dolls of wax and clay and piercing them with pins; he assists her as she sweats a patient to rid him of the death spirit. In an epiphany, he realizes that the owl is an amalgam of Ultima's soul and the local native saint, the Virgin of Guadaloupe. In the summer of 1947 at his grandmother's deathbed, he finds her ready for a new incarnation in the next world.

To justify the boy's questions about occultism, Ultima explains that a wise old man gave her the owl to do good, not to thwart human destiny. She instructs Tony on stripping her room and burning her store of curatives after her death. After promising to bury the owl at a forked juniper tree, he begs a blessing. With her customary pagan benevolence, Ultima replies:

> I bless you in the name of all that is good and strong and beautiful, Antonio. Always have the strength to live. Love life, and if despair enters your heart,

> look for me in the evenings when the wind is gentle and the owls sing in the hills, I shall be with you. (ibid., 247)

Carefully, Tony leaves her corpse, buries the bird, and places a stone on it to protect it from predatory coyotes.

Critics have hailed Anaya's *Bless Me, Ultima* for its compassionate examination of conflicting cultural expectations, motivational tensions, controlling metaphors, and dream sequences. In one vision, Tony experiences the beginnings of his people's history:

> In my dream I flew over the rolling hills of the llano. My soul wandered over the dark plain until it came to a cluster of adobe huts. I recognized the village of Las Pasturas and my heart grew happy. One mud hut had a lighted window, and the vision of my dream swept me towards it to be witness at the birth of a baby. (ibid., 4)

With hope for the future, the family rubs earth from the valley on the infant's forehead and surrounds his bed with "the fruits of their harvest so the small room smelled of fresh green chile and corn, ripe apples and peaches, pumpkins and green beans." (ibid.) The significance of their rituals reflects the agrarian roots of Anaya's Hispanic-American *bildungsroman,* the first of a trilogy that includes *Heart of Aztlán* (1976) and *Tortuga* (1979), winner of the Premio Quinto Sol award. In 1996, he followed with *Rio Grande Fall,* a post-frontier mystery-suspense novel that reprises the motifs of the earthly leader warring against witches and of the beneficent *curandera,* whose eyes look past modern-day Albuquerque to both past and future. (Anaya 1972, 1996; Blair 1991; Bruce-Novoa 1980; Brunvand 1996; Burns and Ives 1996b; Cabeza de Baca 1989; Calderon 1986; Candelaria 1985; Chavez 1984; Gonzáles-Trujillo 1989; Heyne 1992; Jones 1990; Klein 1992; Larson 1979; Lattin 1986; Ramos 1996; Vasallo 1982; Wood 1973)

⚑ ASIAN AMERICANS ON THE FRONTIER ⚑

After the discovery of gold in California, a new immigrant population streamed onto the frontier from Asia. In cities, along the Sierras, and into the desert territory and the Pacific Northwest, Chinese newcomers made their own niche as laundry workers, longshoremen, seamstresses, cooks, house servants, call girls, field hands, and day laborers for railroads, mines, and construction. One of the most famous white frontiersmen to write about the precarious position of Asians in the West was Bret Harte, who collaborated with Mark Twain to produce *Ah Sin, the Heathen Chinee* (1876), an unsuccessful stage play. In 1870, Harte had toyed with the theme of anti-Asian prejudice in "The Heathen Chinee," also called "Plain Language from Truthful James," a narrative poem published in the *Overland Monthly.* Later issued in an illustrated monograph, the poem was twice set to music. Harte created the wily Chinese cardsharp during a period

Chinese emigrants arrived in large numbers beginning with the California gold rush in 1849 and in even greater numbers as workers for the Union Pacific, the western segment of the transcontinental railroad begun in 1869. Perceived as a threat to job security, whites attacked Chinese immigrants and destroyed their homes and businesses. Bret Harte and Mark Twain wrote about a cardsharp named Ah Sin; now Asian Americans are telling their own story.

of labor unrest when white workers feared competition from the high number of immigrant laborers who worked for minimal wages on railroad construction crews. Harte's sinister Ah Sin has his own say in "Ah Sin's Reply," which the poet published anonymously. In the humorous rebuttal, the Chinaman claims to have sound reason for having wax on his fingers, which he used to mark cards, and declares that some odd cards inadvertently worked their way up his sleeve from his pocket.

Harte's wit at the expense of maligned Asians belies a serious prejudice that jeopardized their work, freedom, and lives. In her prologue to the novel *Land of the Iron Dragon* (1978), Alida Young accounts for bigotry and hate crimes as a matter of job insecurity. Cries in the night of "The Chinese must go!" evoke a strength of character in immigrants who intend to remain only long enough to get a stake. Ignorant frontier myths of Americans who could strike Asian men dead with a glance compounded by Native American stories of giant serpents that swallow an entire human in one gulp are less cruel than accidents with black powder and nitroglycerin or the callousness of entrepreneurs toward the expendable "John Chinaman." To Young's character, Lim Yan-sung, the joy of waving a handmade dragon flag in celebration of the completed rail line dissolves into despair at the sight of thousands of unappreciative white observers at the newly opened Union Pacific Railroad. During the hoopla of the Golden Spike Ceremony on May 2, 1869, Lim ponders, "How is it possible to forget ten thousand of us?" (Young 1978, 207) According to Young, a century later, the hundred-year anniversary party made no effort to correct the slight to Asian Americans.

The Japanese, too, share the frontier dream of success. Lauren Kessler's *Stubborn Twig: Three Generations in the Life of a Japanese American Family* (1993) describes a similar boom-and-bust of illusions among the Yasui family. The buoyant enthusiasm of would-be settlers buds into an Eldoradan dream. The gullible read and swallow empty promises on brochures:

> America is a veritable human paradise, the number one mine in the world. . . .
> Gold, silver and gems are scattered on her streets. If you can figure out a way
> of picking them up, you'll become rich instantly to the tune of ten million and
> be able to enjoy ultimate human pleasures. (Kessler 1993, 8)

Departing from the sparse 20-cents-a-day jobs in their homeland, Japanese laborers give in to high-pressure recruiters offering free steerage passage to Tacoma or Seattle. Their lack of sophistication contributes to a generation of exploitation, disillusion, and exclusion.

From the point of view of a female immigrant, Ruthanne Lum McCunn particularizes the experience of Asian immigrants with *Thousand Pieces of Gold* (1981), a biography of Lalu Nathoy, a field hand born in China in 1853. Lalu's captors snare her into slavery and hustle her into a California ghetto, where they deliver her to a flesh peddler's lair:

> The Gold Mountains they had described was not the America she would know.
> This: the dingy basement room, the blank faces of women and girls stripped

of hope, the splintered boards beneath her feet, the auction block. This was her America. (McCunn 1981, 102)

McCunn's realism compounds the initial shock of Lalu's abduction with dismaying episodes. Fortunate to have survived the trip, she learns that others are not so lucky. Shipped in padded crates among loads of dishes or shoved into coal bins, victims of the trans-Pacific slave trade die at sea or are so maimed by jarring against the raw confines of their hiding places that they are salable only as damaged goods. Many are shelved in holding pens until they starve or die of their injuries. Lalu is saddened to compare her safe arrival with the plight of the unlucky. She demands, "What does that change except my price?" (ibid., 103)

In McCunn's re-creation of inhumane barter, Lalu passes from marketplace to Hong King, the seedy aged barkeep of an Idaho mining camp, where she quickly doubles his business. After hours, she provides him sexual release. Renamed Polly, she steels herself to the life of a comfort girl, dreams of her white friend Jim, and hoards any bits of gold dust that escape Hong King's sharp eyes. The technicalities of his hold over her gnaw at her peace of mind. McCunn indicates that language barriers, uneven administration of the law, dishonest judges, and the threat of deportation shackle Polly as firmly as the leg irons on a Guinea slave or the leash on a performing monkey. In forbidding thoughts of home, she ponders, "What would her mother say if she knew her daughter had been forced to submit to an old man's feeble, humiliating rutting?" (ibid., 119)

The first biography of an Asian-American pioneer woman, *Thousand Pieces of Gold* takes shape without histrionics. The multiple disasters that threaten Polly replicate the myriad difficulties of all frontierswomen, even free whites, but her slavery to grasping males eclipses the expected hardships accompanying settlement in the West. In a tense poker game, she changes hands like a sack of gold dust:

> "I have nothing else," [Hong King] said at last. Charlie nodded casually toward Polly. "Stake the girl. . . ." Without a word, Charlie turned over his hidden card: two of clubs, a full house. He had won. (ibid., 156–157)

As McCunn illustrates, the exploitation of women in a male-dominated microcosm stigmatizes her far worse than the shame of prostitution on a city street. Charlie Bemis's winning hand does not free Polly from the ignominy of traded property. She must acclimate to wifedom over time.

In much of Polly's story, McCunn focuses on the needs of the moment. Polly strops a razor and extracts a bullet from her husband's jaw, rescues him from a burning cabin, treats the "spitting blood" disease that she knows is incurable, and tenses to the dull thud of his body in a mountainside grave. Into her seventies, she holds together Polly Place, the ranch that Charlie helped her build. Her possessions come at a fearful price:

> Feeling cheated, she took out the papers she had stuffed inside after Charlie died. Brittle with age and too much folding, they crackled as she spread them out. Her wedding certificate. Her certificate of residence. The mining claim for

the ranch. The papers for which Charlie had been willing to give up his life. The papers she would gladly surrender to bring him back. (ibid., 285)

At her death in 1933, Polly Bemis leaves a legacy of woman's work: binding her breasts for nightly entertainment at the bar, pouring herbal tea into the mouths of the sick, nailing up curtains to keep out prying eyes, chopping chicken for croquettes, and tugging porcupine quills from Teddy, her dog. McCunn dignifies Polly's frontier experience with an attention to detail that refuses to let a lifetime of love and drudgery pass unlauded.

A strong, realistic voice from young adult literature comes from Laurence Yep, a native of San Francisco's Chinatown and the multiple award-winning author of *Dragonwings* (1975) and its prequel, *Dragon's Gate* (1992). Both books anticipate the mechanization of the West—first, through flight; second, through the completion of the Transcontinental Railroad. In both historical novels, the author looks through youthful eyes at the promise of the frontier and the frustration of immigrants who yearn to share in the nation's wealth, but who falter on the threshold of the American dream. In *Dragonwings*, the eight-year-old speaker, Moon Shadow, wrestles with an approach-avoidance complex. He longs to see America, "Land of the Golden Mountain," but realizes that Windrider, his father, has already committed himself to seek his fortune in a demon land:

> There was plenty of money to be made among the demons, but it was also dangerous. My own grandfather had been lynched about thirty years before by the mob of white demons almost the moment he had set foot on their shores. (Yep 1975, 1)

Acknowledging the boy's quandary in facing an ebullient but treacherous new society, Yep follows him through the difficulty of getting to know his father, functioning among vicious gangs of white boys, and recovering from an earthquake.

In an afterword, Yep explains that the inspiration for *Dragonwings* came from a historical figure, Chinese aviator Fung Joe Guey, who accomplished his dream and flew a homemade biplane outside Oakland on September 22, 1909. The motivation for Yep's fictional kite maker, the all-male Tang clan, and Windrider's man-sized kite springs not from adventure but from a desire to right the wrongs of history. Yep declares that he wanted his novel to quell media stereotypes—"Dr. Fu Manchu and his yellow hordes, Charlie Chan and his fortune-cookie wisdom, the laundrymen and cooks of the movie and television Westerns, and the houseboys" from comedy—that serve as impediments to white America's understanding of Chinese Americans. (ibid., 247–248) (Gardner 1995; Kessler 1993; Lamar 1977; McCunn 1981; Yep 1975, 1992; Young 1978)

See also Harte, Bret; prospecting; *Roughing It*; Twain, Mark.

AUSTIN, MARY HUNTER

A regional poet, playwright, folklorist, reformer, ecologist, and lecturer, Mary Hunter Austin, native of Carlinville, Illinois, determined in girlhood not to adopt the sissy behaviors expected of girls. After the deaths of her father, Civil War veteran Captain George Hunter, from malaria and her sister Jennie from diphtheria, Austin endured the disapproval of her mother, Susannah Savilla Graham Hunter, a stiff-backed, pinch-faced Methodist fanatic who prodded Mary to conform to the expected norm and who wished that Mary rather than Jennie had died. From chronic solitude, Austin developed a oneness with self that helped her overcome loneliness and alienation. She attended classes at Blackburn College in 1884 and the State Normal School at Bloomington in 1885, then returned to Blackburn to complete a science degree.

In adulthood Austin continued to reject the conventional role of handmaid and the oppressive narrow-mindedness of fundamentalist religion and small towns. With her mother and brother Jim, she homesteaded in the southern portion of California's Joaquin Valley and discovered a purposeful solitude that accommodated wide expanses of desert and a clean, spare form of beauty. As a poet, she recognized that authenticity in art derives from the rhythms of everyday happenings. She gathered impressions from friendships with Indian women and chance encounters with shepherds, drovers, Hispanic laborers, wagoneers, miners, and innkeepers. From these gleanings, she wrote a variety of fiction and nonfiction, such as her poem "Going West" (1922), which predicts that, when she immerses self in the smell of sage and the view of encircling mountains, "something in me that is of them shall stir." (Austin 1987, 18)

After her marriage to teacher and grape grower Wallace Stafford Austin in 1891, Mary Austin lived near Bakersfield and cared for Ruth, their retarded daughter, whom she eventually placed in an institution in Santa Clara until the girl's death in 1914. Austin resented the fact that her husband knew that he carried a defective gene causing mental handicap. The marriage foundered for this and other reasons: her husband failed to satisfy her physical and intellectual needs, and he was incapable of supporting a family. When he abandoned her temporarily at a boardinghouse, she moved to a humbler inn and took a job as cook to pay the rent. Regret tinged her life and colored the male-female relationships of her stories, which depict women as bold seekers and pathfinders and men as taciturn, abject, thick-headed, or irresponsible.

In 1892, while her husband was serving as superintendent of schools in Lone Pine, Austin began teaching at the Methodist Academy at Bishop and a public school in Los Angeles. She made up stories and poems to please students, for example, her wittily feminist nature verse:

Ladybug, ladybug, fly away home.
The scale bug is down in the orchard alone,
He is eating his way to the topmost limb,
Ladybug, ladybug, go and eat him! (Austin 1928, 214)

The obvious symbolism of the withdrawn male, chewing his way upward, describes Austin's opinion of her husband, who remained coolly detached from her aims. The instruction to the ladybug suggests a sublimated urge to do violence to Wallace, whose lack of compassion kept Austin off-balance, never sure of finances, and devalued as wife, artist, and individual.

Mary Hunter Austin, a homesteader in California's San Joaquin Valley, became an astute observer of her surroundings. After moving to Lone Pine, on the edge of the Mojave Desert, she wrote *The Land of Little Rain*, published in 1903.

While Austin recuperated from a series of health crises, arts patron Ina Coolbrith encouraged her to send a short story, "The Mother of Felipe," to the *Overland Monthly*, which paid $3 per page for the submission. Influenced by the works and independent vision of Sarah Orne Jewett, Louisa May Alcott, and Harriet Beecher Stowe and encouraged by the friendship of Charlotte Perkins Gilman and by Willa Cather's novels about Nebraska, Austin pleased herself by writing distinctively female-centered fiction, verse, and essays. She befriended Indian women and developed resilience, pragmatism, and mysticism by studying them and other stoic desert dwellers. She produced a chapter on Native American writing for the *Cambridge History of American Literature*. Throughout her career, she published short works and serialized longer ones in *Land of Sunshine, American Boy, Youth's Companion, Harper's, Outwest, Young Woman Citizen, Forum, Everygirl's Magazine, Nation, American Mercury, Cosmopolitan, Century,* and *St. Nicholas*.

Austin crafted mature frontier vignettes in *The Land of Little Rain* (1903), an evocative, lyric examination of interrelated forms of life on the Mojave Desert. The work, considered her masterpiece, was serialized in *Atlantic Monthly*. It pioneered new territory in its appreciation of the Ute, Paiute, Mojave, Navajo, Comanche, Papago, and Shoshone. In a bare-bones perusal of the landscape, she notes the effects of rare showers on broad wastelands, which are swept with wind and sculpted into "essays in miniature." (Austin 1903, 3, 5) Of the human creativity spawned by the desert, Austin describes the beauty of baskets made by Seyavi, a dweller in a twig-lined wickiup whom she compares to Deborah, wisewoman of the Old Testament. Austin detects strength in the lone native crafter and surmises: "Every Indian woman is an artist,—sees, feels, creates, but does not philosophize about her processes." (ibid., 168–169)

Austin's works display her ambivalence toward life. She is capable of vigorous commentary on *vaqueros*, herders, and the '49ers of Jimville, Bret Harte's town. Yet, an austere, languid, contemplative mood dominates her essays up to the final chapter, "The Little Town of the Grape Vines," where she watches Hispanic natives celebrate the September 16 holiday. The unity of the collection rests in the moving eye of the narrator and her appreciative glance at native mores. She surmises that desert complacency actualizes a Darwinian principle: compromise with the harsh land and its demands on the spirit.

Encouraged by the book's success, Austin produced 250 short works and 30 book-length titles, including a collection of short fiction, *The Basket Woman* (1904); the novels *Isidro* (1905) and *Santa Lucia* (1908); and a rhetorical play about a Paiute medicine woman, *The Arrow-Maker* (1910), all set in Hispanic California. In *Lost Borders* (1909), Austin identifies with an English character who heals citified ailments by abandoning urbanism and moving to the desert:

> Saunders had drifted about from water-hole to water-hole, living hardily, breathing the driest, cleanest air, sleeping and waking with the ebb and flow of light that sets in a mighty current around the world. He went up in summer to the mountain-heads under the foxtail pines, and back in winter to watch the wild almond bloom by Resting Springs. He saw the Medicine dance of the Shoshones, and hunted the bighorn on Funeral Mountains, and dropped a

great many things out of his life without making himself unhappy. (Austin 1987, 46)

Austin studied the elements of health and concluded that the strongest bodies and spirits derive from a lifelong harmony with the earth. She applied the concept to her own adaptation to the West and spent hours studying the desert herbal treatments administered by shamans and wisewomen.

From an interest in education evolved Austin's book of fables, *The Trail Book* (1918), and a juvenile collection of nature verse, *Children Sing in the Far West* (1928), her only poetry anthology. The latter is a skillfully illustrated and annotated text, the result of her concern that American children of her day knew more about Grimms' fairy tales and other European lore than about the experiences, myths, songs, riddles, landmarks, and beliefs of frontier America. Richly interwoven with euphony, alliteration, stout rhythms, and imaginative phrases, poems like "Whisper of the Wind," "Rain Song of the Rio Grande Pueblos," "In Papagueria," "Furryhide," "Dormidera," "Fire Drill Songs," and "Glitterskin" invite children to experience the joy of word music. Mythic and insightful in style and characterization, "Western Magic" expresses the absence of fairy-folk in desert lore:

> There's no dew anywhere for them to drink
> And no green grass to make them fairy rings . . .
> There are no fairy-folk in our Southwest,
> But there are homes where prairie dog and snake,
> Black beetle and tecolote owl
> Between two winks their ancient forms will take.
> (Austin 1928, 55–56)

To assure children of the worth of the southwestern milieu, she entices them toward the strong "naturist" elements of its culture: the sun and the "mothering earth," who tells "of older things than fairy-folk." To entertain young listeners, she sings the "Song of Western Men," an energetic paean to Cabeza de Vaca, Coronado, the *conquistadores*, Kit Carson, and Zebulon Pike. With a flourish, she implores, "God send us their like again." (ibid., 126)

Austin's popularity followed her to Europe and the East Coast, where she joined feminists Emma Goldman, Ida Tarbell, and Margaret Sanger in championing women's rights and campaigning for birth control. Marital stress caused her to desert her husband and take up residence with the artists of Carmel, where she set up a studio in a wickiup and associated after hours with some of the West's prominent literati, including Ambrose Bierce, Jack London, and John Muir. While recovering from nervous collapse, she joined an art colony in Santa Fe; in Taos, she gained insight from friendships with poet and novelist D. H. Lawrence, arts patron Mabel Dodge, photographer Ansel Adams, and desert artist Georgia O'Keeffe. She represented New Mexico at the Second Colorado River Conference and pressed Congress to protect water resources on Pueblo lands. Dependence on writing, activism, cooking, and gardening helped Austin develop security, overcome depression, and express her disaffection for modern influences that were reshaping American families.

During the final decade of her life, spent peacefully at La Casa Querida, her adobe house in Santa Fe, Austin studied Indian culture, particularly storytelling and healing. Her last novel, *Starry Adventure* (1931), and story collection, *One-Smoke Stories* (1934), contain her most intense southwestern fiction. Before her death from heart disease in 1934, she published *Earth Horizon* (1932), a semiautobiographical novel. She was cremated. A procession on horseback bore her ashes up the Sangre de Cristo slopes and placed them in a rocky niche on Mount Picacho. A friend scratched her name on the cement that sealed the crevice. Her private papers reside in the Huntington Library. Franklin Walker published a collection of her early fiction in *Mother Felipe and Other Early Stories* (1950). Although Austin earned the praise of Sinclair Lewis, Mark Van Doren, and Van Wyck Brooks, her work was largely overlooked until the feminist movement of the 1970s. (Austin 1903, 1928, 1932, 1987; Blain et al. 1990; Buck 1992; Davidson and Wagner-Martin 1995; Dobie 1996; Ehrlich and Carruth 1982; Kunitz 1942; Pierce 1965; Sherr and Kazickas 1994)

See also Bierce, Ambrose; Cather, Willa; Harte, Bret; Lawrence, D. H.; London, Jack.

BIERCE, AMBROSE

Frontier newspaperman, critic, columnist, poet, and writer of supernatural and boisterous adventure stories, Ambrose Gwinett Bierce crafted a wealth of short stories. Many of his most popular titles defy his era's taste for realism by exploiting gothic motifs and affirm his reputation for misanthropy, violence, and black humor. Others re-create subtle, ironic vignettes from Shiloh, Murfreesboro, Chickamauga, the siege of Atlanta, and Sherman's march to the sea, which he knew from wartime experience. His flamboyant style, psychological twists, and sardonic wit anticipated a number of American writers, including Robert Penn Warren, Conrad Aiken, Flannery O'Connor, Sherwood Anderson, Carson McCullers, Nathanael West, Gertrude Atherton, and William Faulkner. To his credit, Bierce is sometimes listed as the Swiftian satirist who sharpened H. L. Mencken's pen.

A native of Meigs County, Ohio, Bierce, born in 1842, was the ninth living child of Marcus Aurelius and Laura Sherwood Bierce and the thirteenth to bear a given name beginning with A. He spent part of his youth in a log cabin on Horse Cave Creek. In 1851, his family moved to a farm on Walnut Creek and later to Warsaw and Elkhart, Indiana. Tired of farming and the belittling and regimentation of his Calvinist parents, he apprenticed as a printer for an abolitionist paper, the *Northern Indianian*. He derived most of his education from reading until he was 17, when his uncle Lucius Verus Bierce paid his tuition to Kentucky Military Institute. Bierce thrived on military field strategy and cartography, but his studies came to an end during their first year after a wayward student torched the school.

Like Erich Remarque, Mariano Azuela, and Ernest Hemingway, Bierce developed point of view from battlefield engagements, during which he familiarized himself with split-second delineations between life and death. To escape the over-strict discipline of his midwestern home, he enlisted as a drummer in the 9th Indiana Infantry at age 19 and was commissioned a map officer and report writer. He fought at the Battles of Cheat Mountain, Missionary Ridge, Lookout Mountain, and Girard Hill, where he was honored for rescuing a fallen comrade during a siege. He was shot in the head at the Battle of Kennesaw Mountain in Tennessee and recuperated at a Chattanooga hospital, yet continued to suffer flashbacks, headaches, and fainting spells.

Bierce resigned his commission as brevet major near the end of the war to manage captured and abandoned lands in Selma, which he describes in "Down in Alabam'." During Reconstruction, he left the job to assist a Treasury Department expedition under General William Hazen in seizing Confederate cotton. His return to war-torn lands unsettled him and, in the eyes of Southerners, placed him on a par with corrupt carpetbaggers. He fled west in 1866 as an engineering attaché assigned to map and inspect army posts from Nebraska to Fort Benton, Montana, a grueling journey through Indian country that he recounts in "Across the Plains."

Like others disillusioned by war and dismayed when the army reclassified him a lieutenant rather than a captain, Bierce sought his fortunes in the West by joining his brother Albert in California. He got a new start in San Francisco working as a night watchman at the U.S. Mint. As a creative outlet, he sketched political cartoons and edited the *News-Letter*. Admirer Bret Harte published Bierce's first sketch, "The Haunted Valley," a ghost tale, in the *Overland Monthly*. The story is Western in setting and dialect and pairs a pun-rich grave marker— JO. DUNFER. DONE FER.—with a baleful tomb message:

AH WEE-CHINAMAN.
Age unknown. Worked for Jo. Dunfer.
This monument is erected by him to keep the Chink's
memory green. Likewise as a warning to Celestials
not to take on airs. Devil take 'em!
She Was a Good Egg.
(Bierce 1984, 121)

Written in the form of tall tale, the story observes the form's conventions of dialect, superstition, and secondhand reporting. The focal character, bitter grogmaster "Whisky Jo" Dunfer, lashes out at Easterners who "are a mile-and-a-half too good for this country, and . . . don't catch on to our play." He complains that newcomers who "don't know a Chileño from a Kanaka can afford to hang out liberal ideas about Chinese immigration," but he commiserates with insiders about the necessity of "[fighting] for his bone with a lot of mongrel coolies." (ibid., 118) The story ends with the complaint of a crazed loser in a love triangle. He tells the narrator that he avoids Jo's vengeful spirit and mourns "the woman who loved him better than she did me!—me who had followed 'er from San Francisco, where 'e won 'er at draw poker!" (ibid., 126)

Bierce developed his grasp of narration and satire from his years as a reporter for the *Californian, Alta California, Golden Era,* and *News-Letter and California Advertiser*. A strong influence on Pacific Coast writers, he was a colleague of Western lore experts Bret Harte, Joaquin Miller, and Mark Twain and earned the nicknames "The Devil's Lexicographer," "The Wickedest Man in San Francisco," and "Bitter Bierce" for the harsh cynicism of his short sketches. At the age of 29, Bierce married Mary Ellen "Mollie" Day, daughter of a wealthy mining engineer. Bierce's family settled temporarily in London, where he submitted fiction to *Figaro* and *Fun* and edited *The Lantern*. Mollie sailed back to the United States, leaving her husband to his writing. Under the pen name "Dod

Ambrose Bierce, a contemporary of Mark Twain and Bret Harte, disappeared in Mexico in 1913.

Grile" he published three collections of short works: *Nuggets and Dust Panned Out in California* (1872), *The Fiend's Delight* (1872), and *Cobwebs from an Empty Skull* (1874).

When asthma endangered his health, Bierce returned to California for a reunion with his wife, infant daughter Helen, and sons Day and Leigh in San Francisco. He served as editor, critic, and columnist for the *Examiner, Wasp*, and *Argonaut*. To gain solitude from a full house that grew onerous after his troublesome mother-in-law moved in, he withdrew to the Bohemian Club. For a short period, he left home on a whim, working as an agent for the Black Hills Placer Mining Company in Deadwood, South Dakota. When that job ended, he rode shotgun for Wells Fargo in the Dakota Territory.

Once more in California, Bierce was pressed by low finances. He holed up in a hotel and composed "One of the Missing," one of his finest war pieces, which he sold to *The Wave*. The story was the beginning of his fame. In 1887, he signed on with young William Randolph Hearst, a budding newspaper giant and strong supporter of Bierce's iconoclastic writings. After his marriage failed, Bierce wrote his column, "The Prattler," from his residence in St. Helena and later from Aurora, California, where he eased chronic shortness of breath by avoiding big-city pollutants. He rose to national fame and earned a reputation as the Samuel Johnson of the West and arbiter of literary culture in the greater San Francisco area.

Bierce's style grew uncompromisingly acid after the death of his estranged wife and the loss of his sons from dueling and alcoholism. His relationship with his married daughter was cordial but distant. He pedaled a bicycle into the hills and read Epictetus, drawing strength from classical stoicism. Frequently overwhelmed with wheezing and insomnia and enshrouded in black moods, he adopted as his motto "Nothing matters" but worked as though he had a deadline to meet. Before the end of the century, he published the translation of a German romance, *The Monk and the Hangman's Daughter* (1892), which was serialized in the *Examiner* in 1893; satiric verse in *Black Beetles in Amber* (1892); two collections, *Tales of Soldiers and Civilians* (1891) and *Can Such Things Be?* (1893); and an Aesopic collection, *Fantastic Fables* (1899).

While muckraking for Hearst Publications, Bierce was dispatched to Washington, D.C., in 1900 as an antirailroad lobbyist and a correspondent for the *Examiner* during hearings on fraudulent dealings by the Central and Southern Pacific Railroads. To an adoring audience, Bierce ridiculed entrepreneur Leland Stanford as "£eland $tanford" and lambasted the "Rail Rogues," who petitioned Congress to cancel company debts. Still actively producing droll commentary and thriller fiction, Bierce contributed to the New York *Journal* and *Cosmopolitan*. Before retiring, he published poems in *Shapes of Clay* (1903); a collection of essays, *Shadow on the Dial* (1906); and *The Devil's Dictionary* (1906), a classic compendium of 500 mordant aphorisms in the form of cunning definitions reissued as *The Cynic's Word Book*. He put much effort into combing through scrapbooks and memorabilia for his final publication, *Collected Works* (1912), a 12-volume set comprising a quarter of his life's work.

At age 71, Bierce set out to tour major sites of the Civil War, wander New Orleans, and visit old military buddies. Perhaps seeking a noble death, he was drawn to the Mexican Civil War. While observing General Pancho Villa's revolutionary force, he disappeared in the winter of 1913–1914. In his last letter from Chihuahua, dated December 26, 1913, he looked forward to a romantic demise:

> stood up against a Mexican stone wall and shot to rags, please know that I think it a pretty good way to depart this life. It beats old age, disease, or falling down the cellar stairs. To be a Gringo in Mexico—ah, that is euthanasia! (Bierce 1994, iii)

Historians surmise that he was killed at the siege of Ojinaga in January 1914.

Like Edgar Allan Poe and Guy de Maupassant, Bierce composed emotionally jarring verse, wry reflections, and pointed short thrillers. Some seem detached from physical locale, yet many of his poems and stories fit the outback insouciance and remote settings of the West. The characteristic lacerating style earned the writer the enmity of the frivolous, self-important, and notorious because he named or clearly identified California's most ignoble politicians, social matrons, clergy, snake-oil sellers, and eccentrics. Bierce's humorous narrative "Mr. Fink's Debating Donkey" echoes the backwoods, knee-slapping delivery of Mark Twain's frontier hoax tale, "The Celebrated Jumping Frog of Calaveras County." In reply to an egotistical prattler, William Perry Peters, the tedious dialect voice of Ebenezer Fink of the Rancho del Jackrabbit, settles the question of which is better, hearing or sight. After Fink's mule enters the room, the old codger exclaims:

> . . . Gents, I heern o' this debate
> On w'ether v'ice or y'ears is best the mind to elevate.
> Now 'yer's a bird ken throw some light upon to that tough theme:
> He has 'em both, I'm free to say, oncommonly extreme.
> He wa'n't invited for to speak, but he will not refuse
> (If t'other gentleman ken wait) to exposay his views.
> (Bierce 1963, 27)

Fink cuts a string that binds a stone to the mule's tail and releases the animal's pent-up brays. A dozing woman jolts to attention and flees; Peters is lofted through a window and abandons his aims to educate the town of Muscatel.

Less slapstick is Bierce's allegorical verse play, *Birth of the Rail*, set at midnight on the Dutch Flat Stage Road in 1862. Three brigands—Happy Hunty, Leland the Kid, and Cowboy Charley—celebrate the stage line, which delivers likely marks to the West and robs them more skillfully than bushwhackers:

> . . . Instead
> Of stopping passengers, let's carry them.
> Instead of crying out: "Throw up your hands!"
> Let's say: "Walk up and buy a ticket!" Why
> Should we unwieldy goods and bullion take,
> Watches and all such trifles, when we might

Far better charge their value three times o'er
For carrying them to market? (ibid., 107)

In the midst of their plotting, Leland hears a crackling in the chaparral. Sootymug, sobriquet of Satan, saunters up and joins the trio's deviltry. Happy, who obviously knows Sootymug's purpose, snorts, "Here's more damned competition!" (ibid., 109) In typical Bierce style, the poem quickly establishes its satiric thrust and ends without didactic comment.

Similar in tone and format, short stories glean Bierce's Western memories, including "The Stranger," set among the rattlers and horned toads of Tucson, and "The Death of Halpin Frayser," which focuses on a native of St. Helena. Bierce returns to the Western milieu of the California gold rush for "The Secret of Macarger's Gulch," the first-person account of a quail shooter who runs across an abandoned miner's shack in 1874. In the foothills of the Sierra Nevada, the hunter spends a night at the ruined chimney, dreams of a Scottish couple in Edinburgh, and awakens to certainty that the dream family once lived in the hut. A year later in Sacramento, the speaker learns of the unexplained violent death of Janet MacGregor, whose husband was suspected of murdering her at their Macarger Gulch home by smashing her skull with a pick. Wise locals stay clear of the gulch lest they incur Macarger's ghost and suffer its wrath.

Some of Bierce's work has been adapted to film. Short versions of *The Little Story* (1967), *Man and Snake* (1972), *The Boarded Window* (1973), *The Return* (1976), *Parker Adderson, Philosopher* (1977), *The Coup de Grace* (1978), and *One of the Missing* (1978) gained little attention compared to the most evocative screen adaptation, *Occurrence at Owl Creek Bridge,* a black-and-white short produced by Robert Enrico in 1962. Columbia TriStar Pictures filmed a moderately successful study, *Old Gringo* (1989). Based on a fictional romance adapted from *The Old Gringo* (1985), written by Carlos Fuentes, Mexico's renowned twentieth-century novelist, the film depicts Bierce as reclusive and enigmatic, possessed of a fading masculinity that longs to leave a "good-looking corpse." (Fuentes 1985, 199) Despite quality performances by stars Jane Fonda, who plays the old maid gringa Harriet Winslow, and Gregory Peck as the aging American writer, the movie contributes nothing to the outsized legends of either Pancho Villa or Ambrose Bierce. (Bierce 1963, 1984, 1994, 1996, 1996a, 1996b, 1996c, 1996d, 1996e; Ehrlich and Carruth 1982; Fuentes 1985; Grenander 1971; Gullette 1996; Hart 1983; Kirsch and Murphy 1967; Kunitz and Haycraft 1938; Lamar 1977; Morris 1995; O'Connor 1966; Trent et al. 1946; Wiggins 1964)

See also "The Celebrated Jumping Frog of Calaveras County"; Harte, Bret; Miller, Joaquin; Twain, Mark.

BILLY THE KID

The West's most notorious outlaw, Billy the Kid, a nickname derived from his usual alias of William H. Bonney, grew from New Mexico vigilante into frontier legend—a Faustian demon concocted from outsized embellishments in dime novels, news stories, and the *National Police Gazette*. News sources quote Billy's boast that he had killed a man for each year of his life. Additions to the Billy the Kid crime motif derive from radio, television, and stage, notably Walter Woods's melodrama, *Billy the Kid* (1903) and the Broadway version, produced three years later. Mythic details began in lurid novels and expanded with Walter Noble Burns's *The Saga of Billy the Kid* (1926). Cinema makers delighted in the legendary juvenile and produced *Billy the Kid* (1930), *The Outlaw* (1943), *Son of Billy the Kid* (1949), *One-Eyed Jacks* (1961), and *Sam Garrett and Billy the Kid* (1973).

A New Yorker whose parents moved to Coffeyville, Kansas, in 1862, Henry "Billy the Kid" McCarty was born to Kathleen and William H. Bonney on November 23, 1859, and lived to age 21, a surprising feat for a desperado sought by a ranching syndicate of assorted thugs and an implacable lawman. According to hazy data, Billy began killing in 1871 because a roustabout insulted his mother. After moving to Tucson, Arizona, and working as a cowboy under his stepfather's name, William Antrim, he answered to "the Kid," a reflection of his diminutive height. In Fort Grant, Arizona, he shot a bully, blacksmith Frank P. "Windy" Cahill, on August 25, 1877, left town, and resurfaced in Mesilla, New Mexico, as William H. Bonney, small-time rustler.

With luck and skill, Billy continued battling oppressors and lawmen for four more years; however, the list of victims appears well padded by gossips and glorifiers. Employed by cattleman John Chisum during the Lincoln County War, Billy joined the Regulators, a vigilante gang, and stalked the waylayers of John Tunstall, an English merchant who sided with Chisum against small ranchers. In the struggle for rights to range land in 1878, Billy murdered Sheriff William Brady and his deputy, George Hindman. From two well-documented battles with Lawrence Murphy's hired guns, Billy earned respect from the law-of-the-gun element. The feud sieges ended with Billy's incarceration and escape. Because Chisum refused to pay for Billy's services and Governor Lew Wallace reneged on a promise of pardon, Billy rustled cattle. He was arrested a second time and condemned to hang for Brady's murder. He shot two guards and escaped again. In Fort Sumner, New Mexico, Sheriff Patrick Floyd "Pat" Garrett cornered Billy in a darkened room of a ranch house and shot him dead before Billy could fire. According to news sources, citizens rejoiced that the wayward delinquent was no longer at large.

In 1882, Garrett yielded to public pressure and published a biography of Billy, ghostwritten by Ash Upson, who claimed to have lived at Billy's mother's boardinghouse. Garrett's work ostensibly credits him with his rightful share of virtues, but epitomizes Billy as a punk, a social cancer, and a disorderly free agent bent on violence and doomed to die of the same. Garrett reflects on the fatal one-sided shoot-out:

> It will never be known whether the Kid recognized me or not. If he did, it was the first time, during all his life of peril, that he ever lost his presence of mind, or failed to shoot first and hesitate afterwards. He knew that a meeting with me meant surrender or fight. (Garrett 1954, 148)

Born Henry McCarty in 1859, Billy the Kid, also known as William H. Bonney, poses in a tintype photograph. His brief, violent life ended at age 21 when he was gunned down by lawman Pat Garrett. His life has provided grist for plays, books, and movies.

A decorous conclusion details Billy's funeral at Fort Sumner July 15, 1881, where he was fittingly laid out and buried in the local cemetery without any looting or mutilation of his body.

After its opening at the New Star Theatre in New York City, Walter Woods's four-act play, *Billy the Kid* (1906), profited from Billy fever with its stagy melodrama, which sold out audiences for 12 years. Billboards touted the lurid fictions that surrounded his brief life:

See: The Famous Bandit Horse, "Silver Heels."
The Battle in the Dark.
The Hairbreadth Escape of Billy the Kid.
The Kiss Auction.
The Soul Stirring Bravery of the Boy Bandit.
The Famous Broken Heart Saloon. (Woods 1940, xv)

A welter of emotion sweeps Act I to a grand gesture: Billy, wrongfully accused of robbing his father's safe, stands over his mother's corpse and vows, "You who have plotted my destruction shall live to hear the outlaw you have created. Go, and leave me with my dead." (ibid., 217) The second act, set three years later at the Broken Heart Saloon, casts Billy in the role of defender of women after he disrupts the auction of a kiss from Nellie Bradley. Wooden exchanges with classic no-goods like saloon owner Boyd Denver have Billy uttering trite pronouncements: "We will stand beside my mother's grave and you will tell me the truth . . . You shall go with me though the whole world tried to stop you." (ibid., 228)

The overplayed conclusion to Billy's story forms a set piece: Denver, pleading for his life, faces an implacable Billy, who is determined to avenge his parents' deaths. Nellie, Billy's girl, tries to intervene. He reveals to her his decision to seek justice and embrace the role of outlaw. Compromised by his choice, he acknowledges that lawmen will give him no rest from pursuit and will probably finish him. The resolution is a total fiction laced with tongue-in-cheek piety: after Denver discloses that he is really Billy's father, the young hero pretends to humble himself before God and await punishment for hounding an innocent man.

Woods's dark humor recasts a historical figure as a wronged man set free by the martyrdom of a villain. By offering Denver his coat and hat, Billy sets him up for a barrage of gunfire from the unseen bounty hunters outside. The play provides a new twist on the legend of the short-lived gunman by suggesting that authorities accept Denver's body as Billy, leaving him and Nellie to "wander down life's pathway together, where the sun shines always." (ibid., 255) The sensationalized plot, which alternates pity, terror, and jubilation, concludes with poetic justice—Billy, no longer stalked and tormented, recedes into obscurity with his girl. A form of denial, the melodrama rescues the appealingly boyish gunslinger from the violent death that history records as truth. (Burns 1926; Dobie 1996; Garrett 1954; Lamar 1977; Love 1988; Milner et al. 1994; Steckmesser 1965; Tatum 1982; Woods 1940)

See also law and order.

BLACK ELK

One of North America's most respected native seers and medicine men, Black Elk made literary history with his oral biography, *Black Elk Speaks: The Life Story of a Holy Man of the Oglala Sioux* (1932), which critics have labeled a "North American Indian bible." Historian John G. Neihardt sought him out as the native authority on the tribe's "pipe religion." Because Black Elk spoke no English, he transmitted the work orally to his son, Benjamin Black Elk, a teacher and lecturer. Ben translated the narration for Neihardt's daughter Enid to take down in shorthand. Neihardt completed the work and supplied photographs of their multiple work sessions. In 1953, anthropologist Joseph Epes Brown expanded Black Elk's lore with *The Sacred Pipe*, a summary of Sioux liturgy and ritual.

A cousin of Crazy Horse, Black Elk was a shaman of the Oglala Sioux, one of seven subgroups of the Western Teton who spoke the Lakota dialect and who vigorously resisted the western settlement that threatened tribal lands. He was born on the Powder River, Wyoming, in December 1863 (or possibly 1862). Named Hehaka Sapa, he was the fourth male in his family to bear this name, which means "Black Elk." His father was wounded at the Fetterman Massacre at Fort Phil Kearney on December 21, 1866, a unified action of Arapaho, Sioux, and Cheyenne warriors against the construction of a fort on holy ground in Dakota Territory. As a child, Black Elk fought his friends in mock battles and seemed destined for an ordinary life. Singled out by dreams and visitations from the spirit world, at age nine he realized that these omens were readying him for a holy calling to restore the Sioux faith. As *wichasha wakon*, or tribal priest, under Chief Red Cloud, Black Elk vowed to uplift and hearten his beleaguered people. This altruistic goal burdened him with a bittersweet outlook of hope and despair. He prayed that *Wakan Tanka*, the Great Mysterious One, would continue to guide him with divine inspiration. He received a vision foretelling that he would establish a Sioux utopia, symbolized by the sacred hoop. Fearful of the metaphysical power bestowed by the Great Spirit, he withdrew from others to commune with the supernatural voices of six Indian grandfathers and with skyriders holding aloft fiery spears. Lest he alarm his family, he concealed an unsettling sequence of out-of-body flights into heaven.

Four years after his vision, Black Elk was felled by an unexplained weakness in his limbs. For 12 days, he remained in a comalike trance. Calling him Younger Brother, the spirits who controlled him promised that he could depend on a titanic power, "the cleansing wind," to cure illness and renew his nation's heart. When he revived, an aura encircled him. He ate little and stayed in isolation to familiarize himself with the otherworldly presence. He received instruction in history and lore from Whirlwind Chaser, Black Road, and Elk Head, Keeper of the Sacred Pipe. By the time Black Elk reached his mid-teens, the augury came true: after considerable fasting and prayer, he developed healing skills. In 1876, he survived the Battle of the Little Big Horn, yet he was often troubled by surging emotions and fear. He and his family joined Crazy

Horse's faction. Upon the leader's death, they followed Sitting Bull's party to Canada and back to Fort Buford, North Dakota.

After the family settled on the Pine Ridge Reservation, South Dakota, in 1886, Black Elk began consulting with individuals who sought his wisdom and comfort. His hope wavered when he realized that European settlers were destroying Native American traditions. Whites—whom he called *wasichus*—slaughtered whole herds of migrating buffalo, stripped the hides, and left the meat to rot. These same frontiersmen and squatters usurped Indian land, fenced in grasslands for their livestock, and pillaged nature in their stampede toward gold fields. In late middle age, he joined a troupe of Sioux dancers in Buffalo Bill Cody's Wild West Show and performed for Queen Victoria, whom the Sioux named "Grandmother England." The next year, he was too ill to perform and lived with a generous French family before returning to Pine Ridge. He was dismayed to find his tribe dwindling from drought and hunger. His father lay dying; his brother and sister were already dead.

> Supported by a strong mother, Sees the White Cow, Black Elk exerted his healing power. The tribe learned that Wovoka, a Paiute mystic, had learned from the Great Spirit that there was another world coming, just like a cloud. It would come in a whirlwind out of the west and would crush out everything on this world, which was old and dying. In that other world there was plenty of meat, just like old times; and in that world all the dead Indians were alive, and all the bison that had ever been killed were roaming around again. (Neihardt 1993, 233)

At first, Black Elk doubted the authenticity of Wovoka's vision that the earth would return to its former serenity and bounty. During the messianic ecstasy that swept Plains tribes into lengthy ritualistic Ghost Dances, Black Elk changed his opinion. He made new contact with the spirit world and experienced out-of-body flight. Dancers put on holy shirts said to ward off bullets. They smeared red paint over their faces, shared the medicine pipe, and circled the dying tree of life.

Fearful that Indians were planning a unified retaliation against them, whites rose up against the ceremony, quelling the Sioux renaissance. On December 29, 1890, cavalry massacred Big Foot's encampment at Wounded Knee, South Dakota. In the struggle between the black cavalrymen and the Lakota Sioux, Black Elk suffered a slice to the abdomen, which his uncle bandaged with strips from a blanket. Fearless in his oneness with the afterlife, he declared, "Help me on my horse! . . . It is a good day to die." His uncle rejected his acquiescence to martyrdom and reminded him that he was meant to guide the Sioux.

At the conclusion of *Black Elk Speaks,* the aged shaman describes how women and children's corpses lay in the mud. He comments, "A people's dream died there." (ibid., 270) Left to freeze, the bodies formed grotesque shapes as a winter blizzard layered them with snow. Dr. Charles Eastman, a Sioux physician, examined the remains, which military personnel interred in mass graves. Black Elk believed himself a failed spokesman and grieved over the erosion of Plains traditions and culture. He abandoned hope for the future haven that warmed his dreams:

Everywhere there were drying racks full of meat. The air was clear and beautiful with a living light that was everywhere. All around the circle, feeding on the green, green grass, were fat and happy horses; and animals of all kinds were scattered all over the green hills, and singing hunters were returning with their meat. (ibid., 242)

He concluded that the one-sided slaughter had forever sapped the strength of his people. To Neihardt, he related his pessimism and disillusion, which preceded a retreat to the spirit world. Overwhelmed by defeat, he prayed, "In sorrow I am sending a feeble voice, O Six powers of the World. Hear me in my sorrow, for I may never call again. O make my people live!" (ibid., x) The plaintive voice echoed others who believed that Native Americans would soon be engulfed by white society and would yield to the vigorous culture and religion of white Protestants.

Twenty years after this momentous collaboration, Black Elk spoke a second time, passing on the oral traditions that mentors had entrusted to him in youth. In 1953, Black Elk saw the completion of six years of interviews with anthropologist Joseph Epes Brown, who composed *The Sacred Pipe*, an account of the Seven Rites of the Oglala Sioux. While sharing a ceremonial smoke on an Assiniboin pipe offered by Brown, the old man, ragged and blind, indicated that his inner sight had predicted the arrival of Brown, whom he had happily anticipated. In a rough-hewn cabin near Manderson, South Dakota, Black Elk spoke through his bilingual son about the dismaying malaise that had settled on his people:

Most people call it a "peace pipe," yet now there is no peace on earth or even between neighbors, and I have been told that it has been a long time since there has been peace in the world. There is much talk of peace among the Christians, yet this is just talk. (Brown 1989)

With some hope of a future harmony among peoples, he dedicates his efforts on a second book to "an understanding which must be of the heart and not of the head alone." In a single paragraph, he concludes his preface with a simple statement about the creator, whom he knows as the Great Spirit, a parallel of the Judeo-Christian god.

Black Elk's narrative repeats the tradition of the sacred pipe, a method of holy communion with the almighty that a mysterious female messenger bestowed on Chief Standing Hollow Horn at an undesignated point in prehistory. The sheathed pipe occupies a place of honor and serves as the focus of a seven-stage ritual that accompanies prayer to the Sioux god, familiarly known and revered as "Grandfather." At the end of the messenger's instruction, she is transformed into a buffalo calf and is later called White Buffalo Cow Woman. According to Black Elk, the Lakota continue to revere the mythic origin of the pipe and turn to it for comfort from personal grief, guidance during coming-of-age ceremonies and the sacred Sun Dance, and solace during hard times. (Brooke 1989; Brown, Dee 1970; Brown, Joseph Epes 1989; Collier 1947; Deur 1972; Dobie 1996; Neihardt, Hilda 1995; Neihardt, John G. 1993; Patterson and Snodgrass 1994; Snodgrass 1995a; Steltenkamp 1993; Waldman 1990)

See also Custer, George Armstrong.

BLACK HAWK

The famed Sauk medicine man, orator, and chief, also called Makataime-shekiakiak, Black Hawk, descendant of chiefs, held the trust of his people through one of the most destructive periods of racial strife during the Eastern Indian wars. Born of noble ancestry in the village of Saukenuk near Rock Island, Illinois, in 1767, he fought Osage and Cherokee in his mid-teens. After the wartime death of his father, Pyesa, Black Hawk assumed a high honor as keeper of the medicine bundle. Under Tecumseh, he fought for the British during the War of 1812 and was dismayed that unfair treaties permitted white encroachment on native lands. Black Hawk's honor contrasts the venality of his rival, Keokuk, who agreed to cede ancestral territory in exchange for land west of the Mississippi River. Black Hawk remained with his band and lived on rich bottomland adjacent to white squatters. White divisions bombarded the area on June 25, 1831; Indian residents withdrew across the Mississippi.

In 1903, Frank E. Stevens published *The Black Hawk War,* a white version of the man and the period. According to Stevens's text, White Cloud, the prophet who supported Black Hawk's political career, called for a resurgence of Indian traditions that buoyed the spirits of Black Hawk's 2,000 followers, who believed that the ghosts of past heroes would rally to their cause. On April 5, 1832, Black Hawk formed an alliance between Sauk and Fox. Anticipating aid from the English in Canada, he led them back toward Saukenuk village and beyond to seek help from the Winnebago and Potawatomi; both tribes preferred peaceful acquiescence and refused to join Black Hawk's confederacy. A premature shot from whites ended truce talks on May 14; Sauk braves won the skirmish later called Skillman's Run.

Protracted sieges led by General Winfield Scott forced Black Hawk's people into tenuous living conditions in the swamps; many collapsed from hunger and disease. His band suffered a serious defeat at the Battle of Bad Axe. On August 1, 1832, after whites fired on a white flag of truce, Black Hawk led a rapid retreat from Wisconsin to the Mississippi River. Combined attacks by whites and Sioux massacred 300 of the noncombatants who remained behind. Three weeks later, he and White Cloud surrendered to government officials at Fort Crawford in Prairie du Chien, Wisconsin, where Black Hawk was confined to barracks in ball and chains. He chafed under the dishonor and spent idle hours making pipes. A visit from Keokuk and some traders relieved the tedium. They delighted him with a gift of dried venison. On September 21, 1832, he signed the Black Hawk Purchase, which yielded his rights to 50 million acres of ancestral grounds in exchange for a reservation in Iowa and a government annuity of $1,000.

After months in prison at Fort Monroe, Virginia, Black Hawk and his two sons were released. In disgrace for bad advice to his tribe, he was escorted to Washington, D.C., for a meeting with President Andrew Jackson. Throngs gathered to cheer his arrival. Government officials allowed his release under Keokuk's supervision in Iowa in exchange for Black Hawk's retirement from tribal duties. Shortly before his death on October 31, 1838, in Iowaville, Illinois, he posed for a portrait. Grave robbers placed his skeleton on display in the Historical Society Building in Burlington, Iowa, which was destroyed by fire in 1855. A 50-foot statue of Black Hawk marks the site of Saukenuk in Oregon, Illinois.

In 1833, Black Hawk dictated *The Autobiography of Black Hawk* to interpreter Antoine LeClaire. The brief work, told in native idiom, describes the Sauk's coming-to-knowledge of the dangers of Fort Madison and its cannon. In addition to chronicling the events of war with white soldiers, Black Hawk also explains native courtship:

> He goes to the lodge when all are asleep (or pretend to be), lights his matches, which have been provided for the purpose, and soon finds where his intended sleeps. He then awakens her, and holds the light to his face that she may know him—after which he places the light close to her. If she blows it out, the ceremony is ended, and he appears in the lodge next morning, as one of the family. If she does not blow out the light, but leaves it to burn out, he retires from the lodge. (Black Hawk 1994, 35)

The ritual continues with flute playing, by which the young man indicates which girl he wants as a wife. Black Hawk claims that his people thoroughly discuss felicity of living arrangements rather than allow their youth to marry hastily like whites and live in misery. Courtship ends with the crane dance, which lasts several days.

A crucial segment of Black Hawk's apologia is the myth of the corn woman, who presented the Sauks corn, tobacco, and beans, and his core belief that land cannot be sold. In his philosophy, the Great Spirit gave tribal grounds for native peoples to live on and cultivate. According to tradition, if Sauks desert the land, it is open to any other person to settle and maintain. He asserts his concept of ownership: "Nothing can be sold but such things as can be carried away." (ibid., 42) Black Hawk accuses whites of violating sacred Indian traditions by plying them with whiskey and cheating them while they are drunk. Anguished by the outcome of his complaints to Indian agents, he comments sagely, "How smooth must be the language of the whites, when they can make right look like wrong, and wrong like right." (ibid., 43)

In a thoughtful discussion of American cities, Black Hawk describes his carriage ride to New York and a favorable impression of architecture, railroads, ships, steamboats, and a hot-air balloon. Crowds present friendly faces, handshakes, and small gifts. At a reception, he marvels at fireworks, which remind him of a prairie fire. On the return trip, Black Hawk is eager to take charge of the tribal medicine bag, a symbol of his prestige. He is mortified to learn that he must follow Keokuk's direction.

The final paragraphs of Black Hawk's autobiography concern his opinions about an end to Negro slavery. After some thought, he suggests that free states remove black males to slave states and that the president buy all female slaves in slave states and sell them to people in free states. The end of the propagation of slaves will halt servitude of blacks. Generously he offers to take any unwanted servants to help Sauk women grow corn. In his eagerness to depart for the hunting grounds, Black Hawk urges "village criers" to publish a rebuttal of false accusations that the Sauk kill white women and children. He hopes that all who shake his hand will know it is a hand that has never been raised against noncombatants. (Black Hawk 1955, 1994; Drake 1851; Graymont 1972; Gurko 1970; Lamar 1977; Patterson and Snodgrass 1994; Straub 1996; Waldman 1990)

See also oratory, Native American.

BOJER, JOHAN

A literary colleague of O. E. Rölvaag, Johan Bojer (pronounced boi' yuhr) was a Norwegian novelist who observed the effects of American pioneer life on Scandinavian emigrants during his visit to the plains in 1923. Sometimes called an American author by adoption, Bojer has been compared to Harold Bell Wright as a novelist of piety. Like Rölvaag and Willa Cather, Bojer analyzed the physical and mental hardships that compounded the difficult task of homesteading on the prairie, where nature was as great an adversary of enterprise as loneliness and self-doubt. In a time of harsh realism, skepticism, and disillusion, he imposed on his subjects a guarded optimism. His masterly Norwegian-American saga, *The Emigrants* (1924), was written in Norwegian, but has entered the canon of American frontier literature in its standard English translation, completed by A. G. Jayne in 1925.

Bojer was no stranger to hard work. He was born in poverty and shame in Orkeskalsøren, Trøndelag, on March 6, 1872. The illegitimate son of a servant, he was fathered by a businessman and lived with foster parents, who worked the land of the Rein estate, which overlooked the Trondheimsfjord. Bojer grew up in sight of the homes of prosperous families, who stood before him as a challenge and a reminder of his limited economic and educational circumstances. He was an outdoorsman from childhood and studied at Dybdahl's country school, to which his father paid tuition. Steeped in the mores of the agrarian-fishing community, he understood the cycles and demands of industry that must rely on the whim of nature. After serving in the army for three years and attending an army business school in Trondheim, he worked at fishing and selling for an exporter in the Lofoten Islands before attempting freelance technical writing for an ad agency. Influenced by free public lectures on literature and by his vast reading in Henrik Ibsen, Emile Zola, Victor Hugo, Guy de Maupassant, and Bjørnstern Bjørnson, he began writing professionally at the age of 24. Because he was willing to suffer poverty while building a reputation, he referred to himself as a literary tramp.

In 1902, Bojer migrated to Paris on a modest bequest from his father and, for five years, worked as a newspaper correspondent. At ease among a coterie of expatriate writers and artists, he dispatched articles to Norwegian journals and, during his free time, indulged bohemian tastes in books and art. After traveling to other countries, including the United States, France, Italy, Denmark, Holland, Belgium, Germany, and England, in 1907 he settled his wife,

Ellen Lange, and their son and three daughters in Norway, but continued to think of France as his literary home. His output spanned more than a half century and extended to short fiction, verse, plays, articles, letters, and novels. He produced *A Procession* (1896), *The Eternal Strife* (1900), and *Mother Lea* (1900) before attaining respect from the French academy for *The Power of a Lie* (1908). In addition to *The Emigrants,* his best-known fictional works include *The Prisoner Who Sang* (1913), *The Great Hunger* (1918), *The Last of the Vikings* (1921), *The Everlasting Struggle* (1931), *Folk by the Sea* (1931), *The King's Men* (1940), and *Skyld* (1948).

Although Bojer supported no political party, he studied social and political forces in the lives of ordinary people and produced deep, philosophical works that have been characterized as novels of ideas. *The Emigrants* displays Bojer's idealism in his depiction of human efforts to subdue a hostile environment. Set in the American West in the late nineteenth century, the novel describes a mismatched band of settlers who leave Norway by steamer to follow Erik Foss, their leader, to America, where they establish the Nidaros Settlement. Among the pioneers are Jo Berg, a teacher and ne'er-do-well; the well-meaning Skarets, Kal and Karen; Per Föll, a young worker given to depression; and Ola Vatne, a jolly fiddler and farm laborer just out of prison on charges of setting fire to his employer's property. The cause of Ola's discontent is evident in his shipboard marriage to his employer's daughter, Else, a pampered darling and member of the landed gentry. Another odd pair of emigrants are Föll and his new wife, Anne Gunnarsdatter Ramsöy, a spinster who has conceived a child by her madcap lover, Klaus Broch, a doctor's son. Amid local gossip and speculation, the eight adult emigrants and four children ready for the journey and board the passenger liner at the Bergen quay.

Bojer describes his settlers as constantly working for a few more dollars to offset their expenses. In their first home in Wisconsin, the emigrants scrimp and work—the men at a lumber mill, the women at cooking and domestic chores—to increase their savings. By the next spring, they have come to know each other like family and they set out by rail to Northville in the Dakota Territory, which was officially established in 1861. The group then braves the wild grassland in five prairie schooners. Foss directs them to the Red River Valley, a likely stretch of virgin plain that he had visited on his earlier journey to America. Along the way, Bojer blends the good with the bad: over undulating sweeps of grassy loam rich with earthy fragrance, they keep watch for rattlesnakes. Their ponderous oxen plod past the skeleton of a buffalo, a reminder of the virtual extinction of wild herds that once roamed the plains in great number. In the privacy of her thoughts, Else ponders the decision to marry beneath her status and makes the best of her lot by singing "Oh, Susanna, oh! don't you cry for me!" (Bojer 1991, 73)

Bojer connects the Norwegians to American plains history by commenting on the desolate road they travel:

> It struck them now for the first time that they had got so far out into the wild prairie that they could no longer see a soul. Every trace of man had vanished.

Up to now they had followed two ruts worn by the wagons of the Hudson's Bay trappers who every year sent their caravans across the plains of the West. Now even these had disappeared. They stood stockstill, gazing at the scene. (ibid., 77)

Upon arrival on a lush sward, each of the five families selects a parcel from Erik's platte map. The author continues to probe their varied motivations and characters by contrasting the style and speed with which they settle in, harvest grass for fodder, and cut squares of sod to frame huts. Anne and Else discuss their concerns about childbirth so far from a doctor or midwife. Petty social distinctions that once separated them seem unimportant in the new land, where they need each other and where they share the hymns and folklore of Norway to stave off homesickness.

Disasters pile up alongside lighter moments in Bojer's realistic recounting of an incipient community. Karen overcomes dizziness and fear after she spies the brownie that brought luck in the old country. Her daughter Siri presides over the formal banns and wedding for a bull and cow. Bojer swells to terrifying proportions a formidable foe—a prairie fire that drives geese, ducks, cranes, hares, coyotes, and hissing rattlers ahead of its path. Kal halts his plowing and gazes in confusion. To him, "it looked as if the plain were on fire beneath the surface; little tongues of flame burst out here and there, then a huge sheet of flame leaped high into the air." (ibid., 127) Using plowed fire brakes and counter fires, the emigrants survive and struggle to reunite children with their parents in the wake of disaster. They draw together, overjoyed that their homes and livestock are spared and awed by the random destruction that flashes on its way over the horizon.

Bojer endows Erik Foss with the vision that prairie tradition expects of a pathfinder. He foresees that the Dakota plains will become "one of the richest corn-growing lands in the world," yet he must acknowledge that pioneers pay dearly for success. He fears that they cannot hold out against more disasters. Coming upon stripped human skulls arranged in a semicircle, he recognizes the burden of leadership on chiefs of the Plains Indians. He mutters, "Now I know!" (ibid., 137) The omens come true: Else confronts an Indian who boldly enters her living quarters and steals a tobacco box before departing from her hut. Foss threatens to oust Ola, the "rum dog," for squandering his money and bullock in drinking and gambling. Jo Berg, the schoolmaster, teaches the children from newspapers and a few books and wrestles with the historic truths that the Vikings were really pirates and that Christianity "was beaten, hacked, and branded into people, that those missionary kings were simply butchers and knaves." (ibid., 157) Without stint, each emigrant faces troubles and threats to peace of mind that grow out of proportion as a result of the isolation and estrangement of foreigners.

Bojer invokes irony to express the random fate of the group's experimental community. Foss, the sheepherder who ponders the destiny of his little band, dies of gangrene after pursuing his livestock over frozen turf. Lead of the remaining homesteaders passes to Morten Kvidal, who had staggered in vain over the prairie for six days in search of help for Foss. In the role of purchasing agent, he journeys to town and hears of new waves of settlers:

> Farmers from the Eastern States had sold out and were moving westward, drawn by the lure of the prairie. For a long time the settlers had mistrusted the open country, where they could get neither timber nor fire-wood; but now they had changed their minds. After all, it was tempting to go where there were no stones or tree stumps to clear away, and you could put in the plow at once. (ibid., 173)

On his return with proof that others favor their experiment, he encounters more troubles. Per Föll, who finds his wife entertaining a bachelor and falls into a "fit of the sulks," wanders the wild and is reduced to insanity. (ibid., 246) He languishes in a madhouse until his death, when he is buried alongside Erik Foss as the Norwegians' second fatality.

By telescoping time and covering the passage of years in less detail, Bojer rushes toward the end of the first generation of the Nidaros Settlement. He contrasts the old and new countries after Morten returns to the fatherland. Local expectations of wealth and prestige require that the returning Norwegian play the part of the American entrepreneur, but he keeps to himself the bad news about Per. Before he returns to America, his brother Simen writes that North Dakota has achieved statehood, which occurred in 1889. Morten arrives in Dakota with Bergitta, his new wife. His settled band works at establishing themselves as American citizens. Their church draws other settlers. The author introduces a shift from altruism to greed after Kal Skaret grows wealthy from broad acreage planted in grain. He becomes a miser and conceals enough wheat to keep his family from starving in hard times.

Bojer focuses more strongly on Morten, whose experiences express the bittersweet joy of leaving home and succeeding in a foreign land. In old age, he continues to lead the Nidaros Settlement, although he grows too feeble to farm and departs from the agrarian community to work as a railroad agent and banker. After his wife dies and the explosion of a carbide lamp blinds him, solitude overwhelms him. He longs for the old country and listens to his grandson read aloud during his dark hours. He returns to Norway and finds his relatives dead. To Bojer, the duality of the emigrant's life defines Morten's existence: "If you came back, you wanted to leave again; if you went away, you longed to come back. Wherever you were, you could hear the call of the homeland." (ibid., 351) The family's Norwegian property remains intact, but he realizes that his children and future lie in America. In a bright vision, he sees a woman sowing. From the land springs a vigorous crop of young men and women. At last, he understands the identity of the sower and the purpose of the sowing.

Bojer acquired an international coterie of supporters in the 1920s and earned international acclaim for his sweeping, epic approach to folk life and to his depth of description. Champions John Galsworthy and Rabindranath Tagore listed him among the era's most acute portrayers of human passions and foibles, both of which help to shape the pioneer experience in *The Emigrants*. However, because of Bojer's intense scrutiny of a full panoply of social and religious issues, the critics of his native land relegated him to mediocrity, chastising him repeatedly for lack of style, shallow characterization, and incomprehensible motivation. His last publications were autobiographical: *Apprentice* (1942) and *Journeyman* (1946). He died in Oslo on July 3, 1959, 30 years after his talents had peaked. Critics have labeled him a congenial humanist significantly out of touch with the modern era, and his impact on American frontier literature remains occluded by the wooden translation of his Norwegian text and by the greater reputation of fellow Norwegian O. E. Rölvaag, whose *Giants in the Earth* overshadows Bojer's work. (Bojer 1974, 1991; Gad 1974; Klein 1981; Kunitz 1942; Magill 1958; Smith 1947)

See also Cather, Willa; Rölvaag, O. E.; Wright, Harold Bell.

BOONE, DANIEL

The prototypical frontiersman, Daniel Boone is a formidable icon of American strength, an emblem of foresight. No other name rings so true to the national image of the trailblazer. His exploits are the stuff that folklore feeds on. He set the example for the Boy Scouts of America, an early version of which was known as the Sons of Daniel Boone. So much has been written about his life, leadership, and adventures that historians surmise that his canon grew at the storyteller's whim, for colorful stories about other woodsmen and Indian fighters sounded better when linked to the famed Kentucky settler.

Boone came from a Quaker family of skilled crafters and traders prominent in North Carolina, Kentucky, Pennsylvania, and Missouri. He is usually portrayed in fiction as a simple, semiliterate woodsman and hunter. However, the stereotype of the two-fisted Indian fighter is too confining to accommodate his service as a statesman, land speculator, and leader. Born November 2, 1734, the sixth of the 11 children of Squire and Sarah Morgan Boone, he lived in a log farmhouse in Exeter, Pennsylvania, then moved with his peripatetic family to the Shenandoah Valley in 1750 and south two years later to the Yadkin Valley, North Carolina's western frontier, where his brother Squire owned farmland. Boone's teen experiences include sharpshooting, hunting, tracking, and driving wagons for General Edward Braddock's forces at Fort Duquesne in Pittsburgh.

Although Boone received little education, he bettered himself by learning wilderness skills. In 1756, he married Rebecca Bryan, mother of their ten children, and settled in Rowan County, but he often left home to explore as far south as Pensacola, Florida. Boone learned from John Finley of the beauties of "Kentucke." Ostensibly for Rebecca and the children, he built four more homes along the Yadkin River, the last at Halmans Ford (southeast of Boone, North Carolina). Lengthy hunting expeditions into the Blue Ridge Mountains over a nine-year period brought him to Abingdon, Virginia, and closer to Kentucky.

Boone's assistance in maintaining Anglo-Indian relations cast him in the role of administrator in 1774 when a local Cherokee tribe sold 20 million acres to the Transylvania Company in exchange for $50,000 worth of goods. Boone headed the wagon train that ferried the merchandise west to Watauga. Another task put Boone in charge of the defense of Fort Dobbs (Statesville, North Carolina) before he planned his first trip to Kentucky. While following Warrior's Trace, a Cherokee war trail to northern tribes now immortalized as the "wilderness road," he arrived in pristine country teeming with game. In his mid-eighties, he is quoted as saying:

> I have traveled over many new countries in the great Mississippi Valley; I have critically examined their soils; their mineral wealth; their healthful climates; their manufacturing situation; and the commercial advantages given them by nature. I have discovered where these endowments were given most bountifully in many localities, singly and in groups, but I have never found but one Kentucky—a spot of earth where nature seems to have concentrated all her bounties. (Botkin 1944, 279)

The land resolved his quandary: how to roam free and hunt game while bearing the family man's responsibility. The answer lay in the abundant animal life and peaceful meadows of the Cumberland Gap. Reunited with his family after a three-year absence, he resolved to settle them in Kentucky.

After selling their property and assembling a train of five families, the Boones moved northwest, losing six settlers to Indian attack on the way. Among them was one of Boone's sons. The inauspicious beginning temporarily halted resettlement. In 1775, a group of investors hired Boone to mark a trail to Kentucky and build a fort that developed into Fort Boonesboro near Harrodsburg. To preserve his holdings, he fought Shawnee along Licking River and recovered from them his daughter Jemima and two other females, an event that served as the model for action in James Fenimore Cooper's *The Last of the Mohicans*. In 1778, Boone, too, was captured at a salt lick and held from February until September. During his residence among tribe members, Chief Blackfish came to value him and adopted him as a replacement for his dead son. To prevent Blackfish from raiding his fort, Boone escaped to rally the community, which survived a two-week siege. Following a year's retreat to North Carolina, he set out in 1779 to build a new settlement, Boone's Station, near Athens on the Kentucky River. In forcing back the frontier, he paid a continual price of vigilance against Cherokee attacks, which killed his brother Edward in 1780 and his son Israel in 1782.

A tall, lanky, ruggedly handsome man, Boone served the state militia as lieutenant colonel during the Revolutionary War and was elected to the Virginia legislature in 1781, 1787, and 1791. When peace was assured, the Boone family moved to Maysville, Kentucky, where Daniel opened a tavern and worked part-time as county surveyor and land agent. Already renowned for pluck and optimism, he learned of his first biography, *The Adventures of Col. Daniel Boon [sic], Containing Narrative of the Wars of Kentucke* (1784), a romanticized story written by Pennsylvania schoolteacher and land speculator John Filson. Boone was flattered by the melodrama, which includes absurdly flowery dialect, such as this unlikely citation:

> Thus situated, many hundred miles from our families in the howling wilderness, I believe few would have equally enjoyed the happiness we experienced. I often observed to my brother, You see now how little nature requires to be satisfied. Felicity, the companion of content, is rather found in our own breasts than in the enjoyment of external things: And I firmly believe it requires but a little philosophy to make a man happy in whatsoever state he is. (Rose 1995)

In 1789, Boone moved his family to Point Pleasant on the Ohio River, where he earned his living by supplying the military. A poor businessman, he abandoned contracting and returned to hunting at his new home in Charleston, West Virginia.

Advancing age did not halt Boone's wanderlust. In his late sixties, he was arrested for debt and suffered a serious hunting accident. He continued to push west to Femme Osage, Missouri, where he received a land grant, accepted Spanish citizenship, and was appointed syndic by the Spanish governor. He lost most of his claims after the United States acquired the land through the Louisiana Purchase, but successfully petitioned Congress for 850 acres near St. Louis, Missouri, in 1814. Late in his life, he held a judgeship in St. Charles County, Missouri, where he was living with his son Nathan when he died on September 26, 1820. The bodies of Rebecca and Daniel Boone were moved to Frankfort, Kentucky, in 1845.

In 1813, Daniel Bryan, a distant relative and champion of Daniel Boone, ignored the fact that Boone and his followers fled the fussy refinements of civilization and its onerous taxes. The poet chose to extol him with *The Mountain Muse: Comprising the Adventures of Daniel Boone; and the Power of Virtuous and Refined Beauty*, an ambitious epic poem composed in high Miltonic style. Crediting the unlettered woodsman with bestowing enlightenment on Kentucky, Bryan proclaims the reign of freedom, science, and religious truth, which counterbalance the dangers of cruelty, death, and superstition. He lauds "the Glowing Guardians, fill'd with views sublime/Their lofty minds, their enterprising power awak'd" and honors Boone's enterprise in bringing "Politic Wisdom" to "Columbia." (ibid.)

A flood of Boone material—both erudite and down-to-earth—continued through the nineteenth century. The works typify the era's tendency toward long, involved titles. The year of Boone's death, Samuel L. Metcalfe published *A Collection of Some of the Most Interesting Narratives of Indian Warfare in the West, Containing an Account of the Adventures of Daniel Boone, One of the First Settlers of Kentucky* (1820), in which the author casts Boone as a skilled negotiator and defender of settlers from wilderness perils. Two decades later, J. B. Jones wrote *Wild Western Scenes; A Narrative of Adventures in the Western Wilderness, Forty Years Ago; Wherein the Conduct of Daniel Boone, the Great American Pioneer, Is Particularly Described* (1841), a frontier thriller replete with heroic deeds. In 1851,

Frontiersman Daniel Boone wrote best-selling memoirs and anecdotes.

George Caleb Bingham accentuated the prevailing reverence for Boone's heroism with a dramatic painting depicting the arrival of settlers to Kentucky via the Cumberland Road. Vivid chiaroscuro shows Boone in the lead and Rebecca sidesaddle on his horse in a Madonna-like pose. The dark, forbidding landscape implies that the settlers moved resolutely through danger and dispelled the gloom of the wild by importing the light of civilization. In 1854, Timothy Flint published *The First White Man of the West, or the Life and Exploits of Col. Dan'l. Boone, the First Settler of Kentucky; Interspersed with Incidents in the Early Annals of the Country.* In prose and verse, Flint lauded the settlement of Boonesboro, which he proclaimed "the garden of the West" in token of its Edenic qualities. (ibid.)

In addition to biographies, the majority of overviews of the early frontier feature the prototypical figure of the Kentucky woodsman. W. H. Bogart comes close to conveying a believable image of Boone in *Daniel Boone and the Hunters of Kentucky* (1857). Bogart is hesitant to claim that Boone intentionally blazed a trail or built a segment of Western civilization. To prove his point, he stresses the nation's need for a hero, who was invented out of frontier episodes that suited the purpose of the mythmaker. A regressive step in Boone biography appeared in 1884 in Edward S. Ellis's *The Life and Time of Col. Daniel Boone, Hunter, Soldier, and Pioneer,* which returns to the image of the wise, honest woodsman, led by God to establish America's right to the frontier. Theodore Roosevelt's *The Winning of the West* (1889) credits Boone with the love of solitude in the wild and with furthering the expansion of white settlement far from the seaboard, thus weaning the nation from ties with Europe. In addition, Boone was the model for Natty Bumppo, the virtuous loner of Cooper's Leatherstocking Tales.

In the twentieth century, Boone's myth holds steady, particularly among the young. Stewart Edward White's inspirational biography *Daniel Boone: Wilderness Scout* (1922) tempted young boys to elevate their sights by following the revered trailblazer's example. In contrast to the monumental Boone, poets Rosemary and Stephen Vincent Benét depicted him as a destroyer in *A Book of Americans* (1933) with an enigmatic four-line stanza:

> When Daniel Boone goes by, at night,
> The phantom deer arise
> And all lost, wild America
> Is burning in their eyes.

More often positive than denigrating, the Daniel Boone legend has served notable outdoor dramas, particularly Jan Hartman's *The Legend of Daniel Boone* in Harrodsburg, Kentucky, and Kermit Hunter's *Horn in the West* (1952) in Boone, North Carolina, which describes Boone's role in aiding settlers during social and political turmoil that accompanied the Revolutionary War. (Benet and Benet 1933; Botkin 1944; "Daniel Boone" 1996; "Daniel Boone: American Pioneer" 1996; Faragher 1995; Gislason 1996b; Lamar 1977; Rose 1995; Waldman 1990; Wilson and Ferris 1989)

See also Cooper, James Fenimore; Hunter, Kermit; theater of the frontier.

BORLAND, HAL

Famous for his young adult novel, *When the Legends Die* (1963), Hal Borland earned a reputation for the sympathetic treatment of a difficult subject: the coming-of-age of a young Indian in a bicultural plains society. Borland was a multitalented writer alternately identified as nature and conservation activist, radio and film scriptwriter, poet, polemicist, editor, columnist, and freelance fiction writer. Born May 14, 1900, in Stirling, Nebraska, he claimed ancestors who had helped to populate the American plains. As he describes in his autobiography, *High, Wide, and Lonesome* (1956), his parents, William Arthur "Will" Borland and Sarah Clinaberg Borland, were homesteaders. In 1910, the family settled in remote Brush, Colorado, and struggled with debt after extensive family illness depleted their savings. In the worst of times, his mother parceled out their meals from pots of beans simmered over a cow-chip fire.

Borland learned from his father the trade of editor and master printer. After the family bought a newspaper in Flagler, he entered the U.S. Naval Reserve and attended the University of Colorado from 1918 to 1920, studying chemical engineering and English. In his early twenties, he wrote for United Press and King Features Service. After earning a degree in journalism from Columbia University, he migrated among newspaper offices in Salt Lake City, Carson City, Fresno, San Diego, and Marshall, Texas, and served in varied capacities at the Denver *Post*, Flagler *News*, Stratton, Colorado, *Press*, Philadelphia *Morning Sun*, Philadelphia *Morning Ledger*, Torrington, Connecticut, *Register*, Brooklyn *Times*, and *New York Times*. From books published under the pseudonym Ward West, Borland gained critical praise for his Thoreauvian descriptions of topography and animals in the wild. He was named director of the Rocky Mountain Writers' Conference in 1955. Two years later he was honored by the Secondary Education Board and won the Westerners Buffalo award for his autobiography.

In 1963, the Reader's Digest Book Club featured *When the Legends Die*, Borland's classic story of alienation. Focusing on the identity crisis of Thomas Black Bull, a Ute who progresses from misfit schoolboy to national rodeo star, Borland inverts the usual Western by moving his developing character east. The only son of a native couple living on Bald Mountain near the Arboles Reservation in southwestern Colorado, Tom is secure. An idyllic expedition takes the family hunting, fishing, berry picking, and smoking meat. Because their actions violate reservation rules, Tom's father, George Black Bull, an unsophisticated sawmill worker, ends their life in the wild and moves to Pagosa to save for the family's return to the reservation. But the father's murder of a thief forces his wife, Bessie, to flee to an abandoned bear den on Horse Mountain with five-year-old Tom, where the family lives the traditional Ute life. Fearing arrest, George Black Bull remains out of sight in the wild and uses the oportunity to supervise his son's education in native survival skills. Following the example of George and Bessie, Tom grows wise in native husbandry:

> [George] taught the boy to set snares for rabbits. Then, when the drifts lay
> deep and the cold shriveled the rocks and shrank the days, she kept the stew

pot full and simmering. She made winter moccasins and winter leggings and shirts, and when she had done these things she wove baskets. And she told the old tales and sang the old songs. (Borland 1989, 19)

Borland elucidates how the white world begins its insidious intrusion on Tom's family. Blue Elk, an Indian emissary and troublemaker, insists that the couple marry and have Tom baptized. The complexity of biculturalism overcomes Tom after his parents die and he enters a restrictive reservation school at Ignacio. Borland parallels Tom's dilemma with an episode in which authorities force him to free his pet bear. Tom begins a pattern of rebellion and running away. He finds that Blue Elk has ended Tom's ties with home in the wild by burning the Black Bull family's lodge:

[Tom] stood among the ashes and whispered his sorrow chant, not even saying it aloud. For small griefs you shout, but for big griefs you whisper or say nothing. The big griefs must be borne alone, inside. (ibid., 70)

On his last flight from authority, he, like the bear, is overpowered and returned to the agency in shackles. He fails at paperwork and plowing, but excels at cobbling, leather work, and basketry. To assure Tom a trade, the school dispatches him to the tutelage of Albert Left Hand, a sheepherder.

The serendipitous rise in Tom's fortunes comes from a trip to Bayfield to trade hides. Red Dillon admires Tom's horsemanship and hires him to break broncos on a ranch in New Mexico. Red's opportunism becomes clear after he forces Tom to throw competitions. For several seasons, Red squires Tom across the southwestern rodeo circuit, alternately winning and squandering Tom's winnings on liquor. After he establishes a name for himself as Tom Black, he abandons Red and competes honestly, but earns a reputation for riding horses to death. Stardom gives place to a downward spiral as Tom loses his sense of self and is badly injured at Madison Square Garden. The name "horse killer" violates the reverence for nature that he learned in the wild.

At a crucial point in Tom's maturity, Borland returns him to the Southwest. While recuperating, Tom courts Nurse Mary Redmond, who teaches him to walk again and attempts to set him up in his own apartment. Out of step with the East, Tom bolts for Pagosa, takes a herding post on Horse Mountain, and relearns the old ways by weaving a basket, stalking a cinnamon bear, and recalling the songs, superstitions, and legends of childhood. Borland forces his character to undergo a transformation that reacclimates him spiritually and emotionally to the wild. He strips the residue of white culture from him like layers of an onion. For the first time comfortable with his adult native self, Tom reflects on his coming-of-age:

Now he knew that time lays scars on a man like a chipmunk's stripes, paths that lead from where he is now back to where he came from, from the eyes of his knowing to the tail of his remembering. (ibid., 215)

At home in the land where his father taught him the strengths of manhood, he acknowledges the Ute self that he had denied. He accepts past events that shaped him, for "They are the ties that bind a man to his own being, his small part of the round."

In 1972, Twentieth Century-Fox filmed *When the Legends Die,* starring Richard Widmark and Frederic Forrest. From 1967 to 1978, Borland edited *Audubon Magazine* and published his last memoir, *A Place to Begin: The New England Experience.* He and wife Barbara moved to an isolated spot near Salisbury, Connecticut, on the Housatonic River, far from the misery and confinement of city life. At his death from emphysema on February 24, 1978, Borland had won the Meeman award for conservation, Interpretive Naturalists award, an Outstanding Science Books for Children award, John Burroughs Medal for nature writing, an honorary doctorate from the University of Colorado, the president's tribute, and a tribute from the *Congressional Record.* He left his manuscripts to Yale University's Beinecke Library. A nature trail in Sharon, Connecticut, honors his passion for the outdoors. (Adkins 1968; "Author" 1978; Bell 1984; "A Bit" 1964; *Books for Children* 1966; Borland 1956, 1963, 1989; Carlsen 1967; Devlin 1964; "Farewell" 1978; "Hal Borland" 1978; Perkins et al. 1991; Snodgrass 1995b)

See also Native Americans in literature.

BROWN, DEE

One of America's most distinguished authorities on the West, Dee Alexander Brown is a noted storyteller and author of 30 adult and juvenile works of fiction, history, and chronicle, most of which focus on either the Civil War, Native Americans, or the American frontier. As he explains in his autobiographical *When the Century Was Young* (1993), he feels a greater kinship with the nineteenth century, the time of Buffalo Bill Cody, Teddy Roosevelt, "Mrs. George Armstrong Custer, and real cowboys and Indians, including Hollow-Horn Bear, the Sioux chief whose face appeared on a postage stamp after his death." (Brown 1993, 9) Brown's ability to resituate his spirit in the past has proved a blessing to history and literature, for his patient, reflective studies of significant moments in the white settlement of the Plains has produced some of the most influential commentary on Indian and cavalry history.

An iconoclast, Brown has enjoyed a 40-year career as an archivist, teacher, and humanitarian who departs from the accepted notions about America's past. His most impressive chronicle, *Bury My Heart at Wounded Knee: An Indian History of the American West* (1970), challenges established notions of manifest destiny and condemns a favorite era of American lore as rampant imperialism and the cause of displacement and manifold miseries to a targeted population of native tribes. The book has earned prominence among multicultural classics as a reputable reference source and the first of a deluge of retrospectives on American Plains settlement from a nonwhite point of view. While contemplating the westering movement, Brown surmised that writers centered on white immigrants in the West to the exclusion of an equal number of Indians who were making the same move, although under duress rather than by choice. After intense research among speeches, maps, duty rosters, treaties, and memoirs on both sides, Brown concluded that an American epic needed writing.

He added that his perusal of military reports reflects falsification in the number and significance of army victories over Native Americans.

Brown's open-mindedness on race relations with Indians began in boyhood. The son of lumberman and sawyer Daniel Alexander and Lula Cranford Brown, he was born February 28, 1908, in Alberta, Louisiana. After his father's death, the family settled in Stevens, Arkansas. When he was four years old, his maternal grandmother, Elizabeth Cranford, recounted episodes of the Civil War and narrated adventures of Brown's great-grandfather, who hunted with Davy Crockett. Along the way, she taught Brown reading, the impetus to a love of source material and research that became a career.

In his mid-teens, the family lived with an aunt in Little Rock, Arkansas, where Brown attended high school. In his spare time, he haunted the public library and the baseball park and developed a friendship with Moses Yellowhorse, an Osage pitcher who threw him balls to trade for tickets to home games. Friendship with an Indian altered Brown's attitude toward stereotypical shoot-'em-up movies. After learning to set type, he and his cousin bought a handpress and published a four- to eight-page newspaper, which preceded his work as a cub reporter for the Harrison, Arkansas, *Times*. At a time when he had no interest in college and intended to become a professional printer, he began writing for fun and sold his first published title, a baseball story, to *Blue Book*, a dime pulp thriller magazine, for $100. He moved on to library work in Conway, Arkansas, where, as a student aide, he first shelved and cataloged historical documents.

While Brown was studying at Arkansas State Teachers College in the mid-1930s, his mentor, Dean McBrien, taught him to value primary sources. Brown learned to carry research to the original photo, map, diary, manuscript, or report by locating early documents in libraries, private collections, or state historical and genealogical societies. Put off by the slow pace of interlibrary loan and the inefficiency of the Smithsonian Institution, National Archives, and Library of Congress, he preferred searching shelves, a haphazard process enhanced by background knowledge, instinct, and luck. To encourage Brown, McBrien hired him to drive his Model T Ford on summer junkets to Indian reservations, where Brown studied the physical setting and interviewed survivors of the Indian wars either directly or through reliable interpreters. While working as an assistant librarian at the U.S. Department of Agriculture in the mid-1930s, he attended George Washington University and earned a degree in library science.

During a stint as librarian at a research center in Beltsville, Maryland, Brown submitted published short stories to McIntosh and Otis, two New York literary agents. They suggested that he attempt longer works. He supplied them with a satire on Washington bureaucracy; however, he completed the work at the end of 1941, when pro-government sympathies ruled out anything derogatory about FDR's administration. The failure of his first effort proved negligible. Three decades after his grandmother told him stories of Davy Crockett, Brown crafted the unpublished episodes into a novel, *Wave High the Banner* (1945), a deliberately cheerful, patriotic work. He portrays the legendary frontiersman as energetic, noble, and dedicated to the task of moving civilization west. In a song he sings to himself while he marches along, Crockett sounds the credo of the American cavalier:

Droop not, brother, as we go
Over the mountains, westward ho,
Under boughs of mistletoe
Log huts we'll rear.

In lusty masculine style, the verse concludes with the pioneer's watchword: "keep our rifles ready, boys, Aha!" (Brown 1945, 12) The call turns to a desperate cry in the final chapter when Crockett, Abram Henry, and brave Texans face the surge of General Antonio Santa Anna's warriors over the barricades of the Alamo. Though clumsy and overcharged with drama, the novel reveals attention to historical detail, Brown's greatest strength.

Brown's service in the army during World War II prefaced a significant turning point in his immersion in frontier history. During basic training at Camp Forrest, Tennessee, he quizzed an expert, Major James Warner Bellah, on Indian guerrilla war tactics. (Ironically, after the war, as Brown was developing his own expertise in Western lore, Bellah was entertaining the public with screenplays for "Fort Apache" (1948), "She Wore a Yellow Ribbon" (1949), and "Rio Grande" (1950), all John Ford film classics.) As a member of the 80th Infantry, Brown fought in World War II and formed a friendship with army mate Martin Schmitt, a librarian, editor, and curator. Inspired by their mutual enthusiasm for the frontier, especially antique photos of Western events, they co-authored three books: *Fighting Indians of the West* (1948), *Trail Driving Days* (1952), and *The Settlers West* (1955).

After the war, Brown moved to the Technical Information Branch Library of the army's Aberdeen Proving Ground in Maryland to manage classified archival data for the War Department. During his 26-year post as agriculture reference librarian and, from 1962 to 1975, as professor and research specialist at the University of Illinois at Urbana-Champaign, he earned a master's degree while working in the country's third largest university library. While editing *Agriculture History,* he squirreled away cartons of file cards in no particular order and drew on them for a variety of articles on Western themes for *American History Illustrated, Esquire, Christian Science Monitor, Civil War Times, Southern Magazine,* and *Hinterland.* He admits that he used his private trove to write Westerns such as *Yellowhorse* (1957) for profit, although one of his works, *Galvanized Yankees* (1963), lost him money. The book grew out of Brown's research from a rare autobiography by an army volunteer and is prized as the first serious treatment of Confederate soldiers who enlisted in the Union army after being captured.

A more profitable venture was *The Gentle Tamers: Women of the Old Wild West* (1958), which cites the contributions and mishaps of known and obscure frontierswomen: rodeo rider Tillie Baldwin, temperance activist Carry Nation, gunfighter Rose of Cimarron, teamster Arizona Mary, teacher Martha Summerhayes, Ute captive Josephine Meeker, suffragist Clarina Irene Nichols,

Wyoming Justice of the Peace Esther McQuigg Morris, Virginia City madame Julia Bulette, cross-dressing soldier Loretta Valasquez, actresses Lola Montez and Lotta Crabtree, memoirist Elizabeth Custer, and Donner party victim Virginia Reed. The illustrated work enumerates diverse bits of information about women during the westering movement:

> They traveled westward not only in covered wagons but on river boats, in army ambulances, in jolting railway cars, aboard sailing ships to Panama and by muleback across the Isthmus, or around Cape Horn to San Francisco, and some of them even walked, pushing handcarts before them. (Brown 1958, 14–15)

According to Brown, nineteenth-century prudery hampered women by requiring pantaloons, slips, and modest dresses. Eventually, women freed themselves from Eastern customs and, clad in pants and boots, adapted to the dangers of Indians, snakes, and rugged country. The author cites a poignant grave marker for one victim, who is commemorated only as "Woman." (ibid., 17)

Brown credits women for the advent of cleanliness and order on the frontier and also with the foundation of cities, three strides he believes men would have left undone. Of this concerted effort to civilize, he muses:

> It was the males themselves, of course, who brought about the destruction of their lusty frontier hegemony. The very nature of their disheveled way of life precluded any organized division of labor among themselves. . . . No male was willing to hew wood, draw water, cook meals, or wash clothes for the other males. The habitations of these womanless men resembled pigsties and became favored haunts of fleas, rats, and other vermin. (ibid., 295)

Although Brown tends to portray women as a domestic commodity, *The Gentle Tamers* sold well to male and female readers, then rebounded to fame during the early days of the feminist movement.

In 1962, Brown returned to male-oriented Western history with *The Fetterman Massacre* (originally titled *Fort Phil Kearny: An American Saga*). A grueling recreation of events leading up to America's second major military wipeout, the history details the elements of the 1866 disaster after Sioux, Cheyenne, and Arapaho braves annihilated all 80 cavalrymen under the command of Lieutenant Colonel William J. Fetterman. Brown probed untapped sources—letters, eyewitnesses, and court testimony from a congressional investigation of Colonel Henry B. Carrington's role in the debacle. Critics lauded Brown for fairness and objectivity in exposing imaginative newspaper accounts as lies and in citing an inflammatory letter from the legendary frontiersman Jim Bridger predicting that "these Indians will not respect any treaty until they have been whipped into it." (Brown 1962, 217)

While working days, Brown labored nightly researching original documents, letters, treaty council records, newspaper articles, and journals and composing a new history of the plains. Dismayed that Westerns cast mostly European Americans as the main characters and relegated Indians to scenery, Brown focused on the dissension arising after native families were displaced from their homes and shoved onto reservations in remote spots and under unlivable conditions. He determined that the Indian diaspora deserved its own chronicle. The villains, in Brown's assessment, were hordes of government minions, fur traders, miners, entrepreneurs, ranchers, and land and railroad barons who demonized Indians as godless, bloodthirsty savages intent on scoring a kill. In recounting familiar episodes of frontier violence, he honored native leaders and warriors for battlefield strategy and for a bold, last-ditch effort to protect their families and hold on to hunting rights on ancestral lands.

Influenced by the mystical quality of Indian lore and by his reading of Lewis and Clark's diaries, John Dos Passos's *USA*, and Sherwood Anderson's slice-of-life midwestern stories, Brown wrote *Bury My Heart at Wounded Knee*, taking his title from the last line of Stephen Vincent Benét's poem "American Names." He became an adept spokesman for Native Americans. In interviews and subsequent writing, he disclosed a reprehensible motif of opportunism and treachery by Indian agents and the self-serving Bureau of Indian Affairs. He disclosed unpunished acts of desecration, arson, rape, infanticide, murder, and theft committed by settlers against Indian tribes inhabiting prime grazing land. In an overview, Brown described the westering movement as catastrophic for the Indians—an egregious misapplication of the white reverence for personal freedom. Stripping the era of glamour, he condemned white plains heroes for violence and greed and upbraided historians for romanticism and rationalization of wrongful acts.

Public reaction was swift and intense. Media interest in Brown's muckraking forced a nationwide reexamination of the settlement of the American West, which he depicts as a blatant land grab and unprecedented genocide. Scores of journals and newspapers published heated arguments about patriotic bias, racial superiority, and revisionism. Individuals accused Brown of exonerating savagery by belittling Western heroes such as General George Armstrong Custer, General William T. Sherman, and Colonel John Chivington and questioning the governance of Presidents Abraham Lincoln and Ulysses S. Grant.

Brown's supporters countered that his evenhanded study of the Native American point of view is a necessary correction of an era of chauvinism, missionary zeal, jingoism, and double-talk regarding Indian rights. His inclusion of interviews, oral biography, and evidence gleaned from 270 unpublished photographs of cavalry brutality encouraged historians to reevaluate pompous texts that heap honor on some of America's most duplicitous, genocidal military leaders. He also calls to account unscrupulous newspaper hacks intent on satisfying reader demand for bloody sagas from the West. Overall, reviewers admit that his study of native attitudes toward frontiersmen and cavalry set a precedent for historical analysis.

Brown followed *Bury My Heart* with a less severe chronicle, *Hear That Lonesome Whistle Blow: Railroads in the West* (1977), an exposé of railroad corruption. A repetition of his traditional themes, the chronicle cites multiple examples of white entrepreneurs discounting and overriding Indian rights to valuable land. He justifies Sitting Bull's angry backlash after work crews overran the Yellowstone Valley:

> The reason the surveyors had come into this area was that the owners of the Northern Pacific Railroad had decided to change its route, abandoning the line through previously ceded lands and invading unceded lands without any consultation with the Indians. (Brown 1977, 205)

These and other unflattering comments about arrogant rail owners and public policy so enraged the Association of American Railroads and Union Pacific that officials refused Brown access to their private library.

Brown next produced two novels, *Creek Mary's Blood* (1980), a blend of first- and third-person accounts of a female Georgia raider and of the forced exodus of members of her family to Western reservations, and *Killdeer Mountain* (1983), a less successful fictional study of a cavalry hero who fights the Sioux. Readers bought both, but *Bury My Heart at Wounded Knee* continued to draw the most critical attention. It began to appear on reading lists for high school and college courses in American history and was reissued in 1990, the centennial of the Wounded Knee Massacre. An eloquent blend of history and philosophy, Brown's famed reassessment of the Old West remains his masterwork. Now in his late eighties, he still writes about the frontier and challenges illusions of Western glory, which he characterizes as an attempt to rid North America of its aboriginal population. (Bevilacqua 1981; Brown 1945, 1958, 1962, 1970, 1977, 1993; Chepsiuk 1991; *Contemporary Authors* 1994; Courtmanche-Ellis 1978; Dahlin 1980; Lamar 1977; Waldman 1990)

See also Bury My Heart at Wounded Knee; Carrington, Henry B.; Crockett, Davy; Custer, George Armstrong.

🔯 *BURY MY HEART AT WOUNDED KNEE* 卐

A reflective treatise surveying the era following Lewis and Clark's expedition from South Dakota to Washington State, Dee Brown's noteworthy Western chronicle recounts white America's historical pattern: westering, trailblazing, profiteering, and subjugating and exterminating Native Americans. At the same time that European Americans were evolving a frontier mythology of the sodbuster, teamster, rancher, fur trader, mountaineer, riverboat gambler, prospector, hired gun, cavalryman, dance-hall queen, and cowpuncher, the white world was systematically plundering the aboriginal canon, restructuring history to fit Protestant orthodoxy, and obliterating the sacred grounds, craft and pictographic history, and territorial rights of native peoples. Indian contributions to oratory, poetry, myth, legend, biography, chronicle, fiction, theater, song, and hymn ebbed in a market glutted with dime thrillers, Wild West shows, and news hoaxes. Brown concludes, "This is not a cheerful book." (Brown 1970, xviii) He justifies the dismal data as an aid to understanding the squalor and despair of modern Indians.

In the opening chapter, Brown initiates a system of timeline and direct quotation followed by historical summary. He quotes Tecumseh's rhetorical question: where are the Pequot, Narragansett, Mohican, and Pokanoket, all extinct tribes who "have vanished before the avarice and the oppression of the White Man, as snow before a summer sun." (ibid., 1) Brown backtracks with a summary of the first meeting between Europeans and aborigines: Christopher Columbus initiates the looting and extermination of indigenous peoples with his misdirected voyage to India, a failed treasure hunt that unwittingly connects with the Taino on San Salvador. Unaware of the cultural significance of his find, Columbus believes he has located "Indians." The Spanish label them heathens and use their animistic rituals as an excuse to plunder and rape while ostensibly saving their souls through proselytism and baptism. Aborigines learn from experience that white adventurers are dangerous, particularly Indian fighter Andrew Jackson, who exerts presidential power to banish tribes from the East.

Dee Brown's disclosure of trickery and dishonor lists chronologically the misdeeds of some of the great Indian fighters of American lore, beginning with General Winfield Scott, who uproots the Cherokee in 1838 from ancestral homelands along the East Coast and sets them on a disastrous death march to the West. Politicians rationalize the despoliation of Indian territory as manifest destiny. The post–Civil War push of settlers gradually robs Indians of valuable land and forces them into shrinking plots of worthless desert and wilderness. Systematic military pressure precedes the alliances of the greatest Native American leaders: Crazy Horse, Sitting Bull, Gall, Spotted Tail, Dull Knife, Roman Nose, Satanta, Kicking Bird, Quanah Parker, Mangas Colorado, Geronimo, Cochise, Manuelito, Ouray, Captain Jack, Chief Joseph, Red Cloud, and Wovoka, the failed messiah. Both pathetic and thrilling in its prospectus, the chronicle depicts the best of times and the worst of times for some of America's notable Indians.

To characterize nineteenth-century racism, Brown outlines despicable events: Kit Carson forces Navajo sheepherders and farmers from Four Corners, Arizona, southeast to Bosque Redondo, New Mexico; the cavalry removes the Santee Sioux to Dakota Territory. Counter to these and other defeats run the victories of Red Cloud and Crazy Horse, who oppose the Bozeman Trail, which violates Indian territory by rationalizing a string of forts to protect white settlers on the way west. Generals Phil Sheridan and Joseph West restore the upper hand to the army by massacring Black Kettle and his peaceful band at their camp on the Washita River and by murdering Mangas Colorado, an Apache chief. By detailing repeated treaty infractions and denouncing Washington's failure to curb the military's killer tactics or to mete out fair judgment against frontier imperialism, Brown justifies mounting hostility on the plains.

According to Brown's logic, the most misunderstood white hero of the Indian wars is Custer, who faces a united plains force in all-out war. By luring him into a trap, Sioux and Cheyenne surround and slaughter his troops in 1876 at the Battle of the Little Bighorn, the climax of Brown's history. In a direct quote from Red Horse, these soldiers became foolish, many throwing away their guns and raising their hands, saying "Sioux, pity us; take us prisoners." The Sioux did not take a single soldier prisoner, but killed all of them; none were alive for even a few minutes. (ibid., 296)

Military retaliation for the slaughter forces other tribes into desperate situations. After the murder of Crazy Horse and the capture of Chief Joseph in 1877, more Indians die from hunger and disease. Brown depicts Dull Knife's band as desperate enough to contemplate mass suicide. At Fort Keogh, whiskey, boredom, and hopelessness demoralize Cheyenne captives, but bureaucrats fear that liberating potentially dangerous Indians will jeopardize the frontier economy. The most dramatic attempt at stabilizing the West is the hunt for Geronimo, the nation's most notorious—and most successful—guerrilla warrior. Brown describes his capture and incarceration in Florida as the nadir of Indian hopes for fair treatment.

In one of the rare humorous episodes of Western history, Sitting Bull accepts an invitation to speak at the completion of the Transcontinental Railroad. In his native tongue, he castigates whites, but the translator deliberately obscures his message. In a formal apologia for the Sioux, Sitting Bull makes a practical suggestion:

If a man loses anything and goes back and looks carefully for it he will find it, and that is what the Indians are doing now when they ask you to give them the things that were promised them in the past. (ibid., 425)

Sitting Bull explains that he feels hatred because whites treat his people like beasts. Brown returns to the dire tone of earlier chapters by stressing the indignity of Sitting Bull's role in Buffalo Bill Cody's Wild West Show, which brought catcalls of "Killer of Custer" from the audience.

According to *Bury My Heart at Wounded Knee*, Wovoka's messianic influence and the resultant Ghost Dance of 1890 are the beginning of the end for plains tribes. After multiple losses of lands and leaders, the ultimate blow falls at Wounded Knee. A pitiable photo of Big Foot frozen in death agony precedes an ironic benediction: on the chancel of the Episcopal mission chapel where survivors recuperated stretches a holiday banner: "PEACE ON EARTH, GOOD WILL TO MEN." Brown closes with Black Elk's pessimistic mysticism: "the nation's hoop is broken and scattered. There is no center any longer, and the sacred tree is dead." (ibid., 445, 446)

Brown's masterpiece provoked a surprising mix of academic criticism, pro and con. A cause célèbre among pro-Indian scholars for its journalistic objectivity, *Bury My Heart at Wounded Knee* insists that Americans come to terms with frontier policies of stolen land and broken promises. The work remains a best-seller, both in its original form and in Amy Erlich's abridgment for young adult readers, entitled *Wounded Knee: An American History of the Indian West* (1974). Reviewers praise Brown for meticulous authentication, including clothing, weapons, and mounts; interpretation of native remarks; even the seating arrangements, discourtesies, facial expressions, and gestures of hostile negotiators. Some laud the book's objectivity; others declare that Brown's one-sided sympathy with Indians betrays his nation's aims in civilizing and settling the West. Many find the chapter divisions chaotic and repetitive and the episodes cluttered with too many difficult Indian names. Movie, television, and cassette makers and book clubs vied for rights to the book. *Time* magazine proclaimed *Bury My Heart at Wounded Knee* one of the year's best books; New York Westerners gave Brown a Buffalo award. (Bevilacqua 1981; Brown 1970, 1974; Chepsiuk 1991; *Contemporary Authors* 1994; Courtmanche-Ellis 1978; Dahlin 1980; Lamar 1977; Waldman 1990)

   See also Brown, Dee.

THE CALL OF THE WILD

A classic adventure story loved by readers both young and old, Jack London's *The Call of the Wild* (1903) surveys a sweep of frontier terrain. Along the grueling Yukon and eastern reaches of Alaska, the great-hearted dog Buck abandons domestication and returns to the wild. Opening in the warm environs of California's Santa Clara Valley, the story describes a gentle pet pampered into a "sated aristocrat." (London 1964, 13) He lazes about and basks in the solicitude of Judge Miller and his family. An unforeseen abduction thrusts Buck onto a wagon, then aboard a truck and a ferry steamer, and into the grasp of a man with a club. London masks the man's name and face beneath a rain of blows that reduce the 140-pound St. Bernard-Scotch shepherd to quivering rage. From Seattle, Buck journeys north across the Queen Charlotte Sound to Dyea, the waterfront town on the Alaskan strip where Buck first samples snow, feels the pull of harness, and learns the hard truth of coexistence with snapping, quarreling sled dogs.

London centers the story within Buck's limited point of view. Gazing out at snow-heaped horizons, he tempers his racing feet to the rhythm of a nine-dog mail sled and to the hearty humor of Perrault, a French-Canadian mail carrier, and his good-natured partner François, who pays $300 in government money for a dog that is "one in ten t'ousand." (ibid., 59) The story centers on stamina, survival, and native wit, the three traits that make Buck a valuable work animal to the hardy wilderness tamers of the Western Hemisphere's northern territory. Speedy coverage of the mail route flashes place names like Sheep Camp, Scales, Chilkoot Divide, and Lake Bennett, echoing Buck's brief glimpse of stopping places along the unforgiving outback he must comprehend and endure to remain alive.

A skilled raconteur, London alternately terrorizes and appeases the reader with the romance and menace of the Northwest:

> With the aurora borealis flaming coldly overhead or the stars leaping in the frost dance, and the land numb and frozen under its pall of snow, this song of the huskies might have been the defiance of life, only it was pitched in minor key, with long-drawn wailings and half-sobs, and was more the pleading of life, the articulate travail of existence. (ibid., 48)

London's metaphor of the song connects the ancient melody to the breed itself and dates its plaintive air to a time "when songs were sad." Built on the cries of primordial dog-fathers, the song stirs the trace memory, drawing Buck "through the ages of fire and roof to the raw beginnings of life in the howling ages." (ibid.)

Buck's precipitous retracing of evolution lures him into perpetual jeopardy. The proof of danger lies within the circle of the story's myriad campsites: wicked jaws tear Curly to bits, rival dogs threaten instant slaughter over scanty rations of salmon, wild marauders rip and chew dog flesh to stave off hunger, and mad Dolly lies dead, her cranium split with one blow of her keeper's club. By the time the team has pushed up Thirty Mile River and arrived at Five Fingers, Buck has lacerated his footpads, his four slim connectors with the icy path. In a show of love and empathy, his master covers his paws with handmade rawhide moccasins hacked from the tops of his own boots.

London's infrequent gentling scarcely relieves the overall tone and atmosphere of raw strength pulling against the leads, of wearied sinews curled in a snowbank for a night's rest. Buck and his teammates reach Dawson a good deal wiser and greatly brutalized by the savagery of the wild. After launching out on the same fearful trail, he lapses into reveries of a distant era, a time when shaggy cave dwellers warmed themselves at the fire. A flick of the whip yanks him back from the dreamy past into the precarious present. Deep into Yukon Territory, the pack hauls the Salt Water Mail over endless, repetitive routes. Proud Dave, Buck's predominant teammate, is courageous but done for. Past argument from his handlers, he chews his rival's traces and demands reinstatement at the wheeler's post. The shot that ends Dave's misery signals another leg of the interminable 1,200-mile run.

When London's humans interact with beasts, they tend to display extremes of behavior. François and Perrault are kind and perceptive; Hal and Charles, the new owners, are too ignorant of sledding to look out for their animals. Persistent mismanagement, beatings, fatigue, and feedings of frozen horse-hide reduce Buck to a near-death lethargy:

> His muscles had wasted away to knotty strings, and the flesh pads had disappeared, so that each rib and every bone in his frame were outlined cleanly through the loose hide that was wrinkled in folds of emptiness. It was heartbreaking, only Buck's heart was unbreakable. (ibid., 80)

His rescuer, John Thornton, gradually restores Buck to his former robust self with daily application of patience and concern. In delight that the dog responds, John exclaims, "God! you can all but speak!" (ibid., 88) In return, Buck tenders his loyalty and wins a bet at the Eldorado bar by breaking out a 1,000-pound load. After Indians kill John, Buck, hard-muscled and self-sufficient, has no choice but to retreat into the uncharted wild to the terrain of the elusive past:

> Deep in the forest a call was sounding, and as often as he heard this call, mysteriously thrilling and luring, he felt compelled to turn his back upon the fire and the beaten earth around it, and to plunge into the forest, and on and on, he

knew not where or why; nor did he wonder where or why, the call sounding imperiously, deep in the forest. (ibid., 91)

At the end of the metamorphosis, London pictures Buck as "a great, gloriously coated wolf, like, and yet unlike, all other wolves," ripping the throat from a Yeehat chief and receding into the wilderness lore as a ghost dog. (ibid., 125)

By drawing on beast fable as a means of describing the frontier, Jack London invigorates reader interest in animal lore and in the Alaskan and Yukon outback. He blends the background of the 1897 gold rush with his own experiences in the Klondike. A sure-footed spinner of tales, he easily navigates faint trails, hunting lodges, way stations, and ice-rimmed coastline, all destinations he saw and internalized during his few months of prospecting in the northern wild. His memories of winter temperatures of 30 below, snarling predators, blinding snowstorms, and treacherously soft ice enumerate the most formidable barriers to human pioneers in the subarctic landscape. The overall effect has earned a lasting admiration for London, both as writer and frontiersman. (Beauchamp 1984; Franchere 1962; Hedrick 1982; "Jack London" 1996; Labor 1974; Labor and Reesman 1994; London, Jack 1964, 1965, 1980, 1982, 1991, 1992, 1996a, 1996b; London, Joan 1990; Lundquist 1987; Moore 1996; O'Connor 1964; Perry 1981; Sinclair 1983; Snodgrass 1991, 1995a; Stone 1978; Tavernier-Courbin 1994)

See also Alaska and the Yukon; London, Jack.

CAPTIVITY MOTIF

A common scenario in frontier literature involves capture, usually Indians seizing white women and children, the focus of *The Indian Captivity of O. M. Spencer* (1995) and the central plot of Janice Holt Giles's fictional *Hannah Fowler* (1956). Other uses of the motif cover abductions between Indian tribes, kidnap by and of Hispanics, and enslavement of Asians into railroad press gangs and prostitution, as depicted in Ruthanne Lum McCunn's *Thousand Pieces of Gold* (1981). Kidnap plots date to two classic first-person experiences from Puritan New England: Mary White Rowlandson's *Narrative of the Captivity and Restoration of Mrs. Mary White Rowlandson* (1682) and John Williams's *The Redeemed Captive Returning to Zion* (1707). Of the abduction of Rowlandson and her three children, which preceded three months with the Algonquin in New Hampshire, she comments sensibly that she would

choose rather to be killed by them than taken alive . . . [yet] when it come to the trial my mind changed; their glittering weapons so daunted my spirit, that I chose rather to go along with those (as I may say) ravenous beasts, than that moment to end my days. (Rowlandson 1985, 82)

The intrigue, melodrama, and allure of these stories—particularly the possibility of rape, sexual torment, or forced marriage—influenced James Fenimore

Cooper's *The Last of the Mohicans* (1826), which exploits the titillating possibilities of sex between Cora, the dusky Anglo-West Indian daughter of a white military leader, and Magua, a lusty forest brave.

In *Kit Carson's Autobiography* (1926), the famed trapper and guide describes his role as guide of a party seeking to recover the wife and small daughter of James M. White, abducted by Jicarilla Apache from a wagon train in October 1849. The trail, marked by items of Mrs. White's clothing, lead to the Indian camp. An exchange of fire gives the Indians time to kill Mrs. White before they escape. Carson reports, "She had been shot through the heart with an arrow not more than five minutes before. She evidently knew that someone was coming to her rescue." He surmises that she was making her escape at the time of her death, but adds that "the treatment she had received from them was so brutal and horrible that she could not possibly have lived very long. Her death, I think, should never be regretted by her friends." (Carson 1966, 133–134) This ambivalence toward captives marks both fiction and nonfiction accounts with a Victorian squeamishness toward atrocities to females.

Despite—or perhaps because of—the overtones of sexual abuse, rape, and torture, captivity literature has remained surprisingly popular. One famous narrative, *Captivity of the Oatman Girls: Being an Interesting Narrative of Life among the Apache and Mohave Indians* (1859), by Rev. R. B. Stratton, relates the hardships of the family of Mary Ann and Olive Ann Oatman, who were traveling to California with a party of Mormons led by James C. Brewster. The abduction occurred during the winter of 1851 as the family pushed on toward the Gila River in Mexican territory. After surviving the slaughter of most of their family, the girls undergo a forced march 350 miles to Mohave Valley. Olive reports:

> When I could not be driven, I was pushed and hauled along. Stubs, rocks, and gravel-strewn mountain sides hedged up and embittered the travel of the whole day. *That day* is among the few days of my dreary stay among the savages, marked by the most pain and suffering ever endured. I have since learned that they hurried for fear of the whites, emigrant trains of whom were not unfrequently passing that way. (Stratton 1983, 127)

The melodramatic style of the Rev. Stratton appealed to readers who satisfied their curiosity about life on the Great Plains with lurid stories of kidnap, mutilation, and enslavement.

Stratton's emphasis on the girls' innocence and the savagery of their captors reaches a peak after the Indians join some Apaches. He describes the latter as "selfish iron-hearted fiends, glutting over a murderous, barbarous deed of death and plunder." (ibid., 167) His gloating condemnation of Mohave agriculture climaxes in a sermonette on white achievements. Speaking through Olive, he exhorts, "It was a remembrancer, and reminded us of home, (now no more ours,) and placed us in a nearness to the customs of a civilized mode of life that we had not realized before." (ibid., 172) The girls are stripped to the waist and endure terrors, as well as the humiliation of facial tattooing:

> They then pricked the skin in small regular rows on our chins with a very sharp stick, until they bled freely. They then dipped these same sticks in the

juice of a certain weed that grew on the banks of the river, and then in the powder of a blue stone . . . and pricked this fine powder into these lacerated parts of the face. (ibid., 183)

The girls think of home and sing hymns to strengthen their resolve against panic. After famine kills Mary Ann, Olive wishes for death, but survives to be reclaimed at Fort Yuma five years later. In his didactic conclusion, Stratton attacks Native American morality. He declares all Indians to be lazy, unambitious, war-loving, disrespectful of marriage, and contemptuous of whites, especially white women. Stratton's zealous pursuit of Christian piety obscures the story of Olive and Mary Ann but offers the reader an intimate portrait of frontier sanctimony and racism.

Featured in young adult fiction by Conrad Richter in *The Light in the Forest* (1953) and by Scott O'Dell in *Streams to the River, River to the Sea* (1986) and *Sing Down the Moon* (1970), the captivity motif envigorates action by manipulating a variety of escape and chase plots, as in *Sing Down the Moon*, in which an Indian girl, who is sold into servitude by Hispanic slavers, flees from a church darkened for a pre-Easter tenebrae service and gallops over the trail homeward on stolen horses. A more cerebral study of abduction appears in McCunn's *Thousand Pieces of Gold*, in which Lalu, a Chinese woman kidnapped and forced into prostitution at an Idaho mining camp, secretly builds a cache of gold and dreams in vain of being rescued by Jim, her white lover. Unlike McCunn's straightforward novel of servitude and longing, the poignant scenario in Conrad Richter's *The Light in the Forest* depicts a complex social issue of white society's rejection of a captive child returned from Lenni Lenape foster parenting to a frontier settlement rife with animosity toward Indians. Whereas McCunn's Lalu battles captivity among racists, Richter's True Son prefers captivity among Indians to a return to his pious, judgmental white relatives.

The alliance of the captivity motif with racism colors "The Captive," a vital, sexually charged short story by Kentuckian Caroline Gordon, which she collected in *The Forest of the South* (1945). The first-person narrative precedes the kidnap of a mother with the cold-blooded murder of her children. The Cherokee attackers, Mad Dog and Crowmocker, bash the children with tomahawks and hustle Jinny Wiley, the protagonist, onto the trail. To facilitate rapid travel, an annoyed brave deliberately smashes the brains from her suckling infant and tosses the corpse aside. Along the way, Jinny struggles to keep up but is hampered by bloodied feet, fatigue, and sorrow for her family. The ghoulish vision of her daughter Sadie's fair-haired scalp swings from a captor's belt, reminding Jinny that she, too, may lose her life in some grisly fashion.

Gordon's breathless pacing moves the story toward some unknown rendezvous deeper in the Kentucky woods. Balanced against the kind attentions of the elderly Crowmocker are leers from Mad Dog, a barbarous brave whom Jinny suspects of wanting her for a wife. After the column pushes its way uphill and through dense bracken, it arrives at "the biggest rockhouse ever I seen," a dialect reference to a cave. (Gordon 1952, 874) As fall approaches, Jinny takes her mind off her abductors by singing folk songs and thinking about the two suitors who courted her in girlhood, but the return of Mad Dog reminds her of

Captivity and abduction is a recurring theme in Western literature. James Fenimore Cooper's *Last of the Mohicans* (1826) recounts the capture of the Munro sisters during the French and Indian War. Here, the sisters unsuccessfully fend off their abductors in a scene for the 1936 film version of Cooper's classic story.

his menace. Gordon describes his face in the colors of passion and death:

> His eyes was black in the circles of paint. His tongue showed bright between his painted lips. The red lines ran from his forehead down the sides of his cheeks to make gouts of blood on his chin. A devil. A devil come straight from hell to burn and murder. (ibid., 881)

A flagrant phallic symbol echoes his insidious presence, fierce masculinity, and ritual paint: near a barren rises a large elm peeled and painted to resemble a monster rattlesnake coiled about it. These realistic details heighten the terrors that carry Jinny to the rim of despair.

Evanescence, a characteristic of Gordon's fiction, intensifies the ins and outs of hope. Jinny's faint chance of rescue by frontiersman Tice Harmon or by Crowmocker ends abruptly as the older Indian sweeps a collection of brooches into his buckskin bag and accepts the trade: loot for the woman. Brusquely, he turns from her, reminding her that a white woman deserves no sympathy. Dreams of a white boy the Cherokees torture and burn and fantasies of Lance Rayburn, Jinny's former suitor, disturb her sleep. Gordon's feminist theme takes hold of the falling action after Jinny accepts responsibility for her own reclamation and flees on foot down the creek toward a settlement. The suspenseful flight from pursuing Indians takes her to a blockhouse, where she must scream her name over the roar of water and beg to be helped across the stream and into the gates. An elderly white man strings together logs with grapevine and begins poling Jinny across the stream to safety. To her faltering rescuer, Jinny snorts, "Go on and pray, you old fool, . . . I'm a-going to git across this river." (ibid., 889) The final sentence, which has Jinny thanking luck, tweaks the reader, who shares Jinny's relief and knows that luck played no part in her rescue.

Written in the same era as Gordon's short story, Janice Holt Giles's *Hannah Fowler* (1956) depicts the multiple problems of a lone woman on the frontier. Kentuckian Hannah Moore is long-legged and stout and eligible, three worthy attributes of a woodsman's wife. Because of her father's sudden death on the trail, she arrives at Fort Pitt with little choice but to marry a local man. After selecting Tice Fowler, she manages well at their crude forest homestead with a small daughter and another child expected within weeks. When Indians capture her, kill the stock, and burn her house, she recalls Tice telling her Daniel Boone's advice to captives, "act as natural as you kin, like you wan't botherin' none at all about bein' took. Jist go on like they was folks you was used to, do the best you kin, be cheerful-like, don't be stubborn or sulky." (Giles 1956, 181) The advice fails to quell the turmoil of fears and regrets in Hannah, whose mind frames images of her husband pursuing the captors. On her return, Hannah's pent emotions force to consciousness her fear of rape: "Tice, she thought, with a rush of choking, fierce emotion, was the *best* man. Oh, she would have died had that Cherokee laid a hand to her!" (ibid., 214) (Burns and Ives 1996a; Giles 1956; Gordon 1952; Lamar 1977; McCunn 1981; Miguel 1996; O'Dell 1970, 1986; Richter 1953; Spencer 1917; Stratton 1983)

See also Asian Americans on the frontier; *The Light in the Forest*; O'Dell, Scott; Richter, Conrad.

CARRINGTON, HENRY B.

A villain in George Bird Grinnell's *The Fighting Cheyenne* (1915), a dupe in J. W. Vaughn's *Indian Fights: New Facts on Seven Encounters* (1966), and a noble soldier in Dee Brown's *The Fetterman Massacre* (1962) and *Bury My Heart at Wounded Knee* (1970), Henry Beebee Carrington (1824–1912), army officer during the Bozeman Trail war, remains a puzzle in Western cavalry history. His own writing offers a chilling glimpse of Western warfare and the passions on both sides that compel whites and Indians to desperate fighting. A native of Connecticut and a graduate of Yale, at age 24 he opened a law office in Columbus, Ohio. At the beginning of the Civil War, he entered the state militia as an adjutant general and helped stock the Union army with trained recruits from Ohio and Indiana. Carrington's service in the field began in 1865, when he was dispatched west to join the 18th Infantry Regiment of Indian fighters and was stationed at Fort Reno, Wyoming. After guarding the Powder River Road in 1866, he joined guide Jim Bridger and journeyed up the Platte River for treaty negotiations with Sioux Chief Red Cloud at Fort Laramie. He also facilitated stabilization of the Bozeman Trail to assure safe movement of plainsmen and miners west to Wyoming and Montana. Carrington's building of the road during peace talks caused Red Cloud to snub him and the Sioux to withdraw from the fort to continue attacks against trespassers on traditional Indian hunting grounds.

Carrington's role in establishing Forts C. F. Smith, Montana, and Phil Kearny, Nebraska, precipitated a siege state by Arapaho, Cheyenne, Oglala, Brule, Hunkpapa, and Miniconjou bands. Because of lack of battlefield experience, his wartime performance was weak and discipline lax. His most famous frontier service occurred on December 21, 1866, during the Fetterman Massacre near Fort Kearny. Carrington ordered Captain William Judd Fetterman to lead a relief detachment to aid a stalled wood convoy laden with lumber for the completion of the fort. The situation preceded a disastrous ambush by the allied forces of Red Cloud, Crazy Horse, Hump, Gall, Rain-in-the-Face, and their 2,000 braves. Against orders, Fetterman proceeded beyond Lodge Trail Ridge; he, two other officers, two civilians, and 79 enlisted men from the 18th Infantry and 2nd Cavalry died in the attack. The Indians lost 200 braves and suffered heavy casualties. A blizzard interrupted the army's efforts to bury their dead, capture Sioux stragglers, and collect evidence at the scene. An investigation turned up contradictory conclusions concerning Fetterman's obedience to command. In disgrace for negligence, Carrington—whom some considered a political scapegoat—bore full blame and withdrew to minor commands at Fort McPherson, Nebraska, and Fort Sedgewick, Colorado. After retirement at age 46 following a hip injury, he taught military science at Wabash College. He returned to public service in 1889 to assist in negotiating peace with the Flathead and in settling Plains Indians on Montana reservations.

In 1884, eight years after Custer's disastrous battle at the Little Bighorn, Carrington composed *The Indian Question, an Address*. Reprinted in 1909, the pamphlet contains his side of the Fetterman Massacre, which was the beginning of Red Cloud's War, the only U.S. Cavalry defeat during the Plains Indian wars. Carrington clearly defines the war as a clash of races and predicts, "The inferior must perish." (Carrington 1909, 5) In view of the truncation of game trails by railroads, his evaluation of conditions is compelling:

> Since the Indian cannot profitably make long expeditions, as in former times, he clings to these last, these best hunting grounds, with more than the tenacity of a party contractor to existing treaties. Fast as the mountain streams declare to the avaricious gold-hunter that gold is there, so fast comes fresh to the red man, the warning that, worse than the contracting iron chamber of romance, an inevitable doom is surrounding heart and home. (ibid., 7)

Carrington illustrates Indian desperation with details from the Fetterman Massacre, after which braves scalped, mangled, and removed the muscles from the dead to prevent them from functioning in the afterlife.

Laced with generalizations about Indian society, the pamphlet moves from communication problems with unsophisticated Sioux to a negative portrayal of the male's treatment of his squaw:

> The squaw is the slave. Her mission is to cut wood, cook food, make arrows, tan hides, and do everything that is menial. Her skill with knife, bow, and axe is very great, and in defence of their village, the women and boys are no mean enemy. (ibid., 10)

The stereotyping increases with Carrington's depiction of native males as tyrants, gamblers, liars, thieves, rovers, idlers, deceivers, and boilers of dogs. With a grudging admission of the natives' proficiency and strength, he concludes, "The whole drift of the Indian life is in the direction of struggle."

Drawn once more to the horror of Fetterman's debacle, Carrington gives an eyewitness account of the mutilation that occurred within a half hour of the massacre. He recounts multiple arrow wounds, from which blood flowed down grooves in the shafts. According to the official report, which follows Carrington's speech:

> Eyes torn out and laid on the rocks, noses cut off, ears cut off, chins hewn off, teeth chopped out, joints of fingers cut off, brains taken out and placed on the rocks with members of the body, entrails taken out and exposed, hands and feet cut off, arms taken out from sockets, eyes, ears, mouth, and arms penetrated with spearheads, sticks, and arrows. (ibid., 16–17)

He interviewed Red Cloud for a philosophical discussion of mutilation and learned that Sioux religion sanctioned dismemberment. Carrington shores up his report with a citation from Chief Joseph and with honor to Dull Knife, whom fellow Sioux castigated for remaining true to his white comrades. These examples suggest that he tried to know his enemy well and that he admired Sioux single-mindedness and courage. (Brown 1970; Burns and Ives 1996a; Carrington 1909; Lamar 1977; Waldman 1990)

See also Bury My Heart at Wounded Knee.

CATHER, WILLA

One of America's premiere prairie realists, Willa Sibert Cather devoted much of her serene pastoral writing to diverse reflections of agrarian life, religious outreach, and immigrant culture of the Midwest and Southwest. Her canon of Americana is rooted in the prairie and graced with the spectacle of desert crag and rugged arroyo. She adorns human scenarios with the commonplace faith and good works of rural people. Partially because of the feminist movement, biographies and critiques of her works have undergone late-twentieth-century reexamination and they have found broader influence on college and university reading lists.

Born in the community of Gore near Winchester, Virginia, on December 7, 1873, Wilella (shortened to Willa) was the eldest of the seven children of frontier farmer and financier Charles Fectigue and Mary Virginia Boak Cather. She was educated by her grandmother Boak at home, Willow Shade, where she learned five languages, including Greek and Latin. Uprooted to her uncle and grandparents' farm on the Nebraska plains, she left behind Back Creek Valley, part of Virginia's graceful Shenandoah range. Of her family's move in 1884, in the final decade of true pioneer settlement, she recalled that the myriad French-Canadian, Bohemian, German, Swiss, and Scandinavian dialects overwhelmed the sound of English. The open range, which she later called "shaggy grass country . . . as naked as the back of your hand," threatened an erasure of self. (Bohlke 1986, 23) The displacement changed her from a sheltered southern child into a tough, self-possessed plainswoman.

Because Cather's father failed at agriculture, he resettled his family in the town of Red Cloud, a railroad and marketing center of 2,500 residents, and sold real estate and insurance. Cather made the town a frequent fictional setting, alternately named Black Hawk, Frankfort, Sweetwater, and Moonstone. Her nostalgic reminiscence pictures the spare existence in the backwoods of the Nebraska Divide where "Willie" Cather rode her pony to visit Scandinavian, French Catholic, German, Russian, or central European neighbors or to the grave of Chief Red Cloud's daughter. Whenever possible, she enjoyed plays, musicals, and readings in the classics with a local storekeeper. On warm afternoons she brought her siblings to the Republican River to play on an island near the mill dam and to read aloud from Matthew Arnold's "Sohrab and Rustum" and Alfred Tennyson's *Idylls of the King*. In the distance, the children viewed prairie dog towns and the sod huts described in *My Ántonia* and the gleaming furrows of *O Pioneers!* The long waving grass stirred by the wind reflected moonlight, just as it did in her story "Neighbour Rosicky."

An ambitious female for her day, Cather hoped to become a surgeon. At age 15 she abandoned the female persona, dressed in men's work clothes, and cropped her hair to become William Cather, an imaginary brother who received "his" mail at the local post office. She moved to Lincoln in 1890 to enroll at the Latin school; abandoning pre-med courses, she completed a degree in classical language and literature from the University of Nebraska. After an English professor submitted her essay to the *Nebraska State Journal,* Cather was hypnotized by the sight of her name in print. From experience as associate editor of two campus literary magazines, she initiated a career in fiction based primarily on her life in the West.

A columnist and drama critic for the *Lincoln State Journal* her junior year, Cather continued writing for newspapers and magazines after she graduated and moved east to Pittsburgh, where she enjoyed the literary and musical stimulation that Nebraska lacked. She edited, reviewed drama, and wrote for the *Home Monthly* and the *Pittsburgh Leader* and taught English and Latin at Central High School from 1895 to 1896 and at Allegheny High in 1901, where she chaired the English department. Sharing her life with Isabelle McClung and later with Edith Lewis, Cather lived for a year in France, but returned to the United States to spend most of her adult years on the East Coast. She joined the editorial staff of *McClure's* magazine as an associate in 1906 and encountered literary lions, including Thornton Wilder, G. K. Chesterton, John Galsworthy, and H. G. Wells. Her colleague, Sarah Orne Jewett, warned her that magazine

Willa Cather, 1873–1947

work would erode creativity and urged her to choose writing over security. Cather, who was weighted down with editorial work and considering giving up fiction, realized that she had been "trying to sing a song that did not lie in my voice." (ibid., 37)

Cather took Jewett's advice. She vacationed at her brother's home in Winslow, Arizona, and in Taos, New Mexico, and then returned to the East to inaugurate the second stage of her literary career. She recognized a major flaw in her earlier writing, the neophyte's reliance on strings of adjectives. To rescue her work from immaturity, she cut to the base elements, avoided obvious heroes and generalities, and began drawing on mental pictures, which she recorded in clear sense impressions. Of these, she remarked that the material dated to her childhood, "gathered—no, God save us! not gathered but absorbed—before I was fifteen years old." (ibid., 43) In adulthood, she returned to Nebraska to refresh her memory and to reconnect with the vigor and promise of the Plains. An example of her improvement occurs in "On the Divide":

> Near Rattlesnake Creek, on the side of a little draw stood Canute's shanty. North, east, south, stretched the level Nebraska plain of long rust-red grass that undulated constantly in the wind. To the west the ground was broken and rough, and a narrow strip of timber wound along the turbid, muddy little stream that had scarcely ambition enough to crawl over its black bottom. (Piekarski 1988, 13)

The refocusing of Cather's writing on sense impressions gelled into clearer pictures of Midwest settings in which her characters came to life.

In a Greenwich Village apartment near Washington Square, Cather worked hard and long over each text, writing two to three hours daily and revising each draft three times. Her first novel, *Alexander's Bridge* (1912) was successful enough to free her from editorial work for *McClure's*. She followed with *O Pioneers!* (1913), an optimistic novel dedicated to the beauty of Nebraska, which, up to that time, had received little notice in fiction. She succeeded with *The Song of the Lark* (1915), *One of Ours* (1922), and *A Lost Lady* (1923), the touching story of the entrancing and daring wife of Captain Forrester, one of the "men who had put plains and mountains under the iron harness." (Cather 1972, 169) Some critics consider her best work to be *Death Comes for the Archbishop* (1927), a study of faith and commitment. *My Ántonia* (1918), one of her most nostalgic pieces, lauds compassion, charity, and acceptance of outsiders, three virtues that eased the hard, isolated immigrant life. In addition to novels, Cather contributed short fiction and poetry to *Cosmopolitan, Youth's Companion, Harper's, Collier's, Woman's Home Companion, Smart Set, Atlantic, Ladies' Home Journal, Commonweal,* and *Scholastic*. Her most frequently anthologized story, "Paul's Case," details the motivation and method of a teenage suicide.

Throughout her career, Cather gave well-received public addresses on writing and the prairie. One of her impassioned speeches called upon Nebraskans to preserve hedges, honey locusts, and especially cottonwoods, which the post-pioneer era was decimating and replacing with soft maple. In praise of the virgin landscape, she pled:

> I am not asking them to plant more, but to let stand those great trees that are dear to the pioneers. Their faculty of drawing moisture makes the cottonwoods needed in low places along the roads to take up water which would otherwise form a slough. On high barren pasture land, where nothing else will grow, the cottonwood will thrive. (Bohlke 1986, 40)

Much as Twain had chided America for emulating Europe in mannerisms and speech, Cather admonished Nebraskans to stop copying Eastern cities and to maintain the natural beauties of the prairie landscape.

Like the cottonwood, writing also sprang from Cather's natural surroundings. In a generalized observation, she noted with characteristic vigor, "A book is made with one's own flesh and blood of years. It is cremated youth. It is all yours—no one gave it to you." (ibid., 50) After a lengthy run of literary successes based on her vision of the West, Cather, who suffered neuritis and chronic wrist pain, grew more reclusive. She grew despondent over the deaths of friends and family members, retired briefly to Cherry Valley, New York, and died unexpectedly April 25, 1947, in Manhattan of a cerebral hemorrhage. She was buried in Jaffrey, New Hampshire, where she had spent summers.

Cather's collected works were published in 1941; and her critical essays, *The Kingdom of Art* (1893–1896), in 1966, featuring commentary on the American novel and on the writings of Katherine Mansfield and Sarah Orne Jewett. Posthumous publications remained true to the prairie residents whom she immortalized (and supported during the Depression by sending money to stricken Nebraska farm families). Written in her characteristic unembellished style, her canon proves the wisdom of light structuring to avoid the forced style and contrived dialogue and plotting that she disliked in trendy modern fiction.

Until Cather's death, her novels found their way into cinema only once. She disliked movies and despised the melodramatic screen version of *A Lost Lady*, which was filmed in 1934 starring Barbara Stanwyck. In 1929, Cather, a champion of print fiction, wrote her antimovie credo in a letter to the Omaha *World-Herald*:

> Only living people can make us feel. Pictures of them, no matter how dazzling, do not make us feel anything more than interest or curiosity or astonishment. The "pity and terror" which the drama, even in its crudest form, can awaken in young people is not to be found in the movies. (Tysver 1991, 11A)

After her books became public domain, *O Pioneers!* was filmed for television, starring Jessica Lange as Alexandra, and premiered on *American Playhouse* May 17, 1991. Reviewers praised the screenplay for its faithful rendering of Cather's style and tone, but fans complained that Cather's will stated unequivocally that her works were to be read, not viewed.

A literal and literary pioneer, Cather received worthy tributes: the *Prix Fémina Américaine*, selection as one of *Good Housekeeping*'s 12 notable American women, and honorary doctorates from her alma mater as well as from the University of Michigan, University of California, Yale, Princeton, Smith,

Creighton, and Columbia. Her canon received favorable commentary from critics H. L. Mencken, Katherine Anne Porter, Maxwell Geismar, Lionel Trilling, and Edmund Wilson. Cather was surprised to receive the 1930 Pulitzer Prize of $1,000 for *One of Ours,* a wholesome novel that judges felt displayed the high standards of American manners. She also earned the 1927 Howells Medal from the American Academy and Institute of Arts and Letters for *Death Comes for the Archbishop.* That same year, Sinclair Lewis declared that his Nobel Prize for literature should have gone to Cather, whom he characterized as Nebraska's foremost citizen. (Blain, Grundy, and Clements 1990; Bloom and Bloom 1962; Bloom 1986b; Bohlke 1986; Brown, E. K. 1987; Buck 1992; Byrne and Snyder 1980; Cather 1947, 1972, 1977, 1991; Cowie 1951; Davidson and Wagner-Martin 1995; *DISCovering Authors* 1993; Dobie 1996; Drabble 1985; Ehrlich and Carruth 1982; Goring 1994; Hazard 1927; Hornstein 1973; Kunitz 1942; Lamar 1977; Lee, Hector 1975; Lee, Robert Edson 1966; Magill 1958; Milner et al. 1994; "North Side" 1996; O'Brien 1986; Piekarski 1988; Robinson 1983; Sherr and Kazickas 1994; Tysver 1991; Whitman 1992; Woodress 1982)

See also *Death Comes for the Archbishop; My Ántonia; O Pioneers!*

CATLIN, GEORGE

Artist and observer George Catlin (1796-1872) was one of the most influential gatherers of Plains lore, which he compiled at the height of Native American culture. He captured Indian life and philosophy in his graphic journals and documentary paintings and, in vain, attempted to preserve his observations for all time. A native of rural Wilkes Barre, Pennsylvania, Catlin had thrilled to Indian lore from boyhood. He was fifth of the 14 children born to Putnam and Polly Catlin, a white woman kidnapped by Indians in 1778 and returned that same year. He learned to fish, hunt, and paddle a canoe with enough skill to enable him to survive in the wild.

After studying for the bar in Litchfield, Connecticut, Catlin opened a law office in Lucerne, Pennsylvania, and practiced for two years, then abandoned his profession for art. In 1823, he opened a studio in Philadelphia and began painting portrait miniatures on ivory, including New York Governor DeWitt Clinton and Red Cloud, the Seneca orator. The next year, Catlin was intrigued by a visiting entourage of Indians. During the removal of native tribes to the West, he resolved to paint portraits of every tribe. He visited local reservations and sketched Indian delegations visiting Washington, D.C. For his enthusiasm and skill, he earned a prestigious place in the Philadelphia Academy of Art, but turned from formal European-style painting to the task of recording the life and customs of the threatened Native American.

In 1830, Superintendent of Indian Affairs William Clark introduced Catlin to native groups visiting St. Louis. Two years later, Catlin traveled with easel, canvas, and paints up the Missouri River to the Dakota Territory on the *Yellowstone,* the private steamer of the American Fur Company. From there he journeyed by canoe to Fort Union in present-day Montana and remained for three months. He sketched Sioux, Blackfoot, Assiniboin, Ojibwa, Crow, Paw-nee, Mandan, Cree, and others and produced a variety of portraits, including one of Black Hawk, leader of the Sauk and Fox. The next spring, he pushed west over the Oregon Trail to Fort Laramie, Wyoming, and south to Salt Lake, Utah. The experience so seized his fancy that he envisioned a national game park to preserve

> in their pristine beauty and wildness, in a *magnificent park,* where the world could see for ages to come, the native Indian in his classic attire, galloping his wild horse, with sinewy bow, and shield and lance, amid the fleeting herds of elks and buffaloes. . .

all part of the spectacular Western landscape that Catlin painted along the Yellowstone River. (Catlin 1989, vii) In 1834, he and his wife, Clara, crossed the West on his way to study the Comanches in Texas. A planned military expedition with Henry Leavenworth and Henry Dodge ended abruptly after Catlin con-tracted fever. He persisted in his study of native subjects in 1835, when he settled in southwestern Minnesota and painted Winnebago, Menominee, and Keokuk, civil chief of the Sauk and Black Hawk's old rival. The next year, Catlin visited the steatite quarry at Pipeston, Minnesota, the only source of the soft red stone used for peace pipes. The site was a phenomenon of nature that tribes held jointly as neutral territory. In his honor, the substance was renamed catlinite.

From contact with 48 tribes, Catlin became expert in ethnology, particu-larly the ways of the Mandan, who shortly died out from their first exposure to smallpox. He sketched dress, customs, and rituals of tribes from Central America to the Alaska coast and painted Osceola, the Seminole chief imprisoned in Fort Moultrie near Charleston, South Carolina. In hopes of establishing a national archive called Catlin's Indian Gallery, he circulated his notebooks, 600 paint-ings, and thousands of beaded tunics, ceremonial robes, feathered headdresses, drums, teepees, medicine bags, clubs, pipes, and other artifacts in the United States, Belgium, France, and England. In a feverish schedule requiring unpack-ing, displaying, and lecturing, he moved from place to place, enthralling lis-teners with his stories of life with the Indians.

Despite assistance from Daniel Webster, Jefferson Davis, and Henry Clay, Catlin failed to stir Congress to underwrite a national Indian museum. Fearful that voters would mock the expenditure of $60,000 on pictures of "savages," officials shelved the proposal. His dream ended in 1852 when his collection was seized to pay debts incurred in transporting and erecting the display. He tramped over South America in search of gold, but returned up the Pacific Coast with no nuggets to finance his dream. In his absence, Henry Rowe Schoolcraft had spitefully reproved Catlin for publishing inaccurate informa-tion about Mandan rituals, thus lessening the likelihood of convincing Con-gress to build a museum.

Catlin withdrew from family and friends to a tenement in Belgium and painted in isolation. In his last months, deaf and crippled, he resided in a private studio at the Smithsonian Institution and continued to paint and petition

Congress for money. The tenor of the post–Civil War era energized the drive for more money for forts and cavalry to ward off Indian attacks. Few supporters wanted an Indian museum. Broken in health and spirit, he ceased working. At his death in Jersey City, New Jersey, in 1872, what originals survived haphazard storage passed to numerous American galleries, notably the American Museum of Natural History in New York City and the National Gallery and the Smithsonian Institution in Washington, D.C.

Catlin's riverscapes, portraits, animal studies, linecuts, and ink sketches and portraits of men, women, and children illustrate his six eyewitness accounts: *Letters and Notes on the Manners, Customs and Condition of the North American Indians during Eight Years' Travel amongst the Wildest Tribes of Indians of North America* (1841), the outgrowth of his 21 dispatches to the *Spectator* and the *Daily Commercial Advertiser; North American Indian Portfolio: Hunting Scenes and Amusements of the Rocky Mountains and Prairies of America* (1844); *Catlin's Notes of Eight Years' Travels and Residence in Europe* (1848); *My Life among the Indians* (1867); *Okeepa, a Religious Ceremony, and Other Customs of the Mandans* (1867); and *Last Rambles amongst the Indians of the Rocky Mountains and the Andes* (1868). Displaying the appreciation and excitement of Meriwether Lewis and Francis Parkman, Catlin marveled at the pageantry and grandeur of native life and proclaimed the Plains Indians "the finest looking, best equipped, and the most beautifully costumed of any on the Continent." (Haverstock 1973, flap copy)

Like poet Henry Wadsworth Longfellow, sociologist Henry Rowe Schoolcraft, naturalist John Muir, and novelist O. E. Rölvaag, Catlin longed to preserve as much of American history and culture as he could. At the same time that he observed ceremonies and rituals and sketched scenes of native home life and hunting parties, he realized how the fragile aboriginal society would fare within another decade of settlement and government control. He wrote in 1832 of his aims:

> with a light heart, inspired with an enthusiastic hope and reliance that I could meet and overcome all the hazards and privations of a life devoted to the production of a literal and graphic delineation of the living manners, customs, and character of an interesting race of people, who are rapidly passing away from the face of the earth—lending a hand to a dying nation, who have no historians or biographers of their own to portray with fidelity their native looks and history; thus snatching from a hasty oblivion what could be saved for the benefit of posterity, and perpetuating it, as a fair and just monument, to the memory of a truly lofty and noble race. (Catlin 1989, 3)

He claims to have met around 400,000 individuals, none of whom ever cheated, robbed, ill-treated, or threatened him. To his amazement, they lived without lock and key and readily embraced him as a medicine man. At parting, they entrusted him to the care of their Great Spirit, whom they depicted as a God who accepted all people.

Among Catlin's written observations are comments on a variety of native topics. He recalls dining on dog meat, watching runners deliver an invitation or spread news, and observing the loading of women and toddlers on the backs of ponies. He describes the smoking of skins, wooing rituals, setting up of lodges, burial sacrifices, rainmaking, head flattening, ball games, and the self-torture ceremony that accompanies the annual Mandan Bull Dance. He corrects misconceptions about Indian ways and comments that, because natives are accustomed to dealing with white traders, they are inclined to think all white people are cheats and liars and act accordingly when confronted by a white outsider. Catlin's fear that disease and alcoholism will further jeopardize Indian society colors his objective reportage with compassion and respect for life. (Boorstin 1965; Catlin, 1965, 1989; Dobie 1996; Haverstock, 1973; Lamar 1977; Longfellow 1993; McCracken 1959; Milner et al. 1994; Patterson and Snodgrass 1994; Trent et al. 1946; Waldman 1990)

See also Black Hawk; Longfellow, Henry Wadsworth; Muir, John; Oregon Trail; Parkman, Francis.

⚅ "THE CELEBRATED JUMPING FROG OF 卐 CALAVERAS COUNTY"

A creative effort that marks the shift in Mark Twain's career from journalism to fiction, "The Celebrated Jumping Frog of Calaveras County" dates to an actual frog contest that Twain learned about during the winter of 1864–1865. While visiting Bret Harte in Calaveras County, California, Twain stayed at Angels Camp, a quartz-mining center in the hill country of the Sierra Nevada Mountains, and listened to a version of the story told by Ben Coon, barkeep at the Angels Hotel. When Twain returned to work in San Francisco as correspondent for the *Virginia City Territorial Enterprise,* he composed "Jim Smiley and His Jumping Frog," which was offhandedly published on November 18, 1865, as filler for the New York *Saturday Press,* a weekly famous for publishing the humor of Josh Billings and verse by Walt Whitman. The story achieved immediate success. Passing through reprints and several editings, it has been alternately retitled "The Notorious Jumping Frog of Calaveras County" and "The Celebrated Jumping Frog of Calaveras County," its most familiar version, which was the title of Twain's first collection of short fiction, published in 1866.

A framework narrative told by Simon Wheeler (a mask for Mark Twain), the story recounts the gulling of a gambler by an unnamed stranger. Opening on the visitor's search for a boyhood friend, the Reverend Leonidas W. Smiley, the questioner encounters Simon, a voluble yarn spinner, dozing at a barroom stove and listens to a rambling tale about Jim Smiley, a lucky bettor who usually wins. Smiley nabs a frog, names him Dan'l Webster (for the U.S. secretary of state), and spends three months "educating" him into a champion jumper and flycatcher. When a stranger seems interested in a bet on how far Dan'l can jump, Smiley wagers $40. The crux of the story is Smiley's foolish departure to find an opponent. In the meantime, the stranger loads Dan'l with quail-shot.

The frontier humor that buoys the story from tale to art introduced Twain's Eastern readers to a basic Western trait—exaggerated anecdote. According to Simon, the frog focus of the story could "nail a fly every time as fur as he could see him." Simon describes Smiley [singing] out, "Flies, Dan'l, flies!" and quicker'n you could wink he'd spring straight up and snake a fly off'n the counter there, and flop down on the floor ag'in as solid as a gob of mud, and fall to scratching the side of his head with his hind foot as indifferent as if he hadn't no idea he'd been doin' any more'n any frog might do. (Twain 1985, n.p.)

Counter to Smiley's bragging runs the offhand interest of the "stranger," a standard figure in frontier literature. Without great effort, the newcomer allows Smiley to outsmart himself by setting out to find a competitor for Dan'l, leaving his prize jumper unguarded for the stranger to freight before the match.

Twain lightly spices the jump scene with humor. At the moment of truth, the stranger's frog hops off, leaving Dan'l to "[hyst] up his shoulders—so—like a Frenchman, but it warn't no use—he couldn't budge; he was planted as solid as a church, and he couldn't no more stir than if he was anchored out." (ibid.) Smiley is perplexed and notices that the recalcitrant frog "'pears to look mighty baggy, somehow." The story trails off after a call from outside distracts Simon, who returns to tell about Smiley's "yeller one-eyed cow that didn't have no tail, only just a short stump lik' a bannanner."

Twain's story proved livelier than he had imagined possible. The jumping frog caught the attention of a Greek professor, who located a Boeotian frog story written 2,000 years previous to Twain's version. On July 15, 1872, another round of retelling added two more stylized frog stories after Twain published for the *Revue des Deux Mondes* "Madame Blanc's" translation in French and then "restored to the English after martyrdom in the French." In the Gallic restatement, Smiley's boast drops its dialect twang, which Twain renders verbatim with French punctuation: "—Mon Dieu! répond Smiley, toujours d'un air dégagé, elle est bonne pour une chose à mon avis, elle peut batter en sautant tout grenouille du comté de Calaveras." (ibid.) The fun of Twain's linguistic exercise is the retranslation from idiomatic French to a literal English that is both absurd and entertaining: "My God!" respond Smiley, always with an air disengaged, "she is good for one thing, to my notice (à mon avis), she can batter in jumping (elle peut batter en sautant) all frogs of the county of Calaveras." The end of the tale winds down in macaronic Franglais: "When Smiley recognized how it was, he was like mad. He deposited his frog by the earth and ran after that individual, but he not him caught never." (ibid.) (Bloom 1986a; Davis and Beidler 1984; Emerson 1985; Kaplan 1966; Lyttle 1994; Rasmussen 1995; Ridge 1993; Robinson 1996; Shalit 1987; Thomas and Thomas 1943; Twain 1985; Wexler 1995)

See also Roughing It; Twain, Mark.

CLARK, WALTER VAN TILBURG

Like Jack Schaefer, his contemporary, Walter Van Tilburg Clark was an unlikely person to write a classic deglamorized Western, *The Ox-Bow Incident* (1940), a psychological study of the lynch mob. Written during the rise of fascism in Germany, the book demonstrates a universal theme—that lawfulness resides in individuals as well as in communities. In his novel, cowboy society polices itself via common consent. Consequently, the citizens, whether active or passive, must answer for a quasi-legal triple hanging, a merciless execution and serious miscarriage of justice, which Clark typified as "a kind of American Nazism." (Calder 1975, 122)

A native Easterner who came to love the Sierras, Clark was born in East Orland near Bangor, Maine, on August 3, 1909. He was the oldest of the four children of Euphemia Murray Abrams and Walter Ernest Clark, an economist and president of the University of Nevada. Clark began publishing short fiction, verse, and illustrations in *The Clark News* in early childhood, which he spent in West Nyack, New York. He enjoyed chess, camping, and hiking as well as informal socializing with a variety of people. After his family moved to Reno, Nevada, in 1917, he preferred Western history above other bodies of information because he could become more personally involved in its lore. He used the area as the setting of his second Western, *The City of Trembling Leaves* (1945), an autobiographical coming-of-age novel.

A product of the Reno public schools, Clark graduated from the University of Nevada with an M.A. in literature in 1932 and obtained a second M.A. in philosophy from the University of Vermont two years later. From 1936 to 1945, he served as basketball coach and English and drama teacher in Cazenovia, New York, and coached tennis and headed the English department in Rye, New York. A peripatetic career as professor of creative writing took him to San Francisco State College and Stanford University's writers' workshops, as well as the state universities of Nevada, Iowa, Utah, Montana, Wyoming, California, Illinois, Missouri, Washington, Oregon, and Arkansas. He earned honors as a lecturer in writing at Wesleyan University and Reed College.

Describing his choices of residence, Clark once remarked that he hated cities and crowds. To him, urban life, where animal passion was curbed by zoo and leash, was devoid of real freedom. He preferred the open air of farm, shore, mountain, and prairie. In addition to his growing-up years in Nevada, major influences on his character were books: classic mythology, frontier and Indian sagas, the Bible, and adventure tales of King Arthur and Robin Hood. These works inclined him toward Western fiction, where personal responsibility flourished outside the tight confines of citified law and order.

The Ox-Bow Incident, which established Clark as a major fiction writer, earned widespread praise as the prototype of the objective Western novel. An adventure story that reflects Arthurian-style peacekeeping, the novel pursues the theme of frontier lawlessness as it impinges on the lives of a group of individuals. The story opens in the early spring of 1885 in a fictional town with the evocative name of Bridger's Wells and covers a brief span of hours from one morning to sunset of the next day. Like Greek tragedy, the interwoven actions occur in rapid order and build to a climax that permanently alters the behaviors and self-perception of an entire town.

Told by outsider Art Croft, an unremarkable cowboy and partner of Gil Carter, the plot opens in town, where the two range riders anticipate their first poker-and-whiskey outing at Canby's saloon since winter isolated them with their cattle herd. Inclement weather mimics the coming dilemma as dark, threatening cloud cover and wind propel a brief snowstorm that shuts out the outside world and, like a spotlight on a stage, focuses attention on a circumscribed field of action. Looming violence overtakes Gil, who gets into a fistfight because he makes suspiciously heavy bets and wins. The bartender halts the fracas by rapping Gil on the head with a bottle. A preface to later disunity, the use of force to quell discord mirrors the work of the lynch mob.

The main event follows a tightening of atmosphere: seasonal weather teeters on the raw edge of early spring and feeling is running high following the rustling of 600 cattle. Under a sky mottled with passing clouds, young Greene gallops in to report that Larry Kinkaid was found shot about noon. Like a dismaying news bulletin, the vision of the murder galvanizes locals. Art comments, "You could no more believe that Kinkaid was dead than you could that a mountain had moved and left a gap in the sky." (Clark 1968, 30) The irony of his comment holds off until the falling action, when townspeople discover that they have trusted faulty information.

As talk turns ugly, Clark explores the ethics of mob justice. Frena Hundel, an hysterical bystander, goads the men to vindicate Kinkaid, whom she liked. The contemplative voice, Arthur Davies, argues for restraint and due process of law. Osgood, the local minister, turns the situation into a grimly prejudicial pulpit opportunity:

> Let us not act hastily; let us not do that which we will regret. We must act, certainly, but we must act in a reasoned and legitimate manner, not as a lawless mob. It is not mere blood that we want; we are not Indians, savages to be content with a miserable, sneaking revenge. We desire justice, and justice has never been obtained in haste and strong feeling. (ibid., 33)

Uncertain when faced by opposing sentiments, locals seek a clear mandate uncluttered with high-flown oratory. The author indicates that, on the frontier, action appeals to Westerners, who have abandoned the more rational East with its abstract discussions of right and wrong for a land of direct action. In subsequent scenes, Osgood's gratuitous dig at Indians attains increasing irony.

Clark builds the pro-posse momentum into the evening hours, depicting the arrival of night as a symbol of the darkness of soul in the 27 men and 1 woman who ready themselves for group vengeance. The only available authority figure, Judge Tyler, warns that vigilantism is illegal and that temporary deputation is insufficient legality for their purpose. Against his admonition, Jenny "Ma" Grier's example carries more weight. A female in men's garb, she espouses a macho philosophy by disdaining churches and sermons and adopting an anti-intellectual stance:

> Art, you're gettin' worse every day. . . . First you let the reverend there give you prayin' faith, and then you let Tyler argue you into drummin' up business for him. It's them books, Art, them books. (ibid., 78)

A blend of motherhood and pseudorationality, Ma is a force too long respected to be shoved aside. Rather than agree with the unmanly preacher and allow Ma to outdo his manhood, Art opts to join the posse.

Rumor, the origin of the town's uproar, fuels the mob's choice of direction. Amigo claims to have seen rustlers driving around 40 cattle. Intending to rid the area of stock thieves, the mob departs down the stage road toward Pike's Hole and through a treacherous pass that leads to Ox-Bow, an isolated valley. The author uses topography to represent the force of the majority as they stampede naysayers toward a narrow consensus. A foreshadowing of false logic occurs when Jimmy Carnes, the stage guard, shoots into the dark toward a suspected highwayman. The bullet, like random evil emerging from the dark, nicks Art in the shoulder.

An extended pattern of chiaroscuro occludes the rising action, which follows the conventions of the quest motif. Through spits of snow, the group proceeds toward Ox-Bow. A few hours before daylight, they encounter their quarry, Donald Martin, Alva Hardwick, and Juan Martinez, who sleep at their camp near an abandoned farm. Interrogation of the trio is a muddled affair; on strength of the recovery of Kinkaid's gun, the mob resolves to hang the three before dawn. Martin's death is a struggle. Farnley finishes him with a single shot. Ostensibly done with their mission, members bury the bodies and drive the cattle back to Drew's ranch. The simplistic closure reveals the group's miscalculation of their act.

The return to Bridger's Wells, Clark's Western forum, reconnects mob participants with the truth. Kinkaid is bandaged but still alive. Martin told the truth about the purchase of cattle. The impact of the night's violence sinks in. At the same time that Art rests from his injury, Gerald Tetley, a contemplative and guilt-ridden posse member, becomes the fourth victim by hanging himself from a beam in his father's barn. The jangled pattern of opinions and advice prevails. Davies, the major holdout against lynching, unburdens his conscience. Clark comes dangerously close to intruding on his characters with Davies's pathetic confession. Quivering against Art's bed, he laments:

> All a great, cowardly lie. . . . All pose; empty, gutless pretense. All the time the truth was I didn't want it to come to a showdown. The weakness that was in me all the time set up my sniveling little defense. I didn't even expect to save those men. The most I hoped was that something would do it for me. (ibid., 210)

Art concludes that the group didn't need a Christ, "all it had needed was a man." (ibid., 211) After Major Tetley falls on his sword Roman-fashion in grief for his son, the tentative tink-tink-a-link of the meadow lark begins to cleanse the evening air of rancor. Gil and Art retreat to the escapist mindset that fueled much of the settlement of the West: sickened by their part in the night's murderous work, they look forward to leaving Bridger's Wells.

Concerning his first novel, Clark wrote that he intended to confront formulaic Westerns and to breach conventions that confined frontier writing to a stale, predictable pattern. After *The Ox-Bow Incident,* he resigned from teaching and devoted himself to freelance writing. He published *The Track of the Cat* (1949), *The Watchful Gods, and Other Stories* (1950), and numerous pieces of short fiction and articles for *Saturday Review, Holiday, Western Review, Pacific Spectator, Chrysalis, New York Times, New Yorker, Nation,* and *New York Herald Tribune.*

Although he won few notable honors, he did receive the 1945 O. Henry Memorial award for "The Wind and the Snow of Winter," a poignant story about an old-timer from the Comstock days who anticipates seeing friends in Gold Rock but finds them long dead and the town modernized. Clark also earned an honorary degree from Colgate University in 1957. At his death on November 11, 1971, his first novel remained a classic in the frontier canon.

As a screen vehicle, Clark's cerebral, heroless Western earned mixed response. Directed by William Wellman and starring Henry Fonda, Henry Morgan, Jane Darwell, Anthony Quinn, Dana Andrews, and Mary Beth Hughes, the critically successful screen version won a 1943 Oscar nomination for best picture, but fared poorly at the box office. Reviews point to the unwieldy cast size, which confused the viewer with too many points of view. Wellman's cinema version of *The Track of the Cat* (1954) was also only marginally successful. (Blacker 1961; Calder 1975; Cawelti 1970; Clark 1968; *Contemporary Authors* 1994; Ehrlich and Carruth 1982; Folsom 1966; Lamar 1977; Magill 1958; Milner et al. 1994; Sarf 1983; Westbrook 1969)

See also Schaefer, Jack Warner.

CODY, BUFFALO BILL

Iowan Colonel William Frederick Cody, alternately labeled a hoax and the archetypal frontier plainsman, is claimed by Cody, Wyoming, setting of the Cody centennial. Born February 26, 1846, he was part of a westering family who moved to Kansas. After Indians killed his father, he supported his mother and sisters as a teamster for a freight company and as a railroad messenger. In his teens, he was hired by Jack Slade to ride for the Pony Express. Western writer Ned Buntline initiated a series of adventure stories about Cody in the *New York Weekly* in 1869, starting with "Buffalo Bill, the King of the Border Men." William Lightfoot Visscher, author of *The Pony Express: A Thrilling and Truthful History* (1908), claims to have met Cody at the Trans-Mississippi Exposition in Omaha in 1898. In decorative style, Visscher exults, "He passed through many a gauntlet of death in his flight from station to station, bearing express matter that was of the greatest value." (Visscher 1980, 44) The text presents the story in energized dialogue and anecdotes. Visscher emphasizes Cody's self-congratulatory voice, claiming that a round-trip of 322 miles from Rocky Ridge to Red Buttes was the "longest Pony Express journey ever made."

Renowned more for hunting buffalo than for delivering mail, Cody provided meat to railroad crews. While serving as a guide and scout for the army during the Indian wars, he earned a Medal of Honor. In the final chapters of his short, action-rich autobiography, *The Adventures of Buffalo Bill* (1904), he describes the backlash following Custer's defeat at the Battle of the Little Big Horn. As a scout for General Wesley Merritt's select horsemen, Cody engaged Yellow Hair (inaccurately reported as Yellow Hand), a Cheyenne chief, before he could unite with Sitting Bull and Crazy Horse. Cody describes the two-man

Former enemies now actors, Buffalo Bill Cody poses with the Sioux chief Sitting Bull in a South Dakota studio in 1891. Both men led legendary lives in the mid-1800s, Sitting Bull as a leader of his people and participant in the 1876 Battle of the Little Big Horn, and Buffalo Bill as a Pony Express rider, scout, and showman.

battle, in which both fire from their mounts, then face off on foot. Cody claims that luck favored him: "He reeled and fell, but before he had fairly touched the ground I was upon him, knife in hand, and had driven the keen-edged weapon to its hilt in his heart." (Cody 1904, 80) The action ends with Cody jerking the war bonnet from his head and slicing off his scalp. Jubilant, he waves his trophy and shouts to Merritt and his men, "the first scalp for Custer." (ibid., 81)

After organizing the fast-paced Buffalo Bill Cody's Wild West Show in 1883, Cody became a world figure. Visitors crowded his tents to see roping, sharpshooting, trick riding, and contrived scenarios involving longhorns, elk, buffalo, log cabins, stagecoaches, forts, and American Indians. Poet Carl Sandburg immortalized the spirit of the Buffalo Bill Wild West Show in the longing of Johnny Jones, the focus of the poem "Buffalo Bill," in which a young boy aches to see the great slant-eyed showman. Sandburg pleads,

> Come on and slant your eyes again, O Buffalo Bill. Give us again the ache of our boy hearts. Fill us again with the red love of prairies, dark nights, lonely wagons and the crack-crack of rifles sputtering flashes into an ambush. (Coleman 1932, 89)

For 30 years, the spectacle toured the United States, Canada, and Europe, helping to fuel foreign stereotypes that Americans were primarily prairie hunters and pioneers. The French idolized Cody for introducing them to the "peau rouge" or "redskins."

Cody was famous for generosity and for investing in mining and land projects. In the 1890s, he homesteaded on the southern fork of the Shoshone River in Yellowstone, Wyoming. He and fellow entrepreneurs dug irrigation lines to water tracts of land, which he sold to individual ranchers. The growth of the area surged after he provided tourists a spur line of the Burlington Railroad and the Irma Hotel, Buffalo Bill's Hotel in the Rockies. The end of his life found him bankrupt and disillusioned. He died on a visit to his sister in 1917 and was buried in Colorado rather than his beloved Wyoming. Friends chartered the Buffalo Bill Historical Center, a major draw for Western aficionados. The center boasts the Cody Firearms Museum, Plains Indian Museum, Buffalo Bill Museum, and Whitney Gallery of Western Art, a collection of the great names in Western painting, featuring works by George Catlin, Charles Russell, and Frederic Remington. (Burns and Ives 1996a; Cody 1904; Coleman 1932; Downes 1996; Driggs 1935; Lamar 1977; Rainey 1996; Visscher 1980; Waldman 1990)

See also Catlin, George; Custer, George Armstrong; Oakley, Annie.

COOPER, JAMES FENIMORE

James Fenimore Cooper belongs at the head of any list of American frontier writers. The father of the American historical novel and the sea romance, he is also one of the nation's prominent travel writers and social commentators. Born in Burlington, New Jersey, on September 15, 1789, in the year of the first Continental Congress, he was the eleventh of the 12 children of Otsego County judge and congressman William Cooper and Elizabeth Fenimore Cooper. Within months of his birth, the Coopers moved to the frontier and settled on 40,000 acres at the headwaters of the Susquehanna River. William Cooper built the family mansion, Otsego Hall, at a crude hamlet in upper New York State. Later, the town was named Cooperstown to honor his role in property development and to acknowledge his pioneer's handbook, *A Guide in the Wilderness or the History of the First Settlements in the Western Counties of New York* (1810), descriptive advice intended for investors. From locals and visitors to Cooperstown, young Cooper heard the oral lore of hunters and woodsmen, which later formed the basis of his Leatherstocking Tales, a lasting literary monument to the frontier.

As the son of a privileged, wealthy Quaker family, Cooper received private tutoring under Thomas Ellison, an Episcopal rector of St. Peter's Church in Albany, and entered Yale at age 14. In his teens, even though he excelled in Latin, he rebelled against the study of Hebrew and the classics. Fiercely independent, he was dismissed from Yale in his third year for setting a powder charge that burst the lock of a classmate's door. To contain James's high spirits and end his time wasting, William Cooper enlisted him in the navy as a common sailor. In 1806, Cooper shipped out aboard the *Stirling* to England, served on the *Vesuvius*, and traveled to Lake Ontario to the construction site of the brigantine *Oneida*, part of the Great Lakes fleet. In two years he was commissioned a midshipman and earned assignment to the *Wasp* as its recruiting officer. His enthusiasm for the sea ended in ennui in 1811; he married Susan Augusta De Lancey, an aristocrat of similar background to the Coopers, and resided for three years at Angevine Farm at Mamaroneck before settling at Cooperstown.

After a political enemy murdered his father outside a tavern with a blow to the head, Cooper inherited $50,000 and managed the family estate. In 1817, he used family money to establish Fenimore Farm near Scarsdale. In his spare time, he dabbled in local politics and performed volunteer service for the American Bible Society. He and his spendthrift siblings soon ran through their father's money. Following the deaths of his five older brothers, he became the squire of Otsego Hall and supported their widows. To retire family debts, Cooper's wife challenged him to earn money by emulating Jane Austen's domestic romances. He published *Precaution* (1820), an undistinguished, gentrified idyll set in England and replete with sententious elegance. He admitted that the novel was conventional and derivative and set out to write something more original.

To accommodate American settings, themes, and rhythms, Cooper altered his style to imitate Sir Walter Scott's Waverly series and wrote a Revolutionary War–era thriller, *The Spy* (1821). Described from the point of view of Harvey Birch, a voluble peddler infiltrating British loyalists to learn information for the colonists, the suspenseful patriotic novel was a critical and financial triumph in the United States and Europe. Success as the nation's first historical novelist brought Cooper respite from bankruptcy, an honorary degree from Columbia University, and a clutch of fans, colleagues, and cultural leaders, who met regularly as New York's Bread and Cheese Club. Among them were poet William Cullen Bryant and inventor Samuel Morse.

After Cooper published two novels, *The Pilot* and *The Pirate,* in 1823, he launched the Leatherstocking Tales, a quintet of adventure novels featuring sharpshooter Nathaniel "Natty" Bumppo, a frontier veteran of years with Moravian missionaries ministering to the Delaware of Pennsylvania and with the Pawnee on the Plains. Natty is a composite figure drawn from the biography of Daniel Boone and from famous woodsmen whom Cooper knew and admired. The fictional wilderness scout passes through five incarnations: Deerslayer, Hawkeye, Pathfinder, Leatherstocking, and the aged trapper. In all forms, Natty is an elusive figure who chooses not to disclose his past. Like the mysterious code hero of subsequent movie and TV Westerns, he says little about his origins and keeps to himself.

Written out of chronological sequence, the Leatherstocking series begins with *The Pioneers or, The Sources of the Susquehanna* (1823), which depicts the forebears of Cooperstown's residents. Cooper's optimism toward the frontier arises early in the panoramic description of New York's lake district:

> The mountains are generally arable to the tops, although instances are not wanting where the sides are jutted with rocks, that aid greatly in giving to the country that romantic and picturesque character which it so eminently possesses. The vales are narrow, rich, and cultivated; with a stream uniformly winding through each. Beautiful and thriving villages are found interspersed along the margins of the small lakes, or situated at those points of the streams which are favorable to manufacturing; and neat and comfortable farms, with every indication of wealth about them, are scattered profusely through the vales, even to the mountain tops. (Cooper 1968, 13)

The conflict that powers the plot lies not in vales, lakes, or farmland, but in the hearts of the main characters, who live worlds apart in their attitudes toward God, virtue, ambition, and human relations.

For personae of the novel, Cooper recasts his father as Judge Marmaduke Temple of Templeton and ends the life of the first Native American literary hero, Chingachgook, also called John Mohegan, who expires after singing a ritual death song in the aftermath of dramatic forest fire. Cooper focuses on the ethnic differences that separate woodsmen and townspeople, didactic white clergyman and sage animist. As the Indian speaks his last to Natty Bumppo, he makes a pointed discovery: on the path to the happy hunting-grounds, he discerns "no white skins," only "just and brave Indians." (ibid., 588) Natty clings to the stiffening hand and laments that life has grown cumbersome for him because the wild has retreated in the distance as settlers move onto the landscape that once was the hunter's domain. He disdains the wholesale slaughter of pigeons for sport and complains, "There is scarcely a tree standing that I know, and it's hard to find a place that I was acquainted with in my younger days." (ibid., 591) To return to natural law, Natty leaves the settled area and pushes farther west.

The second of the series, *The Last of the Mohicans* (1826), turns on a hardy chase motif that evolved from reader feedback on *The Pioneers.* Set among the

Huron near Lake Champlain, the novel draws on Jonathan Carver's *Travels through the Interior Parts of North America* (1778) and David Humphrey's *Essay on the Life of the Honorable Major-General Israel Putnam* (1788). For maximum excitement, Cooper capitalizes on the abduction motif and on the unrequited— and socially repugnant—love between Cora Munro and Uncas, the last Mohican. Uncas, known by the French phrase *Le Cerf Agile* (the spry stag), is the enemy of Cooper's darkest villain, Magua, *Le Renard Subtil* (the cunning fox), a challenger for the hand of Cora. Daring to press the issue of miscegenation, Cooper resorts to a tragic turn of plot that suppresses the attraction between the swarthy young female and the vigorous Mohican brave by killing both. The final chapter depicts Uncas's funeral, where "They pronounced him noble, manly and generous; all that became a warrior, and all that a maid might love" (Cooper 1989, 366), as though according him in death the qualities that society discounted in his life.

The third Leatherstocking novel, *The Prairie* (1827), a tribute to virgin landscape, brings the Leatherstocking saga to its end. The plot carries the aged Natty Bumppo from the spoiled, oversettled woodlands to the pristine Western prairie, where he braves the dangers of hostile Plains tribes to trap alone. The style is less romantic and more contemplative, filled with ponderous and at times elegiac passages in which Cooper appears to consider the future of the nation as settlement passes from the Eastern coast to the trans-Mississippi region and beyond. He surmises:

> In the pursuit of adventures . . . men are ordinarily governed by their habits or deluded by their wishes. A few, led by the phantoms of hope and ambitious of sudden affluence, sought the mines of the virgin territory; but by far the greater portion of the emigrants were satisfied to establish themselves along the margins of the larger water-courses, content with the rich returns that the generous, alluvial bottoms of the rivers never fail to bestow on the most desultory industry. (Cooper 1958, 3)

Thus, Cooper bids farewell to the Eastern woods in anticipation of virgin land in the West with its rolling prairie, determined pioneers, and "vehicles, loaded with household goods and implements of husbandry," preceding their livestock as they seek the "Eldorado of the West." Yet, the advance of white settlers to the plains does not guarantee a utopia. Adding to the uncertainty of human expectations in unknown lands is the slender promise extending from bleak, untried turf that bears little resemblance to the lush meadows, forest resources, and deep harbors of the East Coast.

Wistful and perhaps a little homesick, Cooper completed *The Prairie*—his favorite of the five Leatherstocking Tales—while he and his family lived among ostentatious notables in France. Reflecting on America, he appears to mourn the end of an era, when settlement of the frontier challenged the ideal of Natty Bumppo. The story replicates Cooper's characteristic antitheses: capture and rescue, nobility and savagery, faith and betrayal. For details of Western life, the author—who had no experience on the Western frontier—relied on popular source material, particularly the Lewis and Clark journals, as well as John

Heckewelder's *Account of the History, Manners, and Customs of the Indian Nations Who Once Inhabited Pennsylvania and the Neighboring States* (1819) and biographies of Daniel Boone. Cooper appears to construct his novel from a series of vignettes, which he limns on paper as though he were arranging characters and props in a setting for a cinematic tableau. The resulting staged drama invites the imagination, yet robs the reader of a fully realized, three-dimensional scenario.

After a 13-year hiatus, Cooper returned to his frontier series to write the final two volumes: *The Pathfinder: or The Inland Sea* (1840) and *The Deerslayer* (1841). The former combines the dash of sailing on Lake Ontario with the serenity of the forest, which is threatened by the French and Indian Wars. Like Adam in Eden, hero Natty is ambivalent toward solitude. At the close of a rather limp love triangle, another man wins the girl and the pathfinder glides into the wild with a regretful toss of the head, but no backward glance. Familiar, yet elusive, the legendary hunter retains his appeal: "a being of great purity of character and of as marked peculiarities." (Cooper 1964, 384) In *The Pathfinder*, he earns the sobriquet Leatherstocking, the symbolic rough, unfinished exterior that sets him apart from both the more polished, educated Easterner and the bare-legged Indians he befriends.

Cooper concluded the Leatherstocking Tales with *The Deerslayer*, the earliest view of Natty Bumppo and a tribute to the unshakable Christian and man of the forest. Set in Otsego in 1760, the novel idealizes Cooper's New York and the wilds beyond:

> A bird's-eye view of the whole region east of the Mississippi must then have offered one vast expanse of woods, relieved by a comparatively narrow fringe of cultivation along the sea, dotted by the glittering surfaces of lakes, and intersected by the waving lines of rivers. (Cooper 1980, 10)

To the author, the spectacular beauties of the frontier display the structured cycles of nature, ordered by the Creator "with a sublime precision." The hero, Deerslayer, at age 24, lives a treasured harmony and dresses and acts the part of one who passes his days "between the skirts of civilized society and the boundless forest." His encounters with danger and with the love of Judith Hutter challenge his complacency, yet these threats to his lifestyle wed him inextricably to the code of the frontier loner. A solitary resident of the wilderness cosmos, Deerslayer embraces celibacy as an unavoidable element of his peripatetic adventures.

Overall, the Leatherstocking series is uneven in quality, style, and philosophy. Natty Bumppo, though civilized and mannerly, lives an asocial existence in the no-man's-land that divides white settlements from native villages. Representing neither colonist nor Native American, Cooper's hero is an escapist. A champion of the forest, he nonetheless withdraws into self rather than involve himself in the East Coast's irreconcilable conflicts over settlement of Indian lands. By nature detached and objective, he has little at stake with either faction in an era of potentially cataclysmic confrontation. It is to Natty's advantage that the decisive battles over America's manifest destiny were still a quarter century away.

Of the five Leatherstocking Tales, *The Deerslayer* ranks best for structure but suffers from geographic and factual inaccuracy. The novel is understandably less popular than the action-packed *The Last of the Mohicans*, with its engrossing themes of retribution and unrequited romance. The classic figure of Natty Bumppo reflects the qualities of the epic hero and of the *chevalier* and Grail Seeker of Arthurian convention. He pairs well with Chingachgook, the noble savage idolized by François Chateaubriand and Jean-Jacques Rousseau. By blending the Mohican's Native American wisdom and woods lore with Natty's Christian principles of fraternity and morality, the Leatherstocking saga epitomizes the pathfinder's dedication to honor, decency, and respect for nature and humanity.

Taken singly or together, the Leatherstocking Tales comprise Cooper's most lasting contributions to American prose and to the pioneer ideal. He was the first major spokesperson to acknowledge the influence of the frontier on American character. In addition to frontier novels, he produced *Lionel Lincoln* (1825), the first of a short-lived series to be called *Legends of the Thirteen Republics*. He also wrote *The Wept of Wish-Ton-Wish* (1829), *The Water-Witch* (1829), *The Bravo* (1831), *The Heidenmauer* (1832), and *The Headsman* (1833). Comfortably well off from royalties, in 1826 he assumed the post of U.S. consul at Lyons and toured Holland, Germany, Italy, Switzerland, Belgium, France, and England. While living in Paris, he kept his thoughts on home and continued composing on American themes. His popular works earned as much as $20,000 annually in royalties and underwrote tuition to good schools for his son and four daughters. His style and subject matter found favor with his idol, Sir Walter Scott, as well as literati of later periods—Johann von Goethe, George Sand, Alexandre Dumas, O. E. Rölvaag, Joseph Conrad, and William Makepeace Thackeray. French novelist Honoré de Balzac summarized Cooper's contribution to literature in his toast to *"le grand écrivain américain."*

The notoriety that attaches to Cooper's works did not shield him from changes in the public's tastes and politics. After the market for colonial literature waned, in 1833 the Cooper family returned to New York, where their aristocratic views met serious challenge from Jacksonian egalitarians. Further deterioration of Cooper's reputation derived from his polemics, *Notions of the Americans* (1828), *Letter to His Countrymen* (1834), and *The American Democrat* (1838). He turned next to travelogues and histories: *History of the Navy of the United States of America* (1839), *The Two Admirals* (1842), *Ned Myers* (1843), and *Lives of Distinguished American Naval Officers* (1845). His last fiction—*Wyandotte* (1843), *Satanstoe* (1845), *The Chainbearer* (1845), *The Redskins* (1846), and *The Crater* (1848)—were poor in comparison to earlier triumphs because Cooper used them as pulpits for dogmatism and outlets for anger. Although he shared the popularity of the Knickerbocker Group, which included the beloved Washington Irving and William Cullen Bryant, he annoyed Americans and Europeans by criticizing American and French culture and politics. Because he seemed out of touch with his homeland, he was mocked by detractors, embroiled in libel suits, and disillusioned with the progressive alteration of his beloved frontier. A frequent litigant, he successfully sued New York *Tribune* editor Horace Greeley in 1842 for publicly deriding him, but the triumph only intensified public scorn. As ineptitude and melodrama plagued his fiction, Cooper produced defensive monographs, which did nothing toward reestablishing his former popularity. Incapable of dispelling the aura of chauvinism, cattiness, and dilettantism, he feared that, except for the Leatherstocking Tales, his published works would sink into oblivion. Consequently, he capitalized on his one strength: vigorous championship of the trailblazer's spirit.

Despondent and misunderstood, Cooper clung to an outmoded eighteenth-century vision of America until the end. He died in Cooperstown on September 14, 1851, and was buried in Christ Church Cemetery. At his death, he was honored as the father of the American historical romance; later criticism extended the honors by naming him forerunner of Hawthorne, Melville, and Western novelists Zane Grey, Louis L'Amour, Conrad Richter, and Owen Wister. However, modern analysts temper respect with a frank admission of weakness. In general, Cooper's clumsy love plots, ornate philosophical commentary, one-dimensional minor characters, and Continental stereotypes of the noble pioneer repel modern readers. His illogic netted a travesty, *Muck-a-Muck*, by Bret Harte, and provoked the scorn of Mark Twain, whose essay, "Fenimore Cooper's Literary Offenses" (1895), is eternally paired with *The Deerslayer*. The hint of physical attraction between his idealized males and winsome females, especially those of different races, social levels, and cultures, causes Cooper to shy away from honest human passion. He distances himself from true characterization by contriving wooden, sententious dialogue and tedious digressions. His retreat into nature lore and cliff-hangers is a sham refuge that further demonstrates his inability to touch on the realities of frontier life. He had planned a sixth novel to place Natty in the American Revolution, but abandoned the project after he wearied of his series.

Despite the author's eventual disaffection for Leatherstocking, numerous literary tributes and memorials perpetuate the pathfinder's mystique. Fans of the gallant, swift-footed Uncas still make pilgrimages to Tschoop's burial mound in Bethlehem, Pennsylvania. Tourists seek Lake Glimmerglass, Cooper's Cave in Glens Falls, and the tomb of trapper Nathaniel Shipman, the model for Natty Bumppo, who is buried in Hoosick Falls, New York. A few pursue another possible Natty, Ephraim Webster, who is buried in the Onondaga Valley Cemetery in Syracuse. Their persistence attests to the uniqueness of Cooper's heroes. D. H. Lawrence defied an academic tradition of devaluing Cooper by lauding his frontier myth in *Studies in Classic American Literature* (1923), which ushered in a new era of Cooper criticism. Two versions of *The Last of the Mohicans* have reset the drama for the screen: a 1936 edition starring Randolph Scott, and Warner's 1992 color spectacular, starring Daniel Day-Lewis and Madeleine Stowe. It is curious that the latter screenplay, a flawed rewrite of Cooper's original, avoids the subject of Uncas's love for Cora Munro by energetically restructuring the plot to suit Hollywood's preference for violence and mayhem over love.

Cooper himself has become an international icon of frontier lore. His daughter Susan, born in 1813, extended the life of the Leatherstocking series by supplying late-nineteenth-century editions of his works with authentic preface material. At Lakewood near Cooperstown stands a statue of Natty Bumppo; a seated statue of Cooper resides in Cooper Park. In France, Pierre Jean David carved a portrait bust of the author and Hector Berlioz named a musical composition, *Le corsaire rouge*, after Cooper's *The Red Rover* (1827). Fenimore Cottage, the Cooper home and current headquarters of the New York Historical Association, houses documents, paintings, and original manuscripts; other memorabilia reside at the Beinecke Rare Book and Manuscript Library at Yale University. (Clymer 1969; Cooper, James 1963, 1964, 1968, 1980, 1989; Cooper, William 1970; Dekker and McWilliams 1973; Folsom 1966; Franklin 1982; Grossman 1949; Hazard 1927; Kelly 1984; Ladd 1996; Lamar 1977; Levine 1989; Long 1990; Motley 1988; Rainey 1996; Ringe 1988; Spiller 1991; Spiller and Blodgett 1949; Thomas 1987; Trent et al. 1946; Walker 1962; Wallace 1986)

See also Boone, Daniel; Harte, Bret; Irving, Washington; *The Last of the Mohicans;* Twain, Mark.

COWBOYS IN LITERATURE

The romanticized story of the Western cowboy is perhaps the most resilient myth of the frontier. Retold in countless anonymous verses, dime novels, sensationalized newspaper articles, children's literature, radio and TV programs, Hollywood movies, and advertising, the life of the Western cowpuncher has evolved into a familiar stereotype—rider of horses, wearer of chaps, shooter of rifles, roper of longhorns, and breaker of broncos. Vachel Lindsay immortalizes the cowboy's hapless range colt in his poem "The Broncho That Would Not Be Broken." Born free on the prairie, the spirited animal bursts into its prance for the entertainment of its pursuers, but ultimately loses the fight against its conqueror, the cowboy:

> In that last afternoon your boyish heart broke.
> The hot wind came down like a sledge-hammer stroke,
> The blood-sucking flies to a rare feast awoke. . . .
> Then you died on the prairie, and scorned all disgraces,
> O broncho that would not be broken of dancing. (Coleman 1932, 314)

The cowboy won out over his animal opponents, but, as immortalized in frontier convention, achieved an impermanent truce with his nemeses—sheepherders, nesters, mechanization, and the obdurate barbed wire.

An early historian of Plains lore as well as a Pinkerton detective, storekeeper, and peace officer, Texan Charles A. Siringo produced the first bestselling cowboy autobiography, *A Texas Cowboy, or, Fifteen Years on the Hurricane Deck of a Spanish Cow Pony* (1885), a classic work that has remained in print for over a century. He also wrote *The Cowboy Detective* (1912), *Two Evil Isms: Pinkertonism and Anarchism* (1915), *A Lone Star Cowboy* (1919), *A Song Companion of a Lone Star Cowboy* (1919), *A History of Billy the Kid* (1920), and *Riata and*

FRANK LESLIE'S ILLUSTRATED NEWSPAPER

No. 1322.—Vol. LI   NEW YORK, JANUARY 29, 1881.   [Price 10 Cents.

Cowboys led what urban readers imagined as a romantic life of freedom on the open prairie, a simple life of hard work with a good horse and occasional hardships with nature or Indians. Magazines, such as *Frank Leslie's Illustrated Newspaper*, pictured here, published stories and sketches that fueled the myth.

Spurs (1927) and billed himself as "an old stove up cow puncher who has spent nearly a life time on the great western cattle ranges." (Siringo 1950, xiii) He spent 20 years on the range, including stints in Tascosa, Indianola, and Tulerosa and on the Chisholm Trail. He claims to write for money, but his love of the range is obvious. He has an eye for detail, as demonstrated in this passage on the loss of animals during a hard year:

> To give you an idea how badly cattle died that winter I will state that, at times, right after a sleet, a man could walk on dead animals for miles without stepping on the ground. This, of course, would be along the bay shore, where they would pile up on top of one another, not being able to go further, on account of the water. (ibid., 56)

The mild exaggeration suggests that Siringo is a facile raconteur skilled with the typical Western tall tale. His knowledge of good times, hard times, and contemporary lingo are obvious from the fair sprinkling of Western jargon, for example, maverick, bulldog, grit, breaks, rifle pits, itchy-footed, dragoon pistol, chuck wagon, Joe-dandy, bed ground, round-up, cutting, draw, blue coats, and bucking monte, a saloon pastime that claimed much of the cowboy's end-of-trail pay.

To the end of the first edition of *A Texas Cowboy*, Siringo added seven addenda, each a detailed aspect of cowpunching that he deemed worth the mention. He discusses the overhead involved in wintering and delivering cattle, starting up, and maintaining water rights. In an extensive summary of the cow pony's life, he strikes to the heart of grueling, gritty labor: "The bridle is put onto you, and then your lazy master picks up the dirty, hard saddle blankets—which have not been washed for a month—and throws them over your raw and swollen back." The harsh tone extends to pity for the equally wretched cowboy, who, out of sympathy for his mount, may "throw up a paying job rather than ride one of those poor sore-backed brutes." (ibid., 210–211) Siringo concludes that there should be a law making it punishable by hard time to abuse, neglect, or override the weary cow pony.

One of the most irresistible of cowboy memoirs is Andy Adams's *The Log of a Cowboy: A Narrative of the Old Trail Days* (1903). A drover who turned to freelance writing about the Old West, Adams sold stories to magazines before publishing his reflective journal, an overnight success. He delineates the geographic movements of herds and comments on a restful break from a journey:

> Our long hours in the saddle, coupled with the monotony of our work, made these supply points of such interest to us that they were like oases in desert lands to devotees on pilgrimage to some consecrated shrine. We could have spent a week in Ogalalla and enjoyed our visit every blessed moment of the time. (Adams 1975, 275)

Adams toys with atmosphere, expertly limning the shift in mood among plainsmen. On his return to regular herd duty a few days before Christmas, he notes that a worker of Shanghai Pierce's livestock accidentally shot and killed himself when his horse reared, causing his gun to discharge. Blending sweet with sour in frontier fashion, Adams turns from the respite of a few days in town to contemplation of a suitable monument. In a clump of cottonwoods, mourners fence off the grave with a square pen; a flat headstone and mound stones protect the body from animal predators. In a tree, the carved letters of the victim's name preserve his memory. Adams adds, "There was nothing different about this grave from the hundreds of others which made landmarks on the Old Western Trail, except it was the latest." (ibid., 276)

The lethal incident provokes campfire philosophers. Rod Wheat declares, "You can't avoid it when it comes, and every now and then you miss it by a hair." Fox reserves his pity "for a mother or sister who might wish that he slept nearer home." Flood wishes that he had been on guard so that he could have missed the gloomy stories. An outrider named John Officer returns to camp and declares he can make doughnuts, which he calls "bear sign." The next morning, gloom dissipates as Officer puts in a full day of doughnut making. The treat that some haven't tasted since boyhood draws men from other outfits, one from 25 miles away. Once more in good humor, Adams confides, "This luck of ours was circulating faster than a secret amongst women." (ibid., 283) The gorging and reminiscing continues until the cattle get jumpy and the cowboys hit the saddle to earn their keep through an all-night drizzle. (Adams 1975; Burns and Ives 1996b; Lamar 1977; Rainey 1996; Siringo 1950)

See also Gipson, Fred; law and order; Love, Nat.

CROCKETT, DAVY

A noted scrapper, yarn spinner, and pathfinder in his own day, Colonel David "Davy" Crockett survives in America's Western lore as a symbol of independence, martyr of the Alamo, and colorful frontier myth. At the height of his political career, the growing legend of his frontier exploits spawned numerous primitive penny broadsides and newspaper features; a smash-hit stage parody, James Kirke Paulding's *The Lion of the West* (1831), which mimics Crockett in the character Kentucky Colonel Nimrod Wildfire; and a contrived biography, Mathew St. Clair Clarke's *The Life and Adventures of Colonel David Crockett of West Tennessee* (1833), reprised in its second printing as *Sketches and Eccentricities of Colonel David Crockett*. Crockett countered Clarke's faulty work and other scurrilous caricatures of himself by hiring Thomas Chilton to help him compose his folksy dialect reflection, *Narrative of the Life of David Crockett of the State of Tennessee* (1834), one of the nineteenth century's most popular autobiographies. Composed in Washington on February 1, 1834, his preface summarizes his spirit of frontier independence: "Most authors seek fame, but I seek for justice,—a holier impulse than ever entered into the ambitious struggles of the votaries of the *fickle, flirting goddess.*" (Crockett 1834, 3) He published two more works the next year—*An Account of Colonel Crockett's Tour to the North and Down East* and *The Life of Martin Van Buren, Hair-Apparent to the "Government," and the Appointed Successor of General Jackson,* a derisive biography.

Crockett's writings offer sparse but definitive details of his life. The grandson of North Carolina homesteaders and son of John and Rebecca Hawkins

Crockett, he was born the fifth son of nine children on August 17, 1786, in Tennessee. Crockett mentions with pride that his father was a veteran of the Battle of Kings Mountain. His family had moved from Virginia over the Smoky Mountains to the rough community of Rogersville, where hostile Creeks killed his paternal grandparents, wounded his uncle Joseph, and took his uncle James prisoner for a year and a half until an older brother could ransom him for an undisclosed sum.

When Crockett was ten, his family opened an inn on the Abingdon-Knoxville road, where he worked at odd jobs. Of this frontier establishment, he writes: "His tavern was on a small scale, as he was poor; and the principal accommodations which he kept, were for the wagoneers who traveled the road." (ibid., 22) He admits that he was an indifferent student and that offers of work enticed him to run away. He accepted short-term jobs as herdsman, wagoneer, and farm hireling and enjoyed shooting matches in his spare time. After losing his first sweetheart to a rival, he married Mary "Polly" Finley in 1806, whom he supported by farming and selling wild game and hides. Six years later, he made his initial overtures to the West by resettling his wife and two sons, first in Lincoln County, then in Franklin, Tennessee.

Service as a scout with Andrew Jackson's men in the Creek Indian war of 1813–1814 and as an infantryman with Major Russell's mounted sharpshooters introduced Crockett to Alabama and Florida. Near Ten Islands on the Coosa River, he saw action at an Indian town and describes the horror of Indian fighting:

> We now shot them like dogs; and then set the house on fire, and burned it up with the forty-six warriors in it. I recollect seeing a boy who was shot down near the house. His arm and thigh was broken, and he was so near the burning house that the grease was stewing out of him. In this situation he was still trying to crawl along; but not a murmur escaped him, though he was only about twelve years old. So sullen is the Indian when his dander is up, that he had sooner die than make a noise, or ask for quarters. (ibid., 88–89)

He concludes on a grislier note: the hungry Indian fighters discover a potato cellar under the burned house. Although the bodies exuded oils, seasoning the potatoes "like they had been stewed with fat meat," the victorious soldiers feast on them, then turn to beef hides for meat.

On his return to civilian life, Crockett shifted from fighter to pioneer. After his wife died following the birth of a daughter, he married a widow, Elizabeth Patton, collected a sizable dowry, and added her son and three daughters to his family. The Crocketts traversed Lawrence County in search of a homestead. He departed alone to Alabama, came down with malaria, and was reported dead before the end of his convalescence and surprise return to Tennessee. Settling down once more, he served as a local magistrate, town commissioner, and colonel of the militia. His commentary on frontier justice indicates his low level of literacy:

> I improved my handwriting in such manner as to be able to prepare my warrants, and keep my record book, without much difficulty. My judgments were never appealed from, and if they had been they would have stuck like wax, as

> I gave my decisions on the principles of common justice and honesty between man and man, and relied on natural born sense, and not on law, learning to guide me; for I had never read a page in a law book in all my life. (ibid., 135)

While challenging Dr. William E. Butler in a run for the state legislature, Crockett made his first political address. He reports that he "choaked up as bad as if my mouth had been jam'd and cram'd chock full of dry mush." (ibid., 141) He amused the public with mocking stump speeches that glorified Butler's grandiose lifestyle. This strategy of reverse psychology caused voters to perceive Crockett as a model of the common man and to revile Butler as a self-serving plutocrat.

Crockett won a seat in the state legislature. The event coincided with a low point in his fortunes, when a flood destroyed his gristmill, which fed his distillery. Impoverished by the loss, he took consolation in his wife's sensible counsel:

> She didn't advise me, as is too fashionable, to smuggle up this, and that, and t'other, to go on at home; but she told me, says she, "Just pay up, as long as you have a bit's worth in the world; and then every body will be satisfied, and we will scuffle for more." This was just such talk as I wanted to hear, for a man's wife can hold him devilish uneasy, if she begins to scold, and fret, and perplex him, at a time when he has a full load for a rail-road car on his mind already. (ibid., 145)

After making a new start on the Orion River, he recalls the difficulties of living in the wild without a fence to keep out "wild *varments*" and of feeding his family on the meat of ample deer and ten bears shot in the spring of 1822. Juggling home and called sessions of the legislature, he earns a reputation as "the bear hunter, the man from the cane." (ibid., 167)

In 1827, Crockett was elected to the U.S. House of Representatives. Subsequent periods in and out of office and a grassroots canvass of Whigs for support of a presidential run interspersed his woods career with politics. Championing the Democratic platform, he initially supported Jacksonian policies, then shifted his stance when he realized he was expected to rubber-stamp Jackson's every whim. In his signature frontier humor, Crockett declared, "I wouldn't take a collar around my neck with the letters engraved on it, MY DOG. Andrew Jackson." (ibid., 171–172) Crockett denounced the popular president for initiating the Indian bill, a stringent policy that proposed resettling the Cherokee, Choctaw, Creek, and Chickasaw west to Indian territory over what was later called the Trail of Tears. Crockett concluded his autobiography with a fierce declaration:

> I am now here in Congress . . . what is more agreeable to my feelings as a freeman, I am at liberty to vote as my conscience and judgment dictates to be right, without the yoke of any party on me, or the driver at my heels, with his whip in hand. (ibid., 210)

The remainder of his life, Crockett energetically opposed Jacksonian policies for their corruption, favoritism, and insincerity toward the working man.

Crockett's freewheeling philosophy, irrepressible witticisms, and low-key politicking prefigures the stump style of Abraham Lincoln. In a fiery address on congressional finances, Crockett proposed that he single-handedly clear out "the hull nest o' your political weasels." He offers to "work Uncle Sam's farm, till I restore it to its natural state o' cultivation, and shake off these state caterpillars o' corruption." (Crockett 1996, 1) His homespun grammar, idiom, and choice Crockettisms, such as "bodyaciously," "helliferocious," "riproarious," "fairation," "tetotaciously," and "obflisticated," endeared him to voters who functioned at the same level of illiteracy.

After Crockett's tenure in the Tennessee House of Representatives ended in defeat, he launched a series of seven *Crockett Almanacks* (1835–1838) in which he departs from the straightforward narration of his autobiography to play the unassuming backwoods dupe. One of the most read frontier publications in the years following his death, the almanacs feature fellow congressman Ben Harding as Crockett's sidekick. The homely southwestern jests, teasing, stunts, cliff-hangers, outrageous farce, and rambunctious tall tales reflect a backwoods trend toward exaggeration of dangers, hoaxes, and exploits that reached its height in the Paul Bunyan tales.

Crockett's self-styled heroism ranges beyond hyperbole to humor. A rustic prodigy from childhood, he describes himself as oversized at birth and thriving on a diet of whiskey and rattlesnake eggs. He claims to "run faster,—jump higher,—squat lower,—dive deeper,—stay under longer,—and come out drier, than any man in the whole country." (Crockett 1987, xxix) He introduces himself to voters as "half-horse, half-alligator, a little touched with the snapping-turtle." (Derr 1993, 19) In a marathon bluster, he declares,

> I can outlook a panther and outstare a flash of lightning: tote a steamboat on my back and play at rough and tumble with a lion, and an occasional kick from a *Zebra*. Goliath was a pretty hard colt but I could choke him.—I can take the rag off—frighten the old folks—astonish the natives—and beat the Dutch all to smash—make nothing of sleeping under a blanket of snow—and don't mind being frozen more than a rotten apple. (Crockett 1987, xxviii)

In print, the facets of his life reach epic heights—the prettiest wife, ugliest dog, roughest horse, keenest knife, truest friend, and most dependable rifle, which he called Killdevil. The publication of these stretchers caused ill-humored detractors to spread unfounded rumors of Crockett's gambling, philandering, corruption, cowardice, and disloyalty.

The Crockett canon of "ring-tailed roarers" demonstrates the frontier version of the trickster motif. Boisterous and calculating, he applies his wits to outsmarting "mud turkles," bears, grizzlies, catamounts, pirates, and Indians. In the anecdote of his courtship of Zipporina, he attributes trickery to the woman. When a miner from Wisconsin tries to beat Davy's time with "Zippy," she covers herself with a bearskin and leads him into the forest:

> It was alfired dark, and so he couldn't tell a great black bear that Zippy had driven along before her from Zippy herself. So he went up to the bear, and the

feller put his arms around the varmint's neck, and it stood right up on its hind legs, and give him a most beautiful hug. (ibid., 14)

The wooer shouts, "Don't hug me quite so hard, dear Zipporina! Oh! Oh! Zippy-Zip-Zip, you will choke me with your love." The miner, ripped and torn by the bear's claws, deserts his beloved and flees back to Wisconsin. He warns other beaux not to court women along the Mississippi, "for the gals up that way loved so hard they would have squeezed his bowels out if he hadn't got away from them."

At the age of 49, Crockett, along with companions William Patton, Lindsey Tinkle, and Abner Burgin, arranged an expedition bound for San Antonio, Texas, with the intention of moving his family farther west. To his detractors at the bar, Crockett remarked, "Since you have chosen to elect a man with a timber toe to succeed me, you may all go to hell and I will go to Texas." (ibid., xxiii) Eight weeks before his death, he wrote a glowing letter praising Texas as "the garden spot of the world" and hoping for a seat on its constitutional committee. He concludes, "I am rejoiced at my fate. I had rather be in my present situation than to be elected to a seat in Congress for life. I am in hopes of making a fortune yet for myself and family, bad as my prospect has been." (ibid., xxiv) Typically optimistic, Crockett applied to the Texas adventure his lifetime philosophy, "Be sure you're right, then go ahead." (ibid., xxxv)

The buoyance of Crockett's can-do spirit precedes a dramatic, unexpected death. According to the diary of eyewitness José Enrique de la Peña, Crockett and five or six other survivors of the siege of the Alamo were tortured, bayoneted, and then shot on March 6, 1836, after the group's surrender to the Mexican troops of General Antonio Santa Anna. The diarist reports that all died nobly without complaint or plea for mercy. A romanticized biography, Richard Penn Smith's *Colonel Crockett's Exploits and Adventures in Texas* (1836), sold well in the months following Crockett's death, when public sympathies increased the demand for his frontier lore.

A popular stage version of the frontiersman's legend pushed actor Frank Mayo into stardom. In 1872, Mayo, a veteran of the San Francisco and Boston circuits, premiered in Frank H. Murdoch's five-act melodrama *Davy Crockett*, a romance that stresses frontier values, strength, and determination over Crockett's illiteracy. Drawings of stagings show Davy in fringed leggings, buckskin tunic, and coonskin cap. The long-barreled flintlock, powder horn, and knife belt common to the era complete the standard woodsman's attire. Essential to the play's romantic appeal is the contrast of the frail, adoring heroine dressed in ultrafeminine attire with panniered skirt and bonnet.

A review of the noble characterization of the woodsman appeared in the New York journal *Spirit of the Times* on March 14, 1874. Brimming with praise for the character's humanity, the critique lauds the pairing of a rough-hewn hero with Eleanor Vaughn, the faultless heroine whom he saves from freezing in a blizzard. Davy survives a mauling by wolves and appears at the crucial moment to rescue Eleanor from Neil Crampton, who forces her into marriage by blackmailing her guardian, Major Hector Royston. Because Eleanor has given her word, she remains betrothed to Crampton. Mayo played the role of Davy so well that he could not escape it and grew to loathe the part that expanded from dime novel to classic idyll.

Twentieth-century versions of the Crockett legend surfaced with the nation's interest in past heroes. In 1945, archivist-historian Dee Brown published *Wave High the Banner*, a novel formed of research, legend, biography, superstition, folklore, songs like "Who Will Shoe Your Pretty Little Foot," and the stories his grandmother told him. The novel limps along, impeded by lame, unimaginative dialogue:

> "Old Hickory says he aims to strike another blow afore winter. But I know how you boys feel. I got a family back home myself."

> "We don't need to kill every last one of the Creeks," said David. "I figure we've taught 'em their lesson now." (Brown 1945, 136)

Unlike earlier tellings, Brown's dialogue avoids heavy dialect and places in Crockett's mouth the kind of language indigenous to Brown's own background.

Walt Disney's television series, *Davy Crockett, King of the Wild Frontier*, in 1954–1955, crystallized for its family audience a romanticized vision of Crockett, starring Fess Parker, who wore the stereotypical frontiersman's costume—fringed buckskin sleeves and leggings and the famous coonskin cap. The role and its multiverse musical ballad stretches the facts with extreme adulation for a defender of democratic principles and for a woodsman skilled in riflery and good-natured joshing. The screen version depicts Crockett as well mannered, philosophical, and gifted with an adventurous spirit that may have proved his undoing. Quick to quip in the face of danger and to speak his patriotism in simplistic aphorisms, the TV mountaineer-turned-war hero fights bears; carouses with Mike Fink, the legendary riverboatman; and dies valiantly at the Alamo while battling overwhelming odds. ("Ballad" 1996; Beatty et al. 1952; Blair 1944; Blankenship 1931; Botkin 1944; Brown, Carolyn 1987; Brown, Dee 1945; Brunvand 1996; Burns and Ives 1996b; Coad and Mims 1929; Crockett 1834, 1987, 1996; "David 'Davy' Crockett" 1996; Derr 1993; Ehrlich and Carruth 1982; Hewitt 1959; Lamar 1977; Milner et al. 1994; Neuendorf 1995; Patterson and Snodgrass 1994; Waldman 1990)

See also Brown, Dee.

CUSTER, GEORGE ARMSTRONG

An ambiguous hero of the American West, General George Armstrong Custer (1839–1876), leader of the disastrous Battle of the Little Big Horn, has inspired a vast body of conjectural literature. A lackluster West Pointer in the class of 1861, he earned a reputation for flawed character and boyish exhibitionism, epitomized by his collections of demerits and his shoulder-length blond curls. As a result of Custer's service to the Army of the Potomac, General Philip

George Armstrong Custer, poses in uniform, full length.

Sheridan promoted him to brigadier general of volunteers in 1863. Distinguished at the Battle of Gettysburg for holding back General Jeb Stuart's forces, Custer seemed to overcome his early lack of promise with zeal for the military, decisiveness in battle, and audacious courage in the face of overwhelming odds.

Custer achieved notoriety at the Washita River massacre of Black Kettle's village in western Oklahoma on November 27, 1868. Custer led the surprise charge on reservation grounds at dawn, but drew criticism for abandoning Major Joel Elliott's party, which the Cheyenne wiped out two miles from the battle. Reassigned to the Dakota Territory in 1873, Custer's regiment patrolled the Yellowstone and Black Hills areas, where the rush for gold exacerbated a decline in Anglo-Sioux relations. During this tense period of constant alert and skirmishes with the enemy, Custer shaped his forces into a crack team of Indian fighters. He was accused of abusing and callously overtaxing his men in a 55-hour march of 150 miles. Although his punishment called for suspension, he maintained his command.

Writing at night by dim lantern light, Custer penned field dispatches for *Galaxy* magazine and produced a detailed memoir, *My Life on the Plains* (1874), covering a 34-month period from January 1872 to October 1874. The narrative discloses some of the overblown bravado that critics have attached to the author's personality. For example, he describes a rough-and-tumble buffalo hunt engaged to test his dogs, Blucher and Maida:

> Blucher seized him by the throat, Maida endeavored to secure a firm hold on the shoulders. The result was that Blucher found himself well trampled in snow, and but for the latter would have been crushed to death. Fearing for the safety of my dogs I leaped from my horse, who I knew would not leave me, and ran to the assistance of the stag-hounds. Drawing my hunting-knife and watching for a favorable opportunity, I succeeded in cutting the hamstrings of the buffalo, which had the effect to tumble him over in the snow, when I was enabled to despatch him with my pistol. (Custer 1962, 294)

This passage sets a tone of dash and daring that carries over to his description of the Battle of the Washita, which his book attempts to justify.

Custer's account of the attack is a suspenseful narration detailed down to the smell of fire and the crisp winter night during which his troops creep forward at the direction of Osage scouts. At the last moment, Custer calls for the band to play "Garry Owen" and enters a lively scrap with Cheyenne warriors armed with rifles and bows and arrows. In his version, the troopers are under orders to attack warriors only. He excuses the deaths of noncombatants with consummate logic:

> In a struggle of this character it is impossible at all times to discriminate, particularly when, in a hand-to-hand conflict such as the one the troops were then engaged in the squaws are as dangerous adversaries as the warriors, while Indian boys between ten and fifteen years of age were found as expert and determined in the use of the pistol and bow and arrow as the older warriors. (ibid., 336)

In close tussle with an Indian youth, Major Benteen is forced to shoot the boy to halt his attack on the major's person and mount. Custer follows this event with a description of a squaw leading a white captive, whom she stabs with a knife as the cavalry presses to the center of the village. Custer exults, "The next moment retributive justice reached her in the shape of a well-directed bullet from one of the troopers' carbines." (ibid., 340)

Custer recounts a serious situation as a sizable party of mounted Indians in war dress forces his regiment into heated conflict. This distraction compromises the cavalry's effectiveness and overtaxes their energies as they superintend the wounded, prisoners, and a moiling herd of 800 wild ponies. Justifying his actions with a battlefield maxim, he decides "to do that which his enemy neither expects nor desires him to do." (ibid., 352) To deprive the war party of its wealth and means of transportation, he orders his men to shoot the ponies. At this dramatic point, Mah-wis-sa, Chief Black Kettle's sister, intervenes. She claims to have warned the male authorities of the village of an impending disaster and requests that Custer treat the helpless women and children with compassion. As token of her esteem of the "big chief" of the whites, she leads a teenage Indian girl to Custer, calls on the Great Spirit, and conducts an impromptu marriage ceremony.

Obviously, Custer skillfully salts his text with the type of detail that wins the sympathies of readers. As his men remove their coats to execute the ponies, warriors capture the uniforms and shoot Custer's dog, Blucher, with an arrow. A male Indian seeking warrior status gallops toward Custer and, as proof of competence, flourishes "an entire scalp, fresh and bleeding." (ibid., 368) A young bugler sits patiently while an army surgeon cuts free a barb and withdraws an arrow that pierces the boy's skull. The stoic bugler produces a scalp from his pocket and boasts that he killed his attacker with his revolver. The battlefield memoir draws to a close with Custer's premature claims of success and visions of a "comparative peace and immunity from Indian depredations" as he reconnoiters unexplored territory. (ibid., 608)

A complex and much maligned figure in American history, Custer died on June 26, 1876, at the Battle of the Little Big Horn, at the height of the Plains wars, which pitted the cavalry against a combined force of Cheyenne, Comanche, Arapaho, Kiowa, and Sioux. In the analysis of Louis L'Amour in *The Education of a Wandering Man* (1989), the Indians might have bested the entire cavalry if they could have solved the problem of acquiring food and ammunition. Since they lived off the land and made their own weapons, the assembly of large numbers of warriors depleted game and wood so rapidly that they had to move on or break into small autonomous bands. The constant jockeying for supplies and victory kept councils busy deciding strategy, which, in defiance of Custer, worked well.

For the cavalry and the Plains Indian, the massacre at the Little Big Horn ended an era. According to General Oliver Otis Howard's *Famous Indian Chiefs I Have Known* (1908), Custer's debacle energized the military in the West to break up Indian strongholds and defeat the most militant chiefs, especially Sitting Bull, Gall, Spotted Eagle, Lone Wolf, Lame Deer, and Crazy Horse. In the East, the one-sided clash produced national controversy over the leadership of the impulsive, attention-seeking cavalry officer. A hearing in February 1879 failed to clear up questionable commands that suggest gross misconduct on the part of Custer, who hoped to wreath himself in glory to assure his candidacy for the White House.

A firsthand testimony to Custer's role in the Plains Indian wars appeared in print in 1947. Dictated to Frazier and Robert Hunt by First Sgt. Charles Windolph, a former army deserter and six-year veteran of the famed Seventh Cavalry, the book was published under the title *I Fought with Custer: The Story of Sergeant Windolph, Last Survivor of the Battle of the Little Big Horn.* Concise and even-handed, the text bears no ill will to Custer. Seventy years after the fact, Windolph claims to have buried Custer and his brother Tom on a ridge bordering the battleground. In the opening paragraphs, he declares:

> People call it "The Custer Massacre." It wasn't any massacre; it was a straight, hard fight, and the five troops who were with Custer simply got cut to ribbons and every last white man destroyed. (Windolph 1947, 2)

Windolph accompanied Captain Will Benteen through naked, scalped, and mutilated corpses of the regiment's 210 men before arriving at the knoll where Custer's corpse lay. Windolph describes it as untouched "save for a single bullet hole in the left temple near the eye, and a hole on his left breast." A few feet away, Tom Custer's body was grossly carved. The only survivor was Comanche, Captain Keogh's horse, which recovered from seven wounds and lived until 1891.

Windolph accords Custer the benefit of the doubt for dividing his forces and concludes, "the gods themselves were against him. It was the Indians' day. Their one and only day." (ibid., 113) An addendum to the text declares that Cheyenne chiefs guarded Custer's corpse against Sioux mutilators to display to all that the Cheyenne had conquered their great enemy. Stripped of watch, pistols, and personal effects, the body lay in "beaded buckskin shirt, plain trousers and high cavalry boots." (ibid., 221) In the words of eyewitness Jim Gatchell, there were no signs of powder marks, which would substantiate claims that the general committed suicide. Custer and his men were neither captured nor tortured. Their wounds resulted from "war clubs, arrows, lances or bullets."

Nearly a decade after Custer's death, Elizabeth "Libby" Bacon Custer produced lively, supportive books about her husband's career, notably *Boots and Saddles: Life in Dakota with General Custer* (1885), which she followed with *Tenting on the Plains* (1887) and *Following the Guidon* (1890). In her first work, she recounts journeying to the Dakota Territory and spending days with her husband in pleasurable camping, fishing, hunting, and riding. As the danger from Indians increases, Custer is dispatched to capture Rain-in-the-Face, a Hunkpapa Sioux war chief who is accused of murdering a white surgeon. She describes the colorful dress of the Indian party that comes to Fort Lincoln to petition for his release. Her shift to the plaintive lines of "Nearer My God to Thee" accompanies the return of the wounded after the Little Big Horn. Before breaking off her narrative, she comments, "From that time the life went out of the hearts of the 'women who weep,' and God asked them to walk on alone and in the shadow." (Custer 1961, 222) The overt piety and sentimentality of her autobiography derive from the somber nature of the scene that preceded her widowhood.

In one of myriad fictional histories and screen retellings of Custer's career, Tom Berger's *Little Big Man* (1964) describes the events of the Plains Indian wars as straightforward genocide. While the strutting Custer strides up and down in smart riding boots, a corporal remarks, "He is a real son of a bitch, ain't he? Goddam, I'd pay the Cheyenne what put a bullet in his brass heart." (Berger 1964, 269) The narrator, Jack Crabb, who serves the Seventh Cavalry as a teamster, attempts to warn Custer of the danger awaiting him along the meadow the Indians call "Greasy Grass." Custer condescends to Jack, then swaggers off with a self-defensive air:

> I have been called impetuous. I resent that. Everything that I have ever done has been the result of the study that I have made of imaginary military situations that might arise. When I become engaged in a campaign and a great emergency arises, everything that I have ever heard or studied focuses in my mind as if the situation were under a magnifying glass. My mind works instantaneously but always as the result of everything that I have ever studied being brought to bear on the situation. (ibid., 399)

Jack, who was reared by Cheyenne, realizes the strategy that draws Custer toward an ambush and concludes,

> Well, I expect Custer was crazy enough to believe he would win, being the type of man who carries the whole world within his own head and thus when his passion is aroused and floods his mind, reality is utterly drowned. (ibid., 404)

In the heat of bullets, arrows, and falling men and horses, Custer stalks the battlefield with military posture, firing his Bulldog pistols from the "classic stance he must have learned at West Point, elbow bending like a steel hinge, forearm rigid." (ibid., 414)

Berger capitalizes on Custer's picayune attention to the military ideal. Robotic and fanatic under fire, Custer withdraws into fine-line quibbling. Near the end of the attack, he ignores the desperation around him and chatters idiotically:

> It is to be regretted that the character of the Indian as described in Cooper's interesting novels is not the true one. Stripped of the beautiful romance with which we have been so long willing to envelop him, transferred from the inviting pages of the novelist to the localities where we are compelled to meet him, the Indian forfeits his claim to the appellation of the *noble* red man. (ibid., 418)

Demented with arrogance and paranoia, Custer cues the bugler to summon Benteen's men. Among fallen forces already stiffening in death, Custer continues his animated pacing, muttering to himself, "Benteen won't come. He hates me." His death results from a single clean shot to the chest. Jack Crabb remarks, "I had finally accepted the fact that he was great." (ibid., 420–421) (Berger 1964; Burns and Ives 1996b; Custer, Elizabeth 1961; Custer, George 1962; Howard 1989; Lamar 1977; L'Amour 1989; Waldman 1990; Windolph 1947)

See also Cooper, James Fenimore; Howard, Oliver Otis.

DEATH COMES FOR THE ARCHBISHOP

Based on the lives of Bishop Jean Baptiste Lamy and Father Joseph Machebeuf, Willa Cather's episodic historical novel, *Death Comes for the Archbishop* (1927), lauds the purity, idealism, dedication, and selflessness of French missionary priests in the Southwest. She drew on her 1912 vacation in New Mexico and Arizona and a return trip to Taos in 1916 for background material on animistic ritual, Catholic missions, and the *conquistadores* to flesh out the fictional account of two devout men who brave the hostile frontier to bring Christianity to a multicultural society. In her reflections on the Hispanic church architecture of New Mexico, she recalled that the artistic representations of martyred saints, death, and the grieving virgin were more pitiable and terrifying in remote adobe churches of the mountains than in the more accessible chapels of the valleys. The magnitude of human suffering during the area's settlement touched her deeply, particularly the uneven partnerships in interracial marriages, enslavement of Indians and Hispanics by whites, and Kit Carson's displacement of the Navajos from Four Corners during the Long Walk. Cather gained personal satisfaction from researching the sites and from writing *Death Comes for the Archbishop*. She realized almost from the time the manuscript was completed that it would be well received.

The story, set in New Mexico and Arizona between 1858 and 1888, chronicles the fieldwork of the fictional Father Jean Latour, a scholarly, citified French prelate who makes a painful yearlong journey from Ontario to his new assignment as bishop of Santa Fé. As he crosses the rough arroyos on his way to a loosely formed frontier diocese, Cather's description of the landscape emphasizes its remoteness and the blend of desert menace and beauty:

> Low brown shapes, like earthworks, lying at the base of wrinkled green mountains with bare tops,—wave-like mountains, resembling billows beaten up from a flat sea by a heavy gale; and their green was of two colours—aspen and evergreen, not intermingled but lying in solid areas of light and dark. (Cather 1947, 22)

The arrival precedes an even longer trek south because local renegade priests, led by an apostate, Father Martínez, reject Bishop Latour and force him to journey to Agua Secreta in Durango to secure written proof of his authority. After he takes his rightful post, the bishop plants the area with fruit trees, a symbol of the nurturing he brings to hungering spirits.

Bishop Latour and Father Joseph Vaillant, a practical, energetic vicar, work together to extend Christianity to local peasants. Their names—literally, "John the Tower" and "Joseph the Valiant"—suggest the author's admiration for their strength and courage. On returning to Santa Fé, Bishop Latour hears the rich tone of the Angelus. Father Vaillant narrates the story of the bell, a legend that connects the relic to Moorish assaults on Spain. The bell is dated 1356 and, like the bishop, arrived over a toilsome path—from Mexico City by oxcart. During a journey to Mora through the Truchas Mountains, Bishop Latour and Father Vaillant encounter Magdalena, a crazed woman. They learn that her husband, Buck Scales, a snake-featured villain, has abused her and murdered their three children. A Missourian identifying himself as Kit Carson offers her refuge with his Mexican wife at their adobe home. Carson commiserates in private, "I used to see [Magdalena] in Taos when she was such a pretty girl. Ain't it a pity?" The bishop assesses Carson to be a man of "standards, loyalties, a code which is not easily put into words." (ibid., 77, 75) The two, who are a little over 40 years old, become firm friends.

Cather conveys the diverse requirements of a missionary's calling. Over a lengthy career of good works, Bishop Latour—assisted by Jacinto, an Indian guide from the Pecos pueblo—aids refugees; suspends Padre Gallegos, a back-sliding priest; and establishes a girls' school, Our Lady of Light, run by five Sisters of Loretto. As the school takes shape, Magdalena, rehabilitated from her bad marriage, keeps house and manages the kitchen. Cather depicts her flowering in a Christian atmosphere with an image of her feeding a flock of doves, which "caught the light in such a way that they all became invisible at once, dissolved in light and disappeared as salt dissolves in water." (Woodress 1982, 409) The image identifies two aspects of Magdalena's redemption: her devotion to humble chores and the work of the Holy Ghost at one with her becalmed spirit.

The author, impressed by the physical and spiritual expanses that separate humans on the southwestern desert, emphasizes that miles of rugged terrain frequently separate the missionary duo. After Father Vaillant assumes the post of parish priest in Albuquerque, Bishop Latour travels by mule to his bedside to help him recover from measles. When a blizzard threatens, Jacinto guides the bishop to a hidden ceremonial cavern in the cliffs of the Pajarito Plateau and builds a pungent fire with piñon branches. Jacinto leads the bishop to a crevice, from which issues a vibration:

> He told himself he was listening to one of the oldest voices of the earth. What he heard was the sound of a great underground river, flowing through a re-sounding cavern. The water was far, far below, perhaps as deep as the foot of the mountain, a flood moving in utter blackness under ribs of antediluvian rock. It was not a rushing noise, but the sound of a great flood moving with majesty and power. (Cather 1947, 130)

At Jacinto's request, the bishop keeps the river a secret, but ponders the fact that whites and Mexicans understand little of Indian religion, which, like the river, flows deep in native spirits and nourishes vulnerabilities that lie beneath their fierce exteriors. After locating Father Vaillant, Bishop Latour welcomes Kit Carson, who delivers venison to the stricken man and helps the bishop and Jacinto transport Father Vaillant to Santa Fé.

Cather varies the mood toward the end of the novel by portraying a heart in conflict. On a wintry night in December 1859, the bishop lies in bed contemplating the essence of failure. Cather's compassionate description of his ministry pinpoints the source of discontent:

> His prayers were empty words and brought him no refreshment. His soul had become a barren field. He had nothing within himself to give his priests or his people. His work seemed superficial, a house built upon the sands. His great diocese was still a heathen country. (ibid., 211)

The enormous task of gentling a demanding parish diocese threatens to engulf him. In spiritual torment, he sets out in the snow and finds Sada, an elderly Mexican woman who has been enslaved for 19 years by the Smiths, a Protestant family from Georgia given to mocking Catholic worship. Cather ends the episode with the power of faith: after the bishop reassures the old slave, joins her in prayer, and hears her confession, he offers her a religious medal of the Virgin to treasure in private. By uplifting Sada, he finds peace in a one-on-one ministry, the job for which he was trained.

The novel follows decades of the careers of the protagonists, who advance from basic parish developers to higher posts—Bishop Latour to Archbishop and Father Vaillant to Bishop of Colorado. Alone in Santa Fé, Archbishop Latour struggles as his job grows burdensome for an aging minister cut off from his partner. After dreaming of spending his last years in Auvergne, France, he willingly retires outside Santa Fé, where he endears himself to the community by building a cathedral. He falls ill with a fever and cough in 1888 and requests, *"Je voudrais mourir à Santa Fé"* (I want to die in Santa Fé). Wrapped in Indian blankets to protect his fragile heart, he receives the prayers and love of local worshippers who have profited from his commitment and faith. At his death, common folk have already decked him in the mantle of sainthood.

Cather salts the novel with Western history pocked with violence—Father Junipero Serra's frontier missions in California, the visitation of the Virgin of Guadaloupe, and Kit Carson's misguided assistance of the army in driving Navajos on a forced march from the Canyon de Chelly to Bosque Redondo. One episode tells of Father Lucero, an elderly priest who struggles to protect a cache of $20,000 in gold against a brigand, whom he stabs to death. In an event set in 1859, Father Vaillant returns from surveying territory granted to the United States by the Gadsden Purchase. Under Bishop Latour's care, he recuperates from malaria and chafes to return to Tucson to recover lost Catholics. He tells of entering a terrifying black canyon with a Pima convert who showed him "a golden chalice, vestments and cruets, all the paraphernalia for celebrating mass." (ibid., 207) The sacred objects attest to an Apache attack on a mission long before. Such vivid details anchor Cather's story in the unsettled times when isolated Native Americans first confronted outsiders.

Critics remark on several unusual facets of *Death Comes for the Archbishop*. A moving example of Catholicism in action, the story was written by a non-Catholic. Cather, who was Episcopalian, appears to have studied New Mexico and its history with such intensity that she returned to the East to write not only of the racial groups on the rugged land, but also their understanding of an unknown religion conveyed by missionaries. Because the author creates a dignified, unembellished text growing out of substantial characters, touches of humor, and suspenseful action, the story has become a classic. (Blain, Grundy, and Clements 1990; Bloom and Bloom 1962; Bloom 1986b; Bohlke 1986; Buck 1992; Byrne and Snyder 1980; Cather 1947; Davidson and Wagner-Martin 1995; *DISCovering Authors* 1993; Drabble 1985; Ehrlich and Carruth 1982; Goring 1994; Hornstein 1973; Kunitz 1942; Lamar 1977; Lee 1975; Magill 1958; Milner et al. 1994; "North Side" 1996; O'Brien 1986; Robinson 1983; Sherr and Kazickas 1994; Woodress 1982)

See also Carson, Kit; Cather, Willa; *My Ántonia; O Pioneers!*.

🖾 DIARIES, MEMOIRS, AND JOURNALS 🖾 OF THE FRONTIER

The wealth of first-person narratives, diaries, daybooks, letters, logs, and journals is a valuable adjunct to frontier literature, particularly for readers seeking authentic details. Historians and writers of fiction draw on these unembellished personal narratives for multiple and varied sources of frontier conditions and lore. Examples include the firsthand experience of whites among southwestern Indians found in *Through Indian Country to California* (1854), John P. Sherburne's diary of the Whipple expedition, and the life of a soldier in H. H. McConnell's *Five Years a Cavalryman or, Sketches of Regular Army Life on the Texas Frontier, 1866–1871* (1889). Typical vignettes cover hunting adventures, observations of birds and fish, make-do methods of cookery and food preservation, first aid and herb gathering, care of livestock, and travel details unavailable from any other source. Reputable sources recount the various routes by which westering parties made their trek: in 1849, Jane McDougal writes of a voyage by steamer from the East Coast and across the Isthmus of Panama to California; three years later, Mary Stuart Bailey made her way over the California Trail, which Helen Carpenter traversed by oxcart in 1857; following established southwestern trails were Harriet Bunyard in 1869 and Maria Shrode the next year. Filled with daily laundry and cooking chores, commonplace occurrences and pastimes, encounters with Indians, and prevailing fears and attitudes, these diaries and journals alternately corroborate and refute derivative sources, which often mold facts into sensational or titillating pseudohistory.

A modest collection of letters and journal entries by Catherine Parr Traill, an English children's author and pioneer in the outback near Peterborough, Ontario, enlivens a slim personal narrative, *The Backwoods of Canada* (1871).

Composed from 1832 to 1835, the text contains practical information for the immigrant homesteader. She describes a method of clarifying maple sugar, sealing a vinegar vat with tar or laundry soap, raising bread with hops or bran, pickling beans and cabbage with maple vinegar, and making soft soap and candles. Her optimism for success in the New World culminates in a toast to Canada, which she calls "the land of hope: here everything is new; everything going forward." (Traill 1966, 7) She declares it impossible for "arts, sciences, agriculture, manufactures to retrograde; they must keep advancing; though in some situations the progress may seem slow, in others they are proportionally rapid." Her numerous books—written as lucid, pragmatic guides for the emigrant female—won her a strong following throughout North America. An example of her concern for other homesteaders is her commentary on cholera, which fells a disproportionate number of "the poorer sort of emigrants. Many of these, debilitated by the privations and fatigue of a long voyage, on reaching Quebec or Montreal indulged in every sort of excess." (ibid., 26) She balances her own cheerful outlook with frank admission that other stories of the frontier are less sanguine and often tragic.

Vermont Quaker Thomas C. Battey, author of *The Life and Adventures of a Quaker among the Indians* (1875), demonstrates the unique situation of missionaries and teachers spreading Christianity among Native Americans. Frequently serving as a mediator during racial clashes, Battey moves from Iowa to the Wichita Agency in Oklahoma to teach Caddo Indians, who fondly refer to him as Thomissey. In addition to his brief biographies of significant figures on the frontier, he describes the death of Ten Bears, an influential Comanche chief. Battey seems disconcerted that braves desert their leader and leave him to die alone. He comments:

> This appears to be the prevailing custom among the wild Indians; when a person becomes old and feeble, so as to become in their estimation burdensome, they are neglected; and when sickness and death come upon them, they are sometimes abandoned to die alone; hence a life of barbarity, if not ended by violence, usually ends in cold neglect, without comfort, without sympathy, and without hope. (Battey 1972, 90–91)

Battey seems surprised by the difference between the before and after of a Comanche death. Upon Ten Bears's passing, relatives cut themselves, wail bitterly, and collect household items and clothing to bury with the old chief. Their final tribute is the burning of his lodge.

Eight months after his residency with the Caddo, Battey assumes a similar role as school principal at the Kiowa Agency. When the Modoc War breaks out, he brings together federal peace commissioners with Kiowa chiefs and defuses a potentially fierce situation. During the ceremony accompanying the solemn task of peacemaking, Battey describes Lone Wolf's "making medicine," a ritual involving brushing the ground, laying wormwood and cedar leaves and lighting them afresh with coals, then wafting smoke toward the naked body as a gesture of obeisance to the Great Spirit. Battey performs a service to frontier history by recording the speeches of Lone Wolf and Kicking Bird, both prestigious voices in the peace faction, and the corresponding remarks by white leaders Thomas Wistar and J. E. Rhoads.

Like Battey, Major General Ethan Allan Hitchcock preserves unwritten Indian lore and ethnography in an unassuming journal, *A Traveller in Indian Territory*, composed in 1842 and published in 1930. In this extended narrative filled with first-person insights into Native American customs, Hitchcock, a native of Vermont and descendant of the patriot Ethan Allen, reveals the value of a questioning mind. In the vigorous, precise, scholarly voice of a skilled reporter, he records eyewitness accounts of horse thievery, sacred fire, marriage and widowhood, and rituals such as the Green Corn Dance. In one entry dated January 1842, he relates a horseback ride to Arkansas where he writes in pencil the story of Milly Francis (1802–1848), a legendary Creek-Seminole martyr whose life parallels that of Pocahontas. In 1817, during the First Seminole war, Francis's father, the prophet Hillis Hadjo, also called Josiah Francis, ordered the immolation of a military prisoner, Captain Duncan McKrimmon, whom tribesmen captured while he fished on the Apalachicola River. He was tied to a stake and readied for execution. In Hitchcock's words:

> Milly heard a war whoop and going to the place found that two Indians had a young white man tied and perfectly naked; other Indians came around and Milly described the white man . . . looking anxiously around as if to ask if there was no one to speak for him and save his life. (Hitchcock 1996, 103)

Before the tinder was lighted beneath his feet, Milly declared herself ready to die if her sacrifice would save his life. At her insistence, the chief granted a reprieve. McKrimmon gained his release on condition that he shave his head and live as a tribesman. He remained with the Seminole two years, then was sold as a slave to Spaniards.

Hitchcock seems intent on portraying Milly Francis realistically by presenting the facts of her story as she dictates them rather than repeating the touched-up version that had circulated for a quarter century. During his interview with Milly, she strips the story of romantic implications by insisting that she had no intention of marrying McKrimmon, even though he returned and proposed to her. Because of Hitchcock's interest in her courageous act, he supported her request for relief of the tribe's poverty and gained for her a pension of $96 a year. As was often the case with federal funds owed to Indians, the money was never allocated. Milly died in Muskogee, Oklahoma, where she is proclaimed a native heroine decorated by Congress with a medal.

A similar fascination with Indians colors the writings of attorney Lewis Henry Morgan, a hobby sociologist who produced journals and reports as a part of fieldwork in Kansas and Nebraska among a prodigious number of tribes—the Oto, Dakota, Omaha, Shawnee, Missouri, Ottawa, Ponca, Gros Ventres, Minnetarees, Potawatomi, Crow, Delaware, Mandan, Miami, Wyandotte, and Ojibway. During Morgan's meetings with distinguished Indians, he encountered Ely Parker, a Seneca chief and aide to General Ulysses S. Grant. Parker assisted Morgan in researching *League of the Ho-de-no-sau-nee or Iroquois* (1851), a study of native kinship. Morgan's subsequent work, *The Indian Jour-*

nals, 1859–1862 (1959), a scholarly ethnology, covers a variety of subjects relating to social order, health, travel, craft, language, religion, and work. One useful description is a discourse on pemmican, a blend of grease and buffalo meat that hunters and travelers carry in sacks to feed them on the trail. Morgan's recipe explains how to dismember the buffalo, cure the meat in the sun and over coals, then flail large pieces into fragments to mix with suet. His precise measure declares that meat from three buffaloes and fat from six animals produces 100 pounds of pemmican, which Indians sell to the Hudson Bay Company for six cents per pound. He concludes, "We have had it daily on the boat. Not bad eating." (Morgan 1959, 141)

An Ojibway memoir, Basil H. Johnston's *Indian School Days* (1989), recounts the placement of the author in his youth at a coed Jesuit boarding school in Spanish, a small town on Lake Huron's northern shore. Among friends bearing the nicknames of Half Chick, Ti Blue, Harpie, and Boozo, in 1939, Jake Johnston is forced to go to "Spanish" because of his lack of a father and his mother's inability to curb his mischief. He summarizes one of the school's two main purposes: to train Indian young people for jobs in tailoring, milling, blacksmithy, shoemaking, tinsmithing, painting, carpentry, baking, cooking, plumbing, welding, gardening, sheep and swine herding, animal husbandry, and poultry care. He adds, "Alas, while there were some accomplished chicken farmers and shoemakers, no graduate went into business; the trades for which we had been trained were rendered obsolete by new technology." The other purpose of the reclamation process was to foster piety through prayer. However, Johnston quips, "all the prayers, masses, novenas and benedictions could not overcome the natural resistance of most boys to a career in holy orders." (Johnston 1989, 26–27)

From the perspective of the early twentieth century, frontierswoman Elinore Pruitt Stewart, a native of Fort Smith, Arkansas, collected and published *Letters of a Woman Homesteader* (1914) and *Letters on an Elk Hunt* (1915), a series of first-person anecdotes about her life on the Utah border in Burnt Fork, Wyoming. A *Wall Street Journal* book reviewer describes her lavishly detailed letters as "a warmly delightful, vigorously affirmative chronicle." (Stewart 1988, flap) Although isolated on a cattle ranch in 1909, she takes joy in prairie splendor: "It was too beautiful a night to sleep, so I put my head out to look and to think." (ibid., 11) Stewart's contemplative nature enhances the lyricism of her style, yet she avoids gushiness by balancing realism and humor. Her catalog of Christmas treats proves the frontier menu heartier than drier sources claim: she names a spread of geese, hams, hens, doughnuts, rye bread, coffee cake, fruitcake, seeds, nuts, fruit, and jelly. In a droll scene in which locals tweak a Yankee tenderfoot, she cites their dialogue:

> The punchers hurriedly made their beds, as they did so twitting N'Yawk about making his between our tent and the fire. "You're dead right, pard," I heard one of them say, "to make your bed there, fer if them outlaws comes this way they'll think you air one of the women and they won't shoot you. Just us *men* air in danger." (ibid., 168–169)

These lighthearted scenarios suggest that Stewart's wit and good nature buoy her during her residence on the northwestern frontier. A passage from *Letters on an Elk Hunt* displays another side of her observations after she finds a cow elk bled to death and the tracks of "the faithful little calf. It would stay by its mother until starvation or wild animals put an end to its suffering." (Stewart 1979, 112) The evidence nauseates her. She agrees with her husband that "bunch shooting" is likely to wound an animal and leave it writhing for hours or days, a method too hit-or-miss for decency. (Battey 1972; Burns and Ives 1996b; Hitchcock 1996; James 1993; Johnston 1989; Lee 1966; Morgan 1959; Myres 1991; Sherburne 1988; Stewart 1979, 1988; Waldman 1990)

See also Oregon Trail; prospecting.

DOBIE, J. FRANK

Popular Texas folklore collector and writer of frontier life and history, James Frank Dobie is called the "Story Teller of the Southwest." The scion of Texas settlers, he was born in Live Oak County on September 26, 1888, and grew up in Alice, 40 miles from Corpus Christi, where he hunted deer and game birds for his family's table. He worked as a journalist for the Galveston *Tribune* and the San Antonio *Express* while pursuing a Ph.D. at Southwestern, Columbia, and the University of Texas. After service as a gunnery officer in World War I ended his career as a high school teacher, principal of Alpine Public School, and college dean, he married Bertha McKee, his lifelong love, and settled on his uncle Jim Dobie's ranch in Los Olmos. Among the *vaqueros* of south Texas, he felt at home and recorded the stories, verse, and songs of the Spanish.

At a time when Southwest lore carried no academic cachet, Dobie ignored trends and turned himself into an expert at unwritten southwestern literature. At age 33, he returned to teaching while writing articles on the Old West for *Country Gentleman, New Mexico, Arizona Highways, Southwest Review, Natural History, Outdoor Life, Vogue, Saturday Evening Post, New York Herald Tribune, Magazine of the South, Frontier Times, American Gun, Texas Game and Fish,* and other periodicals. Before it was fashionable to champion the fragile ecology of the open range, Dobie challenged federal programs encouraging the extermination of the prairie dog, coyote, and other predatory animals and wrote knowledgeably about rattlers, jackrabbits, whitetails, grizzlies, coyotes, panthers, wolves, skunks, and roadrunners. Fired from his role as maverick professor of the University of Texas, he continued to write a newspaper column on frontier tradition and pursued his political agenda while publishing *A Vaquero of the Brush Country* (1930), *Coronado's Children* (1930), *The Longhorns* (1941), *Guide to Life and Literature of the Southwest* (1943), *Tales of Old-Time Texas* (1955), *Cow People* (1964), and *Some Part of Myself* (1967), a memoir of his teaching days. At his Paisano Ranch outside Austin, Dobie welcomed colleagues, served the Library of Congress as a consultant on American history, and supported the work of the Texas Folklore Society. He accepted an honorary doctorate from Cambridge

Texan J. Frank Dobie, 1888–1964

and, a few days before his death in Austin in 1964, received from Lyndon Johnson the Presidential Medal of Freedom.

Dobie earned his reputation for colorful exaggeration and meticulous scholarship. His love of a romantic yarn is evident in *Apache Gold and Yaqui Silver* (1928), a collection of stories about prospectors and lost mines culled from long interviews with Nat Straw, an elderly retired prospector eager to share his stories of mining folklore. Dobie's paean to the Western horse, *The Mustang* (1934), is studded with anecdotes, such as his picture of the Spanish equestrian: "In contrast to Arabian warriors, *caballeros* preferred riding stallions to mares as more powerful and proud. In battle some of their war stallions bit and kicked the barbarous Indians." (Dobie 1952, 22) In *The Ben Lilly Legend* (1950), Dobie re-creates the legendary career of a famed Alabama tracker and bear and panther hunter who stalked game over Mississippi, Louisiana, Texas, and Mexico, at one time serving Teddy Roosevelt as chief huntsman. The dash of Dobie's stories spotlights a night that Lilly, wearied by quarrying a female bear, sleeps by its carcass. He awakens to a curious muzzle and growl and empties his rifle in the dark. Unperturbed, Lilly goes back to sleep. The next day, he locates the well-drilled corpse of the male, which had come in search of its mate.

A spirited, wholehearted craftsman, Dobie does not turn squeamish in the face of bloody subjects. In *The Ben Lilly Legend*, he specifies not only game kills but Lilly's weapons and differentiates between Western six-shooter hunters and southerners like Lilly, men known as "Big Knives," who carried the Bowie knife, "The bloodiest instrument ever utilized in American bloodletting." (Dobie 1978, 57) Alongside pictures of Lilly's knives is the history of the huntsman's curiosity about smithy shops, where he reshaped files, rasps, springs, and other steel objects into knives. Dobie compares Lilly's weapons to the Mexican machete and gentleman's hunting knife. He tempered the blades of his killing and skinning knives to break rather than bend and cooled them in panther oil to a "drake-neck" color, then hafted them with buckhorn. Meticulous about its shape, Lilly claimed to need a knife that gouged rather than plunged in. He wanted a two-edged blade so sharp from tip to haft "that if he got it inside a bear it would cut in any direction he pulled or twisted it." (ibid., 61) (Carmony 1992; Dobie 1952b, 1978, 1990, 1996; Ehrlich and Carruth 1982; Lamar 1977; McVoy 1940)

EXPLORERS OF THE FRONTIER

To European explorers of the fifteenth and sixteenth centuries, the entire Western Hemisphere was a frontier that beckoned to adventurers across the Atlantic with a promise of the unknown. The first reports on the New World attest to the excitement and curiosity of men who dared to sail to an unknown land to map routes and landfalls, take in the sights, study native flora and fauna, meet and convert indigenous peoples to Christianity, establish colonies and forts, and search out valuable resources and treasures. This body of work, composed by some of the most prestigious male voices of presettlement times, comprises a separate wing of frontier literature. Suited to the explorers' tasks, exploration literature took shape in nonliterary form—letters, ships' logs, scientists' daybooks, personal journals, formal reports, overviews, market studies, and maps—and covers scientific, sociological, topographical, religious, economic, and demographic concerns.

Christopher Columbus, who in his declining years thought of himself as the *Christoferens colombo* or the dove that carried Christ across the sea to the New World, recorded in his journal a day-by-day account of his fleet's encounters in the Caribbean isles. His saintly purpose notwithstanding, Columbus comments on Thursday, October 11, 1492:

> When we stepped ashore we saw fine green trees, streams everywhere and different kinds of fruit. I called to the two captains to jump ashore with the rest, who included Rodrigo de Escobedo, secretary of the fleet, and Rodrigo Sánchez de Segovia, asking them to bear solemn witness that in the presence of them all I was taking possession of this island for their Lord and Lady the King and Queen, and I made the necessary declarations which are set down at greater length in the written testimonies. (Columbus 1992, 94)

The high-handedness of his assumption of control over the land contrasts with the naiveté of his greeters. Naked islanders swim to his ships to offer parrots, balls of cotton thread, and darts. He sizes up native seacraft, which are simple, hollowed-out canoes propelled by paddles. Two days later, on October 13, 1492, he records: "I kept my eyes open and tried to find out if there was any gold, and I saw that some of them had a little piece hanging from a hole in their nose." (ibid., 95) The statement bodes ill for the Taino and Arawak, who suffer depredations for the sake of gold caches that existed only in Columbus's dreams.

In the boom years of North American exploration, Spaniard conquerors, inflamed by similar hopes of abundant gold, were overwhelmed by Montezuma's gifts, which he presented to Hernan Cortéz out of a misapprehension that the explorer was the god Quetzalcoatl. According to William H. Prescott's account in *History of the Conquest of Mexico* (1843), in 1520 Aztec ambassadors entered the general's pavilion and, making gestures of reverence, displayed atop delicate mats

> shields, helmets, cuirasses, embossed with plates and ornaments of pure gold; collars and bracelets of the same metal, sandals, fans, *panaches* and crests of variegated feathers, intermingled with gold and silver thread, and sprinkled with pearls and precious stones; imitations of birds and animals in wrought and cast gold and silver, of exquisite workmanship; curtains, coverlets, and robes of cotton, fine as silk, of rich and various dyes, interwoven with featherwork that rivalled the delicacy of painting. There were more than thirty loads of cotton cloth in addition. (Prescott n.d., 174–175)

Along with these examples of artistry and craft, Montezuma's emissaries proffered an upturned Spanish helmet heaped with golden grains and circular engraved plates as large as carriage wheels wrought out of gold and silver. Prescott notes that the fine quality of the gifts far surpassed Cortéz's dreams. In an introductory letter to Spain's king, now lost, Cortéz is said to have composed a gift catalog, which opens with "a hundred ounces of gold ore, that their Highnesses might see in what state the gold came from the mines." (ibid., 197)

Intending to join Cortéz, a Spanish grandee, Alvar Núñez Cabeza de Vaca, arrived in Florida in 1528 and struggled on to east Texas, where he, an Arab slave, and two fellow adventurers survived the arduous journey, which killed the rest of their party. Cabeza de Vaca lived among Indians before setting out for the Southwest, where he covered much of southern Texas, Arizona, New Mexico, Sonora, Durango, and Chihuahua. In *The Castaways* (1555), he briefly describes the long journey, which brought him into contact with Calusa, Timucua, Apalachee, Pensacola, Karankawa, Caddo, Atakapan, Coahuiltecan, Jumano, Concho, Pima, and Opata. The text is spare, leaving out details that might have explained more clearly his method of travel and survival techniques.

Subsequent writers have drawn on the drama and romance of two cultures in conflict—one seeking treasure, the other trying to survive. In C. Falkenhorst's historical fiction, *With Cortéz in Mexico* (1892), the treachery of Montezuma's leaders results in the king's assassination after a sharpshooter fires an arrow from an elevated position. Cortéz's men shield the fallen king, but protection comes too late.

> The more the king recovered his consciousness, the more clear did it become to him that he had drained the bitterest dregs of his life-cup. He, the famous ruler of Tenochtitlan, had been despised by his own people! They no longer recognized him as their king; they followed another who, more courageous

than he, advanced, weapon in hand, to meet the enemy who had so suddenly appeared in the midst of the kingdom. (Falkenhorst 1892, 117–118)

The novelist's depiction of the irreversible upheaval that accompanies the meeting of Spanish explorer with Aztec chief ends in silence. Montezuma is so overcome by his people's fickle shift of loyalty that "he did not reply by a syllable to the words of consolation offered by the surrounding men." (ibid., 118) The fictional scene reflects what history holds as truth—the abrupt and barbarous slaying of a native king for no other reason than greed.

A sixteenth-century reflection on Cortéz's depredations of the Aztecs derives from the chronicle of Friar Diego de Landa, who wrote *Relación de las cosas de Yucatan* (1566), later translated and published as *Yucatan before and after the Conquest*. According to Landa, religious fanaticism among the conquerors fueled the destruction of 5,000 idols and 27 hieroglyphic scrolls. His work is the primary source of details about Aztec ritual and sacrifices, calendars, commerce, clothing, diet, agriculture, architecture, and learning. His section on self-mortification resembles Julius Caesar's revulsion at Druid immolations in the *Gallic Commentaries*. Landa lists the stripping of skin from around the ear, body perforation, slit tongues, and penis mangling. In his words, ritual killings reached a height of atrocity unheard of in European experience:

> They threw the dead body rolling down the steps, where it was taken by the attendants, was stripped completely of the skin save only on the hands and feet; then the priest, stripped, clothed himself with this skin and danced with the rest. This was a ceremony with them of great solemnity. (Landa 1978, 49)

In some ceremonial killings, the victim was sanctified at the altar and the flesh consumed. Priests claimed the most sacred parts—hands, feet, and head. The extensive preparation and blood-fest accompanying sacrifice influenced D. H. Lawrence's *The Plumed Serpent* (1926), which describes a similar selection of a victim to be groomed, reverenced, and then slain in honor of a diety.

Contemporaneous with Landa's writings are the contrasting commentaries of geographer, intelligence officer, and publicist Richard Hakluyt and of Bartolomé de Las Casas, an opportunistic despoiler of Cuba who changed his ways and converted to the Catholic priesthood. In "Divers voyages touching the discovery of America, and the Ilands adjacent unto the same" (1582), one of the mammoth collection of travel narratives by Richard Hakluyt, the author exults in the "fertile and temperate" land, a good omen of profit for English colonizers. In *The Principal Navigations, Voyages, and Discoveries of the English Nation* (1589), an overview of early voyages to North America, he demonstrates his eye for data; for example, he notes that the aborigines of New Spain are, for the most past, naked and that their king wears a crown knitted of feathers. Of the first voyage to Virginia, he comments:

> The soile is the most plentifull, sweete, fruitfull and wholsome of all the worlde: there are above foureteene severall sweete smelling timber trees, and the most part of the underwoods are Bayes and such like; they have those Okes that we have, but farre greater and better. (Hakluyt 1958, 291)

Recounting Spanish conquest and exploration in the New World, William H. Prescott compiled *History of the Conquest of Mexico*, published in 1843, and a companion work *History of the Conquest of Peru*, published in 1847, from original sources housed in Spanish archives.

Of the welcome extended from the people of Raonoak Island [*sic*], he notes that Chief Granganimo's wife and brother ran to meet the English landing party. The people drew the tender to shore and carried the visitors on their backs to spare the European clothes and shoes from sand and salt water, then set out a feast in their honor. These details were meant to prepare European occupation forces for the lay of the land and tenor of the people so that colonial enterprise could proceed swiftly and smoothly to the benefit of the British crown.

To increase his knowledge of expeditions, Hakluyt interviewed mapmakers, bureaucrats, merchants, captains, and sailors and learned minutiae about the magnates of exploration: Sir Francis Drake, Sir Humphrey Gilbert, and Martin Frobisher. Hakluyt's usefulness to Sir Walter Raleigh as a propagandist derives from his encyclopedic list of selling points for English military installations in the New World, which were intended to stop the Spanish from subduing the continent for their own enrichment and to supplant their head start in North America with English plantations and trading zones. In addition to Hakluyt's considerable published canon, he translated Antonio Galvano's *Discoveries of the World* (1601) and Hernando de Soto's *Virginia Richly Valued by the Description of Florida* (1609). The combined impetus of his writings contributed significantly to the success of the East India Company.

Unlike Hakluyt, historian and cleric Bartolomé de Las Casas, the "Defender and Apostle of the Indies," lost his stomach for opportunism. A native of Seville, he was inspired by Columbus's triumph in the New World and completed training in theology, which prepared him for his voyage to Hispaniola in 1502 with Nicolás de Ovando. Rewarded with an *encomienda*, or power over native press gangs, he developed a sympathy for the "poor of Christ," renounced his commission, left the plantation, and journeyed to the Vatican to take priestly vows. Serving as chaplain in the field, he crusaded for human rights, petitioned for laws to control the extremes of overlords, and established a benevolent test colony to actualize his theories of humane administration. The failure of the experiment sapped his moral energy; he withdrew to a Dominican monastery to agonize in private. In virtual seclusion, he composed *A History of the Indies* (1532), his witness to Spain's failed mission in the New World. Like Josephus, chronicler of the Jews during the Roman Empire, Las Casas rued his own part in conquest and determined to publish a record of "simple naked truths" that the world could neither deny nor ignore. (Las Casas 1992, xxxvii)

Spain's racist policy of subjugation so enraged Las Casas that he left the quiet of his cell and publicly warred against government-sponsored pacification of Indians, an illegitimate military venture he claimed might lead to punishment from heaven for the decimation of innocents. His growing influence with the crown resulted in promotion to Bishop of Chiapas, Mexico. Before his death in 1566, he published *A Short Account of the Destruction of the Indies*, a scathing denunciation of the *conquistadores*. The fervid, bitter protest informed true Christians of the outrages natives suffered at the hands of ruthless goldseekers:

They extended their reign of terror far inland, plundering and devastating whole provinces, killing or capturing the people who lived there in much the same way as we have seen happening elsewhere, torturing chiefs and vassals alike in order to discover the whereabouts of the gold . . . they contrived to depopulate, between 1529 and today, an area of over four hundred leagues which was once as densely inhabited as any other. (ibid., 31)

Las Casas's indignation fuels his eloquent jeremiad, which charges royalty with complicity in the lofty manner of Nathan the Hebrew priest chastising King David. Las Casas castigates the conquerors for holding onto ill-gotten wealth by devious means. With fierce righteousness, he thunders,

Now they have sheathed their swords and no longer murder the natives on sight, they have got into the habit of killing them slowly with hard labour and the imposition of other intolerable and totally unmerited vexations. (ibid., 129)

In a doom-laden finale, he mourns that such fortune hunting has cost the surviving Indians their freedom, property, and dignity. Such iniquity "brings dishonour on the name of God and on that of the King." (ibid., 130)

The high point of Western exploration journals comes from William Clark and Meriwether Lewis, American surveyors dispatched by President Thomas Jefferson in 1804 with a specific task: "to explore the Missouri River, and such principal stream of it as . . . may offer the most direct and practicable water communication across this continent." (Snyder 1970, 11) A roster names their 4 sergeants, 2 interpreters, 24 privates, 7 soldiers, 10 boatmen, and, in a footnote, the Shoshone interpreter Sacajawea and Clark's slave, York, the first black to travel the western route to the Pacific. Setting out by water, portage, and land from Mandan territory in North Dakota, they moved west over the Missouri, Snake, and Columbia Rivers to the Pacific Ocean, where they established a base camp and viewed a beached whale. During their encounters with incredulous Indians, Clark unwisely lit his pipe with a magnifying glass. The implied power of this unknown method of producing fire strained relations with the Indians until Sacajawea appeared. The journal notes that she "confirmed those people of our friendly intentions, as no woman ever accompanies a war party of Indians in this quarter." (Lavender 1988, 283)

An equally controlled, scholarly perusal of North America appears in the ingenuous commentary of Capt. James Cook, who added more to Europe's knowledge of the Pacific than any other navigator or cartographer. *The Explorations of Captain James Cook in the Pacific as Told by Selections of His Own Journals, 1768–1779* (1729–1779) reports on his observations as he journeyed from New Zealand and Tahiti northeast to the Sandwich Islands and on to the American Northwest. On a mission to New Albion in April 1778, he discovered the coast around Nootka Sound to be deadly in foul weather. His trek to Alaska and through the icy cape into the Arctic Sea provided the world its first details about the topography of the northern shores and the unlikelihood that anyone would locate a Northwest Passage, which he had failed to find. Overall, his acquaintance with Hawaiians and his descriptions of the plants and animals of the area are invaluable.

The acclaimed *Voyage of the Beagle* (1839) echoes the excitement of early explorers through the daybooks of Charles Darwin (1809–1882), the era's foremost naturalist. On the volcanic Galapagos Islands, an archipelago lying 500 to 600 miles from the West Coast of America, Darwin discovered a closed community of animals that inhabited their own cosmos. Unhampered by the greed, lust for conquest, and religious piety that spurred earlier explorations, he examined birds, turtles, and lizards. He seemed astonished that the Pacific island birds had not learned to avoid human touch. Darwin concluded that the introduction of "any new beasts of prey" can wreak havoc before the creatures adapt to their new predator and develop protective instincts that will make them fly away. (Darwin 1989, 290) (Burns and Ives 1996b; Cabeza de Vaca 1993a, 1993b; Columbus 1924, 1969, 1988, 1992; Cook 1971; Darwin 1989; Falkenhorst 1892; Ferdinand 1992; Greene 1963; Hakluyt 1826, 1954, 1958, 1962; Hopkins 1969; Landa 1978; Las Casas 1992; Lavender 1988; Lewis and Clark 1922, 1953; Patterson and Snodgrass 1994; Prescott n.d.; Snyder 1970; Villiers 1967)

See also Hawaii; naturalists.

FERBER, EDNA

A multifaceted novelist, playwright, and autobiographer, Edna Ferber holds an honored spot as a popular chronicler of America's coming-of-age. She produced one of frontier literature's vivid sagas, *Cimarron* (1929), the fictionalized story of the Oklahoma land rush and the triumph of materialism over spirit. Skilled in portraiture, she wrote visual feasts that provided Hollywood with material for 20 films and Broadway with two stage adaptations, *Show Boat* and *Saratoga*. The recipient of degrees from Adelphi College and Columbia University and a member of the National Institute of Arts and Letters, Ferber produced works that American servicemen have carried on the battlefield, schools recommend for student readers, and critics list among the literary achievements of Jewish and feminist authors.

Born of Hungarian-Jewish descent on August 15, 1887, in Kalamazoo, Michigan, Ferber was the second of two daughters of Julia Neumann and merchant Jacob Charles Ferber. After her family settled in Appleton, Wisconsin, her father opened a mercantile store. He moved to Ottumwa, Iowa, to establish Ferber's Bazaar, but shortly went blind from atrophy of the optic nerve. Ferber internalized daily doses of Jew-baiting and taunts of "sheeny." When family resources foundered, the Ferbers went to Chicago and moved in with Edna's maternal grandparents. She abandoned hopes of studying drama and, after graduation from Ryan High, worked as the first newspaperwoman for the local *Daily Crescent*, from which she was fired for indulging her love of fiction. A vigorous reporter, she migrated to the Milwaukee *Journal* and the Chicago *Tribune* and served as a civilian war correspondent for the U. S. Army Air Force. In her mid-twenties, Ferber worked herself into nervous collapse and launched a career in fiction as an antidote to depression. From the publication of *Dawn O'Hara* (1911), she advanced to a Pulitzer Prize–winner and best-seller, *So Big* (1924), filmed in 1925, 1932, and 1953. *Show Boat* (1926), a popular romance set on the Mississippi River, was the nucleus of a stage musical, film, and radio series and the source of popular songs, notably "Old Man River," a plaintive slave ballad popularized by baritones Paul Robeson and William Warfield.

With the publication of *Cimarron*, Ferber achieved stardom for dramatizing the opening of the state of Oklahoma. She drew material about the frontier giveaway from the Oklahoma State Historical Library collection in Oklahoma

City. Her heroine, Sabra Venable, exemplifies the pioneer woman's spirit of adventure by marrying Texan Yancey Cravat, a beguiling but unstable criminal lawyer. The rumor that surrounds him derives from the romance of the West:

> They say he has Indian blood in him. They say he has an Indian wife somewhere, and a lot of papooses. Cherokee. They say he used to be known as "Cimarron" Cravat, hence his son's name, corrupted to Cim. They say his real name is Cimarron Seven, of the Choctaw Indian family of Sevens; he was raised in a teepee; a wickiup had been his bedroom, a blanket his robe. (Ferber 1981, 321)

Identified with the unruliness of the unsettled West, Cravat earns contempt from local champions of law and order and bigots for upholding Indian rights in his paper, the Wichita *Wigwam*, which inaugurates its editorial page with deliberate bait: "Will the Blue Blood of the Decayed South Poison the Red Blood of the Real Middle West?"

The central event of the story occurs in 1889, when Cravat moves to free land in Oklahoma, "a wilderness made popular in an hour" where cities spring up by the thousands "where the day before had been only prairie, coyotes, rattlesnakes, red clay, scrub oak, and an occasional nester hidden in the security of a weedy draw." (ibid., 322) Ferber creates an energetic, star-driven dreamer who regales his wife and in-laws with the story of his gallop on an Indian pony over land open to settlers. Within the mad dash, he sees a girl fall, her pony lamed by two broken forelegs. While he gallantly halts to finish off the pony, the girl seizes his mustang and races on to secure a choice quarter section. Following the rules of the chase, "she leaped from the horse, ripped off her skirt, tied it to her riding whip . . . dug the whip butt into the soil of the prairie—planted her flag—and the land was hers by right of claim." (ibid., 329)

Ferber stresses the oversell that accompanies many of the frontier dreams of instant wealth and future contentment. Over the objections of the staid Venables, Cravat takes Sabra and the boy Cim to a "brand-new, two-fisted, rip-snorting country, full of Injuns and rattlesnakes and two-gun toters and gyp water and desper-*ah*-dos! Whoop-*ee!*" (ibid., 332) His joy and bravado express themselves in the lethal lashing of a rattler with his whip and the gladsome singing of three verses of a cowboy song:

> Hi rickety whoop ti do,
> How I love to sing to you.
> Oh, I could sing an' dance with glee,
> If I was as young as I used to be. (ibid., 343)

Woven into these authentic details are events from history that Ferber considers vital to the plot, for example, the arrival of horses to the Western Hemisphere. She describes the wide variety of mounts as descendants of "the equine patricians who, almost 400 years before, had been brought across the ocean by Coronado or Moscoco to the land of the Seven Cities of Gold." (ibid., 353)

On his downhill slide into alcoholism and self-pity, Ferber's male protagonist wraps himself in moral outrage and defends in court and editorial the

Edna Ferber, 1887–1968

beleaguered Indian. Yancey blasts any hope of appointment to the governorship of Oklahoma with his steel-pointed retort to racists:

> Herded like sheep in a corral—no, like wild animals in a cage—they are left to rot on their reservations by a government that has taken first their land, then their self-respect, then their liberty from them. The land of the free! . . . What hope have they, what ambition, what object in living? Their spirit is broken. Their pride is gone. (ibid., 435)

Ferber's didacticism swamps the plot. Sabra fights the crassness of the West and of her hard-drinking husband, driven senseless by his obsession with pioneer days. When she finds Cim clutching the green button of a peyote plant and chanting an ethereal ritual song, she lashes out at escapism, whether into the Old West or the religious dreams of native worshipers. After she is elected congresswoman, she reunites with Cravat, who dies muttering a line from *Peer Gynt*: "Wife and mother—you stainless woman—hide me—hide me in your love!"

For good reason, Ferber feared that melodrama and diatribe overshadowed the purpose of *Cimarron*, which escaped the notice of readers and critics. She complained:

> I was bitterly disappointed. *Cimarron* had been written with a hard and ruthless purpose. It was, and is, a malevolent picture of what is known as American womanhood and American sentimentality. It contains paragraphs and even chapters of satire, and, I am afraid, bitterness, but I doubt that more than a dozen people ever knew this. (Gilbert 1978, 42)

True to her misgivings, critics wrote the novel off as colorful regionalism and Western romance. Praise from notable fans, Rudyard Kipling and Clark Gable, helped to blunt her dismay. Kipling wrote,

> Of course it's melodramatic, but then so was (and so is) Oklahoma and how well she describes the merciless pressure of the respectable women pulling their men folk into line—like mothers chasing up bad boys which, indeed, I suspect all men are. (ibid.)

As though protecting her fiction from defamation, Ferber reviled the simpering 1931 and 1960 film versions, the first starring Irene Dunne and Richard Dix, the second featuring Glenn Ford and Maria Schell. The travesty of a television series, *Cimarron Strip*, a stereotypical Western that debuted in fall 1967, heightened her dismay that packagers failed to read the novel for its historic and thematic merits. Her despair spilled over into mockery of Willa Cather, a contemporary female whose success as a chronicler of the prairie exceeded that of Ferber and others who had set out to write its story.

Many of Ferber's novels, short stories, plays, movie scripts, and autobiographies impressed critics with one major strength: attention to detail, which she acquired by traveling over the setting and imagining herself as a native during exciting times. For information about logging days, Ferber interviewed veteran woodsmen for *Come and Get It* (1935). Two subsequent romances— *Saratoga Trunk* (1941) and *Giant* (1952)—were successful novels and panoramic films, the first set in New York and the second in Texas, both of which she studied on foot and in original manuscripts and maps. *Giant* captivated readers with the love story of Leslie Benedict, bride of a Texas cattle baron whose possessiveness threatens his family and their way of life. The novel covers four decades of Texas history—including a wry scene in which guests at a *barbacoa* eat a roasted steer's head—and predicts the state's eventual struggle with plutocracy, greed, and racial discrimination. *Great Son* (1945), one of Ferber's less-known pioneer novels, takes place in the Northwest and features the history of Seattle and Alaska. In preparation for writing, she traveled the Pacific Northwest and Alaska from Pacific shores to the Arctic Circle and concluded, "It isn't a land for sissies." (ibid., 142) She used five years' worth of experience and note taking to write the backdrop for *Ice Palace* (1958), a semisuccessful novel that has been lauded as the "*Uncle Tom's Cabin* of Alaska Statehood."

At her death from stomach cancer on April 16, 1968, Ferber was collecting material for a novel on Indians. She had already compiled notes on firsthand hikes through the Southwest desert, visits to pueblos, and interviews with Apache, Navajo, Pima, Papago, and Hopi. Lines from her notes resonate with the energy of her quest to understand without Hollywoodizing:

> Mysterious? No, it wasn't mystery that baffled me, any more than a rock is mysterious. It gives back no response, but that does not necessarily give one the effect of a mystery unsolved. The rock is simply there—a rock. Perhaps there is a vein of pure gold in it, once you've split it. But more likely it is just a rock. (ibid., 27)

Looking back at the Indians' dominance of North America, she marveled that for 45,000 years, aborigines lived in harmony with nature, which they idolized as the earth mother. Without written language, vehicle, cook pot, or permanent dwelling, Indians seemed content to live on a vast, breathtaking continent and to leave it as pristinely beautiful as they had found it. There is evidence in Ferber's identification with Indians that she had felt from childhood the ostracism of Jews in the Midwest and that her own self-defense took shape in novels that championed the underdog. (Blain, Grundy, and Clements 1990; Buck 1992; Ferber 1945, 1981; Gilbert 1978; Gislason 1996a; Kunitz 1942; Lamar 1977; Rainey 1996; Sackett 1996)

See also Alaska and the Yukon; Cather, Willa.

GERONIMO

The story of Geronimo stands out in southwestern history as the single most compelling biography of a native leader. Arguably America's most cunning guerrilla warrior, Geronimo was a shaman and military expert for the Nedni branch of the Chiricahua Apache. He was born to a noble family in southern Arizona near the Gila River in June 1829. His grandfather, Chief Mahko, who died before Geronimo was born, had been a noted war leader. In childhood, Geronimo was called Goyathlay or Goyakla, meaning Yawner. At age 17, he gained a place on the warrior council and traded a herd of ponies for Alope, the first of his eight wives.

In adulthood, Geronimo settled in Arispe in Sonora, Mexico, and was 29 years old before he saw his first whites. He assisted his brother-in-law Juh in leading the tribe against Mexican slavers, missionaries, and settlers at a time when Apache scalps were prized by the Mexican government, which offered $50 each for adult scalp locks and $25 for a child's scalp. Under the command of Cochise, Geronimo, along with Mangas Colorado and Victorio, raided mining camps, stagecoaches, and ranchers and villagers of the Mexican uplands. Swift, decisive, and bold, he avenged the 1858 unprovoked massacre of his mother, wife, and three children by attacking the Mexican village of Kaskiyeh. Among the cries of his victims he heard worshippers begging mercy from Saint Jerome, called Hieronymus. From the name he adapted his own name, which he pronounced Hispanic fashion with a softened G. His hatred for the Mexicans determined his actions for nearly 40 years.

The U.S. Army was dispatched to end Apache raids and to make the Gila Trail safe for whites traveling west from El Paso and Santa Fe through Tucson and Yuma to California. A clever deceiver, Geronimo was expert at setting up ghost camps to draw pursuers away from his location. When apprehended, he used his wiles to escape and taunted would-be captors at close range. In 1876, the Chiricahua were forced to settle in the Gila Mountains at San Carlos, Arizona. In vain, Geronimo petitioned President Grant to allow him to return to his homeland in Arizona to die and be buried among his ancestors. He fled south to Mexico with his followers, but was recaptured and returned to the hated reservation.

The call-up of reserve troops after the shooting of Nakaidoklini, the Apache prophet, on August 30, 1881, restored Geronimo's band to a state of siege from their camp in the Sierra Madre Mountains. Treacherous Apaches working for the cavalry captured him once more. In 1883, Geronimo, Mangas Colorado, Naiche, and the rest of the Chiricahua Apache were cast into prison on the San Carlos reservation and bound with leg chains. Under the power of General George Crook, his old nemesis, Geronimo spoke boldly. According to *Life of Tom Horn, Government Scout and Interpreter* (1904), the wily chief complains that the life of an outlaw condemns to death too many people on both sides of the conflict. The prospect of watching more people die in vain distresses him:

> I have grown old on the war path, and what have I accomplished? Only this: today I stand before you as a supplicant. Today I am going to ask of you what I, the proud war chief of the Chiricahua tribe, never thought to ask of any white man. I ask you to take me to the Reservation, and there to do with me as you see fit, and as your judgment says is right for you to do. (Horn 1964, 131)

The speech is well received, but the military leaders doubt that he intends to go meekly to prison. The next day, Geronimo's men leave to round up the rest of the Chiricahuas, a move that makes Crook and his officers look like inept fools. According to army scout Tom Horn, once more local settlers fear Apaches on the loose.

Two years later, rumors of a plot to try Geronimo for a capital offense caused him to join his cousin, Jason Betzinez, and a half-brother, White Horse, in a daring jail break. On May 17, Geronimo led 144 Apaches back to their secret camp. Public outcry forced the government to mount a huge Anglo-Mexican search mission, which outnumbered Geronimo's band 100 to 1. Recaptured by Crook on March 25, 1886, at Canyon de los Embudos, Mexico, Geronimo signed a surrender that exiled his tribe to Florida for two years, yet reunited Apache families that had been parted by earlier arrests. On the way to the reservation, unexplained shooting broke out, confusing Geronimo; he escaped again. He was taken in Skeleton Canyon by General Nelson A. "Bear Coat" Miles, dispatched in chains by rail, and imprisoned at hard labor with 450 Apaches at Fort Pickens, Florida, where malaria, tuberculosis, and suicide decimated their number.

In 1894, Geronimo, then in his sixties, was shuffled to the Mount Vernon Barracks in Vermont, Alabama. There he encountered General Oliver Otis Howard, the renowned one-armed Civil War veteran and Indian fighter, who wrote a chapter about him in *Famous Indian Chiefs I Have Known* (1906). By order of President Grover Cleveland, the military settled the Apache with Comanche and Kiowa inmates at Fort Sill, Oklahoma, where Geronimo joined the Dutch Reformed Church. Domesticated in old age, he grew melons and vegetables and raised horses. He begged officials to allow his people to return to Arizona, but the public fear of his past history and the difficulties of coordinating settlement terms with Mexico doomed his efforts.

An attraction to readers of Wild West lore, Geronimo remained in demand, becoming one of the most photographed of the notorious Southwest desert warriors. He sold trinkets, photos, and his signature for a dime or a quarter in Omaha at the 1898 Trans-Mississippi and International Exposition, in Buffalo at the 1901 Pan-American Exposition, and as part of a Wild West show in St. Louis at the 1904 Louisiana Purchase Exposition. The following year, he rode in President Theodore Roosevelt's inaugural procession. The last great native leader to surrender to the military, Geronimo longed to die a free man, but died instead in the Fort Sill hospital on February 17, 1909, of pneumonia after a fall from his horse.

At age 75, Geronimo dictated his autobiography, *Geronimo's Story of His Life* (1906), to translator S. M. Barrett and, in hopes of fair treatment of Apaches after his death, dedicated the work to Theodore Roosevelt. Barrett sheds light on Geronimo's admiration for the president in the introduction:

> Accordingly I wrote to President Roosevelt that here was an old Indian who had been held a prisoner of war for 20 years and had never been given a chance to tell his side of the story and asked that Geronimo be granted permission to tell for publication, in his own way, the story of his life, and that he be guaranteed that the publication of his story would not affect unfavorably the Apache prisoners of war. (Geronimo 1989, xiv)

After the president's immediate sanctioning of the project, Barrett set to work, employing Asa Deklugie as native intermediary. Although Geronimo was weakened from pneumonia, he was faithful to his word and kept appointments to relate installments of his past.

Beginning with a brief history of Apaches and their subtribes, Geronimo's story tells of his widowed mother's decision to remain with her son. With stoic control, he narrates the events of the massacre that took his family without warning and of his meeting with the council that decided to depart without burying the dead:

> I stood until all had passed, hardly knowing what I would do—I had no weapon, nor did I wish to fight, neither did I contemplate recovering the bodies of my loved ones, for that was forbidden. I did not pray, nor did I resolve to do anything in particular, for I had no purpose left. (ibid., 45)

In a state of trauma, he fasts on the retreat from their camp and talks with the others. Eloquent in his memory of grief, he comments, "none had lost as I had, for I had lost all." (ibid., 46) The blood oath that he swears over the dead fuels his hatred throughout his career as Apache guide and leader.

In 1929, Britton Davis, formerly a lieutenant with Troop L, Third Cavalry, at Fort Russell, Wyoming, determined to counter the fiction that was passing for Western history by writing *The Truth about Geronimo*, a dry documentary containing communiques among army officials. He establishes his objectivity by stating that Indians are "a race of fellow human beings whose many fine qualities we have been too prone to becloud under hate and misunderstanding." (Davis 1929, xvii) After introducing his book with details of Coronado's meeting with the Apache in 1541, Davis carries his brief overview up to 1885, the year he joined the campaign to capture the old chief. His factual account of the cavalry's ragged attempt to subdue Geronimo's band includes a map of the campaign, which extends from the common border of Arizona and New Mexico south an equal distance into Sonora and Chihuahua, Mexico. Davis acknowledges the chief's skill in eluding the army for 18 months while sustaining 35 males, 8 youths, and 101 women and children on goods and livestock stolen from whites. In infrequent but deadly confrontations, Geronimo's men killed 75 settlers, 12 friendly Apache, two cavalry officers, eight troopers, and around 100 Mexicans. With the military man's cold accuracy, Davis emphasizes that Geronimo lost 11 from his band, *not one of whom was killed by regular troops.* (ibid., xv) Almost as an afterthought, Davis offers the single most important compliment to the wily Apache, "who was never *captured* by anyone." (ibid., xvi)

Three decades after Britton Davis published his account, Jason Betzinez, Geronimo's cousin, contributed valuable details omitted from the autobiography by publishing *I Fought with Geronimo* (1959), his eyewitness account of the Geronimo Wars and negotiations with General Crook that resulted in exile of Apaches to Florida. Of Geronimo's clairvoyance he relates an event that happened at Casas Grandes:

> We were sitting there eating. Geronimo was sitting next to me with a knife in one hand and a chunk of beef which I had cooked for him in the other. All at once he dropped the knife, saying, "Men, our people whom we left at our base camp are now in the hands of U.S. troops! What shall we do?" (Betzinez 1959, 113)

None question the statement, for they had seen Geronimo's prophecies come true on other occasions. Betzinez remarks that seven days later, the event came true, leaving him to marvel at Geronimo's second sight.

Betzinez's description of guerrilla tactics clarifies Geronimo's methods, explains how he supported his band by trading stolen livestock, and details fierce shootouts with Mexican pursuers. As proof that Geronimo made the best deals for the good of his people, Betzinez recounts Geronimo's retort to a carping Mexican that the U.S. Army offered supplies and shelter, whereas Mexicans had never done anything to alleviate Apache suffering. On the train trip east, Betzinez recalls public curiosity about the flagrant Apache bandit:

> We stopped at many stations along the way where hundreds of white people gathered to stare at us to see what kind of wild creatures had made so much trouble in Arizona and New Mexico.... During the night the train crossed the Rio Grande, passed through Albuquerque, and plunging through a tunnel, left the mountains behind. We saw the last of the Rockies at noon when we stopped for lunch. (ibid., 142)

One fervid warrior, Massai, tried to stir others to revolt, then fled alone and retraced his route to Arizona, a formidable task in settled country where he knew no one and had no directions, food, or weapons for the journey. (Today, two landmarks honor his spirit—Massai Point and Massai Canyon, Arizona.)

Betzinez recalls Geronimo in his last years as a peaceful man. Dishonored and despised after falling victim to alcohol, he earned an unjust reputation for reckless violence and vicious reprisals. One source of inaccuracy was the stream of media interviews, which unscrupulous journalists padded with lies, such as the fabrication that his coat was made of 99 human scalps. Long before his death, Geronimo had become a standard exhibit at fairs, parades, and pageants—a national curiosity, like a bear in a zoo. (Betzinez 1959; Burns and Ives 1996b; Davis 1929; Geronimo 1989; Grafton 1992; Horn 1964; Howard 1989; Lamar 1977; Patterson and Snodgrass 1994; Stockel 1996; Straub 1996; Waldman 1990; Wetherill 1992; Wexler 1995)

See also Bury My Heart at Wounded Knee; Howard, Oliver Otis.

GIPSON, FRED

One of young adult literature's classic storytellers, Fred Gipson, author of *Cowhand: The Story of a Working Cowboy* (1948) and *Old Yeller* (1956), captured the rhythms of work and idiom common to frontier Texans. A native of Mason, Texas, born February 7, 1908, he lived on a ranch and halfheartedly studied journalism at the University of Texas. After reporting for the Corpus Christi *Caller* and the San Angelo *Times*, he began writing novels, television scripts and screenplays, and articles for *Reader's Digest*, *Liberty*, and *Collier's*. His first success was *The Fabulous Empire: Colonel Zack Miller's Story* (1946) and his first major award-winner was adult fiction, *Hound-Dog Man* (1949). Other frontier publications include *Big Bend: A Homesteader's Story* (1952), coauthored by J. O. Langford, and three works of young adult fiction, *The Trail-Driving Rooster* (1955), *Savage Sam* (1962), and *Little Arliss* (1978). For his appealing tales, Gipson earned the Maggie award, William Allen White Children's Book award, First Sequoyah award, and the Northwest Pacific award.

For the biographical *Cowhand*, Gipson chose a typical west Texas ranch worker named Ed "Fat" Alford, a squat, thick-necked bulldogger who can "rope a cow out of a brush patch so thick that a Hollywood cowboy couldn't crawl into it on his hands and knees." (Gipson 1953, vi) The author characterizes Fat as knowledgeable, handy with a rope or two-cycle engine, skilled at odd jobs, and tolerant of extremes of weather and circumstance. Born on the Texas-Oklahoma border in 1901, Fat, like previous generations of Westerners, determined in his early teens to escape hard scrabble farming for even harder herd work. He moves to trans-Pecos territory, a thrilling locale that becomes his home:

> It's a fantastic country. High, bald ridges. Wide mesquite flats. Crawling desert sands. Gushing springs, some hot, some cold. Salt lakes. Grassy swags. Greasewood slopes. Flat-topped mesas. Deep tortuous canyons. Great desert plains sweeping up to pine-studded mountains, and the mountains standing blue in the distance. (ibid., 9)

In his depiction of the area's history, Gipson tempers enthusiasm for piñon country with the violence of past scraps between Indians and Mexicans, squatters and ranchers, and lawless and law-abiding. For all the protracted squabbling over land and water rights, the eventual developers of ranch land possess a rough, barely tenable terrain. Daily fare keeps Fat "worse broke than the Ten Commandments" as he vies for work against usurping wetbacks, who will labor at half the pay. (ibid., 179) In the end, he acquires a small toehold of his own near Wildhorse Springs, New Mexico, the same gritty bronc-buster's paradise that he fled to in boyhood.

Equally readable is *Big Bend*, a memoir illustrated with photos of the countryside. It follows Langford, a sickly, malaria-wracked Mississippi homesteader, by buckboard from Alpine, Texas, along the Rio Grande to Tornillo Creek. At Hot Springs, a healing resort, he constructs a flat-roofed rock home that looks out on dry, rugged country. He earns a meager living selling bales of chino grass, hand-braided quirts and whips, and pelts from the beavers, foxes, raccoons, skunks, and opossums he traps along the trail. The isolation of his small family ends abruptly with a threatened raid of bandits. The false alarm sends the narrator to the 14th Cavalry at La Noria. The next threat—a revolt in Mexico—uproots the Langfords from Big Bend. Fourteen years later, they return to their homestead, build a store, and open a post office. In the interim, the pristine frontier alters to accommodate automobile travel and an increase in settlement. No longer insulated from Eastern civilization, Langford mourns that "the brightness seemed gone from the land." (Langford and Gipson 1973, 154)

Better known for his frontier classic, *Old Yeller*, Gipson achieved a steady popularity among young adult readers. His work succeeded both in book form and in the 1963 Walt Disney film version, for which he coauthored the screen play. The film starred a quality cast—Dorothy McGuire, Fess Parker, Tommy Kirk, Kevin Corcoran, and Chuck Connors. Its first-person narrative depicts the struggle of Travis Coates, a 14-year-old farm boy compelled to head a pioneer family during the late 1860s. While Papa Coates earns "cash money" by driving cattle from Salt Licks, Texas, to market at Abilene, Travis shoulders chores, plowing with Jumper the mule and supplying game for his mother and little brother Arliss. Papa's predeparture warning weighs heavy on Travis's mind:

> Now, there's cows to milk and wood to cut and young pigs to mark and fresh meat to shoot. But mainly there's the corn patch. If you don't work it right or if you let the varmints eat up the roasting ears, we'll be without bread corn for the winter. (Gipson 1956, 3)

From dealings with "loafer wolves, bears, panthers, and raiding Indians" common to wild frontier settlements, Travis concludes that local cattlemen have no choice but to leave their wives and children in charge: "they needed money, and they realized that whatever a man does, he's bound to take some risks." (ibid., 2, 4)

Perhaps unintentially, Gipson's picture of the frontier wife and mother honors an admirable figure battling a daunting, unrelenting panoply of challenges. As Travis's backup, Mama Coates displays fortitude and a cool head for emergencies and on-the-scene decisions. With no recourse to professional medical care, she threads a hair from the mule's tail and sews up Old Yeller's wounds after he is gored by a wild range hog. Because they must slaughter livestock too close to the house and water supply to leave to vultures, she drags the carcasses away and burns them. When a mad wolf threatens, she knocks it away from Old Yeller with a chinaberry pole and offers to shoot their watchdog when she and Travis recognize the threat of rabies. During her multiple labors, Travis comments on her expertise at frontier cures:

> Mama nearly ran herself to death, packing fresh cold water from the spring, which she used to bathe me all over, trying to run my fever down. When she wasn't packing water, she was out digging prickly-pear roots and hammering them to mush in a sack, then binding the mush to my leg for a poultice. (ibid., 90)

The combination of crippled teenager, wounded dog, knot-headed mule, and worrisome small son to superintend deprives her of sleep and forces her to improvise, such as the drag that she ties to Jumper to keep him out of the corn. In Travis's words, "Altogether, Mama sure had her hands full." (ibid., 91)

In his father's absence, the boy learns from a tough female who not only works hard but also soothes her children's fears of wilderness terrors. In the end, however, Gipson awards the role of sage to the father. Papa's gift of a "cat-stepping blue roan" is welcome yet not wonderful enough to counter the execution of Old Yeller. Papa remarks on the cruelty of life, then adds

> But it isn't the only way life is. A part of the time, it's mighty good. And a man can't afford to waste all the good part, worrying about the bad parts. That makes it all bad. . . . You understand? (ibid., 116)

The lesson sinks in. In a week or so, Travis's funk gives way to humor and exasperation. Little Arliss once more strips naked and frolics in Birdsong Creek, source of the family's drinking water. Along with him is the "bread-stealing speckled pup," the image of its father, Old Yeller.

The blend of nature's savagery and bounty forms a realistic but satisfying tapestry of farm life on the Texas frontier. Travis's humorous run-ins with the "big ugly slick-haired yeller [stray]" grow from grudging acceptance to admiration after Old Yeller saves Arliss from a bear. Gipson balances the warmth of the boy-dog relationship with the harsh truth of plains life. Death is ever-present, whether an outgrowth of the hunt for food or the protection of territory, in predatory wolves or vultures that feast on carcasses, from pea vine or hydrophobia that can madden cattle and dogs, or the grisly death of Bell from the snapping fangs of a disembodied rattlesnake head. When Papa evaluates the events that have pressed his family to the ends of energy, resources, and courage, he affirms Travis's manhood. (Carlsen 1967; Dobie 1996; Gillespie and Lembo 1967; Gipson 1953, 1956, 1993; Langford and Gipson 1973; "Review" 1956; Sackett 1996)

GREEN, PAUL

North Carolina's most prominent playwright, creator of the symphonic drama, and progenitor of the historical outdoor drama movement, Paul Eliot Green excelled in varied styles of drama and criticism over his lengthy career. A native of Harnett County near Lillington, North Carolina, Green, born March 17, 1894, grew up on a cotton farm. His familiarity with agrarian values and rhythms tinged his work with authenticity, in action and in the characterization and voicing of rural folk, whom he represented with games, folk cures, superstitions, religious beliefs, aphorisms, and traditions. Even in the spring preceding his death in 1981, he still planted a garden and grew cuttings and flowers.

The son of progressive cotton farmer William Archibald and organist Betty Byrd Green, Green grew up in a rich lineage of English and Scots settlers of the Cape Fear region. His family tree boasted a maternal grandfather, William Byrd, who composed hymns and taught singing, and a paternal grandfather, Judge John Green, who cultivated a plantation with slave labor and supported education. The last of six children, Green was a voracious reader and attended a one-room school and Buie's Creek Academy. At age ten, he suffered osteomyelitis and had to learn to write left-handed.

To pay for his study of philosophy at the University of North Carolina, Green played professional baseball and served as principal of the Olive Branch School near Kipling, North Carolina. His college years abruptly ended for a stint in the army during World War I. Returned in 1919 from action in Flanders and France, where he served as a lieutenant in the American Expeditionary Force, Green came under the influence of notable drama teacher Frederick H. Koch, a member of the University of North Carolina faculty. A newcomer to stage fare, Green wrote instinctively rather than from experience and produced comedy, fantasy, parable, and tragedy. His first play, *The Last of the Lowries* (1920), dealt with the demise of a gang notorious in eastern North Carolina. Other college-era titles derive from similar sources: *The Miser, A Farm Tragedy,* and *The Old Man of Edenton, A Melodrama of Colonial Carolina.* Green's alliance with Koch enriched the influential teacher's campus after Green, his most promising student, published folk plays and became the first recipient of the Sir Walter Raleigh award for imaginative literature by a North Carolinian.

Central to Green's canon of 30 one-act plays are the religion, traditions, and mores of working-class and agrarian whites and blacks, including bootleggers, mill workers, tenant farmers, and hillbillies. Southern mountain dialect enriches his canon, particularly the antifundamentalist comedy *Quare Medicine* (1925) and *The No'Count Boy* (1925). In the former title, Old Man Jernigan defeats his priggish daughter-in-law Mattie, a pro-missionary, anti-tobacco meddler who dominates his son Henry. In pity, Old Jernigan looks toward Henry and mutters, "Poor soul, not at peace in his own household, going about like a man with the mulligrubs, can't sleep, can't eat, worried, worried down to the ground." (Green 1956, 110) Doctor Immanuel delivers his Universal Remedy, which he advertises with a jingle:

Two dollars a bottle, two dollars,
Going at two dollars,
Are you weak and heavy laden,

Sore distressed, sad distressed?
It will cleanse of evil passion,
Restore your bowels of compassion,
Accidents, diseases chronic—
The marvelous Egyptian Tonic. (ibid., 116–117)

After the elixir restores "manly courage" and rids Henry of Mattie's henpeck-
ing, Jernigen exclaims, "Well, I be durned if I ever seed the beat!" (ibid., 128)

At an early peak in his career, Green earned a Pulitzer Prize for his first
full-length drama, *In Abraham's Bosom* (1927), a folk play composed in dialect
and produced in New York for a disappointingly short run. Green's subsequent works—*The Field God* (1927), *The House of Connelly* (1931), and *The Laughing Pioneer* (1932)—thrived on New York stages. His antiwar drama *Johnny
Johnson* (1928), cowritten with Kurt Weill, was produced in Finland; and in
Hollywood he wrote for Warner Brothers and MGM the screenplays *Voltaire*
(1933), *State Fair* (1933), and *Cabin in the Cotton* (1943). While in Germany on a
two-year Guggenheim fellowship, Green came under the influence of Alexis
Granowsky's Yiddish repertory theater and experimented with people's pageant, spectacle, or interlude, blending ballet, dialogue, pantomime, poetry, film,
lighting, and music in *Tread the Green Grass* (1932), *Roll, Sweet Chariot* (1934),
Shroud My Body Down (1934), and *The Enchanted Maze* (1935). In 1941, he returned to conventional drama with *Native Son*, a collaborative effort with author Richard Wright.

Green's famed historical plays began with *The Lost Colony: A Symphonic
Drama in Two Acts* (1937), an austere blend of music and drama that details Sir
Walter Raleigh's role in England's doomed first settlement. Subsequent his-
torical works include *The Highland Call* (1939), a biographic glimpse of Flora
MacDonald, legendary rescuer of Bonnie Prince Charlie and settler among
North Carolina's tobacco planters; *The Common Glory* (1947), a tribute to Thomas Jefferson; *Faith of Our Fathers* (1950), a study of George Washington; *The
17th Star*, a celebration of Ohio's admission to the Union; and *Wilderness Road*
(1955), an outdoor drama set among the pioneer stock of Berea, Kentucky.
Green's contributions to folk theater and his dedication to human equality
earned him an American Theatre Association award, Theta Alpha Phi Medallion of Honor, Frank Porter Graham Civil Liberties award, North Carolina Dra-
matist Laureate, Albert Schweitzer Medal, three Freedom Foundation medals,
three honorary degrees, Distinguished Citizen of North Carolina, and selection as a Rockefeller Foundation lecturer. In 1978, the Paul Green Theatre was
dedicated at the University of North Carolina in Chapel Hill. From his incep-
tion of the outdoor theater came the Department of Dramatic Art and the Extension Division, which has aided 55 fledgeling folk theaters since 1963. (Adams
1951; Beatty et al. 1952; Charles 1996; Green 1937, 1956; Hoyle 1956; "The Lost
Colony" Playbill 1990; *North Carolina Authors* 1952; Spearman 1953; Stick 1983;
Walser 1956; Wynn 1990)

See also Hunter, Kermit; the lost colony; theater of the frontier.

GREY, ZANE

The quintessential author of adult and juvenile Western novels, Zane Grey was an Easterner enthralled with America's frontier. His famed shoot-'em-ups were the product of an active imagination whetted by a detailed study of history and a thorough familiarity with the arroyas, buttes, and desert expanses that became his fiction landscape. For 40 years, he entranced readers with a two-fisted brand of Westerns that formulated the world's image of "Out West." Today, Grey's books are a standard feature in bookmobiles, paperback shelves, school lockers, prison libraries, and barrack and firehouse book collections—wherever predominantly male readers congregate. His titles find favor with workers and professionals alike, and outspoken fans include the late President Dwight Eisenhower and Western movie star Randolph Scott.

Born in Zanesville in southeastern Ohio on January 31, 1875, Grey grew up under the curse of a prissy, girlish name, Pearl Zane Gray, spelled American-style with an *a*. As the great-grandson of a Revolutionary War hero, he de-served better and subsequently altered his name to a genteel, discreet Dr. P. Zane Grey when he opened his first dental office. His family heritage allied him with the trailblazer of Zane's Trace, later known as the National Road, which, by 1833, offered safe transport to the Great Migration from Cumberland, Maryland, over Ohio and Indiana to Vandalia, Illinois. As the fourth of the five children of Alice Josephine Zane and Dr. Lewis M. "Doc" Gray, a dentist and itinerant evangelist, Grey received a comfortable middle-class upbringing. He enjoyed camping and fishing and read widely from the adventure fiction of Daniel Defoe and James Fenimore Cooper, but reaped his father's ire for scribbling a short story on a scrap of wallpaper, which his father destroyed.

Dr. Gray disdained writing as an unmanly pursuit. He preferred that his sons take up sports. Under the nickname "Pitchin' Pearl," Grey excelled at baseball. He was scouted while playing for Baltimore, Ohio, and, after comparing the records of local colleges, agreed to sign with the athletic department of the University of Pennsylvania. At the age of 21, he earned a D.D.S. degree and, for seven years, dutifully practiced dentistry in Lackawaxen, New York, under the guidance of his father. He was known as a quick-wristed drawer of teeth; his reputation with the drill and impression plate was merely satisfactory.

From the beginning, Grey's dental office took second place to his writing of historical romance, which he explored in his early teens with his first story, "Jim of the Cave." He broke into print in 1902 with the publication of "A Day on the Delaware" in *Reaction* magazine. In the self-published historical romance, *Betty Zane* (1903), he told the story of his great-grandfather, Colonel Ebenezer Zane, founder of Wheeling, West Virginia, and of his great-aunt Elizabeth "Betty" Zane. A forerunner of the doughty plainswoman, she assisted defend-ers of Fort Henry, North Dakota, by transporting gunpowder from storage to the fort while dodging fire from Indian attackers. The success of the romance gave him the confidence to resign from dentistry, marry Lina Elise "Dolly" Roth, and write Westerns full-time, a career change bolstered by strong reader re-sponse to his next two novels, *Spirit of the Border* (1906) and *The Last Trail* (1909).

Zane Grey, 1875–1939

Aided by Colonel C. J. "Buffalo" Jones, a game warden in Yellowstone Park and former guide and hunter, Grey traveled to Kanab, Utah, and Grand Canyon and Flagstaff, Arizona, and interviewed wagoneers, Mormons, Indians, ranch hands, miners, and other likely folk to people his novels. He grew adept at interweaving plots with elements of Americana—southwestern dialects, the quick draw, bronco busting, long gallops over brutal terrain, hoarded bags of gold dust, revenge plots, and a pastiche of hidden sin in the lives of darkly handsome, brooding protagonists. He wrote Jones's biography, *The Last of the Plainsmen* (1908), which contains searching passages that assess the strengths and challenges of the West. Near the book's conclusion, while the characters stalk a mountain lion, the character looks out on

> the noblest and most sublime work of nature. The rim wall where I stood sheered down a thousand feet. . . . From Point Sublime to the Pink Cliffs of Utah there were twelve of these colossal capes, miles apart, some sharp, some round, some blunt, all rugged and bold. (Grey 1978, 287)

Grey's descriptives reach for specific topographical and botanical nouns: chasms, turrets, mesas, domes, parapets, escarpments, cliffs, tables, saguaro, and piñon thicket. The excited cries of the hunters sound a celebratory anthem to the wilderness that anchors Jones's biography.

Under the influence of Owen Wister's *The Virginian*, Grey attempted to carry the love story to a mature level. He earned a handsome living from *The Heritage of the Desert* (1910) and his most famous Western, *Riders of the Purple Sage* (1912), written on the scene in Dove Creek, Colorado. The strength of *Riders of the Purple Sage* lies in the tension between the heroine, Jane Withersteen, a staid Mormon, and her rescuer, Lassiter, a battered gunfighter and former Texas Ranger. Lassiter strikes fear in Elder Tull, the Mormon patriarch who seeks to add Jane to his bevy of wives. Grey pioneered the female point of view in a genre that had previously focused on violence in a man's world. As he describes his heroine, she is not the silver-screen stereotype:

> Jane's vanity, that after all was not great, was soon satisfied with Lassiter's silent admiration. And her honest desire to lead him from his dark, blood-stained path would never have blinded her to what she owed herself. But the driving passion of her religion, and its call to save Mormons' lives, one life in particular, bore Jane Withersteen close to an infringement of her womanhood. (Grey 1940, 122)

Grey places his male and female characters in untenable buyouts, showdowns, ambushes, and squeeze plays that require bold action. In a distinctly Western microcosm, his personae act out Darwin's survival of the fittest, thus assuring the American frontier the best of the breed to gentle the land and keep it safe from a variety of evils, often the greed of land grabbers and thieves. Writing for proletarian tastes, Grey succeeded by stressing the virtues of the iron-willed settler, rancher, and cowboy who are willing to risk all for the preservation of frontier independence.

Early on, Grey preferred Western historical romance as his métier for novels. He returned to historical figures, selecting Mexican revolutionary Pancho Villa as the central figure of his next novel, *Desert Gold* (1913), which ranks only so-so by Grey experts. The publication of his horse classic, *Wildfire* (1917), ended Grey's pulp era and resituated him among "slick" authors. In 1918, he wrote an international classic, *The U. P. Trail*, an ambitious vehicle for his story of the Union Pacific Railroad's role in Western settlement. Grey's sincere interest in humanism and the frontier West shows in a poignant preface. He cites from Robert Louis Stevenson's *Across the Plains* (1892), which reproves how the top-hatted millionaires

> pushed through this unwatered wilderness and haunt of savage tribes; how at each stage of the construction roaring, impromptu cities, full of gold and lust and death, sprang up and then died away again, and are now but wayside stations in this desert; how in these uncouth places Chinese pirates worked side by side with border ruffians and broken men from Europe, gambling, drinking, quarreling, and murdering like wolves. (Grey 1918, n.p.)

Readers approved Grey's new direction. In the 1920s, his take per book reached $80,000. Wealth and freedom from office tedium enabled him to tour memorable frontier sites, particularly Oak Tree Canyon, Arizona, the setting for *Call of the Canyon* (1924), and Robber's Roost in the Badlands of Utah, where Butch

Cassidy's gang once holed up from the law. Grey retained the name of the hideout in *Robber's Roost* (1932).

In addition to a steady production of Western novels, Grey continued writing articles and stories about baseball and fishing, an avocation that lured him to the world's best fishing holes, both salt and fresh. While angling for marlin and shark, he broke deep-sea fishing records. A blend of avid writer and fisherman, he pursued work and hobby wherever he traveled, including Australia, Tahiti, Ecuador, New Caledonia, New Zealand, and his vacation home in Avalon on the island of Santa Catalina. While living in a cabin outside Grants Pass, Oregon, he composed "Tales of Freshwater Fishing" (1924), a serial for *Field and Stream*, and "Shooting the Rogue" (1926), a series about the Rogue River for *Country Gentleman*. On a fishing trip to Long Key, Florida, in 1934, he wrote *Code of the West* in five weeks.

At their three-story manor in Altadena, California, Dolly reared their daughter Betty and two sons, Loren and Romer, and furthered her husband's career by correcting errors in rhetoric and grammar and by advising her beloved "Z.G." on contracts. Although he lived apart from her on his fact-finding trips and yearlong voyages aboard his yacht, he valued her as agent, friend, and mate, especially during his bouts of depression and self-doubt. Overall, he produced 61 books in his lifetime; 17 more were published after his death from heart disease on October 23, 1939, in Altadena. Of his 78 titles, 43 were serialized in an astonishing list of publications: *Popular Magazine, All-Story Cavalier, Outdoor America, Izaak Walton Monthly, Munsey Magazine, Blue Book, Ladies' Home Journal, McCall's, Collier's, Physical Culture, American Boy, American Magazine, Pictorial Review, Cosmopolitan,* and the New York *Daily News*. In the 1920s and 1930s, spin-off writers such as Max Brand and Ernest Haycox emulated the Grey formula for Westerns and contributed to a spate of horse-and-rider fiction in hardback and magazine serials. Into the next two decades, Hollywood based 104 films on Grey's plots; *Zane Grey Western Theatre* introduced his stories to television audiences. Millions around the world thrilled to his broad range of melodramatic horse operas, but *Riders of the Purple Sage* remained the favorite.

At the center of Grey's stories stands the code hero, patterned after a mythic figure. Masculine and toughened by battle scars, he is a self-determined survivor and defender of right, goodness, and women. At the same time that he battles for a square deal, he suppresses the violent streak in his makeup until social or political circumstance demand action rather than reason. In some of Grey's impassioned dialogue, he allows the romantic thrust to destroy verisimilitude and weaken the hero, as with this farewell in *Quaking Asp Cabin* (1934):

> "Go away. Leave me peace in retribution. . . . But if you have any manhood, you will let this terrible deed—this fruit of our passion—be a turning point in your life."
>
> "Manhood! Am I my brother's keeper? I want *you*, Blue. You, my woman, else I'll go to hell!" (Grey 1988, 343)

When played out in movies, these overblown exchanges put legs and faces on Grey's idealism. Even though critics derided soupy sentiment, fans accepted the convention of heightened emotions and selfless platitudes, which became a Hollywood standard during the heyday of saddle soaps.

Two themes resonate through Grey's literary jaunts about the West: the demand for law and order and the replacement of played-out Eastern ethics with vigorous, morally upright Western values. The loner, tinged with melancholy and pressed into physical combat, serves a community or individual by quelling anarchy and restoring peace. Skill with weapons readies the hero for the quest. Like King Arthur bearing Excalibur into battle or St. George squaring off against the dragon, Zane Grey's man faces adversity with assurance that past experiences have prepared him for the next scrape. To balance these staunch, romanticized cavaliers, Grey juxtaposes the code heroine, the female who has departed from Eastern priggishness, but whose hardening in the West resides within the precincts of decency, womanliness, and decorum.

Grey's characters build their strengths by interacting with the rugged wilderness, the Western terrain that he loved and respected for its toughening of national character. He revered Western history and depicted it accurately in accounts of, for example, the wars between sheepherders and cattlemen in *To the Last Man* (1921), embattled Indians in *The Vanishing American* (1922), and the buffalo culture in *The Thundering Herd* (1923). His immersion of human figures on the horizon colors *Blue Feather* (1934), one of his many novellas. He orchestrates the steadily increasing cadence into a symphony of landscape and emotion:

> That ragged slope was to Blue Feather as a multitude of enemies, every rock of which seemed a foe to spurn. He ran, he leaped. He set the avalanches rolling. He might have been pursued by the winged spirits of those who had died with twisted minds. That league-long slope of talus, ending in the red gorge, was as a short space of thin air to the Nopah. No feat of endurance in any game he had ever played, no race he had ever run to the plaudits of the clan, could compare to this descent alone, seen only by the spirits, driven as he was by his tortured conscience. (ibid., 47)

Parallel to Grey's love for the pristine wild runs his passion for the real people who tamed the frontier by matching its rigor with their own hardihood. Proclaimed a testimony to America's resilience, Zane Grey Westerns continue to enlighten generations on the romance of the frontier. (Calder 1975; Ehrlich and Carruth 1982; Grey 1918, 1940, 1970, 1978, 1988; Griner 1995; Gruber 1970; Janke 1996; Lamar 1977; Milner et al. 1994; O'Neil 1979; Rainey 1996; "Riders" 1996; Ridge 1993; Wexler 1995)

See also Cooper, James Fenimore; Mormons; Wister, Owen.

GREY OWL

A unique figure on the deteriorating North American frontier, Grey Owl (Wa-sha-quon-asin), a naturalist and tramper of the woods of Quebec, Ontario, and

Alberta, was a dashing but ominous figure among Canadian storytellers and early conservationists. An outsider and loner, he bore the stigma of the half-breed Ojibway drifter and augmented his reputation for romantic entanglements with posturing and pranks, which he flaunted with the call of the owl, his verbal signature. Grey Owl joined the Canadian Expeditionary Force and fought with the Black Watch in the trenches of France in 1915 and 1916. Crippled in the right foot and suffering diminished lung capacity, he convalesced in Hastings, England, and married Constance Ivy Holmes, but he returned to Ontario in 1917 alone.

In his settled years, Grey Owl published a series of five books on the Canadian wild, then launched a popular lecture campaign throughout England to draw attention to the ravages of mining, trapping, roads, and logging on Canada's forests, streams, and countryside. Lovat Dickson, his publisher and biographer, characterized the zeitgeist that marked the times:

> It was the mid-thirties when Europe was stumbling towards another war. This voice from the forests momentarily released us from some spell. In contrast with Hitler's screaming, ranting voice, and the remorseless clang of modern technology, Grey Owl's words evoked an unforgettable charm, lighting in our minds the vision of a cool, quiet place, where men and animals lived in love and trust together. So great was the demand for his healing presence that we had to bring him back in 1937 for a second tour. (Dickson 1975, 14)

After Grey Owl's return to the lecture circuit, the pace of two or three public appearances per day weakened his lungs and wearied him with insomnia and longing for the wild. He returned to Canada and accepted a position as honorary ranger in Riding Mountain National Park and Prince Albert National Park. He died April 13, 1938, in Prince Albert, Saskatchewan.

Within hours of Grey Owl's death, Dickson began to assemble disturbing data unmasking the hearty half-breed and proving that he was actually English. Born George Archibald Stansfeld "Archie" Belaney in Hastings on September 18, 1888, he was the product of a bizarre marriage between amateur taxidermist George Belaney, Sr. and his 14-year-old sister-in-law, Katherine Verona "Kitty" Cox. After his father deserted the family and returned to an American residence in Bridgeport, Florida, Archie spent his boyhood in the charge of a dictatorial grandmother and a doting aunt. To escape the pressures of petticoat rule at home and school, he read pulp fiction and dreamed of becoming an Indian. He lived out puerile fictions in backyard tents and drew other children into his fantasy. At age 15, he emigrated to Canada, worked as a forest ranger, then gradually assumed the name, dress, and behaviors of a roguish native canoeman, guide, and hunter.

To clarify questions about Grey Owl, Dickson relied on those who knew him best. Of the women in his life, the one most suited to Grey Owl's elusive comings and goings was Anahareo, a teenage Iroquois love mate he met in 1925. The couple roamed the wild, built a cabin on a remote lake site, and invested time and publicity in Jelly Roll, a motherless female beaver they raised from infancy. Dickson cited in part from Anahareo's autobiographical works— *My Life with Grey Owl* (1940) and *Devil in Deerskins* (1972)—as well as from letters and interviews with Grey Owl's aunt and mother for the careful re-structuring of details about the noted woodsman. Apart from the biography's detective work, Grey Owl's five books give a clearer understanding of the inner man.

In his gentle children's story, *Sajo and the Beaver People* (1935), written for his and Anahareo's daughter, Shirley Dawn, Grey Owl creates Gitchie Meegwon (Big Feather), a graceful, keen-eyed character too similar to the author for coincidence. The loving father and brave—a strong paddler, like Grey Owl—sits erect in his yellow canoe, which one newsman described as a trusty mount that parallels the plains horse of the Sioux. With pictorial idealism faithful to the stereotypes he read in boyhood, Grey Owl portrays himself in braids and fringed buckskins "smoked to a rich brown, and altogether he looked a good deal like those Indians you see in pictures." (Grey Owl 1991, 8)

Central to the text of *Sajo and the Beaver People* is the idea of frontier purity before the arrival of white settlers and despoilers. Pines flank the river's edge. In their overhanging limbs rest robins, blackbirds, and canaries. As though lured by a feast of the senses, the narrator adds, "The air was heavy with the sweet smell of sage and wild roses, and here and there a hummingbird shot like a brilliant purple arrow from one blossom to another." (ibid., 9) Although such idyllic nature lore is often compared to Henry David Thoreau's *Walden* and John Muir's *My First Summer in the Sierra,* Grey Owl's text lacks the spirituality of the transcendentalist and the mysticism of the conservationist. He ennobles elements of the woods that offer sustenance, survival, peace, and benevolence, yet he avoids investing the wild with the unnecessary freight of religious interpretation.

Scenes from *The Men of the Last Frontier* (1931), an action-packed memoir, place Grey Owl among virile adventurers, far from the polluters of streams and burners of virgin forests. Within the sound of Indian drums, he studies signs and interprets the trail ahead. Content in his canoe, he thrills to the rapids that hazard the way downriver:

> None but those who have experienced it can guess the joyous daredeviltry of picking a precarious channel at racing speed between serried rows of jagged rocks, spiteful as shark's teeth. Few may know the feeling of savage exultation which possesses a man when the accumulated experience of years, with a split-second decision formed after a momentary glimpse through driven, blinding spume into some seething turmoil, and a perfect coordination between hand and eye, result in, perhaps the one quick but effective thrust of the paddle or pole, that spells the difference between a successful run, and disaster. (Grey Owl 1972, 71)

The call of nature is a death-dealing challenge that refreshes Grey Owl during his numerous departures, when he drops from sight to wrap himself in solitude. In defense of his erratic, unpredictable nature, he claims the Indian's right "not to be judged by the standards of civilization." (ibid., 209) Cloaked in the mythic oneness that aborigines share with the eagle and a welcoming carpet of buffalo grass, Grey Owl joyfully tosses off the torpor of the settlement;

forgets "the price of eggs, champagne, and razor blades"; and exhilarates mind and body with hard river travel. In the bush, he reverts to private views and "secretly communes with his omnipresent deity," the unnamed animistic presence that cannot thrive among railroads, dams, housing developments, and sawmills. (ibid., 213, 212)

Written four years after *The Men of the Last Frontier*, Grey Owl's autobiography, *Pilgrims of the Wild* (1935), is a fluent, engaging source of those facets of his later life that he chooses to publish, particularly his acquired distaste for killing:

> I had long ago invested the creatures of the forest with a personality. This was the inevitable result of a life spent wandering over the vast reaches of a still, silent land in which they were the only form of animate life, and sprang from early training and folklore. Yet this concession gained them no respite, and although I never killed needlessly and was as merciful as was possible, under the circumstances, the urge of debts to be paid, money to spend, and prestige to be maintained, lent power to the axe handle and cunning to the hands that otherwise might have faltered on occasion. (Grey Owl 1990, 24)

The turning point that altered Grey Owl from trapper to activist was the demise of the beaver, which had once been plentiful in Ontario forests. During conferences with bands from Simon Lake and Grand Lake Victoria, he warned that the wilderness would turn to wasteland if the beaver died out. He looked back remorsefully, "The exuberant recklessness of my earlier days was past and gone, those lonely, wild and heedless days in the vast and empty silences, when I had been sufficient unto myself, leaving death behind me everywhere." (ibid., 48) (Dickson 1975; Grey Owl 1972, 1990, 1991, 1992; Story 1967; Wallace 1963)

See also Muir, John.

HARRIOT, THOMAS

A prominent English astronomer and geographer, and the founder of the English school of algebra, Thomas Harriot (or Hariot) was one of the earlier chroniclers of Virginia history. Born in St. Mary's parish in 1560 and educated at St. Mary's Hall, Oxford, he graduated at age 20 and became an agent and scientific consultant in the London office of promoter and colonizer Sir Walter Raleigh. In 1585, Harriot served as Sir Richard Grenville's navigator and as cartographer for Raleigh's Virginia expedition. On his return a year later, he wrote *A Briefe and True Report of the New Found Land of Virginia,* an unadorned, informative quarto.

The book demonstrates Harriot's attention to duty and his meticulous observations of the voyagers, who set out to study Virginia's natural resources and aborigines and to map the territory. The report opens with a succinct listing and description of valuable commodities: silk grass, flax, hemp, alum, pitch, tar, rosin, turpentine, sassafras, cedar, walnuts, berries, fur-bearing animals, iron, copper, pearls, sweet gum, dyestuffs, medicinal earth, and cane. The second part details native plants and root crops, such as maize, apples, chestnuts, grapes, mulberries, acorns, and cushaw, that could be grown for profit. Harriot concludes with beasts, fowl, fish, and turtles, but refrains from making subjective comments on how or why Raleigh should harvest these natural resources for profit.

The most interesting of Harriot's reconnaissance is a summary of human resources and the possibility of natives "troubling our inhabiting and planting" of the Virginia colony. (Harriot 1972, 24) He surmises that Indians are a primitive race:

> a people poore, and for want of skill and judgement in the knowledge and use of our things, doe esteeme our trifles before thinges of greater value: Notwithstanding in their proper manner considering the want of such meanes as we have, they seeme very ingenious. (ibid., 25)

His left-handed compliment spotlights native crafts and wit and the Indians' willingness to please. Harriot projects an easy future for the English colonists, who can civilize and evangelize native peoples from their belief in Mantóac to the "true religion."

A second edition of *A Briefe and True Report,* published by Richard Hakluyt and grandly dedicated to Raleigh, contains sketches drawn by colonist John White. Theodor de Bry engraved the sketches and had the text translated into Latin, French, and German as a multilingual segment of his *America* series, a treatise on the New World. The appended map of Virginia shows a shoreline protected by a string of outer islands, expansive inlets to the north and south, deep water harbors, and a long river that branches east and west some 25 leagues inland. Captioned drawings depict male and female dress, adornments, and hairstyle front and back for all ages and comments on native delight in bow hunting and fishing.

Detailed drawings of canoe making, fish grilling, table manners, towns, idol worship, tattooing, ritual rattles, and dancing offer glimpses of native customs. Harriot seems mildly bemused by the conjurers, who "shave all their heads savinge which they weare as others doe, and fasten a small black birde above one of their ears as a badge of their office." Of the aboriginal style of one-pot cooking, he reports that "their woemen fill the vessel with water, and then putt they in fruite, flesh, and fish, and lett all boyle together like a galliemaufrye, which the Spaniarde call, olla podrida." (ibid., 54, 60) The combined report of Harriot and de Bry provided Raleigh with cartographic and historical information for his *History of the World.*

Harriot's report appears to have served Raleigh's political aims by establishing the value of Virginia colonization after the disastrous Lost Colony incident of 1586 cost the lives of settlers and most of Raleigh's investment and reputation. Harriot's careful assessment of economic promise in the New World arrived in print during England's shift of interest from colonizing to defeating the Spanish in their dominion at sea, which the English accomplished in 1588 with Sir Francis Drake's scuttling of a vast armada.

Before the publication of *A Briefe and True Report* in 1588, Harriot joined Raleigh's colony in Ireland, where he lived in an abbey. Ten years later, Harriot joined the staff of William Percy, Earl of Northumberland. As a result of the Gunpowder Plot, both Harriot and his patron were imprisoned in the Tower of London. Unlike his patron, Harriot gained release and retired to Syon, where he conducted experiments by telescope and charted phases of the moon, sunspots, and Jupiter's satellites. After an eight-year struggle with nasal cancer, he died July 2, 1621. His heirs published his advances in shipbuilding, fluids, arcs, magnetic variance, projectiles, logarithmic interpolation, algebraic notation, and binary numbers under *Artis Analyticae Praxis ad Aequationes Algebraicas Resolvendas [A Practical Analysis of Solving Algebraic Equations]* (1627). His unpublished papers have yielded data on the Algonkian language and useful seventeenth-century scientific observations, including letters to Johannes Kepler on optics, maps of the moon's surface, and studies in refraction and on comets and telescope construction. Harriot's Virginia report remained in circulation for decades and was frequently bound with other data pertinent to the Virginia frontier. (Harriot 1972; Hart 1983; "Thomas Harriot" 1996)

See also the lost colony.

HARTE, BRET

Bret Harte, a master raconteur and one of the triad of frontier wits with his contemporaries Artemus Ward and Mark Twain, earned a reputation for drollery and melodrama with his most famous short works: "The Luck of Roaring Camp" (1868) and "The Outcasts of Poker Flat" (1869). Like other seekers of fortune, Harte bore the freight of failure in the East in his ambitious migration to California's mining camps. Born in Albany, New York, on August 25, 1836, Francis Brett Harte (who later dropped the second t from his middle name along with his first name) lost his chance for formal education after his father's death in 1849, but he taught himself by reading the well-stocked family library. When his mother moved the family to California seven years later and remarried, Harte worked as teacher, printer, wagoneer, law clerk, Wells Fargo guard, and laborer at Angel's Camp, Jackass Hill, and other boom-and-bust locations until he learned the printing trade.

A skilled typesetter, Harte worked on a weekly newspaper in Yreka and found steady work at the San Francisco *Golden Era,* a respected West Coast literary journal. He began composing mining camp vignettes, short fiction, and frivolous verse, such as "Plain Language from Truthful James," the tall tale of the "heathen Chinee," Ah Sin, who shucks two Caucasian cardsharps in a game of euchre.

One of Harte's first successful romances, "M'liss: An Idyll of Red Mountain," was serialized in December 1860, then returned to print in 1863 in a lengthened version that ran for three months. A sentimental morality tale, it depicts the love of the schoolmaster in Smith's Pocket, California, for Melissa Smith, the illiterate teenage daughter of a local ne'er-do-well who commits suicide. A contrast of painfully crude dialect and high-flown narration, the story is transparent and poorly conceived, although Harte produces verisimilitude in rowdy frontier behaviors and rudimentary frontier mores. It was an awkward beginning, but promised better fiction to come.

At age 23, Harte found suitable work as an editorial assistant for the Union, California, *Northern Californian.* He earned a reputation for crusading journalism with his report of a massacre of Mad River tribesmen who gathered for a celebration. Against the prevailing racism of local newspapers, he risked reputation and job with an editorial calling for military action against mob violence in Humboldt Bay. Beneath an unflinching headline—INDISCRIMINATE MASSACRE OF INDIANS—WOMEN AND CHILDREN BUTCHERED—he described skulls crushed with axes and elderly women lying in blood and brain tissue. (O'Connor 1966, 45) Published February 29, 1860, the editorial roused brigands, who smashed the newspaper office and threatened to lynch Harte, who was forced to flee town by steamer.

In the mid-1860s, Harte married Anna Griswold, fathered two boys, Griswold and Frank, and assumed the post of secretary of the U.S. branch mint in San Francisco. He helped launch the *Californian,* a literary weekly in which he published a feature on a frontier Independence Day in 1866:

The celebration of the day was opened with cheerful energy by a neighbor with a four-pounder. Apparently under the impression that his remoteness from the city limits justified him in an extra vigor of expression, he for a long time held a terrible pre-eminence in the neighborhood, dominating over all other sounds to that extent that the Chinese crackers of my children, albeit they were extra size, sank into puerile insignificance. (Twain and Harte 1991, 38–39)

Harte amuses his readers by clarifying the obvious: the 49ers who stayed to settle the West maintain an out-of-proportion holiday exuberance that surpasses children's joy in color and uproar. The July Fourth cannoneer attests to a zany exhibitionism, perhaps as an antidote to the spartan lifestyle of miners and camp followers far from the social controls of East Coast civilization. Harte's choice of humor as his métier derived from a meeting with frontier humorist Artemus Ward and from the country's need for an uplift from Civil War gloom.

The *Californian*'s successor, the *Overland Monthly*, was one of the West's most prominent periodicals and locators of talent. Harte, as editor, published the work of new writers, including Ambrose Bierce's "The Haunted Valley" and four chapters of Twain's best-selling humorous travelogue, *Innocents Abroad* (1868), and showcased his own stories. His signature local color introduced a gallery of classic Western types: the good-hearted floozy, dashing duelist, faithful sidekick, toughened frontiersman, profane stage driver, eminent lawman, carping Bible-thumper, gawking gossip, witty road agent, and chivalrous card-sharp. In "The Luck of Roaring Camp" (1870), the birth of a child to Cherokee Sal, the camp's only woman, draws an entourage to the babe that parodies Bethlehem's shepherds admiring the baby Jesus:

As the procession filed in, comments were audible,—criticisms addressed, perhaps, rather to Stumpy, in the character of showman,—"Is that him?" "mighty small specimen"; "hasn't mor'n got the color"; "ain't bigger nor a derringer." (Harte 1992, 3)

In their wake piles up a collection of gifts: silver tobacco box, doubloon, silver-mounted navy revolver, embroidered handkerchief, diamond stickpin and ring, Bible, gold spur, teaspoon, surgeon's shears, lancet, £5 banknote, and $200 in coin. Harte's attention to detail holds steady through the flood that sweeps away Kentuck and Tommy Luck. The story ends with the precipitate demise of man and baby, "drifted away into the shadowy river that flows for ever to the unknown sea." (ibid., 9) Like life and fortune in the California goldfields, no one in Harte's story pockets a sure thing, not even the innocent.

In the same year, Harte produced "The Outcasts of Poker Flat," a companion piece with "The Luck of Roaring Camp" and usually named with it as his most paradoxical short stories. The denizens of Poker Flat boost Harte's ragtag character list to a height of idiosyncrasy: the predatory Mother Shipton, the Duchess on her mule, the saintly Piney, and the gambler Oakhurst, an enigmatic figure whom critics identify as Harte's fictional vision of himself. As his earlier writing portends, Harte allows sentiment to overwhelm this tableau of self-denial and sacrifice. "The Outcasts of Poker Flat" trumpets tolerance in

Bret Harte, 1836–1902

the pairing of two juxtaposed female corpses, one pure and one a sinner—a pictorial statement about idealized extremes of virtue.

Similar in its pairing of light and dark is "Tennessee's Partner," a spare, predictable morality tale of comrades, one a despicable drunk and highwayman, the other his long-suffering mining associate. The highwayman goes to the gallows; his "pard" buries his remains and grieves for the loss. The loyalty of the simple-witted survivor holds firm until death, when the two partners reunite as ghosts. For all its faults, Harte's sentimental story produces substantial glints of meaning, as with the dying man's cry to his mule on the way to reunite with Tennessee's ghost, "How dark it is! Look out for the ruts,—and look out for him, too, old gal." (ibid., 28) The theme of camaraderie wins out over personal scores to settle and the narrow meanness that turns Tennessee's trial into mob justice. Harte demonstrates the unity of an unlikely pair whose rough existence in a mining camp milieu brings out the best and worst in men.

In 1870, Harte moved to Chicago to edit the *Lakeside Monthly,* which failed because of his last-minute hesitance to support a suspiciously shaky operation. He settled at Newport, Rhode Island, and published *The Poetical Works of Bret Harte,* an uneven collection of spirited but often turgid and fussy verse that belies its Southwest origin. The best example of overwriting is "Poem," his tribute to California on its admission into the Union on September 9, 1864. The eight-stanza paean rises to sonorous heights, then sinks to triviality with a comment on the climate:

> For this, O brothers, swings the fruitful vine,
> Spread our broad pastures with their countless kine:
> For this o'erhead the arching vault springs clear,
> Sunlit and cloudless for one half the year. (Harte 1902, 35)

The strain on Harte to produce phalanxes of couplets forces him into uninspired metrical corners and inappropriate choices of diction and rhyme, such as the closing duo, which owes much to Longfellow: "Lo! the far streamlet drinks its dews unseen, And the whole valley wakes a brighter green."

Harte's ragbag approach to the collection suggests that he was a poor editor of his own efforts and needed a stronger, more objective hand to jettison the derivative and replace them with worthy originals. An egregious mix, "The Mission Bells of Monterey," a weak, sentimental piece that emulates Poe's "The Bells," stands alongside a tedious parody, "The Ballad of Mr. Cooke," with its thirteen rhymes for "Cooke": overlook, forsook, nook, shook, snook, Horne Tooke, book, brook, undertook, rook, crook, Chinook, and mistook. In contrast to these forced, sophomoric chimings, Harte includes "The Old Camp-Fire," an ode to the natural beauty of the redwood forest and Indian Springs. The poem succeeds in its pure, untrammeled settings, which reflect the West's promise, before the arrival of "chimney, spire, and roof" and the intrusion of railroad and telegraph. ("Poetry of Bret Harte" 1996, 2–3)

Biographical poems reflect Harte's interest in the makers of history. "California's Greeting to Seward," for example, lauds the "world-worn man we honor still." In another view of California's past, Harte creates an obscure figure for "Don Diego of the South," a dramatic monologue in the style of Robert Browning's "The Bishop Orders His Tomb in St. Praxed's," which the poet sets in the refectory of Mission San Gabriel in 1869. (Harte 1902, 25) The latter sparkles with Harte's characteristic incidental humor by acknowledging, "The Don loved women, and they loved him. Each thought herself his *last* love! Worst, Many believed that they were his *first!*" (ibid., 93–94) More successful than his sentimental poems, "Don Diego of the South" thrums with the vigor and elan of the Hispanic West, an area Harte knew well.

Opposed to the coarser dialect writers of his day, such as Joaquin Miller, whom he disliked and barred from the *Overland Monthly,* Harte often chose *thee* and *thou* and refinements of the East Coast aristocracy over the vernacular of Westerners. The emphasis on drawing room niceties destroys poems like "Grizzly" with pretentious couplets such as "Shambling, shuffling plantigrade, Be thy courses undismayed!" ("Poetry of Bret Harte" 1996, 7) Also ineffective is "Madrono," the hero whom Harte characterizes as "Captain of the Western wood, Thou that apest Robin Hood!" (ibid., 8) In the few poems where Harte avoids these anachronisms of finishing school English, he produces gems such as "Coyote," a desert denizen he classes as a vagabond, beggar, and marauder, "A foor-footed friar in orders of gray!" (ibid., 9–10) Such touches of Horatian satire rescue his more memorable verse from the predictable rhymed pap common to nineteenth-century journals and dance hall tunes.

Unlike Twain, his multitalented colleague, Harte lost momentum in midlife. His popularity netted him a $10,000 contract with *Atlantic Monthly* and a full schedule of lectures, but the quality of his work suffered after he left the Western milieu and settled in New York and later in Boston. In 1876, he published a frontier play, *The Two Men of Sandy Bar,* and collaborated with Twain on *Ah Sin, the Heathen Chinee* (1876), a four-act stage version of his story "The Heathen Chinee." The merger of two egotistical writers—one rising and one failing—ruined the play and ended a friendship. Harte left his wife and children and moved permanently to Europe. He served in the U.S. embassy in Crefeld, Germany, in 1878 and lived in Glasgow as ambassador to Scotland, from 1880 to 1885.

In self-imposed exile with his mistress, Madame Van de Velde, Harte concealed his homesickness and career disappointments and avoided family and American visitors, except for the few, such as Hamlin Garland, who came with letters of introduction. Harte was unable to duplicate the spirit of his frontier writings. In the years before his sudden death from throat cancer in Camberely, England, on May 5, 1902, he produced derivative stories, such as a suspenseful romance about an abandoned Mestiza child in "At the Mission of San Carmel," in *The Story of a Mine and Other Tales* (1877), *A Protégée of Jack Hamlin's and Other Stories* (1894), and *Condensed Novels* (1902), a reprise of parodies he had published in magazines. To the detriment of his reputation, he degraded his work to mediocre fiction writing for London hacks.

In Mark Twain's posthumous autobiography, unflattering anecdotes and lengthy character sketches of Harte lambaste him unmercifully for a laundry list of flaws, including dandyism, sarcasm, and indecent public behavior. In a rolling diatribe, Twain says:

There was a happy Bret Harte, a contented Bret Harte, an ambitious Bret Harte, a hopeful Bret Harte, a bright, cheerful, easy-laughing Bret Harte, a Bret Harte to whom it was a bubbling and effervescent joy to be alive. That Bret Harte died in San Francisco. It was the corpse of that Bret Harte that swept in splendor across the continent. (Twain 1959, 127)

Enlarging on this unrelenting accusation, Twain quotes William Dean Howells, who cites Harte for meanness, shabbiness, and dishonesty. At the end of patience during Harte's lengthy stay as a houseguest, Twain recites a tirade he delivered to Harte for ridiculing Olivia Twain and for being a "born bummer and tramp." (ibid., 298) Overall, Twain seemed more disgusted with an absentee father and unfaithful husband than with a skilled writer who wasted his talent. (Dobie 1996; Folsom 1966; Harte 1883, 1896, 1902, 1991, 1992; O'Connor 1966; "Poetry of Bret Harte" 1996; Rainey 1996; Rasmussen 1995; Twain 1959; Twain and Harte 1991)

See also Bierce, Ambrose; Miller, Joaquin; theater of the frontier; Twain, Mark.

HAWAII

The exploration and commercialization of the Sandwich Islands precedes by centuries any notion that the area would receive full status as one of the United States. Yet, as an extension of the frontier, the area tantalized writers and visitors, luring the likes of Mark Twain and Jack London, both of whom were captivated by its graceful beaches and welcoming warmth. The first expert to write about Hawaii was Captain James Cook, the renowned Scotch-English navigator. A meticulous, dutiful "company man," Cook wrote *The Explorations of Captain James Cook in the Pacific as Told by Selections of His Own Journals, 1768– 1779*, a thorough report on his three voyages to the South Seas. His clear, impersonal style and depth of perception impressed scientists, who marveled at the breadth of his knowledge and interests.

Traveling aboard the *Resolution*, a slow, blunt-nosed, shallow-draft vessel, the expedition moved northeast from Bora Bora, Tahiti, in December 1777. Cook reached Hawaii on January 18, 1778, and named the high-peaked island chain the Sandwich Islands for his patron, the Earl of Sandwich. The captain demonstrated his sincere concern for shipboard health by commanding his men to avoid sexual encounters with island women, particularly the men already suffering "the venereal." (Cook 1971, 217) The captain himself disembarks to trade with the natives and admire their handsome demeanor and beautiful garments made of bark cloth. He comments on the likelihood that Hawaiians are familiar with iron from the flotsam of Spanish shipwrecks, which regularly washed ashore. In summing up the value of the islands to European merchants and conquerors, he concludes that Spain has an easy access from the coast of New Spain.

Cook's voyage up the West Coast of North America to Alaska placed him in the Arctic Sea in April 1778, when he decided to return to Hawaii to refit the

Resolution. After extensive study of the waters of North America, on February 14, 1779, he again sought the familiar Kealakeakua Bay, where he trod on the islanders' hospitality by hastily burying a seaman who died on board. The Hawaiians, angry that the feeding of so large a crew unjustly impoverished them, withdrew their former welcome. Theft of a boat for its nails and iron fittings resulted in an ugly set-to between white sailors and a handful of natives. According to Captain King, who completed the unfinished log, Cook was attempting to stave off mounting violence, which had already cost lives on both sides. When he turned to the ship to halt firing of muskets, a Hawaiian knifed him in the back. In recent times, the publication of his journal along with his personal maps and charts has revealed to scholars and readers the monumental task he accomplished, even though he failed to locate the fabled Northwest Passage over the polar ice cap.

One century later, during Hawaii's cultural renaissance, King David Kalakaua's *The Legends and Myths of Hawaii* (1888) dispelled the notion that the island chain is a savage realm. The introduction recaps four major challenges of the nineteenth century: the arrival of Captain Cook with proof that Hawaii was a backward, isolated nation; the post-1786 influx of alien missionaries, explorers, and traders, who adulterated the simple ecosystem with multiple plants, seeds, livestock, and philosophies; diseases such as measles, leprosy, and scarlet fever, which endangered the Hawaiian strain among the melange of hardy races that inhabited the islands and competed for power and ownership; and Liholiho's destruction of temples and renunciation of traditional idols and taboos separating the sexes in 1819. Kalakaua's writings inform both Hawaiians and the outside world of the nation's derivation from Polynesians fleeing Sumatra and Java and their sojourn in the Fiji group. He appends a royal genealogy beginning in A.D. 1095 and including all leaders to his own time. In a wistful prediction, Kalakaua fears that

> year by year their footprints will grow more dim along the sands of their reef-sheltered shores, and fainter and fainter will come their simple songs from the shadows of the palms, until finally their voices will be heard no more for ever. (Kalakaua 1972, 64)

So widespread is American influence on culture, religion, and trade that Kalakaua correctly assumes that the green fields of his homeland "will pass into the political . . . system of the great American Republic." (ibid., 65)

Following the same epic movement of southern Pacific Polynesians from Nuku Hiva to the shores of the Sandwich Islands, James Michener's *Hawaii* (1959) concentrates on one challenge: the arrival of missionaries, whose coming forever alters the mores, lifestyle, and contentment of the aboriginal population. Abner Hale, a caricature of the self-aggrandizing religious fanatic, berates Hawaiians for sexual behaviors that shock and disgust him. Nettled that the royal family and their subjects expect brother and sister to marry, Hale goes into a private tirade worthy of an Old Testament patriarch, calling "Floods! Winds from the hills! Pestilence! Destroy this place!" (Michener 1959, 332) Unknown to him, measles, an epidemic worthy of the blood-fed goddess Pele, strikes the bay city of Lahaina in 1832. The efforts of Dr. John Whipple make no inroads against the suffering and dying of feverish islanders, who bathe their wracked bodies in the surf. Noelani, the surviving princess, bitterly accuses Hale of withholding true sympathy and charity from the people whose souls he tries to save.

Interspersed in Michener's narrative are lengthy passages of history. He accounts for the destruction of native lands and people as settlers press in, eager to force Hawaiians into press gangs to work cane and pineapple plantations or to enhance trade along the flourishing docks. While wrestling with the issue of miscegenation, Dr. Whipple, a more humane settler than Hale, questions the priggish anti-Hawaiianism of his fellow ministers. He declares that when Captain Cook discovered the islands, "he estimated their population at four hundred thousand. That was fifty years ago. Today how many Hawaiians are there? Less than a hundred and thirty thousand." (ibid., 285) Whipple deduces that the continued spread of consumption will doom the natives. "Sick with God," he withdraws to attend a meeting in Honolulu where sanctimonious white church leaders censure a minister for marrying a Hawaiian girl. The spectacular film version of Michener's *Hawaii* was completed in 1966 with Max von Sydow, Julie Andrews, Richard Harris, Jocelyn La Garde, and Gene Hackman in starring roles. Praised for its humanism, the film earned Oscar nominations for cinematography, the music of Elmer Bernstein, the song "My Wishing Doll," and La Garde's role as the island's queen. (Cook 1971; Kalakaua 1972; Michener 1959; Rasmussen 1995; Sackett 1996; Villiers 1967)

See also explorers of the frontier; London, Jack; Twain, Mark.

⚑ HISPANIC AMERICANS ON THE FRONTIER ⚑

White America's disdain for nonwhite populations extends to premodern eras in which Asian, Native American, and Hispanic writers received little credit for their creation of frontier literature. With the advent of multiculturalism, white Americans have discovered the writing skills of such artists as Mariano Azuela, Carlos Fuentes, Laura Esquivel, and Sylvia Lopez-Medina. Their acute analyses of Anglo-Chicano relations throughout the shifting loyalties of the Mexican Revolution pose fresh perspectives on the unrest that rocked Central America and the states north of the U.S. border.

A beloved warrior, humanitarian, and altruist of late-nineteenth-century Mexico, Mariano Azuela empathized with peasant hardships both as physician and writer and was proclaimed the foremost novelist of the revolutionary era. He treated the indigent and disenfranchised in his clinic and chronicled their miseries over a 40-year writing career. His canon covers Mexico's political landscape from Porfirio Díaz's demise to the end of Lázaro Cárdenas's presidency. A member of the middle class, Azuela was born to poor ranchers on January 1, 1873, in Lagos de Moreno, Jalisco, in southern Mexico. A writer since his first year of college, he produced short fiction and sketches before completing pharmacy and medical school at the University of Guadalajara in 1899. After marrying Carmen Rivera, mother of their ten children, he set up practice in Lagos, was elected mayor in 1911, and, in 1914 and 1915, served Jalisco as education minister.

Eight years into his medical practice, Azuela began writing essays, book reviews, and novels of social conscience. He portrayed the unjust regime of dictator Porfirio Díaz, who bilked the peasants of land that his followers coveted. The spokesman for the bottom and least salvageable echelon of the military during the Mexican Revolution, Azuela wrote from the point of view of the soldiers' doctor. Unlike Jack Reed, who observed the grim aggression of folk hero General Pancho Villa, or Ambrose Bierce, who chose to exit his life on the frontier by following the romantic but doomed Villa, Azuela joined the general as a field surgeon under the command of Julián Medina.

After Venustiano Carranza's forces defeated Villa's "Golden Boys" in 1915, Azuela fled to El Paso, Texas, where he lived the expatriate life while awaiting better times in his homeland. In retrospect, he produced a masterwork, *Los de abajo: Novela de la revolucion mexicana* [*The Underdogs: A Novel of the Mexican Revolution* 1915]. Overlooked at first, it was serialized in *El Paso del Norte*, a local Spanish-language journal with a limited readership. In the late 1920s, during a reprise of revolutionary-era fiction, *El Universal Ilustrado*, a Mexico City news daily, introduced the novel to a new generation of readers eager to learn about the revolution. The text, translated into English and illustrated by José Clemente Orozco, was published in 1929 and found immediate favor with an international audience, both as a novel and as the basis for a play and film.

The Underdogs is a realistic study of ignorant men fighting a complicated war. It discloses the squalor of prerevolutionary Mexican peasants and the poignance and waste during a fruitless national slaughter for unclear goals. The novel opens in Moyahua in central Mexico around 1914 with the military emergence of Demetrio Macías, a stout-hearted but illiterate native farmer from the mountains of Jalisco. By following leader Francisco Madera, Demetrio rids himself of his oppressor, Don Mónico, a member of the repressive gentry. Azuela emphasizes the isolation of unschooled bandits under the leadership of their peer, who abandons his wife and infant son to provoke a headlong clash with federal soldiers. Demetrio's sharpshooters achieve some impressive wins for the rebels.

A focal motif in the novel is the serendipitous rise of peasant leaders to power and prominence. Because he aids General Pánfilo Natera, Demetrio receives a battlefield promotion to colonel in the regular army. He leads a charge for Villa and, in the headiness of combat, performs the improbable: he disables a machine gun by lassoing it. The dizzying string of victories ends after Natera reports that Villa has changed the course of the revolt by warring against Carranza, his former ally. Demetrio, who is unsophisticated in politics and too confused to know for whom he fights, is unsure of his worthiness to lead.

As the polemics of war deplete the army's spirits, *The Underdogs* depicts the cost of long seasons of violence and the waste of Mexico's agricultural

Armed Mexican women, likely followers of Pancho Villa, pose for a postcard photographer during the revolutionary era, 1910–1917. The photographer scribbled "women waiting for a job" on the photograph.

resources. After *Federalistas* overwhelm Villa at Celaya, Demetrio and his rag-tag unit retreat down a dismaying trail strewn with aimless folk depleted by hunger and apathy. Along a roadway lined with graves, crippled veterans curse the outlaw chief; Demetrio's soldiers break ranks and challenge discipline. Azuela turns to irony to express the futility of Demetrio's sacrifice: two years after his precipitate departure, he sinks to defeat at the same site where he first met victory.

In austere glimpses that outline the bold, absurd, and malefic aspects of war, Azuela sketches in miniature the cost of rebellion to the band of backward Mexican rebels. The leader's decisive moves highlight the gutsy courage of untrained, ill-equipped, and poorly mounted mountaineers. Their joking disregard for imminent death proves them foolishly dedicated to Demetrio, and by extension, to Villa. As Azuela pictures them,

> The soldiers sang, laughed, and chattered away. The spirit of nomadic tribes stirred their souls. What matters it whither you do and whence you come? All that matters is to walk, to walk endlessly, without ever stopping; to possess the valley, the heights of the sierra, far as the eye can read. (Azuela 1962, 148)

Beyond the rewards of camaraderie, self-actualization, and loot, the warriors risk all to rid themselves of petty land barons. Darkly comic flashes in Azuela's narrative ridicule weary victors relaxing on a dung heap, teasing a turncoat by pretending to provide him a priest for last confession, or hauling camp followers and tequila to hotel rooms. From a brief taste of battlefield pleasures, Azuela's folk heroes churn downhill into the creeping viciousness that subsumes their courageous gesture toward liberation. In an enveloping cycle of cynicism and lawlessness, they doom themselves.

Azuela obviously writes from experience of the myriad faces of war. Just as Stephen Crane patched together a montage of Henry Fleming's exploits during the Civil War in *The Red Badge of Courage,* Erich Maria Remarque sketched Paul Baumer's indoctrination into trench warfare in *All Quiet on the Western Front,* and Ernest Hemingway cataloged the ineptness of ignorant guerrillas in *For Whom the Bell Tolls,* Azuela discloses the insanity of the juggernaut. He conveys the waywardness of the cause through the raving poet Valderrama:

> Villa? Obregón? Carranza? What's the difference? I love the revolution like a volcano in eruption; I love the volcano because it's a volcano, the revolution because it's the revolution! What do I care about the stones left above or below after the cataclysm? What are they to me? (ibid., 136)

The romance of war swiftly peaks. Azuela's backcountry warriors degenerate from ebullient heroes to truculent looters and self-promoters. On a controlled canvas, he paints their varied moods as they observe the collapse of the dream.

The Underdogs reveals the protagonist as a simple man too lacking in vision to cope with command. After an unforeseen success, the bandits turn into swaggering, liquor-loud carousers who sprawl on town squares, vilify landowners, menace women, gamble, and shower bullets on the unwary. Lacking leadership and self-discipline, they violate townspeople, demand service and refuse to pay for it, and cavort with frowzy prostitutes, who join them in ransacking the manor houses of their former overlords. In one mansion, Demetrio's looters paw through jewels and boil roasting ears over a fire fed by leather-bound volumes of the classics rifled from the don's library. Blondie, a depraved soldier, shoots at a mirror and dehumanizes a captive by leading him dog-fashion on a leash and starving him to death.

Unwilling to glorify Mexico's rebellion, Azuela typifies the post-victory revelry as an added onus to the poor. Beset by rebels and federals, the natives—

including Demetrio's wife and infant—flee to the hills from whatever army ravages their land. To the outlanders, Demetrio puts a new face on villainy no less opportunistic than Don Mónico and his ilk. After anarchy destroys Mexico's agrarian economy, both military and civilian populations go hungry. With nothing to buy, roisterers squander sacks of worthless cash and deal in stolen goods. Peasant males have little choice but to claim loyalty to each passing band. To prevent the recruit-hungry bands from forcing them to join, the men who remain on the farm cower in their hiding places and wish the plague of liberators a hasty exit.

The Underdogs makes no exceptions in allotting wartime sufferings. The falling action tears down Demetrio's brigands one by one. Three commit suicide. The leader himself bears the burden of shame leveled by disillusioned veterans and cripples. As the federal army approaches the Juchipila canyon, undisciplined freebooters disobey Demetrio, leaving him defenseless and vulnerable. Even Valderrama, the mad prophet, withdraws to safety. For good reason, Azuela builds up a protagonist whom he must tear down. Exalted far above his worth to the army, Demetrio, a skilled marksman, rises by luck from peon farmer to colonel to general. Ringing huzzahs from regular forces and villagers give place to an echo in his head: "I don't know why." He loses momentum, direction, and initiative. To the general's questions about loyalty, Demetrio lamely replies that he does what he is ordered and marches home through craggy sierras over his own Via Crucis, the symbolic "Way of the Cross." A year after capturing Zacatecas, the band returns to Juchipila on the feast day of the Sacred Heart of Jesus. The metaphor contrasts the peasants' sincere veneration of Christ to their loathing of Demetrio's boorish gunslingers.

Azuela presses the image of godliness in the final scene, which takes Demetrio back to the canyon of Juchipila where he first outshot a large band of Federalistas. Within two years, Demetrio has wearied of war and yearns for simple agrarian chores. A heavy irony accompanies his view of the valley, blissful with silvery clouds and the frolic of colts on the mountaintops. Like their nomadic ancestors, the wretched returnees march through a freshened valley. Death comes as gracefully and inexorably as the sickle to stalks of wheat. Demetrio makes the most of his final moments. Like Jacob, the biblical patriarch, he lays his head on a stone and takes aim. The home shot that ends his career mixes gunsmoke with the chirp of locusts and the call of doves. Unshaken by human violence, cows chew their mouthfuls. Azuela pictures his fallen hero, inert like a sacrifice to the gods, with eyes "leveled in an eternal glance." (ibid., 147)

After peace returned to Mexico, Azuela soured on the self-serving opportunists who robbed and ravaged the peasants they set out to free. To uplift and better understand the Mexican underclass, he set up a practice in a Mexico City barrio. In 1949, he received the National Prize for Literature. At his death from a heart attack on March 1, 1952, he was interred in Mexico City in the Rotunda des Hombres Ilustros. Eight years after Azuela's death, Alí Chumacero completed the author's unfinished autobiographical novel Madero (1960), which was published along with a three-volume set of his complete works. Critics have lauded Azuela's minimalism and the stream-of-consciousness technique that synthesizes the mental processes of troubled soldiers, but the author's murky symbols, didacticism, and frequent digressions have weakened his influence.

With similar flashes of photographic brilliance, authors Carlos Fuentes, Laura Esquivel, and Sylvia Lopez-Medina disclose the alternating success and failure of frontier Mexico's struggle to rule itself. Fuentes, an international star for his outpouring of short fiction, novels, and plays, has developed a coterie of followers on the eight university campuses where he teaches creative writing. To his pupils, he has commented, "We have to assimilate the enormous weight of our past so that we will not forget what gives us life. If you forget your past, you die." (Solomon 1992, 450) In his historical novel *The Old Gringo* (1985), the author looks at the Mexican Revolution through the eyes of American schoolmarm Harriet Winslow, an old maid who toys with the war's danger as an antidote to spinsterhood. Her captivation with a Mexican rebel and a courtly, enigmatic American author challenges her stability, just as lawlessness and revolt threaten to topple Mexico. An international best-seller and subject of a moderately successful 1989 film, the colorful, violent novel netted Fuentes a *Los Angeles Times* Book award nomination, the Miguel de Cervantes Prize from the Spanish Ministry of Culture, and renown for being the first Latin author listed on the *New York Times* best-seller list.

Deriving momentum from the same era, Laura Esquivel's *Like Water for Chocolate* (1991) swirls one of her frontier characters from a backwater ranch into the maelstrom of Mexican unrest. In comic folk style, she characterizes Gertrudis's capture by Juan, a hot-blooded bandit overcome by the romantic aroma guiding him to an unspecified tryst. Esquivel exults in the freedom and carnality of the girl, stripped for a makeshift outdoor shower:

> Naked as she was, with her loosened hair falling to her waist, luminous, glowing with energy, she might have been an angel and devil in one woman. The delicacy of her face, the perfection of her pure virginal body contrasted with the passion, the lust, that leapt from her eyes, from her every pore. (Esquivel 1991, 51)

In contrast to Tita, her repressed sister, Gertrudis opens her body to Juan, an army captain who has battled desire in long months of mountain fighting and who whisks her away without comment; the two consummate their instant attraction on his galloping horse. Of reports of the bizarre mating, Esquivel notes, half in jest, "That is the way history gets written, distorted by eyewitness accounts that don't really match the reality." (ibid., 52)

Esquivel pursues the theme of freedom of expression during Gertrudis's return. Tita, still shackled to the kitchen, observes the extravagant licentiousness of her sister, who closes her eyes as she sprawls in the salon, savors a cup of chocolate, and draws on a cigarette:

> Gertrudis, perfectly at her ease, was regaling them with fantastic stories of the battles she'd been in. She had them openmouthed, as she told them about the first firing squad she had ordered, but she couldn't contain herself. (ibid., 176)

Representing the violent uprooting of a ranch rose, her example typifies the rebellion of frontier maidens who are caught up in revolutionary fervor. While dancing gracefully to *"Jesusita in Chihuahua,"* she sways with hitched-up skirt to Juan's brilliant playing of the norteño accordion. Before departing from her lovesick sister, Gertrudis consoles her and strengthens her resolve, then departs amazon-style to attack Zacatecas.

Less precipitate than Esquivel's Gertrudis is the elopement of Rosario Carras in Sylvia Lopez-Medina's *Cantora* (1992). In her Chihuahua home in 1904, 14-year-old Rosario, darling of an aristocratic hacienda, confronts a patriarchal fiat that determines whom she will marry. While secretly meeting in a distant cave with Alejandro Pérez, an outlaw-class messenger carrying military dispatches from Francisco Madero to Pancho Villa, Rosario loses her heart and virginity and eludes the grasp of her dictatorial father, Ramón. The pair's flight 200 miles west to Hermosillo in the Sierra Victorino Mountains thrusts Rosario into a kind of freedom that extends rewards as it brandishes ill fortune. Violence robs her of a gallant husband and leaves her with a family to feed. To authenticate the setting and personae, the author salts the text with significant social and economic terms: *caballeros, campesinos, curanderas, duenna, indios, mestiza, padre, patrón, revolucionarios, rurales,* and *pobrecita,* meaning "poor little thing."

In each of the three twentieth-century novels detailing the lives of women in frontier Mexico, the authors express a contemporary feminist theme—the empowerment of women. All three females languish in an Old World society where choice is the province of men and where women are left with the obligation to obey. On the frontier, Harriet Winslow, Gertrudis, and Rosario escape not only narrow provincial mores but also limited self-concepts that tie them to a rutted pattern of female existence. Rather than spin their wheels in self-defeat, the trio adopt a frontier attitude toward challenge and grasp an alternative lifestyle that juxtaposes their rebellion alongside the masculine paradigm of the man of action. Gertrudis, the most androgynous of the three, walks, talks, and smokes like a man to prove her self-actualization. Harriet and Rosario, whose ambivalence indicates their fear of so great a leap from the role of female handmaiden, take measured steps in the direction of empowerment and pay the price of hesitation. (Azuela 1962; Ecchevarria 1993; Esquivel 1991; Estrada 1979; *Hispanic Literature Criticism* 1989; Langford 1971; Leal 1971; Lopez-Medina 1992; "Mariano Azuela" 1996; Martinez 1980; Rigg 1977; Robe 1979; Solomon 1992; Spell 1968; Ward 1978)

See also Bierce, Ambrose; Reed, John.

HOWARD, OLIVER OTIS

A Congressional Medal of Honor recipient, humanitarian, and major peacemaker in nineteenth-century American military history, General Oliver Otis Howard performed varied service during the tense era of Indian resettlement.

From his experiences came three first-person narratives about the frontier: *Nez Perce Joseph* (1879), *My Life and Experiences among Our Hostile Indians* (1907), and his most popular work, *Famous Indian Chiefs I Have Known* (1908). Born in 1830 in Leeds, Maine, Howard was a graduate of Bowdoin College. He gained a reputation for Christian piety and distinguished himself in combat as an army ordnance officer and in classes at West Point, where he was teaching mathematics at the outset of the Civil War.

In June 1861, Howard entered active service in the Union army and rose to the rank of brigadier general by the age of 35. He was wounded in the Battle of Fair Oaks the next year. Despite the amputation of his right arm, he maintained command of a regiment at Gettysburg, fought at Bull Run and against Stonewall Jackson at Chancellorsville, and joined General William Tecumseh Sherman on his brutal march to the sea. After Lee's surrender at Appomattox, President Andrew Johnson gave Howard control of the Freedman's Bureau, a government agency created to ease newly freed slaves into society during Reconstruction.

In 1867, Howard founded Howard University to educate rehabilitated ex-slaves and was serving as university president five years later when President Ulysses S. Grant dispatched him to the Arizona Territory to establish peace with the Chiricahua Apache, who manned a stronghold in the Dragoon Mountains and, for ten years, had besieged white settlers. In 11 days, Howard—known to the Indians as "One-Armed Soldier Chief"—charmed the Apache with courtesy and negotiated a verbal agreement with Cochise, chief of the militant guerrilla band. Along with scout and mail courier Thomas J. Jeffords, known by the Apache name of Taglito, Howard located the Chiricahua in Apache Pass on the Mexican border, where Cochise agreed to protect the road from hostile Indians. At Howard's insistence, Jeffords was named Indian agent.

Two years later, a new assignment placed Howard at Fort Lapwai, Idaho, where he failed to achieve an equally quick truce among Indians of the Pacific Northwest and was humiliated by critics who thought him too liberal with hostile tribes. As with the Chiricahua, he performed the task as peacemaker with Chief Joseph, the prophet Toohoolhoolzote, Ollikut, White Bird, and Looking Glass of the Nez Perce from the Wallowa Valley, all of whom the government was relocating to the Lapwai Reservation. Howard disapproved of confiscating the Indian lands but was dutifully determined to carry out government policy. When the Indians balked at removal from ancestral lands, he had the prophet arrested for obstructing peace talks and ordered Chief Joseph to obey presidential orders in one month or face military action and confiscation of his livestock. Because the Nez Perce refused and ambushed a column at White Bird Canyon, Howard challenged them in skirmishes in Canyon and Clearwater, Idaho.

Howard remained in command when militants from the Bannock, Umatilla, Cayuse, and Paiute tribes bolted from a native reserve at Fort Hall, Idaho. He led forces from Fort Boise against Buffalo Horn, Egan, and Oytes. In 1879, after rebels from the Bannock and Shoshone known as the Sheepeaters attacked prospectors on the Salmon River, Howard compelled the holdouts to surrender and rejoin the main body of natives at Fort Hall. It was at the end of this episode at his quarters in Vancouver Barracks that Howard wrote his first major work, *Nez Perce Joseph: An Account of His Ancestors, His Lands, His Confederates, His Enemies, His Murders, His War, His Pursuit and Capture* (1879). In the preface, Howard introduced Eastern readers to his overtly Christian attitude toward "the Indian problem" and termed the military role in resettlement "necessarily arduous and unpopular." (Howard 1972, iv)

In the overview, Howard presents Joseph as deceptively even-tempered but iron-willed. The upheaval that caused the Joseph War Howard blames on the period "when our people first began to jostle the then quiet holders of the soil in this region of the far West." (ibid, 2) He corrects the inadequacies of Washington Irving's account of the Nez Perce as given in *The Adventures of Captain Bonneville, U.S.A.* (1837) and pinpoints in military fashion the exact location of the tribe's homeland. At the end of his detailed relation of the cavalry's pursuit of Joseph, Howard credits the chief with quick-witted strategy "not often equalled in warfare." (ibid., 273) Ever the optimist, Howard concludes that Joseph's good qualities, to the national good, should be turned "from savagery to civilization." (ibid.)

After a brief appointment as superintendent of West Point Military Academy, Howard set out for the plains states in 1882 to command the Department of the Platte. He returned east in 1886 and headed the northeastern command. His experience in the Indian wars and his belief in assimilation, education, and Christian evangelism made him the likely choice to champion Indian rights and the liberation of Apaches from a Florida prison. Over a lengthy process, Howard, aided by General George Crook, gained the Indians' release and their resettlement at Fort Sill, Oklahoma.

Turned reformer, lecturer, children's book author, and memoirist in retirement in Burlington, Vermont, Howard made a useful contribution to the era of plains Indian wars. Labeled the military leader with the most personal experience with Indians, he produced illustrated articles for young adults on 30 Native American chiefs: Osceola, Billy Bowlegs, Pasqual, Antonio, Antonito, Santos, Eskimenzeen, Pedro, Miguel, Cochise, Manuelito, Captain Jack, Fernandeste, Sitka Jack, Anahootz, Chief Joseph, White Bird, Looking Glass, Moses, Winnemucca, Toc-Me-To-Ne, Mattie, Chief Egan, Lot, Red Cloud, Sitting Bull, Washakie, Homili, Cut-Mouth John, and Geronimo. Even though he grew up on blood-and-thunder tales of Indian massacres, Howard wrote a positive remembrance of Native Americans, *Famous Indian Chiefs I Have Known*. Coauthored by his daughter-in-law, these capsule biographies appeared serially in *St. Nicholas* magazine from November 1907 through October 1908. The collection has become a staple in plains histories and studies of Indian lore.

Obviously, Howard's paternalism is out of date and some of his conclusions naive, yet his dignified representations of great Native Americans ennobles leaders whom dime novels have traditionally viewed as deceivers, killers, and scalpers. An example of his fairness is the depiction of Manuelito, who made a good impression by riding up on his horse, dismounting, and greeting Howard in Spanish. The text pictures Manuelito as pragmatic and patriotic:

He asked me to appoint 20 Navajo Policemen and dress them in United States uniform, for then every Indian would know them and every white man would respect them. He asked me to give them the same pay as soldiers and then they would be proud and obey their leader and there would be no more trouble from the Navajos. (Howard 1989, 147)

Howard recalls his review of Manuelito's troops, dressed in "grand army cords and tassels, blue blouses and belts with two pistols to show their authority." (ibid., 148) Howard determines by the display of parade dress that Manuelito had become a man of peace.

As demonstrated in the heavy-handed final chapter, Howard's didacticism intrudes on his narrative. A proponent of replacing native religion, customs, and education with white equivalents, he rejoices that Geronimo in old age abandons his Apache ways:

Geronimo was taken to the Omaha and Buffalo Expositions, but he was sullen and quiet, and took no interest in anything. Then at last all the Apache Indians were sent west again to the Indian Territory near Fort Sill, Oklahoma Territory, and here Geronimo began to go to church and became a Christian Indian. (ibid., 362)

Howard's inability to pity the humiliated old chief on display among "Filipinos from Manila, the Boers from South Africa, or the Eskimos from Alaska" places him in the philosophy of his time, which saw Plains Indians as relics of a lost past and objects of missionary zeal. Howard's summation shortchanges young adult readers with its gratuitous remark that Geronimo was "happy and joyful, for he had learned to try and be good to everybody and to love his white brothers." (ibid., 364) (Brown 1970; Hopkins 1994; Howard 1972, 1989; Lamar 1977; Waldman 1990)

See also Brown, Dee; Geronimo; Irving, Washington; Winnemucca, Sarah.

HUNTER, KERMIT

A contemporary and colleague of playwright Paul Green, Kermit Hunter, himself a pioneer of outdoor drama, has provided 40 American communities with historical spectacles based on local events and personalities. Because his works appeal to grassroots dramatic groups, he has been called the most widely performed playwright in the United States. Born October 3, 1910, in McDowell County, West Virginia, Hunter attended Emory and Henry College before earning a B.A. from Ohio State University. During his undergraduate years, his verse won the Vandewater Poetry Prize. He studied piano at Julliard and won the West Virginia Young Artist's Contest in piano. After touring Europe and working in journalism, he earned an M.A. and doctorate in dramatic arts from the University of North Carolina. For his unusual gift in the arts, he received a Joseph Feldman Playwriting award and Rockefeller and Guggenheim fellowships. He managed the North Carolina Symphony, taught English at the University of North Carolina and at Southern Methodist University, and played church organ for 15 years. For his service as lieutenant colonel of the army infantry as assistant chief of staff of the Caribbean Defense Command in Panama during World War II, he received a Legion of Merit.

An energetic, forceful scholar and appreciator of the arts, Hunter lectured in the United States and Europe, authored the "university theatre" section of the *Encyclopaedia Britannica,* and served as dean of the school of arts at Southern Methodist University. Throughout his varied career experiences, he has maintained one obsession, the creation and performance of historical drama. He wrote 25 plays in the form of outdoor spectacle, including *Walk toward the Sunset,* the story of the mysterious, swarthy Melungeon clan of the Ozarks; *Unto These Hills,* a pageant of Cherokee history from 1540 to 1842 featuring the story of Tsali, a Cherokee martyr; *Forever This Land,* a study of Abraham Lincoln's formative years, performed in Petersburg, Illinois; *The Trail of Tears,* portraying the social chaos caused by the removal of Cherokees from tribal lands in the East to a reservation in Oklahoma; *The Bell and the Plow,* an epic drama based on the altruism of Father Eusebio Kino and featured in Tucson, Arizona; *Voice in the Wind,* a survey of Florida history; *Chucky Jack,* the story of Revolutionary War hero John Sevier, performed in Gatlinburg, Tennessee; and *Honey in the Rock,* a dramatization of H. L. Davis's novel about the pioneers who settled Oregon.

One of Hunter's most significant contributions to frontier literature is *Horn in the West* (1952), a paean to Daniel Boone that runs annually in summer stock in Boone, North Carolina. Over a million visitors have seen the play. Depicting the ideals of godliness and freedom, the text deviates from the technical structure of *The Lost Colony,* Paul Green's prototype of outdoor spectacle, by focusing more on drama than pageantry. Narrated by a balladeer, the play lauds the westward movement. The plot features the revolt of a group of pioneers against the regulators of Hillsboro in Alamance County, North Carolina. Brawling against Redcoats, the players act out the story of Dr. Geoffrey Stuart, a visiting Tory physician who, during the colonial unrest of 1771, alters his allegiance and joins the pioneers. Fleeing across the Blue Ridge Mountains, he dwells with local folk and begins to question his loyalty to England's King George III. When Indians threaten, the mountaineers turn to Daniel Boone, an experienced frontiersman, empire builder, and symbol of American ideals.

The central event of the play describes the Battle of King's Mountain in October 1780, when John Sevier makes a stand against General Patrick Ferguson's Tory troops. Stuart's family departs from him in support of the libertarian Carolinians. His son Jock joins in the fight against tyranny, is arrested, and awaits hanging when his father comes to his aid. As the physician clings to the last shreds of loyalty to the Crown, his resolve collapses after British soldiers ransack the Morganton home of William Morris in violation of laws dating to the Magna Carta. The price of Stuart's coming to knowledge is high: he determines that he is an American rather than an Englishman, but the shift in loyalty costs him his home and son. Downplaying his loss, the playwright concludes with the greater theme of American independence.

Hunter's skill with southern mountain dialect and his knowledge of colonial history invigorates the predictable plot, which covers ground known to most Americans. Like other masters of the outdoor drama, he blends the British military hierarchy with a Cherokee fire dance, square dancing, and frontier humor. Long before feminism revitalized women's roles in significant events, Hunter stressed the part of Nancy Ward, daughter of a British officer and Cherokee mother. Ward's role as ambassador during troubled times brought her the privilege of sitting with the council of chiefs and the power to pardon prisoners under sentence of death. (Charles 1996; Correll 1961; Gillett 1952; " 'Horn in the West' " 1990; Hoyle 1956; Hunter 1967; *North Carolina Authors* 1952; "Outdoor Drama" 1996; Spearman 1953; Walser 1956)

See also Boone, Daniel; Green, Paul; the lost colony; theater of the frontier.

IRVING, WASHINGTON

A classic storyteller, historian, and observer of picturesque landscapes and human idiosyncrasies, Washington Irving was one of America's first originals. A frail man with an active imagination, he endured frequent medical treatment for tuberculosis and sought rest cures that gave him the leisure for introspection and evaluation of human nature. Defying a persistent cough and lung weakness that threatened constraints on his career, he flourished as a notable diplomat and as the father of the American short story. Irving produced a cornucopia of romantic tales, history, sketches, plays, a novel, biographies, essays, vignettes, miscellanies, and conservative satires. His fame on both sides of the Atlantic places him in a category with Mark Twain, Ambrose Bierce, Bret Harte, and James Fenimore Cooper, who also entertained European as well as American readers with frontier lore.

Irving was proud to be a first-generation New Yorker. He was the last of 11 children born to Sarah Sanders and William Irving, a prosperous hardware dealer and no-nonsense Scotch Calvinist, in lower Manhattan on April 3, 1783, in the final week of the American Revolution. In honor of the nation's father, he bore the name of George Washington. A known scamp, Irving preferred prowling the wharf, watching amateur theatricals, and investigating legends and ghost sightings to attending classes at Benjamin Romaine's private school, which his father chose to tame and settle him. When players set up at a local theater, like the fictional Huck Finn he climbed out his bedroom window to catch the final act. Irving's unimpressive academic record, particularly in math, prohibited admission to Columbia University.

After privately studying law and clerking for attorney Brockholst Livingston, in 1802 Irving worked as a stringer for his brother Peter's newspapers, *The Corrector* and *The Morning Chronicle*, for which Irving published the droll letters of Jonathan Oldstyle, Gent., a satiric examination of manners and attitudes of New Yorkers in the style of *The Tatler* and *The Spectator*. From 1804 to 1806, Irving lived in France and recovered from consumption. He made rigorous side trips through Europe that took him to public hangings, the ballet, troop departures for the Napoleonic Wars, and the pirate-infested shores of Sicily. He returned with extensive journal entries animated with the people and events he encountered, especially dance, opera, theater, street festivals, and social interaction.

On his return to New York, Irving opened a Wall Street law firm with his brother John, but took little interest in the profession. Attracted to writers, Irving, along with brothers Peter and William and brother-in-law James Kirke Paulding, dubbed themselves the "Nine Worthies" and founded *Salmagundi; or, the Whim-Whams and Opinions of Launcelot Longstaff, Esq. and Others,* a short-lived satiric journal named for a spicy meat sauce. They produced 20 issues during 1807 and 1808 under the pseudonyms of Anthony Evergreen, Jeremy Cockloft the Younger, Will Wizard, and Pindar Cockloft, Esq. Similar to the waggish writings of Joseph Addison and Sir Richard Steele, the journal concentrated on informative, whimsical, and witty caricatures, travesties on America's earliest presidents, and essays on New Yorkers. In the editor's words, the staff took to heart the mission of satire: "to instruct the young, reform the old, correct the city, and castigate the age." (Malia 1983, 20)

Irving preferred broad-based humor. To the delight of New York insiders, he challenged his colleagues to spoof "the fairest, the finest, the most accomplished, the most bewitching, and the most ineffable beings that walk, creep, crawl, swim, fly, float, or vegitate [*sic*] in any or all of the four elements." (ibid.) Audience favorites were the concocted letters of the fictional Mustapha-Rub-a-Dub Keli Khan, who purported to inform friend Asem Haachem of political opinions of the era. Assorted jabs skewered the elite Ding Dongs and Sophie Sparkles, self-indulgent rakes, windy backbenchers, busybodies, and bombastic actors. His touch remained incisive but light and rarely didactic.

Irving's literary career took an inauspicious turn shortly before he published America's first comic burlesque, a spoof of the historical guidebook entitled *A History of New York, from the Beginning of the World to the End of the Dutch Dynasty* (1809), later referred to as "A Knickerbocker's History." The work is a melange of fact, satire, puns, mock heroism, irony, caricature, and buffoonery spoken through the fictional persona of Diedrich Knickerbocker, a Dutch pedant whose name came to personify New Yorkers. In Book II, Irving describes the arrival of voyagers to Manna-hata, a verdant island, where flows the Shatemuck River, later called the Mohegan. With mock-serious scholarship, Irving follows the settlement of the area and the rise of the Dutch city of New Amsterdam under the hand of empire-builder Peter Stuyvesant, who inveigles natives to assist him by plying them with alcohol.

In October 1809, Irving extended the humor of his comic frontier history by taking out an ad in the *Evening Post* describing Knickerbocker and requesting information about his whereabouts, then wrote letters to the editor indicating that a curious book in the old gentleman's handwriting had been located in his room. Although Irving's lighthearted satire brought raves from critics and titters from readers, Dutch residents were not amused at a lampoon of the governor of New Amsterdam, whom Irving characterized as five feet six in height, five feet six in girth, and bearing "the appearance of a beer barrel on skids." (Irving 1978, 85) During the stressful time when Irving came under fire from irate readers of Dutch ancestry, he suffered the double loss of his father and fiancée, Matilda Hoffman. Their deaths precipitated the darkest period of his life.

Grief undermined the author's energies. Irving retired briefly to tutor the children of Judge William Van Ness at Lindenwald in Kinderhook, New York, the setting of the notorious ride of the headless horseman. As a partner in P & E Irving, the family cutlery trade, Irving traveled to Washington, D.C., where he petitioned Congress to assist the flagging New York market. During the War of 1812, he divided his time between serving as attaché to Gov. Tompkins and editing the *Analectic Magazine,* a Philadelphia-based journal rife with the author's patriotism and bemusement at varied citizen responses to the war years. Although he disliked editing, he earned $1,500 annually and kept up a column and critical articles as part of his duties.

At age 33, after the deaths of his mother and eldest brother William, Irving unintentionally chose the life of the expatriate author. He settled in Liverpool, England, as representative for the foundering family trade at the Goree Arcade. When the company went bankrupt, he visited his brother-in-law in Birmingham, West Midlands, to relieve chronic melancholia. Forced to write for a living, Irving became America's first professional author, completing *The Sketch Book of Geoffrey Crayon, Gent.* (1818), an entertaining, seven-part serial, and followed with *Bracebridge Hall, or the Humourists: A Medley* (1822), a monetarily successful collection of comic vignettes, ghost stories, travelogues, essays, supernatural tales, and reflections. These vivid beginnings contain his three most famous stories, "The Spectre Bridegroom, A Traveller's Tale"; "Rip Van Winkle," set in the mountains around Kaatskill [Catskill], New York; and "The Legend of Sleepy Hollow," a darkly humorous legend of superstition and cruelty to the weak. The latter two stories preserve Irving's most famous caricatures: Ichabod Crane, the scrawny, diffident Yankee schoolmaster and butt of local pranksters; Dame Van Winkle of the scalding tongue; and Rip Van Winkle, a tattered ne'er-do-well who ventures from his village into the mountainous, ghost-ridden frontier. The author's spirited fun at the expense of henpecked husbands extends to Rip's henpecked dog Wolf, who "was as courageous an animal as ever scoured the woods; but what courage can withstand the ever-during and all-besetting terrors of a woman's tongue?" In her presence, the cowering beast wilted and "sneaked about with a gallows air, casting many a sidelong glance at Dame Van Winkle, and at the least flourish of a broomstick or ladle he would fly to the door with yelping precipitation." ("Washington Irving" 1979, 5)

The public's taste for droll, irreverent lampoons brought Irving instant fame and the friendship and respect of Sir Walter Scott, Thomas Moore, and George Byron. In Paris, Irving wrote stage plays in collaboration with John Howard Payne. Irving settled in London and worked in the Reading Room of the British Museum while composing *Tales of a Traveller* (1824), a critically disastrous blend of 32 short pieces published under his real name and including more of Knickerbocker's anecdotes and a brief mention of the legends of the pirate Captain Kidd in the acclaimed "The Devil and Tom Walker." In the latter, the author halts a gripping Faustian allegory of a man's deal with an ominous, dark Satan to interject a quip about the protagonist's wife. A parallel of Rip Van Winkle's shrewish mate, Irving surmises that Tom's wife is a match for the devil.

Following the poor critical reception of *Tales of a Traveller,* Irving's failed courtship of Mary Shelley, and appointment to an insignificant government post in London, the author sank into depression. A lengthy sojourn as minister to Spain sparked his interest in translation, biography, and history. He abandoned satire and wit to write *The Life and Voyages of Christopher Columbus* (1828), a serious work that accuses the New World discoverer of abusing and enslaving Caribbean Indians. Irving moved rapidly into a romance, *A Chronicle of the Conquest of Granada* (1829), published as the work of Fra Antonio Agapida, one of the author's many pen names. Restored to good humor, Irving published *Voyages and Discoveries of the Companions of Columbus* (1831), a literary treatment of history that rounds out his Iberian period. For his works on Columbus, the adoring Spanish awarded him membership in the Real Academia de la Historia.

At age 49, Irving found himself in great demand. In England he received a history medal from the Royal Society of Literature and an honorary degree from Oxford. On return to New York in 1832, he discovered his work in vogue in the East and on the frontier. His name was as well known among readers as those of Ichabod Crane, Knickerbocker, and Dame and Rip Van Winkle. President Andrew Jackson honored Irving at a formal dinner in the presidential mansion. Irving capitalized on his popularity with *The Alhambra* (1832), an architectural guide collected with miscellaneous Spanish sketches and a satire on King Boabdil, the tearful, ineffectual Spanish monarch.

At the suggestion of Johann von Goethe, Irving turned from European subjects to a closer study of home. A monthlong trek for a fact-finding commission took him and naturalist John James Audubon west to study locations for the resettlement of the Cherokee nation. They visited Indian mounds in Missouri, rode horseback across the prairies, and traversed the Ohio, Missouri, and Mississippi Rivers by steamer. Irving traveled with General William Clark and Sam Houston, studied bee-hunting techniques, and explored Cherokee, Kickapoo, Osage, Sioux, Shoshone, Crow, Creek, and Blackfeet territory. Nights around the campfire and days on buffalo hunts where wild duck flocked overhead whetted his urge for the outdoors and for conversations with trappers, hunters, and rangers. He admired settlers, whose log homes and fences he describes in architectural detail and whose menus he lists as "ham, fried chicken, eggs, milk, honey, delicious butter, boiled maize, and hot wheaten bread." (Irving 1944, 18) In one Creole woodsman named Antoine, Irving perceives a "Gil Blas of the frontiers . . . a notorious braggart and a liar of the first water." (ibid., 51) Irving enjoys hearing him "vapor and gasconade about his terrible exploits and hairbreadth escapes in war and hunting."

Five thick notebooks and a hand-lettered map of the trip supplied Irving with splendidly detailed material for three titles: *A Tour of the Prairies* (1835), a somewhat romanticized narrative of Indians and buffaloes on the plains; the second, *Astoria* (1836), summarizes and justifies John Jacob Astor's monopoly

Washington Irving, 1783–1859

of the fur trade in the Northwest; the last, *The Adventures of Captain Bonneville, U. S. A.* (1837), is a romantic tale of Benjamin Bonneville, Paris-born mountaineer and army officer who trapped for fur in the Rockies. The triad, known as his *Western Journals,* was still popular over a century later.

During Irving's subsequent steamboat journey down the Mississippi, he recorded his interest in a Creole village, which he reports is more faithful to the Old World than enclaves of other nationalities. As adherents to tradition, locals keep their homes in pristine condition with no thought to modernization or enlargement. Irving's regard for an old black retainer results in a comparison of Negro slaves with Native Americans:

> He was the politest negro I met with in a western tour, and that is saying a great deal, for, excepting the Indians, the negroes are the most gentlemanlike personages to be met with in those parts. It is true they differ from the Indians in being a little extra polite and complimentary. (ibid., 174)

The pleasure of a hearty Creole community forces Irving into a melancholy mood, for he doubts that any community can remain so true to its forebears and so indifferent to "the almighty dollar," as demonstrated by municipal plans to turn surrounding forest into lots, a canal, and two railroads. (ibid., 179) He complained:

> Lots doubled in price every week; every body was speculating in land; every body was rich; and every body was growing richer. The community, however, was torn to pieces by new doctrines in religion and in political economy; there were camp meetings, and agrarian meetings; and an election was at hand, which, it was expected, would throw the whole country into a paroxysm. (ibid., 47–48)

Nostalgic for the isolated hamlets that once dotted the bayous and riviera, he mourned with others who admired the unique Louisiana frontier: "Alas! with such an enterprising neighbor, what is to become of the poor little creole village!" (ibid., 48)

More ambassadorial appointments returned Irving to Spain and England as cultural liaison into his mid-sixties, when he rejected further political offices. He retired to Sunnyside, his country estate on the Hudson River near Tarrytown, New York, with his niece Sarah Paris. In these settled years, he wrote *The Lives of Mahomet and His Successors* (1850) and *Wolfert's Roost and Miscellanies* (1855), which describes the frontier west of Manhattan, the home of "a race of hard-headed, hard-handed, stout-hearted yeomen, descendants of the primitive Nederlanders." (Irving 1855, 16)

Still productive until his death from heart failure at Irvington, New York, on November 28, 1859, Irving conducted research, managed the library of John Jacob Astor, and contributed sketches and essays to *Knickerbocker Magazine.* His last great work was the critically acclaimed five-volume national epic, *Life of Washington* (1859), a somber effort meant to laud the nation's past. Irving was buried in Sleepy Hollow Cemetery. Although rarely published in their entirety, his works have remained fresh and charming, filled with the candid admiration of a literary patriot. (Bowden 1981; Carlsen 1979; Cowie 1951; Eagle and Stephens 1992; Ehrlich and Carruth 1982; Hart 1983; Hazard 1927; Irving n.d., 1851, 1855, 1944, 1978, 1981, 1983, 1987; Lamar 1977; Lee 1966; Malia 1983; Miller 1989; Ruland and Bradbury 1991; "Washington Irving" 1979)

See also Jefferson, Joseph, III; "Rip Van Winkle"; theater, frontier.

ISHI

One of the most poignant stories of late-frontier genocide derives from the stoic testimony of Ishi, a wandering Yahi tribesman of the Yana nation in California. He was the last survivor of his tribe and spent the final four years of his life at the Museum of Anthropology of the University of California. Born in 1861 or 1862, he recalled the massacre of his village by miners in 1864 and the local real estate boom that followed the arrival of the railroad to the north end of the state. After the death of his mother in 1911, Ishi, bereft of cultural and lingual ties, collapsed at a corral outside Oroville and huddled from jeering onlookers until the sheriff rescued him and placed him in protective custody.

Safely lodged with anthropologist Alfred Kroeber in San Francisco, Ishi accepted the museum's sponsorship, ate white people's food, wore their clothes, and learned to tell time by a clock. Throughout his friendship with Kroeber, the staff, and museum patrons, he refused to reveal his real name, a ceremonial title conferring mystical protection. He answered to the Yahi word for *man* and became a living museum display. He crafted tools and weapons and taught visitors the Yahi way of starting fires, fishing, hunting, cooking, and healing. In 1914, he led Kroeber and an associate into Yahi territory to demonstrate the use of the sweat lodge and sacred tobacco and to disclose the hiding places of his tribe before their discovery.

In Theodora Kroeber's young adult biography, *Ishi, Last of His Tribe* (1987), the Yahi tribe of the Yana nation dwindles to the boy's widowed mother, paternal grandparents, and uncle, a female cousin on his mother's side, and another adult male named Timawi. They shelter in the forests, canyons, and meadows near Mount Lassen in northern California while Tehna-Ishi ("Bear Cub Boy") learns Yahi ways, conceals his footprints, and observes the *saldu*, the Yahi word for encroaching whites, who ride the train to the West in search of gold. Ishi learns ritual and woods lore and plays with his cousin Tushi while anticipating the rites of manhood, which require him to fashion a bow and arrows of juniper wood tipped with obsidian. Three years later, he pursues the trail of the Yahi to relive the death of his father, a brave killed by 20 white miners, who raided Mill Creek twice in fall 1864.

Ishi's dreams prepare him to leave his homeland, ride the monster train, and swim in the ocean. To the boy's bemusement at the omens, his uncle comments, "I do not know what your dream means, but it is a Power Dream. Follow the Way, and in the moons to come you will learn its meaning." (Kroeber 1987, 45) Multiple tragedies leave Ishi and his mother isolated on a narrow ledge above Mill Creek. His mother dies a month later; Ishi faces the unthinkable—a life without friends, family, culture, religion, or native language. After a bear claws his shoulder, he wanders the valley for three years, unable to focus on a purpose for living. Finally, he collapses, starving and dazed alongside a slaughtering pen, where the Oroville sheriff handcuffs him and locks him in a jail cell.

In Kroeber's telling, Ishi adapts well to the twentieth century, seeing for the first time a trolley car, multistory building, and the Pacific Ocean. A poignant moment comes at the museum, where he discovers two baskets made by Tushi and weeps with homesickness. He ponders, "These are the Little One's baskets—but this kind *saldu*, my Friend, was not among those who came to Wowunupo [Mountain]. I saw their faces; I heard their voices; his was not one of them. How do these baskets come here?" (ibid., 176–177) The curator explains that the compassionate white man who first found Ishi's mother brought the baskets to the museum and tried to locate the Yahi and their well-hidden rock ledge. Later, an anonymous donor—or perhaps a looter—returns Ishi's bow and arrows, quiver, and knife that were stolen by white invaders.

Kroeber, aided and advised by linguist Thomas Waterman, took down Ishi's words, stories, songs, and tribal customs in copious notes and received Ishi's approval to publish a book about the Yahi. At his death, Ishi received an appropriate Neolithic burial, with his arrows and bow, a basket of acorn meal, ten pieces of dentalium shell, a box of shell bead money, tobacco, three rings, and obsidian flakes. He was cremated and his ashes interred in a Pueblo jar in Mount Olivet Cemetery. To acquit Ishi's debt to the hospital for treatment of his tubercular condition, his friends sent $260 to the dean of the medical school. His physician wrote a suitable epitaph:

> He closes a chapter in history. He looked upon us as sophisticated children—smart, but not wise. We knew many things, and much that is false. He knew nature, which is always true. His were the qualities of character that last forever. He was kind; he had courage and self-restraint, and though all had been taken from him, there was no bitterness in his heart. His soul was that of a child, his mind that of a philosopher. (Kroeber 1962, 237–238)

In addition to Kroeber's language and anthropological studies and articles, his wife, Theodora, won a silver medal from the Commonwealth Club of San Francisco for her young adult biography and for its adult version, *Ishi in Two Worlds* (1962). (Kroeber 1962, 1987; Patterson and Snodgrass 1994; Waldman 1990)

JEFFERSON, JOSEPH, III

One of America's independent actors in the school of realism, Joseph Jefferson III perfected a life's role as Rip Van Winkle, the beloved hillbilly of Washington Irving's story. From the character's debut in 1859 to the end of Jefferson's life in 1905, the actor answered as readily to "Rip" as to "Joe." Jefferson, who sought natural grace in his characterizations, was willing to perform in a tent or on a hay platform if the audience would sit still for a production. The rise of Jefferson's name among frontier promoters and acting troupes suggests that he took seriously the task of developing stage skills and that sporadic failures and setbacks made no lasting dent in his self-confidence. The name Jefferson became so irrevocably linked with the comedy and pathos of Rip Van Winkle that the actor is considered a significant contributor to author Washington Irving's literary longevity.

A Philadelphian born February 20, 1829, Jefferson came from tested stage stock: the great-grandson of an actor in David Garrick's Drury Lane company; grandson of comic star Joseph Jefferson (1774–1832), progenitor of one of America's first prominent acting lineages and founder of a respected American troupe; and son of talented actor and scene painter Joseph Jefferson II and Cornelia Frances Thomas, a French exile residing in the West Indies. The younger Jefferson, who grew up next door to the family playhouse in Washington, D.C., debuted at age four in blackface and became an audience pleaser with his first efforts as a strolling player. In late boyhood and his early teens, Jefferson's wanderings took him from Albany to the Midwest, South, and West and then on to Mexico—a pioneer player traveling across America's entertainment beginnings rather than its legendary trails.

Written at the urging of novelist and critic William Dean Howells, *The Autobiography of Joseph Jefferson*—a perceptive reflection on stagecraft, travel, and fame serialized in *Century Magazine* from November 1889 to October 1890—reveals a vibrant, demanding trade requiring grace, charm, talent, and luck. Jefferson recalls in his memoirs the *Pioneer,* a sail-rigged packet traversing the Erie Canal, a Noah's ark affair filled with Jeffersons rather than animals. Travel by sledge in the Midwest resulted in the scuttling of scenery and baggage after the ice gave way; a sandbar saved the lot, which had to be dried and spruced up before the next opening night. He recounts:

Mildew filled the air. The gilded pasteboard helmets fared the worst. They had succumbed to the softening influences of the Mississippi, and were as battered and out of shape as if they had gone through the pass of Thermopylae. (Jefferson 1964, 38)

He reports that the exigencies of frontier theater followed the troupe across Illinois, from Burlington to Quincy, Peoria, Pekin, and Springfield. Once, they were usurped from the stage by a languorous herd of pigs; another time, in the midst of antitheater religious frenzy, the Jefferson family escaped jail through the courtroom drollery of a young Springfield attorney named Abraham Lincoln.

After his father's sudden death in a yellow fever epidemic in 1842, Jefferson partnered with his actress mother and continued the trek, this time as man of the house and troupe leader. Like a Johnny Appleseed of the theater realm, he sowed the seeds of national stagecraft on keelboat and small-town stages from Albany to Dubuque, Chicago, Galena, Memphis, Mobile, Galveston, Houston, and into Hispanic territory as the U. S. Army marched west and south. In the colorful social mix of Matamoras, Mexico, he describes gambling in a saloon:

Of course there was a heavy risk to life and property in such a place, as the frequenters of the "Grand Spanish" were more numerous than select, and, to paraphrase an old saying, "when the rum was in, the knife was out." Several times the firm had dodged under the counter to escape contact with a stray bullet, and on one occasion the offending coffee-urn had been fatally shot. (ibid., 59)

At the end of this rough-and-tumble escapade, Jefferson returned to New York to join Chanfrau's National Theater. After his marriage to actress Margaret Clement Lockyer in 1850, he toured England and France.

Jefferson's early successes as Doctor Pangloss in Colman's *The Heir-at-Law* and 150 performances as Asa Trenchard in Tom Taylor's *Our American Cousin* were minor in comparison to audience adoration of Dion Boucicault's rewriting of *Rip Van Winkle*, which Jefferson premiered at London's Adelphi Theatre in 1865. A believer in the worth of drama, he kept a record of his impressions of the frontier just as his audiences filled letters and journal entries with their memories of his stage wizardry that transformed him from middle-aged Rip to an old man. A notable honor to his skill is found in Willa Cather's *My Ántonia*, in which the speaker recalls drama and music that highlighted his college years in Lincoln, Nebraska. Listed along with presentations of *Camille* and *Norma* as memorable artistic experiences is the actor Joseph Jefferson.

To create the idiosyncratic part of Rip Van Winkle, so suited to his personality, good humor, and wit, Jefferson and Irish impresario-playwright Dion Boucicault had cobbled together an amalgamation of three earlier comedies based on Irving's short story from *The Sketch Book of Geoffrey Crayon, Gent.* (1818). One of the actor's more endearing traits was his insistence on clean lines, which he trimmed or bowdlerized to suit the tastes of the house. His declaration of frontier family values stands out in an age of naughty-nice daring: "[Playgoers] are for the time imprisoned, and have no choice but to see and hear your ill-breeding. You have no better right to be offensive on the stage than you

Nineteenth-century actor Joseph Jefferson III made a career through portraying Washington Irving's character Rip Van Winkle in Western theaters.

have in the drawing-room." (ibid., xiv–xv) His assessment of the audience's standards rang true. Over four decades, upgraded versions of *Rip Van Winkle* kept the play fresh and enjoyable at the same time that they adapted the starring role to the actor's aging body.

After his wife's death in February 1861, Jefferson recovered his health by performing the part of Rip in San Francisco and by touring the warm climes of Australia, Tasmania, Peru, and Panama. In London, his last adaptation ran 170 nights, followed by packed performances in Paris, Glasgow, and Belfast. Of Jefferson's immersion in the role, critic Henry Austin Clapp claimed, "Mr. Jefferson can point, it seems to me, to but one work of supreme distinction, the solid and single product of his life, the masterpiece of our stage,—the figure of the immortal Rip." (Coad and Mims 1929, 208) It is little wonder that stage historians consider Jefferson's "Rip Van Winkle" a national institution. (Brockett 1968; Coad and Mims 1929; Hartnoll 1983; Jefferson 1964; Malone 1933; *National Cyclopedia* 1967; Quinn 1938; Roberts 1962; Walser 1956)

See also Irving, Washington; *My Ántonia;* "Rip Van Winkle"; theater of the frontier.

A self-starter and a traveling man, author Louis Dearborn L'Amour shaped and invigorated the Western novel of the mid-twentieth century. A native of Jamestown, North Dakota, he traced his genealogy to a French-Irish beginning and a long line of pioneers. In boyhood, he thrilled to stories of a grandfather who lost his scalp to the Sioux. His family tree names 33 writers, the most famous being François René, Vicomte de Chateaubriand. L'Amour was born on March 28, 1908, to veterinarian and deputy sheriff Louis Charles and Emily Dearborn LaMoore (he later respelled the surname). He was an adventurer given to assembling crystal radios, electroplating, reading about Marco Polo, and imagining the adventures of his great-grandfather at the Little Crow Massacre of 1862. He picked up Western Americana from a variety of sources, such as data about six-shooters from Dodge City lawman Bill Tilghman. At age 12, L'Amour financed a new bike by working as a messenger boy for Western Union. From his father he gained two preparations for successful manhood: lessons in boxing and an appreciation for classic literature. His favorites ranged from Shakespeare and Voltaire to the outdoors adventures of Robert Louis Stevenson, Jack London, Rudyard Kipling, and Robert Service.

In 1923, hard times forced the LaMoores to the Southwest and later to Klamath Falls, Oregon. To spare his family the financial burden of his upkeep, L'Amour dropped out of school at age 15 and traveled the West, picking up short-term jobs as timberman, dockworker, caretaker at the Yoba Copper Mine, roustabout for the Hagenbeck-Wallace Circus, farm laborer, and orchard man. He toured the Pacific Rim on the *Steelworker* and the *Steadfast*. As a merchant seaman, he knocked about the waterfront bazaars of Singapore, familiarized himself with much of the West Indies, and returned to the United States to pursue boxing. On his own, he read widely about the American frontier and polished a repertory of oral tales and poetry recitations for the entertainment of friends.

In 1935, L'Amour sold a short story, "Anything for a Pal," to *True Gang Life* for $6.43. After studying tales and short fiction from around the world and reading up on the West in works by Frank Dobie, Wild Bill Hickok, and other frontiersmen, he launched his career in Western fiction with magazine articles and serials published under his pseudonym, Tex Burns. When World War II began, L'Amour chose tanks over infantry. After serving in Germany as an army lieutenant in the 3622 Transportation Corps, he worked as a book reviewer and published memoirs of Asia, a volume of verse, and detective and boxing thrillers.

In 1950, L'Amour published his first novel, *Westward the Tide*, and wrote at a three-a-year pace for three decades. As Tex Burns, in 1951 and 1952 he produced four of his Hopalong Cassidy series; under Jim Mayo and his own name, he pursued Western themes and settings from the early settlers to Indians and Westerners of the 1880s. He drew on his 10,000-volume library of maps, personal papers, diaries, and over 1,000 biographies of gunslingers to publish frontier essays, screenplays, television scripts, and 62 Western novels, which provided Hollywood with plots for 33 movies. His short stories and articles appeared in 80 publications, including *Saturday Evening Post*, *Story*, *Argosy*, and *Collier's*. For this gargantuan body of work, his wife Kathy aided him in assuring authenticity, the quality most praised by critics.

L'Amour won readers to his distinctive style by composing as though he were reading a story aloud. His most successful titles include *Guns of the Timberland* (1955), *The Burning Hills* (1956), *Silver Canyon* (1956), and *Shalako* (1962), all set on the American frontier. A favorite in print and on the screen is *Hondo* (1953), L'Amour's first title published under his real name. A graphic depiction of Apache savagery, the novel features Hondo Lane, a half-breed cavalry dispatcher, in what John Wayne proclaimed the best Western he ever read. A tense narrative, *Hondo* derives complexity from the biracial background of the hero, who utilizes his Indian upbringing to help him track and slay two villainous Apaches. The 1953 screen version stars John Wayne in the title role opposite Ward Bond and Geraldine Page, who earned an Oscar nomination for her portrayal of the widow protecting her son from Indians.

Because of L'Amour's interest in psychology and motivation, his villains and heroes depart from stereotypical extremes and blur the lines between good and bad. Most of his characters stick to their jobs, however involved or difficult. They profess no more than an everyday self-esteem and accept without murmur the rough justice indigenous to the frontier. A well-constructed example of L'Amour's study of human adaptability occurs in *Conagher* (1964), a novel that lauds a courageous plains widow, Evie Teale. Suddenly husbandless, she earns her living cooking for stage drivers and their passengers while she rears Ruthie and Laban, her stepchildren, on a dismal, grassless plot of ground. Evie expresses her yearning in an innovative form of creative writing: she composes a scattered diary on strips of paper and ties them to tumbleweeds. One of her most poignant lines describes the constraints of isolation: "Sometimes when I am alone I feel I will die if I do not talk to someone, and I am alone so much." (L'Amour 1979, 112) The brief missive reveals a soul so starved and troubled that she cares nothing for discretion and willingly opens her heart to whatever eyes happen upon the drifting plaint.

L'Amour matches Evie's wistfulness and courage with a suitable male protagonist, Conn Conagher, a 35-year-old veteran of the Civil War, Indian fighter, wagoneer, and construction worker with 22 years invested in dead-end jobs. The standard range warrior, he lives the impermanence of the cowboy drifter who had "punched cows from the Musselshell in Montana to the Rio Fuerte in Sonora" and claims only "whiskey friends":

> He was a loner—he had always been a loner. He was as covered with spines as any porcupine. He was cantankerous and edgy. Outwardly easy-going, he shied away from people, wary of the traps surrounding people that could lead to trouble. Yet once in trouble, he knew of no other way than to fight it out to a finish. (ibid., 130)

Sharing much of the taciturnity and persistence of Jack Schaefer's Shane, Conagher pieces together a liveable philosophy: "To be a man was to build something, to try to make the world about him a bit easier to live in for himself and those who followed." Neither pedantic nor self-absorbed, he allies himself with the West's doers, the people who "planted a tree, dug a well, or graded a road." (ibid.) His one-liners resonate with a wisdom not far removed from cynicism. On a wintry night, he stumbles into Evie's kitchen and allows her to spoon soup into his mouth, but asks for no assistance beyond the warmth of the hearth and bedding for his horse. According to Conagher's stoic credo, "a man who has to ask for help better not start out in the first place." (ibid., 170)

In L'Amour's Western microcosm, Conagher is the likely mate for Evie. The obvious pairing must wait for Conagher to fend off Apaches, rustlers, and a surly no-good named Kiowa Staples, and for Evie to observe the propriety of following up on her husband's disappearance. While she subsists on barren acreage, loneliness presses her to string out more heart-cries on tumbleweed. To Conagher, the source of the unnamed writer's discontent has to be the pervasive prairie solitude: "Lonely people, who looked at horizons and wondered what, or who, was beyond them, people hemmed in by distance, people locked in space, in the emptiness . . . prisoners, they were." (ibid., 150) L'Amour extends a kind of grace over the two figures who labor and survive on the same spare, far-flung horizon. The wistful made-for-TV version of *Conagher* that aired in 1991 stars a balanced cast of Sam Elliott, Katharine Ross, Ken Curtis, and Barry Corbin and is dedicated to L'Amour.

As he proves in scenes featuring runaway stages, bar brawls, cattle branding, and fireplace cookery, L'Amour was a master of authenticity. Unlike Owen Wister, Jack Schaefer, Walter Van Tilburg Clark, and Zane Grey, L'Amour constructed his stories from alternating segments of action and technical digression rather than involved dialogue or love plots. He covered the fine points of gunsmithy, lost mines, longhorns, range wars, and marked cards, and narrated minihistories of people and places that figure in the westward movement and in other stirring periods of history. His detailed side notes grew so intricate that readers sometimes lost the continuity of story lines while absorbing the local color and geography that run through them, such as descriptions of the days of piracy on North Carolina's coast in *Fair Blows the Wind* (1978) and the mechanics of drilling, crushing rock, and setting off explosive charges in *The Comstock Lode* (1981). L'Amour's fictional Sackett family served him well as

Louis L'Amour, March 23, 1983

the impetus for an 18-novel saga. Through its multiple episodes, he covers most of Western history, beginning with the departure of the patriarch from England to arrival in North America, crossing the Blue Ridge Mountains of Tennessee and the Carolinas, and settling the West. In his last published work, *The Sackett Companion: A Personal Guide to the Sackett Novels* (1988), he outlines and explains the series. The panoramic saga was the nucleus for *Sackett*, a television miniseries.

Along with writing, L'Amour lectured on Western topics at the Universities of Southern California and Oklahoma and Baylor University. His most prestigious awards are the Congressional Gold Medal, the Presidential Medal of Freedom, and an honorary doctorate from Jamestown College. At his death from lung cancer on June 10, 1988, he had sold more books and produced more best-sellers than any of his contemporaries. His daughter Angelique compiled a posthumous tribute, *A Trail of Memories: The Quotations of Louis L'Amour* (1988). His autobiography, *The Education of a Wandering Man*, which was completed the next year, presents the formidable reading list by which L'Amour taught himself the art of literature. (Calder 1975; Goldfarb 1995; Janke 1996; Lamar 1977; L'Amour 1953, 1961, 1978, 1979, 1983, 1988, 1989; Milner et al. 1994; Rainey 1996)

THE LAST OF THE MOHICANS

The second of James Fenimore Cooper's five-part Leatherstocking Tales, *The Last of the Mohicans* (1826) is one of the most treasured works in the annals of frontier literature and Western film. The novel presents a young Hawkeye, the focal character, in varied views: mythic frontiersman, the sharpshooter and fighter known as "long rifle," tracker, strategist, rescuer, diplomat, Christian, and comrade. Trained in the Delaware woods and dressed in camouflage gear of "hunting-shirt of forest green, fringed with faded yellow, and a summer cap of skins which had been shorn of their fur," he is self-disciplined and alert to the "lurking enemy." (Cooper 1989, 21) On a chance encounter with an English party escorting two white girls to a reunion with their father, Commander Munro, Hawkeye eludes a twofold menace: the Marquis de Montcalm with his 10,000 French soldiers and Magua, a malcontented native scout who attempts to betray the English to the Iroquois. Stressing chiaroscuro in his play of light on dark, Cooper says of Magua:

> The colors of the war paint had blended in dark confusion about his fierce countenance, and rendered his swarthy lineaments still more savage and repulsive than if art had attempted an effect, which had been thus produced by chance. His eye, alone, which glistened like a fiery star amid lowering clouds, was to be seen in its state of native wildness. (ibid., 8)

Hawkeye, who disdains the villain's tomahawk as a symbol of savagery, is well equipped for either challenger with knife and rifle and knowledge of the exigencies of woods warfare.

Cooper supplies *The Last of the Mohicans* with realistic detail drawn from his family's experience on the frontier. Set in colonial New York State along the headwaters of the Hudson River during the third year of the French and Indian wars, the dramatic action opens in July 1757. Hawkeye—backed by Uncas, the last of the Mohicans, and his noble father Chingachgook—guides the whites to a romantic shelter under a waterfall in a double cave. Cooper sets the elder man apart with an authentic detail:

> His closely shaved head, on which no other hair than the well known and chivalrous scalping tuft was preserved, was without ornament of any kind, with the exception of a solitary eagle's plume that crossed his crown and depended over the left shoulder. (ibid., 21)

The trio fights a desperate battle against hostile Indians, who capture the women. After Hawkeye rescues them, the group journeys north to an escarpment overlooking Fort William Henry, where they observe a military panorama—a lopsided engagement between Montcalm's force and the badly outmanned English, who cling to their battlements until they are forced to call a truce. An initially peaceful takeover of the English camp results in one of Cooper's famous violent clashes in which a mother is tomahawked, her child's brains bashed out, and Uncas scalps an enemy Oneida brave.

Cooper tempers the bloodier vignettes with an improbable rescue. After the Munro girls are captured a second time, Alice's suitor, Major Duncan Heyward, poses as a shaman and attends a dying Huron woman in a cave. A conjuror decked in a bear skin accompanies Heyward and reveals himself to be Hawkeye in disguise. Subsequent plot conventions call for chase scenes, near misses, a shooting match, a gallant offer to barter Cora out of an odious marriage with Magua, Uncas running the gauntlet, and his revelation of a bit of Native American exotica—a turtle tattooed as a talisman and identification mark on his chest. The final struggle takes place on a lofty crag, where Hawkeye fells Magua with a single shot from his rifle, Killdeer. The unlikely stop-action view reveals Magua hanging onto a root and shaking his fist in defiance of Hawkeye, then tumbling headfirst into space:

> The arms of the Huron relaxed, and his body fell back a little, while his knees still kept their position. Turning a relentless look on his enemy, he shook a hand in grim defiance. But his hold loosened, and his dark person was seen cutting the air with its head downward, for a fleeting instant, until it glided past the fringe of shrubbery which clung to the mountain, in its rapid flight to destruction. (ibid., 360–361)

The kinetic detail of this scene is typical of Cooper, who captures the physical fall as though he were filming it with a camera.

A significant theme in Cooper's developing love plot is the negroid West Indian heritage of Cora Munro, a tough, swarthy half sister of Alice, a tender, fair-skinned beauty who frequently swoons. In contrast, Cora, pragmatic and strong when threats menace her younger sister, bears up against misadventures of nature and human violence. As a half-breed, she shares the ostracism that forces Magua from his tribe. Because she is unacceptable as a wife for Heyward, the author sacrifices her in a desperate scene that frees his plot from the taboo of miscegenation. Her dramatic pose in white robe with arms extended to the heavens precedes a lyric cry of contrition and self-abnegation, "I am thine! Do with me as thou seest best!" (ibid., 359) Pliant in the final moments before she is stabbed, Cora yields to the social forces that deem her unworthy.

Cooper, a man of propriety and order, speaks through his fictional persona Eastern society's distaste for interracial unions. Cora's murder precedes a sober funereal tableau rich in poetic significance—the parallel violent deaths of Cora and Uncas, last of the Mohicans. Even then, Hawkeye, aloof and unattracted to either female, rejects his Mohican friend, who, although faithful and beloved, remains a pagan red man. With a shake of his head, Hawkeye denies Cora union with Uncas in the afterlife. To Commander Munro's insistence that God ignores sex, rank, and color, Hawkeye declares such sentiment a violation of nature.

The final paragraphs turn from racial matters to the concerns of the older generation. Chingachgook sits immobile before the chill remains of his son, then calls out with Homeric grandeur:

> Thy feet were like the wings of eagles; thine arm heavier than falling branches from the pine; and thy voice like the Manitou when he speaks in the clouds . . .
> Pride of the Wapanachki, why has thou left us? (ibid., 368)

While he and other mourners honor Cora and Uncas, Delaware maidens sing praise hymns. Serving as a chorus, Chingachgook and the wise Tamenund, a revered elder statesman, look ahead to clashes with white settlers and the end of aboriginal domination of the Eastern woodlands. The two men leave the frontier in the hands of the good and noble Hawkeye. Cooper concludes the novel with a nod toward worthy whites and a gesture of farewell to the idealized noble savage, embodied in Uncas.

A controlling metaphor in the novel links ancient Mediterranean culture and the New World. The white music instructor—named David after the Hebrew psalmist and warrior king—intones the hymnody of the Old Testament. In amusement, Alice cries, "The man is, most manifestly, a disciple of Apollo . . . and I take him under my own especial protection." (ibid., 16) The importance of David lore to the novel extends to Hawkeye and Uncas, the soulmates who parallel the friendship of David and Jonathan from the Bible. Cooper emulates David's cry of woe for Jonathan in II Samuel 1:17–27 in Hawkeye's confession of loyalty that ends Chapter 25:

> I have heard . . . that there is a feeling in youth which binds man to woman closer than the father is tied to the son. It may be so. I have seldom been where women of my color dwell; but such may be the gifts of nature in the settlements. . . . I have fou't at his side in many a bloody scrimmage; and so long as I could hear the crack of his piece in one ear, and that of the Sagamore in the other, I knew no enemy was on my back. (ibid., 280)

The motif of blood brothers sharing mortal danger uplifts the action and eases the grief of the final scene. In a beneficent gesture, Hawkeye reaches over the racial chasm to Chingachgook and receives him as surrogate parent. The two shed mutual tears. Tamenund's benediction rounds out the scene: "It is enough. . . . Before the night has come, have I lived to see the last warrior of the wise race of the Mohicans." (ibid., 374) (Clymer 1969; Cooper 1963, 1964, 1968, 1980, 1989; Dekker and McWilliams 1973; Franklin 1982; Kelly 1984; Ladd 1996; Levine 1989; Motley 1988; Rainey 1996; Ringe 1988; Spiller 1991; Thomas 1987; Wallace 1986)

See also captivity motif; Cooper, James Fenimore.

LAW AND ORDER

A fascinating subject to Eastern American and European readers, justice in the West got off to a raw and often bloody start and filled pages of personal narrative, novels, short stories, verse, plays, and movie and television scripts with engrossing tales and reflections. The core motif derived from a single truth: people who migrated beyond police and military control had to formulate pragmatic methods of righting wrongs, guarding property, and reclaiming stolen goods, livestock, and real estate. The confrontations between whites and Indians, farmers and free range advocates, gunmen and warrant servers, and vigilantes fighting horse thieves, rustlers, child abductors, and claim jumpers produced a variety of scenarios that permeate frontier literature, ranging in severity from the one-on-one threat of a schoolyard knuckle match in Edward Eggleston's *The Hoosier Schoolmaster* (1871) to the summary execution of rustler Juan Flores featured in Lillian Zellhoefer White's poem "Hangman's Tree" to the threat of genocide in Howard Fast's *The Last Frontier* (1941).

For all its mayhem, the West was disconcertingly open about its misdeeds. An example of candor highlighted with swaggering bravado comes from Jim McIntire's *Early Days in Texas: A Trip to Hell and Heaven* (1902), which chronicles a checkered past:

> I have stolen and robbed; I was sold for murder in New Mexico, and brought a good price, but was exonerated. I have killed Kiowa and Comanche Indians by the score, and skinned them to make quirts out of their hides; and I once killed and skinned a squaw and made a purse of her breast, which I carried for nine years. (McIntire 1992, 113)

The confessor balances his sins with claims that he was charitable, even altruistic to the hungry and destitute. Defensively, McIntire adds that he had to sleep in a cemetery and hide in a vault when he was "a wolf and the hounds were hunting me." With frontier sangfroid, he summarizes that he survived "a very busy life from boyhood."

Much of frontier lore glows with admiration for the brigands who carried out their felonies with panache. In 1933, William Rose Benét published *Golden Fleece*, a verse collection containing his ballad "Jesse James." Written in folk song style, the poem breaks up straight narrative with cries of "Roll on, Missouri" and "Missouri down to the sea." The dialect description of James stresses his strong-arm intimidation of an outlaw clan and puerile grandstanding by twirling a Colt .45 in public. A sardonic commentary on the strutting bandit's exhibitionism, the poem mimics his loud demand for jewels from victims and the farewell call to his gang, but myth making replaces the narrative voice at the poem's end, when Jesse rides into the sunset, tearing up trees like Hercules and smoking the ground with his pinto at a gallop. Tying the outlaw to Americana, Benét pictures him as an icon:

> Jesse James wore a red bandanner
> That waved on the breeze like the Star Spangled Banner;
> In seven states he cut up dadoes.
> He's gone with the buffler an' the desperadoes. (Benét 1965, 287)

As though transforming Jesse from flesh into legend, Benét avoids the gory death of the "sooper-human" bandit and allows him to vanish in a blaze of light.

Theodore Roosevelt

Among some otherwise commonplace autobiographies are names and events that have typified similar examples of Western lawlessness. Marquis James weaves into his memoirs, *Cherokee Strip* (1945), the rise of the James and Younger gang and William Clark Quantrill's Raiders. He links the paradox of these famed outlaws to their organic growth within Western culture:

> In 1867 it was hard to catalogue the James and the Younger brothers. Although fugitives, they were not outlaws in the minds of most Missourians of southern sympathies. Their prolongation of the War Between the States found sincere apologists: that conflict could have no satisfactory end until the James brothers had caught up with the northern rogues in uniform. (James 1993, 191–192)

The author describes the outlaws' first daylight assault on a bank, which occurred in Liberty, Missouri, on February 14, 1867. Within three months, Quantrill and the James brothers carried their patterned crimes to Lexington, Savannah, and Richmond, Missouri, and extended their daylight affrontery to trains. Because of a spate of copycat robberies, historians have labored to separate the work of lesser thugs from the refined thievery of Quantrill's men, led by Jesse James.

Western crime did not exclude amateurs. As described in James Michener's *Texas* (1985), a monumental historical novel, a mounting stream of "land hungry" settlers was likely to vent annoyance at weariness, long days on the trail, and thwarted expectations by killing any beast, fowl, or human that stood in the way of ambition. Mattie, a landless Tennessean, pursues a vision of property across Arkansas and beyond:

> Many people like Mattie poured into Texas, and no better description could be fashioned. She was tired, dead tired of being pushed around, and when she picked up that rifle in the Neutral Ground and killed the renegade, she felt that she was protecting her right to acquire land when she crossed over into Texas. (Michener 1985, 209)

Restrained by her husband, she ceases striking at obstacles and returns to the all-consuming quest: "This was an exploration toward paradise, and she knew it."

Riddled with misinformation, stereotypes, and outright lies, media representations of the Old West milk events for their glamour, building Billy the Kid, Tom Horn, Wild Bill Hickok, Belle Starr, John Wesley Hardin, and the gunfight at the OK Corral into fantasy. The brittle, romanticized brutality of pulp fiction and B movies so misleads the public that many of the real stories of law and order have lapsed into footnotes of history. An eyewitness who sought to stop the creation of outlandish myth was Lula Parker Betenson, resident of Circle Valley, Utah, and descendant of devout Mormon pioneers. Her brother, Robert LeRoy Parker, better known as Butch Cassidy, headed the Wild Bunch, a gang of rustlers. In *Butch Cassidy, My Brother* (1975), she complains that sensationalizing writers made no effort to document details:

> The stories became wilder and wilder. My brother was given credit for robberies which were committed at almost the same time, but many hundreds of miles apart, in the days of horseback travel. He would certainly have needed wings—and we know he was no angel. (Betenson 1975, xii)

According to a letter written by a local high school principal and added to the preface, Cassidy's outlawry deserves to be studied in light of the zeitgeist— the spirit of times when outlaws traveled from Canada to Mexico, receding into tolerant backcountry where settlers tended to think of their enemies as the cattle baron, banker, and railroad agent. As threats to a way of life, the growing menace from opportunism disturbed men like Butch, whose libertarian philosophy set decent folk above the land developer and industrialist in a democratized reversal of the feudal lord over vassals.

Deadlier than Butch Cassidy, Texan John Wesley Hardin, one of the most vicious killers in the annals of the West, figures less prominently in gun-and-chase lore. Hardin shot an average of two men annually from 1868 to 1878, the decade that saw the rise of his notoriety as a gunslinger. In his novel, *The Pistoleer* (1995), James Carlos Blake, winner of the *Quarterly West* Novella award, depicts Hardin's egotism in his meeting with Peckinpah, plucky reporter for *The Police Gazette*. Peckinpah proposes to introduce Hardin as "the most famous pistolero in the West." Hardin rejects the term as "too damn Mexican." Peckinpah reels off a string of possibilities: "Gunfighter? Shootist? Pistolman? Mankiller?" (Blake 1995, 347) At the sound of "Wild Bill the Prince of the Pistoleers," Hardin chooses the same sobriquet because it sounds "properly American." Peckinpah further inflates his puffed-up image with "the *King of the Pistoleers*."

Violent from an early age, Hardin was reputed to have carried a pistol in childhood and to have stabbed a schoolmate during recess. In defense of his violent escapades, he penned a classic autobiography replete with drinking, brawling, and flights from justice, *The Life of John Wesley Hardin as Written by Himself,* published in 1896, a year after his death in El Paso, Texas. Tight, well paced, and dotted with dialogue prissily expunged of swear words, the book reads like the discourse of an educated writer skilled at describing motivation and action. To establish authenticity, Hardin inserts appropriate idiom and standard Western jargon, e.g., Ku Kluck Klan, crack-a-loo, seven-up and euchre, six-shooters, taken the drop on, throw up your hands, squared me. The overall effect is one of on-the-scene reportage with Hardin as the central news maker.

The creation of the noted "hard case" begins with Hardin's birth to a cultured mother and a father who rode circuit for the Methodist Church. Despite his refined background, Hardin, a die-hard racist, courted confrontations with blacks. While successfully teaching school in Navarro County in 1969, he works hard at justifying violence against an unnamed troublemaker, a "most insulting and bulldozing Negro bully":

> In those times if there was anything that could rouse my passion it was seeing impudent Negroes lately freed insult or abuse old, wounded Confederates who were decrepit, weak, or old. There were lots of those kind in the country in the sixties, and these Negroes bullied both them and even the weaker sex whenever they had the advantage. Frequently I involved myself in almost inextricable difficulties in this way. (Hardin 1961, 15)

Repeated face-offs against bullies and bad-mouth enemies suggest that Hardin cultivated his fame for letting his gun do the talking. In the case of the alleged black offender, Hardin curries sympathy for the recently defeated South and disguises himself as an old man to lure the bully into a fight. Hardin claims to have removed his mask, drawn on the black man, and given him a chance to pray for mercy. According to Hardin's version of the incident, threat of retribution reformed the bully on the scene. Hardin adds, "That Negro afterwards became one of the best citizens of that county." (ibid., 16)

The latter portion of Hardin's slim autobiography retreats from post–Civil War vengeance to the settling of scores between law-abiding citizens and lawless vigilantes. In his description of an escalating range war, Hardin depicts himself as a drover doing his job despite a series of hostile encounters, threats, and violent confrontations. During a drinking spree in Comanche, his friends encourage him to quit the bar. In a charged atmosphere, Hardin sets up the classic street showdown:

> I turned around and faced the man whom I had seen coming up the street. He had on two six-shooters and was about fifteen steps from me, advancing. He stopped when he got to within five steps of me . . . and scrutinized me closely, with his hands behind him. (ibid., 92)

On hearing someone say, "Look out, Jack," Hardin draws and fires on Charles Webb. Both men are injured, Webb critically, but Hardin is still able to cover a second potential assassin and halt the gun battle. He concludes this arbitrary duel by turning himself over to the sheriff and requesting protection from an incipient lynch mob. After his escape, pursuit builds to a suspiciously one-sided manhunt: Hardin versus 500 searchers and a party of Texas Rangers. He maintains that he was slick enough to evade them all, leave money for his wife and daughter, and swear an oath over his dead brother's grave. The taut narration builds momentum as Hardin gallops away to resurface unharmed in New Orleans.

One of the least understood chapters of popularized Western outlawry derives from the Earp-Clanton feud, a standard issue in fiction, biography, and film. In a journal entry dated "Tombstone, 1894," novelist Owen Wister comments on this complex series of events. He found the famed Arizona border town a depressing place and debates the best point of view to adopt in retelling the details. He describes the feud as the outgrowth of the killings of Billy Clanton and Frank and Thomas McLowrey on November 26, 1881. Wister sizes up the two sides with an epic touch: a catalog of warriors in the style of Homer's roll call of fighting men in the *Iliad*. Wister begins with "Earp Brothers 5: James, Virgil, Wyatt, Morgan, and Warren." Individual description records Wyatt as

> more refined than the rest. Dresses in excellent taste—handsome man. Gambler, cold, etc., brains of the outfit. Consulted on all occasions. Does not know the taste of liquor and only occasionally smokes a cigar. (Wister 1958, 214)

On the opposing side, Wister lists the Clantons as Ike, Phineas, and Billy, residents of San Pedro outside Tombstone. Not newcomers to violence, the boys are in a retaliatory mood following the death of "old man Clanton," whom Mexicans murdered.

According to Wister, the height of the many-sided feud began March 15, 1881, after robbers held up the stage bound from Tombstone to Benson. The tenor of the times requires greater attention to law and less winking at the frequent acts of lawlessness that the Clantons have assumed was their right. To assure his election as sheriff of Pima County, Arizona, Earp precipitates the final clash by offering Ike Clanton $1,000 to induce Billy Leonard and Harry Head to show themselves near Tombstone so Wyatt can shoot them. The convoluted story involves Doc Holliday's claim that he saved Earp in a confrontation in Dodge City, Kansas. Holliday precipitates a showdown by publicly branding Billy Clanton a cow thief. Earp accuses Clanton of selling out his friends. In a street face-off, Holliday and Wyatt, Morgan, and Virgil Earp confront Clanton and his companion, Frank McLowrey. In the shoot-out, Billy Clanton and Tom and Frank McLowrey die on the scene; Virgil and Morgan Earp are wounded. The sheriff arrests the Earps; despite testimony that they shot men with their hands in the air, the Earps are exonerated. In a lengthy retelling, Wister concludes with the events of March 18, when an assassin shoots Morgan during a game of pool. Three days later, Wyatt and Doc flee to Colorado after murdering Frank Stillwell, a deputy sheriff whom they believe shot Morgan in the back. In Wister's account, conspiracy, hearsay evidence, and criminal misuse of firearms contribute to the illicit pattern of retribution in frontier Arizona.

In 1927, Stuart N. Lake began soliciting interviews for Wyatt Earp's authorized biography, *Wyatt Earp, Frontier Marshall*. After Earp's death in 1929, Lake consulted with his widow, Josephine Sarah Marcus Earp, who excised sensational elements, particularly the subtitle—*Gunfighter*. Lake appears to have sided with Earp and his brothers because they were better educated and less vicious than the seedy, ignorant Clantons and murderous McLowreys. In gatling gun style, Lake peppers his text with short sentences:

> "Look out, Doc!" Morg called, shooting as he lay.
> McLowery's, Holliday's, and Morgan Earp's pistols roared together. Doc winced and swore. Frank McLowery threw both hands high in the air, spun on his bootheels, and dropped on his face. Morg got to his feet. Morgan's bullet had drilled clear through Frank McLowery's head, just behind the ears; Doc's had hit the outlaw in the heart. (Lake 1994, 297)

Precise details of the carnage typify Lake's protracted retelling. He rationalizes the Earps' actions by revealing the large amount of cash the outlaws had brought to the battle. He surmises that the money proves that they planned to exterminate the "Earps and Holliday and ride for Old Mexico to stay until public resentment subsided." (ibid., 300) The account stretches on with details of the two-day display of the bodies under a sign reading "MURDERED IN THE STREETS OF TOMBSTONE."

Glenn Shirley's *Belle Starr and Her Times: The Literature, the Facts, and the Legends* (1982), a scholarly biography and overview of frontier justice, corroborates Wister and Lake's data on the peacekeeper's difficulty in upholding the law. Shirley describes the ill-famed Belle Starr, former consort of Cole Younger and Blue Duck, after she settled in Indian territory with husband Sam Starr. After leading a feisty band of horse thieves, she faced Judge Isaac Parker, Arkansas's hanging judge, and was remanded to a Detroit prison. The journey to Illinois exasperated her captors. She dropped objects out of the wagon and took advantage of their deference to her sex to annoy them. According to an interview:

> She had been alone in her tent eating her dinner when the side blew up, disclosing the guard seated on the outside, his pistol in his scabbard, with his back toward her. It was but the work of an instant for her to seize the pistol; she intended to kill the guard, liberate the other prisoners, her husband and herself. Unfortunately for the success of her plans . . . the timely arrival of the officers saved the day. (Shirley 1990, 153)

In Shirley's biography, Belle weeps with rage after she is disarmed and chained. He rounds out the story of her rough life with a description of her assassination. She died in ignomy, shot in the back by an unknown assassin on her way home from Fort Smith, Arkansas. Over her tomb, the family placed a white marble headstone inscribed with a quatrain:

> Shed not for her the bitter tear,
> Nor give the heart to vain regret.
> 'Tis but the casket that lies here;
> The gem that filled it sparkles yet. (ibid., 261)

Typical of nineteenth-century piety and sentimentality, the epitaph borders on humor from the contrast between the heinous crimes that attach to her past and the delicacy of the Starr family's "gem."

In his sturdy biography of Sam Houston, *The Raven* (1929), Marquis James corroborates the writings of Lake and Shirley by depicting Texas as a thriving hotbed of lawlessness. Americans who choose to populate Mexican lands southwest of Indian territory know before they immigrate that living outside the law will require homesteaders, squatters, and ranchers to defend their own. The Texas spirit thrums with romance and daring:

> People who had anything to lose stayed at home. The Redlands and the unauthorized settlements about Galveston Bay entitled Texas to the picturesque fame acquired in those early days. "Hell and Texas!" took its place in the vocabulary of the thirties as a mild cuss word; a loose expression or Texas would have been mentioned first. (James 1929, 197)

James appends a humorous bit of local idiom: "When a citizen disappeared from his home community under cloudy circumstances he was said to have G. T. T.—Gone to Texas." However, the devil-may-care of James's anecdotes obscures the fact that life outside the law was haphazard, often fatal.

Within this milieu of rebellion, street dueling, robbery, rustling, ambush, and backshooting grew the tradition of the stalwart Texas lawman. An eyewitness account of frontier police work comes from James B. Gillett's *Six Years with the Texas Rangers, 1875–1881* (1921). Members of the state law enforcement agency were dispatched to railroad and oil boomtowns, border squabbles, and trouble spots to enhance local sheriff departments in bringing to justice bandits, rustlers, and rampaging gangs. Gillett's factual and decidedly racist account of the Salt Lake War, the role of the Apache chief Victorio, and border skirmishes with Mexican bandits attest to the single-mindedness of Texas lawmen, who earned modest wages and had to furnish their own horse, uniform, and equipment. He reports that, after 1877, each ranger bore a Winchester rifle, a Colt .45, two cartridge belts, and a bowie knife. Constantly on call over a wide territory, Gillett and his fellow rangers boast that they are ready for duty, rain or shine, and exult, "We live in the saddle and the sky is our roof." (Gillett 1976, 21)

A defense of harsh frontier methods of preserving Western law and order comes from a surprising source. In a central chapter of *Ranch Life and the Hunting Trail* (1888), Theodore Roosevelt outlines his personal experience with law enforcement. During a brief stint as deputy sheriff of the Dakota Territory, he earned $50 for recovering his own flat-bottomed scow. In a separate incident, he records an informal connection with two amiable Texans whom he identifies as fugitives from justice, one an accessory to murder and the other a witness. The men had become involved in an isolated land war in the wilds of New Mexico, which Roosevelt grandly characterizes as

> a quarrel between two great ranches over their respective water rights and
> range rights,—a quarrel of a kind rife among pastoral peoples since the days

when the herdsmen of Lot and Abraham strove together for the grazing lands round the mouth of the Jordan. (Roosevelt 1983, 88)

For all his bonhomie, Roosevelt cannot explain away the virulence of Western vengeance, which he sees escalate from minor episodes of stampeding of cattle at watering spots to burning camps and fighting to the death with guns and bowie knives. These personal squabbles also set off racist feuds between Anglo cowboys and Mexican *vaqueros*. On the verge of open warfare, Roosevelt indicates that the only redress is a sheriff's posse and threats of military intervention.

Roosevelt declares such sporadic periods of violence a natural outgrowth of the free and easy life in the Southwest. He acknowledges that various degrees of lawlessness disrupt peace and require "vigilance committee work." (ibid., 90) In defense of vigilantism, he states:

> In such a society the desperadoes of every grade flourish. Many are merely ordinary rogues and swindlers, who rob and cheat on occasion, but are dangerous only when led by some villain of real intellectual power. The gambler, with hawk eyes and lissome fingers, is scarcely classed as a criminal; indeed, he may be a very public-spirited citizen. (ibid.)

Roosevelt adds that confrontations in saloons erupt into gunfights, an eventuality that requires gamblers to practice marksmanship and be willing to shoot to kill when the occasion demands. One scenario from frontier hooliganism is the three-day carouse that concludes cowboys' six months of herding cattle. Having wasted their wages on women, whiskey, and games of poker and three-card monte, they often resort to hearty roistering, letting off steam by shooting heels from boots or knocking heads in a local dance hall. One episode that the author observed involved a sour-tempered cowpuncher who rode his horse into a hotel, shot up glass ornaments, then tossed down a roll of cash to cover the owner's loss.

Apart from the drunken horseplay of such cowboys, Roosevelt categorizes more dangerous types of criminal behavior. Claim jumpers he labels as blackmailers who may terrorize a foreigner but never an experienced Westerner. He adds, "They delight to squat down beside ranchmen who are themselves trying to keep land to which they are not entitled, and who therefore know that their only hope is to bribe or to bully the intruder." (ibid., 93) The author relegates horse thieves to a higher level of culpability than cattle thieves, who usually butcher a steer only in winter, when wild game may not be available. In reasoned discourse, he explains that horses are valuable to frontiersmen and become, therefore, marketable booty. Armed bands in search of horse thieves tend to locate them in league with highwaymen and no-goods and to administer a summary punishment, usually hanging or shooting. In contrast to livestock thieves, man-killers may be less harmful, having been forced into a shoot-out. As fugitives, they are obliged to live on the run, forever watching to the rear for lurking avengers. Of his own experience with backshooters, Roosevelt claims,

I can recall but one man killed in these fights whose death was regretted, and he was slain by a European. Generally every one is heartily glad to hear of the death of either of the contestants, and the only regret is that the other survives. (ibid.)

Because this picture of frontier justice comes from a respected citizen and eventual president of the United States, it implies that the law of the gun is a predictable feature of territory that is still being civilized.

According to Roosevelt's *Rough Riders* (1902), it is from the ranks of action-ready cowboys in Arizona, New Mexico, and Oklahoma that Lt. Col. Theodore Roosevelt recruited his Rough Riders, a troop of mostly Western desperadoes and former ranch hands who fought in Cuba and earned the respect of Americans for their courage and patriotism. He writes in his journals: "They were a splendid set of men, these Southwesterners—tall and sinewy, with resolute, weather-beaten faces, and eyes that looked a man straight in the face without flinching." (Roosevelt 1990, 15) He admires the dynamism and grit of his regiment of plainsmen, whom he describes as "accustomed to handling wild and savage horses" and skilled with rifles and living in the open.

In comparison with the Southwest, the situation on the northern frontier was no less unruly. According to *The Bootlegger's Lady* (1984), a biography of pioneer Edith Julia Bronson, the family of outlaw Fred Frye set out from North Dakota to Albreda, British Columbia, on a 2,000-mile trek to Fred's lumbering job cutting ties for the railroad. Bronson, Frye's tenacious wife and mother of his nine children, lost patience with his skirt-chasing, bootlegging, and brutality. In 1915, the untenable situation in Bronson's home threatened the lives of wife and mother as Frye's whiskey madness raged out of control:

Fifteen feet away, Fred stooped by the bed, reaching for the shotgun. The intensity of sensation increased within Edith, her ears ringing. She lifted the long rifle toward the tormented husk of her husband. When the sights aligned on his head, she squeezed the trigger. (Sager and Frye 1993, 117)

The spree of family violence ends with Edith killing Fred, who had raved "I am God" and plotted to murder the family and shoot himself. The authors cite newspaper accounts and cross-examinations of witnesses at Edith Bronson's trial. After she is exonerated for her actions, she returns to her job cooking for loggers. The authors shore up their defense of the wronged wife by listing her good deeds—fighting forest fires and killing a wolf.

A source that puts a positive spin on lawlessness compiles the desperado broadsides and jail ballads first recorded by John Lomax. In his autobiography, *Adventures of a Ballad Hunter* (1947), Lomax describes the southwestern balladeer's fascination with felons like Johnny Harty, Quantrill, Sam Hall, and Jim Haggerty. A favorite of Lomax were songs about Sam Bass, an Indiana native who became a Texas cowboy and hard-riding drover. A jolly, vigorous brigand who enjoyed his freedom, at age 17 Bass made a name for himself as a pistolero and bank robber who rode with Frank and Jesse James and the Younger boys, robbers of the Union Pacific Railroad. Betrayed to Texas Rangers during a holdup at a Texas bank in 1887, Bass was fatally shot at age 27. According to the song that commemorates his career:

> Sam met his fate at Round Rock, July the twenty-first,
> They filled poor Sam with rifle balls and emptied out his purse.
> Some say [Sam's betrayer's] got to Heaven, there's none of us can say;
> But if I'm right in my surmise, he's gone the other way.
> (Lomax 1947, 57)

Lomax claims that this authorless broadside sprang from locals, who followed Bass's freebooting lawlessness and celebrated his Robin Hood–style generosity to poor nesters. This gloomy but data-filled fragment of Texas history perpetuates the legend in 11 stanzas. Still admired by visitors, Bass's gun and holster reside at the University of Texas Museum. His reputation as a good-hearted rakehell outlives the number of people he shot and the places and people he robbed.

In retrospect, Lomax describes the song of Sam Bass as "mysterious and unknown as the Texas grasses that grow above his grave, rustling and whispering in the Texas northers that sweep through them on long wintry nights." (ibid., 58) The ambiguity of the gunman's notoriety parallels Louis L'Amour's fiction, which pairs outlaws with lawmen who are as unprincipled and disrespectful of the law as the villains they shoot or hang. Described in verse seven of "Sam Bass," Texas Ranger Thomas Floyd is less admirable than the men he stalks. In a jab at Floyd, the composer declares:

> Sam had another companion, called Arkansas for short,
> Was shot by a Texas ranger by name of Thomas Floyd;
> Oh, Tom, he's a big six-footer and thinks he's mighty fly,
> But I can tell you his racket—he's a dead-beat on the sly.
> (Lomax and Lomax 1968, 127)

The singer's calculated insults to betrayers escalate in the last three verses, in which Sam is left at the mercy of the vengeful law while Jim Jackson flees the scene. The song wishes on Jim "a scorching . . . when Gabriel blows his horn." (ibid., 128)

In the style of frontier ballads, twentieth-century horse operas, cowboy movies, and television Westerns flaunt the tension and violence of the street shoot-out. The mounting urgency of gunman facing gunman down a dusty, wind-swirled expanse powers the mundane Western novel, such as Luke Short's *Ride the Man Down* (1942). As a bystander yells, "Don't do it, Joe. Don't do it," the main character presses on: "[Bide] reached for his gun and pulled it up hurriedly and shot, and he saw Kneen slap both hands sharply on the counter as he was brushed sideways and fell to his knees." The familiar fictional motif presses for a retaliatory shot, which is only seconds away: "Then he saw Kneen's gun come up and Bide hurried. He shot twice, and then he saw Joe's gun pointing at him, saw it fire." (Short 1942b, 245) The drawn-out verbal description prefigures Hollywood's slow-motion camera, which rivets eyes to the screen for the slight hesitation before one—and sometimes both—of the shooters falls.

In the last decade of the twentieth century, Pulitzer Prize–winning author Larry McMurtry escapes such lineups of white hats and black hats by adopting a pragmatic attitude toward exigencies of frontier law and order. In reconstructing the standoff between Texas livestock thieves and Mexican ranchers, he narrows the distance between justice and opportunism. *Lonesome Dove* (1985)—a smash novel that spawned a 1989 CBS-TV miniseries, popular video, and sequel, *The Streets of Laredo* (1993)—showcases two endearingly rough-cut characters, Augustus "Gus" McCrae and Captain Woodrow F. Call, former Texas Rangers turned quasi-respectable livestock agents. Living an easy distance north of likely pickings, the two ride out of their rough adobe on Hat Creek by night to raid Pedro Flores's herd, tended by *vaqueros*. McMurtry examines border rustling through the eyes of Newt, the youngest and least-tried member of the rustling party, who ponders the vagaries of respect for rights and property:

> It was puzzling that such a muddy little river like the Rio Grande should make such a difference in terms of what was lawful and what not. On the Texas side, horse stealing was a hanging crime, and many of those hung for it were Mexican cowboys who came across the river to do pretty much what they themselves were doing. (McMurtry 1985, 125)

Further muddying the issue is Newt's hero worship of The Captain, a stern proponent of retribution for horse thieves. That Call and his crew can heist a whole herd is incomprehensible to the boy. Newt's deduction sums up much of the appeal of shoot-'em-up lore: "if you crossed the river to do it, it stopped being a crime and became a game."

In the style of Louis L'Amour, McMurtry smudges the line between law-abiding and lawless. He builds on the affability of his protagonists before testing them with a more vexing legal question: the culpability of their ex-associate, Jake Spoon, who joined the Suggses, a low-life bunch with a yen to torment nesters. The enormity of their crime of murdering, then hanging and burning the corpses of guileless sodbusters eats at Jake, but not enough to separate him from his companions. In judgment of Jake, Gus speaks the ready quip of the lawman: "Ride with an outlaw, die with him." (ibid., 572) The code of on-the-scene apprehension and punishment turns momentarily light with Jake's acceptance of a lynching, "I'd a damn sight rather be hung by my friends than by a bunch of strangers." (ibid., 575) With cavalier grace, Jake spurs his horse and swings slack in the noose before Gus can order his execution. The self-administered hanging strikes Gus as admirable. He remarks, "he died fine." (ibid., 576) (Benét 1965; Betenson 1975; Brunvand 1996; Blake 1995; Dobie 1996; Eggleston 1903; Gillett 1976; Graff 1996; Hardin 1961; Horn 1964; James 1929, 1993; Lake 1994; Lee 1975; Lomax 1947; Lomax and Lomax 1968; McIntire 1992; McMurtry 1985, 1991; Michener 1985; Morris 1979; Roosevelt 1983, 1990; Rottenberg 1996; Sager and Frye 1993; Shirley 1990; Short 1942b; Steckmesser 1965; White 1965; Williams 1982; Wister 1958)

See also Billy the Kid; Geronimo; *Roughing It;* Schaefer, Jack Warner; Wister, Owen.

LAWRENCE, D. H.

One of the surprising sources of Western literature, David Herbert Lawrence, famed novelist, poet, and playwright from Eastwood, Nottinghamshire, England, was a resident and fan of Taos, New Mexico. Like other artists, he used the area's history and lore as a source of regional subjects and themes. Born of working-class parents on September 11, 1885, Lawrence received teacher training at Nottingham University College in 1906 and taught at Croydon, Surrey. After publishing verse and short pieces, he achieved fame in 1912 with *Sons and Lovers,* the novel that prefaced his lifetime of interest in female protagonists and womanly vulnerabilities and strengths.

During World War I, for which Lawrence was declared unfit, he married Frieda von Richthofen Weekly. Military surveillance and suspicions about her father, Baron von Richthofen, caused the Lawrences to move frequently. They first settled in Chesham, Buckinghamshire, where he published *The Rainbow, Amores, Women in Love,* and *Twilight in Italy.* After traveling through much of Europe and living in Sicily, Sardinia, Germany, Capri, Ceylon, the Antipodes, Australia, New Zealand, and Tahiti, the Lawrences moved to an adobe lodge at Del Monte Ranch near Lobo Mountain in 1922. In the relaxed Southwest, he anticipated rest, recovery from exhaustion, and the stimulus of an art colony. To secure maximum warmth, he wintered in Chapala and Oaxaca, Mexico, then recuperated on the ranch after tuberculosis depleted his energy. During his frequent changes of residence, he formed numerous attachments to women, thus fueling marital anguish at home.

In 1923, Lawrence published a varied verse collection, *Birds, Beasts and Flowers.* A potpourri of his travels and experiences, his poems reproduce delicate images of life in the Southwest. In "Eagle in New Mexico," which he ties to Taos, he explores the beneficent and doom-laden dichotomy of ancient legend and asks:

> When you pick the red smoky heart from a rabbit or a
>   light-blooded bird
>
> Do you lift it to the sun, as the Aztec priests used to lift red
>   hearts of men? (Lawrence 1974, 148)

The last poems accentuate the separation between the vitiated East and the invigorated West, where the American eagle lays its "golden egg." In the final selection, labeled "Ghosts," Lawrence returns to the fearful dreams of the indigenous desert people with "Men in New Mexico" and an image of Penitentes lashing their bloody flesh in a fruitless effort to awaken themselves from dreams of the past.

Lawrence's experience in New Mexico and his study of ancient Mexican and Indian cultures were the impetus of *The Plumed Serpent* (1926) and "The Woman Who Rode Away," a novel and story he completed after moving to Florence, Italy, in 1925. *The Plumed Serpent* sets jaded European values against the mystery and allure of the Aztecs. The protagonist, widowed Irishwoman

D. H. Lawrence, 1885–1930

Kate Leslie, sojourns in Sayula, Mexico, and is moved by the fervid dance of villagers, who anticipate that Quetzalcoatl, the plumed Aztec god, will be reincarnated on earth. The emerging cult, which centers on the apocalyptic delusions of Don Ramón, attracts Kate to General Cipriano Viedma, who believes that he has become the war god, Huitzilopochtli. Don Ramón conducts the pagan ceremony uniting Kate and Cipriano. She envisions herself as Malintzi, mate of the war god, but rebels against the masculine power over her: "Horrible, really, both Ramón and Cipriano. And they want to put it over me, with their high-flown bunk, and their Malintzi. Malintzi! . . . I am sick of these men putting names over me." (Lawrence 1992, 370)

Viscerally drawn to the cult, Kate grows fearful of its power, which supplants Catholicism in the local church. She yearns for escape to a traditional Piccadilly Christmas scene with holly and presents. She realizes that white America, like the church, has never stamped out the aboriginal past and will one day syncretize with the dark blood of its native ancestry. As revolution spreads in the province, she longs to return to Ireland, but realizes that the pull of the cult comes not from Cipriano but from her own dark duality. Lawrence depicts her yielding to primitive sexuality, symbolized by a snake disappearing into a hole and peering out at her like a self-satisfied Satan.

A similar theme of unspeakable savagery, passion, and coercion empowers "The Woman Who Rode Away," Lawrence's tale of a 33-year-old married woman, mother of two, fleeing her confining marriage and her husband's mine by climbing to a Chilchuis Indian retreat high in the mountains of Mexico. She joins a religious outpost restricted to males and lives under benign house arrest. Dosed with an emetic and plied with honeyed drinks, over a period of weeks she perceives her volition draining away, replaced in part by hallucinations and heightened sensibility. Her male captors allow her to observe a ritual in the square below:

> Men with naked, golden-bronze bodies and streaming black hair, tufts of red and yellow feathers on their arms, and kilts of white frieze with a bar of heavy red and black and green embroidery round their waists, bending slightly forward and stamping the earth in their absorbed, monotonous stamp of the dance. (Lawrence 1976, 568–569)

A parallel of Kate Leslie, she succumbs to "primeval symbols" and ponders the biblical "handwriting on the wall," a doom-laced foreboding of doom.

The inevitable denouement follows a steady barrage of hints. On the shortest day of the year, when the sun is at its lowest influence, the cacique presides over ritual sacrifice. The protagonist, stripped of a blue-and-white blanket, lies naked on a stone before a single icicle and awaits death from the upraised obsidian knife. Lawrence overwhelms the character with the traditions of primitive culture that replicate a universal struggle between male and female. The victim, an earthly equivalent of the moon, cedes her life to the predominant males of the ancient culture, symbolically atoning for her husband's silver mine, an affront to wilderness gods.

A segment of "The Spirit of Place," an exegesis on freedom in Lawrence's *Studies in Classic American Literature* (1923), casts light on these characters who flee from one bondage into another. He asserts that freedom and escape from control are not synonymous:

> Men are free when they are in a living homeland, not when they are straying and breaking away. Men are free when they are obeying some deep, inward voice of religious belief. Obeying from within. Men are free when they belong to a living, organic, *believing* community, active in fulfilling some unfulfilled perhaps unrealized purpose. Not when they are escaping to some wild west. (Lawrence 1969, 440)

When applied to Kate Leslie and the unnamed woman who flees to the Chilchuis, the statement illuminates the process of discovering what Lawrence terms "the deepest self," the unconscious maturity that lies below an obstinate surface show of will. While fettered to peripheral beliefs, which he calls a "false dawn," the self has no communication with the wholeness in the spirit, a deep-flowing stream which, he claims, leads to human destiny.

Near the end of his career, Lawrence tired of marital discord and left his failed Eden in New Mexico, but he continued to blend southwestern lore and themes into his writings. He completed the reflective *Mornings in Mexico* (1927) and published his most controversial work, *Lady Chatterley's Lover* (1928), a challenge to free-speech laws, while living in Europe. Restless and desperate as his strength ebbed, he begged to leave the hospital and died of tuberculosis in Vence, France, on March 2, 1930. Five of his posthumous works were published by 1935, the year his ashes were interred in the chapel of Kiowa Ranch in New Mexico. (Burgess 1985; Champion 1989; Fay 1953, Kunitz 1942; Lawrence 1969, 1974, 1976, 1992; Tindall 1939)

THE LIGHT IN THE FOREST

Set at Fort Pitt during a historic release of Indian captives in 1764, Conrad Richter's realistic young adult novel, *The Light in the Forest* (1953), derives its energy and historical significance from the struggle between Pennsylvania settlers and the forest Indians who tried to oust them from tribal lands. The story draws its motivation from a dramatic betrayal described in Francis Parkman's comprehensive history *The Conspiracy of Pontiac* (1851). The fictional version depicts the tragic no-man's-land inhabited by whites who were kidnapped by Indians, then reclaimed, returned, or traded back to white families. Unwelcome among racist whites after acculturation to native ways, these victims found themselves isolated from both groups.

True Son, the symbolic name of Richter's teenage character, grows up from age four in the family of Quaquenga and Cuyloga, a Lenni Lenape couple living on the Tuscarawas River. A fictional representation of Parkman's description of whites adopted by Indians, True Son has known acceptance and love.

In Parkman's words, "[Indians] nurture them with the same tenderness and indulgence which they extend, in a remarkable degree, to their own offspring." (Parkman 1991, 789) As might be expected from a child torn from a loving home, True Son is content with his upbringing, fights reclamation by the Butler family, who know him as Johnny, and eludes Colonel Henry Bouquet's company. After locating his rebellious foster son, Cuyloga admonishes, "Now go like an Indian, True Son. . . . Give me no more shame." (Richter 1953, 3) The march of Bouquet's detail east across the Susquehanna River to Fort Pitt ends in humiliation when True Son tries to escape and captors force him back on his horse, tie him down, and deliver him to his natural father, Harry Butler.

Richter stresses realistic details of True Son's arrival to indicate how much the boy must learn and how deeply his birth family resents his native language and ways. As John Cameron Butler, he enters his first two-story house and meets his hostile Aunt Kate and admiring brother Gordie. To counter a closed, stuffy bedroom and confining clothes, True Son sleeps on his bearskin at an upstairs hearth and rejects a suit and boots. Conversation with two racist uncles, Wilse and George Owens, reminds him of the Peshtanks' raid on a Conestogo village and subsequent atrocities committed against Indians in the Lancaster jail. True Son seeks common ground by reminding his uncles that whites derive words like tomahawk, wigwam, and Susquehanna from the Delaware language. He claims that his father Cuyloga taught him the Lenni Lenape words for God. Uncle Wilse retorts, "I can't stand that! You mean this heathen Indian, Cuyloga, who stole Johnny and claims to be his father, talks about God before he goes out and murders Christian men and women!" (ibid., 43) Wilse claims that butchery and genital mutilation were appropriate measures to halt the breeding of more Indians.

Contrasts between white schools and churches and Indian dependence on the outdoors and the rule of the Great Spirit trouble True Son. His invalid birth mother, Myra Butler, encourages him to emulate Parson Elder, whom the boy knows as Colonel Elder, captain of the Peshtanks. To the parson's insistance that True Son be baptized a Christian and give up bad practices, he retorts, "My father don't swear. He tells me never swear. It's the white man's lie." (ibid., 62) To the boy's worried mother, Elder confides, "It will take some effort . . . But time is on our side." (ibid., 64)

At the novel's climax, True Son rejects white socialization and lies ill with a malaise that Dr. Childsley's bleeding cannot cure. Richter accounts for the boy's difficult case:

> Cut them up, and the heathen had the same organs and muscles as civilized peoples, even to the exact shape and size of their bones. The blood they hemorrhaged was as rich and red as any white man's, but there were obscure primitive tendencies and susceptibilities in the aboriginal race, and they weren't helped by the superstition lurking in the dark and hidden recesses of the untutored mind. (ibid., 65–66)

Uncommunicative and passive, the boy wills himself to die. The arrival of Half Arrow, an old friend, restores his spirit. The two flee Paxton, slip past Fort Pitt, steal a canoe, and return to the Lenni Lenape by crossing the Muskingum River, where True Son reunites with his beloved foster parents.

Richter's story concludes with a test of True Son's loyalty. When the tribe sends a war party to avenge the murder of Little Crane, whom Uncle Wilse Owens shot in a Paxton orchard, True Son accompanies his father and other braves. He dresses in pantaloons and shirt and poses as a decoy to the white crew of a flatboat. As the family poles the awkward craft near him, True Son changes his mind when he spies a young boy on board. Recalling his white brother Gordie, True Son frenziedly warns the family of the ambush. Captured, bound, and tried for treason, he is exiled from the Lenni Lenape. Cuyloga severs kinship ties with a harsh warning:

> This is the parting place. This is where the path must be closed between us. My place is on this side. Your place is on that. You must never cross it. If you come back, I cannot receive you and they will kill you. (ibid., 116)

Unwelcome in either culture, the unclaimed boy stands alone on the road to Paxton and cries out, "Then who is my father?"

The pathos of True Son's longing for a Lenni Lenape identity elucidates Richter's depiction of an era in which a clash of cultures alienated innocent people and perpetuated hostilities to no purpose. The fictional True Son questions the purpose of repatriating kidnap victims who had lost connection with their birth family. Despite his physical likeness to the Butler clan, he renounces his white blood in favor of a loving native family that supports the ongoing war against white encroachment. As fruitless as True Son's lament, the Lenni Lenape struggle to stem the westering tide is doomed to a relentless daily battle against a growing wave of settlers who accept genocide as a way to safeguard their community. (Barnes 1968; *Contemporary Authors* 1994; *Dictionary of Literary Biography* 1984; Edwards 1971, Gaston 1965; Kunitz 1942; LaHood 1975; Leisy 1950; Parkman 1991; Richter 1953, 1965; *Something about the Author* 1972; Stuckey 1966; Wagenknecht 1952; Ward and Marquardt 1979)

See also captivity motif; Parkman, Francis; Richter, Conrad; *The Sea of Grass*.

LOMAX, JOHN

A pioneer among lecturers on the Southwest and among collectors of Western lore, John Avery Lomax originated the concept of preserving work and field songs, ballads about outlaws, canal boat chanteys, tracklayers' plaints, spirituals, rotgut blues, and prison chants indigenous to North America. Like Mark Twain, Frank Dobie, and Mary Hunter Austin, Lomax championed an authentic creativity that sprang from American experiences in shanties and lumber and rail camps, on barges and chuck wagons, at harvest dances and card games, among *vaqueros* and desperadoes, and along trails to pioneer settlements, campsites, and cattle centers. To Lomax, imitations of European style and content said nothing about the American point of view. His nationalistic anthologies have influenced writers of frontier literature, providing them with titles, verse, and metaphors as familiar as "John Henry," "Casey Jones," "Days of Forty-nine," "Sweet Betsy from Pike," "Starving to Death on a Government Claim," and "Whoopee-ti-yi-yo, Git Along, Little Dogies."

A native southerner and son of Susan Frances Copper and James Avery Lomax, a farmer, Lomax was born in Goodman, Mississippi, on September 23, 1867. In 1869, his family moved 500 miles west to northwest Texas by mule and ox wagon. A treasured narrative by his mother tells how the family made a new start on the Bosque River, at a point on the Chisholm Trial, over which drovers moved their herds from San Antonio to Wichita and Abilene, Kansas. Influenced by Western lore and folk tunes, he was fascinated by cowboys and memorized the words and melodies of their songs. After studying for one year at Granbury College, he taught at Weatherford College for six years before continuing his education at the University of Texas. In his spare time, he continued searching out the unusual and true among the wry and witty lines of cowboy folk songs.

During his tenure as an instructor at Texas Agricultural and Mechanical College, Lomax impressed the college president, who arranged for him to attend Harvard, where Lomax completed an M.A. in English in 1907. With financial aid and encouragement from a scholarly circle of folk collectors, he returned to the West to polish his impressive portfolio of cowboy songs. Drawing on these, he published a best-seller, *Cowboy Songs and Other Frontier Ballads* (1910), and followed with *Songs of the Cattle Trail and Cow Camp* (1917). The former compilation, which reappeared in revised form in 1938, elucidates the mobile cattle puncher's values of independence and individuality. His choices adhere to the paradigm of impersonal narrative songs without date or author that circulate orally through a homogeneous group.

Much of Lomax's canon bears the piquance, easy sociability, and frontier ribaldry found in the writings of Mark Twain, Bret Harte, Davy Crockett, Artemus Ward, Joaquin Miller, and Robert Service. In "Hell in Texas," the songwriter claims that tarantulas, cactus thorns, steer horns, and rattlesnakes are gifts of the devil. The rich natural lore includes the bronco steed, centipede, wild boar, and black chapparal as essentials to hell's decor. The fillip that concludes the second stanza adds:

> He planted red pepper beside all the brooks,
> The Mexicans use it in all that they cook;
> Just dine with a Greaser and then you will shout,
> "I've Hell on the inside as well as the out!" (Lomax 1947, 60–61)

Lomax laces his potpourri with similar humorous and scurrilous references that are racist and sacrilegious. Less rambunctious songs, like "Goodbye, Old Paint" and "Home on the Range," a favorite of Teddy Roosevelt, reflect a nostalgia for past times on the prairie when it was free and open land. Lomax's most plaintive songs punctuate mournful stanzas with the eerie yodel of the cowboy riding guard late at night and crooning animal lullabies to placate a restless herd.

Typical of Lomax's concern for folk is his interest in dirt-level English, as spoken by Tom Hight in "Starving to Death on a Government Claim." Tom, an "old bach'lor" sodbusting in Greer County, narrates his situation:

My clothes are all ragged, as my language is rough,
My bread is corndodgers, both solid and tough;
But yet I am happy and live at my ease
On sorghum molasses, bacon, and cheese. (Lomax 1965, 261–262)

A victim of the Homestead Act of 1862, Tom Hight determines to quit his cheap shelter, escape brutal extremes of weather, and "travel to Texas and marry me a wife/And quit corndodgers the rest of my life."

In the 1930s, Lomax recovered from the death of his wife and from physical and financial collapse by collaborating with his son, John Lomax, Jr., who drove the Ford and helped his father make camp. On a subsequent journey funded by Macmillan Press, Lomax traveled with his son Alan, then a teenager. The duo combed the South for the emotional cries and rhythmic chants of chain gangs, dispirited prisoners, levee stevedores, saloon keeps, lumberjacks, cardsharps, stage drivers, buffalo skinners, well diggers, and native blues singers. Their recordings resulted in *American Ballads and Folk Songs* (1934). During this monumental project, Lomax encouraged the work of Huddie "Leadbelly" Ledbetter, a fresh, innovative lyricist who was serving a sentence at the Angola Prison Farm in Louisiana. Lomax became the national folklore editor for the Federal Writers' Project, an effort that compromised his true sentiments about the underpinnings of national songs. The remainder of his career was spent at the Library of Congress, where he managed the Archive of Folk Music and added 10,000 recordings to the collection. His last three works—*Negro Folk Songs as Sung by Lead Belly* (1936), *Our Singing Country* (1941), and *Folk Song U.S.A.* (1947)—preceded a revival of interest in blues and native folk tunes. Lomax insisted that American balladeers spoke the commonalities of the West, which reflect a longing for freedom and the challenge of the violent frontier. Shortly before his death from cerebral hemorrhage in Greenville, Mississippi, on January 26, 1948, he published his autobiography, *Adventures of a Ballad Hunter* (1947), a salute to the vigor, diversity, and distinctive flavor of Americana. (Botkin 1944; Brunvand 1996; Dobie 1996; Hazard 1927; Lamar 1977; Lomax 1947, 1965; Lomax and Lomax 1968; Trent et al. 1946; Wexler 1995)

See also Austin, Mary Hunter; Dobie, J. Frank; law and order; Twain, Mark.

LONDON, JACK

Jack London was America's chronicler of adventure and conflict on the bleak, exhilarating Yukon frontier. In naturalistic tales and novels, he wrote the story of the Northwest's gold rush. Unlike writers of camp yarns and wilderness reportage, he often concentrated on animals, who form the bulk of his casts of characters in works such as *The Call of the Wild* (1903), *White Fang* (1904), and his masterpiece short story, "To Build a Fire" (1900). By contrasting human problem solving with the instinctual behaviors of dogs, wolves, and their quarry, London expressed nature's unrelenting laws of survival.

Born in San Francisco on January 13, 1876, John "Jack" Griffith was the illegitimate son of an Irish astrologer, William Henry Chaney, and his mistress, Flora Wellman, a psychic, who had abandoned her disapproving Ohio family to live a Bohemian fantasy. She defied her lover's demand that she abort her child, but her resolve concealed a suicidal bent that jarred her peace of mind. Although she married eight months later, her son grew up stigmatized, fragile, and introspective. At age two, he and his stepsister Eliza weathered deadly bouts of diphtheria. At age five, he was adopted by his stepfather, grocer John London, and lived on a struggling truck farm near Colma, California. He transcended poverty by reading Rudyard Kipling, Sir Walter Scott, and other adventurers and voyagers and by sailing his sloop, the *Razzle Dazzle*, purchased with money he earned at odd jobs in a cannery, bowling alley, jute mill, and ice wagon. In his teens, he quit school so that he could search Oakland's waterfront for his biological father.

Dissatisfied and poorly supervised, London teetered on the edge of delinquency. The director of the Oakland Public Library helped him escape ennui and the potential for crime by encouraging him to read the classics. After giving up prowls with wharf thugs, London found work patrolling the oyster bay. At age 17, he sailed to Japan, Siberia, and Hawaii on the *Sophia Sutherland* to hunt seal, a quest that provided material for his novel *The Sea-Wolf* (1904). His first published story, "Typhoon off the Coast of Japan," won a contest sponsored by the San Francisco *Morning Call*. In his late teens, he joined Kelly's industrial army of the unemployed and protested poverty, the burden of his childhood. Living among hoboes, in 1894 he was arrested for vagrancy in Niagara Falls, New York, and served a month in jail.

Within a year, London finished his high school education and worked brief stints as a newspaper carrier, longshoreman, coal stoker, canner, jute mill operator, and laundryman. An Oakland bartender, impressed with London's keen intellect, provided tuition for the University of California at Berkeley. In class, London dressed poorly and jolted his peers with encyclopedic knowledge of *The Communist Manifesto,* Karl Marx, Friedrich Engels, Friedrich Nietzsche, Charles Darwin, and social philosopher Herbert Spencer. He acquired the basics of a degree in philosophy and set out to put his ideals into action. Inflamed by socialism, he was arrested at age 20 for anticapitalist oratory in downtown Oakland, the city he referred to as a mantrap and in which he ran unsuccessfully for mayor in 1901 and 1905.

During his formative years, London stocked his writer's memory with observations of the last frontier—the Klondike goldfields of northwestern Canada, where he settled on the Stewart River and prospected during the autumn and winter of 1897 and 1898. Along with other seekers of adventure in an unspoiled land, he and his brother-in-law, Captain J. H. Shepard, sailed on the *Umatilla* and trekked 2,000 miles north from Dyea Beach over Chilkoot Pass and the White

Horse Rapids. The winter among other snowed-in Klondikers enlivened London's imagination with the realities of wilderness survival, but earned him almost nothing from prospecting.

Achy and lame with scurvy, London gave in to the demands of health and rafted down the Yukon River to the Pacific Coast aboard a three-man houseboat. He retold his experience in "From Dawson to the Sea," published in *The Illustrated Buffalo Express*. The experience proved monetarily fruitless, but the whetting of his taste for a male-centered domain invigorated his hard-edged narratives. Assimilation of the macho code, dog and Indian lore, and the society that sprang up around mining camps fed his writing until his death. He got a promising start in magazine fiction from Bret Harte, editor the *Overland Monthly* and a respected supporter of frontier writers, and turned out a prodigious amount of fiction for the *Atlantic Monthly, Black Cat, Harper's, Youth's Companion, Collier's,* and *Century.* The discipline of regular writing, revision, and submissions set him on a routine of composing 1,000 words per day for the remainder of his life.

In 1900, London published two volumes in one year—his first novel, *Daughter of the Snows,* and a collection of adventure lore, *The Son of the Wolf: Tales of the Far North.* Settled for the first time into a rewarding career, he married Bessie Maddern and fathered two daughters, Joan and Little Bess. Quickly soured on living with a whining, insecure woman he didn't love, he fled to England, immersed himself in social conditions, and turned from Yukon tales to social and political commentary. His most incisive work, *The People of the Abyss* (1903), presented a stark overview of slum life. After his return to the United States and marriage to Charmian "Mate" Kittredge, their happy domesticity returned him to stability and contentment at Beauty Ranch, a rural retreat near Glen Ellen in California's Sonoma Valley. To bankroll an extensive ranching operation encompassing livestock, grain, vegetables, and fruit, London wrote his masterpiece, *The Call of the Wild* (1903), and its companion piece, *White Fang* (1906). The former, which was serialized in the *Saturday Evening Post,* brought a flat return of $750. Both earned London international stardom.

The Call of the Wild introduces John Thornton, one of London's fictional "ideal men." Acquainted with living off the land, John retains his humanity in brutal conditions and rescues Buck, the mighty sled dog, through love, understanding, and patience. Buck, London's epitome of survival of the fittest, is himself a pioneer, although not by choice. After his abduction from a cushioned life in the Santa Clara Valley of California, he tentatively confronts new challenges:

> Every hour was filled with shock and surprise. He had been suddenly jerked from the heart of civilization and flung into the heart of things primordial. No lazy, sun-kissed life was this, with nothing to do but loaf and be bored. Here was neither peace, nor rest, nor a moment's safety. All was confusion and action, and every moment life and limb were in peril. There was imperative need to be constantly alert; for these dogs and men were not town dogs and men. They were savages, all of them, who knew no law but the law of club and fang. (London 1964, 25)

The transformation of Buck into a predatory canine concludes the story on a folkloric note with Indian rumors of a mighty ghost dog.

In *White Fang,* London retraces the pattern of *The Call of the Wild* by transporting the wolf-dog from the frontier to the tranquil Santa Clara Valley. The unremitting shifts in setting turn the wolf into a deranged loner before reshaping him into a house pet. The sequel displays London's strengths: diction, suspense, phrasing, characterization, and action. At the novel's core lie universal themes and symbols, particularly the play of light on dark and the contrast between predator and family dog. After rescue from brutal exploitation, White Fang is still a newcomer to trust when he senses that his new owner is withdrawing. The wolf crashes through the cabin window of the steamer *Aurora,* a symbol that perpetuates the influence from White Fang's unfettered puppyhood. Still enamored with the theme of social justice, London has White Fang stalk the villain Hall through the foreboding dark on behalf of Weedon Scott, his man-god.

London maintains the demands of the wild in the final chapter of *White Fang.* In the pivotal scrap, White Fang demolishes the trappings of civilization, "snarling and growling, and . . . a smashing and crashing of furniture and glass" before being felled by three bullets. (London 1980, 304) The newly tamed wolf conquers a cunning convict but nearly succumbs to pain, shock, and blood loss. The attending surgeon doubts that he has one chance in 10,000 of survival. In a protracted stupor, White Fang rebattles old ghosts, the high moments of his early life in the wild. London rewards readers with a Disneyesque finale: a touching view of the resilient hero, tottering out of confinement to welcome a litter of "a half-dozen pudgy puppies playing . . . in the sun," the author's promise that White Fang's toughness and determination will endure. (ibid., 310)

In 1908, London published in *Century* magazine what has become American literature's most anthologized story, "To Build a Fire," later collected in *Lost Face* (1910). The spare, moody narrative describes the departure of a luckless traveler from the standard Yukon Trail in 75-below temperatures where spit crackles on the air like gunfire. Contrasted with his dog, the unnamed protagonist—a *che-cha-quo,* or neophyte northman—ignores the advice of an oldtimer, goes out alone in perilously cold weather, and loses all by one misstep into a snow-covered spring. In a simple line, London states the fatal lapse: "He had forgotten to build a fire and thaw out." (London 1965, 106)

The musher's maddeningly awkward attempt to curl stiff fingers about matches and tinder builds false hopes. In one swift twitch of the overhanging spruce, nature defeats his efforts when the rising warmth loosens a blob of snow onto the fire, extinguishing it before he can warm himself. In contrast to the man's floundering, his nature-wise dog perceives looming tragedy. As day draws to a close, he watches with "a certain yearning wistfulness in its eyes, for it looked upon him as the fire-provider, and the fire was slow in coming." (ibid., 108) The ineluctable penalty for carelessness is death, a recompense exacted by the elements, the villain of the story. In a last glimpse, London juxtaposes his characters: the dog, well coated with fur and protected by instinct, trots away, leaving the unfortunate human to drift into eternal sleep.

During this period, London also published *The Sea Wolf* (1904), *The War of the Classes* (1905), the autobiographical *Martin Eden* (1909), *Burning Daylight* (1910), *The Iron Heel, Revolution and Other Essays* (1910), *The Valley of the Moon* (1913), and *John Barleycorn* (1913). Overall, he produced 50 books and hundreds of stories as well as a respectable portfolio of speeches and thousands of letters. Earning up to $75,000 a year as the most-read author of his time, London achieved lasting success but mishandled his money. To supplement royalty income, he lectured and wrote for West Coast newspapers and for *Colliers* and *Cosmopolitan*. In nonfiction works that empathize with the poor and downtrodden, he drew on firsthand knowledge of illegitimacy, alcoholism, and the opiates he took to stem kidney and back pain. From a two-year sea voyage about the South Pacific in the *Snark,* a homemade ketch, he derived an article about life in the leper colony that he visited in Hawaii. In 1913, London neared bankruptcy from medical problems and the loss of his manor house to arson. The last years of his life, marred by depression and chronic rheumatism, cost him both health and peace of mind. On November 21, 1916, he died of uremia and an overdose of morphine, which some biographers label as suicide. His ashes were interred by ranch workers and a few friends at a private ceremony at Beauty Ranch. (Beauchamp 1984; Franchere 1962; Hedrick 1982; "Jack London" 1996; Labor 1974; Labor and Reesman 1994; London, Jack 1964, 1965, 1966, 1980, 1982, 1991, 1992, 1996a, 1996b; London, Joan 1990; Lundquist 1987; Moore 1996; O'Connor 1964; Perry 1981; Rainey 1996; Sinclair 1983; Snodgrass 1991, 1995b; Stone 1978; Tavernier-Courbin 1994)

See also Alaska and the Yukon; *The Call of the Wild;* Harte, Bret.

⟨⟩ LONGFELLOW, HENRY WADSWORTH ⟨⟩

Master poet of vigorous, sonorous epic verse, Henry Wadsworth Longfellow was so well liked in England that he became the only American honored with a bust in Poet's Corner of Westminster Abbey, the burial place of England's finest writers. Much of his fame rests on mythmaking, as represented in two popular frontier narratives. The first, *Evangeline, a Tale of Arcadie* (1847), is a verse epic based on the thwarted romance of Emmeline Labiche, who was separated from her fiancé Louis Arceneaux during the Acadian diaspora along the Bay of Fundy, Nova Scotia. The second, *The Song of Hiawatha* (1855), is a fictionalized version of Iroquois lore taken from major sources: the sociological studies of Henry Rowe Schoolcraft, portraits and landscapes in George Catlin's *North American Indian Portfolio* (1844), Catlin's *Letters and Notes on the Manners, Customs and Condition of the North American Indians* (1841), and the 1849 novel *Dacotah, or Life and Legends of the Sioux around Fort Snelling* (1849), by Mary H. Eastman and illustrated by her husband, Seth Eastman. Famed for his romanticism and interest in Native American traditions, Longfellow dramatized the two masterworks with the same striking elements—vivid nature images and intense rhythm. Both *Hiawatha* and *Evangeline* have remained the most anthologized of his poetry.

Longfellow's background aided him in introducing Americans to the epic qualities of their history. Born on February 27, 1807, the son of attorney and congressman Stephen Longfellow and Zilpah Wadsworth Longfellow, a member of New England's aristocracy, the poet was the descendant of Puritans and grandson of Peleg Wadsworth, a general in the Revolutionary War. Longfellow grew up in his grandfather's three-story house in Portland, Maine, and entered Portland Academy at age 3. In childhood, his mother read to him from classic mythology and epic tradition. His favorite character was Don Quixote. At age 13, he published his first verse in the Portland *Gazette*.

In 1826, near the end of his senior year at Bowdoin College, Longfellow rejected his father's advice to enter the legal profession and made the choice between law and letters by accepting America's first chair in modern languages. After earning honors, he took three years to refine his knowledge by conducting a walking tour of France, Spain, Germany, and Italy. Ready to achieve his aim of becoming America's poet laureate, he returned home fluent in Swedish, Dutch, Finnish, Spanish, French, German, Italian, and Portuguese. He assumed the role of professor and librarian, produced America's first French and Spanish textbooks, and translated European classics into English. He also published poems and scholarly essays for the *North American Review, American Monthly Magazine, United States Literary Gazette, New York Ledger,* and *New England Magazine.* Foremost in his career was a desire to be the poet who acquainted Americans with their unique traditions.

Maturity brought contentment and fame as well as tragedy to Longfellow. He married childhood friend Mary Storer Potter, began concentrating on poetic technique, and, at age 28, was awarded the Smith professorship in modern language and belles lettres at Harvard University. This honor afforded him a second opportunity to study world epic on sabbatical in Europe. During the couple's journey to the Netherlands in 1836, Mary Longfellow died unexpectedly in Rotterdam of puerperal fever, a common cause of death to women following childbirth. Dismayed and lonely, Longfellow returned home a widower, settled at Craigie House in Cambridge, and resumed his role as a brilliant lecturer and mentor. He published *Voices in the Night* (1838), his first poetry collection, and an anthology of Western verse, *The Poets and Poetry of Europe* (1845). Subsequent publications include a semiautobiographical romance, *Hyperion* (1838); *The Village Blacksmith* (1840), a nostalgic reflection on one of his New England ancestors; *Ballads and Other Poems* (1841); *Poems on Slavery* (1842), which verbalized his abolitionism; and *The Belfry of Bruges* (1847).

Longfellow became a best-selling author and the first American to earn a living from writing verse after he composed *Evangeline*, a narrative romance he adapted from colleague Nathaniel Hawthorne. The idyll models classic dactylic hexameter, the six-beat meter of Homer's *Iliad*. Longfellow reshaped the central figures as Gabriel Lajeunesse and Evangeline Bellefontaine, symbolic names redolent with youth and beauty. The action, based on the historic deportation of French males from the reclaimed salt marshes of Acadia during the British settlement of Halifax in 1755, begins with the farmworkers' dramatic clash with English overlords, who force rural French Acadians to swear fealty to the British Crown. On the day of their betrothal, the couple are parted during *le grand dérangement* and forced into exile. Evangeline speaks a naive optimism: "Gabriel! be of good cheer! for if we love one another, Nothing, in truth, can harm us, whatever mischances may happen!" (Longfellow 1951, 67) She swoons as the reddening sky dramatizes the burning of Grand-Pré and the destruction of their hopes of return.

Longfellow heightens tension by having the two embark on separate ships with 6,000 refugees. Evangeline begins questioning any who might know where the English have dispersed other Acadians. In May, she and her companion, Father Felician, board a raft propelled by Acadian oarsmen and depart from the Ohio River toward the Mississippi River and Louisiana, the place where Gabriel was last sighted. Longfellow describes the beauties of the wild:

> Onward o'er sunken sands, through a wilderness sombre with forests,
> Day after day they glided adown the turbulent river;
> Night after night, by their blazing fires, encamped on its borders.
> Now through rushing chutes, among green islands, where plumelike,
> Cotton-trees nodded their shadowy crests, they swept with the current,
> Then emerged into broad lagoons, where silvery sandbars
> Lay in the stream, and along the wimpling waves of their margin,
> Shining with snow-white plumes, large flocks of pelicans waded. (ibid., 77–78)

On a serene landscape, Evangeline sweeps into the Bayou of Plaquemine, Louisiana. Ironically, she covers territory Gabriel has recently traversed. As she sleeps, the oarsmen sing Acadian tunes; in the distance they hear a blend of animal calls: "the whoop of the crane and the roar of the grim alligator." (ibid., 80)

Readers acquainted with Longfellow's loneliness following his wife's death recognize the source of his emotion. Near-misses recur as Evangeline and Gabriel search for each other along the Mississippi River; repeatedly, she senses that her love is near. When Basil reports Gabriel's departure for Ozark trapping grounds, she weeps and turns her eyes toward the town of Adayes, the place from which his party embarked. In the night, the oaks whisper, "Patience!" and the verdant meadow sighs, "Tomorrow!" (ibid., 93) The poet touches lightly on Gabriel's westward journey over the Oregon River and south to the Spanish Sierras and teases the imagination with Evangeline's sighting of his campfire at a distance. Tender yearning compels his protagonist to follow each lead, however unlikely, and to remain hopeful of a reunion.

Essential to the characterization is the saintliness of Evangeline, who takes time from her search to comfort a Shawnee woman whose Canadian husband was murdered by Comanches. The Shawnee's tales of phantom lovers chill Evangeline's heart. Six days after Gabriel's departure, she arrives at a Jesuit mission and waits until autumn, when he plans to return. Through fall, winter, and spring, she keeps her vigil, then gives up and follows him to the Saginaw River, where she finds his lodge tumbled to ruin. In a pathetic conclusion, Evangeline journeys through Quaker country; she reunites with her beloved, now a helpless old man. At his bedside in a Philadelphia almshouse, she witnesses his death from plague. After she, too, dies, the pair lie in unmarked graves, far from their Acadian roots.

Hymnodic and euphonious, the verse glides like a wandering voyager over much of frontier majesty. From the Gaspereau River in Nova Scotia, Longfellow guides his heroine past slave cabins and plantations, through the spiced scent of magnolia under willow boughs to Opelousas and onto the plains, thundering with herds of buffalo and circled above by vultures. Westward, she passes Hispanic herdsmen, relaxes to the music of Michael the Acadian fiddler, searches graveyards, and journeys to the isolated Western abode of a generous-hearted Black Robe, then back to Eastern cities. The conclusion on a Sunday morning in the "city of brother love" closes the poem in an appropriate setting—a colony founded on principles of tolerance. Briefly reunited with Gabriel, she intones a pious prayer, "Father, I thank Thee!" Like many immigrants to the frontier, Evangeline and her love die far from home and recede into the earth, leaving little trace of their lives and hopes.

Longfellow's pastoral tragedy took two years to write and polish. Filled with beneficent Americana, it draws on legend and local color as well as Audubon's bird studies, travelogues, maps, art, and eyewitness accounts for descriptions of the wilderness, which the poet had never visited. Longfellow de-emphasizes dangers and stresses the comfort that nature imparts to wanderers. He is particularly drawn to the majestic canopy of American trees: stands of cedar, the cathedral-like arches of cypress boughs, grand oaks, chinaberries, mimosa, and shady groves draped with vines and mosses. For its winsome grace and wholesome theme, *Evangeline* won American readers and flourished in Europe, where it was translated and widely quoted. The loyal and constant Evangeline is commemorated by statues in Grand-Pré, Nova Scotia, and St. Martinville, Louisiana.

The security of Longfellow's reputation as a master poet and man of principle and refined taste gave him the courage to resign his professorship in 1854 and to work full-time on verse. He intended to elevate American traditions to a noble position equivalent to the *Chanson de Roland, El Cid, Lusiad, Niebelungenlied, Beowulf,* and other Western heroic verse. For a better understanding of American Indians, he studied John Gottlieb Ernestus Heckewelder's *Account of the History, Manners and Customs of the Indian Nations,* and the *Algic Researches* (1839) and the five-volume *Historical and Statistical Information Respecting the History, Condition and Prospects of the Indian Tribes of the United States* (1857), both works of Ojibwa specialist Henry Rowe Schoolcraft, illustrated with engravings by Seth Eastman. Longfellow reshaped the information into *Hiawatha,* an artistic, imaginative American epic, the first literary use of Native Americans as significant subject matter. He chose his subject from the fusion of a tribal god with the semilegendary Hiawatha, a late-sixteenth-century Mohawk who founded the Iroquois League, a five-nation intertribal governing body that influenced American democracy.

To suit a dignified theme and subject, Longfellow chose trochaic tetrameter, the rhythm of the *Kalevala,* the Finnish epic. Striding forth in four pulsing drumbeats of short-long, short-long meter, the book-length poem foretokens a messiah among the Ojibwa—the coming of Hiawatha, a prophet and states-man sent by the master of life, Gitchie Manito, to enrich tribal life and establish peace. For this purpose, the poet fashions a chivalric, contemplative hero, a pathfinder endowed with gentility, sensitivity, and sagacity. A mediator similar to Moses and King Arthur, Hiawatha leads his people from the savagery of a warring society to a higher level of civilization.

Crucial to Longfellow's theme is the stabilization of the Ojibwa. The poem depicts the ritual of peace as the smoking of the sacred calumet, which was made from steatite or catlinite, the sacred red stone quarried from Pipestone, a section of Minnesota that tribes worked jointly. *Hiawatha* describes how the hero teaches people to grow maize and gather and apply the medicinal herbs that grow along Lake Superior at Iron River, Wisconsin. He urges them to set down their cures and lore in pictographs:

> Nor forgotten was the Love-song,
> The most subtle of all medicines,
> The most potent spell of magic,
> Dangerous more than war or hunting;
> Thus the Love-song was recorded,
> Symbol and interpretation. (ibid., 104)

At the end of his lecture on the importance of securing Ojibwa history in picture writing, Hiawatha asks that his people learn the "heart within a circle," the symbol of the receptive spirit that lies unprejudiced and ready to absorb instruction.

Conflict brought about by Chibiabos the mischief maker and by the deaths of Hiawatha's companion Kwasind and wife Minnehaha weighs heavily on the hero. Canto XX mourns the fever that accompanies famine. It describes how Minnehaha

> Lay down on her bed in silence,
> Hid her face, but made no answer;
> Lay there trembling, freezing, burning
> At the looks they cast upon her,
> At the fearful words they uttered. (ibid., 143)

In grief, Hiawatha flees from her side and roams the forest calling her name. At her grave, he instructs her not to return to pain and toil but to await his transition from earth to the land beyond.

Shortly before Hiawatha's death, Longfellow introduces a highly idealized motif of the white settler. Iagoo the traveler foretells the arrival of a great-winged canoe. He describes to unbelieving listeners the hundred white-faced Europeans sailing over bitter waters vaster than any they can imagine. Longfellow envisions an era of unity as woodlands ring with axe blows and smoke floats over valleys and lakes. In reference to the Indian wars, he mentions that nations will be scattered in the westward sweep, "Like the cloud-rack of a tempest, like the withered leaves of Autumn." (Longfellow 1993, 153) After the Black Robe chief arrives in Ojibwa territory, he pronounces a Christian blessing, wishing "Peace of prayer, and peace of pardon, Peace of Christ, and joy of Mary!" (ibid., 156) Thus, the poet sends his hero to heaven after the tribe is safely Christianized.

Longfellow's view of an Iroquois golden age and an afterlife blends animism, epic lore, and the Christian concept of the hereafter. Sometimes called the Indian Edda, *The Song of Hiawatha* echoes the influence of it and other European epics, particularly the *Kalevala*, Homer's *Iliad* and *Odyssey*, the Norse *Niebelungenlied*, Virgil's *Aeneid*, and Torquato Tasso's *Jerusalem Delivered*. The charm and serenity of the earthly Indian idyll, set on the Iron River in Wisconsin, foretell a time of Native American progress and harmony yet is freighted with prophecy of the eventual loss of land and power to European settlers. Based on oral tradition, *The Song of Hiawatha* was an unparalleled favorite of children and adults for half a century. Parodists continue to mimic the poet's skill with rhetorical devices by adapting the repetition, parallelism, alliteration, and THUMP-thump of strings of trochees into humorous applications.

Longfellow followed his successful *Hiawatha* with two of his best-received works, *The Courtship of Miles Standish* (1855), based on his family ancestors, John and Priscilla Alden, and *Tales of the Wayside Inn* (1863), which included "Paul Revere's Ride." Composed of varied themes and plots, *Tales of the Wayside Inn* resembles the plan and arrangement of Geoffrey Chaucer's *Canterbury Tales*. At the height of his creativity, Longfellow married his landlord's daughter, Frances Elizabeth "Fanny" Appleton, and spent the remainder of his life in Craigie Hall, home of his and Fanny's three daughters and two sons. In the twentieth year of a harmonious marriage, his wife was fatally injured while packing family memorabilia. The sealing wax caught fire in her hands and ignited her dress. Longfellow, grieved by personal tragedy and by the outbreak of the Civil War, took solace from writing verse and traveling Europe while polishing his translation of *The Divine Comedy*, which introduced unschooled Americans to Dante.

For his imitation of European styles, themes, and motifs, Longfellow received accolades from both sides of the Atlantic, honorary degrees from Oxford and Cambridge, and membership in the Spanish Academy and the Russian Academy of Sciences. Both Queen Victoria and the Prince of Wales invited him for visits, and foreign guests in New England sought him out as a high point of their American tour. For a century after his death on March 24, 1882, at his home in Cambridge, Massachusetts, his works remained a strong influence on school curricula. Speakers committed his verse to memory for declamation at formal events. Today, his Victorian optimism, inoffensive gentility, and fervid nationalism seem dated alongside the harsher, more strident realism of the twentieth century, yet teachers return to his lines for models of eloquence. (Brooks 1940; Dexter 1972; Kennedy 1972; Longfellow 1951, 1993; Patterson and Snodgrass 1994; Rabe 1996; Ruland and Bradbury 1991; Trent et al. 1946; Wagenknecht 1986; Westbrook 1988; Williams 1964)

𝔽 THE LOST COLONY 𒀭

A much-debated episode from North Carolina history, the Lost Colony names an ill-fated settlement: the "Cittie of Ralegh" on Roanoke Island in the vast Pamlico, Albemarle, Roanoke, and Croatan Sounds that separate the bulk of North Carolina from the Outer Banks, a thin strip of offshore islands. After Queen Elizabeth chartered Sir Humphrey Gilbert to found a New World colony in 1578, he died on the return voyage from Newfoundland. In 1584, his half brother, Sir Walter Raleigh, renewed the royal charter. The settlement got off to a promising start in the spring of 1585 with Simon Fernando, a pilot of good reputation, leading the fleet west from Plymouth harbor. The group established Fort Raleigh on Roanoke Island in June 1585 with Ralph Lane as governor. As described by Arthur Barlowe, captain of the second of the original fleet, in a formal report to Raleigh, the newly colonized land—referred to as part of Virginia, an unsurveyed land mass named for Elizabeth I, the virgin queen—was sweet-smelling, overrun with grapes, and echoing with the calls of cranes. He assured his English master that rabbits, deer, and fowl offered an abundance of food and that tall stands of cedar provided wood for building and fuel. At this point in English colonial history, success seemed certain.

A pair of sources, Richard Hakluyt's *The Principal Navigations, Voyages, and Discoveries of the English Nation* (1589) and the undated *Discourse of Western Planting,* offer general information about the colony's harbor, landfall, and resources, which he apparently gathered from Barlowe and Captain Philip Amadas after their return voyage in 1585. However, the prospects of a flourishing New World colony failed to convince Queen Elizabeth to invest in the venture, which entered the second stage in 1585 with seven ships, supplies, and 15 men under the command of Sir Richard Grenville. The next year, storms and limited supplies compelled the settlers to abandon Fort Raleigh and leave with Sir Francis Drake, who was returning from the West Indies to England by way of the Roanoke colony. When Grenville reached the fort, he found it empty. He left men and supplies and departed for England. On May 8, 1587, 115 voyagers left England to settle in the colonies. They reached Fort Raleigh on July 22 and discovered the remains of Grenville's crew, whom hostile Indians had killed. The colonists stayed on the island and built the city of Raleigh around the fortress. On August 18, Virginia Dare, first English child born in the New World, was welcomed to the colony and baptized six days later. By August 27, Governor John White had returned to England for supplies.

During England's war with the Spanish, which ended in 1588 with the defeat of the Spanish Armada, the mother country lost contact with the settlers of Roanoke Island. For unknown reasons, around 1587 the remaining colonists disappeared. Pirates impeded White on his return voyage to Roanoke. In 1590, searchers led by White found only fragmented clues, including the famous three letters—CRO—on a tree growing out of a dune on the island's north end. White comments,

> We passed toward the place where they were left in sundry houses, but we found the houses taken down and the place very strongly enclosed with a

high palisade of great trees, with curtains and flankers very fortlike, and one of the chief trees or posts at the right side of the entrance had the bark taken off and five feet from the ground in fair capital letters was graven CROATOAN without any cross or sign of distress. ("Before Jamestown" 1990, 5)

White anticipated the cross as a prearranged symbol of danger or attack. In its absence, he assumed that the colonists had departed in peace to the Outer Banks. A storm forced him toward the West Indies before he could launch a wider search. Additional information comes from Thomas Harriot's *A Briefe and True Report of the New Found Land of Virginia* (1590), which gives a full account of Indian traditions, religion, hunting and fishing, homes, dress, and customs. Additional details gleaned from Governor White's skillful drawings affirm studies of native villages but supply little useful information about the missing English settlers.

In 1602, after the Queen abandoned the royal experiment in the New World, Raleigh mounted a private hunt for survivors, whom White deduced had moved to a Croatoan settlement near Cape Hatteras. George Percy of the Jamestown colony reported in 1607 that he saw a blond-haired, fair-skinned Indian boy on the James River; a similar smidgen of evidence in Captain John Smith's *True Relation of such occurrences and accidents of noate as hath hapned in Virginia since the first planting of that Collony* (1608) offers secondhand information about a Pamunkey king who saw men in Ocanahonan wearing English clothes. A second report from a chief in Weramocomoco attests to settlers owning brass and building walled dwellings like those at the Roanoke fort. Other seventeenth-century details crop up in letters, memoirs of crosses carved on trees, and reports of gray-eyed and book-educated people among the native population.

Based on these events, Paul Green's historical drama, *The Lost Colony* (1937), is America's longest-running outdoor play. The drama is performed for six weeks each summer on the site of the first landings on Roanoke Island in Manteo, North Carolina. The text honors the 350th birthday of Virginia Dare, who had played through his memory alongside "rotting ribs of many a ship, the disappearing records of struggle and death." (Adams 1951) In the text, 118 colonists (identified in a prefatory list broken down into assistants to Governor White, male colony members, female colony members, and children) exhibit familiar English names, particularly Browne, Chapman, Colman, Dare, Harris, Johnson, Jones, Little, Taylor/Tayler, and Wyles. In the opening scene, set on Roanoke Island in summer 1584, their voices join in three stanzas of "O God that madest earth and sky," a praise anthem typical of seventeenth-century hymnody, which precedes the minister's prayer and a salute to the pioneer:

O lusty singer, dreamer, pioneer,
Lord of the wilderness, the unafraid,
Tamer of darkness, fire and floor,
Of the soaring spirit winged aloft
On the plumes of agony and death—
Hear us, O hear!
The dream still lives,

It lives, it lives,
And shall not die! (Green 1937, 4–5)

Against a theatrical background with the chorus in period costume, a character known as the historian appends the brief note that the English-speaking settlers intend to colonize the New World. Led by explorers Philip Amadas and Arthur Barlowe, they had left the homeland in April 1584 and alighted on Roanoke Island three months later, when local tribes were harvesting corn.

Following a pantomime of the Indian tribe receiving news of the arrival of strange white people, the historian describes how Wanchese inflamed the settlers' desire for treasure with a report of riches at the head of the Roanoke River. Manteo disputes the report, yet he and Wanchese are selected to bear the news of treasure to England. After meeting with the queen, Raleigh, and interested parties in spring 1585, the group recruits 108 English citizens for a voyage that splits forces between Roanoke and Jamestown, a colony established to the north on the James River. Commander Ralph Lane enslaves the Indians and murders Wingina, an innocent tribesman. Tensions between the tribe and colonists destroy the original settlement.

Green alternately lightens and darkens the atmosphere as he unfolds the events that shape Carolina history. In May 1587, Raleigh sends a replacement colony of 121 from Plymouth, which arrives July 23 at the barren fort and reclaims it for England. The colonists claim as a propitious sign Virginia Dare's birth on August 18 to Ananias and Eleanor White Dare, daughter of Governor White, but an Indian ambush two days later proves otherwise. Manteo, who is baptized in the Christian faith, defends the English. During Governor John White's absence to ferry provisions from England, hardship depletes the colony. The survivors depart for Croatoan, leaving their destination carved on a tree. Green surmises that the remaining few were killed by Spanish adventurers, died on the journey, or were assimilated by Indians.

Although more recent historical, archival, and archeological inquiry has elucidated previous misconceptions, Green's version remains unchanged. Researches have denounced as hoaxes a spurious booklet and the scattering of rocks carved with VWD [Virginia White Dare] and known as "Virginia Dare's diary" and have discredited evidence that the English settlers fell victim to the Spanish. Plausible theories explaining the group's disappearance cluster into three possibilities: resettlement on the Outer Banks, where survivors of the fort's decline either starved, were slain by Wanchese's men alone or in conjunction with Powhatan's forces, or were swept away by offshore storms and hurricanes; departure as planned to Chesapeake Bay and settlement on Lynnhaven Bay near Norfolk, Virginia; and embarkation by boat to the Atlantic Ocean, where the ill-prepared few are presumed capsized and drowned. Current conjecture favors a blend of possibilities: that some colonists may have rejoined English families on the Chesapeake Bay, some may have moved inland to Lumbee settlements on the Lumber River, and a small party may have remained to tell Governor White of the colony's move and settled with Manteo's people at the town of Croatoan. Historians conclude that most probably died of disease, accident, or exhaustion. (Adams 1951; Arner 1985; Bayly 1989; "Before Jamestown" 1990; Charles 1996; Green 1937; Harriot 1972; Smith 1967; Stick 1983; Waldman 1990; Walser, 1956; Wynn 1990)

See also Green, Paul; Harriot, Thomas; theater of the frontier.

LOVE, NAT

One of the few black cowboys to leave a memoir of frontier life, Nat Love is the author of an informative if inflated autobiography, *The Life and Adventures of Nat Love, Better Known in the Cattle Country as Deadwood Dick* (1907), which he claims to be a "true history of slavery days, life on the great cattle ranges and on the plains of the 'wild and woolly' west, based on facts, and personal experiences of the author." Born into slavery in June 1854, he was a native of Davidson County, Tennessee. He lived on Robert Love's plantation near Nashville in a log cabin that he pictures in a pen-and-ink drawing. He records little about his father, a plantation foreman and Union army carpenter, or his mother, a kitchen domestic and weaver. He names Jordan and Sally as his older siblings and recalls that emancipation left his family destitute but eager for literacy.

After hiring out to neighboring plantations, Love worked his father's tobacco fields. His father's death left him accountable as head of the family; he found work six miles from home and earned $1.50 per month. He got a second job breaking colts, the beginning of a career as a horseman and ranch hand. His uncle took his place as head of the family in 1869 so that Love could migrate to Dodge City, Kansas. With pride, he recalls that his boss supplied "a saddle, bridle and spurs, chaps, a pair of blankets and a fine .45 Colt revolver." (Love 1988, 41) On the initial ride toward the Texas panhandle, he encountered 100 Indians in war paint, who stampeded his party's herd of horses.

Love's reminiscence is a testimony to determination. While employed in Texas at the Duval Ranch and later at the Gillinger Ranch in Arizona, he mastered roping, branding, and marksmanship and claims to have taken part in gun battles with outlaws. In addition, he learned Spanish, a skill that increased his value as a herdsman among *vaqueros*. During branding season, he worked alongside many cowboys "who lived, ate and often slept in the saddle, as they covered many hundreds of miles in a very short space of time." (ibid., 47) Work took him to Montana, Wyoming, the Dakotas, and Nebraska, where he served his employer by battling horse thieves and more Indians.

The height of Love's career came on July 4, 1876, at a rodeo in Deadwood, South Dakota, where he earned the nickname "Deadwood Dick." He describes winning with straightforward boast:

> I roped, threw, tied, bridled, saddled and mounted my mustang in exactly nine minutes from the crack of the gun. The time of the next nearest competitor was twelve minutes and thirty seconds. This gave me the record and championship of the West, which I held up to the time I quit the business in 1890, and my record has never been beaten. (ibid., 93)

Rider and roper Nat Love, also known as Deadwood Dick.

At the time of his victory in the arena, the news of General George Armstrong Custer's defeat was just reaching Deadwood, heightening fears of an Indian revolt. The return trip took Love through hostile territory, but he maintains that his party gave little thought to "bloodthirsty redskins." (ibid., 95)

Love's insouciance proved his undoing in October 1876, when he was captured by Indians in Yellow Horse Canyon after being shot in the leg and using up his ammunition. His captors dressed the wound and adopted him into their tribe, which he does not identify. He participated in the medicine dance and married a chief's daughter, who brought him a dowry of 100 ponies. After a daring night departure, he returned to work in Dodge City, then rode to Junction City over the Haze and Elsworth Trail. It was during this period of employment that he claims to have known William H. Bonney, alias Billy the Kid, who drank with him in a saloon in Antonshico, New Mexico. Love confirms Billy's story that he shot men who worked for John Chisholm [Chisum], the employer who cheated him of his wages. Love remarks that the last time he saw Billy, "he was laying dead at Pete Maxwell's ranch in Lincoln county, New Mexico, having been killed by Pat A. Garret." (ibid., 121)

Unlike many life stories of the West that end in failure, disappointment, or death, Love's autobiography concludes with success and optimism. He worked 20 years as a drover and wrangler throughout the American Southwest and Mexico and earned a reputation for recognizing cattle brands, hunting buffalo for ranch meat, and performing fancy lariat and riding tricks. At age 46, he fell in love in Mexico:

> I saw a handsome young Spanish girl standing in the yard and I suppose I fell
> in love with her at first sight, anyway I pretended to be very thirsty and rode
> up and asked her for a drink. (ibid., 125)

After she followed him on the trail, they married and, in 1890, settled in Colorado. Love took a job on the Denver and Rio Grande Railroad at $15 per month as a Pullman porter, one of the professions that offered the most upward mobility to black males. At age 54, he completed his autobiography, which he dedicated to his mother and his wife, Alice.

Much of Love's autobiography appears to draw on the frontier convention of the tall tale. He claims that horses were shot out from under him and that his body survived numerous bullets, one of which passed through him and killed his mount. In the final chapter, he boasts that he knew Buffalo Bill, Kit Carson, Frank and Jesse James, Kiowa Bill, and Yellowstone Kelley. Love's moralizing, astonishing deeds, and bold assertions of on-the-scene knowledge of much of the West's history suggests that he had a failing for romance, a standard feature of frontier literature. (Estell 1993; Love 1988; Low and Clift 1981; Stewart and Ponce 1986)

See also Billy the Kid; Custer, George Armstrong.

MILLER, JOAQUIN

A Western original, Joaquin Miller took his pen name from the California out-law Joaquin Murietta. Born Cincinnatus Hiner (or Heine) Miller, he jettisoned his given name and took on the persona of the "Sweet Singer of the Sierras" and the "Byron of Oregon," the state he claimed to have popularized in verse. As a frontiersman, he tried numerous lifestyles—squaw man, preacher, vigilante, prospector, entrepreneur, lawman, editor—before settling into writing. One of the era's neglected regionalists, he briefly maintained his reputation for verse, fiction, and editing before critical opinion turned against his derivative style and relegated him to a back bench behind Mark Twain, Jack London, Ambrose Bierce, and Bret Harte.

Facts of Miller's early life are muddled by half-truths and falsifications. The son of Quaker farmers Hulings and Margaret DeWitt Miller, he was born on March 10, 1839 (or possibly 1837 or 1841), on a farm near Liberty, Indiana, although he later claimed that his birth took place while his family's wagons were in transit over the Oregon Trail. When his family decided to relocate on better farmland in the Willamette Valley of Oregon in 1852, he was not yet a teenager. Two years later, Miller and another boy traveled south to work the California gold mines on the Klamath River. During the Battle of Castle Crags, a fight between Modoc Indians and the homesteaders of Mt. Shasta in June 1855, Miller survived the passage of an arrow through his face and into his neck. Subsequent failure at prospecting near Squawtown left him homesick and miserable. He wrote four stanzas, hoping to give up his diet of "chile beans, shortbeef, and rusty bacon" and to quit the "mud and mire and rain." In mock-serious desperation he concludes, "I havent half the chance to get back there/ Than I have to go to hell sir." (Frost 1967, 23)

The undocumented events of Miller's adult life are interwoven with more mistakes, hearsay, lies, and "stretchers." He claimed to have journeyed on William Walker's expedition to Nicaragua and back up the Pacific Coast to Mt. Shasta, where he lived for two years among the Digger Indians with his Native American wife Paquita and daughter, Cali-Shasta. For two months, he studied law at Columbia College in Eugene, Oregon, then returned to Shasta City, where he was jailed for mule theft. He sawed through a barred window, leaving behind a saucy note laced with scripture. A scrape with the law in 1860 left a

Poet Joaquin Miller

constable wounded in the arm by a single rifle shot from Miller. A bench warrant put a price of $2,000 on his head for assaulting an officer.

Miller taught school in Clarke, Washington, and studied law with an attorney before resuming prospecting, this time in Oro Fino, Idaho, where no warrant awaited him. Around 1861, he financed a home, bought the Eugene *Democratic Register,* and, from his mining success, founded an express business linking Millersburg, Idaho, and Walla Walla, Washington. After selling out to Wells Fargo in 1862, he married poet Theresa "Minnie Myrtle" Dyer and turned full-time to journalism. Still aggrieved at his brother's death in the Civil War, Miller wrote a pacifist poem, "After All," which mourned a "nameless grave in the battle-field," and used his newspaper to express antiwar and secessionist sentiments. (ibid., 30) Because local Unionists accused him of treason, he labeled them lurking Federal spies. His paper ceased publication after it was denied passage through the U.S. mail.

Because of his leadership of a posse against hostile Indians in 1866, Miller regained respectability. He was elected judge of Grant County, Oregon, and presided over the court of Canon City, Colorado, where he also served as mayor and minister. During this part of his lengthy writing career, he submitted poems to the prestigious *Overland Monthly* and asked that the journal publish his poetry collection. Editor Bret Harte rejected Miller's efforts because of their illiterate dialect and theatricality. In dismay, Harte warned, "Let this informal and well-meaning attempt at criticism take the place of a notice in the 'O. M.'" (O'Connor 1966, 108)

Unfazed by Harte's ungenerous critique, Miller produced two verse collections, *Specimens* (1868) and *Joaquin et al.* (1869) and sent the latter to the *Overland Monthly* for a formal critique. The central poem of the second volume features rhymed couplets detailing the death of the real Joaquin, a cardsharp and highwayman whom Miller invests with the glamour and hardihood commonly found in heroes of dime novels and exaggerated journalism. Critics surmise that the figure is Miller's fantasy, a cardboard hero decked with Hollywood trappings. Harte, as he indicated in earlier correspondence, had no taste for the "florid dramatics" of Miller's subsequent works and noted that the poet's "neck is generally clothed with thunder, and the glory of his nostrils is terrible." (ibid.) This public laceration galled Miller late into his career, even though he was published in the *Overland* after Harte resigned.

In 1870, Miller turned his attentions from the West at the same time that he enlarged its myth. Dressed in buckskins, red flannel shirt, high-top boots, bear cape, and sombrero, he toured Europe and satisfied the European's mental picture of frontier picturesqueness. In England, he squired around his old nemesis, Bret Harte, and led a pilgrimage to Charles Dickens's tomb. In treks across South America, he gained a reputation for exhibitionism, eccentric behavior, and Byronic posing. Onstage, he accentuated public recitations with puffs from oversized cigars and related personal anecdotes that bore the stamp of episodes pilfered from cheap Western fiction.

While abroad, Miller published verse collections—*Song of the Sierras* (1871) and a suspect Western memoir, *Unwritten History: Life among the Modocs* (1873)—

both embraced by French and English audiences. He wrote a novel, *The One Fair Woman* (1876), and an anti-Mormon drama, *The Danites in the Sierras,* which debuted on August 22, 1877. Based on the theme of law and order, family, and wilderness beauty, it became one of the West's most popular stage dramas and fared well in Great Britain. Less successful were three plays published in 1881: *Forty-Nine, Tally Ho!,* and *An Oregon Idyll.*

Divorced and remarried to New York heiress Abigail Leland, Miller separated from her and lived in a rustic lodge in Washington, D.C., a tourist attraction for which he penned "To My Log Cabin Lovers." After his return to the West, his widowed mother, Margaret Miller, came to live with him and his daughter at "The Hermitage, Oakland Heights," his Oakland, California, ranch. Still eager to publish, he served as associate editor of *The Golden Era.* During the Klondike gold rush of 1897, he visited the Yukon, crossed the Chilkoot Pass, and earned $6,000 for dispatches printed in Hearst newspapers. After traveling as a correspondent in the Sandwich Islands for the *Overland Monthly* and covering the Boxer Rebellion in China, he lectured on his experiences. A determined showman, he dressed for the occasion in fur parka, mukluks, and vest buttoned with gold nuggets. He broadened his canon with a protest novel, *Shadows of Shasta* (1891), about the displacement of Indians from ancestral lands; *The Building of the City Beautiful* (1893), a utopian romance; and *The Illustrated History of Montana* (1894). He died in Oakland on February 17, 1913, and was cremated at his estate.

Known as the "Poet of the Sierras," Miller produced six picturesque verse collections that helped to introduce Eastern readers to the raw edge of the mining camp and the grandeur of West Coast scenery. Critics accuse him of being a mythmaker, of falling in love with his roguish poetic persona, and of creating the mystique of "Joaquin" to replace the mundane "Cincinnatus." Among his memorable nature works are "Dead in the Sierras," "Yosemite," "By the Sun-Down Seas," and "California's Cup of Gold," an eight-line stanza that praises the beauty of the California poppy, "the gold that knows no miser's hold." ("Poetry of Joaquin Miller" 1996, 3) His melodramatic narrative, *Joaquin Murietta,* an overlong, macho action poem, contrasts the freedom and grandeur of the Sierras with the bloodred hand of the young *bandito,* who survives betrayal and rides south to safety in Mexico with his sweetheart. Perhaps more appealing to readers of frontier verse is the heroic "Columbus," which depicts the brave captain urging his men, "Sail on! sail on! and on!" (Ehrlich and Carruth 1982, 419) (Crystal 1995; Ehrlich and Carruth 1982; Frost 1967; Hart 1983; Hazard 1927; Lamar 1977; Miller 1922; Nevins 1955; O'Connor 1966; "Poetry of Joaquin Miller" 1996; Rasmussen 1995)

See also Bierce, Ambrose; Harte, Bret; London, Jack; Mormons; Oregon Trail; Twain, Mark.

MOMADAY, N. SCOTT

Teacher, philosopher, writer, storyteller, and Native American sage, Navarre Scott Momaday has evolved into a significant literary voice of the late twentieth century. A spokesperson for Native American history on Ken Burns's and Stephen Ives's PBS-TV series *The West*, Momaday moves with erudition and efficiency over the troubled terrain of Western history, speaking without malice of the American destruction of the buffalo and the plains tradition. A Kiowa and a gifted professor of comparative literature, he writes of the past as though he is recalling his own life. His works stand at the forefront of the Native American renaissance.

Momaday connects his obsession with clan and kin relations to two influences: childhood memories of his paternal grandparents, Mammadaty and Aho, and his mother's revolt against the assimilationism of Haskell Institute, the government-run Indian boarding school she attended. Born February 1934 in Lawton, Oklahoma, to Mayme Natachee Scott and Alfred Momaday, he remains close to the animistic traditions of the Kiowa through the naming ceremony at Devil's Tower, where his step-grandfather Pohd-lohk named him Rock-Tree Boy. He attended grade school in Hobbs and in Jemez, in the high country of New Mexico, where his parents taught, and completed high school at a Virginia military academy. His scholarly studies include degrees from the University of New Mexico and Stanford and, in 1975, an unprecedented Fulbright lectureship in Russia in American Literature.

Momaday won a Pulitzer Prize for his first novel, *House Made of Dawn* (1968), a compassionate study of Abel, an orphaned Indian youth who labors to bridge the chasm between his Indian upbringing and the white world. The sequel, *The Way to Rainy Mountain* (1969), illustrated by Momaday's father, is a poetic montage that juxtaposes segments of Kiowa history with myth and with Momaday's childhood memories. Momaday's sense of place compels him to reconstruct the tests of his people's unity that mark the end of the Kiowa's golden age: a prophetic meteor shower in 1833, the famine of 1848–1849, the burning of the ceremonial teepee in 1872, pressure by the army in 1874, and the last Sun Dance of 1888. One of the calendric series of winters that stands out in Kiowa memory, the 1834 visit by plains artist George Catlin, resulted in the portrait of a handsome warrior, whom Momaday wished he had met.

The intense portraits of Momaday's grandparents become one with Kiowa history, which ends with enforced residence at the Fort Sill reservation. In a grasp at hope, he recalls how his Grandmother Aho turned meat in her skillet and how she leaned on her cane when she walked. He beatifies her at prayer as she stands by her bed, stripped to the waist, her hair unbraided and resting on her shoulders like a shawl. He says, "I do not speak Kiowa, and I never understood her prayers, but there was something inherently sad in the sound, some merest hesitation upon the syllables of sorrow." (Momaday 1969, 10) Recalled near the end of her life, the pose encompasses the last of Momaday's visions of her.

A multidimensional writer, Momaday has published and illustrated *In the Presence of the Sun: Stories and Poems 1961–1991* (1992), which features striking shield drawings as visual tokens of Plains Society's flair for war. A feast of images, reminiscence, history, and polemics, his mature work bests earlier stirrings blended with Western lore—*The Gourd Dancer* (1976), *The Names* (1976), and *The Ancient Child* (1990). A trenchant spokesperson for Native American art and being, Momaday has suffered a fragmented reputation that began to take shape during the rise of multiculturalism in public schools and universities. Much sought as a speaker and anthologized in textbooks in the late 1980s and 1990s, he appears to have overcome the tag of native writer to take his rightful place among humanists. (Bode 1993; Lamar 1977; Milner et al. 1994; Momaday 1968, 1969, 1992; Roemer 1988; Trimble 1973; Van Deventer 1992; Velie 1982; Woodard 1989)

MORMONS

The Mormon saga is a unique component in the history of the American West. A story of pioneer spirit compounded with religious zeal, the movement of individual wagon trains toward the Mormon enclave in Salt Lake City is the driving force of *Winter Quarters, The 1846–1848 Life Writings of Mary Haskin Parker Richards* (1996), one of the many diaries composed by frontier women. A religious refugee from Chaigley in Lancashire, England, Richards traveled to the transitional lodgings on the Missouri River, then crossed Iowa during a period of great travail and disease for her fellow Latter Day Saints. Of the epic journey she writes:

> Never shall I forget the feeling that shriled through my Bosem this day. while parting with all my dear Brothers & Sisters. and all my kindred who were near & dear to me by the ties of nature. and expecialy my Dear Sick Sister and her companion. who needed my assistance. to travil to a distant Port. from there to venture upon the wide Expanded Ocean. behind wich to wander in a strange Land in wich I should be a stranger. (Richards 1996, 1)

She grieves at the separation that takes her husband back to England to enter the Mormon mission field. Her one hope is to reunite with her parents, who had already arrived in Utah.

In contrast to Richards's intense, moving journal, non-Mormon writings vary from curious to unsympathetic to overtly hostile. Early on, Mormons attained a reputation for odd behavior and for setting themselves apart from other settlers of the West. The folklore of Mormon country bears markings of a distinct culture of educated middle-class and professional-class Westerners. Over 150 versions of the story of the Three Nephites have surfaced in Utah from 1855 to the present, evidence that unnamed messengers of Christ wander North America in unassuming guise, visiting the sick and lonely and receiving human hospitality, primarily from isolated women. According to the Book of Mormon, III Nephi 19:4, the three aged men received their commission directly from Christ. Typically, in payment for a meal, refreshment, or a stopping place on their journey, they work miracles, such as curing a sick infant, and then vanish. Parallels of the immortal Wandering Jew and Christian saints, they bless, uplift, rescue, heal, and spread goodwill. Self-perpetuating because they reflect Mormon values, the stories of the beneficent Nephites have regenerated with such modern versions as the ghost hitchhiker in the desert.

According to Thomas Farnham's judgmental commentary, *Travels in the Great Western Prairies* (1839), Mormons differentiated themselves from other Americans by claiming to be God's saints, endowed with the promise of inheriting the earth. This purported high-handedness strained relations with Missourians, whose backlash of 1838 derived from loss of timber and crops, which Mormons stole as their rightful share of the "bounty of God." Tongue in cheek, he adds:

> For whenever they took corn from fields in possession of the world's people, they not only avoided exciting unholy wrath by allowing themselves to be seen in the act, but, in order that peace might reign in the bosoms of the wicked, even, the longest possible time, they stripped that portion of the harvest field which would be last seen by the ungodly owner. (Farnham 1983, 5)

This thinly veiled accusation of deception and pilfering depicts the sojourners as sneak thieves deserving of public scorn and retribution. Accordingly, locals, adhering to earthly law, denounced the "Prophet Joe" (Joseph Smith) and waged the Mormon Wars to rid themselves of crop-stealing pests. In mock biblical language, Farnham derides their wooden storehouse, which vigilantes raided to retrieve stolen goods. The outbreak of violence sent Mormons on their way west to a more hospitable locale.

From personal studies, Farnham questions Smith's claim that a divine source, the Angel Moroni, revealed buried coded manuscripts to him in 1823, which he extricated in 1827 and translated into the Book of Mormon in 1830. According to Farnham, the Mormon scripture is actually a novel written by Rev. Solomon Spaulding, a Dartmouth graduate and resident of New Salem, Ohio, who supposedly completed the text in 1812. Farnham asserts that Sidney Rigdon copied the work and that Joseph Smith elevated it to holy scripture and used it to "[build] up a system of superstition," which Farnham compares to Islam. (ibid.) The extreme condemnation in Farnham's discussion weakens his arguments, which are founded on deep-seated bigotry.

Written nearly four decades after Farnham's *Travels in the Great Western Prairies*, one of the unique dialect plays of the West illustrates the prejudice settlers continued to bear against Mormons in the second half of the nineteenth century. Joaquin Miller's *Danites of the Sierras* (1876) succeeded both in the West and in England, where it debuted in 1877. Riddled with simplistic generalizations about the devout, the play depicts ingenuous and corrupt characters, the extremes of the moral continuum. Saccharine in the style of Bret Harte's "The Outcasts of Poker Flat," the sanctimonious conclusion focuses on the Widow, a strong, nature-loving female whose goodness influences mob-oriented miners. She is so imbued with piety that her presence blunts the zeal of frontier vigilantism, which threatens imminent destruction to two groups of outsiders, the Mormons and Washee Washee, the lone Chinese resident.

A dominant motif of *Danites of the Sierras* is the resilience of anti-Mormon suspicion. Act I opens in a haunted house where the Danites, a secret protective agency of the cult, reputedly assassinated three miners from Hannibal, Missouri. Miller's exposition implies that the victims had participated in the lynching of Joseph Smith, which occurred at a jail in Carthage, Illinois, on June 28, 1844. In an awkward blend of bathos and heavy-handed villainy, the play explores the current of justifiable vengeance that compels the Danites to stalk the "hundred masked men that killed the Mormon Prophet, Joe Smith" and jeopardized the Mormons' peaceful western migration. According to the Judge, "the Danites hunted 'em down, every one, even away out here in the heart of the Sierras." (Miller 1922, 383) Modeled on the stereotypical "hanging judge," he suspects people who live apart from general society and categorizes missionaries of all types as "hungry, Bible-howlin' varmints, I do believe." (ibid., 384) The Parson interjects his hostility in a parallel generalization: "Oh, I know the white choker gentry. They will have the best in the land and pay nothing. They never miss a meal and never pay a cent." (ibid., 386) The Judge decides to declare the missionary guilty and execute him summarily, without investigation or jury trial.

Miller creates tension through an obvious pairing of literary foils. When the missionary in question arrives, the benevolent Widow, a kind-spoken, upbeat woman, offsets local prejudice with ingenuous goodness. She lauds the industry of local miners, whom she typifies as "the pure gold from the earth." (ibid., 388) She welcomes the Parson to preach at every service, thus winning his love, which he conceals until the last act. The diversion of vigilantes refocuses the Judge and his henchmen on a more obvious victim, Washee Washee, a limp Asian caricature further weakened by his penchant for brandy and his seriocomic pidgin English: "Melican man no comee. No catchee Chinaman. Melican man he no comee. Chinaman he no go." (ibid.)

Miller's plot rushes to a melodramatic clash between bullying whites and Washee Washee, an easily identified minority whom they intend to hang. The intervention of the saintly Widow halts their conspiracy. Like the medieval saint who walks unscathed amid evil, she lifts the rope from his neck; the mob stands back as though cowed by her goodness. Selecting the least reprehensible of the pack, the Widow declares her love for Sandy, a simpleton saint, and offers to marry him. Speaking the pap common to sentimental stage melodrama, Sandy agrees that they should conduct a legitimate courtship. He declares, "It's a man's place to brighten a woman's name, not to tarnish it." (ibid., 392)

Miller's jangled plot complications produce more titillation than believable action. After Billy Piper swoons in fear that the vigilantes have marked him as a Danite, the Widow loosens his collar and discovers that Billy is female. When the Widow falls into the hands of the mob, she looks at the beauty of the Sierra night and comments that "nights like this were not made for sleep." (ibid., 394) The Danites attack her and stab her along with her sleeping infant, the first migrant baby born in the Sierras. The Judge leads the mob after Billy, but Sandy intercedes in the name of his blameless wife. In the final act, Bill Hickman, leader of the skulking Danites, intimidates Billy, but before the Mormon hit men can strike, the miners rip off the Mormons' fake beards, expose them as murderous religious fanatics, and hang them.

Miller's play advances with such banality and choplogic that its popularity with frontier audiences is puzzling. The author leaps from admiring the beauties of the Sierras to condemning rough-hewn frontier justice, thus altering the atmosphere of the play and leaving considerable doubt as to the underlying mission of locals bent on finding someone to execute. Overall, the exaggerated accusation of Danite blood-lust wrongs Brigham Young's followers, most of whom sought a peaceful settlement in a land isolated from persecutors. The playwright himself admitted, "I have always been sorry I printed [the play], as it is unfair to the Mormons and the Chinese." (ibid.) The author's lame commentary on the Mountain Meadows Massacre and the "Missouri mob that butchered Joseph Smith and his brother Hiram" raises the question of Miller's understanding of the complexities of Mormon history. His obsession suggests that he exploited a muddled issue by stirring a mixed pot of animosities ranging from hatred of Chinese immigrants, Digger Indians, and Mormon vigilantes to disdain for missionaries, child killers, loners, and cross-dressers.

A lighter form of humor comes from Artemus Ward, the pen name of Charles Farrar Browne, who developed along the same career path as Mark Twain—from printer to journalist to wit. Less enduring than the creative Twain, Ward assumed the persona of traveling barker and wrote humorously misspelled essays and letters on varied topics. In addition to writing, Ward appeared in *Under the Gaslight*, a post–Civil War traveling show based in Wilmington, Delaware, featuring a stage set complete with railway tracks, engine, and cars. At the Egyptian Hall in London, he starred in *Among the Mormons*. To those in the audience who might miss Western jokes, he offered to call on the citizens of London and explain any jokes they might have misunderstood.

On a visit to Salt Lake City, Ward wrote that he feared to get too close because a certain humorous sketch "had greatly incensed the Saints." (Ward 1939, 390–391) He had written in mock illiteracy:

> I girded up my Lions and fled the Seen. I packt up my duds and left Salt Lake, which is a 2nd Soddum and Germorer, inhabited by as theavin' & on principled a set of retchis as ever drew Breth in eny spot on the Globe. (ibid., 392)

On closer examination of Mormons, Ward was surprised to find them more cosmopolitan than he had assumed, as demonstrated by their love of theater and orchestral performances. As he peruses the congregation, he discovers:

> The congregation doesn't startle us. It is known, I fancy, that the heads of Church are to be absent to-day, and the attendance is slim. There are no ravishingly beautiful women present, and no positively ugly ones. The men are fair to middling. They will never be slain in cold blood for their beauty, nor shut up in jail for their homeliness. (ibid., 391)

No longer terrified of Danites, Ward delights in watching Brigham Young dancing at a sprightly ball and withdraws his "wholesale denunciation of a people I had never seen."

Late-nineteenth- and early-twentieth-century Western writers sustain frontier prejudice and curiosity about Mormon lifestyles and accomplishments. In 1893, novelist Owen Wister wrote an anecdote to his mother about peculiarities of a Mormon bishop who has been in hiding for polygamy in his day, on account of nine wives; he has forty-seven children and can't read or write but signs contracts and letters with an X. He is 74 and the other day had twins. Now don't you see that it's quite impossible to preserve any proportion? (Wister 1958, 192)

As an example of Western anomalies, Wister cites the example of plural wives as proof of the change that occurs in visiting Easterners, who must adjust expectations to the norms of the West.

Zane Grey, an admirer of Wister, utilized notes and observations he had made of Mormons in several Western novels, notably *The Heritage of the Desert* (1910) and his masterpiece, *Riders of the Purple Sage* (1912). In the latter, Grey expands the theme of religious hypocrisy to cover greed, violence, and lust. His patriarchal villain, Elder Tull, presses the heroine, Jane Withersteen, to become head wife of his coterie of mates. The tenor of evil and coercion threatens to overwhelm Jane and her ranch hand. Only the intervention of Lassiter, Grey's range-riding hero, can save Jane from Mormon predators. In revivals of Grey's novel on screen and for television, the duality of stalwart Mormon pioneers and their corrupt leaders lends a Mafia-esque air to the superstructure of the Utah-based church.

Grey's intense novel at first precipitated rejection and second thoughts. The Frank A. Munsey Company and *Harper's* feared a backlash among Mormon communities. Within weeks, *Popular Magazine* added its veto to the stack of rejections. In a decisive move, Grey insisted that *Harper's* vice-president read the manuscript. His favorable response led to publication and phenomenal success for Grey's classic work. A few critics accused Grey of promulgating a negative stereotype that his audience too willingly accepted as historical fact. The majority found too much to praise to condemn the author for depicting Mormons as the heavies.

A perception of Mormons as inherently evil and manipulative surfaces in Thomas Wolfe's *A Western Journal* (1939). He enters Mormon country with preconceptions about "Mormon coldness, desolation—the cruel, the devoted, the fanatic, and the warped and dead." (Wolfe 1967, 39) He expends a major portion of his observations on the frontier atmosphere of Mormon farmland, which lies in the "saline citric flatness paleness of the lake . . . semi barren ridges, and a strip of arid land." (ibid., 40) The sudden appearance of ample orchards, vineyards, and "greenery, lushness, watery fertility, the like of which was never seen before" flanks the eight-gabled Mormon temple. At a distance, Wolfe admires

a magic valley plain, flat as a floor and green as heaven and more fertile and more ripe than the Promised land then down and winding down the lovely canyon and cattle, horses, and houses sheltered by the trees, and then below the most lovely and enchanted valley of them all—the great valley around Logan—a valley that makes all that has gone before fade to nothing—the very core and fruit of Canaan. (ibid., 42)

The paradox of the blessed-cursed atmosphere causes Wolfe to marvel at a fecundity that he did not think possible in the midst of a crusty, parched desert.

Less pictorial is Thomas Berger's *Little Big Man* (1964), which presents the pathetic situation of Amelia, a teen prostitute in a lurid sin den in Kansas City. Oblivious to the implied comparison between prostitution and polygamy, the girl snuffles and narrates her early life in Salt Lake City in a respectable family. She describes how her mother married in her teens to a notable Mormon and adds:

> You would know the name right off if I was to tell it. Now, outside folks have a funny idea about Mormons on account of the number of wives they take, but I tell you that is the reason why you won't find a den of iniquity like this in Salt Lake. . . . All we did was work and pray from early in the morning until night. (Berger 1964, 303)

Unaware of the humor she generates with the depiction of Mormons as opportunists and female despoilers, Amelia explains that Woodbine, a neighbor with "only six wives," wanted to add her to the household. Dismayed, she ran away, spurning the opportunity to join model Mormon women in harem-style family life. As Amelia describes her self-perceived shame: "whereas instead of a device of pleasure to any man who comes down the road I would have been an honored Mormon wife." Narrator Jack Crabb, a frontier sage despite his lack of experience with women, comments that such hard-luck stories are common to women of easy virtue, all of whom claim to have come from "good families."

In 1956, Austin and Alta Fife attempted to dispel the faulty notion of Mormonism by collecting a volume of Mormonia, *Saints of Sage and Saddle*. The study of Mormonism and its abhorrence of European mores opens on the epic trek west, which concluded July 24, 1847, with the arrival of the Saints in the Great Salt Lake Valley. The Fifes cite favorite marching songs: "Ye Saints Who Dwell on Britain's Shore," "And Should We Die before Our Journey's Through," and a salute to the handcarters, "As on the Road the Carts Were Pulled." In acknowledgement of churchmen who slaughtered anti-Mormon settlers at the Mountain Meadows, the Fifes express the church's pervasive fear of the military and cite six verses of the "Mountain Meadows Massacre," a frontier ballad composed by soldiers at Fort Bridger, Wyoming. The words shame Mormons "in Indian colors all wrapped," who massacred the party traveling in 30 wagons. The song concludes with blame centering on the church president, Brigham Young. Another grouping of frontier drollery demonstrates tunes arising from outrage at the practice of polygamy. One song, "Wish I Was a Mormonite," chortles "fifty wives are just the thing the flesh to mortify." Again, Brigham Young, "a shepherd of a heap of pretty little sheep, and nice fold of pretty little lambs," rises above other Mormons as the chief villain. (Fife and Fife 1956, 121, 125) (Arrington and Haupt 1973; Berger 1964; Crystal 1995; Ehrlich and Carruth 1982; Farnham 1983; Fife and Fife 1956; Frost 1967; Hamilton 1916; Hart 1983; Herron 1939; Hutchinson 1963; Lamar 1977; Lee 1949; Miller 1922; Nevins 1955; O'Connor 1966; "Poetry of Bret Harte" 1996; Rasmussen 1995; Richards 1996; Schlesinger 1971; Walser 1956; Ward 1939; Wister 1958; Wolfe 1967)

See also Grey, Zane; Harte, Bret; Miller, Joaquin; Oregon Trail; Twain, Mark; Wister, Owen.

🔣 MOUNTAINEERS, HUNTERS, AND TRAPPERS 🔣

One of the most engaging eras of Western settlement profits from the romantic literature about mountaineers and trappers who roamed the outback and made their living off the wild. Primarily free agents, men such as Jim Beckwourth, Daniel Boone, Joe Meek, Davy Crockett, Jim Bridger, Manuel Lisa, John C. Fremont, Milton and William Sublette, and Kit Carson looked the part of frontiersmen in buckskins and fur hats. Traveling in the days before motor vehicles, they carried the minimum of equipment—canteen, powder and shot, tomahawk, knife, pistol, and rifle. By drawing on their primitive gear plus packets of dried fruit, jerky, and pemmican, they earned a reputation for a rugged survivalism that required pluck, knowledge of the terrain, and the ability to adapt to all forms of danger, whether beast, Indian, accident, or act of nature.

An example of adaptability appears in the opening paragraphs of *Kit Carson's Autobiography* (1926). On his first foray from home, 15-year-old Carson watches an amateur medic amputate the arm of Andrew Broadus, a fellow expeditioner who accidentally discharged his rifle into his right arm:

> The doctor set to work and cut the flesh with a razor and sawed the bone with an old saw. The arteries being cut, to stop the bleeding, he heated a kingbolt from one of the wagons and burned the affected parts, and then applied a plaster of tar taken off the wheel of a wagon. The patient became perfectly well before our arrival in New Mexico. (Carson 1966, 5–6)

In similar concise manner, Carson tells of a trek from the San Francisco River to Sacramento, for which his party was to garner supplies. Because game was scarce, the men valued three deer, the only animals to be found. On the advice of local Indians to beware parched land ahead, he adds, "we took off [the skins] in such a manner as to make tanks for the purpose of carrying water." (ibid., 11) On the trail ahead, streams and springs proved so scarce that Carson and the others took turns guarding the little water their skins would hold.

Carson's succinct style is a rarity among the more florid tales of mountain expeditions. A puzzling account of woods lore, Virginian David H. Coyner's *The Lost Trappers* (1847), blends fact and fancy in a classic study of the pursuit of pelts. The story, derived in part from Ezekiel Williams's journal, claims that, out of 20 trappers departing up the Missouri River in 1807, only three survived. Two of them went west; Williams, the third, paddled south on the Arkansas River and returned to Missouri in 1809. Coyner claims that Williams lived primarily off the meat of trapped beaver, the tail of which he considered a "great dainty":

> He separates it from the body of the beaver, thrusts a stick in one end of it, and places it before the fires with the scales on it. When the heat of the fire strikes through so as to roast it, large blisters rise on the surface, which are very easily removed. The tail is then perfectly white, and very delicious. (Coyner 1995, 75)

Williams notes that the trapper recycles much of his prey, saving the testicles to use as bait. He keeps containers of semen and musk to cover human scent.

While setting a trap, he baits the jaws with a scented stick, which protrudes a few inches above the water. Placement is crucial, for the beaver must entangle itself, sink to the bottom, and drown. Williams claims that if the beaver struggles ashore, he may bite off his leg and flee.

In 1914, Osborne Russell, a sailor from his teens, published his own share of woods adventures in *Journal of a Trapper.* According to his narrative, he leaves New England in 1834 to join Nathaniel Wyeth's trapping expedition to the Rockies, take up with the American Fur Company, and later set out on his own from a base camp at Fort Hall. His memories of Jim Bridger, Joe Meek, and the Sublette brothers supply specifics from a crucial era in Western economic history before the demise of the beaver and the flow of westering traffic ended the trappers' monopoly on the wild. A standard feature of trapper lore is the annual rendezvous, a meeting of mountain men at a traditional gathering spot. Russell recalls the blend of American, Canuck, Dutch, Scottish, Irish, English, Indian, and half-breeds who arrive to gamble, settle old scores, and swap stories of the past year.

The twentieth century has produced its own memoirs of mountaineering. In 1900, Captain William F. Drannan, an acquaintance of Kit Carson, John Fremont, Jim Beckwourth, and Jim Bridger, published *Thirty-One Years on the Plains and in the Mountains or, The Last Voice from the Plains.* Paralleling the autobiographies of other trappers, he unfolds an account of an adventurous wilderness career beginning when he fled Tennessee at age 15 to seek his fortune. His travels take him and sidekick Johnnie hunting for wild turkey and buffalo, visiting the chief of the Arapaho. They journey south to Mexico City, north to Carson's wedding in Taos, and west among notorious gamblers in San Francisco. A chapter on Drannan's appointment to the lead of a wagon train contains the instructions he passes to greenhorns who are unused to circling wagons in Indian country:

> By having each wagon numbered every man knew his place in the train, and when it was necessary to correll [sic], one-half of the teams would turn to the right and the other half to the left. Each would swing out a little distance from the road and the two front teams—numbers one and two—would drive up facing each other. (Drannan 1900, 314)

With the teams facing the center and the wagon backs pointed outside, passengers and livestock are safer from attack and stampede than if they allowed the animals too free a range. Drannan completes the exercise by appointing scouts and guards and electing a sergeant. When the train reaches the South Platte River, Drannan is forced to kill nine Sioux and scalp them. To a squeamish female, he justifies his barbarism: "I told her that the Indians did not fear death, but hated the idea of being scalped." (ibid., 322) His forthright trail techniques color much of his writing and explain how he survives a lengthy list of harrowing episodes.

Virginian James Clyman, a contemporary of Kit Carson and William Drannan and a member of William Ashley's second expedition, recorded his observations in *Journal of a Mountain Man* (1840). He claims to have read

Shakespeare, saved fur trader William Sublette from freezing in a blizzard, discovered the South Pass through the Rockies, advised the Donner party not to get caught in the wintry passes of the Sierra Nevadas, and sewed up Jedediah Smith's ear after a grizzly clawed it. Of the latter event, Clyman writes in semi-literate English:

> Grissly did not hesitate a moment but sprung on the capt taking him by the head first pitc[h]ing sprawling on the earth he gave him a grab by the middle fortunately cat[c]hing by the ball pouch and Butcher K[n]life which he broke out but breaking several of his ribs and cutting his head badly none of us having any su[r]gical Knowledge what was to be done one Said come take hold and he wuld say why not you so it went around. (Clyman 1984, 22)

Although unskilled in grammar and rhetoric, Clyman proves equal to trail first aid. He stops the bleeding along Smith's left eye and ear where the bear had "laid the skull bare to near the crown of the head leaving a white streak whare his teeth passed."

Similar life-threatening adventures in the life of John George "Kootenai" Brown, heroic Pony Express rider, trapper, and fisheries officer of southwestern Alberta, Canada, enliven *Kootenai Brown, Canada's Unknown Frontiersman* (1996), an adventure biography written by William Rodney. According to Rodney, Brown, who was born in 1839, earned a reputation for daring and physical stamina that equaled the exploits of Beckwourth and Bridger. In anecdotal style, Brown details a meeting with Sitting Bull, the famed Sioux chief, who captured Brown and his pal near Strawberry Lake during a regular mail run from Fort Stevenson to Fort Totten. After establishing that his companion is Sioux and Brown's mother a Santee Sioux, Brown recalls:

> Sitting Bull ordered us to get off our horses and when we did he had us stripped as naked as the day we were born. They took everything, dispatches, mail, guns, horses, clothes. . . . Some of the young bucks began yelling "Kash-ga, Kash-ga," meaning kill them, kill them. Sitting Bull raised his hand and shouted, "Don't be in a hurry, we'll make a fire and have some fun with them." (Rodney 1996, 79)

Fluent in the native language, Brown understands and anticipates slow torment Sioux-style, with bits of burning pine pitch stuck to the body. While Sitting Bull holds a council to determine the best method of killing the captives, the pair roll down an incline, sprint for the cattails along the lake, and brave clouds of mosquitoes on their way back to the fort.

Brown's hunting lore provides a vivid glimpse of prairie times when buffalo were plentiful. He describes the pursuit of a herd, accomplished by a long line of mounted Metís and white hunters who await the signal from the leader:

> It was some experience for a new hunter—dust flying, horns clashing, buffalo bellowing, men yelling, and all going at top speed. The buffalo dare not stop as the rest of the herd would trample over them. There was hardly ever a drive in which someone was not hurt. (ibid., 100)

Brown adds that each hunter had to skin and transport meat unless the hunt was a general drive, when all quarry became common property. He also details the selection of particular animals to provide the best robes, blankets, and lariats. Danger, too, was shared among mountain men, who cultivated a group mentality to avoid falls and overloading firearms, a miscalculation that caused "two or three hands blown off or a few fingers mutilated by guns exploding."

Fictional hunters and trappers reflect the influence of historical frontiersmen. In *Centennial* (1974), James Michener creates a compelling figure, Pasquinel, the dark *coureur de bois* from late-eighteenth-century New Orleans, who trades with the Indians, offering beads and silver, yard goods and blankets in exchange for furs. Michener builds the mystique of his mountaineer with the rumors that tend to cluster about hunters who conceal personal information:

> He dressed like an Indian, which was why men claimed he carried Indian blood: "Hidatsa, Assiniboin, mebbe Gros Ventre. He's got Injun blood in there somewheres." He wore trousers made of elk skin fringed along the seams, a buffalo-hide belt, a fringed jacket decorated with porcupine quills and deerskin moccasins—all made for him by some squaw. (Michener 1974, 173)

The blend of exotica and shame of the "squaw man" hovers about Pasquinel, who maintains an Indian wife, Clay Basket, while he works the Missouri River and travels among Cheyenne, Arapaho, and Ute as he earns his fortune in the Rockies. To equip his character for social gatherings, Michener shapes him into a teller of tales and a congenial dinner guest among the likes of Lewis and Clark and Thomas Jefferson. (Burns and Ives 1996a; Carson 1966; Clyman 1984; Coyner 1995; Drannan 1900; Lamar 1977; Michener 1974; Oglesby 1963; Rodney 1996; Russell 1965)

See also Boone, Daniel; Crockett, Davy; Grey Owl.

MUIR, JOHN

North America's preeminent mystic, mountain climber, naturalist, and conservationist, John Muir instructed Americans with lyrical writings enriched by his passion for natural beauty. His work influenced Congress to set aside 148 million acres for public parks by passing the Yosemite National Park Bill of 1890, which names Yosemite and Sequoia as national reserves. In Muir's honor, in 1908 Congressman and Mrs. William Kent donated a virgin redwood grove outside San Francisco in Marin County, California, to the Department of the Interior. The tract, renamed Muir Woods National Monument, comprises 354 acres of virgin *Sequoia sempervirens* only 17 miles north of San Francisco. Native to the woods and to Redwood Creek are trees over 240 feet high and colorful stands of evergreen and lady fern, black-tailed deer, steelhead trout, and silver salmon. The treasure of the forest is *Sequoiadendron giganteum*. Dubbed "the Big Tree," it is the largest organism alive on the planet, which Muir declared a forest masterpiece. For preserving Yosemite's Big Tree and conducting other public service crusades, he earned the title "father of the national park system."

Named California's greatest citizen in 1976, Muir was a legend among explorers and outdoorsmen. Central to his interests were nature's virtuoso performances—snow crystals, sea squalls, glaciers, mountaintops, granite slides, falling water, bee pastures, and his favorite, verdant forests—"God's first temples," which he visited in Siberia, Australia, New Zealand, Canada, and throughout the United States. (Tolan 1990, 37) A godly man who supported Darwin's theories of evolution and survival of the fittest, he believed that God's works inspired human observers, but he declined to put human life above any other aspect of nature. Inspired by Emerson and Thoreau, he formulated a personal philosophy based on wonder at natural splendor and often declared that beauty is as necessary to nourishment as bread. In 1916, combined efforts begun by Muir secured the National Park Service as a permanent part of America's guardianship of natural beauties, particularly virgin western and northwestern forests.

A willowy, smooth-muscled outdoorsman with a full bushy beard, Muir was the eccentric of the conservation movement. A native of Dunbar, a fishing port in East Lothian, Scotland, Muir was born April 21, 1838, in the family lodgings over their feed and grain shop on High Street. He emigrated in 1849 with older siblings Sarah and David and their parents, Ann Gilrye and Daniel Muir, who interrupted nightly study with cheerful news: "Bairns, you needna learn your lessons the nicht, for we're gan to America the morn!" (Melham 1976, 30) The family built a log cabin on Fountain Lake near Portage, Wisconsin, where the Muirs dug a well and removed stumps to make way for the plow. Largely without the assistance of Daniel, who preferred proselytizing to grubbing tree roots out of the ground, the children and their mother wrested an 80-acre farm from virgin, thin-soiled forest, then added a second tract at Hickory Hill, which required the same drudgery to accommodate a family grown from five to ten members.

Tied to the land by Daniel's ambition, Muir was largely self-taught and well read. He had to smuggle books about the explorations of Mungo Park and Alexander von Humboldt and the poetry of John Milton and William Shakespeare past his Calvinist father, a mean-spirited religious extremist who allowed only the Bible on his shelf. In his spare time, Muir whittled mechanical devices out of local wood and gained media attention by carving from pine a series of whimsical timepieces, pendulums, thermometers, barometers, locks, counterweights, mechanical bed, scholar's desk, table saw, and sawmill, which were displayed at the 1860 Wisconsin agricultural fair in Madison. Estranged from the Puritan work ethic, he disdained money and chose to put his gizmos to work for personal delight and use rather than to sell them to manufacturers.

In 1861, Muir worked his way to the University of Wisconsin. He spent two years studying Latin, Greek, math, chemistry, and physics and communing with the flora and fauna of Lake Mendota. Penniless except for tuition money he earned by teaching elementary school, he lived primarily on graham crackers and milk until penury led to illness and his father relented and sent him $90. As the Civil War worsened, Muir considered going to medical school, then opted for a lifelong series of walking tours, beginning in 1863 with a hike over Iowa and Illinois and eventually extending over much of the Western Hemisphere. His hatred of war inspired a second jaunt. When conscription into the Union army became a possibility, he fled into Canada, worked at the Trout & Jay sawmill and rake handle company, and remained in self-imposed exile until 1866. After a whirling drive belt tossed a file point into his right eye and diminished the sight of his left eye for a month, he turned down a job offer for a supervisor's post and ended his evolving career in mechanical engineering. His tramps in the wild became both a life's work and a spiritual quest.

While compiling meticulous notes, pressing specimens, and cataloging aspects of nature, Muir subsisted largely on odd jobs and short-term employment, such as his work as an efficiency expert in Indianapolis at the Osgood, Smith & Company carriage parts factory. At age 30, he traveled solo down the Mississippi River to points south and kept a daybook of his observations. On the way, he spied indolent millers and composed a vignette about people who shun what Muir called "over-industrialized society":

> On Sundays you may see wild, unshorn, uncombed men coming out of the woods, each with a bag of corn on his back. From a peck to a bushel is a common grist. They go to the mill along verdant footpaths, winding up and down over hill and valley, and crossing many a rhododendron glen. The flowers and shining leaves brush against their shoulders and knees, occasionally knocking off their coon-skin caps. The first arrived throws his corn into the hopper, turns on the water, and goes to the house. After chatting and smoking he returns to see if his grist is done. Should the stones run empty for an hour or two, it does no harm. (Muir 1992, 36)

In like manner, Muir took his travels lightheartedly. After passing through Tennessee's Cumberland range and alongside the Hiwassee River in the Carolinas to Georgia's Chattahoochee, he camped in a Savannah cemetery and read Robert Burns's poems until his brother could send money.

Deep in the South, Muir wrote of his affection for Georgians, whom he considered the most hospitable and polite hosts on his journey. He commiserated with the post–Civil War depredations:

> broken fields, burnt fences, mills, and woods ruthlessly slaughtered, but also . . . the countenances of the people. A few years after a forest has been burned another generation of bright and happy trees arises, in purest, freshest vigor; only the old trees, wholly or half dead, bear marks of the calamity. So with the people of this war-field. Happy, unscarred, and unclouded youth is growing up around the aged, half-consumed, and fallen parents, who bear in sad measure the ineffaceable marks of the farthest-reaching and most infernal of all civilized calamities. (Muir 1996, 84)

In October, he took passage on a boat south to Fernandina, Florida, and pushed on to the swamps of Cedar Key, where he documented his symptoms and treatment for malaria and typhoid fever. After a two-month convalescence among palms, palmetto, and live oaks, he was able to test his strength with brief day sails along the Gulf Coast.

In January, Muir sailed to Cuba and Panama. Because there was no steamer to South America, he canceled his planned visit to the Amazon forest and advanced up the Pacific coast to California, which became his adopted home state. While contemplating his roaming, he concluded that the world was not made for humankind. In straightforward contradiction of a theology that reveres "a manufactured article as any puppet of a half-penny theater," he formed his original notions of the creator, who made an interdependent universe from which human beings "may disappear without any general burning or extraordinary commotion whatever." (Muir 1992, 136–137, 140) The trip crystallized for him the focus of his life: to live free of materialism and to champion the wild for both God and humankind.

After working as a ranch hand and herding sheep in his favorite spot—the 500-mile Sierra Nevada chain that Muir called the "Range of Light"—he formulated more clearly a transcendental oneness with nature in a rhapsodic journal reminiscent of the essays of Ralph Waldo Emerson and Henry David Thoreau and the pantheist verse of William Wordsworth. With a symphonic upsweep of immediacy and appreciation of earth's profusion, he proclaimed:

> How deep our sleep last night in the mountain's heart, beneath the trees and stars, hushed by solemn-sounding waterfalls and many small soothing voices in sweet accord whispering peace! And our first pure mountain day, warm, calm, cloudless,—how immeasurable it seems, how serenely wild! . . . Along the river, over the hills, in the ground, in the sky, spring work is going on with joyful enthusiasm, new life, new beauty, unfolding, unrolling in glorious exuberant extravagance,—new birds in their nests, new winged creatures in the air, and new leaves, new flowers, spreading, shining, rejoicing everywhere. (Muir 1988, 142, 18)

In this benign setting, he explored meadows, cascades, rills, boulders, and rocky tors while recalling poems by Percy Bysshe Shelley and verses of scripture. Resting under the skies, he found quiet, spiritual and physical health, and holiness. Prayerful and humble amid all beings, he searched the "divine hieroglyphics" in natural phenomena and admitted that he hoped to meet God in the Sierras.

Muir built a sawmill in Yosemite and, surviving primarily on bread and tea, launched a search for evidence of glaciation. His steady production of ten books and 300 articles for the *New York Tribune, Scribner's, San Francisco Evening Bulletin, Overland Monthly, Harper's, Atlantic,* and *Century* entertained and informed readers with descriptions of Douglas squirrels, water ouzels, snow flakes, pasqueflowers, and hummingbirds. He warned readers that "braggart lords" were destroying nature's sublimity through deforestation, illegal lumbering, dynamiting, hunting, grazing, and other forms of commercial despoliation. After spending six years in the Yosemite Valley, he concluded that the area was created by glacial erosion and joined with Robert Underwood Johnson, owner of *Century* magazine, to lobby for the area's preservation.

In 1879, Muir explored an Alaskan glacier that was later named for him and achieved name recognition with his exploration of Alaska's Glacier Bay. Following marriage to Louisiana "Louie" Wanda Strentzel, a talented pianist, in 1880, he departed from their home in the Alhambra Valley near Martinez, California, for the first of a series of return trips to Alaska. Virtually alone, he explored with a doughty black mongrel named Stickeen, the star of Muir's popular children's book about a dangerous crossing of an ice-sliver bridge over a 40-foot crevasse. After Muir passed over the divide, Stickeen

> pressed his body against the ice as if trying to get the advantage of the friction of every hair, gazed into the first step, put his little feet together and slid them slowly, slowly over the edge and down into it, bunching all four in it and almost standing on his head. (Muir 1996, 6)

Muir's praise of the little dog reflects his reverence for independence and daring, which marked his happiest hours. During extended periods when Muir was home with his wife and two daughters, he constructed a mansion and supervised his father-in-law's fruit and wine ranch, which was profitable but sapped Muir's health. When he appeared glum and dispirited, his wife shooed him out of his "scribble den" for a rejuvenating communion with the wild.

In 1888, Muir's trip to Mount Rainier and subsequent articles sparked the national interest in conservation. In 1892, he ended his connection with the ranch and founded the Sierra Club, over which he presided for the remaining 22 years of his life. The Club became a national movement. Its political influence maintained the security of the Yosemite highlands as a national park. After publishing *The Mountains of California* (1894), he achieved the second coup of his career when Congress added Mount Rainier National Park to the U.S. forest reserves for study and pleasure. As commercial interests began to erode national commitment to the wild, in 1897 Muir published articles to sway the public from short-term profits in land development to long-term conservation. Like his fervid father, he struck out at sin—the sin of wasting natural resources and of living and working in crowded, sooty dwellings to the exclusion of regular communion with the outdoors.

In 1901, Muir produced *Our National Parks,* a work that caught the attention of President Theodore Roosevelt. During a four-day outing in Yosemite, the president listened to Muir's animated sermons on nature. The two collaborated on a national policy of land use and recreation; their plan required them to convince urban Easterners of the need for wilderness for "thousands of tired, nerve-shaken, over-civilized people." (Lamar 1977, 779) Three years later, Congress added the Petrified Forest to its list of national monuments; in 1908, the Grand Canyon joined the park system. It was at this time that Muir published his reflective story "Stickeen" (1909) and two of his most popular works, *My First Summer in the Sierra* (1911) and *Yosemite* (1912). A world traveler, he enjoyed treks to South America and Africa before completing *The Story of My Boyhood and Youth* (1913).

The year before Muir's death, he lost a major battle of nature advocacy. Although apolitical, he defied Gifford Pinchot, head of the U.S. Forest Service, and the utilitarian wing of the conservation movement. Muir orchestrated a flurry of letters, pamphlets, articles, and speeches to prevent the flooding of the Hetch Hetchy Valley of the Tuolumne River. He fumed:

These temple-destroyers, devotees of ravaging commercialism, seem to have a perfect contempt for Nature, and, instead of lifting their eyes to the God of the mountains, lift them to the almighty Dollar. Dam Hetch Hetchy! As well dam for water tanks the people's cathedrals and churches, for no holier temple has ever been consecrated by the heart of man. (Tolan 1990, 53)

Muir had to admit that forces representing the city of San Francisco countered with a cogent argument: to prevent future fires, populous areas had to have a dependable source of water. His friendship with President William Howard Taft kept the splendid area safe from pragmatists, but after Taft's term in the White House, the pristine valley was devalued for its beauty and flooded by the O'Shaughnessy Dam project.

Muir, ill with a chronic cough, sank to his lowest level of disillusion and nearly gave up hope that forests could be rescued from what he called the "money-changers in the temple." After his death from pneumonia in Los Angeles on December 24, 1914, posthumous publication of his visionary prose—*Letters to a Friend* (1915), *Travels in Alaska* (1915), *A Thousand Mile Walk to the Gulf* (1916), *Steep Trails* (1918), *The Cruise of the Corwin* (1935), and *John of the Mountains* (1938)—preserved notes and sketches on some of his most delightful musings about cloud formations, weather, minerals, water courses, plants, and animals, many of which bear his name. One of America's most influential stewards of natural treasures and a persuasive celebrant of natural science, Muir taught by action and words that "No particle is ever wasted or worn out but eternally flowing from use to use." (ibid., 58) He avoided the pose of coat-tail lobbyist and chose instead to mount the public pulpit and declare, "Everything is hitched to everything else." (Naden and Blue 1992, 44)

Muir's works provide an intimate glimpse of the work of the naturalist. When left to solitude, he planted trees; set out on meandering, ascetic tramps; sketched curious shells, fern fronds, and duck feathers; filled 60 volumes with scientific and humanistic study; and relished the splendor of the environment. While cruising in Alaska, he commented, "So abundant and novel are the objects of interest in a pure wilderness that unless you are pursuing special studies it matters little where you go, or how often to the same place." (Muir 1993b, 54) For most of his long and active career, he maintained high spirits, an optimism born of delight in creation. At times, his work bristled against opportunism and thundered with a chronic disaffection for "progress." Throughout hard-fought battles with opponents, he pacified his spirit with expressions and assessments of private moments at his lifelong address, "Earth-Planet, Universe." (Bennett 1975; Brower 1990; Dunham 1975; Gray 1975; Hart 1983; Kunitz and Haycraft 1938; Lamar 1977; Melham 1976; Milner et al. 1994; Muir 1988, 1992, 1993a, 1993b, 1996; Naden and Blue 1992; Ravitch 1990; Ridge 1993; Smith 1965; Tolan 1990; Wood and Chinn 1996)

MY ÁNTONIA

Willa Cather's *My Ántonia* (1926) derives from a graceful, nostalgic study of late-nineteenth-century immigrant culture on the Nebraska plains. An obvious accumulation of real events and characters, the novel grew out of the author's friendship with a Bohemian hireling, Annie Sadilek Pavelka, and from childhood memories of sod huts, poverty, harsh weather, and the hard looks that denoted social exclusion of outsiders. Embedded in the action are Cather's tone poems about a prairie-dog town, an isolated grave, town dances, and the impermanence of efforts to farm virgin land covered in prairie grass and ruled by nature's whim.

Unlike patterned romance, *My Ántonia* unfolds in Cather's characteristic unadorned style, which she called *démeublé*, or unfurnished. Told in first-person narration via a framework—a chance meeting on a hot, dusty train ride across Iowa—the story reunites the speaker with childhood friend Jim Burden, a New York attorney, who is writing a portfolio of memories about their mutual friend, Ántonia Shimerda Cuzak. Around 1910, Burden—a male mask for the author— finishes the portfolio and alters the title from "Ántonia" to "My Ántonia." He seems satisfied with the change, which betrays a bittersweet, youthful crush that clings into adulthood.

The story opens in September in Nebraska to detail the arrival of Jim, a ten- year-old orphan. Cather introduces her setting with lyric appreciation:

> As I looked about me I felt that the grass was the country, as the water is the sea. The red of the grass made all the great prairie the colour of wine-stains, or of certain seaweeds when they are first washed up. And there was so much motion in it; the whole country seemed, somehow, to be running. (Cather 1977, 15)

Similar to the sea in Melville's *Moby Dick* and the river in Twain's *Life on the Mississippi,* Cather's grassland becomes a character itself through its continual change of mood and the firm hold it maintains over plains dwellers. In the final chapter, Jim looks out over the same prairie grass that "used to run like a wild thing across the open prairie, clinging to the high places and circling and doubling like a rabbit before the hounds." (ibid., 371) In adulthood, he finds the same ground channeled with wheel ruts and washed out with rain, perma- nently gashed and scarred like the claw mark of a grizzly.

Echoing the author's childhood, Jim leaves Virginia for permanent resi- dency in Nebraska. On the way to his grandparents' home near Black Hawk, he prefers reading a dime novel about Jesse James to meeting the Shimerdas, an immigrant family who will make a permanent mark on his psyche. Like adult Easterners of his day, Jim appears to stereotype the West as a stage set- ting for action heroes rather than the farmland cultivated by ambitious, hard- working farmers and ranchers. In daily camaraderie with two farmhands, Jake and Otto, he picks up lines from "Bury Me Not on the Lone Prairiee," tales of desperadoes, an anecdote about the sudden death of an Italian miner at the Black Tiger Mine in Silverton, Colorado, and other exotic Western lore.

Significant to Cather's themes are Jim's paternal grandparents, great-hearted farm folk who prosper and share their good fortune with the Shimerdas, an illiterate Bohemian family of six who buy a homestead and get cheated on the price of a stove and plow horses. In multiple episodes, the Burdens pack a hamper for the immigrants, eye the Shimerda girls' beds in holes in the earthen floor of the family's spare sod hut, and respect Mr. Shimerda's reverence for their Christmas decorations. To Jim's consternation at Mrs. Shimerda's covetousness, Grandmother reminds him, "a body never knows what traits poverty might bring out in 'em. It makes a woman grasping to see her children want for things." (ibid., 91)

The pivotal event of Cather's plains novel is Shimerda's suicide and funeral, which sympathetic homesteaders attend. Ántonia's brother Ambrosch shelters at the farm, praying over his rosary until he falls asleep. At the Shimerda barn, the frozen corpse lies waiting for the coffin that Otto crafts:

> The lumber was hard to work because it was full of frost, and the boards gave off a sweet smell of pine woods, as the heap of yellow shavings grew higher and higher. . . . He handled the tools as if he liked the feel of them; and when he planed, his hands went back and forth over the boards in an eager, beneficent way as if he were blessing them. (ibid., 110)

Like their charitable hired men, the Burdens live out the implications of their name—bearing the onus of Christian love and tolerance. They willingly accept the frustration and scorn of Mrs. Shimerda, who demands potatoes and a pot from Emmaline Burden's well-stocked kitchen. Over Mr. Shimerda's grave, Grandfather absolves him of suicide with a simple, eloquent prayer: "Oh, great and just God, no man among us knows what the sleeper knows, nor is it for us to judge what lies between him and Thee." (ibid., 117)

The central figure of the novel, young Ántonia, comes of age while mourning her *tatinek* and playing and studying English with Jim. A quick, firm-willed girl, she impresses local people with her eagerness to work outdoors like a man. Three years after Jim's move to Nebraska, his grandparents resettle in Black Hawk, where Emmaline Burden saves Ántonia from farm drudgery by getting her a job with the Harlings, a Norwegian family. Parallel to Ántonia's young womanhood runs the social and entrepreneurial emergence of Lena Lingard, a lively, ambitious hired girl from Norway who masters dressmaking. Although the girls are companions, Ántonia recognizes the wild, flirtatious streak in Lena that threatens Ántonia's innocent but warm relationship with Jim. Cather refrains from turning the novel into girl-chases-boy by letting the characters develop organically into close friends but unlikely mates.

The crucial event in the novel is the development of local entertainment in the play-starved community after the Vannis set up a tent in town and teach dancing. Local people—Jim included—dance until midnight every Saturday. Some choose the hired immigrant girls as partners, but a definite separation exists between Americans and immigrant girls, whom townspeople consider "a menace to the social order." (ibid., 210) According to the speaker, the variance in mores for young women generates a two-layered society: the poorest American farmers refuse to hire out their daughters; immigrant girls readily accept live-in jobs. Consequently, immigrant fathers prosper and their daughters marry well.

The crisis that arises over weekend dancing discloses a submerged prejudice that refuses to remain hidden. Mr. Harling demands that Ántonia cease dancing. She retorts prophetically, "A girl like me has got to take her good times when she can." (ibid., 108) She quits her job and continues her fast, energetic weekend schottisches. Although Emmaline respects Scandinavian laborers and makes no effort to end Jim's friendship with Ántonia and other outsiders, she weeps at his nightly prowls to the Firemen's dances with girls of shady reputation. At her request, he returns to translating the *Aeneid* in serious preparation for college. The entire community, including Ántonia, champions his determination to gain a professional education, which is too valuable to be jeopardized by frivolity.

In the following action, Cather departs from prairie society to characterize the behaviors of country youths living in a college town. While at the university, Jim escorts Lena to opera and stage plays, grows misty-eyed at a production of *Camille*, and becomes distracted and lax in his studies. After he departs for Harvard to study law, he grows apart from old friends in Black Hawk. On a vacation trip, he learns that, while he was away at school, a cad named Donovan jilted Ántonia, leaving her to rear their illegitimate daughter. That summer, Jim reunites with "Tony" and pities her coarse dress and hard farm labor. Twenty years later, he calls on her in Hastings, Nebraska, where she lives with her ten children and husband Anton Cuzak. The unexpected visit thrills her but accentuates differences in their paths.

One of Cather's slowest manuscripts to take shape, *My Ántonia* has the elements of a classic. Clear, evocative glimpses of an island in the glinting river, kerchiefed women performing endless chores, plum-filled *kolaches,* the crushed head of a rattlesnake, wintry solitude, and springtime wagon rides to town intermix joyous and uplifting times with the melancholy and commonplace vignettes of prairie life. The author gained her reputation for sympathetic views of frontier womanhood through the array of strong female characters who populate the novel. She showcases the widow Steavens's skill at the sewing machine, Tiny Soderball tending an invalid in the Yukon, Lena becoming independent in San Francisco, Mrs. Shimerda shedding her role of farm drudge, Molly Gardener's blue-lettered hotel bus, and Mrs. Harling's energetic piano playing. The vitality of Black Hawk's denizens reinforces the aura of community that draws Jim back home, then disappoints him when he locates few friends from old times.

As myth, the novel shapes the daily toil of homesteaders and the gossip and snobbery of townspeople into a single symbolic tableau. While Jim picnics with the immigrant girls, the conversation turns to Coronado's exploration of Nebraska in search of Eldorado, the legendary city of gold. At the end of his narrative, the group looks toward the horizon and spies a plow that "stood out against the sun, was exactly contained within the circle of the disk; the handles, the tongue, the share—black against the molten red." (ibid., 245) As indomitable as the armor of the *conquistadores* and the axes of frontier settlers, the plow is a formidable yet glorified shape that embodies the plainness, firmness, and singular purpose of Cather's pioneers. (Blain, Grundy, and Clements 1990; Bloom and Bloom 1962; Bloom 1986b; Bohlke 1986; Buck 1992; Byrne and Snyder 1980; Cather 1947, 1977, 1991; Cowie 1951; Davidson and Wagner-Martin 1995;

DISCovering Authors 1993; Drabble 1985; Ehrlich and Carruth 1982; Goring 1994; Hornstein 1973; Kunitz 1942; Lamar 1977; Magill 1958; Milner et al. 1994; "North Side" 1996; O'Brien 1986; Robinson 1983; Sherr and Kazickas 1994; Woodress 1982)

See also Cather, Willa; *Death Comes for the Archbishop; O Pioneers!.*

NATIVE AMERICANS IN LITERATURE

From the beginning, American writers, white and nonwhite, have peopled their literature with a mix of races. In Western literature, the confrontation between whites and resident Hispanics, Asians, and Indians is a given, as undeniable as the enslavement of blacks in the South. In Lansford W. Hastings's valuable pioneer handbook, *The Emigrants' Guide to Oregon and California* (1845), the knowledgeable author describes where and how to locate Indians—or avoid them—and what measures to take to protect wagon trains from attack. Hastings summarizes:

> All of the various tribes, of this country, are found in their aboriginal state of barbarism, as perfectly wild and timid, as the herds of beasts, with which they are surrounded. Upon approaching one of their villages, without their previous knowledge, a scene of most extraordinary confusion, and noisy clamor is presented; all scudding at once, into their earthen houses, not a human soul is to be seen, excepting those who present their heads through the aperture at the apex, of each of the huts, and who are, in a most clamorous and confused manner, drawing upon your humanity and mercy, and begging you to spare them, collectively and individually. (Hastings 1845, 116)

Reliance on such slanderous stereotypes reduced inclusion of Indian characters to a proliferation of absurdities, prime examples being the beatific messiah-chief in Henry Wadsworth Longfellow's *The Song of Hiawatha* (1855), the melodramatic tableaux of Philip Freneau's "The Indian Burying Ground" (1788) and "The Dying Indian" (1784), fastidious Quaker piety that masks anti-Indian sentiments in William Bartram's *Travels* (1791), and the darkly evil Injun Joe in Mark Twain's *The Adventures of Tom Sawyer* (1876). More open-minded writers— notably, William Gilmore Simms, Helen Hunt Jackson, George Bird Grinnell, John Ehle, and Michael Blake—have attempted to understand the psyche and motivations of native peoples to better account for the Indian's prominence in America's view of itself.

One of the most successful to take seriously the study of native characters was Charlestonian William Gilmore Simms. The first fiction writer to treat Native Americans as humans, he fleshed out *The Yemassee: A Romance of Carolina* (1835) with believable Indians, in particular, Chief Sanutee, his wife,

Matiwan, and Occonestoga, their son. One of the most readable of nineteenth-century frontier novels, the book opens in 1715 and focuses on the inevitable clash of cultures that dooms the bucolic lifestyle of this South Carolina tribe. In the opening tableau, husband and wife discuss their wayward son. Sanutee interrupts her hesitant beginning:

> Occonestoga is a dog, Matiwan; he hunts the slaves of the English in the swamps for strong drink. He is a slave himself—he has ears for their lies—he believes in their forked tongues, and he has two voices for his own people. Let him not look into the lodge of Sanutee. Is not Sanutee the chief of the Yemassee? (Simms 1964, 36)

This domestic exchange enlightens the reader to a major fault of colonial whites: their dissemination of alcohol, which was unknown to the Yemassee before the coming of settlers. Overriding her obdurate husband, Matiwan states that she has shared her husband's bed, cooked venison for his guests, and borne him a son. So distraught is Sanutee with his son that he refuses to let Matiwan claim to be the boy's mother.

In the ensuing action, Simms develops fully the character of Sanutee, a father and leader whose personal and civic duties force him to evaluate realistically the quandary of his tribe facing an "intrusive race." From the beginning of Simms's romance, Sanutee acknowledges that the stakes are high for his people, who must accept their doom if they fail to stop whites from overrunning Yemassee land. The author credits him with philosophical foresight and pragmatism in predicting the destiny that awaits his people. Sanutee "knew that the superior must necessarily be the ruin of the race which is inferior—that the one must either sink its existence in with that of the other, or it must perish." (ibid., 39) Wise to the duplicity of the intruder, Sanutee acknowledges that the "Christian (so called) civilization" held both the sword and the sacrament over his people. At first impressed by the English, he had come to fear "the degradation which was fast dogging their footsteps." (ibid., 40)

At the heart of Simms's novel, insidious whites undermine native unity. The burden of a son's profligacy pulls the proud, uncompromising Sanutee from Matiwan, who refuses to abandon Occonestoga. In a pivotal scene, the son confronts the father. With tomahawk raised in defiance, he sings the scalp song and prepares for the one-sided slaughter of the older man when Matiwan screams, causes tribesmen to rush in and arrest her son, then falls at Sanutee's feet. He attends a formal hearing with other dignitaries and sternly rejects pleas to rescue his son from judgment. In a dramatic tableau, women sing the exile's doom: "They know thee no more—they know thee no more." (ibid., 209) Matiwan, unable to bear Occonestoga's protracted agony and the humiliation of having the traditional tribal mark sliced from his skin, strikes him with a hatchet she had concealed in her dress. The novel concludes in a three-way tragedy: the family's grief and shame is revealed for all to judge as Matiwan collapses in Sanutee's arms.

As the West spread beyond the Mississippi River to forts and posts along the trails, military men such as Oliver Otis Howard, George Armstrong Custer, and Richard Irving Dodge began producing the nonfiction memoirs and reflections that fed the East's hunger for factual accounts of Indians. Dodge's *Our Wild Indians: Thirty-Three Years' Personal Experience among the Red Men of the Great West* (1882) exemplifies the ethnocentrism of a white Christian whose revulsion at Indian dress, religion, and customs inhibits objective description. Dodge faults George Catlin for his colorful studies and drawings of plains Indians and rebuts James Fenimore Cooper's creation of Uncas, an admirably moral Indian. Dodge retorts, "no such individual could possibly have existed." (Dodge 1978, 54) To correct the "onstage" quality of fiction, Dodge composes a subjective analysis of Indian mores, sprinkling his text with judgmental terms such as "illiterate," "uncompromisingly hostile," "warlike temperament," "universal lack of fecundity," and "peculiar home attachment." He cites "excellent people . . . who argue that humanity and policy alike point to his extermination as the most prompt and effectual way of solving our Indian problem." (ibid., 67) Dodge rejects genocide but insists that Indians are savage, undisciplined, lawless, and heathen. His solution is to draw them into full citizenship. Like a zealous Paul Revere, he appeals "to the press; to the pulpit; to every voter in the land; to every lover of humanity. Arouse to this grand work." (ibid., 653)

At the beginning of the twentieth century, Thomas Henry Tibbles lived both the native and white lifestyles and wrote a memoir that captures the spirit of Native American life at the height of its threat from white settlers. In 1904, Tibbles—husband of Susette La Flesche, or Bright Eyes, an Omaha painter, lecturer, and activist—penned *Buckskin and Blanket Days,* a classic reflection of his life as a newspaper reporter and peacemaker on the plains. The white son-in-law of Iron Eye, Tibbles was admitted into the tribe through ordeal, which required the initiate to dance while pulling against a thong attached to a sinew in the chest. Central to the text is the role of the Ponca in the Indian exile, which in 1877 dispatched them from their Nebraska homeland to Indian territory in Oklahoma. Tibbles witnesses some of the crucial changes of heart among Indians who supported the messiah craze and danced the Ghost Dance and describes the destruction at Wounded Knee, where victims discovered that their ghost shirts did not deflect cavalry bullets.

A breakthrough in reportage on Native Americans occurred in the late nineteenth century with the writings of Helen Hunt Jackson, George Bird Grinnell, and George E. Hyde. Jackson, a Massachusetts poet, altered her early career focus in 1879 after hearing a lecture by Thomas Henry Tibbles, Susette La Flesche, and Standing Bear, a Ponca chief. Under their influence, Jackson established the Boston Indian Citizenship Association and published two strongly pro-Indian propaganda pieces: *A Century of Dishonor* (1881) and *Ramona* (1894), a novel revealing the sufferings of the Mission Indians of California. The first work, a diatribe issued under the pseudonym H. H., exposes American degradation and brutalization of Indians and challenges the popular stereotype of Indians as savages. In carefully outlined and documented chapters, she cites unimpeachable testimony of broken treaties and disinterest in the plight of Indians, notably Chivington's unprovoked attack on noncombatants at Sand Creek. Her local color novel, a popular title despite its sentimentality and the passionate plea for justice to Native Americans, depicts the dilemma of a Cahuilla girl in southern California who chooses to return to a humble native village in the San Jacinto Mountains rather than continue living on a grand Spanish estate.

Yale-trained anthropologist George Bird Grinnell corroborates Jackson's indictment of racism against Indians. In 1870, he began a series of field trips to the West. In 1874, he accompanied Custer's expedition to the Dakotas; the next year, he toured Yellowstone National Park. Moved to express the unjust treatment that Native Americans suffered at the hands of a string of capricious, deceitful government agents, he launched his writing career. A contributor of articles to *Scribner's, Atlantic Monthly, Forest and Stream, Century,* and *Harper's,* he later drew on biological and ethnological data to produce children's fiction and scientific studies of Indians, including *Pawnee Hero Stories and Folk Tales* (1889), *Blackfoot Lodge Tales* (1892), *The Fighting Cheyenne* (1915), *The Cheyenne Indians* (1923), *By Cheyenne Campfires* (1926), and *Two Great Scouts and Their Pawnee Battalion* (1928). The introduction to *Blackfoot Lodge Tales* typifies Grinnell's altruism:

> The most shameful chapter of American history is that in which is recorded the account of our dealings with the Indians. The story of our government's intercourse with this race is an unbroken narrative of injustice, fraud, and robbery. Our people have disregarded honesty and truth whenever they have come in contact with the Indian, and he has had no rights because he has never had the power to enforce any. (Grinnell 1972, ix)

Enumerating the Indian qualities, Grinnell insists that kindness, affection, hospitality, honesty, and spirituality are the Native American's best traits. Positive reception of Grinnell's first work encouraged him to continue studying Indians from a sympathetic point of view. In addition to native myths, he summarized history and daily life, accounted for the male-female division of camp chores, and described pleasureable activities—jokes, crafts, pipe smoking, gambling, singing, and a game similar to "Button, button, who's got the button?" Grinnell's research assistant, Nebraskan George E. Hyde, used the same scholarly techniques to locate informants and collect testimony and oral history. He completed highly praised annotated studies: *The Pawnee Indians* (1951), *A Sioux Chronicle* (1956), *Indians of the High Plains* (1959), *Spotted Tail's Folk* (1961), *Indians of the Woodlands* (1962), and *The Life of George Bent* (1968), all devoid of the prejudice and racism rampant in earlier writings.

Twentieth-century literature made its own strides toward a fairer presentation of Indians. Popular New York novelist Walter Dumaux Edmonds produced *Drums along the Mohawk* (1936), a work of historical fiction set during the American Revolution. A pastoral quality enhances his description of Deodesote, a Seneca town east of the Genesee River. Set among evergreens and deciduous trees, Gahota's cabin stands near a small vegetable patch, where his white wife Nancy hoes corn, pumpkins, beans, and squash. The specter of army columns inexorably forcing native peoples into the wild dismays all but Gahota, who persists in living the old way with his pregnant wife and his son, Jerry

Log-in-the-Water. Edmonds summons an Edenic picture of Nancy as earth goddess and Gahota as the complacent forest dweller. The short-lived idyll teeters on destruction when racist whites defame women who live as red men's squaws. Three years after publication of *Drums along the Mohawk,* John Ford successfully turned the novel into a color film spectacular, starring Claudette Colbert, Henry Fonda, John Carradine, and Edna May Oliver, who earned an Oscar nomination for supporting actress.

The latter quarter of the twentieth century has produced a deeper study of American racism and ambivalence toward Native Americans as citizens through the history and fiction of John Ehle and Michael Blake. John Ehle, North Carolina author of *Trail of Tears: The Rise and Fall of the Cherokee Nation* (1988), cites journals, government documents, speeches, and other untapped sources in his stirring study of the removal of the Cherokee from the East Coast to Indian territory. Embedded in the diaspora are the stories of Sequoyah, inventor of the Cherokee alphabet; Tsali, a martyr who surrendered to executioners to save his people from displacement; Elias Boudinot, editor of the *Cherokee Phoenix;* Stand Watie, a military leader; and two Cherokee peacemakers, Major Ridge and John Ross. Corroborative information tells of Cherokee ball games, a printing press, burial customs, migrations, and child-rearing practices. Ehle concludes that displacement of the preponderance of five eastern tribes—notably the Cherokee nation—disoriented and disrupted family and town life and resulted in the deaths of 4,000 Indians.

Equally passionate about the racial prejudice of white America's past is Ehle's contemporary, Michael Blake, author of *Dances with Wolves* (1988), a popular novel developed with the help of producer and actor Kevin Costner. Blake's characterization of Lt. John Dunbar, a white trooper on the Western plain who chooses to live with the Comanche, develops a strong transracial motif that follows the protagonist from a Civil War battlefield to a rejection of white ways. With the assistance of Kicking Bird, an admirable holy man, Dunbar is able to shuck the materialism and insensitivity of white society and embrace tribalism and the soul-satisfying spirituality of belonging.

Although Blake's novel and adapted screenplay tread perilously close to stereotype with their re-engineering of the motifs of the captive white girl, buffalo hunt, night attack by Pawnee, and flight from evil cavalrymen, the plot reflects realism in Dunbar's realization of a new kind of pride in manhood. After Dances with Wolves assists his Comanche friends in winning a one-sided battle against Pawnee raiders, he considers the difference between bravery in Civil War battles and the protection of noncombatants from an invader: "This killing had not been done in the name of some dark political objective. This was not a battle for territory or riches or to make men free. This battle had no ego." (Blake 1988, 269) The novel earned Blake awards from the Writers Guild and the Western Writers of America. He also won an Oscar for best adapted screenplay. The cinema version thrived from an astute casting of Native American and white actors, including Graham Greene as the holy man, Rodney A. Grant as Dunbar's best friend, and Mary McDonnell as a former captive who adapts to Comanche standards of wifely behavior. Altogether, the film garnered seven

Academy Awards—best film, director, screenplay, music, sound, editing, and photography—and five additional nominations for best actor, actress, supporting actor, costume, and art direction.

Paralleling these adult titles, sympathetic treatment of Native Americans appears in several classic works from young adult literature. An existential view of assimilation powers Conrad Richter's *The Light in the Forest* (1953) and Hal Borland's *When the Legends Die* (1963). The two protagonists—True Son, the captive son of a Lenni Lenape family, and Tom Black Bull, an orphaned Ute—journey from the wilderness to eastern communities, where they attempt to acclimate to the idiosyncrasies of whites, True Son with his birth family and Tom on the rodeo circuit. A trio of young adult novels by female authors— Margaret Craven's *I Heard the Owl Call My Name* (1973), Elizabeth Speare's *The Sign of the Beaver* (1983), and Jean Craighead George's Newbery Medal–winner, *Julie of the Wolves* (1972)—delineates the strengths of native and white lifestyles. In all five of these works, the authors present a sympathetic study of native customs, such as the syncretism of Anglican faith with native religion in *I Heard the Owl Call My Name,* the wearing of an Inuit good luck charm in *Julie of the Wolves,* and a boy's understanding of manitou in *The Sign of the Beaver.* Far removed from literature that lambastes Native Americans as ignorant savages, these novels attest to impressionable readers that native cultures have much to teach about alternate views of nature, spirituality, family, and humanity.

In contrast to white efforts to justify Indian behaviors or to ameliorate the clash of whites with Native Americans, Indians have spoken eloquently of themselves. Without the awkward piety and ill-concealed patronage common to whites, native writers such as Luther Standing Bear and Charles Alexander Eastman have spoken directly on the subjects of morality and education. Luther Standing Bear, author of *My Indian Boyhood* (1931) and *Stories of the Sioux* (1934), reflects on the selection of a chief, the culmination of training and character building. He describes how the people must approve any young man for a high position, even the son of a chief: "No man must be chosen unless he had shown himself fully worthy of honor and no man would be chosen unless he had the respect and confidence of all the people." (Standing Bear 1988a, 146) Reflecting on the response of Hollow Horn Bear to election as leader, Standing Bear lists the major traits of a chief: gratitude, honesty, reliability, will power, purpose, service, kindness, generosity, and justice. In token of honor, young chief Hollow Horn Bear accepts the pipe of peace, a symbol of entitlement.

Eastman, too, writes about the importance of character to the Sioux. An activist and physician at the Pine Ridge Reservation, he graduated from Dartmouth and Boston University Medical School and composed a substantial amount of tribal ethnology, history, and mythology in four memoirs: *Indian Boyhood* (1902), *The Soul of the Indian: An Interpretation* (1911), *Indian Scout Craft and Lore* (1914), and *From the Deep Woods to Civilization* (1916). The first, a reflection of his boyhood in Minnesota and North Dakota, is a well-structured autobiography filled with details of the grandmother who reared him after his mother's death and the systematic education of an apprentice brave. As a future defender of his people, he valued courage and skill, learned hunting songs and legends, and studied how to survive alone in the wild. Of white misconceptions about Indian youths, he comments:

> It seems to be a popular idea that all the characteristic skill of the Indian is instinctive and hereditary. This is a mistake. All the stoicism and patience of the Indian are acquired traits, and continual practice alone makes him master of the art of wood-craft. (Eastman 1975, 52)

Eastman, who was called Ohiyesa in childhood, studies trees, birds, fish, animals, and the shorelines of lakes with his uncle, who reminds him that the wise hunter is guided by the habits of animals: the moose in low, swampy land, the restless movements of the doe and fawn, and the gray wolf made fierce from hunger. Exposed to endurance training, Eastman learns to cultivate strength, inure himself to hunger and thirst, and remain silent near enemy camps.

Paralleling white children inquiring about Indians, Eastman questions the ways of the Big Knives, who had killed his father and older brothers. His uncle, blending amazement with admiration, admits that white people have created a "fire-boat-walks-on-mountains." (ibid., 280) In addition to trains, Eastman hears an incredible list of accomplishments from the white world: "they had bridged the Missouri and Mississippi rivers, and that they made immense houses of stone and brick, piled on top of one another until they were as high as high hills." (ibid., 281) To temper the boy's impression of greatness, the uncle reminds him that whites enslave blacks, devote themselves to becoming rich, and drive Indians away from their lands. He instructs Eastman on various types of whites: devout missionaries, honorless soldiers, and families who produce great numbers of children. Eastman ends his memoir with the unexpected return of his father, still alive and freed by a pardon from President Abraham Lincoln. The father introduces his son to the white world, which profoundly alters his future.

In subsequent works, Eastman alters the tone and structure of his writing to suit a mature reader. In *The Soul of the Indian*, he delineates topics including relationship to the Great Mystery, family responsibilities, worship, morality, spirituality, and the afterlife. Of barbarism, he asserts that, long before he became Christian, "I knew God. I perceived what goodness is. I saw and loved what is really beautiful. Civilization has not taught me anything better!" (Eastman 1980, 87) He recalls boyhood lessons on silence, the cornerstone of character, which develops self-control, courage, patience, dignity, and reverence. As a model of uprightness, Eastman cites the behavior of Crow Dog, who was found guilty of murder. Because he comported himself like a noble, honorable tribesman, he was allowed freedom from incarceration. Before he was to be executed, he visited his family and traveled unescorted to prison. Because of his actions, authorities reopened the case and exonerated him.

With *Indian Scout Craft and Lore*, Eastman continues his explanation of native skills and behavior. He begins with physical training, study of footprints, hunting with slingshot and bow, trapping and fishing, canoeing, camping, building wigwams, making fire, and sports. In the final chapters of this slim

Charles Alexander Eastman, a Sioux known as Ohiyesa, wrote autobiographical works, including *Indian Boyhood*, 1902, and *From the Deep Woods to Civilization*, 1916.

volume, he returns to his earlier perusal of self-discipline with a discussion of manners. He states,

> The natural life of the Indian is saved from rudeness and disorder by certain well-understood rules and conventions which are invariably followed. Simple as these rules may seem, they have stood the test of time, and are universally respected. (Eastman 1974, 182)

He explains the system of justice and honor that governs a village and the corresponding system of family respect. In the style of ancient Sparta, Eastman and his contemporaries grow up well schooled and wholesome in outlook and expectation. He prides himself on the Indian sense of public service, the core of the ideal communal life. He recalls with pleasure the "happy, rollicking, boy man! Gallant, patriotic, public-spirited—in the Indian is the lusty youth of humanity. He is always ready to undertake the impossible, or to impoverish himself to please his friend." (ibid., 189)

Because of language barriers, some Indian authors have had to rely on whites to write down and publish their works for the white world to read. Memoirists such as Black Elk and Pretty-Shield have published through interpreters, transcribers, and ghost writers. In 1932, Frank B. Linderman—trapper, hunter, and cowboy among the Crow of Montana and author of *Plenty-Coups: Chief of the Crows*—transcribed *Pretty-Shield, Medicine Woman of the Crows,* the story of a lively yet contemplative woman who spoke through Goes-Together, an interpreter who translated both her words and sign language. Eager to tell of native life before the white settler, Pretty-Shield recalls spirited buffalo hunts, games and dolls of her childhood, and duties of the lodge. She and other Crow women picked berries, dug roots, skinned and plucked game, cooked, and cared for their husbands and children. Unlike white women, Pretty-Shield recalls traveling by pack animal, to which she had tied a friend's baby girl named Turtle, who comes untied. To "sign-talker," her name for Linderman, she stresses, "I cannot make you know how quickly my heart fell to the ground, nor how loudly I cried out, 'Stop! Stop! We have lost the baby!' "(Linderman 1972, 67) Joyfully, she finds that a party of braves have recovered Turtle, whom she comforts and returns to her mother.

After relating her girlhood and her marriage to Goes-Ahead, Pretty-Shield recounts vision dreams, wars with neighboring tribes, a visit from Sitting Bull, and the Battle of the Little Big Horn. Near the end of her narrative, she answers questions about the extermination of the buffalo, a calamity that affected all plains tribes. She mourns, "Ahh, my heart fell down when I began to see dead buffalo scattered all over our beautiful country, killed and skinned, and left to rot by white men, many, many hundreds of buffalo." (ibid., 250) As though precipitated by the disaster, disease strikes the children; adults stare fixedly at the empty plains. She blames the trauma to her people for encouraging braves to desert their duties for "white man's whisky, letting it do their thinking." (ibid., 251)

In the middle of the twentieth century, adapted native autobiography, following the model of Paul Radin's *The Autobiography of a Winnebago Indian* and

John G. Neihardt's *Black Elk Speaks*, became more prevalent. To preserve fading memories of what the West was like before white men came, ethnologists and biographers recorded first-person narratives of chiefs, sages, fighters, healers, and priests. In 1972, Richard Erdoes interviewed John Lame Deer, storyteller and medicine man of the Lakota, to produce *Lame Deer, Seeker of Visions*, a parallel to *Black Elk Speaks*. Lame Deer connects himself to the vivid clash of cultures exacerbated by General Nelson A. "Bear Coat" Miles, nemesis of the Sioux, in a version of the Battle of the Little Big Horn that Lame Deer heard from his grandfather, Good Fox. In 1969, ethnographer Charles S. Brant published the reflections of Jim Whitewolf as *The Autobiography of a Kiowa Apache Indian*. Among the mundane facts about kinship and culture are Whitewolf's memories of the Ghost Dance, the feared aboriginal renaissance that impelled white settlers and military leaders to squelch a possible rebellion of the remaining free tribes. The dance involved shaking cow-hoof rattles, stomping and rolling on the floor, and awaiting a vision of Jesus. Whitewolf recalls that the purpose of the dance was to return the dead to earth. Before another Kiowa Ghost Dance could be held, whites suppressed the gathering and warned Whitewolf and other tribesmen that they risked being jailed if they danced again.

Published in the latter portion of the twentieth century, the works of two knowledgeable writers—Ella Deloria and James Sewid—explain the complexities of native society. Against the tide of literature that depicts Indians as a simple, static race that has accomplished little beyond stone-age skills, Deloria heeded the advice of anthropologists Franz Boas and Ruth Benedict and, in 1944, collected cultural material for a Sioux novel, *Waterlily*, which was published posthumously in 1988. The day-to-day detail of Deloria's story establishes an authenticity not found in casual fiction, which often transposes native characters onto white plotlines and places in their mouths and minds unthinkable words and thoughts. Because she stresses sociological detail, the author suppresses the protagonist's story to present in full the role of women in Sioux society before the coming of whites, as in this passage on polygamy:

> Waterlily was, of course, familiar with the idea of plural wives, though there happened to be none in her uncle's *tiyospaye* back home. This was her first opportunity to know such a case intimately and she found it a harmonious household. All the wives cheerfully shared the burdens of the family. They took turns in their husband's affections, and if he seemed to favor one of them overmuch for a time, the others joked about it and let it pass. (Deloria 1988, 167)

Each scene is so packed with the details of kinship, filial duty, and tribal expectations that Deloria all but acknowledges that Waterlily is only a fictional icon representing woman in the greater sense as a means of expressing sex role among the Sioux.

From the Kwakiutl of Alert Bay, British Columbia, comes an equally detailed native study, the Pacific Coast memoir *Guests Never Leave Hungry: The Autobiography of James Sewid, a Kwakiutl Indian* (1989). Before accepting white ways, Sewid and his family lived in a community house and observed traditional customs. He explains the community's complicated clan structure and its rituals, which include the potlatch feast, a lavish giveaway that increases the prestige and honor of the host, who presents blankets, shells, copper jewelry, canoes, money, or tokens to his guests while entertaining them with singing, dancing, food, and oratory. Outlawed by Canadian law in 1921, the custom continued in secret for three decades until its reinstatement as a means of preserving native heritage. Sewid stresses the dancing of the *hamatsa*, a member of a secret men's society who dances naked except for hemlock branches strapped to his body and a jointed animal mask obscuring his identity. Each dancer punctuates ritual gestures and songs about his ancestors with blasts on a whistle and traditional cries. The value of these detailed studies lies in their validation of native customs and beliefs, which fell victim to years of discredit as white land-grabbers justified the usurpation of aboriginal lands and the vilification of native peoples. (Beatty et al. 1952; Borland 1989; Brant 1969; Davidson and Wagner-Martin 1995; Deloria 1988; Dodge 1978; Eastman 1974, 1975, 1980; George 1972; Grinnell 1972; Hyde 1951; Jackson 1931, 1979; Lamar 1977; Linderman 1972; Patterson and Snodgrass 1994; Remington 1994; Richter 1953; Sewid 1989; Simms 1964; Speare 1983; Standing Bear 1988a, 1988b; Tibbles 1957; Waldman 1990)

See also Black Elk; Borland, Hal; Geronimo; Howard, Oliver Otis; *The Light in the Forest*; Momaday, N. Scott; Richter, Conrad; Winnemucca, Sarah.

NATURALISTS

Naturalists comprise a distinct class of writers on the frontier. Unlike travelers and explorers who wrote of conquest, adventure, commerce, and conflict, noted biologists and outdoor lyricists studied the untouched wilds. Their observations of quiet realms of fowl and mammals, fish and reptiles have provided later generations with a reminder of the cost of civilization. Among the most memorable, original, and poetic of testimonies are John Bartram's observations of east Florida in the mid-eighteenth century, Henry David Thoreau's impassioned plea for solitude at his cabin by Walden Pond, John Muir's memories of a California meadow that now lies under dammed-up waters, Grey Owl's energetic conservation in the Canadian heartland, and Mary Hunter Austin's verse extolling the hardihood of desert cactus. Less well known are the works of artist and journalist Samuel Washington Woodhouse and explorer Major Stephen Harriman Long. The former wrote *A Naturalist in Indian Territory* (1992), his journal annotating the 1849–1850 topographical study of the Creek boundary. Long, who led a fact-finding expedition of the trans-Mississippi region to the Rocky Mountains, produced *From Pittsburgh to the Rocky Mountains* (1823).

Significant to the preservation of natural beauty are the notebooks and drawings of naturalist and wildlife artist John James Audubon. More than any other nature artist, Audubon presented the world an unusually sensitive, refined gift of American bird and animal pictures in natural settings. A native of the port city of Les Cayes, Haiti, Jean Jacques Fougère Audubon-Rabin was born April 26, 1784. He was the fourth illegitimate son of John (or Jean) Audubon, a French trader, sugar planter, and former lieutenant in the French navy, and a Creole mother, Jeanne Rabine (or possibly Fougère), who died in 1785. John Audubon and his childless wife, Anne Moynet Audubon, adopted him when he was ten. Educated according to the aristocratic ideal in Nantes, France, he learned dancing, drawing, music, shooting, and fencing and studied birds and taxidermy as hobbies. He took to the sea as a cabin boy, but did not flourish.

The threat of conscription into Napoleon's navy forced Audubon out of France. Trained in art by Jacques Louis David, he emigrated to Mill Grove, his father's estate outside Norristown, Pennsylvania, and learned mine management. In search of opportunity, he settled in Louisville, Kentucky, at the age of 18 and anglicized his name. Five years later, he married Lucy "Minnie" Bakewell, whose uncle helped to establish him in trade. The failure of Audubon's general store and gristmill resulted from his immersion in the outdoors and his eagerness to paint scenes from nature. Bankrupt by 1819, he taught art and painted portraits; his wife worked as a governess. For a few months, he joined the staff of Cincinnati's Western Museum as a taxidermist.

In October 1820, Audubon traveled the Mississippi River by flatboat south to the bayous, canebrakes, and tributaries around New Orleans to collect specimens of wildlife and to paint migratory waterfowl, flowers, fruits, seedpods, and leaves. Until his death on January 27, 1851, he devoted his career to disseminating natural poses of animals and birds. In 1827, he left his family in Bayou Sara, Louisiana, and transported his sketches to England to collaborate with engraver William Home Lizars of Edinburgh. The duo published *The Birds of America* (1838), a monumental four-volume set. Praised for its quality and detail of animal behaviors, the book contains 435 aquatinted plates of 1,055 life-size birds in their natural habitats and sold for $1,050. To underwrite his expensive prints, Audubon obtained subscribers, including the kings of France and England, the Duke of Orleans, Daniel Webster, and the Library of Congress. To lessen the cost of the etched copperplates and increase circulation, he hired J. T. Bowen, a Philadelphia lithographer, to reduce, print, and hand-paint the plates, which Audubon published in 1838 as *Synopsis of the Birds of America*. A thorough text appeared in 1841 in seven volumes as *American Ornithological Biography,* cowritten by Scottish anatomist and naturalist William MacGillivray, who eased Audubon's difficulties with English composition.

Driven from youth to complete his classic collection of wild species, for a half century Audubon traveled North America searching for rare birds to paint. An explorer skilled at observation, he trekked from Florida to Labrador and west to Montana. In 1843, he left Minnie's Land, his home on the Hudson River, and journeyed to the headwaters of the Missouri River. From this mission came *The Viviparous Quadrupeds of North America* (1845), a study of native mammals written in collaboration with John Bachman. Among Audubon's incisive observations on animals and their habitats is this denunciation of the results of still-hunting, one of the most vicious methods of pursuing deer:

John Muir poses with President Theodore Roosevelt on a glacier point above Yosemite Valley, California, in this undated photo. Muir's work persuaded Roosevelt and Congress to pass the Yosemite National Park Bill of 1890, which set aside 148 million acres for parks.

We arrive at the spot where the animal had laid itself down among the grass in a thicket of grape-vines, sumach, and spruce bushes, where it intended to repose during the middle of the day. The place is covered with blood, the hoofs of the deer have left deep prints in the ground, as it bounced in the agonies produced by its wound; but the blood that has gushed from its side discloses the course which it has taken. We soon reach the spot. There lies the buck, its tongue out, its eye dim, its breath exhausted; it is dead. (Audubon 1940, 88)

Deeply moved by the senseless killing of a beautiful forest animal, Audubon expands on the insanity of shooting mammals for the skins and antlers or for sport. His writings and drawings not only preserved the habits and grace of endangered or extinct species but also have exposed the strategems by which human predators cornered and annihilated them.

One of Audubon's essays, "Hospitality in the Woods," lauds a gracious frontier family who befriended him on a dismal, rainy night while the artist was still recovering from yellow fever. In the gloom, he comes upon Willy and Eliza, youthful newlyweds, who welcome him into a log cabin. Audubon notes its scrubbed slab floor, homespun garments hung from logs, fine coverlet, rifle over the chimney piece, and spinning wheel set among rolls of cotton and wool. He quotes Flint's commentary on settling his land along the Mississippi:

> I have cleared a couple of fields, and planted an orchard. Father gave me a stock of cattle, some hogs, and four horses, with two negro boys. I camped here for most of the time when clearing and planting; and when about to marry the young woman you see at the wheel, father helped me in raising this hut. (ibid., 110)

The strength of the family bond assures the couple the love and support of older, more settled parents, aunts and uncles, and siblings. Audubon, who seems to value a warmth that was lacking in his own childhood, extols the couple's good fortune. He ends the sketch with the next morning's courtesies, which include breakfast and a guide back to the main road. Other sketches more sensitive to blacks depict the plight of less-fortunate people: an eloquent runaway slave in a Louisiana bayou, industrious squatters along the Mississippi, and the Mandan, whom both Catlin and Lewis and Clark immortalized in word and picture before their extinction from the smallpox epidemic of 1837.

Audubon's legendary travels surpassed the journeys of Francis Parkman and George Catlin and rivaled the fieldwork of John Muir. Passionate and skilled, he used his talents for the preservation of American wildlife before the invention of the camera. Legends sprang up about his past, one claiming that he was Louis XVII, the lost dauphin of France. Frequent travels and attention to drawing kept him too busy to conduct the numerous conferences that preceded the completion and arrangement of lithographs. In his absence, his sons, Victor and John, represented their father and negotiated with engravers and publishers to reduce the life-size prints to fit on octavos. Freed from the tedium of publishing, Audubon continued his art until the failure of his eyesight in 1847.

Less familiar to American readers is Major Stephen Harriman Long, a Phi Beta Kappan who taught mathematics at West Point and wrote about the western wilderness. In 1823, he led a government survey party to the upper Missouri and Yellowstone aboard a steamer, the *Western Engineer*. Accompanied by a geologist, physician-botanist, zoologist, topographers, and landscape artists Samuel Seymour and Titian Ramsey Peale, the group met with congressional opposition to continued funding and had to replan their expedition. They chose to travel overland to their destination, the source of the Platte River. In addition to paintings of animals, riverscapes, and Indian villages and behaviors, Long's published report contained a variety of nature study. One of his most engaging essays describes the prairie wolf and its relative, *Canis nubilus*.

Another treasure of Long's text is a series of character studies of noted Indians, including Longhair, Red Mouse, Hard-Heart, Bear-Tooth, and Clermont. One of the most outspoken, the Omaha second chief Big Elk, makes a speech to be relayed to the president. At a gift exchange, Big Elk offers jerky for tobacco and regales his visitors with native eloquence. He declares that Indians

> who tell the white people that they love them, speak falsely, as is proved by their killing the white people; but my nation truly love you, they have never stained their hands with the blood of a white man, and this much cannot be said of any nation of this land. (Long 1988, 134)

The pleasantries between Long and Big Elk end with an inspection of a steamer and some curious doodling with iron nails in mercury. Like students in a science lab, the ingenuous Omaha are impressed with white technology. Later, a party returning from a foray on the Sauk dances for the surveyors and gives them a wild cat they had killed on the trail.

Moved by the twentieth century's post-frontier mindset, writers continue to ponder the original beauties of unspoiled land before whites settled America. Edward Abbey wrote "The Second Rape of the West," a poignant essay on nature plunder in *The Journey Home: Some Words in Defense of the American West* (1977). Barbara Kingsolver's *Animal Dreams* (1991) reproduces the anguish of an Arizona community over the steady poisoning of their resources from abandoned tailings at a copper mine. Other works—Wallace Stegner's *The Sound of Mountain Water* (1969), Barry Lopez's *Of Wolves and Men* (1978), Ann Zwinger's *Run, River, Run* (1975), and William Kittredge's *Owing It All* (1987)—return to frontier themes that elucidate the plights of the wild struggling to survive the onslaught of the military, land development, airports, mining, clear-cutting, and industrial waste. (Armstrong 1996; Audubon 1940, 1995; Lamar 1977; Long 1988; Milner et al. 1994; Woodhouse 1996)

See also Austin, Mary Hunter; explorers of the frontier; Muir, John.

O PIONEERS!

Set in the Nebraska uplands, Cather's episodic romance, *O Pioneers!* (1913), was smoothly cobbled together from two short stories, "The White Mulberry Tree" and "Alexandra." The propitious union resulted in one of her most sympathetic novels, a long-lived favorite that placed her among Hamlin Garland, Mari Sandoz, and other of America's foremost midwestern regionalists. The simple story of Alexandra Bergson, a self-possessed Swedish immigrant living in Hanover, Nebraska, prefigures Hester the "imperatrix" in "The Sentimentality of William Tavener" and the force and determination of Ántonia Shimerda, Cather's complex European farm laborer in *My Ántonia* (1926). Slow to find American readers, *O Pioneers!* (1913), which pays homage to a farm woman's resilience, was immediately translated into Czech and later into French, with the author's supervision. It delighted audiences in Norway, where it was serialized in a daily newspaper.

Taking her title from Walt Whitman's poem "Pioneers, O Pioneers!" (1855), Cather opens the novel with "Prairie Spring," an epigraphic hymn to "miles of fresh-plowed soil" and the youthful emotions that presage love and desire. Like Dvorak composing his *New World Symphony,* which elevates the land to the status of hero, the author orchestrates a turbulent opening scene in which the personified Nebraska tableland "[tries] not to be blown away." (Cather 1991, 9) Against this foreboding gale, Alexandra journeys to town with her brother Emil to seek medical advice about John Bergson, their mortally ill father. The symbolic scene foretells Alexandra's adulthood and the determination of her push against two sources of emotional turmoil: gossip and the male-centered thinking of her pigheaded, chauvinistic younger brothers.

Alexandra is a quiet heroine. A sensible daughter, she demonstrates the intelligence and rationality that her siblings lack by selecting promising land on which to make her future. Grandly, Cather pictures her in epic mold:

> For the first time, perhaps, since that land emerged from the waters of geologic ages, a human face was set toward it with love and yearning. It seemed beautiful to her, rich and strong and glorious. Her eyes drank in the breadth of it, until her tears blinded her. Then the Genius of the Divide, the great free spirit which breathes across it, must have bent lower than it ever bent to a

human will before. The history of every country begins in the heart of a man or a woman. (ibid., 42–43)

Surefooted in financial matters, Alexandra insists that her brothers, Oscar and Lou, buy valuable sections from neighbors Linstrum, Crow, and Struble to bring their total to 1,400 acres. With the combined profit, she plans to acquit the mortgage in six years and free her family from debt. Confronted by the brothers' ominous grumbling, she is sweet, attentive, but adamant about her belief that the farm's wheat crop will make them rich.

The transition to financial independence is swift. Within 16 years, Alexandra secures the ambitions of her deceased father, who selected her to supervise his dull, unimaginative sons and to set them an example of resourcefulness and industry. Unlike her beau, Carl Linstrum, whose family returned to St. Louis because they were unable to adapt to the rigors of the plains, Alexandra succeeds and, by empowering herself with money and land, rises to a social plateau too high for Carl to attain. The separation between Alexandra and her love seems permanent after her smug, judgmental brothers insist that Carl, an engraver, is a tramp and a gold digger and that their spinster sister, at age 40, has become a town joke. Carl distances himself from the feuding and asks Alexandra to give him a year in the North to strengthen his finances.

During the tense rising action, Cather echoes the sterility of Alexandra's spirit in an extended image of winter's control over the Continental Divide:

The teeming life that goes on down in the long grass is terminated. The prairie-dog keeps his hole. The rabbits run shivering from one frozen garden patch to another and are hard put to it to find frost-bitten cabbage stalks. At night the coyotes roam the wintry waste, howling for food. The variegated fields are all one color now; the pastures, the stubble, the roads, the sky are the same leaden gray. (ibid., 103)

Nebraska's monochromatic "iron country" symbolizes Alexandra's spiritual hibernation, which she relieves with "her old routine." In loneliness and isolation, she slides into romantic reveries of a man "like no man she knew; he was much larger and stronger and swifter." (ibid., 113) Ironically, the dream ends with the unidentified rescuer carrying her away from the fields, the source of her material success, to undisclosed ecstasy.

The novelist connects the untapped promise of the frontier with the emotional energy that Alexandra suppresses. Out of sight of Oscar, Lou, and disapproving neighbors, Alexandra's feelings become underground torrents, unseen but still churning. A conflict liberates her yearnings and rids her of the brothers' tyranny after she develops modern ideas about farming and sends her younger brother Emil to the university. Oscar and Lou maintain that land should pass to male heirs; she refuses to be bullied and orders them out of the house. A crisis reminds the reader that rashness does not equate with boldness. Emil, the rash young swain, dies while making love to Marie Shabata, a married woman whose husband, Frank, stalks her to a tryst under a mulberry tree and shoots them both. The loss unhinges Alexandra. After regaining sanity, she travels to Lincoln and visits Frank, who is dehumanized by prison. She makes peace with him and promises to seek a pardon. On return to her hotel room, she receives a wire from Carl and sets free the underground stream that no longer needs a dam.

In remarks to the press on the conclusion of *O Pioneers!*, Cather emphasized that the text speaks for itself: Carl Linstrum's return from Alaska as a successful prospector restores the old romance; the lovers enter a controlled relationship free of the fire of Emil's chancy affair and steadied by mutual trust and maturity. A testimony to Cather's admiration for immigrant Swedes and to her love for Nebraska, the novel depicts hearty emotions and ambitions, the basis for the success of the westward movement. Emblematic of careful husbandry, Alexandra's skill at management becomes "a white book, with clear writing about weather and beasts and growing things." (ibid.). The author adds that only "the happy few" pore over such a stodgy, unromantic ledger. Unlike romanticizers of the American pioneer, she applies straightforward narrative to a situation that others might overpaint with melodrama or sensationalism. Dedicated to New England regionalist Sarah Orne Jewett, *O Pioneers!* follows the genre constraints of the memoir, which makes no effort to embellish a good frontier love story. (Blain, Grundy, and Clements 1990; Bloom and Bloom 1962; Bloom 1986b; Bohlke 1986; Brown 1987; Buck 1992; Byrne and Snyder 1980; Cather 1947, 1977, 1978, 1991; Davidson and Wagner-Martin 1995; *DISCovering Authors* 1993; Drabble 1985; Ehrlich and Carruth 1982; Goring 1994; Hornstein 1973; Kunitz 1942; Lamar 1977; Magill 1958; Milner et al. 1994; "North Side" 1996; O'Brien 1986; Robinson 1983; Sherr and Kazickas 1994; Whitman 1992; Woodress 1982)

See also Cather, Willa; *Death Comes for the Archbishop; My Ántonia*.

OAKLEY, ANNIE

Annie Oakley, the star sharpshooter and actress, stands out from other frontier women in a time when females were disenfranchised, second-class citizens. For 50 years, she showcased her skill at turkey shoots, vaudeville, the circus, Buffalo Bill's Wild West Show, and a brief stint with Gordon W. Lillie's Pawnee Bill Historical Wild West Exhibition. Throughout her career, she published articles on shooting and her experiences as a competitor that appeared in the Newark *Sunday Call, American Shooter, New York Tribune, Shooting and Fishing, Shooting Times and British Sportsman, New York Sun,* and *Outlook,* and privately published her autobiography, *The Story of My Life* (1926).

According to her memoirs, the legendary "Little Miss Sure Shot," "The Rifle Queen," and "The Peerless Lady Wing-Shot," Phoebe Ann "Annie" Moses Oakley, daughter of pioneers Jacob and Susan Wise Moses (or Mozee), derived her signature modesty and self-restraint from a Quaker environment. Her parents had abandoned the burned remains of their log tavern in Hollidaysburg, Pennsylvania, in 1855. They moved west to a farm in Drake County, Ohio, where Oakley was born on August 13, 1860, the fifth of eight children. After her father's death from pneumonia and the death of her stepfather, Dan Brumbaugh, the family managed on Susan Moses's meager pay as a county visiting nurse.

It was her mother's decision that Oakley relieve the family of the cost of her upkeep by moving into the county infirmary to live with the aged, handicapped, and insane and attend school with other poor and orphaned children. Skills she learned from the matron, Mrs. Crawford "Auntie" Edington—wool carding, sewing, and fancy needlework—later enhanced her career in entertainment, when she made her trademark costumes herself. Mrs. Edington loved Annie but was compelled to board her with a stranger, who offered to take the girl as a babysitter and domestic. The situation forced the nine-year-old into servitude. She fled the confinement and dawn-to-late-night drudgery to locate Mrs. Edington, who returned the girl to the infirmary. Three years later, Annie reunited with her mother and siblings.

Oakley was cheered to find that Susan Moses had married mail carrier Joseph Shaw and settled in a real home, where she kept a garden and orchard. To relieve the family's debt, Oakley spent her savings from taking in sewing at the infirmary; when that was gone, her younger brother John taught her target shooting. Armed with her father's single-barrel muzzle loader, she was said to behead running quail at 50 yards. Her proficiency turned a profit with the sale of rabbits, squirrels, and grouse and enabled her to pay the mortgage on the family home. Merchants preferred selling her game because she hit the heads and didn't leave shot in the meat. During an 1875 Thanksgiving shooting match in Cincinnati, Annie bested showman "Kentucky Frank" Butler, an Irish emigrant, whom she married the next year. While Butler toured with his sharpshooting partner in vaudeville shows, she remained at home to continue her education.

Oakley's rise to stardom occurred in 1882, after Butler's partner became ill. She substituted and performed at the Crystal Hall in Springfield, Ohio, and was an immediate success. Petite, shy, and refined, but self-confident before an audience, she chose her stage surname from an Ohio town. She cut skirts, shirts, and frontier dresses and sunbonnets from tan cloth and embroidered them in contrasting colors, which matched her dainty gloves. In trim, cinch-waisted outfits and matching gloves and hat, she wowed audiences by shooting apples from the head of a poodle named George. At the end of the routine, Annie, Frank, and the dog took a bow.

Oakley and Butler acted in plays—*Slocum's Oath, Deadwood Dick, Miss Rora,* and *The Western Girl*—and joined Buffalo Bill's show in 1885, where she set up trick shooting with mirrors and animal and human targets and took part in reenactments of bear hunts, stage robberies, Indian attacks, daring rescues, and other stereotypical scenarios from the Old West. She performed with Sioux chief Sitting Bull, who believed that her skill was a gift from the Great Spirit and first called her Watanyi Cicilia, "Little Sure Shot." The show performed for royalty, notables, and politicians, among whom her trick shooting was well known. Oakley loved and trusted Cody and worked without a written contract for 17 years.

Although Oakley and her husband enjoyed the privileges of a private rail car and first-class hotel accommodations, she wearied of continual road performances, wardrobe demands, interviews, parades, practice, and gun care. She exerted considerable energy and polished acting stunts as the Wild West Show opener, for which she shot skeet from a bicycle and a galloping horse. In addition to tours, she performed for exhibitions and silent movies, posed for ads, and served as the company goodwill ambassador at Queen Victoria's Golden Jubilee in 1887 and the World's Columbian Exposition in 1893, where crowds thronged the tents and demanded autographs and a word with the stars.

Oakley's health suffered permanent damage from the pace of performing. In 1888, she had to rest after a tour of Great Britain. In 1893, she and Frank settled into their first home in Nutley, New Jersey, but returned to touring. A railcar smash in Virginia in October 1901 killed many horses and wounded Oakley, who remained in a New Jersey hospital for two months to recuperate from surgery. A worse incident occurred in 1921 near Daytona, Florida, where she was partially paralyzed when a car overturned, fracturing her hip and pulling tendons. The damage to her right leg forced her to wear a steel brace. After Butler accepted a post as skeet-shooting teacher at the Carolina Hotel in Pinehurst, North Carolina, in 1915, she joined him for demonstrations, such as splitting a playing card, shooting a dime tossed in the air, smashing swinging glass balls, or ripping a cigarette from his lips.

During World War I, Oakley and her husband entertained at army camps and raised funds for war charities by displaying their guns, memorabilia, and lavish gifts from fans around the world. Out of fond memories of the children of the Ohio infirmary, she melted gold medals and donated the proceeds to a southern orphanage. She retired to her half sister's home in Dayton, Ohio, in 1925, where fans and old friends dropped in for visits. Before her death from pernicious anemia on November 3, 1926, in Vandalia, Ohio, she wrote out explicit funeral plans and chose cremation rather than burial. Her ashes were stored in a silver loving cup and placed in a family safe. Three weeks later, Frank died. The two were commemorated by a double grave in Brock, Ohio. A life-size bronze statue of Annie in hat, neckerchief, and boots with rifle at rest stands in Annie Oakley Memorial Park in Greenville, Ohio. Artifacts are displayed at the Remington Gun Museum in Ilion, New York, and the National Cowgirl Hall of Fame in Hereford, Texas.

Over her lengthy career, thousands throughout North America and Europe witnessed Annie Oakley's thrilling, action-packed performances. Her name entered English as a slang synonym for a free ticket, punched with a hole like a shot from Annie's rifle. Numerous memoirs and biographies capitalized on her fame. In 1927, Courtney Ryley Cooper conveyed much of the previous generation's Oakley fever in a generous biography, *Annie Oakley, Woman at Arms*, which opens with a warm testimonial from Will Rogers, an old friend and admirer. Cooper portrays Oakley as a tomboy who learned how to put youth and enthusiasm to work to rescue her mother from poverty. To the end of the biography, the author maintains the legend of Oakley's good qualities—devotion, humility, practice, and skill.

Annie Oakley, billed as "Little Miss Sure Shot" in Buffalo Bill's Wild West Show, was a legendary rifle shooter. Oakley earned medals for her marksmanship, wrote articles about shooting, and an autobiography that was published in 1926, the year of her death.

In 1940, Herbert and Dorothy Fields composed *Annie Get Your Gun*, the source of Richard Rodgers and Oscar Hammerstein's classic musical. Irving Berling provided 15 energetic songs. The musical depicts Oakley as an illiterate, love-struck rube whom Buffalo Bill and others easily maneuver. An even less flattering portrait is the grunting, pidgin-talking Sitting Bull, who makes Annie his unofficially adopted daughter. Like a doting parent, he promises, "Annie want Frank. Annie get Frank. . . . Papa Bull dig up money." (Fields and Fields 1952, 69) The authors force him into a stoic, tight-lipped caricature of the real Sioux chief and turn Annie into a conniver. In the nonmusical version, she deliberately fudges in competition against Frank, then closes with her feisty good humor, "If'n ye hadn't [saved the show], I'd a shot ye right in the belly button!" (Fields and Fields 1946, 84)

Opening on Broadway in 1946 for a three-year run, *Annie Get Your Gun* was a high point of the career of Ethel Merman, who starred as Annie and stopped the show with two popular dialectic tunes, "Doing What Comes Natur'lly" and "You Can't Get a Man with a Gun." That same year, the road show starred Mary Martin and preceded Betty Hutton's version of the Annie role in the multimillion-dollar movie, filmed by MGM in 1950 and reprised as a television movie in 1957, starring Mary Martin. Other actresses who have played the popular role of Annie include Geraldine Chaplin, Barbara Stanwyck, and Judy Garland. (Cooper 1927; Fields and Fields 1946, 1952; Kasper 1992; Lamar 1977; McHenry 1980; Milner et al. 1994; Sackett 1996; Sayers 1981; Sherr and Kazickas 1994; Weatherford 1994; *Wild Women* 1994)

See also theater of the frontier.

O'DELL, SCOTT

A lover of nature and history, Scott O'Dell, a top writer of young adult frontier novels, received inspiration from his native Los Angeles, which he described as a "frontier town" as late as 1898, when he was born. The son of Union Pacific Railroad official Bennett Mason O'Dell and May Elizabeth Gabriel, O'Dell loved roaming his home turf on Terminal Island and sought solitude in the California wilds. He read widely and enjoyed schooling at Long Beach Polytechnic High School. On entry to Occidental College, he did not adjust to large classes and preplanned course outlines. For six years, he drifted and chose as he pleased from the offerings of the University of Wisconsin, Stanford, and the University of Rome. Establishing his own academic program, he profited from history, psychology, language, and philosophy—anything that would prepare him to write.

In 1925, O'Dell ended his eclectic studies and began a restless round of jobs, including farmer, technicolor cameraman for the MGM filming of *Ben Hur*, technical director for Paramount Studios, author of a correspondence course in photojournalism, freelance essayist, and book reviewer for the Los Angeles *Times*, *Daily News*, and *Mirror*. After serving in the air force during

World War I, he wrote *Woman of Spain: A Story of Old California* (1934) and published essays in *Mirror News, Fortnight, Saturday Review,* and the San Diego *Independent.* A decade after concentrating on mature readers, he shifted to young adults, whom he saw as more susceptible to themes from history and more likely to identify with real characters.

O'Dell's first major contribution to the young adult canon of fictional biography was *Island of the Blue Dolphins* (1960), a haunting tale of the marooning of a native woman on a craggy Pacific island 10 miles long lying 75 miles off the shore of Santa Barbara, California. Based on a historical account described in *Scribner's Monthly* in 1880, he tells the story of 12-year-old Karana, motherless daughter of Chief Chowig. Russian and Aleut trappers kill the chief while usurping rights to sea otters on the island's teeming shores. The interim chief leaves to seek help. That spring, a ship arrives to take the islanders to the mainland. While looking for her little brother Ramo, Karana realizes that the ship has left without them. Alone after wild dogs kill Ramo, she makes a fortress of whale ribs, dries candlefish for light, and learns to spearfish. While evading Aleut adventurers, she sits in her cave and sews a skirt of green cormorant skins. She survives a tidal wave and earthquake before welcoming rescuers from California and accompanying them to the Santa Barbara Mission.

In an epilogue, O'Dell connects the fictional Karana with the real lost Indian woman, who lived on San Nicolas Island from 1835 to 1853 after a gale drove the *Peor es Nada* out to sea with 20 islanders aboard. Discovered in July 1853 by Capt. Nidever and Father Gonzales after an earlier mission failed to locate her, she lived her remaining years in Santa Barbara. The frontier mission that received her was established by Father Junipero Serra and other Franciscan missionaries, who evangelized natives east of the channel island on which she was marooned. The woman never learned to speak English and communicated by hand signals. Unidentified and unclaimed by local Indians, she was buried in the mission cemetery under the name Juana Maria. Her cormorant skirt is still on display at the Vatican Museum.

Following the success of his first young adult historical novel, O'Dell wrote a tale of conquistadors, *The King's Fifth* (1966), a swift-paced story of Spanish treasure hunters and the Zuñi girl who guides and interprets for them. Although the book won awards, he was displeased with the ambitious scope of the book and moved on to *The Black Pearl* (1967), the brief story of Ramon Salazar of El Paz, Mexico, whom a greedy Spaniard abducts after Ramon retrieves the black pearl from the statue of the Virgin. The story, which is strikingly similar to John Steinbeck's *The Pearl*, is filled with idealism and betrayal. It ends with Ramon's liberation and the return of the pearl to the Madonna.

A decade after composing his award-winning story of the Lost Woman of San Nicholas, O'Dell turned to another strong female survivor of attempted genocide. Bright Morning, a Navajo shepherdess, is the heroine of *Sing Down the Moon* (1970), a fictional account of the Long Walk, the resettlement of Navajo and Apache superintended by Colonel Kit Carson in June 1863 to free the area for white settlers. On the high mesas above Canyon de Chelly, Arizona, O'Dell's heroine hears gunfire and observes a column of "Long Knives," the native name for white cavalrymen from Fort Defiance, who equip their rifles with bayonets. The next day, two Spanish slavers abduct her and a girlfriend to the lowlands, where Bright Morning enters the service of a white woman. Nehana, a Nez Perce slave, helps Bright Morning escape on stolen horses while whites gather for Maunday Thursday services. She rejoins Tall Boy, who is wounded in the shoulder during their flight north, and helps rig a travois to ease his transportation to their homeland.

The first winter of the Long Walk, soldiers routed 8,491 Navajos southeast out of Canyon de Chelly and destroyed farms, burned hogans, slaughtered livestock, chopped down peach orchards, and trampled crops. In O'Dell's version, during the forced march 180 miles southeast to a prison camp outside Fort Sumner, New Mexico, Bright Morning sees thousands of Indians struggle to find food and to survive the epidemics of cholera and smallpox that carry off 1,500, mostly the very young and the very old. At Bosque Redondo, despair deepens as supplies dwindle, crops fail, and idleness provokes quarrels with Apaches. Bright Morning marries Tall Boy in a traditional ritual and moves into a willow lean-to. She bides her time and conceals small portions of food in preparation for escape.

After the birth of a son, the couple flee northwest on horseback to their ancestral home. Bright Morning exults:

> Hidden Canyon was just as I remembered it. The yellow cliffs rose on all sides. The spring flowed from the rock and made a waterfall that the wind caught and spun out over the meadow. On the far side of the meadow was the grove of wild plums, where I had picked many handfuls of fruit. (O'Dell 1970, 119)

When the young family arrives the next spring, the few remaining trees flaunt white and pink blossoms. In a postscript, O'Dell explains that survivors like Bright Morning's family were released four years after their incarceration. Led by Manuelito, a rebel chief, the internees migrated unaided to their sacred homeland.

Another decade passed before O'Dell next wrote of a strong female survivor, *Sarah Bishop* (1980), the fictionalized biography of a girl from Midhurst, West Sussex, England, who was orphaned in Long Island, New York, at the time of the American Revolution. After the battle of Brooklyn Heights, she flees to the frontier to live in a cave on Waccabuc Pond at the edge of European society. The book preceded one of O'Dell's most historically accurate novels, *Streams to the River, River to the Sea* (1986), the fictional account of Sacajawea's assistance in guiding and interpreting for the Lewis and Clark expedition. The famed surveying party left a Mandan village in South Dakota in 1804, reached Fort Clatsop in Oregon Territory on November 7, 1805, and returned by an altered route on September 23, 1806. Like O'Dell's earlier female protagonists, Sacajawea or "Bird Girl," a Shoshone kidnapped by Minnetarees and sold to French trader Toussaint Charbonneau, is a model of loyalty and self-sufficiency. With her newborn son, Jean Baptiste "Pompey" Charbonneau, strapped in a cradle board, she earns the admiration of the expedition's leaders for courage and leadership. They pay her husband $500, but he gives her nothing from their earnings and deserts her for a younger native wife. O'Dell implies that Sacajawea and Clark are attracted to each other but ends the novel on a wistful parting between two people whom society would consider unsuited for marriage.

After a lengthy career, O'Dell, still writing at age 91, died of prostate cancer on October 15, 1989, in Mt. Kisco, New York. He left unfinished *Thunder Rolling in the Mountains* (1992), a fictional story of Sound of Running Feet, daughter of Chief Joseph, who flees white cavalrymen in a failed run for the Canadian border. O'Dell's research into the legend of the Lost Woman of San Nicholas earned him the Nene award, Rupert Hughes award, a Lewis Carroll Shelf award, and his first ALA Newbery Medal. The variety of awards and honors garnered in his half century of publishing includes two more Newberys, Los Angeles Public Library Focal award, Hans Christian Andersen Medal for lifetime achievement, Regina Medal, William Allen White award, German Juvenile International award, honors from the Freedoms Foundation and Parents Choice, and a University of Southern Mississippi Medallion. Three of his 35 published works have been filmed: *The Island of the Blue Dolphins* (Universal Pictures 1964), *The Black Pearl* (Diamond Films 1976), and *The King's Fifth*, his tale of Spanish *conquistadores*, which was the subject of *Mysterious Cities of Gold* (1982), a television animated series. (Fuller 1961; Gallo 1990; Georgiou 1969; Hardacre 1961; Hoffman and Samuels 1972; Kingston 1974; Kirkpatrick 1983; Meigs 1969; O'Dell 1943, 1961, 1967, 1970, 1972, 1980, 1982, 1986; O'Dell and Hall 1992; Roop 1984; Schon 1986; Snodgrass 1995b; Straub 1996; Townsend 1965, 1971; Warfel 1951; Wesselhoeft 1984; Wintle and Fisher 1974)

See also captivity motif; explorers of the frontier.

ORATORY, NATIVE AMERICAN

One of the most ephemeral genres in frontier literature, oratory, especially of Native American speakers, has made a comeback in late-twentieth-century compendia. One of the oldest works of oratory comes from traditional tales of Dekanahwideh, the legendary founder of the Confederate Nations. In explaining the tenets of his constitution, the orator uses a tree as a controlling metaphor. He concludes symbolically by binding a bundle of arrows with deer sinew, "which is strong, durable and lasting and then this Institution will be strong and unchangeable." As a reminder of the unified strengths of the six Confederate Nations, Dekanahwideh predicts, "If any evil should befall us in the future we shall stand or fall unitedly as one man." (Moses and Goldie 1992, 9–10)

Ethnologist Henry Rowe Schoolcraft's *Historical and Statistical Information Respecting the History, Condition and Prospects of the Indian Tribes of the United States* (1857) cites a speech given by the semilegendary lawgiver Hiawatha, founder of the Iroquois League. Before he spoke, a giant white heron swooped down and crushed Hiawatha's daughter, who vanished under the great feathered corpse. In awe of this heavenly omen, all members stepped forward to take a plume to wear during warfare. Hiawatha, shaken by their encounter with the Great Spirit, addressed the members of the five great nations, assigning each a position in the council lodge. He called the Mohawk the first among nations for their might and placed the wise Oneida second. The Onondaga, who were talented orators, were third. To the Seneca, he said, "You, whose dwelling is in the Dark Forest, and whose home is everywhere, shall be the fourth nation, because of your superior cunning in hunting." (Spiller and Blodgett 1949, 883) He concluded with the Cayuga, the people who excelled at agriculture and lodge building. The heart of his message is simple:

> Unite, you five nations, and have one common interest, and no foe shall disturb and subdue you. You, the people, who are as the feeble bushes, and you, who are a fishing people, may place yourselves under our protection, and we will defend you. (ibid.)

Hiawatha warns that individual tribes will be "enslaved, ruined, perhaps annihilated" if they try to survive on their own. He concludes with a reminder that petty tribes vanish in war, but that the great-hearted tribes are remembered and honored in dance and song.

An unusual speech in the Native American canon comes from Pocahontas, one of the few heroines from early times. Cited from 1616 in Plymouth, in the latter stages of her legend, a passage in Samuel G. Drake's *Biography and History of the Indians of North America* (1834) credits her with a high-toned, generous acknowledgment of Captain John Smith. Because Smith did not want to offend her by asking a Powhatan princess to call him father, she willingly embraces the verbal gesture with these words:

> You were not afraid to come into my father's country, and strike fear into every body but myself; and are you here afraid to let me call you father? I tell you, then, I will call you father, and you shall call me child; and so I will forever be of your kindred and country. (Drake 1834, 19)

The style, rhetorical balance, and grace of Pocahontas's speech suits legends that establish her self-possession and spunk. It is unlikely, however, that a preteen, even a Powhatan princess, would speak so stately and mature a sentiment.

An early spokesman, Miantunnomoh, a well-connected young sachem of the Narragansett of Massachusetts, set the tone and motif of Native American oratory with a strong objection to white colonists. The son of Chief Mascus and ally of the Mohegan chief Uncas in the 1630s, Miantunnomoh supported the English cause, particularly Governor William Bradford and Roger Williams. To display fealty, Miantunnomoh warred on the Pequot, then, in the 1640s, appeared to veer from earlier alliances toward an anti-English stance. Developing a bias that remained constant for the next three and a half centuries, he implored Waiandance, a Long Island sachem, to challenge European invaders:

> You know our fathers had plenty of deer and skins, and our plains were full of deer and of turkeys, and our coves and rivers were full of fish. But, brothers, since these English have seized upon our country, they cut down the grass

with scythes, and the trees with axes. Their cows and horses eat up the grass, and their hogs spoil our beds of clams; and finally we shall starve to death! therefore, stand not in your own light, I beseech you, but resolve with us to act like men . . . fall on and kill men, women and children; but no cows; they must be killed as we need them for provisions, till the deer come again. (ibid., 64)

The image of despoilers on native soil permeates Miantunnomoh's rhetoric with a clarity, pragmatism, and concreteness that builds his case.

A more passionate assessment of Indian sufferings at the hands of whites comes from Black Hawk, war chief of the Sauk and Fox, who foresaw the downfall of Indian values. Speaking of himself in third person, he notes the future for Native Americans:

He laments their fate. The white men do not scalp the head; but they do worse—they poison the heart; it is not pure with them.—His countrymen will not be scalped, but they will, in a few years, become like the white men, so that you can't trust them, and there must be, as in the white settlements, nearly as many officers as men, to take care of them and keep them in order.

Fearful that assimilation will rob aborigines of their ethnic qualities, he concludes plaintively:

Farewell, my nation! Black Hawk tried to save you, and avenge your wrongs. He drank the blood of some of the whites. He has been taken prisoner, and his plans are stopped. He can do no more. He is near his end. His sun is setting, and he will rise no more. Farewell to Black Hawk. (ibid., 137)

The dismay and defeat that fuels Black Hawk's speech attests to the decline in native control of the East Coast, when the boundaries of the frontier lay east of the Mississippi River. His impetus and intent parallel the words of several generations of Indian leaders stretching from Iroquois lands over the Continental Divide to California and Alaska.

After being betrayed by Keokuk, his old adversary, Black Hawk grew mellow in captivity. Upon his departure from Fort Monroe on June 5, 1833, he assumed that he would soon die. He intoned a noble benediction:

The memory of your friendship will remain till the Great Spirit says it is time for Black Hawk to sing his death song . . . The Great Spirit has given us our hunting grounds, and the skin of the deer which we kill there is his favorite, for its color is white, and this is the emblem of peace. This hunting dress and these feathers of the eagle are white. Accept them, my brother; I have given one like this to the White Otter. Accept it as a memorial of Black Hawk. (ibid., 139)

Black Hawk's magnanimous gesture bestows an idealistic peace on a nation whom he has loved. As though drawing out his farewell to savor parting moments, he concludes, "When he is far away, this will serve to remind you of him. May the Great Spirit bless you and your children. Farewell."

Although Miantunnomoh and Black Hawk primarily keep to political concerns, other topics stand out as significant subjects of memorable orations. About

White Bear, photographed by John Anderson

1760, a Yazoo interpreter named Monchactape journeyed from the Mississippi valley to Ohio, traditional land of the Iroquois. Venturing farther to the northeast, Monchactape describes in his travelogue:

> I went and viewed the great fall of the River St. Lawrence, at Niagara, which was distant from the village several days' journey. The view of this great fall, at first, made my hair stand on end, and my heart almost leap out of its place; but afterwards, before I left it, I had the courage to walk under it. (ibid., 34)

At the end of five years, Monchactape returned to his people with stories to tell of the Kansa nation, floating villages, and meadows covered in buffalo.

Memorable Native American oratory dating to the birth of American democracy follows the themes of the colonial period. During the American Revolution, the prophet Kanakuk delivered a sermon to General George Clark:

> The Great Spirit said to me you must start from a certain point. This is the point: I have marked it. Then we got to a point that I have marked B and finally to one that I have marked C where the Great Spirit said he would appear. At point B the Great Spirit gave his blessings to the Indians and told them to throw away their medicine bags, not to steal, not to tell lies, not to murder, and not to quarrel. He told them that if they did not do this they could not get on the straight way but would have to go along the crooked path. That path led to an abyss of fire. (Radin 1934, 366)

A strong parallel of the homilies of Cotton Mather and a precursor of the beatific prophecies of Wovoka, Kanakuk's metaphoric injunction contains universal elements of moral behavior. When the Ghost Dance revived these precepts in the second half of the nineteenth century, Wovoka adjured:

> You ask me to plow the ground. Shall I take a knife and tear my mother's bosom? Then when I die she will not take me to her bosom to rest. You ask me to dig for stones! Shall I dig under her skin for her bones? Then when I die I cannot enter her body to be born again. You ask me to cut grass and make hay and sell it, and be rich like white men but how dare I cut my mother's hair? (ibid., 368)

Wovoka's insistent parallelism and rhetorical questions testify to a truth that frontiersmen misunderstood, but that subsequent generations learned the hard way: unlike whites, Indians lived in ecological harmony with the earth mother, whom custom and honor bade them to respect.

Parallel structure also anchors Captain Joseph Brant's austere speech in 1801 to a friend on the death of his mother. A Mohawk ally of the British during the Revolutionary War, Brant speaks in controlled measures, each segment beginning with "Brother," a conciliatory gesture to Brant's white friend. Brant typifies the Mohawk concept of the Great Spirit by noting that the custom of condolence dates to ancient times and permeates all cultures. Fearful that whites will neglect the Mohawk in their time of grief, he extends a ceremonial gift of wampum and pleads "to raise you upon your feet as you formerly used to be for since our late loss it seems you have been confined as one absent." Brant concludes with propriety mingled with affection that he hopes "to strengthen your mind and body that you may not be cast down." (Moses and Goldie 1992, 16)

A compelling example of Native American polemics comes from Red-Jacket (Sagoyewatha), a Seneca chief and acclaimed orator from Buffalo, New York. In 1805, in a debate with a missionary dispatched from the Boston Missionary Society to teach Indians how to worship, Red-Jacket retorts against proselytizing:

> You say that you are sent to instruct us how to worship the Great Spirit agreeably to his mind, and if we do not take hold of the religion which you white people teach, we shall be unhappy hereafter; you say that you are right, and we are lost; how do we know this to be true? We understand that your religion is written in a book; if it was intended for us as well as you, why has not the Great Spirit given it to us, and not only to us, but why did he not give to our forefathers the knowledge of that book, with the means of understanding it rightly? We only know what you tell us about it; how shall we know when to believe, being so often deceived by the white people? (Drake 1834, 79)

Red-Jacket displays skill in logic by countering that white people alone bear the guilt for killing the Son of God. If Jesus had chosen to settle among Indians, Red-Jacket maintains, he would have been well treated.

The subject of life after death permeates Native American philosophy and oratory. In 1811, a noted evangelist, the Prophet, whose ceremonial name was Ellskwatawa and who was a 50-year-old triplet brother of Tecumseh and

Kumskaka from a notable Shawnee family, prophesied after turning from alcohol and warning his fellow Shawnee:

> Don't be alarmed. I have seen heaven. Call the nation together, that I may tell them what has appeared to me . . . [according to two male messengers] the Great Spirit is angry with you, and will destroy all the red men unless you refrain from drunkenness, lying and stealing, and turn yourselves to him, you shall never enter the beautiful place which we will now show you. (ibid., 107)

To entice his hearers, the Prophet describes a beautiful retreat filled with joy and pleasure, an Edenic vision he spread among the Creek along the Wabash.

In 1851, historian Francis Parkman published *The Conspiracy of Pontiac*, an incisive study of Chief Pontiac, the Ottawa combatant in the French and Indian Wars. In Chapter IX, Parkman carefully sets the stage for one of the chief's most significant council meetings. Dressed in scanty loincloth and with his hair flowing down his back, he turned his dark, stern countenance on his hearers and addressed them in a firm, impassioned tone. Parkman noted that his audience encouraged him with "deep, guttural ejaculations of assent and approval." (Parkman 1991, 496)

The speech, gained secondhand from Canadians who interviewed an eyewitness, inveighed against the arrogance, rapacity, and injustice of the English. Pontiac contrasted the English with the French, whom he acknowledged by raising a wampum belt he had received from the king of France. To appeal to the superstitions of his people, the chief related a myth about a Delaware hunter who follows the directions of a female spirit and jettisons his clothing, pack, gun, and ammunition before ascending to the Great Spirit. The creator questions,

> Why do you suffer the white men to dwell among you? My children, you have forgotten the customs and traditions of your forefathers. Why do you not clothe yourselves in skins, as they did, and use the bows and arrows, and the stone-pointed lances, which they used? You have bought guns, knives, kettles, and blankets, from the white men, until you can no longer do without them; and, what is worse, you have drunk the poison fire-water, which turns you into fools. Fling all these things away; live as your wise forefathers lived before you. (ibid., 499)

By assuming the persona of the Great Spirit, Pontiac urges the gathering to take advice from God and to join the French in wiping out the Redcoats. Parkman characterizes the speech as an antiprogressive message shared by Red-Jacket, Tecumseh, and others who view white technology as detrimental to Indians.

According to Parkman's history, when war threatened Detroit, Pontiac addressed his Canadian allies with cunning assurances of brotherhood:

> I am the same French Pontiac who assisted you seventeen years ago. I am a Frenchman, and I wish to die a Frenchman; and I now repeat to you that you and I are one—that it is for both our interests that I should be avenged. Let me alone. I do not ask you for aid, for it is not in your power to give it. I only ask provisions for myself and men. (ibid., 533)

Pontiac concludes his eloquent plea with a promise that, after he succeeds in ejecting the English from the Great Lakes region, his people will return to their villages and watch over the French lest any Indian should wrong them.

At the end of a disastrous era of treachery and disappointment, the French lost their foothold south of the Great Lakes. At an assembly of Indian nations in Detroit, Pontiac makes the necessary concessions and peace initiatives to the English. In a formal opening, he announces that he has "taken the King of England for my father, in presence of all the nations now assembled." (ibid., 833) The chief thanks his new allies for reestablishing the council but boldly disdains the enticement of liquor, a meretricious evil that draws his people to Detroit and precipitates drunken quarrels. Wisely, he condemns liquor for alienating whites and Indians.

One of North America's most stirring pleas for native homelands comes from a speech by Seattle or Sealthl, chief of the Duwamish in Washington State in the mid-nineteenth century. A peacemaker who accommodated the arrival of white settlers to the Puget Sound area, at age 68 he verbally assessed the plight of Native Americans, whom he described as "ebbing away like a rapidly receding tide that will never return." (Seattle 1987, 175) In summation, he deduces that the white man's god allows the decline of Indians because he prefers whites. His explanation of the Native American attitude toward the earth contrasts sharply with that of pioneers: "To us the ashes of our ancestors are sacred and their resting place is hallowed ground. You wander far from the graves of your ancestors and seemingly without regret." (ibid., 176)

Like earlier leaders and savants, Seattle blends political savvy with religious mysticism. His belief in a spiritual home for the souls of dead Indians consoles him. Summarizing the future of the city that was later named Seattle in his honor, he predicts that Americans will never rid themselves of Indians:

> At night when the streets of your cities and villages are silent and you think them deserted, they will throng with the returning hosts that once filled and still love this beautiful land. The White Man will never be alone. (ibid., 176)

He concludes enigmatically that God should be king of the dead, then reverses his statement with his belief about the afterlife: "There is no death, only a change of worlds."

After the post–Civil War push to settle Indians on reservations to make way for more white settlers, Native American speeches moved irrevocably to the subject of Indian removal and loss of traditional lands and freedoms. Known as "White Bear, the Orator of the Plains," Satanta, a Kiowa chief, delivered a personal declaration in 1867 before Satank, Kicking Bird, and U.S. commissioners who assembled at Medicine Lodge Creek, Kansas. Pressed by white negotiators, he reluctantly accepted the Medicine Lodge Treaty, which removed his people to the hated Indian territory. Of his love and loyalty to the prairie, he says, "I love the land and the buffalo and will not part with it. . . . I love to roam over the prairies. There I feel free and happy." However, he accepted the reality that the day of Indian independence had ended. He predicted, "When we settle down, we grow pale and die." (Satanta 1987, 270)

In 1871, Satanta was tried at Fort Sill, Oklahoma, for first-degree murder after attacking a wagon train and killing the occupants. At the end of the proceedings, he spoke to the court that tried him:

> I look around me and see your braves, squaws and papooses, and I have said in my heart if I ever get back to my people I will never make war upon you. I have always been the friend of the white man, ever since I was so high. My tribe has taunted me and called me a squaw because I have been the friend of the Tehannas. I am suffering now for the crimes of bad Indians—of Satank and Lone Wolf and Kicking Bird and Big Bow and Fast Bear and Eagle Heart, and if you will let me go I will kill the three latter with my own hand. I did not kill the Tehannas. (McConnell 1996, 287)

Satanta won the hearts of humanitarians and gained a reprieve, but he was incarcerated for life. His sad conclusion predates his imprisonment in Texas, where, in 1878, at the age of 48, he killed himself by leaping from a window.

Similarly dismayed at his nation's hopeless state, Chief Joseph of the Nez Perce, protector of his tribe's noncombatants, refused to die in a strange land. He led his nontreaty band on a circuitous chase from Dug Bear, Oregon, through the Bitterroot Mountains of Idaho, southeast through Yellowstone National Park in Wyoming, then north to Snake Creek, Montana. On the trail, he cried to his people, "I do not care. I am willing to die! But first, I will kill some soldiers. I shall not turn back from death." (Robbins 1996, 162)

Chased by a Civil War hero, General Oliver Otis "Cut Arm" Howard, and a mass of troopers and volunteers, the Nez Perce put up a gallant front against howitzers and Gatling guns. To end his people's torment, Chief Joseph capitulated to U.S. troops in 1877 only miles from the Canadian border, where he had attempted to flee with 750 tribe members. To his captor, General Nelson A. "Bear Coat" Miles, he made the most beloved and honored native speech, "I Will Fight No More Forever," which is frequently anthologized in textbooks. He states simply the plight of old people and children freezing in the northwest forests:

> My people, some of them, have run away to the hills, and have no blankets, no food, and no one knows where they are—perhaps freezing to death. I want to have time to look for my children and see how many I can find. Maybe I shall find them among the dead. Hear me, my chiefs. I am tired; my heart is sick and sad. From where the sun now stands I will fight no more forever. (Joseph 1987, 271)

A far cry from the picture of the stoic, tight-lipped wooden Indian, Chief Joseph is not too proud to admit that he is weary of carnage and that the toll on his tribe is already more than he can bear.

Twentieth-century literature revived interest in native philosophy. John Ehle's *Trail of Tears* (1988) quotes Onitositaii, a late-eighteenth-century Cherokee chief commonly known as Old Tassel, who defied whites from pushing further into tribal land. He concludes:

> The great God of Nature has placed us in different situations. It is true that he has endowed you with many superior advantages; but he has not created us

to be your slaves. *We are a separate people!* He has given each their lands, under distinct considerations and circumstances: he has stocked yours with cows, ours with buffalo; yours with hog, ours with bear; yours with sheep, ours with deer. (Ehle 1988, 19)

Onitositaii's differentiation between domestic lifestyle versus residence in the wild compels his hearers to understand that the Cherokee must retain rights to open land. Only by traditional means can they supply themselves and their dependents with food and raw materials and maintain their autonomy. (Brown 1970; Drake 1834; Ehle 1988; Horn 1964; Joseph 1987; McConnell 1996; McIntosh 1844; Moses and Goldie 1992; Parkman 1991; Patterson and Snodgrass 1994; Radin 1934; Robbins 1996; Satanta 1987; Seattle 1987; Spiller and Blodgett 1949; Straub 1996; Waldman 1990)

See also Bury My Heart at Wounded Knee; Howard, Oliver Otis.

OREGON TRAIL

The most popular of the westward routes, the Oregon Trail appealed to thousands of seekers and drovers during the 45 years of its use. An area that beckoned the entrepreneur, speculator, prospector, settler, rancher, missionary, and European immigrant, Oregon was the goal of the "Great Migration," a mass phenomenon that changed American history. Verse by James Marshall replicates the cadence of whips, dray animals, and wagon wheels on the way west from Liberty:

Out they came from Liberty, out across the plains,
Two-stepping, single-footing, hard-boiled and easy-shooting
Whips cracking; oaths snapping
    Hear those banjos wail—
Emigratin' westward on the Oregon Trail. (Coleman 1932, 107–108)

Concrete images juxtapose good with ill, placing mud holes and snow crusts alongside Independence Rock and hallelujahs for a glorious sunset. While children are born and men die, the conquerors of the wilderness board their wagons and creak on toward "Free land in Oregon!"

As described in Meriwether Lewis and William Clark's journals, the route was rich in game and fur-bearing animals, dotted with lush pastures, and accessible by navigable waters. The Oregon Trail led to a worthy destination—the Pacific Northwest, a potential center for trade. Early reports from Hall J. Kelley, Kit Carson, Nathaniel Wyeth, Jim Bridger, James Beckwourth, Jedediah Smith, Robert Stuart, Thomas Fitzpatrick, and John C. Fremont precipitated a steady crawl of wagons across the continent on a four- to six-month expedition to prosperity. To most newcomers, Indians along the trail spelled trouble. However, painter George Catlin defied the majority by welcoming opportunities to meet and study Native Americans. On his sojourn west to Oregon, he painted hundreds of portraits and ceremonial scenes, which he used to illustrate three books: *Letters and Notes on the Manners, Customs and Condition of the North American Indians* (1841), *North American Indian Portfolio* (1844), and *Last Rambles amongst the Indians of the Rocky Mountains and the Andes* (1868). His meticulous attention to detail provides ethnologists, anthropologists, and historians with the only remaining eyewitness view of nineteenth-century tribal life among the Mandan, who were decimated by European diseases.

Letters, journals, diaries, and reports document the history of the Oregon Trail. According to Lansford W. Hastings's *The Emigrants' Guide to Oregon and California* (1845) and other handbooks for pioneers, the trail, which received its name from organizers in 1841, officially began at Independence or other of the supply centers in Missouri and covered a series of landmarks: a thousand miles from Fort Kearny, Nebraska, to the treacherous quicksand and tricky currents of the Platte River, to Fort Laramie, Wyoming. Along the way to the North Platte past Split Rock and the end of the Sweetwater River, travelers looked for Chimney Rock, Scotts Bluff, and Independence Rock, landmarks pocked by scratched messages left for stragglers to find. From South Pass, the gateway to Oregon, travelers moved on nearly 300 more miles to Fort Bridger, Soda Springs, Idaho, and Fort Hall on the Snake River. The last leg of the journey was hardest. Beginning at Whitman's Mission on the Columbia River to Fort Walla Walla and west to Mt. Hood and the Willamette Valley, pioneers completed their trek of 2,000 miles. An alternate known as the Applegate-Lassen Road took a lesser number to the Rogue River Valley in southwest Oregon.

Obstacles along the overland route were numerous. Indian tribes were usually peaceful but unpredictable; portages were difficult, rattlesnakes plentiful, and supplies and tools unattainable. Waters often became impassable by the time trains converged at chosen fords. Detours elongated the route, delaying travelers from connecting with land agents and family members and from reaching pastures when their stock needed fattening. During the peak years of the 1840s and the 1850s, approximately 4 percent to 6 percent of travelers died of malaria, pneumonia, cholera, drowning, gunshot wounds, and falls; others wearied of the constant threat of danger, the inconvenience of irregular game as the buffalo became scarce during the winter migration, and the stress of walking alongside heavily laden wagons and oxcarts. Supplanted by stagecoach, rail, and steamer travel, the overland route lost its appeal after the Civil War. Similar migration routes include the Mormon Trail, a trek west from Nauvoo, Illinois, to the Great Salt Lake in Utah, taken by Brigham Young and his followers in 1846 and 1847. Two years later, a path led south to the goldfields of California, a popular destination for speculators and prospectors.

Writing about the nation's spread west came from a variety of hands: *My Journal, 1836*, the diary of Presbyterian missionary Narcissa Prentiss Whitman, who traveled to Oregon with husband Dr. Marcus Whitman, did not arrive in print until long after the family's massacre by the Cayuse in 1847. John C. Fremont published his *Report of the Exploring Expeditions of 1842 and 1843–44* in 1845, but waited until the 1880s to tackle his memoirs. J. M. Shively wrote a descriptive guidebook, *Route and Distances to Oregon and California* (1846), complete with watering holes, fords, and tips on dangerous Indians, who proved to be an overrated hazard of the Great Migration. A Pulitzer Prize–winning novel, H. L. Davis's *Honey in the Horn* (1935), typifies the lives of the pioneers who survived the trail and built the state of Oregon.

One of the most readable and factual of the westward diaries was written by attorney Thomas Jefferson Farnham. He was elected captain of a group of 19 pioneers and kept a daybook while crossing the continent from Independence, Missouri, to the Pacific. After opening a law firm in San Francisco, he published *Travels in the Great Western Prairies* (1841) and *Life and Adventures in California* (1846). His wife Eliza, a staff member at Sing Sing Prison, published her own memoirs, *Life in Prairie Land* (1846). Thomas Farnham's first work (republished as *An 1839 Wagon Train Journal*) begins with an overview of Western exploration and launches into destination, date of departure, and a list of necessaries: bacon and flour, salt and pepper, powder kegs, canvas and oil-cloth, bullets, powder horns, and cap boxes. His description of camping on the trail typifies the westering experience with its agreeable swap of mountain yarns and fireside camaraderie. Yet the constant state of alert causes each adult to sit with rifle at the ready, shooting hand on the breech and barrel resting on the opposite.

On the first week of his journey, Farnham rhapsodizes on pioneering by extolling the healthful qualities of soup made of fresh water and game and consumed over an open fire. He exclaims:

> The exceeding comfort of body and mind at that moment undoubtedly gave it being. It was an emotion of condolence for those of my fellow mortals who are engaged in the manufacture of rheumatisms and gout. Could they only for an hour enter the portals of prairie life—for one hour breathe the inspiration of a hunter's transcendentalism—for one hour feed upon the milk and honey and marrow of life's pure unpeppered and unsalted viands, how soon would they forsake that ignoble employment. (Farnham 1983, 13)

The idealism of Farnham's text falters at less sanguine moments, such as a spartan supper of hardtack and water, then swells anew after hunters snag a buffalo during their stay at Fort William on the Platte River. He reports the cooking of "trapper's butter," a trail term for marrow, which is boiled in water and blood and served with salt and pepper. The second course, "boudies," is made from intestines turned inside out, stuffed with strips of tenderloin, and roasted on sticks over the flame.

Farnham's Oregon Trail lore is rich in observations of Indian life and customs. Beyond the Little Snake River, he reports his encounter with Paiutes, whom he likens to primitive Hottentots and describes as too inept to wield a club. He tells how they winter in holes in the slopes of sand hills, where unidentified slavers trap the youngest tribe members in spring. After fattening their prey, captors transport their human booty to Santa Fe to sell at the slave market. Farnham notes that comely teenage girls bring the best price, $300 to $400. More comfortable tribes are the Snake or Shoshone, whom Lewis and Clark met at the headwaters of the Missouri River. Farnham admires their intelligence and comfortable lodges and lauds them for avoiding alcohol, which clouds their judgment.

Farnham's assessment of the Oregon Trail experience is a spirited narrative ever fresh with side notes, history, anecdotes, and observations about nature, hunting, survival, weather, and commerce. Useful information includes a tidy tabulation of 1831's earnings in pounds, shillings, and pence for the Hudson Bay Company, the local monopolizer of the fur trade:

Animal Skins	Total	Unit Price			Annual Profit		
		£	s	d	£	s	d
beaver	126,944	1	5	0	158,689	0	0
muskrat	375,730	0	0	6	9,393	5	6
lynx	58,010	0	8	0	23,204	0	0
wolf	5,947	0	8	0	2,378	0	0
bear	3,850	1	0	0	3,850	0	0
fox	8,765	0	10	0	4,328	10	0
mink	9,298	0	2	0	929	16	0
raccoon	325	0	1	6	24	7	6
tails	2,290	0	1	0	114	10	0
wolverine	1,744	0	3	0	261	12	0
deer	645	0	3	0	96	15	0
weasel	34	0	0	6	0	16	0

Farnham adds that Hudson Bay stock originally cost 100 pounds and that dividends range upward from 10 percent. His detailed account covers the history of the Missouri Fur Company, Pacific Fur Company, and a Canadian firm, the North-West Fur Company. While camped at Wappatoo Island, he questions the fairness of the Oregon trade, which the British dominate, and lauds the promise of Puget Sound as a port from which traders may sell furs and hides in Asia.

Seven years later, during the height of travel along the Oregon Trail, Francis Parkman wrote *The Oregon Trail: Sketches of Prairie and Rocky Mountain Life* (1849), a literary treasure of early westering writings. A more scholarly work than Farnham's, composed of autobiographical details and dialogue as well as observations and vignettes of Sioux life, Parkman's work, illustrated with his own maps and with sketches by Felix O. C. Darley, throbs with idiomatic exchanges and the excitement of a buffalo hunt. Similar in account to George Orwell's "Shooting an Elephant," the episode describes how the hunter sights and then fires:

> The spiteful crack of the rifle responds to his touch, and instantly in the middle of the bare spot appears a small red dot. The buffalo shivers; death has overtaken him, he cannot tell from whence; still he does not fall, but walks heavily forward, as if nothing had happened. Yet before he has gone far out upon the sand, you see him stop; he totters; his knees bend under him, and his head sinks forward to the ground. Then his whole vast bulk sways to one side; he rolls over on the sand, and dies with a scarcely perceptible struggle. (Parkman 1973, 280)

Parkman explains that the frontiersman has a good chance of bagging a buffalo by stalking the herd to a water hole or over the prairie. The group relies on the expertise of Henri Chatillon, their guide. Parkman adds that even Chatillon has been known to straggle back to camp scratched and covered with prickly pear thorns from the unpleasant task of sliding on his belly across rough turf in hope of a dinner of fresh buffalo steak.

Critics accuse Parkman of taking little interest in the Oregon Trail as the path of Western settlement. These commentaries imply that he was a rich man's son, an elitist and aristocrat who absented himself from travelers and stood outside the arena to make notes for his pet historical project. They are, in part, correct in characterizing Parkman as wealthy and enraptured by the study of the setting and lifestyles of the people he meets on the westward journey. However, these detractors omit a significant difference between Parkman and the average wagoneer: he set out from Missouri as an observer, not a pioneer. Whereas others sold their Eastern holdings and moved west to a new life, Parkman had no intention of leaving Boston permanently. Bent on capturing the moment and returning to his desk to write a permanent record, he signed on for a round-trip. As an eyewitness, he accomplished his aim to preserve for history the sights and events of his 1846 journey.

In the twentieth century, novelist A. B. Guthrie turned the story of the Oregon Trail story into a Pulitzer Prize–winning novel, *The Way West* (1949), the middle title in a historical trilogy that begins with *The Big Sky* (1947) and concludes with *These Thousand Hills* (1956). His skillful text re-creates vignettes of the past, such as women and children walking on the windward side of the wagons

> and probably laughing and chattering and looking for wild flowers tough enough to grow on this dry ridge between the Little Blue and the Platte. It was cactus they'd find, and thistle and low sage standing silverish in the sun. The only flowers they were likely to see were the little yellow-hearted daisies that could sprout from a stone. (Guthrie 1960, 105)

Like the resilient daisies, Guthrie's characters survive wheel replacement and repair, buffalo stampedes, and flash floods strong enough to sweep wagons and their contents into swirling rapids.

The pace of Guthrie's fiction rarely halts for relaxation as pioneers slog through muck, hold to draglines during steep descents, and keep an eye out for dangerous predators. Near the conclusion of the overland haul, Guthrie describes their mounting fatigue during the final cut:

> Here, from Boise to the Dalles, was the windup of the trail, the finish of the test, the yes or no to Oregon. Here by slow wheel tracks at last was being written the answer to a question raised years ago last spring, raised so long ago a man lost its beginning across the plain-peak, sage-tree, sand-rock field of time. He lost it along with places, people and doings remembered from before, so that none of them came real to him and he asked himself if sure enough there was an Independence, a Missouri and a spot he once called home, or were they vapors in his mind. (ibid., 390)

In the end, Guthrie follows his pathfinders to Oregon. He exalts them as "Crossers of plains. Grinders through the dust. Climbers of mountains. Forders of rivers. Meeters of dangers. Sailors at last of the big waters. Nation makers. Builders of the country." (ibid., 434) Filmed by Harold Hecht in 1967, the epic Western starred Kirk Douglas, Robert Mitchum, Richard Widmark, Lola Albright, Sally Field, Stubby Kaye, and Jack Elam in a disappointing cinema extravaganza. (Blain, Grundy, and Clements 1990; Breeden 1979; Catlin 1965, 1989; Coleman 1932; Davis 1992; Farnham 1983; Grafton 1992; Guthrie 1960; Hastings 1845; "History" 1996; Kirsch and Murphy 1967; Lamar 1977; Milner et al. 1994; Morrison 1973; Parkman 1973, 1991; Ridge 1993; Swift n.d.; Unruh 1993; Wexler 1995)

See also Catlin, George; Mormons; Parkman, Francis.

PARKMAN, FRANCIS

America's historian of the early stage of the westering movement, Francis Parkman composed bold eyewitness documentaries of Anglo-Indian relations and produced realistic vignettes of the pioneer era. A devout scholar and reader of French and Italian authors, he abandoned the objective mode of archivism and relied on observation as material for detailed exposition. As he explained:

> The narrator must seek to imbue himself with the life and spirit of the time. He must study events in their bearings near and remote; in the character, habits, and manners of those who took part in them. He must himself be, as it were, a sharer or a spectator of the action he describes. (Bartlett's 1992, 503)

Submerged in the sense impressions of historic events, he became a participant. Such devotion to verisimilitude sustained Parkman over historic ground in search of what he called "faithfulness to the truth," the guiding principle of his most popular writings, *The Oregon Trail: Sketches of Prairie and Rocky Mountain Life* (1849) and *The History of the Conspiracy of Pontiac* (1851).

Born in the Beacon Hill section of Boston on September 16, 1823, Parkman inherited a rich lineage of Americana, including kinship with an Indian fighter, diarist, numerous ministers, and Puritan and Unitarian notables. The elder son among four sisters and a younger brother, he was the grandson of Samuel Parkman, a dynamic merchant, and the son of Caroline Hall and the Reverend Francis Parkman, a Unitarian minister at New North Church. Parkman inherited his grandfather's wealth and lived in the family mansion in Bowdoin Square. Thus, he had the leisure and means to indulge in books, travel, and social events sparked by stimulating conversation with New England Brahmins. In boyhood, he tramped the wild near the farm of his maternal grandparents, Nathaniel and Joanna Cotton Brooks Hall, near Medford, Massachusetts. He rode horseback over faint trails left from the French and Indian War and learned firsthand the natural beauty of New England's White Mountains.

After preliminary tutelage at Mr. Angier's school, Parkman spent winters studying Greek and Roman classics, literature, and math at Chauncy Place School to prepare for Harvard. In college, he studied under master historian Jared Sparks, to whom he dedicated *The History of the Conspiracy of Pontiac*.

Summers left time for canoeing and research in Montreal and Quebec for the project Parkman had outlined at age 18—a definitive chronicle of the French and Indian War. His ambitious plan threatened to swamp him. Before induction into Phi Beta Kappa and graduation in 1844 with a B.A., he suffered physical collapse, traveled to Europe on a fruit boat, and recuperated by touring Malta, Sicily, Italy, Switzerland, France, England, and Scotland. His commencement address, "Romance in America," which presaged the direction of his career, warned of the depletion of nature from lumbering, mining, dams, and defoliation. While pursuing an LL.B. from Dana Law School, he published anonymous sketches and tales in *Knickerbocker Magazine* and organized expeditions to the Alleghenies, Buffalo, and the Great Lakes. Despite his father's insistence, he never sought certification from the bar association.

Newly graduated and enthusiastic about history, Parkman did preliminary research on Pontiac, an Ottawa chief, and met with Henry Rowe Schoolcraft, an authority on Indians. Accompanying a cousin, Quincy Adams Shaw, who was going west to hunt, Parkman set out for St. Louis on April 28, 1846, in the peak years of the "Great Migration" over the Oregon Trail, which began in 1841 and remained the preferred route until stagecoach travel over multiple routes replaced it in 1860. He interviewed mountain men who had direct knowledge of Pontiac and began visiting historic sites via a 1,700-mile trek to Fort Laramie, Wyoming, a former fur trading hub on the confluence of the Laramie and North Platte Rivers. Taking to saddle, rifle, and oar, he followed experienced mountain man and guide Henri Chatillon, whose wife was an Oglala Sioux. Chatillon led the party into Indian territory inhabited by Pawnee brigands, impoverished Potawatomie, Kanzas decked in finery, shave-headed Fox and Sauk, Kickapoo traders, turbaned Delaware and Shawnee, and Wyandotte in Caucasian dress. The party returned in late summer via the Santa Fe Trail to Missouri.

According to his journals, Parkman hunted buffalo, lived among the Sioux, studied the Iroquois League, and interviewed trappers, traders, and woodsmen to supply data for his research on the Oregon Trail. To enliven passages of straight commentary, he name-dropped Daniel Boone's grandson as the supplier of a replacement mule and interlaced description with bits of conversation. In context, Delorier, the colorful killer of 30 grizzlies and cheery muleteer at the rear of the company, salts his orders with blasphemous patois shouts of "*Sacre enfant de garce!*" (Holy child of the bitch!) and hasty commands of "*Avance donc!*" (Get up!) (Parkman 1991, 17, 29) During a quiet moment while rain spatters the tent, Delorier inquires hospitably, "Voulez vous du souper, tout de suite? [Do you want to eat dinner right away?] I can make fire, sous la charette [under the wagon wheel]—I b'lieve so—I try." To this typical Canadian-style "Franglais" Parkman replies good-naturedly, "Never mind supper, man; come in out of the rain." At journey's end, Delorier calls "Adieu! mes bourgeois, adieu! adieu! [Goodbye, my city friends, goodbye! goodbye!] . . . when you go another time to de Rocky Montagnes I will go with you; yes, I will go." (ibid., 45, 340) Such snippets of light-spirited discourse ease Parkman's serious stretches of narrative and inject jaunty breaks in the more painstaking reportage.

After departing from Fort Leavenworth, Kansas, on May 23, Parkman's party reached the famous "legitimate trail of the Oregon emigrants." He describes fellow travelers and enumerates signs of hard traveling—abandoned gear, wolf tracks, sidetracked wagon caravans, and a grave marker for two-month-old Mary Ellis, dated 1845. He describes the sights as his party passes a wagon train:

> children's faces were thrust out from the white coverings to look at us; while the care-worn, thin-featured matron, or the buxom girl, seated in front, suspended the knitting on which most of them were engaged to stare at us with wondering curiosity. By the side of each wagon stalked the proprietor, urging on his patient oxen, who shouldered heavily along, inch by inch, on their interminable journey. (ibid., 56–57)

Parkman assesses the human price of the journey: a woman giving birth in a moving procession of wagons, men cursing and arguing while chasing runaway horses and extricating dray animals from the mire, precipices that terrorize inexperienced teamsters, mourners binding crossed sticks into a funereal crucifix, and families regretting the ill-conceived ambitions that uprooted them from comfortable homes in the East.

Parkman's text comes alive with a pictorial quality, as found in episodes of horse stealing, lost travelers, boiled antelope head for breakfast, buzzards picking buffalo carcasses, a Mormon battalion heading for California, and Indians pulling *travaux* laden with young children, aged parents, and household goods. His keen eye dramatizes the decrepitude of an 80-year-old Sioux woman:

> Human imagination never conceived hobgoblin or witch more ugly than she. You could count all her ribs through the wrinkles of the leathery skin that covered them. Her withered face more resembled an old skull than the countenance of a living being, even to the hollow, darkened sockets, at the bottom of which glittered her little black eyes. Her arms had dwindled away into nothing but whip-cord and wire. Her hair, half black, half gray, hung in total neglect nearly to the ground, and her sole garment consisted of the remnant of a discarded buffalo-robe tied round her waist with a string of hide. Yet the old squaw's meagre anatomy was wonderfully strong. She pitched the lodge, packed the horses, and did the hardest labor of the camp. (ibid., 133)

Like a portraitist, he studies such natives up close by joining their circle and eating from their common pot. When his clothes wear out, Sioux women supply him with a buckskin frock coat, trousers, and moccasins. Ending his expedition with regret, Parkman smokes a parting communal pipe and leaves behind the "savage scenes and savage men" with a yearning to visit again. (ibid., 339)

To the reading public, Parkman acknowledged that rapid change was reshaping the wild into the predictable and subdued backcountry of a growing heterogeneous nation. In the preface to the 1892 edition, he expresses the paradox of westering: as throngs of Easterners pressed on toward new sights, untrammeled farmland, and fresh hunting grounds, they "blighted the charm that lured them." (Parkman 1973, 11–12) By the time that wagons full of "Kentucks" had settled the wilderness, the buffalo was reduced to bones, barbed wire cordoned off open grassland, and the Indian was transformed from the romanticized "Noble Savage" into a worrisome social problem—squalid, illiterate, and hopeless. Parkman closed his monumental work with a scholar's sense of mission: to preserve a moment in history when the West was young, virile, and beckoning.

Anticipating the California gold rush, Parkman serialized his observations of the emigrant movement in *Knickerbocker Magazine* from 1847 to 1849. This series appeared as *The California and Oregon Trail: Being Sketches of Prairie and Rocky Mountain Life*, which was later shortened to *The Oregon Trail: Or a Summer's Journey Out of Bounds*. Although he blamed his publisher for inflating sales by inserting "California" in the title to capitalize on gold rush fever, Parkman was pleased with the edition, which he dedicated to companion Quincy Shaw. The book earned the praise of Herman Melville and was the era's best-selling memoir in a wide field of published journals.

About the time of his marriage to Catherine Scollay Bigelow, Parkman, influenced by the style of William Hickling Prescott, published his first comprehensive chronicle, *The History of the Conspiracy of Pontiac*, which recounts the Indian revolt against British conquest in Canada from 1763 to 1765. His incisive study of drawings, maps, correspondence, rare books and manuscripts, and journals corroborated his notes made at historical sites and interviews with descendants of settlers and veterans of the Indian wars. The overview of a crucial conflict in American history departs from Parkman's more relaxed, day-by-day observations of *The Oregon Trail*. He isolates elements of change in Iroquois governance:

> A close survey of the condition of the tribes at this period will detect some signs of improvement, but many more of degeneracy and decay. To commence with the Iroquois, for to them with justice the priority belongs: Onondaga, the ancient capital of their confederacy, where their council-fire had burned from immemorial time, was now no longer what it had been in the days of its greatness, when Count Frontenac had mustered all Canada to assail it. (Parkman 1991, 460)

The cohesive element of native life is the savvy and audacity of Pontiac, whose power, influence, and energy at age 50 intrigued Parkman. The resulting character study reveals both the chief's commanding traits and the author's prejudice in its emphasis on savagery, fierceness, and treachery. The inevitable clash with whites emerges on paper with cinema-like realism, a vignette of Pontiac brandishing a hatchet, boasting his exploits, and reenacting his ancestral greatness for the edification of his warriors. Parkman pictures him "yelling the warwhoop, throwing himself into all the postures of actual fight, striking [a painted post] as if it were an enemy, and tearing the scalp from the head of the imaginary victim." (ibid., 493)

Parkman reports that the intensity of the power struggle between Indian and white led to a heinous plan to infect tribes with smallpox. He cites correspondence from Colonel Henry Bouquet to Sir Jeffrey Amherst that reveals a plan

> to inoculate the —— with some blankets . . . and take care not to get the disease myself. As it is a pity to expose good men against them, I wish we could make

use of the Spanish method, to hunt them with English dogs, supported by rangers and some light horse, who would, I think, effectually extirpate or remove that vermin. (ibid., 648)

Parkman maintains a respectful objectivity regarding this primitive form of biological warfare. He adds that smallpox did plague the Ohio tribes, but reports "no direct evidence that Bouquet carried into effect the shameful plan of infecting the Indians." (ibid., 649)

A more lethal episode in Paxton, Pennsylvania, features the Reverend John Elder as the leader of local rangers who slaughter 14 helpless Conestogas in a local jail, a scene Conrad Richter used as a motivating force in his novel *The Light in the Forest* (1953). Presented even-handedly as a cultural feud, Parkman's version of the event concludes with a moral debacle: Quaker outrage, a reward for the apprehension of the murderers, and the Paxton killers proclaiming themselves in the right "by reason and Scripture." (ibid., 710) The ensuing tension, according to Parkman, preceded daily violence and a plot against a community of exiled Moravian Indians, who fled to a Quaker refuge. The contretemps between racist vigilantes and religious leaders concluded a year later with the Indians' safe return to the west side of the Susquehanna River, but only after a reprehensible era of prejudice, intimidation, incarceration, and loss to smallpox. He ends his treatise with the betrayal and assassination of Pontiac, who died with a tomahawk buried in his skull. Parkman laments that "neither mound nor tablet" identified the chief's tomb. Bitterly, he concludes: "For a mausoleum, a city has risen above the forest hero; and the race whom he hated with such burning rancor trample with unceasing footsteps over his forgotten grave." (ibid., 846)

Parkman's concentration, eyesight, and vigor were impaired by sensitivity to sunlight, insomnia, dysentery, and the demands of overland travel. He feared that his next book would be his last. In the face of eminent failure, he continued to write with the aid of his wife, his sister-in-law, Mary Scollay, and Quincy Shaw, who read to him and edited his manuscripts in a tedious process that restricted progress at times to six lines per day. He contributed essays on James Fenimore Cooper and women's suffrage to *North American Review* and later wrote letters to the *Boston Daily Advertiser* concerning the Civil War; a journal article, "Exploring the Magalloway," for *Harper's;* and a review for *The Nation.* For relaxation, he traveled to Montreal, Quebec, and Ottawa and wrote a semi-autobiographical romance, *Vassall Morton* (1856), featuring himself as hero and his first sweetheart as the heroine. The combined loss of his three-year-old son, Francis Parkman III, to scarlet fever in 1857 and of his wife the following year after the birth of their second daughter depleted his energies and enthusiasm.

Depressed and withdrawn, Parkman suffered a complex of neurological disorders and feared that he would go mad. He wrote pathetic letters to friends and colleagues outlining heart problems, headaches, sensitivity to light, and arthritic limbs. In 1858, he initiated a two-year trip to eye specialist Dr. Brown-Séquard in Paris for treatment of neurasthenia. By the early 1860s, he was enjoying gardening at his greenhouse on Jamaica Pond and, with care provided by his sister Eliza, began to recover. He was dismayed that Ida Agassiz refused his proposal of marriage and that ill health disqualified him for service in the Union army.

By means of willpower and stern self-control, Parkman returned to full-time writing and published *Pioneers of France in the New World* (1865). The book, which established his place among noted American historians, became the first of seven volumes known collectively as *France and England in the New World*, a biographical-historical epic of the French-English power struggle and military rivalry for the North American frontier. In the introduction, he extolled the virtues of the New World's forebears, who looked out on "vast wastes of forest verdure; mountains silent in primeval sleep; river, lake, and glimmering pool; wilderness oceans mingling with the sky." His romantic view of the first Europeans to visit the continent includes priest, colonist, and soldier, who faced imminent death as they established sovereignty over a wild land.

Parkman added six volumes to the series: *The Jesuits in North America in the Seventeenth Century* (1867), *La Salle and the Discovery of the Great West* (1869), *The Old Régime in Canada* (1874), *Count Frontenac and New France under Louis XIV* (1877), *Montcalm and Wolfe* (1884), and *Half-Century of Conflict* (1893). His key characters are the men of action—Giovanni da Verrazano, Jacques Cartier, Samuel de Champlain, Comte de Frontenac, Pontiac, Louis-Joseph Montcalm, James Wolfe, and René-Robert La Salle—and Native American tribes, including the Algonquin, Huron, and Iroquois. Of the latter, the historian remarks on their lack of written records:

> Memory, therefore, was tasked to the utmost, and developed to an extraordinary degree. They had various devices for aiding it, such as bundles of sticks, and that system of signs, emblems, and rude pictures which they shared with other tribes. Their famous wampum-belts were so many mnemonic signs, each standing for some act, speech, treaty, or clause of a treaty. These represented the public archives, and were divided among various custodians, each charged with the memory and interpretation of those assigned to him. (Parkman 1955, 48)

For his own background data, Parkman retraced the explorations of La Salle and Marquette, visited Nova Scotia and New Brunswick, and maintained a correspondence with experts, who aided his research by obtaining original manuscripts and archival material from the Montcalm family.

Parkman is often described as an aristocrat and pedant, yet is remembered by his peers as the good-natured "Frank" and by young relatives as a great yarn spinner and lover of children, for whom he made up animal stories. A hobby naturalist despite dependence on a wheelchair and crutches to ease his gouty knee, he authored *The Book of Roses* (1866) and collected over 1,000 varieties of roses. He hybridized the *Lilium Parkmanni* and propagated new varieties of delphinium, phlox, and poppy. For his expertise in horticulture, visiting Dutch landscapers sought "Parkman the horticulturist." He served as a professor of botany at Harvard in 1871 until ill health exacerbated by his mother's death forced him to resign. Stricken with appendicitis, he died from peritonitis in Jamaica Plain, Massachusetts, on November 8, 1893. Continued interest in his travels and commentary preceded the publication of his journals in 1947, a collection of excerpts in *The Parkman Reader* (1955), and his letters in 1960.

Parkman's literary skills are, without question, singular to his era. Boyhood readings in Sir Walter Scott, Lord Byron, William Wordsworth, German romantics, and the American romanticism of James Fenimore Cooper and the New England transcendentalists influenced his style and outlook. He profited from a meticulous study of *Moeurs des Sauvage Ameriquains, Comparees aux Moeurs des Premiers Temps [Customs of Savage Americans, Compared with Customs of Ancient Times]* (1724), written by Joseph Francois Lafitau, a historian and Jesuit missionary to the Iroquois south of Montreal. One passage from *The History of the Conspiracy of Pontiac* echoes the effusive nature worship of Ralph Waldo Emerson and Henry David Thoreau:

> . . . it is the grand and heroic in the hearts of men which finds its worthiest symbol and noblest inspiration amid these desert realms,—in the mountain, rearing its savage head through clouds and sleet, or basking its majestic strength in the radiance of the sinking sun; in the interminable forest, the thunder booming over its lonely waste, the whirlwind tearing through its inmost depths, or the sun at length setting in gorgeous majesty beyond its waves of verdure. (Parkman 1991, 792)

Typically controlled in tone and style, Parkman allows this rhapsodic flight of the imagination to nudge him into a rare declamation. Such lapses belie the historian's intent to remain objective. He influenced his famed follower, John Muir, who developed descriptive nature lore into individualized worship and extended paeans to God.

Although accused of melodrama and aggrandizing heroes, Parkman's works offer an organic view of leadership during the displacement of forest and plains Indians from ancestral grounds in the North American wild. The glamor of cultures in conflict at times overpowers his prose, relegating truth, logic, and proportion to a lesser place. Against these flaws stands a clear delineation of national strengths:

> The springs of American civilization, unlike those of the elder world, lie revealed in the clear light of History. In appearance they are feeble; in reality, copious and full of force. Acting at the sources of life, instruments otherwise weak become mighty for good and evil and men, lost elsewhere in the crowd, stand forth as agents of Destiny. (Boorstin 1965, 377)

Such eloquent description of the American identity affirms a dominant theme in national history, which honors the individual as the deciding factor in the foundation of a stable civilization. (Boorstin 1965; Dobie 1996; Ehrlich and Carruth 1982; Farnham 1968; Hart 1983; "History" 1996; Jacobs 1991; Lamar 1977; Lee 1966; Milner et al. 1994; Morrison 1973; Parkman 1955, 1962, 1973, 1991; Story 1967; Trent et al. 1946; Waldman 1990)

See also Boone, Daniel; Cooper, James Fenimore; *The Light in the Forest*; Muir, John; oratory, Native American; Oregon Trail; Richter, Conrad.

POCAHONTAS

A real Indian maiden and the favorite daughter of Powhatan, chief of the Powhatan Indians, Pocahontas was born about 1595. She was sometimes called Pocahunta or Pocahonte, meaning "playful one," although Matoake, Matoax, or Matoaks was her real name. During a tense confrontation near Jamestown in 1607, she encountered Captain John Smith, a captive of her uncle Opechancanough, who opposed English settlements in Pamunkey territory. As Smith's head lay on a stone awaiting the executioner's club, she rescued him. The source of Pocahontas lore, Captain John Smith's *Generall Historie of Virginia, New England and the Summer Isles* (1624), precedes centuries of interest in the famous rescue. In his pragmatic wording,

> After some six weeks fatting amongst those Salvage Courtiers, at the minute of my execution, she hazarded the beating out of her owne braines to save mine, and not onely that, but so prevailed with her father, that I was safely conducted to James towne, where I found about eight and thirtie miserable poore and sicke creatures, to keepe possession of all those large territories of Virginia, such was the weakness of this poore Common-wealth, as had the Savages not fed us, we directly have starved. (Tilton 1994, xv)

Her story, much expanded and adorned in later tellings, has served the curious with the stuff of legend, which writers have applied to plays, tales, biographies, pantomime, and animated film.

The historical significance of Smith's rescue is the establishment of communication between Native Americans and English colonists. Subsequent episodes—her kidnap and house arrest by Captain Argall in 1612, baptism into the Christian faith the following year, and her father's blessing of her marriage to John Rolfe in April 1613—contain uninspiring material for enlargement of the original story. By the time Pocahontas gave birth to Thomas Rolfe in 1615, traveled to England with Uttamatomac and other members of her tribe, visited King James I and Queen Anne, witnessed Ben Jonson's *Masque of Christmas* at Whitehall, and sat for Simon Van de Passe to engrave her portrait, the fame of the Native American princess lost its exotic trappings. Her death from smallpox and burial at the St. George's Parish Church in Gravesend in 1617 abruptly concluded a coming-to-womanhood and acceptance by the English, who had renamed her Rebecka and robbed her of the "rescuing maiden" mystique.

Much of later description mythologizes Pocahontas from a 12-year-old Indian girl to a redemptive being bent on a godly mission. In 1839, Harvard history professor Jared Sparks stated the story in simple terms and commented that the immediacy of the last-minute rescue resembles the intervention of an angel from heaven. This transformation of Pocahontas from Indian female to seraph may have served the Victorian prudery of the time, for if intermarriage between a nonwhite heroine and British nobleman had to be rejected, the solution to such an interracial impasse is the recasting of the heroine from forest Indian to winged savior.

As a source of early national history, the Pocahontas legend appears often in creative works. An example of epic verse occurs in Book IV of Joel Barlow's

Columbiad (1807), an imitation of Virgil's *Aeneid*, in which Christopher Columbus receives a vision of America's future. Barlow compares the rescue of Captain John Smith to the Greek myth of Jason, the outsider who sails the *Argo* to the kingdom of Colchis on the Black Sea and obtains the Golden Fleece by the intervention of Medea, the king's daughter. Just as Medea alienates herself from local people, Pocahontas sides against the Powhatans and with the English.

Poetic transformations tailor Pocahontas to varied uses. In the nineteenth century, "Pocahontas," a Byronic ode by Lydia H. Sigourney, twists the reality of an Anglo-Indian relationship to conform to the polemics of an era that saw the demonization of Native Americans, forced resettlement of Western tribes on reservations, and the genocide of those who refused to be moved. John Esten Cooke's poem "A Dream of the Cavaliers" (1885) romanticizes the legend by altering Smith into "The Knight of the Virgin Queen" and Pocahontas into "a fawn of the forest, with a bearing mild and meek." Crowned with feathers and pearls, Pocahontas, "The Virgin Queen of the West," displays nonwhite features—golden skin and raven curls. The poet labors to negate racial differences by emphasizing "the heart of a Christian hero in a timid maiden's breast." (ibid., 168)

Pocahontas was also the focus of art from this period, notably two works housed in the rotunda of the U.S. Capitol: a relief carved in 1825 by Antonio Capellano, depicting her rescue of Captain John Smith, and a Madonna-like painting by John Gadsby Chapman, "Baptism of Pocahontas at Jamestown, Virginia" (1840). The contrast of these companion pieces suggests a visual realignment of the princess from heroine to convert, a lackluster end to what began as an excitingly romantic, selfless deed. The rigidly Caucasian trappings of "Matoake also Rebecka" of the Booton Hall Portrait, the most familiar likeness of Pocahontas, implies that acceptance of a native maiden required a complete makeover—new name, new religion, and as much English coutour and hairstyle as possible to obscure her racial identity.

The dramatic nature of the Pocahontas legend also fueled frontier theatricals. The first extant play based on the episode of Pocahontas rescuing Smith was Joseph Croswell's *A New World Planted* (1802), which relocates the story from Jamestown to Plymouth; a famous second version, James Nelson Barker's *The Indian Princess or La Belle Sauvage* (1808), premiered at Philadelphia's Walnut Street Theatre. Subsequent stage versions of the Pocahontas character appear in George Washington Parke Custis's *Pocahontas, or The Settlers of Virginia* (1830), Robert Dale Owen's *Pocahontas* (1837), and Charlotte Barnes Conner's *Forest Princess* (1848), plus numerous imitations, which were popular but have not survived in print. Of these playwrights, Custis is most famous, perhaps because George Washington was his foster father. Custis wrote on Native American themes in subsequent plays, *The Indian Prophecy* and *Pawnee Chief*.

Custis's *Pocahontas* received elaborate care in preparation and production at Philadelphia's Walnut Street Theatre, where the work honored George Washington's birthday. The play opens on Smith's arrival to the James River. When Pocahontas receives the news in Scene 2, she proclaims, "Come good, come ill, Pocahontas will be the friend of the English." (Custis 1938, 175) Her speech welcomes white explorers, whom she considers noble visitors from a fair land, and she hurries to entertain them as honored guests. In Scene 3, Pocahontas maintains hospitality toward the English when she encounters Rolfe, who is lost in the woods. When hostilities arise, she takes refuge in the tomb of Madoc, where she overhears her father Powhatan plotting treachery against Rolfe and planning her betrothal to Matacoran. Powhatan prays that the Good Spirit will strengthen her to save Rolfe.

Custis keeps his main character busy at noble tasks. At the beginning of Act III, Pocahontas has paddled her canoe to the English hunting lodge. She warns Smith of the poisoned arrows that will fly at daylight. Returned to her father's palace, she rejects his choice of Matacoran for a husband. She avoids seeing Smith brought in as a captive, but Powhatan insists that she watch the presentation. The text avoids anticlimax by saving the rescue scene to the end of Act III, when Smith stands tough against Powhatan and refuses even a "rusty nail" as ransom.

The final lines heighten the drama with pagan ritual. After executioners place the stone under Smith's head and raise their clubs for the sacrifice, Pocahontas and her friend Omaya plead for mercy; Smith, who expects to die, bequeaths his gold chain to the princess. Powhatan waves his feather fan as a signal to kill Smith. Pocahontas rushes out of the guards' grasp as the sound of English muskets explodes in the background. She proclaims fealty to "the Supreme Being, the true Manitou, and the Father of the Universe." (ibid., 191) At the same time that Powhatan relents, the English announce victory and insist that Pocahontas be betrothed to Rolfe.

Custis's conclusion indicates a need for a partially realistic plot resolution. He saves a noble rebuttal for Matacoran, who claims that his grave shall prove the Indian's rejection of the English. In a gesture of acceptance to the "brave, wild, and unconquerable spirit," Smith lets him go free. Powhatan admits that he must yield to a forced alliance with the English, which his daughter's betrothal symbolizes. In a pat epilogue, the chief claims the privilege of "giving away the bride" and trusts that tales of Pocahontas will remain a long-lived part of stage and library lore. (ibid., 192)

After several decades of such turgid, unnatural theatricals about Indians, Irish comedian John Brougham brought an end to the stylized convention with his satiric burlesque *Po-Ca-Hon-Tas, or The Gentle Savage* (1855), which spoofs wooden characterizations of Native Americans. Of a piece with his other two historical takeoffs—*Columbus el Filibustro* and *Metamora, or The Pollywogs*—the good-natured fun of *Po-Ca-Hon-Tas* strips the legend of dull didacticism and replaces it with one-liners, sight gags, and rollicking humor. Subtitled "An Original Aboriginal Erratic Operatic Semi-Civilized and Demi-Savage Extravaganza, Being a Per-Version of Ye Trewe and Wonderrefulle Hystorie of Ye Renownned Princesse," the play features the music of James G. Maeder and calls for a witty playbill naming Ip-Pah-Kak, Kod-Liv-Royl, Kros-As-Kan-Bee, O-You-Jewel, Oso-Char-Ming, and Lum-Pa-Shuga along with "splicers of main braces, shiverers of timbers, anathematizers of eyes and limbs, promiscuously

Pocahontas

general dealers in single combat and double hornpipes, and altogether, amazingly nautical people." (Brougham 1966, 403)

The play opens with a swipe at Longfellow's *Song of Hiawatha* by imitating the stodgy trochaic tetrameter of the original epic, which Brougham dates to "Anno Gothami, 235." (ibid., 404) The lengthy prologue thumps along like native drums:

> Ask you—How about these verses?
> Whence this song of Pocahontas,
> With its flavor of Tobacco,
> And the Stincweed—The Mundungus,
> With its pipe of Old Virginny,
> With the echo of the Breakdown,
> With its smack of Bourbon whiskey,
> With the twangle of the Banjo. (ibid.)

One performance of the play lacked the female lead. To the cue, "Where is Pokey?," the male actors improvised with silly repartee: "Lost among the icebergs on Broadway; but if she were here she would answer you in this way." For the betrothal scene, King Powhatan hands her beau a broom and urges, "Take her, my boy, and be happy." (Moody, Richard, 1966, 400)

In Brougham's realignment of the Pocahontas-Rolfe relationship to a Pocahontas-Smith love plot, Smith takes a lover's attitude toward the maiden, which Pocahontas reciprocates. Their comic patter reduces the famous rescue scenario to farce:

> Pocahontas: Husband! for thee I *scream!*
> Smith: *Lemon or Vanilla?*
> Pocahontas: Oh! *Fly* with me, and quit these vile dominions!
> Smith: How *can* I fly, beloved, with these pinions?
> (Brougham 1966, 419)

Brougham's witty burlesque gave him the choice role as H.R.H. Pow-Ha-Tan, played opposite the comic Smith in a droll jab at idiotic stage stereotypes. Their give-and-take began to resemble stand-up comedy more than formal stagecraft. After Brougham's classic parody and its improvised puns and comic exaggerations gained popularity, stilted portrayals of Pocahontas became scarce. A half century later, Philip Moeller paid Brougham the playwright's compliment of imitation in 1918 with a rewrite, *Pokey, or The Beautiful Legend of the Amorous Indian.* (Bayly 1989; Brougham 1966; Coad and Mims 1929; Custis 1938; Hughes 1951; Moody, Richard, 1966; Quinn 1938; Smith 1967; Tilton 1994; Waldman 1990; Woodward 1969)

See also Longfellow, Henry Wadsworth.

POETRY OF THE FRONTIER

Frontier poetry is a fruitful source of varied themes and motifs from Western lore. Covering the lusty Southwest humor of Joaquin Miller, lyrical Amerindian songs of Mary Hunter Austin, the Yukon wit of Robert Service, and myriad anonymous poems, pioneer verse displays the energy, contemplation, love of nature, and verve for which America's pathfinders are known. A memorable example, Vachel Lindsay's ode "The Ghost of the Buffaloes," from *The Chinese Nightingale and Other Poems* (1917), expresses in first-person dreamscape the fearful tramp of spirit beasts that haunt the vacant plain. Transporting the dreamer from city comforts, Lindsay places him in "a hut without orchard or lawn." (Coleman 1932, 19) Lodged amid mud-smeared logs, the witness looks into the wildness where "Ghost-kings came headlong, row upon row,/Gods of the Indians, torches aglow." In a final stanza, the poet sends a good night from the nimble cricket, a being symbolizing frailty, yet one that is tough enough to withstand change and survive the lumbering buffalo.

From the beginning, frontier verse has resonated with themes of loss and overtones of racism. Following a protracted season of treachery and revenge in Paxton, Pennsylvania, during which citizens died, jailed Conestoga were slaughtered, and Moravian Indians were exiled, an anonymous Quaker published in Philadelphia "The Paxtoniade" (1764), a tetrameter verse in rhymed couplets imitating *Hudibras* (1662), Samuel Butler's epigrammatic satire. Focusing on O'Hara, a stereotypical Irish mick and descendant of the donkey on which he sits, the poem ridicules vigilante-style injustice to Indians. O'Hara, a Paxton apologist, inflames a mob to requite Indian "Canaanites" who "Did tomahawk, butcher, wound and cripple, With cruel Rage, the Lord's own People." (Parkman 1991, 879) In blathering doggerel, the demagogue concludes that settlers "Should totally destroy the heathen, And never till we've killed 'em leave 'em ."

Pausing for rhetorical effect, O'Hara draws twice on his container of whiskey and returns to the diatribe against "our most anti-Christian foes," whom Quakers coddle with "good warm fires." He calls to arms a coterie of rabble. After breaking his decanter in the heat of oratory, he outlines a plan to ride or march,

> With as much quickness as will suit,
> To where those heathen nothing fearful,
> That we will on their front and rear fall.

The poet's jingling rhymes ridicule the obsessive death squad who intend to eradicate Indians from western Pennsylvania.

More serious in style and tone is a lengthy narrative poem, *The Vision of Columbus* (1787), masterwork of Joel Barlow, who wrote one of the many failed American works that founder from aping European styles and tastes. For all its frailties, the work ennobles the vision of Christopher Columbus and retains its place in the frontier canon for acknowledging the post-Columbian stream of pioneers settling the New World. In Book V, Barlow epitomizes the westering spirit:

> Where the dread Laurence breaks his passage wide,
> Where Mississippi's milder currents glide,
> Where midland realms their swelling mountains heave,

And slope their champaigns to the distant wave,
On the green banks, and o'er the extended plain,
Rise into sight the happiest walks of man. (Barlow 1970, 152)

In ponderous pentameter couplets, the nine-book verse epic predicts that cultivation of the frontier will carry pioneers beyond the Hudson River and Kaatskill Mountains toward glorious horizons. Book VI records the Revolutionary War battles that precede settlement; Book VII foresees that peace will boost the fur and fishing industries and will usher in an era favorable to American arts and invention.

Ornate and stodgy, the book-length poem preceded a revised version, the *Columbiad* (1807), a plodding American epic still shackled to European traditions. Freighted with Miltonic gravity and marred by the court phrases in which eighteenth-century English wits delighted, Barlow's decorous encomium features Columbus, George Washington, and the founders of the democratic ideal. Overall, the verse bears too weighty a load of exalted nature lore and glimmering superlatives and too few sense impressions or realistic details to suggest that Barlow had ventured very far from an armchair or nurtured any notion of the West's true grandeur.

Another lengthy verse epic, Adam Kidd's 1,658-line *The Huron Chief* (1830), struggles under the load of rhetoric, Native American lore, and fussiness that mars its narrative purpose. Composed by a youthful Irish romantic resettled in Canada, the poem is overtaxed with details of Native American customs and history gained from book sources: James Buchanan's *Sketches of the History, Manners, and Customs of the North American Indians*, Alexander Henry's *Travels and Adventures in Canada and the Indian Territories*, Alexander Mackenzie's *Voyages from Montreal on the River St. Laurence*, William Tudor's *Letters on the Eastern States*, and Thomas Jefferson's *Notes on the State of Virginia*. Dotted with allusions to classic verse by Ovid and Horace, the poem, which appeared in the Montreal *Irish Vindicator* in 1830, is too didactic to offer much truth, inspiration, or entertainment.

Attempting to honor a noble native leader murdered by whites, Kidd portrays him as a hospitable, grandfatherly savant who welcomes a lone outsider to Indian territory along Lake Huron. The chief calls pleasantly to the poet:

Stranger! whither wouldst thou stray,
    I wish to guide thy wand'ring feet,
This is not the white man's way,
    Another path we soon shall meet.
I'm the Chieftain of this mountain—
    Times, and seasons, found me here—
My drink has been the crystal fountain—
    My food the wild moose or the deer. (Kidd 1997, 6)

Without rancor, Chief Skenandow invites "the Christian foe-man" to a beckoning sward of untraveled territory, despite past experience with explorers who have challenged the Native American's sovereignty on tribal lands.

In the nineteenth century, verse took a different turn by following shorter forms with less ponderous tone and atmosphere. Novelists pursued the era's convention of appending witty poems or verse commentary to chapters of prose. In Chapter 51 of *Roughing It* (1872), Mark Twain's comic travelogue of his seven years in the Nevada Territory, the speaker, a semiserious version of Twain, offers "The Aged Pilot Man," which he claims to have written for the *Weekly Occidental.* He labels his verse "doggerel" and claims it was "one of the ablest poems of the age." (Twain 1962d, 278) Set on the Erie Canal, the melodramatic burlesque of Samuel Taylor Coleridge's *The Rime of the Ancient Mariner* follows the exploits of Dollinger, an experienced boatman who guides his mules through a vicious storm that terrifies his passengers.

In typical Twain style, the poem amuses with hyperbole and dialect. The plot, written in first person and composed in quatrains, takes the speaker and his parents from Albany by canal barge. Acting against the advice to "snub up your boat," the pilot refuses to halt. The chancy trip so terrorizes the speaker that he exclaims;

> So let us strive, while life remains,
>   To save all souls on board,
> And then if die at last we must,
>   Let . . . I *cannot* speak the word! (ibid.)

The exaggerated dangers of low bridge, shoals, gale winds, and wild spray require the whip boy to cling tight as the passengers interrupt themselves to yell advice:

> "We're all"—[then with a shout,]
>   Huray! huray!
>   Avast! belay!
>   Take in more sail!
>   Lord, what a gale!
> Ho, boy, haul taut on the hind mule's tail! (ibid., 279)

The absurd climax attests to the poet's zany humor—after the canal bed bursts, passengers fear they will never reunite with wives and mothers. More glory accrues to the pilot as he struggles on. The passengers jettison a keg of nails, anvils, gunnysacks, glue, sacks of grain, books, cow, violin, Lord Byron's works, a ripsaw, and a sow. With much geeing and hawing, the barge survives a curve and swings into the wind. An inspired farmer ends the silly voyage by laying a plank from shore to barge; the passengers easily step across to shore. Twain's antiheroic voyage poem implies that journeyers of his era tend to overstate the perils of their undertaking.

Looking back at the era of migration from Europe to North America, Canadian poet Alexander McLachlan composed a more sober narrative paean to "The Emigrant" (1861), a lengthy epic poem of mixed verse forms that honors the strength and foresight of the pioneer. Following a group of Scottish and English emigrants aboard the *Edward Thorn* and across the Atlantic Ocean to the green forests of Ontario, the poet cites the cutting of the first tree, the building of a log cabin, and chilling night sounds from roving wolf packs. The long winter seems less onerous from evenings of shared tales, ballads, and songs around the fireside. An attack by Mohawk and Huron disturbs the forest idyll:

> There was fighting Bill, from Kent
> (Bill was in his element)
> Stalking, like a soldier born,
> With his gun and powder horn;
> Then there was old soldier Hugh,
> With his sword and musket too. (McLachlan 1972, 144)

The battle results from a rivalry between two chiefs, Hemlock and Eagle. Eagle wins in hand-to-hand combat and scalps Hemlock while he's still breathing.

The poem turns from bloodletting to nostalgia as it tells of the last years of the fighter known as Old Donald of Argyle. He recalls the history of his homeland and accepts the comfort of his old hound, Fleetfoot. Weary of the woods, Old Donald dies with his eyes turned homeward, far from the St. Lawrence River. The poet laments:

> And our children, sons and daughters,
> Gone like music on the waters.
> Bring my staff, let us away,
> To the land of mountains grey,
> Never, never more to roam
> From our "native Highland home." (ibid., 155)

The poet, offering a gesture toward "men and times of old," veers in the final seven couplets to the bogus preachers, land despoilers, robbers, and speculators who betray the pure motives of the pioneers. (ibid., 156)

With a similar serious purpose, John G. Neihardt, editor of *Black Elk Speaks* and Nebraska's poet laureate, initiated a series of heroic songs about the westering tradition in 1921. He began collecting material in boyhood while living in his grandparents' sod hut in western Kansas and during sojourns among the Omaha and Sioux. Drawing on journals and eyewitness testimony, he composed his verse, like Barlow's *Columbiad,* in epic style, utilizing heroic couplets that emulate Virgil's *Aeneid*. These Western cycles received moderate critical attention, largely because of their departure from the standard ballad or narrative form. Set in the era of exploration and settlement, Neihardt's verse compares to similar themes in European and Asian literature. Combined under the title *The Cycle of the West,* five verse epics recast separate episodes in frontier history in chronological order:

- *The Song of Three Friends* (1919) and *The Song of Hugh Glass* (1915) cover the 1822 river explorations of General William H. Ashley and his aide, Major Henry, who led a hundred trappers from Missouri to the upper Missouri and Yellowstone, rivers rich in beaver.

- *The Song of the Indian Wars* (1925) brings the westering cycle into greater cultural conflict as white invaders disrupt the ancestral lands of the Sioux, Arapaho, and Cheyenne.

- *The Song of the Messiah* (1935) centers on the 1890 Plains Indian cataclysm—the Battle of Wounded Knee, the most telling blow of cavalry against Native American resisters and the end of the Ghost Dance, a Plains ritual evolving from Wovoka's vision of an Indian renaissance.

- *The Song of Jed Smith* (1941) details the overland struggle of Jedediah Smith, leader of the first white party through South Pass to Salt Lake and on to California.

The unifying factors of Neihardt's verse are his use of dialect, historical and geographical accuracy, and universal themes tempered by the cadences of mountain men. In a duel scene, reminiscent of the game of ombre in Alexander Pope's *The Rape of the Lock*, Will Carpenter, Mike Fink, and Frank Talbeau—title characters in *The Song of Three Friends*—play euchre and seven-up while waiting out a blizzard. The poet builds suspense as luck turns against Fink, who had enjoyed an afternoon's lead. One of the players chortles,

"Mike, I'll bet my head
As how them spades of your'n'll dig a hole!"
And in some subtle meaning of the soul
The wag was more a prophet than he knew. (Neihardt 1993, 62)

The tension rises as Carpenter and Talbeau exult, "You're set! You're in the hole!" The two-part epic of the mountain men emulates much of Homer's central duel of the *Iliad* by setting up an Achilles versus Hector motif. The grim-eyed Fink attacks Carpenter, rending the tent and awakening the other campers. In a ring of jostling, yelling onlookers, Fink puts up a titanic battle, then falls to the softer man, leaving local graybeards to discuss how so uneven a battle could unseat the stronger opponent. For his frontier writings, Neihardt won local honors, including a bust in the capitol and admission to the state hall of fame. Critical acclaim brought him the annual award from the Poetry Society of America for *The Song of Three Friends* and a Gold Scroll Medal of Honor from the National Poetry Center for *The Song of the Messiah*.

Other examples of frontier verse are lighter but no less worthy. One of America's most beloved pair of poets, Rosemary and Stephen Vincent Benét, published a hearty collection of short satiric verse portraits entitled *A Book of Americans* (1933). The chronological list of patriotic and historical poems returns frequently to the Western characters, settings, and themes found in grade school history texts, including French pioneers, Johnny Appleseed, Lewis and Clark, Daniel Boone, Sam Houston, Crazy Horse, Jesse James, and Theodore Roosevelt. Appropriate phrasing typifies each case, as with Johnny Appleseed, orchard planter of the plains:

He has no statue.
He has no tomb.
He has his apple trees
Still in bloom. (Benét and Benét 1933, 48)

The Benéts juxtapose a variety of characters. Of Sam Houston, the poets snicker at his checkered past but acknowledge that "His dreams were huge and his costumes showy/And his private honor bright as a bowie." (ibid., 71) In similar lighthearted fashion, the Benéts describe early explorers Christopher Columbus and Hernando de Soto, ribbing Columbus for his obsession with India and de Soto for the failed search for Eldorado. Spirited verse comments on de Soto:

> He discovered the great Mississippi,
> He faced perils and hardships untold,
> And his soldiers ate bacon, if I'm not mistaken,
> But nobody found any gold. (ibid., 7)

The jolting anapestic meter and the amusing internal rhyme in line three indicate that the Benéts seek a less serious study than history tomes and that they weave into the portraits revealing elements, such as the fact that de Soto probably lost his life as a result of greed.

It is no accident that the Benéts stagger the two exploration poems to fall before and after "Indian," a sardonic commentary on European predators. As they did in "Crazy Horse," the poets credit the French, English, Spanish, and Dutch with arrogance and exploitation. Under false pretense of beneficence,

> They'll kill his deer and net his fish
> And clear away his wood,
> And frequently remark to him
> They do it for his good. (ibid., 5)

The poets conclude that the scalping, burning, violence, and broken treaties that color this period in American history were not the fault of the Indians alone; the pernicious quality of this period of settlement is represented as both reprehensible and sad. The Benéts remind the reader that "discovery" is a misinterpretation on the part of explorers: "They didn't find an empty land. The Indians were *here*." (ibid.)

An unusual glimpse of the blending of European and native cultures occurs in Robert E. Holland's *The Song of Tekakwitha* (1942), a narrative verse patterned in style and meter after Henry Wadsworth Longfellow's *The Song of Hiawatha* (1855). The poem relates a romanticized version of the life of a half-breed Algonquin girl born in 1656 in Ossernenon, New York. Tekakwitha was the child of a Mohawk father and his captive wife. She survived an outbreak of smallpox in 1660 that killed her brother and parents. By tribal law, she came under the care of her uncle, an outspoken critic of Christianity as a religion belonging to white men to the exclusion of other races. In 1676, she welcomed the teachings of Jesuit "Black Robes" and was baptized Catherine (Kateri) Tekakwitha. In the poem, she lisps the *Ave* and learns in secret to venerate the Trinity.

Holland indicates that white missionaries attempted to bridge the gap between races by winning Indians to the Catholic faith. Bruyas, the lead priest, greets the Mohawk hierarchy with a message of universal Christian fellowship:

> Know, O Chieftain, mighty Mohawk,
> Hither come my Brothers Blackrobe,

Here am I to teach you wisdom,
Wisdom of the Holy Spirit—
Not of Frenchman, not of mortals—
Wisdom of the Life Eternal,
Rich reward of God His service. (Holland 1942, 44)

Holland describes how the priest's doctrine touches Tekakwitha's heart. After visiting Les Hospitalières de l'Hôtel-Dieu de Montreal, she resolves to minister to Indians. Following an Easter confirmation, Kateri takes First Communion on Christmas 1677.

According to history, Holland follows the true story of Tekakwitha. The last three years of her life were spent in Caughnawaga, Montreal, in self-exile from natives and whites who disapproved of her reluctance to marry and her refusal to gather crops on the Sabbath. Holland parallels her withdrawal from secular society with the vows of a nun. In humility, she joyously proclaims:

Be my body's food and raiment,
Rich my soul to Him united—
Only God my heart desireth.
So, with vow His virgins say Him,
O my Father, let me seal it:
This my choice of Christ my Bridegroom! (ibid., 125)

She died April 16, 1680, at the Christian Indian Mission of Saint Francis Xavier, Kanawake, where her relics are enshrined. For her piety and good works, she was beatified on June 22, 1932, under the name Lily of the Mohawk. (Barlow 1970; Benét and Benét 1933; *Canadian Writers* 1990; Coleman 1932; Holland 1942; Kidd 1997; Kunitz 1942; McLachlan 1972; Milner et al. 1994; Mogen et al. 1989; Neihardt 1993; Parkman 1991; Story 1967; Turcotte 1996; Twain 1962b; Wallace 1963; Westbrook 1988)

See also Austin, Mary Hunter; Boone, Daniel; Cody, Buffalo Bill; Miller, Joaquin; Parkman, Francis; *Roughing It;* Service, Robert.

PORTIS, CHARLES

Author of *True Grit* (1968), one of the most uproarious adventure novels in the young adult canon of Western fiction, Arkansan Charles Portis (December 28, 1933–), like many American writers, trained in journalism. A veteran of the U.S. Marines and graduate of the University of Arkansas, he wrote for the Memphis *Commercial Appeal* and the Little Rock *Arkansas Gazette,* and for the New York *Herald Tribune* as a reporter and London correspondent. Turning to fiction full time in 1964, Portis applied skillful reportage to three novels: *Norwood* (1966), *True Grit,* and *The Dog of the South* (1979). His background in newspaper work is evident in the economy of words and steady pacing that carry an even flow of events in his fiction.

By mastering semiliterate dialects, witty repartee, first-person narration, and the milieu of frontier Arkansas, Portis achieves a balance of picaresque characterization in *True Grit,* a best-seller that was serialized in the *Saturday Evening Post* beginning on May 18, 1968. Set in Indian Territory, the jumping-off point for the law-abiding East, the story brings together the colorful Marshal Reuben "Rooster" Cogburn, a conceited Texas Ranger named LaBoeuf, and 14-year-old Mattie Ross, a budding ranch accountant who seeks a lawman with grit to help her locate and bring to justice the evil Tom Chaney, her father's murderer. On her first view of Rooster, whom she intends to hire on the basis of his no-nonsense reputation, she is surprised to find "an old one-eyed jasper that was built along the lines of Grover Cleveland." (Portis 1968b, 39–40) An unlikely odyssey takes Mattie, Rooster, and the meddler LaBoeuf across the Arkansas River into the Choctaw nation, a "sink of crime" where brigands flee civilization and flout the law. The only justice is administered by coercion and transport by U.S. marshals, who retrieve the worst of crusty no-goods for trial and hanging in Fort Smith.

Portis is agile in the creation of memorable characters and events. Mattie's obdurate mindset buoys her through difficulties not normally associated with young girls from conservative Presbyterian homes. When adults shortchange her, like an annoyed heiress, she reminds them that her family owns property and demands an explanation for the undeserved ill treatment. On arrival at Fort Smith to identify her father's corpse, she and Yarnell Poindexter, a black farmhand acting as duenna, witness a Western spectacle—a triple hanging superintended by Judge Isaac Parker, the notorious "hanging judge" who figures in numerous pulp Westerns, dime novels, and movies. Mattie gamely sets out from Mrs. Floyd's Monarch boardinghouse on Little Blackie, a pony she wangles from Colonel Stonehill, a devious auctioneer who flimflammed Mattie's father but meets his match with pert, quick-witted Mattie. Throughout the formation of the unusual posse, Mattie manages to get her way by confronting obstacles with threats of lawsuits launched by her champion, Lawyer Daggett, the Ross family attorney.

The episodic final chapters, fast-paced and fraught with suspense, place Mattie and the two lawmen at a shoot-out outside a dugout in the San Bois Mountains, from which they return three outlaw corpses to J. J. McAlester's store. Riding hard, the original threesome enters the Winding Stair Mountains, site of the final confrontation with Chaney and his gang: Lucky Ned Pepper, Greaser Bob, and Harold and Farrell, the Permalee brothers, the younger of whom is daft and imitates the mooing and crowing of farm animals. The bizarre manhunt exposes Mattie to numerous atrocities: Rooster shoots a rat in the back room of Chen Lee's Chinese grocery, Emmett Quincy chops off his partner Moon's fingers with a bowie knife, LaBoeuf shoots Haze and Billy and a horse with a Sharps rifle, and Mattie falls backward from the recoil of her father's Colt dragoon pistol and tumbles into a pit containing a skeleton, Chaney's corpse, and a nest of hibernating rattlers. Portis speeds the return to Fort Smith by having Rooster gallop back with Mattie fretful and semiconscious on his back. He delivers her to Dr. Medill for snakebite treatment. The

Charles Portis published *True Grit* in 1968 and describes protagonist Marshal Rueben "Rooster" Cogburn as "an old one-eyed jasper that was built along the lines of Grover Cleveland." John Wayne won an Academy Award for his portrayal of Rooster Cogburn in the 1969 movie, and Kim Darby played Mattie Ross, who sought to bring to justice her father's murderer, the evil Tom Chaney.

rescue ennobles Rooster, whom Mattie worships for a quarter century and honors with an appropriate burial under a Confederate tombstone.

In vivid caricature, Portis duplicates the spirit of random frontier lawlessness and danger, particularly Rooster's testimony as to the high number of criminals he shoots while bringing them to justice:

Mr. Cogburn: I never shot nobody I didn't have to.

Mr. Goudy: That was not the question. How many?

Mr. Cogburn: Shot or killed?

Mr. Goudy: Let us restrict it to "killed" so that we have a manageable figure . . . Twenty-three dead men in four years. That comes to about six men a year.

Mr. Cogburn: It is dangerous work. (ibid., 44–45)

By the beginning of the twentieth century, the old pattern of law and order gives place to professional, law-based police work. Thus, Rooster's questionable methods of law enforcement end his career.

After Rooster gets himself into the "sorry business" of terrorizing nesters and grangers, Mattie, aged into a testy spinster with a reputation for tightfistedness, takes the train northeast to find him. She encounters aging outlaws Frank James and Cole Younger; from the latter she learns that Rooster has recently died. These events jump the plot from wild times to the sunset years of frontier outrages, when masculine bravado is confined to the tents of a Wild West show. A poster bills Rooster as a rider with the renegade Quantrill and an agent for Judge Parker. The fine print echoes the ballyhoo that lured Easterners to the show:

Scourge of Territorial outlaws and Texas cattle thieves for 25 years! "Rooster" Cogburn will amaze you with his skill and dash with the six-shooter and repeating rifle! Don't leave the ladies and little ones behind! Spectators can watch this unique exhibition in perfect safety! (ibid., 187)

Ironically, Rooster, a genuine Southwest gunman, is a swaggering, corn dodger–eating softie who admires and supports Mattie by allowing her to accompany him into dangerous territory where inexperienced young girls have no business going. His abuse of Little Blackie on the ride to Dr. Medill's office proves that Mattie means a great deal to him, even though he wears the mask of the tough Westerner.

The figures and voices of Portis's comic tour de force fit the screen version so completely that, for the most part, the story line remains the same as the novel. Filmed by Paramount in 1969, the movie features a quality cast of actors: John Wayne as Rooster, Kim Darby as Mattie, and Glen Campbell as the mincing Texas Ranger LaBoeuf. Robert Duvall and Dennis Hopper play roistering members of Lucky Ned Pepper's mail-robbing gang. The movie earned John Wayne an Academy Award and received an Oscar nomination for the title song. The part of Rooster fit Wayne so handily that he reprised the role in *Rooster Cogburn* (1975) opposite Katherine Hepburn. Warren Oates played the part of Rooster in a 1978 television version. (Bernard 1955; Fuller 1968; Greene 1968; Lamar 1977; Portis 1968b; Rhodes 1968; Snodgrass 1991, 1995b; Wolff 1968)

PROSPECTING

The enticement of Western Hemisphere get-rich-quick schemes dates to early Spanish explorers, who set out for the New World in hopes of finding Eldorado, the fabled city of gold. Spread over three centuries, the dreams of a fountain of youth, glittering Caribbean Edens, and the Seven Cities of Gold surfaced in oral tradition, song, and adventurers' journals, a broad swath of literature that includes Richard Hakluyt's *The Principal Navigations, Voyages, and Discoveries of the English Nation* (1589), Voltaire's *Candide* (1759), and Charles Baudelaire's "Un Voyage à Cythère" (1861). Counter to meretricious pipe dreams, Edgar Allan Poe limned an ominous verse romance, "Eldorado" (1849), which carries a colorful knight errant into old age. He bears a visage and demeanor as despairing as the wandering Jew and expends waning strength in frivolous pursuit of a mirage. Through sun and shade, the knight weathers highs and lows of spirit until he must admit defeat. A parallel death figure warns that the search for easy riches lies "Over the mountains of the moon, down the valley of the shadow." (Poe 1962, 246)

Some of the quiet, more introspective studies of frontier gold fever come from women's diaries, often retained in private collections, which were not published until the twentieth century. These eyewitness accounts received a fuller appreciation from the feminist movement of the 1970s, which reevaluated the diaries, letters, and journals that set forth the commonalities of women's lives. Two clear-headed diarists, Sarah Eleanor Bayliss Royce and Catherine Haun, offer candid commentary on the ambience of the California mining milieu. In Royce's *A Frontier Lady: Recollections of the Gold Rush and Early California* (1932), the westering urge causes a traffic jam at the ferry crossing on the Missouri River. On June 8, 1849, a threesome—Sarah, her husband Josiah, and small daughter Mary—set out from Council Bluffs, Iowa, experiencing a cattle stampede and three smashed wheels within days of their departure. Through Digger Indian territory into the Great Salt Desert, the Royces encounter better fortune along the Humboldt River. They cross the Sierras into "Eldorado," where an army of gold diggers stay put only so long as the prospecting produces bright flecks or until news of a better strike attracts them to a likelier vein. Royce presents a sane, balanced account of her misgivings and the growing confidence she develops from day-to-day learning experiences amid the fervid materialism of northern California. By the time the Royces set up a store, she believes they will succeed. Because coin is rare, she accounts for the need of a gold scale and weights to measure gold dust.

With a deft touch, Royce replicates the emotional strain of living in a boomtown. She writes that prospectors from poor backgrounds sink into discontent and despair because of wildly unrealistic expectations of instant, toil-free wealth. Some, she says,

> cursed the country, calling it a "God forsaken land," while a larger number bitterly condemned their own folly in having left comfortable homes and moderate business chances, for so many hardships and uncertainties. (Royce 1977, 87)

She labels the plodders "chronic prospectors," whose outlooks surge upward on continuous peaks of euphoria and who "[keep] the whole community in a ferment." She adds that the corresponding sounds of grief arise from illness and death, often brought on by unwholesome food and filth.

A major theme of the gold rush era is lawlessness, which Sarah Royce covers in "Morals," the fifth chapter of her memoir. While living in a tenement house in San Francisco, she notes that newcomers must seek companions judiciously, for stalkers of the gold-getters lie in wait and attack with no mercy. The easiest prey, those with a shallow sense of ethics, lose their moral habits and religious convictions in moments of excitement and temptation. Some rationalize their compromised consciences as "the California way," as though living in a mining atmosphere condones or excuses immorality. Royce claims that the worst cases are young women and girls introduced to vice through the promise of easy money. She hints at—but priggishly refrains from naming— venereal disease as the wages of sin earned by a neighbor who is unfaithful to her husband. With typical nineteenth-century prudery, Royce ends the chapter with two rhetorical questions: "How can she bear to look back to [the children's] baby-hood? How can she endure to think of the work *she* has wrought into the fabric of California social life?" (ibid., 119)

Paralleling the concise, well-organized writings of Sarah Royce, Catherine Haun, a young bride traveling over the Oregon Trail and south to California, produced *A Woman's Trip across the Plains in 1849* (1992), a diary expressing her belief that a more profitable life lay to the west. In the opening paragraphs, she characterizes the mania that impels trekkers to cross the West in prairie schooners:

> At that time the "gold fever" was contagious and few, old or young, escaped the malady. On the streets, in the fields, in the workshops and by the fireside, golden California was the chief topic of conversation. Who were going? How was best to "fix up" the "outfit"? What to take as food and clothing? Who would stay at home to care for the farm and womenfolks? Who would take wives and children along? (Haun 1992, 166)

She reports that "Advice was handed out quite free of charge and often quite free of common sense" and that the 25 people in the party she joined anticipated selling produce from their ox-wagons at inflated goldfield prices. After traveling 2,400 miles over a nine-month span, Haun arrives in Marysville and is herself a victim of inflation: she pays a dollar for a cabbage and $2.50 for a bear steak. Her husband offsets the high costs by doing legal work for a client at the rate of $150 for drawing up a will.

Prospectors pose for a Denver, Colorado, photographer in the mining district near Leadville where fortunes in gold and silver were made and lost from 1860 to the 1880s. While Bret Harte and Mark Twain mined experiences with humor and hyperbole, women such as Sarah Eleanor Bayliss Royce and Catherine Haun recorded candid observations of the era in their diaries.

The element of chance figures in most commentary on goldfield finances. According to *Audubon's Western Journal* (1850), written by artist John Woodhouse Audubon, son of ornithologist John James Audubon, digging for gold was a gamble that brought a few instant wealth but reduced most to poverty and disillusion. In early January 1850 among the piney hills around Chinese Mines near Stockton, California, Audubon traveled as second in command of Colonel H. L. Webb's California Company, a joint venture of 80 men. When the party reaches a field active with gold seekers, Audubon observes the crapshoot atmosphere of prospecting:

> The uncertainty of digging renders the life of the miner, for profit, that of a gambler, for most of his good luck depends on chance. At times you may see two pits side by side, one man getting two ounces a day, and the other hardly two dollars: we heard of one instance of much greater disparity; two friends working next each other found that at the end of the week, one had an ounce of gold worth about twenty dollars, the other gold worth six thousand dollars. So it goes. (Audubon 1984, 201)

At first, Audubon believes reports that gold is plentiful, but he acknowledges the brutal labor required to separate precious metal from rock. Deserting soupy mud, Audubon withdraws and dissolves his company. The group concludes that they are more likely to make money on land speculation, trade, barkeeping, or Monte-dealing than in prospecting among scattered pockets of ore.

Less fatalistic is the straightforward southern humor of Joseph Glover Baldwin, author of *The Flush Times of California*, a tongue-in-cheek epistle published in *The Southern Literary Messenger* in November 1853. A native Virginian and Mississippi attorney, Baldwin produced sketches of his wanderings to San Francisco, where he ultimately was elected to the California Supreme Court. Composed in the style of the sophisticated essays of Washington Irving's *Knickerbocker's History of New York*, Baldwin touches up hyperbole with an echo of Voltaire's *Candide*. In his description of the effect of a rich strike on Phil Steptoe, he reaches into the humor of the tall tale:

> I saw him the other day driving a dozen Chinamen tandem through Red-River Street. You know their hair hangs in a long queue to the ground: he hitched them to each other by the tails, and sat back in an old sulkey, with head one side and his heels over the foot-board, smoking a cigar, driving them along in a trot. (Baldwin 1966, 24)

With just the right shift, Baldwin reverts to understatement for his conclusion, "I am afraid he will turn out badly." He adds that California's boom times have dwindled to dullness with a few disasters and no more than one hanging a week. In a postscript, he promises to send "a few pounds of bracelets and trinkets by the next steamer." (ibid.)

Much subdued in the aftermath of the California gold rush, Baldwin wrote *Ebb Tide* (1864), a sober social commentary on the effects of gold on California. In his opinion, the discovery of nuggets at Sutter's Mill "opened a new page in the history of the world." (ibid., 44) Recently disbanded soldiers leave the war with Mexico in search of adventure. Baldwin satirizes the dreams of these neophyte prospectors by repeating the type of hearsay that draws thousands from the East:

> The mountain torrents were dammed up by boulders of auriferous rock, and swept nuggets of gold, like oranges, down the tide—while the hills groaned and their huge sides swelled out, pregnant with crude "yellow-boys," only awaiting some Yankee accoucher safely to deliver them of their precious burden. (ibid., 45–46)

To grab their share, swarms of "strong-limbed hoosiers and the adventurous backwoods-men" precede a second tide of European gold seekers, who were loosened by the news "as a quart of molasses loosens [the bowels] of a botts-afflicted horse." (ibid., 46–47)

The goldfields produced more accomplished humorists and chroniclers than Baldwin, notably Bret Harte, Jack London, Robert Service, and Mark Train, all of whom dealt in the rough jests and simmering vengeance plots indigenous to mining towns and camps. In one of the less colorful accounts of Western life in *The Autobiography of Mark Twain* (1924), the author delineates morals and manners in a land gone berserk with lust for gold. He inserts a memory of the one-man operation of a pocket mine, which washes out of a hillside and fans down the slope:

> The rest of his work is easy—he washes along up the mountainside, tracing the narrowing fan by his washings, and at last he reaches the gold deposit. It may contain only a few hundred dollars, which he can take out with a couple of dips of his shovel: also it may contain a concentrated treasure worth a fortune. It is the fortune he is after and he will seek it with a never-perishing hope as long as he lives. (Twain 1959, 300)

After spending the winter months of 1864 and 1865 with three friends and a cat named Tom Quartz at Jackass Hill in Tuolumne, California, in fruitless search for gold, he concludes that the experience of prospecting with jolly companions was "fascinating and delightful." However, he, like John Woodhouse Audubon, discloses chagrin that success in gold panning comes more from luck than expertise.

In the late twentieth century, Louis L'Amour presents a starker picture of silver mining in a historical novel, *The Comstock Lode* (1981). Unlike the wise-cracking Mark Twain, Trevallion, L'Amour's protagonist, lives like a hunted animal:

> As a result he had simply pulled out, had left his claim in the canyon, and had wandered over east and staked another claim in a canyon above Pipe Spring. On the certain theory that a man who makes no tracks leaves no tracks, he stayed where he was, killing an occasional deer, living sparsely and working hard. (L'Amour 1981, 85)

The persistence of boom-time lawlessness dogs prospectors like Trevallion with the threat of claim jumpers and thieves, an unpromising atmosphere less tinged by the amusing local color common to nineteenth-century frontier humorists. (Audubon 1984; Baldwin 1966; Beatty et al. 1952; Blacker 1961; Blain, Grundy, and Clements 1990; Blair 1937; Haun 1992; Lagarde and Michard 1985; L'Amour 1981; Poe 1962; Rasmussen 1995; Royce 1977; Snodgrass 1995a; Trent et al. 1946; Twain 1959; Visscher 1980)

See also explorers of the frontier; Harte, Bret; L'Amour, Louis; London, Jack; *Roughing It;* Service, Robert; Twain, Mark.

RADIN, PAUL

One of the foremost anthropologists and ethnologists of the American Indian, Paul Radin, a German-Russian Jewish immigrant from Lodz, Poland, outlined the workings of primitive society through a meticulous study of the Winnebago of Wisconsin and Canada. He explored the makeup of human nature by searching oral lore and superstitions for recurrent motifs and mores. His signal contribution to the understanding of native peoples is his belief that all people move through a series of self-discoveries as they rise from atavism to civilization. He proposed that, whatever their level of civilization, tribes or clans function in groups disciplined by a complex scheme of moral precepts.

Influenced by scholar Franz Boas, Radin became a historical reporter. He first visited the Winnebago in 1908, completed his doctorate at Columbia University in 1911, and then returned to his lifelong field study of the Winnebago. He published *The Winnebago Tribe* (1916) and *The Autobiography of a Winnebago Indian* (1920), a monumental contribution to anthropology, which he preceded in 1913 by an article published in the *Journal of American Folklore*.

Sam Blowsnake, the speaker of Radin's highly readable *The Autobiography of a Winnebago Indian*, identifies himself as S.B., the nephew of White-Cloud, who predicted that the boy would be unusual. Written in a native syllabary and translated by Radin and interpreter Oliver Lamere, the first-person narrative forms a readable summary of a wayward man's religious conversion. In the narrative, Blowsnake undergoes a puberty ritual, which requires fasting. During hunts with his father, he learns the nature of muskrat, mink, otter, and beaver. At his summer home at Black River Falls, Wisconsin, Blowsnake enjoys the usual exploits of young men and displays evolving manhood by teasing girls. About this time, he is adopted by his grandfather, a medicine man, who allows him to attend school in nearby Tomah.

The account of Blowsnake's elopement with a widow and subsequent secret relationship with two Sioux widows precedes a period of heavy drinking, girl chasing, posturing, and riding a bicycle in a Wild West show at St. Paul. With complete candor he admits that he was immature:

> I claimed to be a great man. I then had two women staying with me as my wives, and, at one time I had as many as four . . . I wasn't serious with any of

them. I lied all the time and I knew how to tell falsehoods. On one occasion four children were born to me and each one had a different mother. (Radin 1963, 27)

Still behaving willfully, he poses as a holy man and travels by train with a man named Peter and two other friends to a Nebraska powwow, where Peter kills a Potawatomie. Blowsnake counts coup and names himself Big Winnebago. Two years later, he is arrested and jailed, then released after he testifies against Peter.

Radin's narrative returns Blowsnake from lawlessness to the charismatic rituals of peyotism. Upon his release, Blowsnake dismays his conservative relatives by joining his parents in Nebraska in the peyote cult, which requires him to disavow traditional Winnebago ritual. At the time of his conversion, he experiences a vision of the road to the spirit land:

> The road was an excellent one. Along its edge blue grass grew and on each side there grew many varieties of pretty flowers. Sweet-smelling flowers sprang up all along this road. Far off in the distance appeared a bright light. There a city was visible of a beauty indescribable by tongue. (ibid., 61)

The vision, a blend of desert cult and Christianity, concludes in his realization that he, like a bound object, has tied himself down with flirtations. He repents and marries a good woman, to whom he is faithful. Radin's production and annotation of this insightful autobiography received worldwide recognition for its revelations on social behavior, tribal wisdom, and cultural clash after the Winnebago began to assimilate white ways.

In 1934, Radin departed from the jargon of the scientist to produce *The Story of the American Indian*, an overview of the aborigines who first populated North America. In the prologue, Radin composes a hypothetical description of the introduction of Monsieur Nicollet, discoverer of Lake Michigan and leader of a French expedition to a Winnebago village in 1634. The lyric re-creation of an evening's entertainment includes Nicollet's viewing of painted deerskins and his captivation by prayers, flute music, and ecstatic singing. At the end of his stay, he has witnessed preparations for and return from a successful war mission. He withdraws from the Winnebago with a personal familiarity with their rituals and with many questions unanswered.

Radin's multifaceted introduction to individual Indian cultures combines scientific observation along with drama, liturgy, myth, and verse. His study of how natives learn about nature forms a compelling narrative, as demonstrated by this beast legend of the hare:

> "I wish a spark would fall upon me." Sure enough a spark fell upon him . . . and this he said to his grandmother when he came flying in: "Rub the fire off from me, I am burning up, my grandmother!" Whereupon truly off from him did the old woman rub the fire. Therefore such was how they came into possession of fire. (Radin 1934, 340)

As Radin's poetic description indicates, the Great God Hare takes the form of an animistic hero of primitive society. Natives worship him just as the Maya of Central America venerate the firebird Quetzalcoatl and the Plains Indians the buffalo. Radin surmises that the various strands of animal myth are essentially identical.

Radin's epilogue describes the "Winning of the West" as the annihilation of the aborigine. More than the *conquistadores* and Spanish and French slavers, he blames white Puritans, who cleared natives from the frontier as they settled New England. European settlers broke the spirit of Native Americans in what Radin terms a "man-hunt." He dramatizes the showdown on the prairie:

> The circle became smaller and smaller; the leaders of the Indians more and more puzzled and desperate. What was to be done? Three possibilities existed: either to make one last stand and drive out the hated and destructive invaders, or incorporate what seemed best in white culture into their own culture, or finally, to give up their old culture and adopt that of the white man. (ibid., 365)

Radin's summation describes the resultant literature of the frontier: the desperate shoot-out, the attempt of settlers to coexist with Indians, or the predictable collapse of Native American values as white culture swept over what remained of a once-proud way of life. Just as Dee Brown concluded in *Bury My Heart at Wounded Knee*, the death of a culture is pathetic and ignoble: survivors flee from soldiers and the carnage caused by machine-gun fire. In the wake of white technology, "women with infants in their arms were shot down after resistance had ceased and when almost every warrior was stretched dead, or dying, on the ground." (ibid., 371)

An adjunct to Radin's study of culture is his appreciation of the cultural role of language. His monograph, *The Genetic Relationship of the North American Indian Languages* (1919), classified the lingual groups of Native Americans into a unified continental language family similar to the Indo-European language tree. Outgrowths of his original research undergird *Primitive Man as Philosopher* (1927), *Method and Theory of Ethnology* (1933), and *Primitive Religion* (1938). Near the end of his career, Radin published *The Road of Life and Death* (1945) and *The Culture of the Winnebago: As Described by Themselves* (1949). It was his last major publication, *The Trickster: A Study in American Indian Mythology* (1956), that assured his position in the study of myth. A string of witty, comic animal fables, the work connects the native trickster tales of the Sioux, Ponca, Assiniboin, and Winnebago with Asian, Mediterranean, and Western lore. It remains a standard reference source as well as the touchstone for popular Native American literature for children.

A peripatetic lecturer in Europe; a teacher at the University of California, Berkeley, the University of Chicago, Kenyon College, Fisk University, and Cambridge University; and head of the anthropology department at Brandeis University, he worked in a variety of scholarly settings and died of heart failure during a lecture. His brilliance and compassion influenced subsequent generations of anthropologists and followers from related fields, including psychologist Carl Jung, critic-historian Mark van Doren, poets Allen Tate and John Crowe Ransom, philosopher John Dewey, and sociologist Lewis Mumford. (Cavendish 1970; Eliade 1987; Radin 1934, 1963, 1972; Sills 1968)

RAWLINGS, MARJORIE KINNAN

A city dweller until her early thirties, journalist Marjorie Kinnan Rawlings first saw Florida on a vacation trip in 1928. After she and husband Charles bought a 72-acre citrus grove in Cross Creek, the wild setting seemed light-years away from her native Washington, D.C., or her recent home in Rochester, New York, where she had written for the *Rochester Journal*. Under the influence of thick palmetto swamps and plentiful wildlife, she began writing regional fiction and published *South Moon Under* (1933), which was nominated for a Pulitzer Prize. Her third work, *The Yearling* (1938), won the award and clinched her place in the National Academy of Arts and Letters.

A sensitive young adult classic, *The Yearling* recounts the coming-of-age of 13-year-old Jody Baxter, the "betwixt and between" man-child of Ora, a harsh mother, and Penny, a more lenient father who has just returned from service in the Civil War. Set on the Florida frontier in the late 1860s, the plot covers the cracker dialect, husbandry, and hardscrabble existence of isolated settlers like Penny on a harsh, yet reassuringly stable, landscape:

> The peace of the vast aloof scrub had drawn him with the beneficence of its silence. Something in him was raw and tender. The touch of men was hurtful upon it, but the touch of the pines was healing. Making a living came harder there, distances were troublesome in the buying of supplies and the marketing of crops. But the clearing was peculiarly his own. The wild animals seemed less predatory to him than people he had known. The forays of bear and wolf and wildcat and panther on stock were understandable, which was more than he could say of human cruelties. (Rawlings 1970, 18)

Like other returning war veterans, Penny embraces the frontier for its raw, clean expanse, which was free of the taint of slavery and a national conflict that killed too many on both sides of the issue.

The story centers on Jody's love for an orphaned fawn, which he and his father raise at their rough outback homestead. Jody names the fawn Flag for the white scut of a tail that flirts and bobbles as the fawn noses about the wild. Amid scrub trees, fetter bush, and sparkle berry, the boy and Flag become inseparable. Central to the story is a prevalent frontier theme—the survival of the strong and the winnowing out of the weak. Jody's friend Fodderwing Forrester was "born peculiar—from the second settin'." (ibid., 137) Misshapen and sickly, he dies suddenly, leaving Jody to mourn his passing. Jody realizes, "This was Death. Death was a silence that gave back no answer." (ibid., 204) The loss presages the flood on Lake George, scarcity of game, and desperation among predatory animals, especially a bear named Old Slewfoot, Rawlings's symbol of the bestial, untamed forces of nature. Penny's insistent stalking of the bear ends in triumph. During the sharing of meat, the feud that erupts with the Baxters' neighbors epitomizes the latent violence and smoldering animosities common to independent frontier homesteaders.

The pivotal scene of Rawlings's novel pits the parents against Jody. Wiser heads instruct the child that he must get rid of Flag before he ruins their garden and jeopardizes the winter food supply. Earlier, Penny had warned his son, "A creetur's only doin' the same as me when I go huntin' us meat . . . Huntin' him where he lives and beds and raises his young uns. Hit's a hard law, but it's the law. Kill or go hongry." (ibid., 43) Ora had long "been sparin'" to make the most of supplies, water, meat, garden vegetables, and local berries and greens. To assure their survival, she shoots the deer. Like the animal execution in Fred Gipson's *Old Yeller,* the death of Flag breaks the boy's heart. Emotional trauma forces Jody to flee his home and seek comfort elsewhere. Rawlings returns him to his family via mailboat. Jody, no longer a child, accepts the ways of the frontier and faces the future as an adult. The 1946 film version, starring Gregory Peck, Jane Wyman, Chill Wills, and Forrest Tucker, won audiences to its pure, unspoiled vision of love between child and pet.

Rawlings expanded her writings to verse, short fiction, and nonfiction. She sold stories to the *New Yorker, Scribner's, Harper's, Atlantic Monthly, Collier's,* and the *Saturday Evening Post.* Most successful of her titles were *When the Whippoorwill* (1940), a collection of short stories, and *Cross Creek* (1942), her anecdotal autobiography, which she followed with *Cross Creek Cookery* (1942). After a divorce, she remained content in Florida and died in St. Augustine in 1953. Her work earned the O. Henry award, a Newbery honor, Lewis Carroll Shelf award, and honorary doctorates from Rollins College and the Universities of Tampa and Florida. (Bigelow 1966; Halliwell 1995; Hart 1983; Magill 1958; Rawlings 1970; Sackett 1996; Stuckey 1966; Wagenknecht 1952)

See also Gipson, Fred.

REED, JOHN

In his zeal to capture the agrarian revolt led by General Francisco "Pancho" Villa on behalf of Francisco Madero, provisional president of Mexico, crusading journalist John Silas "Jack" Reed wrote an eyewitness account of the backcountry war, when Villa rode like a legendary hero among adoring peasants. Villa and Reed had little in common. The son of wealth and privilege, Reed fled his Portland, Oregon, background and Harvard credentials to travel among radical newsmakers. He wrote titillating pieces for *American Magazine, Smart Set, New York World,* and *Metropolitan Magazine,* for the last of which he reviewed the rise of Mexico's revolutionary bandit chief. Before World War I, Reed wrote for *The Masses,* a Marxist workers' journal, and helped establish the Communist Party of the United States. His interest in strikes and organizational efforts by the Industrial Workers of the World preceded his coverage of the Bolshevik Revolution and the rise of Lenin, the subject of his most mature historical journalism, *Ten Days That Shook the World* (1919). A year later, he died of typhus in Moscow at the age of 33 and became the only American to be buried in the Kremlin.

Jack Reed's mystique is inseparable from the cult of youthful exhibitionism. At age 27, he produced *Insurgent Mexico* (1914), a picaresque narrative that opens with his view from the Presidio, Texas, post office roof as he summarizes the defeat of General Mercado's federal army. Looking out on the adobe walls of Ojinaga, a crude frontier hamlet on the Rio Grande, Reed determines to interview Mercado and wades across the river into Mexico. A note from Mercado ends Reed's hope with a terse but courteous threat: "Esteemed and Honored Sir: If you set foot inside of Ojinaga, I will stand you sideways against a wall, and with my own hand take great pleasure in shooting furrows in your back." (Reed 1969, 2) Making the most of good intentions, Reed describes the dusty streets, Spanish church bells, and gutted rooms where "lived the soldiers, their women, their horses, their chickens and pigs, raided from the surrounding country." (ibid., 3) The squalor of Mercado's force suggests that Villa had surprised his opponent and succeeded in demoralizing the Mexican hierarchy and its pro-constitution generals.

Reed's first-person experiences take him on a series of impressionistic episodes, concluding with a spontaneous pastoral play given by peasants. He surveys the lowest levels of society, where peddlers sell the "Gringo" wads of *macuche* in lieu of tobacco and where operatives poison the irrigation ditches, leaving corpses behind as they force their opponents into open warfare. Peasants conduct their lives as best they can by ignoring polemics and following the leader who represents their most pressing needs and interests. One disgruntled balladeer sings:

> I am of the children of the night
> Who wander aimlessly in the darkness . . .
> So I am going to become an American.
> Go with God, Antonia.
> Say farewell to my friends.
> O may the Americans allow me to pass
> And open a saloon
> On the other side of the River! (ibid., 34–35)

Another on-the-scene lyric extols Villa, the illiterate peasant leader who undercuts the rich to equalize the economic divisions between Mexico's upper and lower classes. The song urges:

> Fly, fly away, little dove,
> Fly over all the prairies,
> And say that Villa has come
> To drive them all out forever. (ibid., 75–76)

The last of the ten verses proclaims "Viva Villa and his soldiers!" and warns the wicked to observe the power of rebellion against an entrenched plutocracy. An authoritative voice interrupts the shouts and reads a proclamation dividing haciendas among the peasants, who once served as peons of grandees.

While identifying with the surge of supportive underclass folk, Reed pursues Villa to Chihuahua City, where the general's men present the general a gold medal for heroism. The introduction of the people's hero is unremarkable, reading like the exposition of a novel:

> He was dressed in an old plain khaki uniform, with several buttons lacking.
> He hadn't recently shaved, wore no hat, and his hair had not been brushed.

John Reed, 1887–1920

> He walked a little pigeon-toed, humped over, with his hands in his trousers pockets. (ibid., 114)

The adoring rebel force welcomes his nod and polite acknowledgment of the assembled *compadres;* when the combined army salutes, Reed declares the moment Napoleonic.

Reed studies the formative currents of myth that forge Mexico's frontier hero. He observes Villa sitting unceremoniously for a round of speeches that proclaim him "Friend of the Poor," "Invincible General," "Inspirer of Courage and Patriotism," and "Hope of the Indian Republic." (ibid., 115) With eyes that appreciate the loyalty of commoners, Villa leans forward to reply: "There is no word to speak. All I can say is my heart is all to you." (ibid., 116) This two-sentence reply and a macho spit at the floor serves well the needs of the uneducated, who expect no more of their leader than sincerity and superhuman courage. This style of characterization identifies Reed with the realist school of war coverage that dates to Stephen Crane's *Red Badge of Courage,* an emergence so close to the pageantry and action that the observer blends his person with the colorful elements he describes.

At this point in Reed's discourse, he pauses to append "The Rise of a Bandit," a chapter summarizing Villa's 22 years on the run. A frontier outlaw since he killed a bureaucrat and fled his job delivering milk to Chihuahuans, he compounded his outrage against the establishment by violating the haciendos with multiple episodes of cattle rustling. Carrying a price on his head, Villa moved inexorably toward the outbreak of the Madero revolution. With no sense of his place in history, he displays "the naive simplicty of a savage." (ibid., 117) His criminal record bulges with false reports of stickups, lootings, and train robberies committed by would-be Villas who thrive on the romance of their Mexican Robin Hood. Reed concludes that songs, ballads, verse, and popular legend arise from shepherds, farm laborers, and fans throughout Durango and Chihuahua, from Coahuila to Sinaloa.

In person, the Villa of *Insurgent Mexico* is a loner and ascetic who dresses in humble serape and prowls the night. Since the revolt in 1910, he had endured imprisonment in the penitentiary and taught himself to read and write. Within nine months, he could read newsprint. He escaped to El Paso, Texas, recruited men from the San Andres area, and launched an assault on Mexico. The cavalier's plunge into politics failed because he lacked proficiency with budgets, issuing currency, operating public utilities, and educating his fellow peons. In subsequent fight scenes, he overrides these lapses with the insouciance of a natural leader:

> A whispered, smothered shout of "Viva Villa!" burst from them. On foot, holding a lighted cigar in one hand—for he never smoked—and a bomb in the other, the General climbed the bank of the ditch and plunged into the brush, the others pouring after him. (ibid., 250)

In a clutch of Anglo newsmen huddled in the dark, Reed realizes the power of the moment as Villa defeats the odds and propels his juggernaut against Mexico's wealthy. The irony of the continued success of a ragtag force is the backstage plotting of Villa's revolutionaries to build a new government from the educated rebels. In no session does Villa himself figure on the lists of proposed ministers and military leaders. Excluded from victory, he becomes the expendible warrior, just as the peons have been the expendible settlers of frontier Mexico.

Reed earned mixed critical comments for *Insurgent Mexico* for its lack of objectivity and the panoramic sweep of detail, which oversteps journalism with a poet's passion for lyricism, martyrdom, and emotion. Reed's involvement becomes so personal that he seems to lose sight of his notebook and reach for a rifle. Beyond the scope of his book lies irony: the American betrayal of Villa, who attacked and massacred U.S. citizens at Santa Isabel in January 1916 and in Columbus, New Mexico, the next month. General John J. Pershing failed to corral Villa, who lived in public glory until 1923, when a hired assassin shot him.

Reed's *Insurgent Mexico* preceded publication of a sleeper war novel, Mariano Azuela's Mexican classic, *The Underdogs* (1915), which became popular nearly a decade after its serialization in *El Paso del Norte,* an Hispanic journal published in El Paso, Texas. Azuela's view is a moralistic re-creation of one band of ignorant, undisciplined mountain men who fight as their whim dictates and who lose their momentum after Villa's downfall. More detailed than Reed's version but vastly less sophisticated, the work reduces the leader Demetrio and his men to low levels of savagery. Unlike Reed, Azuela finds little grandeur among the spirited men who turned pathetic munitions and unenlightened farmers into a significant fighting force that crumbles into a disorganized band of carousers after their leader perishes.

Reed's fast-paced life among Greenwich Village liberals and his romance with intellectual artist-writer Louise Bryant was the subject of the film *Reds* (1981), starring Warren Beatty as Reed, Diane Keaton as Louise, and Jack Nicholson as Eugene O'Neill. Beatty, who wrote and directed the film, won an Oscar, as did Vittorio Storaro for photography and Maureen Stapleton for her supporting role as radical feminist Emma Goldman. *Reds* also received Oscar nominations for best screenplay, actor, actress, editing, and supporting male actor. The film introduced a generation of viewers to a writer who has remained on the edge of respectability, particularly after his indictment for sedition during extensive involvement with Communists. (Azuela 1962; Ehrlich and Carruth 1982; Hart 1983; Machado 1988; Reed 1936, 1969; Ruland and Bradbury 1991)

See also Hispanic Americans on the frontier.

RICHTER, CONRAD

Influenced by Franz Kafka, Willa Cather, and early-twentieth-century realism, Conrad Michael Richter portrayed in precise, understated fiction the dialect, rites of passage, work rhythms, and values of the frontier. Departing from the violence and stereotyped characters of dime Westerns, he crafted his view of Americana with a pictorial quality derived from verisimilitude and fine detail.

His work earned him the 1951 Pulitzer Prize for Literature as well as the National Book award, Gold Medal for Literature from the Society of Libraries of New York University, Ohioana Library Medal, National Institute of Arts and Letters grant, and a Maggie award and honorary degrees from Susquehanna University, Temple University, University of New Mexico, Lafayette College, and Lebanon Valley College.

Throughout his career, Richter drew on his family's immigrant strengths. He was a native of Pine Grove, Pennsylvania, a town named by his great-grandfather. Born October 13, 1890, to John Absalom and Charlotte Esther Henry Richter, he gained in childhood a pride in his ancestry, which included Palatine German immigrants, a U.S. congressman, and a hero of the War of 1812. While studying at Susquehanna Academy and Tremont High School, Richter toyed with the idea of majoring in philosophy and religion and entering the ministry, as had his grandfather, uncle, and father, a Lutheran pastor to a coal mining district. Instead of church work, however, he chose literature. After graduation from Tremont High School, he supported himself with a quick succession of jobs in lumbering, banking, retail clerking, door-to-door sales, wagon transport, and farming.

In 1909, Richter joined the staff of the Patton *Courier* and discovered that journalism suited him. From on-the-job training, he evolved an uncluttered journalistic style, which he employed while editing for the Johnstown *Journal and Leader* and the Pittsburgh *Dispatch*. For 15 years, he served a wealthy society matron in Cleveland as private secretary, a post that allowed him to travel. In his spare time, he began publishing short fiction, beginning with "How Tuck Went Home" for *Cavalier* magazine in 1913. The next year, "Brothers of No Kin" for *Forum* magazine earned him the Edward J. O'Brien award of $25. He branched out to a children's series for *John Martin's Book*.

Richter married Harvena Maria Achenbach in 1915 and settled in a historic farmhouse in Harrisburg, Pennsylvania, where his daughter, Harvena, was born. He opened a publishing firm in Reading and produced his first collection, *Brothers of No Kin and Other Stories* (1924), but earned little for his efforts. Undeterred, he spent the major portion of his life reading the histories of Francis Parkman, interviewing eyewitnesses, and researching old newspapers, documents, rare books, maps, battle charts, and unpublished manuscripts. From his stock of data, he composed short fiction, novels, and screenplays. He single-handedly published the *Junior Magazine Book*, a short-lived children's fiction journal, which he supplied with puzzles, poetry, stories, and ad copy.

To bolster his wife's frail health in a warmer climate, Richter resettled his family in Albuquerque in 1928, a year before the Great Crash and financial chaos. The Richters moved into a house near the University of New Mexico campus, where he forced himself to write what would sell for *Elks Magazine, Farm Journal, Blue Book, Country Home, Triple-X Westerns, Ghost Stories, Western Trails, Liberty, Home Magazine,* and *Woman's Home Companion*. He narrowed his interest in Americana to southwestern lore by perusing old newspapers and documents, interviewing survivors of historic events, and composing fiction that reflected his detailed research. As though racing to capture a fading vision of the wilderness, he packed his panoramic studies with intense feelings, conflict, loss, and realism. Readers rewarded the authenticity of his strong, unromanticized male and female characters and applauded the themes of courage and perseverance that permeate his portrayal of the pioneer era. In *Early Americana and Other Stories* (1936), the title story, a nostalgic glimpse of a past time, the protagonist yearns for a moonlit horseback ride on the Staked Plains and visualizes how

> a cloud may darken the face of the untamed earth, the wind in your face will suddenly bring you the smell of cattle, and there beyond you for a moment on the dim, unfenced, roadless prairie you can make out a fabulous dark herd rolling, stretching, reaching majestically farther than the eye can see, grazing on the wild, unplanted mats of the buffalo grass. (Richter 1978, 109)

No less disenchanted with the advance of civilization is "Smoke over the Prairie," a frank characterization of greedy railroad speculators, who plan to lay 800 miles of track over New Mexico's San Blas Plain. In these and other works, Richter stressed the fragile beauty that the Southwest retained, even as predators and developers were making plans for its destruction.

For three years, Richter worked for MGM. In the late 1940s, still faithful to early American retrospect, he returned to his hometown and wrote *The Free Man* (1943), *Always Young and Fair* (1947), and *The Mountain on the Desert: A Philosophical Journey* (1955). *The Free Man* re-creates the immigrant's delight in locating a resting place. According to 18-year-old Henner Dellicker, a fictional indentured worker drawn from Richter's German ancestors, Philadelphia was safe harbor, a reprieve from the roll of an oceangoing vessel: "Throw a bucket over the side and you drew up sweet water." (Richter 1965a, 73) The pictorial imagery of *The Free Man* crackles with confrontations between the idealistic immigrant and the hard-eyed Americans who exploit them:

> What kind of Bible do such read? Do they paste the pages together where it says, "Defend the poor and fatherless, do justice to the needy and afflicted," and that it is better for those who don't give a cup of cold water to little ones that they be taken out and hanged to the highest tree? (ibid., 91)

It is not surprising that Richter's work suited cinema: his young adult frontier classic, *The Light in the Forest* (1953), was filmed in 1958; likewise, *Tacey Cromwell* (1942), his novel about a frontier prostitute, served Universal Pictures as a 1955 feature film renamed *One Desire*; and MGM filmed *The Sea of Grass* (1936), his first best-seller, in 1947.

Richter remained active in his last decade. He produced *The Lady* (1957); *The Waters of Kronos* (1960); a reflection on his father in *A Simple Honorable Man* (1962); *The Grandfathers* (1964); and *A Country of Strangers* (1966), a companion work to *The Light in the Forest* that places Stone Girl, a white female captive (originally named Mary Stanton) of the Lenni Lenape, in the inhospitable milieu of eighteenth-century Pennsylvania and the frontier south of the Great Lakes.

In 1966, "The Trees," "The Fields," and "The Town" appeared under the title *The Awakening Land*. Forming Richter's pioneer trilogy of Sayward Luckett's family living west of the Alleghenies in the late eighteenth century, the works recount the stresses of wilderness life, such as the isolation of the housewife and the tedium of woman's work in a primitive cabin:

> It was a good thing, she thought, to have an excuse for going off from your cabin. A woman got tired of seeing the same big kettle and little kettle every day, the same gourds and chinking board shelves, feeding the same fire and going down for water to the same run. You wanted to drink water sometimes from some other run. (Richter 1940, 69)

The portrait of the family's transition from isolation on the frontier to being part of rural, agrarian Pennsylvania gains vigor from the author's knowledge of woodland plants, cooking, doctoring, storytelling, and singing.

Because Richter wrote slowly and carefully, he took three years to complete the last of the trilogy. The combined work earned critical praise for its authenticity and mythic quality, but it did not enrich his family. Moreover, his disappointment with earlier screen versions of his fiction precipitated his refusal of Hollywood offers to film the trilogy. However, a decade after his death on October 30, 1968, in Pine Grove, the trilogy aired as a television miniseries, which earned Emmy nominations for stars Hal Holbrook and Elizabeth Montgomery. Richter's daughter Harvena further introduced his works to the public by publishing collected stories in *The Rawhide Knot* (1978) as well as his private notebooks, *Writing To Survive* (1988).

Critical opinion places Richter in a prestigious position among America's realists of the heartland tradition, notably Willa Cather, O. E. Rölvaag, Hamlin Garland, and Sherwood Anderson. Reviews stress his depiction of vigorous, rugged characters and his choice of fervor and the westering spirit as dominant themes. To a disciplined artist like Richter, the settler's dedication to daunting struggles was an admirable trait that he credited with shaping character. He believed that challenge and sacrifice rewarded the hardy with a spirituality and community harmony that disappeared with America's industrialization and attendant urbanization and affluence. (Barnes 1968; *Contemporary Authors* 1994; Dobie 1996; Edwards 1971; Folsom 1966; Gaston 1965; Hart 1983; Kunitz 1942; LaHood 1975; Lamar 1977; Leisy 1950; Parkman 1991; Richter, Conrad 1940, 1947, 1950, 1953, 1960, 1965a, 1965b, 1965c, 1966, 1978; Richter, Harvena 1988; *Something About the Author* 1972; Stuckey 1966; Wagenknecht 1952; Ward and Marquardt 1979)

See also Cather, Willa; *The Light in the Forest*; Parkman, Francis; Rölvaag, O. E.; *The Sea of Grass*; short fiction of the frontier.

"RIP VAN WINKLE"

A classic story, "Rip Van Winkle: The Posthumous Writing of Diedrich Knickerbocker" (1819), was first told in Washington Irving's regional short fiction. Irving combines dialect humor and a rural tableau with moral serious-ness to produce a unique, enduring blend. He allies the tale with his comic chronicle, *A Knickerbocker's History of New York,* and connects Rip to history by pairing him with Peter Stuyvesant, Dutch founder of New Amsterdam. By supplying the trappings of oral tradition, especially the convention of the wan-derer in the person of an unnamed voyager up the Hudson River, Irving im-plies that the tale is as rootless as the European lore that arrived with early visitors to the New World and traveled to the Pacific Coast with the pioneers. At story's end, Irving accounts for the tale's perpetuation: Rip, like an Ameri-can version of Samuel Taylor Coleridge's *The Rime of the Ancient Mariner,* feels compelled to relate the story "to every stranger that arrived at Mr. Doolittle's hotel . . . and not a man, woman, or child in the neighbourhood but knew it by heart." (Irving n.d., 366) As Irving predicted, "Rip Van Winkle" has settled into the permanent canon of American lore. The sweet-sad tale of the sleepy lag-gard has appeared in numerous adaptations for stage, animated film, audio-cassette, and television drama.

After the publication of the Washington Irving original, a series of anony-mous stage versions delighted playgoers for half a century. In 1828, Thomas Flynn produced *Rip Van Winkle, or The Demons of the Catskill Mountains! A Na-tional Drama* in Albany, New York. The next year at Philadelphia's Walnut Street Theatre, John Kerr put on a three-act version; unlike ephemeral stagings, this version was printed. Performed by C. B. Parsons, *Rip Van Winkle* moved west of the Alleghenies in 1831 and played to enthusiastic audiences. One of the most resilient published versions is Charles Burke's *Rip Van Winkle, a Legend of the Catskills* (1850); another skillful adaptation is the work of James A. Herne, produced in the 1890s. In 1919, Percy MacKaye produced a stagier version, *Rip Van Winkle, a Folk Opera,* set to music by Reginald Koven.

The frontier's most renowned performer, Joseph Jefferson III, a Philadel-phia comedian and character actor, created his enduring rendition of Irving's Rip Van Winkle in 1865. He developed the transformation of Rip from old to young into a theatrical specialty and touched up the eerie mountaintop scene with ghostly realism. Photos reveal a contemplative, bewhiskered, barefoot man dressed in tattered pants and shirt and carrying an outdated flintlock. Looking out on the audience, his eyes take in the growth and change in a settled valley he once knew as frontier.

The plot, based on a German folktale and restated for American playgoers by Dion Boucicault, focuses on a trusting, underschooled frontiersman from the village of Falling Waters in the Kaatskill Mountains. Rip mortgages his land to Derrick von Beekman, a conniving land-grabber. A symbol of the greed that follows settlers into the wild, Derrick tricks the illiterate mountaineer into signing sale papers that he claims are mortgage agreements. Dame Gretchen Van Winkle accuses Derrick of ruining her husband and attempting to seduce her:

> Ten years ago, this was a quiet village, and belonged mostly to my husband,
> Rip Van Winkle, a foolish idle fellow . . . And you, Derrick—you supplied him
> with the money to waste in riot and drink. Acre by acre, you've sucked in his

land to swell your store. Yonder miserable cabin is the only shelter we have left; but that is mine. Had it been his, he would have sold it to you, Derrick, long ago. (*Rip Van Winkle* 1938, 405)

The familiar characterization of the wayward alcoholic portrays Rip as a cheerful, nonthreatening tippler who fills Nicholas Vedder's chalkboard at the George III inn with marks indicating more drinks on account than the family can repay.

Speaking in Dutch dialect, Rip gladly accepts a free drink, chuckling "I say it's a fine thing—when there's plenty in it. (Ve gates! Ve gates! [Cheers!])" (ibid., 408) He quarrels with his shrewish wife, who beats his hound, Schneider, for the same idleness she loathes in her husband. Accompanied by Schneider, who flees through a window, Rip wanders away during a storm. In Act III, he encounters legendary Dutch seaman Hendrick Hudson, a dwarf, and his spectral bowlers, dressed in seventeenth-century garb and playing ninepins. Rip awaits a greeting and voices his annoyance,

Ain't ye goin' to speak to a feller? I don't want to speak to you, then. Who you think you was, that I want to speak to you, any more than you want to speak to me; you hear what I say? Donner an' Blitzen! What for a man is das? I have been walking over these mountains ever since I was a boy, an' I never saw a queer looking codger like that before. He must be an old sea-snake, I reckon. (ibid., 420)

The soliloquy fleshes out the remainder of the act, with Rip helping himself to the bowlers' keg and muttering about their blatant discourtesy.

Rip drinks so deeply from their store of whiskey that he sleeps away two decades. In Act IV, he awakens unsteadily, complaining, "I must have cotched the rheumatix a-sleepin' mit the wet grass." (ibid., 422) On return to the village, Rip discovers that locals believe him dead and buried. He quips, "Last night, I don't know about the time, I went away up into the mountains . . . when I woke up this morning, I was dead." (ibid., 426) He learns that Derrick has usurped both land and wife and betrothed Rip's daughter Meenie to Derrick's nephew.

The proof of Rip's identity and his far-fetched story of a 20-year sleep is in his pocket—the unsigned deed that Derrick passed off to the illiterate borrower as a loan form. In a tidy denouement, Rip reclaims his land and reconciles with Gretchen. Although he has sworn off strong drink and has been sober—and sleeping—for 20 years, the good-hearted Dutchman ends the play with his typical insouciance when offered a drink, "Well I won't count this one; for this will go down with a prayer." (ibid., 431) Like Coleridge's Ancient Mariner, he takes pipe and cup and tells his tale to friends and family and concludes the play with a toast to the audience. (Bowden 1981; Brockett 1968; Brooks 1944; Coad and Mims 1929; Gassner and Quinn 1969; Hartnoll 1983; Hewitt 1959; Hughes 1951; Irving, n.d.; Jefferson 1964; Malone 1933; Quinn 1938; *Rip Van Winkle* 1938)

See also Irving, Washington; Jefferson, Joseph, III; theater of the frontier.

RÖLVAAG, O. E.

Author Ole Edvart Rölvaag produced America's classic Norwegian-American frontier trilogy, an incisive drama of the transformation of the prairie immigrant into resident farmer. Rölvaag shares the viking heritage of Per Hansa, the main character of *Giants in the Earth: A Saga of the Prairie* (1927), the first title of the trio, which was a Book-of-the-Month-Club selection. The insightful study of Per Hansa's motivation to abandon Norse tradition, acclimate to the prairie, and profit from its bounty results in Rölvaag's major achievement: a profound statement about the pioneer's sacrifice and martyrdom to the land.

According to "The Romance of a Life," the kernel of an incomplete autobiography, Rölvaag's roots parallel those of Per Hansa. He was born in a sod-roofed cottage on the barren, gorse-strewn, peat-bogged island of Dönna, Helgeland, on April 22, 1876. The son of Ellerine Pedersdatter Vaag and carpenter Peder Benjamin Rölvaag, he grew up in a traditional fishing society permeated by melancholy and fanatical piety. Local lore was rich in balladry and supernatural stories of the sea, but residents were largely unschooled. Each winter, Rölvaag and his family worked the waters of the Lofoten Islands near the Arctic Circle, 200 miles from home. An unpromising student who envied his smarter older brother Johan, Rölvaag was nicknamed "the Turk" for his stodgy personality and amused his parents with the intent to become a poet. To prepare himself for an academic career, he poured over the island's meager supply of classic works by European and American masters, notably the Norwegian translation of James Fenimore Cooper's *The Last of the Mohicans*, which he read aloud to fishermen.

Like other settlers of the American West, Rölvaag sought escape from drabness and confinement. After a storm wrecked a local crew on January 25, 1893, he determined to flee the dangers of open-boat fishing, but didn't convince his uncle in America to sponsor him until two years later. At the annual Bjørn fair, his mentor, Kristian Andersen, the captain of the best fleet, tried to tempt him with the offer of a grand new boat. The quandary forced him to examine his motives. In his diary he wrote:

> What was my heart aching for? I honestly didn't know. If I decided to refuse this wonderful offer, what reasonable excuse could I make? You see, I *had* no valid excuse, or none that could be put into words. I just felt that I wasn't fulfilling myself. I wanted to go away, find out what the world was like, and see if I didn't fit in somewhere else. (Rölvaag 1971, xiv)

Against the temptation to become an independent fisherman, Rölvaag was adamant about leaving a circumscribed life on the Arctic Sea. At age 20, he migrated to Elk Point, South Dakota, arriving hungry, penniless, and speaking no English.

In his fictionalized autobiography, *Letters from America* (1912), later published under the title *The Third Life of Per Smevik*, Rölvaag records how the protagonist walks half the night until he crosses paths with other Norwegian immigrants. The character, Peder Andersen Smevik, registers the author's somber leave-taking of Nordland and his grave acceptance of American citizenship:

> When we came here and received our citizenship papers and became Americans, we swore obedience and allegiance to the United States of America; but at the same time we forswore all our citizen's rights in that impoverished land we had left behind—in truth a serious oath! Thus were we adopted. Thus you and I exchanged our Fatherland for a new land. (ibid., 118)

In the next breath, he prays, "Much have I lost, but much I received, perhaps it was best that it happened this way. Thank you then, O God." (ibid., 118–119) His character lists in order of importance the gifts of his new citizenship—work, food, and education. The fourth benefit he extols is civil and religious freedom. As the text swells into an anthem to freedom, he proclaims that the American farmer possesses boundless independence and opportunity, which he pursues on his "genuine pioneer farm."

Rölvaag settled southeast of Sioux Falls and, while attending Augustana Academy, a church school in Canton, worked for three years peddling books and stereopticons and toiling at a farm near Elk Point. His commencement address stated a theme that recurred in his novels and his book of essays, *Concerning Our Heritage* (1922): that Scandinavian immigrants could contribute to their adopted home by drawing on the strengths they carried from the old country. During a period of discouragement, he tried factory, saloon, and restaurant work in Sioux City, Iowa, before accepting the advice of others that he get more schooling. He enrolled at St. Olaf College in Northfield, Minnesota, and studied ancient and modern languages, math, church history, and Norwegian literature. To pay tuition and earn money for an off-campus residence, he stoked stoves, painted walls and fences, worked in the kitchen, and taught at a parochial school in Lime Grove and Church's Ferry, Nebraska, and in Bisbee, North Dakota. He wrote for the school newspaper and yearbook and began a novel, which he described to his future wife through letters. To his surprise, he disproved father Rölvaag's low opinion of his intelligence and graduated with honors. Having obtained citizenship and a promise of a teaching job, he completed a year of postgraduate work at the University of Oslo. For a quarter century, he was a professor of Norwegian literature at St. Olaf. Among his interests were a course on Scandinavian immigration and the formation of the Norwegian-American Historical Association, which he helped to found in 1925.

Rölvaag possessed a vigorous intellect, but his body bore the scars of his early labors on the sea. His health was marred by weak lungs and chronic bronchitis, worsened in 1906 by diphtheria. Impelled by his goal to acknowledge the Norse presence on the frontier, he published six novels, a collection of essays, a Norwegian-English dictionary, and a series of Norwegian readers, handbooks, and a grammar. He edited an anthology of Norwegian-American short stories and vignettes and began writing original works under the pen name Paal Mørck. Three titles—*On Forgotten Paths* (1914), *Two Fools* (1920), and *The Ship of Longing* (1922)—prefaced his three somber fictional masterworks on immigrant life. He intended a fourth novel in the saga but, because of multiple heart attacks and exhaustion, never moved beyond the planning stage. At his death from heart disease in Northfield on November 5, 1931, Rölvaag's fatalistic trilogy, composed of *Giants in the Earth, Peder Victorious* (1929), and *Their Fathers' God* (1931), remained his most popular and influential works. His daughter and three sons brought honor to his reputation, particularly Karl Fritjof Rölvaag, one-term governor of Minnesota and U.S. ambassador to Iceland.

Rölvaag mimics the trials of real pioneers, many of whom went broke, lost their sanity, returned home, or died trying to wrest a living from the stern, inhospitable wild. Dismayed by their narrow outlook, he once called them "dwarf spirits." In a perceptive study of stunted lives, he focuses on the psychological stimuli that beset Per and Beret Hansa, fictional homesteaders from Europe who live the pioneer dream and suffer its nightmares. As the Hansa family caravan approaches its destination, the immeasureable land utters an indecipherable earth call:

> "Tish-ah!" said the grass. . . . "Tish-ah, tish-ah!" . . . Never had it said anything else—never would it say anything else, but it complained aloud every time—for nothing like this had ever happened to it before. . . . "Tish-ah, tish-ah!" it cried, and rose up in surprise to look at this rough, hard thing that had crushed it to the ground so rudely, and then moved on. (Rölvaag 1927, 3)

The animated grass prefigures the morbid complaints of Beret, who suffers the isolation and stagnation of the prairie *hausfrau*. Daily, she battles the outsider's plaintive homesickness that robs her of joy in mothering Anna Marie, Ole, and the infant Peder Victorious. At night she shrouds the windows of their hut with clothing to shut out what Rölvaag terms "The Great Desolation."

Giants in the Earth chronicles the fortunes of the Hansas within a network of emigrants from Nordland, Norway. Peculiar to Rölvaag's view is his differentiation between the experiences of men and women on the Plains. Per Hansa, the hardy outdoorsman, is a fulfilled, satisfied farmer who thrives on labor and who welcomes a 14-hour day. He finds release from restlessness and thwarted ambition in unending day labor performed in merciless extremes of weather. To his wife, however, the perpetual challenge of surviving and raising young ones grows onerous. After grasshoppers deluge the family farm, Beret's brooding settles into the grim channels of Norse Calvinism. Unable to delight in her third child, she founders—her soul sickens, then her mind cracks. Although Beret's mental faculties stabilize, the terrible winter of 1880–1881 kills her husband, whose corpse is found beside a haystack after the thaw. The novel halts at this point, leaving the reader with the ominous implication that Beret will not recover from the loss of her anchor, her fearless, hard-working mate.

Often compared to Willa Cather's *O Pioneers!* and Johan Bojer's *The Emigrants*, Rölvaag's epic novel relates a similar blend of conditions: folkways and mindsets from the old country wrestling the exigencies and demands of the American West that the author terms "heaven's derision." A stark incident describes the Hansas' encounter with Jakob and Kari, a pathetically naive, vulnerable family of newcomers. At the arrival of their caravan:

An irresistible curiosity took hold of Per Hansa; in two jumps he stood on the tongue of the wagon. The sight that met his eyes sent chills running down his spine. Inside sat a woman on a pile of clothes, with her back against a large immigrant chest; around her wrists and leading to the handles of the chest a strong rope was tied; her face was drawn and unnatural. Per Hansa trembled so violently that he had to catch hold of the wagon box, but inwardly he was swearing a steady stream. To him it looked as if the woman was crucified. (ibid., 316–317)

Such faithfulness to realism sets Rölvaag's austere vision apart from the bucolic ramblings of Washington Irving, John Muir's exalted nature sermons, and the sturdy optimism of Francis Parkman. Dramatically severed from the glorified sightings of plainsmen just passing through, Rölvaag's pioneers in the Midwest rapidly lose touch with gilded sunsets and the riffling sough of the savannah.

In addition to the terror of a stark, joyless existence, immigrants like the Hansas must battle onslaughts of Indians and hostile nature. They hear in Jakob's voice the gnawing unrest of their own private thoughts, "No, life isn't easy . . . God! this has certainly been a wandering in the desert for me!" (ibid., 317, 319) As Jakob recounts the story of a dying child treated by an incompetent physician, he concludes with an unbearable memory—his son's rapid decline, the corpse shrouded in a discarded skirt, and burial alongside a stone. Past logic, the grieving father declares that he must return to the grave and recover his son's remains. He defends Kari's ravings with his own misgivings, "but you can imagine how it feels, to leave a child *that* way." (ibid., 321) That night, Beret proves her point to Per Hansa: "Now you can see that this kind of a life is impossible! It's beyond human endurance." (ibid., 323) (Ehrlich and Carruth 1982; Lamar 1977; Magill 1958; Reigstad 1972; Rölvaag 1927, 1955, 1971)

See also Bojer, Johan; Cather, Willa; Cooper, James Fenimore; Irving, Washington; *The Last of the Mohicans*; Muir, John; Parkman, Francis; short fiction of the frontier.

ROUGHING IT

A lengthy blend of travelogue, hoax, Western lore, and frontier humor, Mark Twain's *Roughing It* (1872) holds a special place in frontier literature for its eyewitness account of a seven-year sojourn in the West. Primarily a bildungsroman, Twain's only Western novel moves him on a continuum from essayist, journalist, and storyteller toward fiction writer. As is true with much of Twain's longer fiction, the style and tone of the venture varies as the writer himself moves from excited anticipation to disapproval, disappointment, and cynicism. The speaker, who is Twain in a comic guise of simulated innocence, wears the mask of the naif, the bumbling outsider who falls for a series of artifices before wising up to Western trickery and callousness. Money-making schemes, a disastrous motif in Twain's life, occupy the speaker's energies and fill the loosely structured central chapters with comic vignettes of the inept prospector humbled by experience. Obviously, the exertion, pain, and financial loss cost Twain much more in real life than his frontier novel reveals. Perhaps to save face and recoup his investment, he was able to turn into profit what must have been a rigorous era of struggle and disillusion with the myth of the golden West.

Departing from a brief attempt at soldiering for a Union militia at the beginning of the Civil War, Twain, then aged 25, left military service in July 1861 and traveled with his 35-year-old brother Orion Clemens, who had accepted a position as secretary to the governor of the newly created Nevada Territory. The pair booked passage on a steamer from St. Louis to "St. Joe" in northwestern Missouri, then boarded the overland stage and, for $150 each, rumbled over surprisingly smooth roads from Missouri to Nevada. The three-week journey took them, a meager wardrobe, a stack of government statutes, and an unabridged dictionary over the Kansas plains to Fort Phil Kearny, beyond the Rockies into Wyoming, and past the Great Salt Lake to Virginia City, Esmeralda, and Comstock, the mining heartland in the northern Sierra Nevada Mountains, which border California.

Twain's ebullient joshing pictures the ride from numerous angles: bunking on mailbags, watching drivers sleep while on duty, avoiding a leaky roof, hunting buffalo during a stagecoach breakdown, encountering "hostiles" and Mormon emigrants, and taking in the beauties of the snow-capped Rockies. Described as "young and ignorant," the speaker, an exaggerated rube bearing the name and likeness of Mark Twain, arms himself with a "Smith & Wesson seven-shooter, which carried a ball like a homeopathic pill." (Twain 1962d, 31–32) Moving steadily west on a pleasant jaunt punctuated by puffs on his clay pipe, a talkative female passenger, and a broken thoroughbrace, Twain reaches Nebraska, hunts the fabled "jackass rabbit," and camps in the wild. His discourse on plains cookery includes instructions for digging a hole for a fire and burning chopped sagebrush. He comments, "Such a fire will keep all night, with very little replenishing; and it makes a very sociable campfire." (ibid., 39) In anticipation of refreshment at a "'dobe" way station, he seats himself at a "greasy board on stilts, and the tablecloth and napkins had not come—and they were not looking for them, either." (ibid., 45) Unenthusiastic about sharing a disk of bread, condemned Army bacon, and "slumgullion," a tea of dubious origin, Twain insults a surly hostler by passing up the rustic bill of fare.

Beyond Omaha, Twain continues his gladsome commentary with a brief salute to "the wild sense of freedom," then diverts style and tone to a plaintive study of "the regular *coyote*." A lanky, skeletal creature, the animal bears "a tolerably bushy tail that forever sags down with a despairing expression of forsakenness and misery, a furtive and evil eye, and a long, sharp face, with slightly lifted lip and exposed teeth." (ibid., 49) With a sideswipe at natives, Twain adds, "he will eat anything in the world that his first cousins, the desert-frequenting tribes of Indians, will, and they will eat anything they can bite." He extends the kinship metaphor with another relative, the vulture, an "obscene bird" that duplicates the coyote's loathing of other creatures and "[yearns] to assist at their funerals." (ibid., 52) This sallow note suggests that the witty observer is unable to turn the desert's predatory denizens into the same lively jest that he reserves for the human victims of his satire: Irishmen, Mormons, miners, landladies, bureaucrats, gunmen, judges, and juries.

Pluckier characters uplift ensuing chapters, particularly the "pony rider." Twain describes the undersized horseman as "brimful of spirit and endurance." Downsizing the dangers of desert crossings, Twain quips:

> During the preceding night an ambushed savage had sent a bullet through the pony rider's jacket, but he had ridden on, just the same, because pony riders were not allowed to stop and inquire into such things except when killed. (ibid., 67)

The lethal ambience of the West peaks with the secondhand account of Slade, a rough rider who "killed three savages with his own hand, and afterward cut their ears off and sent them, with his compliments, to the chief of the tribe." (ibid., 71) The speaker and his companions wonder what they will hear next about this checkered character and are not surprised that a band of Montana vigilantes have hanged him.

The bantering tone edged with incredulity and alarm continues when the speaker meets a Mormon "Destroying Angel," a nineteenth-century hit man dispatched by the Latter-Day Saints to kill "Gentiles" who are out of favor with church folk. The speaker enlarges on the subject of Mormon history and violence in appendices A and B, which cover Brigham Young's rise to power and the shameful "Mountain Meadows Massacre," in which a party of churchmen ambushes and kills occupants of a wagon train. Twain makes a sham of objectivity when he describes the cleanliness of the Mormon capital and its lack of drunkards, carousers, and loafers. Criticism of the Mormon Bible, a boring treatise claiming that Joseph Smith "'smouched' from the New Testament and no credit given," comes closer to subjective venom, as does a smirking analysis of the Mormon theocracy. The industrious beehive city follows the rule of Brigham Young, a polygamist whom Twain lampoons in risqué jokes about "hiving together [in] one foul nest of mother and daughters." The butt of the humor is both husband and numerous mates, whom the speaker stereotypes as "poor, ungainly, and pathetically 'homely' creatures." Gleefully, he concludes that marriage to 60 Mormon women is an act of generosity "so sublime that the nations should stand uncovered in [the husband's] presence and worship in silence." (ibid., 98, 97)

On August 14, 1861, the stage crossed the Great American Desert and deposited Twain and his brother in Carson City, the ten-year-old territorial capital eight miles east of Lake Tahoe. According to the novel, during a four-month stay in Carson City, the speaker boards with a dormitory of the governor's retinue at Bridget O'Flannigan's "ranch." Twain demonstrates his skill in turning a minor detail into wickedly funny commentary with a description of the rooming house walls, which are actually canvas or flour sacks stitched into room dividers. At his best when deriding snobbery, he adds that "the common herd had unornamented sacks, while the walls of the aristocrat were overpowering with rudimental fresco—i.e. red and blue mill brands on the flour sacks." The decor swells in opulence with "spittoons and other evidences of a sumptuous and luxurious taste." (ibid., 129)

As the Western tenderfoot, Twain-the-tyro learns by the hands-on method. Settling in, he undergoes a harrowing introduction to frontier pragmatism by staying up all night to play cards after tarantulas captured by his roommates are jostled from their containers by a "zephyr." Later, while idling and taking in the sights, he purchases a Genuine Mexican Plug. In short order, he realizes that the auctioneer has sold him a fire-eater capable of bucking him to perdition and of eating $250 worth of hay in six weeks. With a dig at the naive newcomer, the speaker, by now wary of Western-style practical jokes and chicanery, gives the horse to a likely mark, a "passing Arkansas emigrant." (ibid., 145)

The central portion of *Roughing It* lacks the sparkle of the earlier comedy as the speaker begins his search for instant wealth in the silver fields of Humboldt, Nevada. Twain debunks Eastern lore about nuggets lying in plain view with revealing passages on alkali dust, worthless shafts, grueling labor in a quartz mill, a demolished lean-to on Lake Tahoe, and the despair of a German prospector, who, as survivor of two brothers killed in pursuit of riches, gives up the map to his claim to an Esmeralda prospector, who searches for the site for 12 or 13 years. Likewise floundering, the speaker abandons speculation for journalism. At his new post, he fabricates a droll funeral and a Virginia City cemetery boasting 26 graves occupied by murder victims. He blames local violence for the carnage and observes that "in a new mining district the rough element predominates, and a person is not respected until he has 'killed his man.'" (ibid., 255) The career shift frees the speaker of his compulsion to produce non-stop entertainment. An editorial flair induces him to make social commentary. Of the desperado, he levels a charge of cheapening life during senseless frays and blames "flush times" and rampant vice for fattening the court docket.

The last chapters about Twain's sojourn in the Nevada Territory juxtapose more frontier high jinks with the newsman's realistic commentary. Jumping from an obvious digression—Jim Blaine's tale of the Old Ram—the speaker turns to Virginia City's Chinese residents, whom he characterizes as restrained, sober, literate, thrifty, and industrious. He interrupts a disdainful diatribe on Western-style race prejudice with a pointed news bulletin: a crowd in San Francisco allow some boys to stone an "inoffensive Chinaman to death." (ibid., 292) In a lighter vein, Twain quotes a sanguine line of pidgin English about a lottery:

> Sometime Chinaman buy ticket one dollar hap, ketch um two tree hundred, sometime no ketch um anyting; lottery like one man fight um seventy-may-be he whip, may-be he get whip heself, welly good. (ibid., 296)

Mounted on his editorial soapbox, Twain pontificates about abuse and oppression and charges that exploitation of the Chinese comes from "only the scum," police, and politicians, "for these are the dust-licking pimps and slaves of the scum, there as well as elsewhere in America." (ibid., 296–297) This didacticism, which seems inappropriate to a modern reader, thrived in nineteenth-century journalism and, perhaps, did some good. An unexplained inconsistency is Twain's closed-mindedness toward Indians, whom he habitually accuses of savagery, low morals, and bad hygiene. Even more caustic than the racism in *Roughing It* is Twain's virulent "The Noble Red Man," a sarcastic racist essay published in 1870 in *Galaxy* magazine.

Never at home in an atmosphere laden with homily, Twain lightens up as he exits Virginia City and moves to a job reporting for the *Morning Call* in San Francisco, where women are a rare and welcome sight. He reports as second-hand truth the yarn about a coarse miner who is so astonished to see a little girl in her nanny's arms that he hands over a sack filled with $150 in gold dust for the privilege of kissing the child. The speaker claims to have suffered a similar need for contact with females and asserts that he participated in a peephole observation of a woman tossing flapjacks. His punch line— "she was one hundred and sixty-five years old"—he amends with a footnote, "Being in calmer mood, now, I voluntarily knock off a hundred from that." (ibid., 312)

The scurrilous, often overstated adventures of Twain the cub reporter take up a new setting when he goes on an assignment for the Sacramento *Union* to the Sandwich Islands. From March 7 to July 19, 1866, the speaker reports sailing on the *Ajax* to Honolulu. Delighted by variety, he admires straw, adobe, and "pebble-and-shell-conglomerated coral cottages" and

> cats—tomcats, Mary Ann cats, long-tailed cats, bobtailed cats, blind cats, one-eyed cats, walleyed cats, cross-eyed cats, gray cats, black cats, white cats, yellow cats, striped cats, spotted cats, tame cats, wild cats, singed cats, individual cats, groups of cats, platoons of cats, companies of cats, regiments of cats, armies of cats, multitudes of cats, millions of cats, and all of them sleek, fat, lazy, and sound asleep. (ibid., 340)

The speaker reverts to didactic mode with acerbic digs at missionaries, who subvert the Hawaiian's uninhibited lifestyle with dire warnings about hell and by insisting that Kanaka islanders adopt the Puritan work ethic. Tongue-in-cheek, he observes, "How sad it is to think of the multitudes who have gone to their graves in this beautiful island and never knew there was a hell!" (ibid., 346)

In the Pacific paradise, Twain toured plantations and a volcano, studied native Kanakas, sailed to outlying islands, and pondered the historic impact of Captain Cook and King Kamehameha and his dynasty. The resulting 25 dispatches to the *Union* formed the basis of 16 chapters of *Roughing It*. His ability to bypass first-person observation with an imaginative coterie of quaint companions boosted his reputation as both journalist and fiction writer. After returning home aboard the *America* on October 31, 1866, he reshaped the material into a lecture series, "Our Fellow Savages of the Sandwich Islands," an exotic and appealing frontier locale that was annexed in 1898. The stage monologues played to packed halls in the United States and England and during his one-year around-the-world tour begun in 1895.

Roughing It, a critical success, showcases Twain's forte—liberating the American language from the domination of British English. Employing conversations in dialect, tales, verse, infrequent didacticism, and overall laid-back exposition, he invigorates the dash and drama of episodic narration and lightens the burden of straight reportage. Examples of his informal grammar, hyperbole, conversational cadence, and rhetorical improvisation abound:

- Stagecoaching on the Overland is no more, and stage drivers are a race defunct. (ibid., 125)

- About this time occurred a little incident which has always had a sort of interest to me, from the fact that it came so near "instigating" my funeral. (ibid., 208)

- There were nabobs in those days—in the "flush times," I mean. (ibid., 240)

- The people shaved their heads, knocked out a tooth or two, plucked out an eye sometimes, cut, bruised, mutilated, or burned their flesh, got drunk, burned each other's huts, maimed or murdered one another according to the caprice of the moment, and both sexes gave themselves up to brutal and unbridled licentuousness. (ibid., 371)

A three-sentence coda that winds up the novel in Twain's person-to-person style includes the following: "If you are of any account, stay at home and make your way by faithful diligence; but if you are 'no account,' go away from home, and then you will *have* to work, whether you want to or not." (ibid., 422) (Bloom 1986a; Davis and Beidler 1984; Dobie 1996; Ehrlich and Carruth 1982; Emerson 1985; Kaplan 1966; Lyttle 1994; Rasmussen 1995; Ridge 1993; Robinson 1996; Shalit 1987; Thomas and Thomas 1943; Twain 1959, 1962d, 1996b; Wexler 1995)

See also "The Celebrated Jumping Frog of Calaveras County"; poetry of the frontier; Twain, Mark.

SANDOZ, MARI

A true daughter of the upper Niobrara River in the sand hills of the Nebraska panhandle, Marie Susette Sandoz wrote in fiction and nonfiction large overlapping segments of the history of the trans-Missouri plains. Composing under the name Mari Sandoz, she worked and reworked extensive notes, maps, and sketches to flesh out remarkably vivid studies of the midwestern frontier. She developed a strong attachment to Snake Bite Valley, Indian Hill, Laramie Peak, and other Nebraska landmarks that bound her to the land. Thinking over the wealth of local artifacts, she recalls, "The gravel under my bare feet was black from Indian signal fires, and just below me was the place where our father had led a vigilante gang that hanged a man and let him down alive." (Sherr and Kazickas 1994, 264) Although much of her writing issued from a Greenwich Village apartment, her spirit never journeyed far from the spare landscape of her childhood.

From letters, court records, and memories of her father, Jules Sandoz, a Swiss settler and orchard man, Sandoz chronicled the hardships of her youth, which she had spent under the same sod roof with the most eccentric, litigious curmudgeon of the district. Her biography, *Old Jules* (1935), prefaced a lifetime of probing, corroborating, justifying, cataloging, and setting the record straight on the history of Nebraska. Much of her first book testifies to the foul moods, picked fights, and lacerating word battles that Jules pursued as his daily fare. The biography includes a critical episode in Mari's life—a bitter May morning when she and her brother chased cattle over a snow-laden landscape. She returned home with frostbitten eyes that left her blind on the left side. The visual handicap and her father's disapproval failed to deter Mari from finishing eighth grade, teaching school, studying at the University of Nebraska when she could afford to, and working for the Lincoln *Star*, Nebraska *State Journal*, Nebraska *History Magazine*, and Nebraska State Historical Society.

Having grown up with Sioux neighbors such as He Dog and Bad Arm, Sandoz was a worthy choice of biographer for Crazy Horse, the revered Lakota mystic and warrior chief. Her obsession with fact, her determination to resolve conflicting accounts, and her lengthy discussions of the Indian wars with Crazy Horse's relatives and associates provided a basis for *Crazy Horse: The Strange*

Man of the Oglalas (1942), a meticulous reportage devalued at the time by some literary critics, but much admired by Native American readers and by Western specialists Wallace Stegner, Jack Schaefer, and John G. Neihardt. To authenticate details, she walked Indian trails, slept on the ground, and learned as much of the history as could be recounted in the 1930s. In Washington's Bureau of Indian Affairs, courthouses, museums, and Native American archives in Wyoming and Nebraska, she settled minor points about Crazy Horse's movements, friends, even his facial expressions and filled 5,000 note cards with minutiae. To a colleague she confided her awe at the work in progress: "The story is tremendous with all the cumulative inevitability of a Greek tragedy, and I feel small and mean and incomplete, although I've done my best to get at the truth. If I can only pin it down on paper." (Sandoz 1942, x) This unusual discipline refined and structured the material into a work so highly regarded today among ethnologists that it is widely accepted as the best Native American biography of all times.

Crucial to *Crazy Horse* is Sandoz's understanding of the rapacious Americans who threatened to overrun the territory that the Sioux held dear. She chooses to tell the story from the Lakota point of view. With lyric compassion, she describes the chief's doomed effort to spare the tribe from the pattern of near extermination that Native Americans suffered throughout the United States. Himself a victim of circumstance, Crazy Horse endures the loss of his love, Black Buffalo Woman, and the deaths of his daughter and friends from European diseases. At a climactic moment, Sandoz describes the fruitless Black Hill council at which whites try to strike a deal with the obdurate Lakota, who claim that the land is sacred. To agency messengers, Crazy Horse explains as though talking to children, "One does not sell the earth upon which the people walk." (ibid., 295) Indians treasure the precept, but it falters in the minds of white settlers and soldiers.

Sandoz's canon includes other significant contributions to frontier history. *Cheyenne Autumn* (1953), the story of a Plains band that flees Indian territory in 1878, journeyed in manuscript form from Atlantic Press, to Westminster, Duell, Sloan and Pearce, Dial, Viking, Crowell, Norton, and Scribner's before finding favor at McGraw-Hill. The work, like *Crazy Horse,* re-created for non–Native American readers the unity of Cheyenne village life, religion, culture heroes, and ritual. Sandoz's unique source material netted stronger critical applause than did *Crazy Horse* and was filmed the next year by Warner Brothers, featuring a star-laden cast of non-native actors—Richard Widmark, Carroll Baker, Karl Malden, Dolores del Rio, Sal Mineo, Edward G. Robinson, James Stewart, Ricardo Montalban, Gilbert Roland, Arthur Kennedy, Patrick Wayne, Victor Jory, and John Carradine. Hollywood's demand for stereotyped characters, plot complication, and spectacle distressed Sandoz, who had worked out each scene in historical detail down to weapons, religious symbols, costume, and native idiosyncrasies and behaviors. Despite the film's anachronisms and melodrama, it did not harm her reputation for accuracy.

Removed from the hand-to-mouth struggle of her early years as a freelancer, Sandoz continued to win kudos from critics, scholars, ecologists, and histori-

Nebraskan Mari Sandoz in her New York apartment

ans for her later works, *The Buffalo Hunters* (1954), *The Cattlemen: From the Rio Grande across the Far Marias* (1958), *The Beaver Men: Spearheads of Empire* (1964), and *The Battle of the Little Bighorn* (1966), a slim but monumental tribute to her determination to tell the whole story. Her perception of the fate of the plains undergirded these works with verisimilitude, a quality lacking in her fiction. In 1966, at her death at age 70 from breast and bone cancer, Sandoz had rescued much plains history from neglect, distortion, misrepresentation, and selective destruction. Whether describing the patois of mountain men, land-grabbing of speculators, demise of the buffalo, or raw beginnings of the cattle industry, her writing thrums with realism—the intransigent homesteaders, dynamic investors, publicity seekers like Buffalo Bill Cody, and displaced tribes. Plaintive lines recount the worst of American greed and racism, such as the final lines of *The Buffalo Hunters*:

> On the ridge the Hotchkiss guns began their stuttering fire, but upon the tents and the women and children there, cutting them down, the tents jerking as if alive, with crying coming from the inside, and then going down in smoke, some of them blazing out in the strong grey wind. (Sandoz 1954, 366)

Her incisive prose spotlights the inhumanity of the moment—the flight of the helpless from "blood-heated troopers," who pursued and cut them down with efficiency and dispatch. (Davidson and Wagner-Martin 1995; Ehrlich and Carruth 1982; Lamar 1977; Sandoz 1942, 1954, 1958, 1963, 1964, 1966; Sherr and Kazickas 1994; Stauffer 1982)

⚐ SCHAEFER, JACK WARNER ⚐

Easterner Jack Warner Schaefer earned a lasting place in frontier literature with *Shane* (1949), an enduring Western morality plot derived from the twentieth century's passion for the code hero. A reporter for United Press, the New Haven *Journal-Courier,* Baltimore *Sun,* and the Norfolk *Virginia Pilot,* Schaefer wrote a classic feature story on the clash of sodbusters and cattlemen—a predictable animosity that arose when a new element entered a stable open-range society. Schaefer's acute diction and keen verbs enlarge the theme of tough justice as irrevocably as a banner headline reveals a lead story. Penned by an expert journalist, *Shane* possesses a quiet subtlety, developing a suspenseful plot that imitators adopted as the boilerplate for the "mysterious stranger" of dime novels, television and movie Westerns, and advertising. *Shane* won no significant awards, but it precipitated Schaefer's distinguished achievement award from the Western Literature Association in 1975.

Jack Schaefer was a native of Cleveland, Ohio. Born November 19, 1907, to attorney Carl Walter and Minnie Luella Hively Schaefer, he developed a love of the West from his father, an enthusiast of frontier history. Schaefer earned a B.A. in creative writing and classics from Oberlin College. While conducting postgraduate studies in English at Columbia University, he fled academia after professors ridiculed his intention to study literary themes in cinema. On his own, he pursued Western history. In addition to writing and editing, he worked as assistant director of education at the Connecticut State Reformatory and as an associate of the Lindsay advertising agency. He launched a career in freelance writing, the majority of which he devoted to Westerns. Because he had no direct experience with the West, he studied history, maps, newspapers, and diaries.

Utilizing the spare, clean sentence style expected of journalists, Schaefer began *Shane* as a simple story, then carried it beyond the parameters of short fiction. The novel was first published in *Argosy* as a three-part series called "Rider from Nowhere"; Houghton Mifflin purged it of swear words and repackaged it as a novel. Opening with understated drama, the story is told through the observations of young Bob Starrett, a boy growing up in Wyoming, in the summer and fall of 1889. His initiation into adulthood coincides with the arrival of an enigmatic philosopher and role model—Shane, a remarkable, hard-muscled drifter whose demeanor resembles "the easiness of a coiled spring, of a trap set." (Schaefer 1949, 2)

The novel pictures a glamorous mythic figure suited to the open range, where livestock entrepreneurs profit from extensive grasslands, plentiful water, and no interference from farmers. At a fork in the road, Shane abandons the range and works as a farmhand, allying himself with Starrett, Johnson,

Shipstead, Wright, and the other agrarians who profit from the Homestead Act of 1862. At the Starrett farm, Shane takes the place of Morley, a previous hired hand driven away by Luke Fletcher, the valley's uncompromising cattle magnate. Shane assists Joe, Bob's father, in removing an ironwood stump. The act foreshadows their "unspoken fraternity," a cooperative effort that defeats Fletcher. (ibid., 5) Joe predicts that Fletcher's era of open-range livestock ranching must give way to enclosed pastures, the hated symbol of orderly farming that Fletcher's ilk despises. To Joe, Fletcher's freewheeling style is poor husbandry. Joe maintains that the best way to utilize land efficiently is to balance crops with livestock that are "not all horns and bone, but bred for meat and fenced in and fed right." (ibid., 7)

At one time free of the incumbrances of law and order, Shane had packed a gun—an ivory-handled Colt revolver—the *lingua franca* of Western conflicts. For some unexpressed reason, he has chosen to live a simpler, less violent life. When Fletcher's commitment to a beef contract for the Sioux reservation exacerbates his differences with men like Joe Starrett, Fletcher strikes at Shane at Grafton's saloon, the prototypical setting of Western violence. Through the taunts of Chris, Fletcher's second, the message reaches Joe that the cattle baron intends to get tough. Schaefer intensifies suspense by having the hero avoid trouble, then return to settle the score by breaking Chris's arm. The conflict escalates on a subsequent ride into town, where five of Fletcher's men battle Shane in a bar brawl. Joe joins the fray and brings the odds to two against five, enough for a lopsided victory.

Typical of the Western is the right-versus-wrong confrontation, a demarcation that compels fence-sitters to abandon neutrality. Fletcher's decision to hire gunman Stark Wilson, a "pushing man," turns the range impasse into a life-and-death struggle. After Wilson kills another homesteader in a fast-draw duel, Fletcher presses Joe, the pivotal figure among valley farmers, to accept $1,000 for his holdings, a semicivilized way of ushering Joe and other nesters out of the way of ranchers. The maneuver forces him into a showdown that he is ill-equipped to survive but must accept on behalf of the loose union he represents. In defense of his pride, he proclaims to his wife, "A man can't crawl into a hole somewhere and hide like a rabbit." (ibid., 91)

The heightened threat impels Shane into his gunfighting mode, a beautiful and deadly stance that exposes hidden passions and familiarity with firearms:

> His hands were clenched tightly and his arms were quivering. His face was pale with the effort shaking him. He was desperate with an inner torment, his eyes tortured by thoughts that he could not escape, and the marks were obvious on him and he did not care. (ibid., 100)

Razor-edged and armed with a tooled cartridge belt, holster, and pistol, he bears the menace of an invincible killing machine—well-oiled and suited to its job. In his hand, the six-gun clears the path of double danger from Wilson and Fletcher and establishes Shane's authority among nonviolent home folk.

Schaefer illuminates the role of the lone enforcer, the frontier breed of dispassionate, tight-lipped fighters who make their own right through action rather

Jack Warner Schaefer gave Western literature an enduring character in *Shane,* a novel pub-lished in 1949. Alan Ladd played Shane, seen here with Brandon de Wilde, in the 1953 movie.

than word. Speaking of himself, he declares, "No man need be ashamed of being beat by Shane." (ibid., 103) To retrieve his hero from too macho or boast-ful a persona, the author pictures him as a responsible man who realizes that his actions influence the young. To Bob, Shane explains his attitude toward firearms: "A gun is just a tool. No better and no worse than any other tool, a shovel—or an axe or a saddle or a stove or anything." (ibid., 44) His intrinsic vigilante values are much clearer than his past, which remains cloaked in am-biguity.

By his choice of trigger-powered justice in defiance of anarchy, Shane be-comes the West's version of St. George or Sir Launcelot, the armed aggresser who rids a peaceable community of restraints on its freedoms. Ironically, while salvaging others' rights, he condemns himself to bear the burden of the out-sider. By inference, Schaefer loads the drama with an undercurrent of sexual tension, which surges between Shane and Marian Starrett and threatens to overflow into the action. The gunman comments that he can't acknowledge his attraction for the farm wife without jeopardizing his principles. Still loyal to his employer, Shane knocks him cold and leaves him to Marian's care while he strides, "tall and terrible," toward town. (ibid., 105)

The immediate clash of cattlemen with humbler laborers who work neatly fenced parcels plunges Shane into moral crisis: should he pursue his new image of peace-loving frontiersman or strap on his gun and rescue the innocent settlers from bloody rivalry with greedy, unprincipled stockmen? Opting for the six-shooter, Shane advances face-to-face with Wilson, then nails Fletcher, who lurks in the balcony. In Bob's eyes, the swift draw flashes forth in unified choreography:

> I saw the head lead and the body swing and the driving power of the legs beneath. I saw the arm leap and the hand take the gun in the lightning sweep. I saw the barrel line up like—like a finger pointing—and the flame spurt even as the man himself was still in motion. (ibid., 11)

Shane saves the homesteaders and, impervious to a bullet in the arm, restores the wholesome atmosphere of the valley. In one moment deadly, the next relaxed, he takes his leave, recedes into a silhouette, then departs with a gentle swish.

As Bob sums up the messianic figure, "He was the man who rode into our little valley out of the heart of the great glowing West and when his work was done rode back whence he had come and he was Shane." (ibid., 119) The selfless act precipitates the gunman's self-imposed exile. To Bob he admits that the choice to kill is like a brand on cattle, "there's no going back." (ibid., 113) Unsuited to village life, he must move on, taking no one with him. Unemotional yet tinged with a stoic melancholy, he retreats into the open country from which he came. He leaves behind a growing legend and admiration from Weir, a witness to the shooting who declares, "No bullet can kill that man." (ibid., 115)

Schaefer's powerful yet unassuming adult Western novel produced a classic movie spinoff. *Shane*, the 1953 film from Paramount Pictures, features a steel-banded, taut-jawed Alan Ladd in the title role of the A. B. Guthrie screenplay. A quality cast brings together the talents of Jean Arthur, Van Heflin, Jack Palance, Brandon de Wilde, and Ben Johnson. The picture earned five Oscar nominations, including nods to Palance, de Wilde, Guthrie, and director George Stevens. Photographer Loyal Griggs received an Academy Award for his spare, realistic camera angles, which infused the taut story with vigor and grace.

In later years, Schaefer stuck to Western fiction as his major genre. He published three works in 1953: two novels, *First Blood* and *The Canyon*, and a short story collection, *The Big Range*. At a slower pace, he wrote *The Pioneers* (1954), *Out West* (1955), *Company of Cowards* (1957), and *The Kean Land and Other Stories* (1959). In 1960, he won an Ohioana Book award for *Old Ramon*. His last 15 years of fiction writing includes *The Plainsman* (1963), *Monte Walsh* (1963), *The Great Endurance Horse Race* (1963), *Stubby Pringle's Christmas* (1964), *Heroes without Glory* (1964), *New Mexico* (1967), and *Mavericks* (1967). In 1966, ABC cast David Carradine and Jill Ireland in a limp, derivative television series based on *Shane*. Four years later, William Fraker filmed *Monte Walsh*. Although a solid cast of Lee Marvin, Jack Palance, and Jeanne Moreau starred, the leaden screen version turned the study of aging cowboys into tedium. At his death from heart disease January 24, 1991, at his home in Cerrillos Flats near Santa Fe, New Mexico, Schaefer was ranked among the top Western writers, along with Owen Wister, Walter Van Tilburg Clark, Louis L'Amour, and Zane Grey.

Schaefer's understated artistry had become a classic. Shane, his exotic, one-named gunman, remains the touchstone by which Western heroes are measured. (Calder 1975; Cawelti 1970; *Contemporary Authors* 1994; Janke 1996; Lamar 1977; Milner et al. 1994; Sackett 1996; Sarf 1983; Schaefer 1949, 1967; Slatta 1994)

See also Clark, Walter Van Tilburg; Grey, Zane; L'Amour, Louis; Wister, Owen.

THE SEA OF GRASS ·

The Sea of Grass, Conrad Richter's most popular adult work, is a modest yet passionate novel that portrays in elevated style the standard Western conflict between settlers and herdsmen. Through the author's skillful realism, the novel restores life to the cliché of nesters and cattlemen fighting over open grasslands. In a visionary introduction to the work, Richter recalls riding on horseback in the Sandia Mountains east of his home in Albuquerque and capturing in his notebooks

> a remote and almost endless range green with grass, fenceless, sparsely dotted with grazing cattle and horses, and here and there the glint of sky from some fresh water pond, the whole expanse seemingly uninhabited by man and rolling farther than the eye could reach. (Richter 1965b, xvi)

The primordial grandeur of the plains suggested the title. From this inspired communion with the rippling prairie, Richter began asking himself about the kinds of men and women who would settle the untamed land and master their love-hate relationship with wilderness. The plot did not come easily, but the end result manifests a detachment and flow that parallels the sinuous restlessness of the southwestern grassland.

Told from the reflections of Dr. Hal Brewton, the framework story centers on a huge, ruined ranch, a "rude empire" that once supported 70,000 head of cattle but now lies like a quartered steer on a chopping block. Sacrificing suspense, the nostalgic narrator reminisces about the arrival of Lutie Cameron, a strikingly handsome bride-to-be from St. Louis, to the land where she would be wife and homemaker for Hal's uncle, Colonel James Brewton, an empire builder who lives outside the town of Salt Fork. An unsuitably frivolous woman with city tastes and a flair for fun, Lutie unpins her veil and looks at the parched plain, a brown wave that stretched, "dipping and pitching endless like a parched sea." Hal says that "she stopped as if she had run into barbed wire." (ibid., 7)

Lutie's portentous introduction to the prairie sets the tone and atmosphere; from the inauspicious arrival, she seems cursed by the aridity, solitude, and impromptu violence of southwestern life. At the austere wedding in the ladies' parlor of the Exchange House, Lutie, like a victim at the altar, stands in a harsh stab of sunlight alongside her dignified groom. A pale-skinned, sociable creature, she plants tamarisk and cottonwood for shade, whoops delightedly at her nephew's arrival from boarding school, lightens her hair with diamond dust for a party, and endures the grass-walled prison that denies her gaiety and relaxation. Mrs. Myra Netherwood, a tamed wife taken by Lutie's dazzle, predicts, "She'll settle down once she has babies." In time, the children arrive boy-girl-boy, ending with blue-eyed, cotton-topped Brock Brewton. (ibid., 26)

In a controlled lament, Hal recalls the affair that destroys the Brewton family and turns Brock into a hell-bent outlaw. On the day that Lutie confesses that she is leaving the Colonel, Hal notes that his uncle is away at a roundup, an ironic touch that compares both Brock and his mother to range steers. Hal looks out on the "landlocked harbor" of the town square, thronged with the ominous white canvas tops of immigrants' wagons, emblems of change, and tries to digest Lutie's confession that she's "running off" to "balls and theaters and shaded streets and up-to-date stores and where every day people drive in the parks." (ibid., 33) Hal feels that life has gone out of the ranch, leaving a shell like the brown walls of an abandoned adobe. After Lutie boards the train for St. Louis, Colonel Brewton paces the depot platform for several days to prohibit the departure of Lutie's lover, Brice Chamberlain, a district attorney and presidential appointee who defends Salt Fork's nesters.

As tension mounts in Hal's family, the conflict of homesteader and rancher erupts as more of the sea of grass disappears from the landscape. In the voice of a lord expecting deference from his fiefs, the Colonel rebukes Chamberlain for defending a nester. To justify his point of view, the steely rancher testifies against "that worthless nester Boggs" who is out of place on "my big vega," the open range more than 7,000 feet above sea level. The Colonel accuses the despoiler of plowing up grassland

> to support his family where there isn't enough rain for crops to grow, where he only kills the grass that will grow, where he starves for water and feeds his family by killing my beef and becomes a man without respect to himself and a miserable menace to the territory, then I have neither sympathy nor charity! (ibid., 18–19)

Chamberlain challenges the self-appointed lord of the vega and contends that the Colonel dominates the countryside and denies pity and succor to sodbusters, who regularly arrive by wagon and scratch out meager farms. Believing that cattlemen of the open range should retain their privilege by right of first arrival, the Colonel stands firm against change.

A less fearful change—the death of old Dr. Reid—brings Hal to Salt Fork as its new physician. He lives with the Colonel in the house where Lutie was once the respected mistress. To the dismay of Hal and the Colonel, rumors spread by impertinent nesters link Brock's fair complexion with Brice, his real father. At age 18, Brock shoots a man and, paralleling his mother's desertion, leaves the ranch that restricts him from the excitement of town life. The boy's flight from the law prefaces a spree of holdups, shootings, and cardsharping committed under the alias of Brock Chamberlain, a double insult to his noble, upright father. From the Arizona Territory, Brock flees into the Chiricahua Mountains to hole up with the Wild Bunch. His lawlessness ends with vigilante justice at the hands of homesteaders.

The falling action returns order and discipline to the plains. After Brock dies the desperado's death—from a bullet in the chest—in a deserted nester's shack, his father and Uncle Hal bury him on the Brewton ranch, Cross B, an emblem of the enmity between range men and homesteaders and of the opposing forces that kill Brock. On the return trip, the two Brewtons survey pathetic nester dwellings that dot the arid New Mexico prairie. Out of grief, Lutie Cameron Brewton reappears at the depot and pins back her veil in the characteristic gesture Hal recalls from his first glimpse of her. With vision clear on the life that lies ahead, she reunites with her husband and family and yields to the confining role of frontier wife.

Richter's spare fiction creates a meaningful dichotomy: the internal unrest that plagues Brock is the pull of two fathers: Colonel Brewton and Brice Chamberlain. Symbolic of the struggle between the wilderness and civilization, Brock's death is the sacrifice that results from an unavoidable clash of social strata. Harsh prairie winds and human loss conspire to rob the Colonel of his manly physique. When Lutie returns for her son's funeral, she is stopped by "a weary old man in a gray broadcloth coat too large for his shrunken girth and shoulders, unarmed, his coat-tails spreading behind the cantle, his trousers tucked into boots brown with dust." (ibid., 106) After she calmly returns to the home she deserted 15 years before, he lights his evening cigar and takes up the sentinel's post in the ranch gallery, from which he can see the headstone naming him and Lutie as Brock's parents. To Hal, the Colonel confides that Lutie is "one in a thousand." (ibid., 116)

Although critics accuse Richter of emulating Willa Cather's *A Lost Lady*, the heart of Richter's romantic novel is his own panoramic motif—the despoliation of land. The relentless plains dominate the novel and take on the life of a character. Waving in its perpetual emerald sweep, the land lies vulnerable to homesteaders, whom the ranchers accuse of plowing the fertile sward and ruining its roots, then abandoning their pillage when visions of riches founder. Like gravestones marking failed lives, the nesters' tumbled down lean-tos dot the plains as families give up their dreams and move on. (Barnes 1968; *Contemporary Authors* 1994; Dobie 1996; Edwards 1971; Folsom 1966; Gaston 1965; Kunitz 1942; LaHood 1975; Lamar 1977; Leisy 1950; Richter 1953, 1965b; *Something about the Author* 1972; Stuckey 1966; Wagenknecht 1952; Ward and Marquardt 1979)

See also Cather, Willa; *The Light in the Forest*; Richter, Conrad.

SERVICE, ROBERT

A mild-mannered emigrant from Scotland, Robert William Service—called the "Canadian Kipling," "the Poet of the Yukon," and "the Bard of Canada"—became the frontier's most-quoted poet. Born in Preston, England, January 16,

1874, he was from childhood a reader and reciter of poems, particularly those of Walter Scott and Alfred Tennyson. Service received an undistinguished education in Glasgow public schools and attended evening courses at the University of Glasgow before settling into accounting for the Commercial Bank of Scotland. Bored by the age of 20 and longing for the romantic life of a cowboy, he departed for Canada, crossed from Montreal to Vancouver by train, and roamed the Pacific Coast, the Old West, and Mexico. He continued his work as a teller at the Canadian Bank of Commerce in Vancouver, Victoria, Whitehorse, and Dawson, the center of Yukon action. Impressed by the Yukon setting during the gold rush of 1898, he published *Songs of a Sourdough* (1907) and followed with 13 more volumes of poems and ballads, six novels, and an autobiography.

Service's much parodied, much burlesqued light narrative verse is a jolly blend of macabre stories, tales of malcontents and misfits, episodes of drinking and violence, and the wistful longing for warmer climes, sweet women, and a break from the crusty maleness of the Yukon. His two most cited works—"The Shooting of Dan McGrew" (1903) and "The Cremation of Sam McGee" (1905)—draw on a number of up-north conventions. In the former, the weather is 50 below zero when a dread stranger enters the Malamute Saloon, a real frontier drinking spot in Ester, Alaska, named for mushers' preferred breed of sled dog. The unnamed antagonist plays on winter emotions with his skillful piano music, connecting with the "gnawing hunger of lonely men for a home." The faithful woman "known as Lou" figures in the unfolding melodrama, in which Dan, the "hound of hell," is "pumped full of lead." (Service 1996a)

The structure and laconic narrative of Service's "The Shooting of Dan McGrew" so delighted readers and reciters of narrative verse that it became the target of witty parodists. Journalist and screenwriter Ted Paramore, author of *The Thundering Herd,* spoofed the poem with "The Ballad of Yukon Jake," which was published in *Vanity Fair* in August 1921. The poem served Mack Sennett as the impetus for a silent movie entitled *Yukon Jake.* The poem mimics Service's hard cases, this one called "The Hermit of Shark Tooth Shoal." According to Paramore:

He was just a boy and the parson's joy
(Ere he fell for the gold and the muck),
And learned to pray, with the hogs and the hay
On a farm near Keokuk. (Gardner 1995, 113)

The setting is the same, as are the piano music and eccentric barflies who cluster about the bar in the Malamute saloon. The sexual innuendo implicit in the meeting between Jake and Ruth, a shipwrecked maiden, spools out to the ruination of Ruth, "a maid uncouth" who earns her living singing for fallen men who "rust from the gold and the lust/That sears the Northland soul." The poet's ingenuity in spoofing Service pays tribute to the structure and technical skill of the original.

A vigorous bit of twisted humor, Service's "The Cremation of Sam McGee" tells of a Christmas night when mushers dare the Dawson Trail, fearing death from cold as they strike for Lake Lebarge. The speaker promises Sam, a depressed southerner from Plumtree, Tennessee, that if he dies from exposure, his mate will see that he is cremated. The long haul that follows Sam's death ends with the unnamed musher stoking a fire in an abandoned cabin and tending the flames as the corpse burns. Tempted to check on the progress of Sam's cremation, the speaker opens the door and finds Sam enjoying the warmth and claiming that it is the first time he's been warm since he journeyed north.

In general, these and other Service ballads center on the qualities of the survivor in a part of the world that the poet calls "the cussedest land that I know." (Service 1996a) Throughout "The Law of the Yukon," "The Song of the Wage-Slave," "The Men That Don't Fit In," and "The Parson's Son," the poet capitalizes on truths of the Canadian Northwest—the beauties of the Northern Lights, the lack of women, the misery of outdoor work, and the warped personalities that gravitate toward prospecting and mountaineering. "The Parson's Son" contains the epitome of Service's far-north gothic, the consumption of the son's corpse by malamutes, which gobble his flesh down to the bone.

Service retired in 1908 and lived off his royalties, traveling to Europe, particularly the Riviera, and to Hollywood. While living in a cabin, he produced *The Trail of '98: A Northland Romance* (1911). After working as a correspondent in the Balkans and France for the Toronto *Star,* he left his young French wife, Germaine, and applied to serve in the army during World War I, but was rejected because of heart disease. Undeterred, he found a new route to service in the American Ambulance Unit. The experience supplanted his snowscape Yukon settings with *The Rhymes of a Red Cross Man* (1916), derived from his experiences as an ambulance driver and aid station attendant and dedicated to his brother Albert, who was killed in the trenches. The Kipling-esque style of "The Stretcher-Bearer" presents wartime horrors and camaraderie from the point of view of a cockney field scout who "waves no flag" but insists that "A million 'earts is weighed with woe" as a result of battlefield carnage. (*Canadian Poetry* 1994, 342) While living in Hollywood, Service completed a two-volume autobiography: *Ploughman of the Moon* (1945) and *The Harper of Heaven* (1948). Near the end of his 50-year career, he penned "My Cross," four verses of self-deprecation lamenting the fame of "Dan McGrew," which overshadows his gentled verse of later years. He declares:

> Write of gutter and of grime,
> Of pimp and prostitute,
> The multitude will read your rhyme
> And pay to boot. (Service 1996a, 353)

At his death from influenza on September 11, 1958, in Lancieux, France, he was famous among middle-brow reciters of verse for bumptious rhythm, seedy characters, and roughhouse diction. (*Canadian Poetry* 1994; Ehrlich and Carruth 1982; Gardner 1995; Garnett 1996; Mackay 1995; Service 1948, 1992, 1996a, 1996b; Story 1967; Wallace 1963)

See also poetry of the frontier.

𝄢   SHORT FICTION OF THE FRONTIER   卐

Much of the best in Western fiction is the brief and varied storytelling of some of America's most gifted authors. Names such as Dorothy Johnson, Luke Short, Gertrude Atherton, Mari Sandoz, Conrad Richter, Willa Cather, and Paul Horgan attach directly to the Western milieu. Some are connected directly with a fictional character, such as Clarence E. Mulford and his famed hero, Hopalong Cassidy. Others, notably John Steinbeck, O. Henry, William Faulkner, and Stephen Crane, earn renown for novels, stories, and plays in a variety of settings, some of which include the frontier. Overall, Western plots suit the strictures of short stories and novellas because of the conventions that quickly identify their aims and themes. Motifs such as the arrival of a train to a Western depot in Stephen Crane's "The Bride Comes to Yellow Sky," violent retribution in Dorothy Johnson's "The Man Who Shot Liberty Valance," Latina gossips in Gertrude Atherton's "The Wash-Tub Mail," and the reflections of an old pioneer in John Steinbeck's "The Leader of the People" draw on the reader's familiarity with the idiosyncrasies of the frontier, for example, the small number of women in the bride pool, the use of six-guns and rifles to settle legal questions and attain vengeance, the heady power of gossip for disenfranchised Latinas, and the older generation's obsession with the values and challenges of the westering movement.

Chief among late frontier collections is Hamlin Garland's *Main-Travelled Roads* (1891). A farm boy from West Salem, Wisconsin, turned militant reformer, Garland published short stories in *Arena, Outlook, Ladies' Home Journal, Harper's Weekly,* and *Century* magazines and collected six of his sketches in an anthology ten years after graduating from Cedar Valley Seminary in Osage, Iowa. The book, which appeared in expanded form in 1899, presaged a prolific career in novels, historical fiction, biography, autobiography, verse, essays, reviews, and plays. He also wrote Western romances of little critical value, including *The Captain of the Gray Horse Troop* (1902) and *Cavanagh, Forest Ranger: A Romance of the Mountain West* (1910), both of which were filmed. Long before winning the Pulitzer Prize for *Daughter of the Middle Border* (1921), he lived the disappointments of the rural Midwest on humble farms in Wisconsin, Iowa, and the Dakotas and later received the informal title of "the first actual farmer in American literature." He once reflected:

> Something deep and resonant vibrated within my brain as I looked out upon this monotonous and commonplace landscape. I realized for the first time that the east had surfeited me with picturesqueness. It appeared that I had been living for six years amid painted, neatly arranged pasteboard scenery. Now I dropped to the level of nature unadorned down to the ugly unkempt lanes I knew so well, back to the pungent realities of the streamless plain. (Garland 1995, x)

Having worked as a teacher, carpenter, and land claims agent, he dramatized agrarian life in a series of stories that contrast the beauty and promise of the prairie with the soul-killing labor, poverty, and isolation that numbed settlers to seasonal splendors and robbed them of joy in their accomplishment.

Garland's much-anthologized "Under the Lion's Paw" expresses his distaste for land speculators, whom he saw as brazen opportunists squeezing from poor farmers the small profits that derived from backbreaking toil. The repeated scenes of heads bowed in defeat culminate in the story of Haskins, who, with the aid of a charitable fellow farmer, fights his way up from failure:

> Haskins was in the midst of the terrible toil of the last year. He was walking again in the rain and the mud behind his plough, he felt the dust and dirt of the threshing. The ferocious husking time, with its cutting wind and biting, clinging snows, lay hard on him. Then he thought of his wife, how she had cheerfully cooked and baked, without holiday and without rest. (Garland 1970, 239)

One of the first of early-twentieth-century writers to acknowledge the crushing load on farm wives, Garland depicts Mrs. Haskins as a meager survivor on the brink of collapse, a mother and housewife whose chores spool endlessly into the future, long after her youth is spent, her marriage eclipsed by drudgery.

Because Garland fails to control his anger at the two-pronged pincer that tormented the plowman, his stories boil over with regret and guilt, didacticism and melodrama. A typically overstated vignette from "Up the Coolly" demonstrates the author's lack of subtlety:

> A casual observer would have said, "What a pleasant bucolic—this little surprise-party of welcome!" But Howard, with his native ear and eye, had no such pleasing illusion. He knew too well these suggestions of despair and bitterness. He knew that, like the smile of the slave, this cheerfulness was self- defence; deep down was another unsatisfied ego. (Garland 1995, 75)

Overall, Garland intrudes too heavily into his characters' affairs. He draws his *dramatis personae* from a limited circle of disillusioned wives, failing widows, cheerless youths, ragged toddlers, depressed stockmen, and hapless corn planters who keep an eye to the weather while dreading the inevitable foreclosure that will reduce them from landowners to tenants. The onus of imminent failure dogs his fiction, wearing down the reader with its dismal scenes of tattered overalls, gnarled hands, slow starvation, dismay, and resultant family disharmony. The additional five stories of the 1899 edition add some whimsy and charm, but they fail to break the spell of Garland's credo that the main-travelled road "is long and wearyful, and has a dull little town at one end and a home of toil at the other." He comes back to the same rutted byway, "traversed by many classes of people, but the poor and the weary predominate." (ibid., vi)

Unlike Garland's monomaniac emphasis on poverty, Stephen Crane, a journalist and author of *The Red Badge of Courage* (1895) and one of America's finest realists, views the frontier from a complex blend of viewpoints in his classic story, "The Brides Comes to Yellow Sky." With grace and detachment, he imagines a young woman's introduction to the West. A newlywed couple, Marshal Jack Potter and his unnamed bride, disembark from the train from San Antonio and approach a tense street. There, the town drunk, Scratchy Wilson, in the absence of Potter, threatens the peace. An unforeseen face-off pits an unarmed Potter against Wilson. Suspense drops to nothing when Wilson, pondering the impossibility of a domesticated lawman, ends his lawless spree. Dismayed and disgusted, Wilson acknowledges the change in his old nemesis, "Well, I 'low it's off, Jack . . . Married!" (Crane 1985, 351) Crane utilizes marriage as a symbolic spot of gentility, a move from the frontier to civilization. To Scratchy Wilson, the bride represents another nail in the coffin of the rambunctious Old West.

A contemporary of Hamlin Garland and Stephen Crane, William Sydney Porter quit school at age 15, clerked in a drugstore, and, to recover from chronic lung weakness, moved to a Texas ranch in La Salle County run by Captain Lee Hall, a former Texas Ranger. Hall and other old hands taught Porter the ways and lingo of the Westerner, throwing in the ritual razzing of the tenderfoot. After clerking in a land office and in the First National Bank of Austin, Porter turned to journalism and produced a column for the *Houston Post*. In 1895, he was imprisoned—and later exonerated—for embezzling $4,702.94, which he was accused of spending on his failed magazine, *The Rolling Stone*. For four years, he worked in the dispensary in the Ohio State Penitentiary and published from his cell 14 short stories under the pseudonym of O. Henry, perhaps adapted from frequent calls to a prison cat named Henry. In the last decade before his death from tuberculosis, diabetes, and cirrhosis of the liver in 1910, he lived in New York and wrote for *New York World* and *McClure's* tragicomic vignettes of the sordid underworld, rife with con games, prostitution, gambling, and outright thievery. In his honor, in 1918 the Society of Arts and Letters established an annual memorial award for the best American short story.

O. Henry's collection, *Heart of the West* (1907), contrasts with the hard-bitten fiction of Garland. Softened by love of nature, joy in "boy gets girl" pairing, and a belief in the American dream of freedom and promise in the West, the populist stories celebrate the oral anecdote, which typically ends with O. Henry's favorite ending—the unforeseen zinger. The device concludes "Hearts and Crosses," a story of a proud man who accedes to a proud woman who summons him with a ranch logo, the heart and cross brand. Similar romance plots end love troubles in "The Pimienta Pancakes" and "Cupid à LaCarte," the tale of a weary waitress who disdains men with ample appetites.

Not all O. Henry's stories adhere to a pastoral celebration of love. In "The Caballero's Way," he sets up a triangle involving a handsome blond soldier named Lt. Sandridge, a Hispanic girl named Tonia, and her lover, a Latino outlaw known as the Cisco Kid. Tonia's duplicity succeeds in netting her two beaux, one the hunter and the other the quarry. The Kid seems unlikely to win out over so fetching a hero as a six-footer with a badge. The story winds down to a love note impelling Sandridge to ride to Tonia's *jacal*, shoot the Kid, and end the rivalry. The text indicates that the Kid will try to escape by putting on Tonia's clothes and fleeing the arroyo. Not until Sandridge shoots the scarfed, skirted figure does he realize that the Kid has duped him into executing his unfaithful love. As the Kid rides away, he sings his favorite tuneless lyrics, "Don't you monkey with my Lulu girl."

A post-frontier realist with a similar Tex-Mex flair, Katherine Anne Porter wrote stories that reflect her familiarity with Anglos and Hispanics. Following stints writing for the Fort Worth *Critic* and Denver's *Rocky Mountain News*, she produced her first short work, "María Concepción" (1922), a study of the primitive, instinctual revenge killing of a rival. The main character, ostensibly won to Catholicism but still bound by the amorality of her Indian ancestry, weathers the pain of losing her faithless husband to a younger woman. After María Concepción's child dies, she reunites with her husband, who fought briefly with rebel forces, then deserted and returned home to manage both wife and mistress. María Concepción's brutal killing of his lover jeopardizes her life. Testimony on her behalf weakens the case the gendarmes press in court. Porter depicts her exonerated and once more content with the simple life. A survivor of the frontier's typically vengeful confrontations, she takes charge of her rival's infant and sinks into repose, "aware of a strange, wakeful happiness." (Porter 1965, 21) The story precedes Porter's lengthy career in short fiction, notably *Flowering Judas* (1930), *Pale Horse, Pale Rider* (1939), and *The Leaning Tower and Other Stories* (1944).

More suited to cinema than Porter's works are the Indian stories of Dorothy Marie Johnson, a magazine editor in New York who returned to her girlhood home in Whitefish, Montana, to depict in straightforward fiction the lives of the nineteenth-century Crow and Sioux. Her collection, *Indian Country* (1949), reprises "The Man Who Shot Liberty Valance," published earlier in *The Saturday Evening Post*, and "A Man Called Horse," which she wrote for *Collier's*. The latter is the story of a Bostonian of good birth who journeys to Indian country to live the Western adventure he had read and fantasized about. So poignant is his role in a manless family that he remains longer than he intended and grows in stature and self-esteem because of his compassion for Greasy Hand, his pitiable, maimed foster mother. The 1970 color film version, *A Man Called Horse*, starring Richard Harris, sensationalizes Native American culture by putting Horse through a torture ritual not in the original story. Two sequels—*The Return of a Man Called Horse* (1976) and *Triumphs of a Man Called Horse* (1986)—extend the sadistic spectacle and are travesties of Johnson's simple story.

Two writers of post-frontier short stories—John Steinbeck and William Faulkner—epitomized the frontier myth as it impinged on the twentieth century. Steinbeck, a native Californian, expresses his family heritage through "The Leader of the People," a poignant segment of *The Red Pony* (1938), a Western bildungsroman. The story depicts an old pioneer through the eyes of his son-in-law, Carl Tifflin, who dislikes the old man's repeated stories of the trail west. In contrast, Jody, Carl's son, looks forward to his grandfather's visits and to retellings of history:

> A race of giants had lived then, fearless men, men of a staunchness unknown in this day. Jody thought of the wide plains and of the wagons moving across like centipedes. He thought of Grandfather on a huge white horse, marshaling the people. (Steinbeck 1985, 390)

Jody's pictorial fantasies see "the great phantoms, and they marched off the earth and they were gone." Attempting to halt time, Grandfather recites his memories in a frequent litany. Jody, far removed from the distant past, treasures the stories as his inheritance. The theme of frontier values through the remembered past also fuels Steinbeck's *East of Eden* (1952), a flawed saga of California history.

William Faulkner, one of America's most original spokesmen and the South's most prominent novelist, conveys the attraction of the wilderness in "The Bear," his frequently anthologized story. The focus, Old Ben, a venerable bear that eludes adult hunters, captivates the neophyte stalker, who charts his preteen years in unsuccessful expeditions to the forest. Through the coaching of Sam, his trail mentor, the unnamed boy learns to abandon civilization and immerse himself in primeval nature, the crucible in which his maturity is shaped and tested. No longer a newcomer to the swamp, he develops self-confidence and a hunter's expertise:

> He would find the crooked print now almost whenever he liked, fifteen or ten or five miles, or sometimes nearer the camp than that. Twice while on stand during the three years he heard the dogs strike its trail by accident; on the second time they jumped it seemingly, the voices high, abject, almost human in hysteria, as on that first morning two years ago. But not the bear itself. (Faulkner 1985, 379)

At the threshold of manhood, the boy encounters his quarry, yet fails to shoot it because he discards his gun. Annoyed with himself, he tries to understand his father's explanation, which the father couches in abstractions—"courage and honor, and pride . . . and pity, and love of justice and of liberty. They all touch the heart, and what the heart holds to becomes truth, as far as we know the truth." (ibid., 382) At last, the boy recognizes the truths that he has internalized from the annual hunts—the qualities that the wilderness has identified and strengthened in his spirit.

Part of the twentieth century's Native American renaissance, Leslie Marmon Silko displays skills similar to Katherine Anne Porter's mastery of symbolism, irony, and characterization. Silko interweaves the traditional and cultural elements of Southwestern storytelling and woman-centered myth in poems and short stories that shimmer with possibilities. One of her critically acclaimed works, "Yellow Woman," employs the conventions of abduction lore to explore the physical needs and yearnings of a pueblo dweller. The speaker identifies her lover/captor as Silva, an appealing Navajo cattle rustler whom she meets by the river and accompanies on an overnight sexual encounter that ends with Silva shooting an angry white rancher. The story, richly textured in the allure of the free-flowing river and beneficent desert flowers and in the musculature of horse and man, maintains the anonymity of the characters, who part before arriving at the town of Marquez.

Silko learned from childhood the lore of her hometown, Laguna Pueblo, New Mexico. She has commented that her grandfather's tales of the Yellow Woman and the ka'tsina spirit express a similar paradigm of curiosity, longing, and immediacy. Steeped in mythic episodes typical of the Southwest, her story utilizes a sex-charged encounter as a venue for a bicultural glimpse of female roles and the need to flee the predictable to embrace a short-term liberation from tribal domestication. Moving from the clinging of damp thighs to an inevitable separation, the story takes the wistful narrator back to her home, where the lie of kidnap conceals her unfulfilled need to tap deep currents of physical and emotional desire. (Beatty et al. 1952; Boger 1970; Crane 1985; Faulkner 1985; Folsom 1966; Garland 1928, 1970, 1995; Hendrick 1965; Johnson 1953; Kunitz 1942; Magill 1958; "Pardon" 1958; Porter 1965; Silko 1993; Steinbeck 1952, 1970, 1985; Work 1996)

See also Harte, Bret; Lawrence, D. H.

THEATER OF THE FRONTIER

An offshoot of the English Renaissance, the germ of early New World theater arrived on the *Mayflower* and the *Speedwell* with the first European settlers. Many of the original colonists were well read and had watched Elizabethan drama at Blackfriar's and Shakespeare's Globe Theater but repressed enthusiasm for drama because they disapproved of theatrics. Prejudice, a virulent cargo aboard the adventurers' ships, infected American playgoers with the same suspicions that weakened the English theater. Colonists bore Puritan beliefs that portraying characters tempted viewers into evil and that acting troupes showcased society's immoral dregs by pandering to the lowest standards of behavior—sloth, lying, swearing, blasphemy, mockery, lust, whoring, debauchery, idolatry, and sacrilege. To the south, a fledgling frontier effort, *Ye Beare and Ye Cubb,* presented in 1665 in Accomac County on Virginia's James River, met with prompt and vitriolic legal action against its three male performers. The case came to nothing, but the threat hung in the air as a challenge to future idlers daring to bring England's scourge to those who established communities on the principle of avoiding the mistakes of the Old World.

Similar hostility from Judge Samuel Sewall and Increase Mather squelched May Day pantomimes and banned as sinful dancing, mimicking, processing, playacting, and costuming. Quakers added their own concerns in a formal address to the Pennsylvania Assembly May 22, 1759, complaining that

> a Company of Stage Players are preparing to erect a Theatre, and exhibit Plays to the Inhabitants of this City, which they conceive, if permitted, will be subversive of the good Order and Morals, which they desire may be preserved in this Government, and therefore pray the House to frame and present to the Governor, for his Assent, a Bill to prohibit such ensnaring and irreligious Entertainments. (Coad and Mims 1929, 19)

These antiroyalist, antipapist, antientertainment sentiments prevailed until the gradual tempering of sectarian hostility and fanaticism with less fanatic points of view, notably the egalitarian philosophy found in *American Landscapes* (1925), Hector St. John de Crèvecoeur's six dialogues, which lampoon Puritan hypocrisy in confiscating land from political opponents.

A greater deterrent to frontier drama was a matter of priorities. In the seventeenth century, small, rudimentary theaters flourished in Jesuit communities along the St. Lawrence River as an adjunct to religious instruction, but these efforts were in the minority. Until settlers achieved economic stability, peaceful coexistence with natives, and freedom from agricultural duties, they had neither time nor opportunity to build stages, rehearse scenes, and pause for regularly scheduled entertainment and enlightenment. In the eighteenth century, however, aristocratic tastes developed in the West Indies and among coastal plantation families, many of whom were educated and had traveled in the sophisticated cities of Europe. Money pouring in from lucrative indigo, rice, cane, and cotton markets paid for the lavish stage entertainments that planters missed at their isolated country estates. Posters and program notes list titles of French and English favorites by Molière, William Shakespeare, George Farquhar, Joseph Addison, Thomas Otway, Francis Beaumont and John Fletcher, and William Congreve.

Less than a decade before the Revolutionary War, settlers experienced their first professional presentation: Thomas Godfrey's *The Prince of Parthia* (1767), an imitation of English verse fare that opened in Philadelphia's Southwark Theater on April 24, 1767. Such mimicking of Continental plays remained in vogue until Americans found new topics and motifs to express the adventure of the New World. Settings moved from metropolitan areas to the frontier in George Cockings's *The Conquest of Canada* (1766), Everard Hall's *Nolens Volens; or The Biter Bit* (1809), Joseph Hutton's *The Falls of Niagara* (1823), and Lemuel Sawyer's *Blackbeard* (1824), a political comedy set on North Carolina's outer banks. Other native drama includes James N. Barker's blank verse tragedy, *Superstition* (1824), which ends with a trial for witchcraft set in New England in 1675, and William Dunlop's pictorial *A Trip to Niagara or Travellers in America* (1828), which features a woodsman named Leather-Stocking and contains a diorama in Act II of moving scenery depicting New York harbor, Jersey City, Hoboken, Weehawk, Palisades, Highlands, Buttermilk Falls, West Point at sunset, Newburgh, and the Catskills.

More exotic in locale and events are the plays of the mid-nineteenth century. Robert Bird specialized in Spanish settings with his tragedies *Oralloossa* (1832), set in Peru; *The Broker of Bogota* (1834), written to showcase Edwin Forrest's talents; and *Calavar* (1834) and *The Infidel* (1835), derived from the exploits of Hernan Cortez. Other frontier plays featuring New World settings and themes include Bird's *Nick of the Woods* (1837), which takes place in Kentucky; William Henry Rhodes's *Theodosia, The Pirate's Prisoner* (1846); Dion Boucicault's *The Octoroon* (1859); and Mordecai M. Noah's farce about a male impersonator, *She Would Be a Soldier, or The Plains of Chippewa* (1866), laced with Canuck dialect. Farther from Eastern settings and historical events lie Charles Hoyt's *A Trip to Chinatown* (1891), Augustus Thomas's *In Mizzoura* (1893) and *Arizona* (1899), David Belasco's *The Girl of the Golden West* (1905) and *The Rose of the Rancho* (1906), Dan Marble's *Sam Patch, the Jumper of Niagara Falls* (1906), and William Vaughn Moody's *The Great Divide* (1906), which opens in a cabin in Arizona. In Sonoma, California, Benjamin Webster's *The Golden Farmer* (1847) was the first domestic drama to supplant the miracle plays sponsored by Catholic missions with secular fare.

From their debut, New World stage originals portrayed the emergent individualism of America's playwrights, who felt no need to continue emulating European stage plays. The string of firsts features these:

- An Indian drama, frontiersman Major Robert Rogers's *Ponteach* (1766), which premiered the distinctly American interest in Anglo-Indian relations. Centered on the frontier theme of white treachery against a noble Ottawa chief Pontiac, the play traveled back to England that same year for its publication in London.

- A stage hit featuring a Native American motif, the wildly popular Indian tragedy *Metamora, or the Last of the Wampanoags* (1828), by John Augustus Stone, displayed a Cooperesque quality, a blend of history with a generous dollop of nostalgia and romance. Tinged with a hint of menace, Metamora reminds the audience that he

  has been the friend of the white man; yet if the flint be smitten too hard it will show that in its heart is fire. The Wampanoag will not wrong his white brother who comes from the land that is first touched by the rising sun; but he owns no master, save that One who holds the sun in his right hand, who rides on a dark storm, and who cannot die. (Stone 1966, 226)

  The forceful Wampanoag delivers a curse on his murderers, calling down the wrath of the Great Spirit and wolves and panthers to feast on the usurping white man's bones. This dramatization of the wronged noble savage kept *Metamora* in circulation for four decades and bolstered the career of stage heartthrob and muscle-man Edwin Forrest, who earned a substantial fortune from playing the title role.

- In 1767, America's first satiric opera, Andrew Barton's *The Disappointment, or The Force of Credulity,* ridiculed a frenzy of searches for Blackbeard's pirate trove, a major portion of which supposedly was hidden on the outer banks and inner recesses of the Pamlico Sound on the Carolina coast.

- Nationalism emerged as a dramatic theme with Hugh Henry Brackenridge and Philip Freneau's *The Rising Glory of America* (1771), presented at Princeton's commencement, and General John Burgoyne's *The Blockade of Boston* (1776), acted by his soldiers at a rough log theater in Charlottesville, Virginia.

- Bostonian Royall Tyler's *The Contrast* (1787), America's first original comedy, modeled for theatergoers in New York, Philadelphia, and Baltimore the stereotype of the gawky New England Yankee, a death knell to studied copies of Continental manners, styles, and deportment.

- Samuel Woodworth and John Davies's pastoral opera *The Forest Rose, or American Farmers* (1825) was the first popular musical in America. Actors preferred it for its brisk pace, spirited rural dance, and lively solos, duets, and choruses.

- Anna Cora Mowatt's allegorical satire *Fashion* (1850) spurned the fripperies of Continental dress and decor by asserting the charm of the American frontier. Mowatt puts into the mouth of Trueman her credo:

> When justice is found only among lawyers—health among physicians—and patriotism among politicians, *then* may you say that there is no *nobility* where there are no titles! But we *have* kings, princes, and nobles in abundance—of *Nature's stamp*, if not of *Fashion's*—we have honest men, warm-hearted and brave, and we have women—gentle, fair, and true, to whom no *title* could add *nobility*. (Mowatt 1966, 345)

In the epilogue, Trueman looks to the future for "who knows?—an honest man!" (ibid., 346)

A favorite vehicle of Philadelphia actor and frontier star Joseph Jefferson III, Tom Taylor's *Our American Cousin* (1858) opened at Laura Keene's theater in New York on Broadway and ran 140 nights. In his autobiography, Jefferson states his admiration of the play's naturalistic love scene. After the boy and girl draw apart out of shyness,

> He relates the story of his uncle's death in America, and during this recital asks her permission to smoke a cigar. With apparent carelessness he takes out a paper, a will made in his favor by the old man, which document disinherits the girl; with this he lights his cigar, thereby destroying his rights and resigning them to her. (Jefferson 1964, 148–149)

With such powerhouses as Keene and Jefferson in these subtle roles, the production sparked differences of opinion that erupted on stage, a preface to the play's troubled history.

At Washington's Ford's Theater April 14, 1865, Taylor's work earned dubious fame as the play President Abraham Lincoln and his wife watched while John Wilkes Booth crept behind the first family in their box. Booth brandished a knife, shot Lincoln in the head, and broke a leg by leaping to the stage. He fled but was later caught and hanged. The notoriety of his bold pro-South assassination forever attached to *Our American Cousin* the American reputation for savage weaponry as a means of settling differences. Currently, both the stage and the assassination are commemorated at the Ford's Theater Museum, which features Booth's derringer, the boot that Dr. Mudd cut from Booth's leg, and Lincoln's death mask.

By the latter quarter of the eighteenth century, the first dramatic performance west of the Alleghenies helped to establish Lexington, Kentucky, as "the Athens of the West." Frontier promoters invited troupes from Montreal, Quebec, and Albany. The burgeoning demand for stage shows spread to Indianapolis, Dayton, New Harmony, Cincinnati, New Orleans, Nashville, Springfield, Monterey, Sacramento, and Cheyenne. To actors unfamiliar with Western manners, the sight and sound of shaggy Indian fighters and traders assured the company that frontier audiences would consist of more than the average polite playgoer. N. M. Ludlow recalls finding

> the pit, or parquette of the theater *crowded full* of "river men"—that is, keelboat and flat-boat men. There were very few steamboat men. These men were

easily known by their linsey-woolsey clothing and blanket coats. (Coad and Mims 1929, 137)

To persnickety critics like Ludlow, criticism of the audience outweighed theatrical concerns. The fastidious conditioned themselves to rebel yells, b'ar hunter's yahoos, tobacco spitting, belches, retching, and the rough, crude chortles of frontiersmen who rarely curbed their exuberance.

Like the demands of a mixed, rough-edged audience, styles of permanent and temporary stages and seating varied, depending on the resources of the community:

- In 1716, William Levingston built the New World's first permanent playhouse in Williamsburg, Virginia, for the company sponsored by Charles and Mary Stagg.

- In 1736, Charleston, South Carolina, welcomed the Dock Street Theater, which opened with a comedy by Farquhar.

- A 1769 map of Halifax, North Carolina, features a "Play House," the state's first.

- A functional three-doored facade flanked the first stages in Mobile and Pittsburgh.

- The St. Pierre in New Orleans was lavishly decorated in 1808 with parquet and double tiers of loges.

- A crude one-story building housed St. Louis's original theater, which dates its first productions to 1815.

- William Chapman's floating theater stood atop a simple barge fitted with a gangplank. It traveled the Mississippi and Ohio Rivers in the 1830s.

- Gold rush proceeds underwrote Sacramento's short-lived Eagle Theatre, a makeshift building framed in rough lumber, covered with canvas on the sides and topped with sheet metal for a roof. Its first production, *The Bandit Chief; or, the Forest Spectre*, on October 18, 1849, the building, which suffered frequent floods, stayed in operation until the end of December.

- Citizens of Raleigh, North Carolina, boasted the completion of Tucker Hall in 1867, a show-class building equipped with 11 painted scenes and 26 wings.

The aggrandizement of such late-nineteenth-century frontier stages climaxed in such Palladian beauties as the St. Louis Theater, an elegant four-columned building decorated inside with cherry and mahogany finish details, and New Orleans's First St. Charles and New American Theaters, both architectural ornaments to the city and far removed from the frontier.

American theatrics reached a golden era in the nineteenth century with the stage brilliance of Lotta Crabtree, Edwin Forrest, Charlotte Cushman, Edwin Booth, Ada Rehan, John Drew, Lola Montez, and amateur Sam Houston, secretary of the Nashville Thespian Society and comic in the farce *We Fly by Night*. In 1837, the diary of Joseph Jefferson III, a third-generation stage buff, captured the energy of growing towns where theaters played an integral part in local attractions. Of Chicago he says:

people hurrying to and fro, frame buildings going up, board sidewalks going down, new hotels, new theaters, everything new. Saw and hammer,—saw, saw, bang, bang,—look out for the drays!—bright and muddy streets,—gaudy-colored calicos,—blue and red flannels and striped ticking hanging outside the dry-goods stores,—bar-rooms,—real-estate offices,—attorneys-at-law— oceans of them . . . the new theater, newly painted canvas . . . stuffed seats in the dress circle . . . new drop curtain—a medallion of Shakespeare. (ibid., 167)

As a footnote to history, Jefferson credits attorney Abraham Lincoln with halting the suppression of theater in Springfield by arguing against a religious sect that blocked performances. The acceptance of this and other playhouses as a natural part of Illinois's settlement enhanced the diversity of the West as it grew away from the Puritan beginnings in the Massachusetts colony.

Vigorous frontier theatricals created a demand for strongly American stage plays. A major contender for most popular title of the mid-nineteenth century is George L. Aiken's *Uncle Tom's Cabin* (1852) and its sequel, *The Death of Uncle Tom, or The Religion of the Lowly* (1852), both adapted from Harriet Beecher Stowe's best-selling novel. Two of the first works to draw a religious audience, the plays toured the East and as far west as St. Louis and nurtured the frail concept of "moral drama" among people who usually scorned both sermons and staged entertainment. Uncle Tom remained a standard figure in repertory and traveled to London stages, where audiences clambered for a view of Mrs. Stowe's "pathetic darky."

In contrast to the serious, divisive topic of the abolition of slavery, Augustin Daly's frivolous *Under the Gaslight* (1867) depicted the Easterner's romanticized notion of frontier danger with a truly American stereotype, the victim tied to the railroad tracks and set free as the train pulls round the bend. By incorporating realistic stage machinery, the producer buoyed to stardom Rose Eytinge, who claimed Abraham Lincoln and Secretary of State William Henry Seward as fans. Daly's creation of another stereotype, the Indian villain, powers *Horizon* (1871), a play stressing the difference between Eastern and Western mindsets, a recurrent theme in frontier literature.

Other historical notables and settings assured the West a viable theater of its own. In Nauvoo, Illinois, Mormon leader Joseph Smith assembled a city troupe in which Brigham Young played a prophetic role as the high priest in August von Kotzebue's *Pizarro*. After agitators forced Mormons out of the city, Young continued theatricals in Salt Lake City at the board-and-brush worship center. In two years, popular stage productions found a permanent home in the $100,000 Salt Lake Theater, built in 1861 in Doric style to hold an audience of 1,500. Young was so taken with the art of acting that he put his own daughters in the company as examples to other aspiring actresses and seated himself in the front box in a rocking chair.

In the early-twentieth-century prairie classic, *My Ántonia* (1918), Willa Cather describes the excitement at stage entertainment and the welcome extended to theater troupes arriving in Lincoln, Nebraska, late in the season after their close in New York or Chicago. She mentions a respectable cross section of standard operas—*Rigoletta, Martha, Norma,* and *La Traviata*—along with one of many stage versions of *Robin Hood,* Dumas fils's *Camille,* and James O'Neill playing the lead in Alexandre Dumas's *The Count of Monte Cristo.* She also lists standard American titles: Joseph Jefferson starring in an adaptation of Washington Irving's *Rip Van Winkle* (1859) and Bronson Crocker Howard's Civil War classic, *Shenandoah* (1888).

Perhaps the crowning achievement of stagecraft in the American West occurred in California, where the San Francisco Theater opened over the Parker House Saloon in December 1850, followed by a competitive array of playhouses: the Second Jenny Lind, Baldwin's, Bush Street, Bella Union, Metropolitan, and California Theaters. San Francisco attracted star players and provided a wide range of stage fare to satisfy a divergent—often rambunctious and violent—populace brought together by the California gold rush.

An unexpected failure from the Southwest is that of humorist Mark Twain, who teamed with regional fiction writer Bret Harte to produce a memorable flop, *Ah Sin, the Heathen Chinee* (1876), a four-act comedy that failed in Washington, D.C., and New York because of poorly coordinated revision. Joseph Daly skewered the inept play with his witty criticism:

> The construction of this play and the development of the story are the result of great research, and erudition, and genius, and invention—and plagiarism . . . When our play was finished, we found it was so long, and so broad, and so deep—in places—that it would have taken a week to play it. I thought that was all right; we could put "To be continued" on the curtain, and run it straight along. But the manager said no; it would get us into trouble with the general public, and into trouble with the general government, because the Constitution forbids the infliction of cruel or unusual punishment; so he cut out, and cut out . . . I believe it would have been one of the very best plays in the world if his strength had held out so that he could cut out the whole of it. (ibid., 259)

The debacle of *Ah Sin* left Twain disillusioned with his mentor and stung by Harte's abrupt departure for Europe. In his autobiography, Twain blamed Harte for alienating New York critics and linked his collaborator's name with calumny, idleness, alcoholism, and low character.

The early twentieth century, a more reflective time, introduced many communities to frontier values, customs, and history through local pageants and outdoor drama. The Dakotas produced a series of "prairie plays," including *May-Day,* an anonymous one-act play set in a Puritan settlement in 1658; Howard DeLong's *Barley Beards;* Harold Wiley's comedy *Dakota Dick;* and Ben Sherman's *Me an' Bill,* which recounts the life of a plains herder. Included in Constance D'Arcy Mackay's 1915 collection, *Plays of the Pioneers,* is her historical pageant *The Passing of Hiawatha.* Adapted from the writings of Henry Rowe Schoolcraft, it was the introductory episode of a three-day outdoor festival held in Schenectady, New York. Staged at Union College on a trail used by the Five Indian Nations and set at St. Esprit on Lake Superior in 1670, the play honors the chief of the Onandagas depicted in Schoolcraft's writings. Mackay's verse tableau of Hiawatha's death features music by Coleridge Taylor, the elements of Native American lore—campfire, wigwams, medicine man, flute player, breechclouts, beads, wampum, and warbonnets—and the compelling tom-tom beat of dactylic tetrameter, which marks the epic *The Song of Hiawatha* (1855) by Henry Wadsworth Longfellow (which was also based on Schoolcraft). The play ends in mythic style with the revered chief departing on foot with the Spirits of the Sunset.

At the University of North Carolina, student drama classes produced professional work: Thomas Wolfe's first play, *The Return of Buck Gavin* (1919), about a clan chieftain of the Smoky Mountains; Bernice Kelly Harris's *Ca'line* (1932), in which a character demonstrates how to "clay" a hearth; and Fred Koch, Jr.'s *Wash Carver's Mouse Trap* (1935), a Smoky Mountain version of the trickster, who charges a fee to remove vehicles stuck on his muddy road. One of the most skillful of this era of local-color drama, Paul Green's *The Last of the Lowries: A Play of the Croatan Outlaws of Robeson County* (1920), is a dialect drama that examines the tragic lives of a noted band of mountain outlaws. Green adapted the plot from a story by Mary C. Norment that appeared in an 1875 edition of the Wilmington, North Carolina, *Daily Journal Print.* The plot recounts the decade-long search for half-breed Croatan outlaws who hid from authorities in the Scuffletown Swamp until their deaths in 1874. Green's classic outdoor drama, *The Lost Colony* (1937), is a brooding, introspective study of the English settlement off the Carolina coast. The play launched a national movement characterized by spectacle and pageantry.

On this same subject, William Norment Cox's popular play *The Scuffletown Outlaws: A Tragedy of the Lowrie Gang* (1924) fictionalizes the antiwar beliefs of Scotch-Croatan (Lumbee) half-breed chief Henry Berry Lowrie. A historical figure who protested forced service in the Confederate army, Lowrie speaks the outsider's distrust of the overclass: "I thought ye my friend, a-workin' to help me and the rest, when every other domn white mon was a-workin' to kill us. Mon, ye ha'e been brave, but the brave mon most times gits shot." Cox's re-creation of swamp dialect rings true with local pronunciation of man/mon, creek/crick, liquor/licker, and fire/far, as well as folk verb forms (help, helped/hep, holp).

Other southern dramas appealed to audiences for their re-creation of frontier life. In 1923, Lula Vollmer's *Sun-Up* opened on Broadway with a revenge plot about a North Carolina mountain family who shelter in the Appalachians away from involvement in World War I. Vollmer was less successful with later folk plays, *The Shame Woman* (1923), *The Dunce Boy* (1925), *Trigger* (1927), *The Hills Between* (1938), and *Moonshine and Honeysuckle* (1938). Howard Richardson made an international success of *Dark of the Moon* (1945), a brooding play about frontier witchcraft, which succeeded in New York and toured stages in the United States, Canada, and Europe in its original form and as a ballet performed by the National Ballet of Canada.

Canadian-American history is the focus for seven one-act plays by Hilda Mary Hooke. The first, *Brown Lady Johnson* (1947), is set on the Mohawk River in New York colony near the Canadian border in June 1763. The action portrays the outrage of the haughty Julia MacVicar, a guest of Sir William Johnson, because her hostess is Molly Brant, a Mohawk Indian and Johnson's wife. The story takes place during an attack by Senecas. Johnson introduces his wife with a flourish:

> There have been many times when councils have been shortened and arguments won because Miss Molly was there to keep the peace; but to-day for the first time she risked her own life by going out to face an army of belligerent tribesmen, unknown to her and unfriendly to the authorities, so that this house and its inmates might be protected. Ladies and gentlemen, I ask you to acknowledge the bravest lady in the land—Molly Brant, Lady Johnson! (Hooke 1942, 19)

Molly's grace and hospitality disarm the complaining guest, who joins the hostess in leading the way to dinner.

Subsquent plays by Hooke feature Canadian heroes. In *On the King's Birthday*, Thomas Talbot, colonizer of western Ontario, pauses in dancing the gavotte to fight for the honor of Susanne Johnson, whom a racist aristocrat denigrates because her mother is Molly Brant. The sequel, *The Princess of the Snows*, details the courtship of Talbot and the Princess Amelia, daughter of King George III. The third play of the set, *Here Will I Nest*, features Talbot receiving pioneers at Port Talbot, his log estate overlooking Lake Erie.

Hooke's Long Point legends, a series set on Lake Erie—*The Witch-House of Baldoon, Widows' Scarlet, More Things in Heaven*—depicts the powers of Dr. Troyer against witches and evil. In the first play, an Indian woman curses a pioneer house in Wallaceburg, Ontario, by marking the door with "the Black Magic of the Ojibways." The third play involves the use of a divining rod and sets Troyer's mysterious death to coincide with the shooting of a hawk.

The last in Hooke's series of one-act frontier plays, *Hélène of New France*, pictures the marriage of explorer, geographer, and colonizer Samuel de Champlain with Hélène Boulé, a 12-year-old Huguenot, whom he wed in 1610. During their courtship, he describes the beauties of Canada:

> There is an island in my country, a little green island in the big River Saint Lawrence, near the trading-post where your brother Eustache is now. I shall call it Saint Hélène's Isle, and every time I go past it I shall wave my hand to you. (ibid., 142)

In Scene 2, which takes place in 1624, the year of their parting, Champlain conceals from his wife his imminent departure to stem an Iroquois attack on Quebec. Madame Champlain calmly accepts the dangers of his career in New France and places a candle in the window to signal her acceptance of his departure and her intention to return to Paris.

A national interest in outdoor spectacle and pageantry began with Paul Green's *The Lost Colony*, set on historical location in Manteo, North Carolina, and with Kermit Hunter's *Unto These Hills* (1950) and *Horn in the West* (1952), both faithful to North Carolina's historic settlement. Hubert Hayes wrote a similar study, *Thunderland*, a biography of Daniel Boone produced in Asheville, North Carolina, at the Biltmore Estate's Forest Amphitheatre. Current outdoor dramas based on historical themes and presented on or near the site of significant events offer a panorama of themes and events from American history:

- *Anasazi, the Ancient Ones,* by Sharon Frenon, Framington, New Hampshire
- *The Aracoma Story,* by Thomas M. Patterson, Logan, West Virginia
- *Blue Jacket,* by W. L. Mundell, Xenia, Ohio
- *Cassidy: The Mostly True Story of Butch Cassidy,* by Tim Slover, Vernal, Utah
- *Christy, the Musical,* by Shirley Dolan, Sandy Kalan, and Ken McCaw, Townsend, Tennessee
- *Chucky Jack,* by Kermit Hunter, Gatlinburg, Tennessee
- *The City of Joseph,* by R. Don Oscarson, Nauvoo, Illinois
- *The Common Glory,* by Paul Green, Williamsburg, Virginia
- *The Cross and Sword,* by Paul Green, St. Augustine, Florida
- *Doc Brown: Legend of an Outlaw,* by Homis Shain, Pine Knob, New York
- *First for Freedom,* by Max B. Williams, Halifax, North Carolina
- *The Floyd Collins Story,* by Pat Hayes, Brownsville, Kentucky
- *From This Day Forward,* by Fred Cranford, Valdese, North Carolina
- *The Hatfields and McCoys,* by Billy Edd Wheeler, Beckley, West Virginia
- *Honey in the Rock,* by Kermit Hunter, Beckley, West Virginia
- *Horn in the West,* by Kermit Hunter, Boone, North Carolina
- *The Last Hanging in Pike County,* by Janice Kennedy, Lexington, Virginia
- *The Legend of Daniel Boone,* by Jan Hartman, Harrodsburg, Kentucky
- *Listen and Remember,* by Dare Harris Steele, Waxhaw, North Carolina
- *The Long Way Home,* by Earl Hobson Smith, Radford, Virginia
- *Looney's Tavern: The Aftermath and the Legacy,* by Ranny McAlister, Double Springs, Alabama
- *Micajah,* by Fred Burgess, Autryville, North Carolina
- *The Murder of Chief McIntosh,* by Benjamin Griffith, Carrollton, Georgia
- *Oklahoma!,* by Richard Rodgers and Oscar Hammerstein, Tulsa, Oklahoma
- *The Old Homestead,* by Denmon Thompson, East Swanzey, New Hampshire
- *Oregon Fever,* by Dorothy Velasco, Oregon City, Oregon
- *Pathway to Freedom,* by Mark R. Sumner, Snow Camp, North Carolina
- *Prickett's Fork: An American Frontier Musical,* by Seseen Francis, Fairmont, West Virginia
- *Ramona,* adapted from the novel by Helen Hunt Jackson, Hemet, California
- *Reflections of Mark Twain,* by Terrell Dempsey and Albert Conrad, Hannibal, Missouri

- *Salado Legends*, by Jackie Mills, Salado, Texas
- *Shadows in the Forest*, W. L. Mundell, Harrodsburg, Kentucky
- *The Shepherd of the Hills*, adapted from the novel by Harold Bell Wright, Branson, Missouri
- *The Stephen Foster Story*, by Paul Green, Bardstown, Kentucky
- *Stonewall Country*, by Don H. Baker, Lexington, Virginia
- *Strike at the Wind!*, by Randy Umberger, Pembroke, North Carolina
- *The Sword of Peace*, by William Harcy, Snow Camp, North Carolina
- *Tecumseh*, by Allan W. Eckart, Chillicothe, Ohio
- *Texas!*, by Paul Green, Canyon, Texas
- *Thunder Mountain Lives Tonight!*, by Abbott Fay and Dean Davies, Delta, Colorado
- *The Trail of Tears*, by Kermit Hunter, Tahlequah, Oklahoma
- *The Trail of the Lonesome Pine*, by Earl Hobson Smith, Big Stone Gap, Virginia
- *Trumpet in the Land*, by Paul Green, New Philadelphia, Ohio
- *Turpentine Wine*, by Drue Morris, Destin, Florida
- *Unto These Hills*, by Kermit Hunter, Cherokee, North Carolina
- *Utah!*, by Robert Paxton, St. George, Utah
- *Viva El Paso*, by Hector Serrano, El Paso, Texas
- *The Wataugans*, by Ronnie Day, Elizabethton, Tennessee
- *Young Abe Lincoln*, by Billy Edd Wheeler, Evansville, Tennessee

(Blum 1951; Brockett 1968; Cather 1977; Charles 1996; Clark 1963; Coad and Mims 1929; Gassner 1967; Hart 1983; Hartnoll 1983; Hewitt 1959; Hooke 1942; Hoyt 1955; Hughes 1951; Jefferson 1964; Koch 1922; Lewis 1943; "The Lost Colony" Playbill 1990; Mackay 1976; Moody 1966; Mowatt 1966; *National Cyclopedia* 1967; "Outdoor Drama" 1996; Quinn 1938; Rankin 1965; Rasmussen 1995; Stone 1966; Story 1967; Twain 1959; Vollmer 1938; Wallace 1963; Walser 1955, 1956)

See also Cather, Willa; Green, Paul; Harte, Bret; Hunter, Kermit; Jefferson, Joseph, III; Longfellow, Henry Wadsworth; the lost colony; Mormons; Oakley, Annie; Pocahontas; "Rip Van Winkle"; Twain, Mark.

TWAIN, MARK

America's best-loved humorist, local colorist, and public speaker, Mark Twain had a yen for gadding about and for studying human eccentricity. During his formative years as a fiction writer, he produced *Roughing It* (1962), a richly detailed eyewitness study of the frontier. In addition to capturing the Old West in embellished episodes on stagecoach travel, law courts, saloons, and mining camps, Twain spiced his text with provincial rhetoric and comic spellings patterned after the faux illiteracy of Josh Billings and Artemus Ward. In high spirits, Twain looks on new experiences as a challenge and delight, as in his observation of a pony express rider:

> Here he comes! Away across the endless dead level of the prairie a black speck appears against the sky . . . sweeping toward us nearer and nearer . . . a whoop and a hurrah . . . a wave of the rider's hand . . . and man and horse burst past our excited faces, and go winging away like a belated fragment of a storm! (Findlay 1980, 45)

Twain salted his humor and satire with idioms from workday vernacular, riverboat slang, dialect, and miners' neologism (slambang, doxologer, shebang, slumgullion, sockdolager, fantods, scalawag, shindig, hornswoggle, skedaddle, rambunctious, and ker-plunk), often intermixed in seriocomic elegant prose. A talented mimic, he absorbed the diversity and humor of many parts of the country. An example often cited for its vigor comes from *A Tramp Abroad:*

> I've noticed a good deal and there's no bird, or cow or anything that uses as good grammar as a bluejay. You may say a cat uses good grammar. Well, a cat does—but you let a cat get excited once; you let a cat get to pulling fur with another cat on a shed, nights, and you'll hear grammar that will give you the lockjaw. Ignorant people think it's the *noise* which fighting cats make that is so aggravating but it ain't so; it's the sickening grammar. Now I've never heard a jay use bad grammar but very seldom, and when they do, they are as ashamed as a human, they shut right down and leave. (McArthur 1992, 1058)

The introduction to literature of this and other examples of imaginative semiliterate Mississippi and frontier lingo marked Twain's place as the first spokesman for the American language.

Born Samuel Langhorne Clemens on November 30, 1835, Twain was a native of Florida, a backwoods Missouri community. He was the sixth child and third son of retailer, justice of the peace, and judge John Marshall Clemens and Jane Lampton Clemens, a sweet-natured Virginia aristocrat who taught her family the value of language, laughter, and reverence for living things. In 1839, Twain's family moved to Hannibal and enjoyed idyllic country life. Twain grew up on the banks of the Mississippi River, the escape he hoped would carry him far from his rural beginnings. In dreams of glory as a riverboat pilot in his autobiographical *Life on the Mississippi* (1883), he spoofs his childhood fantasies—"comforting daydreams of a future when I should be a great and honored pilot, with plenty of money, and could kill some of these mates and clerks and pay for them." (Twain 1990, 32)

By age 12, Twain was learning the newspaper business while working for the Missouri *Courier;* in 1852, he published his first piece, "The Dandy Frightening the Squattor," for the *Gazette.* His father's death forced him to leave school at age 18 and formally adopt the printer's trade, which he practiced journeyman-style in New York, Philadelphia, St. Louis, and in Ohio in Cincinnati,

Muscatine, and Keokuk. In daily contact with manuscripts and type for the *Hannibal Journal,* his older brother Orion's newspaper, from 1853 to 1854 Twain wrote under various pen names, including Epaminondas Adrastus Perkins, Josh, and Thomas Jefferson Snodgrass. After learning the complicated river maps and current charts to obtain his river pilot's license in 1859, he signed on the *Paul Jones* as a cub pilot and navigated the Mississippi River for four years aboard several vessels before river travel ceased in late April 1861 during the Civil War.

The war, which destroyed Twain's childhood ambition of piloting a stern-wheeler, threatened his life as well. After enlisting in the Confederate irregulars of Marion County, Missouri, he reconsidered his role in the military; two weeks later, he deserted and joined an increasing throng moving west. With his brother Orion, the newly appointed secretary to the governor of Nevada, he journeyed 19 days by stage from Missouri to Carson City, Nevada. He mined quartz and prospected for silver and gold before giving up get-rich-quick schemes. While low on funds, he wrote letters to the Virginia City *Territorial Enterprise.* In 1862, he joined the staff as sole reporter and freelance writer.

Twain's seven-year residency in the West, recounted in 1872 in *Roughing It,* fuels a first-person narrative blended from journalistic essays, notes, letters, local events, and "stretchers," the frontier term for tall tales. To the delight of readers, he relates a melange of anecdotes too far-fetched to be taken literally but too Twain-like to be dismissed as sheer folderol. His reflections on this period recur in his memoirs, in which he recounts adventures in Esmeralda, now called Aurora, Nevada, where he and Calvin H. Higbie prospected unsuccessfully for silver.

In an 1862 edition of the Virginia City *Territorial Enterprise,* Twain published his first serious tale, "The Celebrated Jumping Frog of Calaveras County." Under his pseudonym for the first time, he launched a career enhanced by friendships with humorist Artemus Ward, journalist Ambrose Bierce, and local-colorist Bret Harte. In 1864, Twain published for the *Californian* "Aurelia's Unfortunate Young Man," a humorous letter from a young woman engaged to a suitor who has had such a run of bad luck that he has lost both legs and arms, an eye, and his scalp, which Owens River Indians removed. That same year, Twain wrote "The Killing of Julius Caesar 'Localized,' " a West Coast election-year version of the Roman dictator's assassination composed as a translation of the fictional *Roman Daily Evening Fasces.* In 1866, he published the fractured verse competition of four inebriated Californians on a steamboat journey to Sacramento:

> Myself—"On London when the tray was low—"
> John Paul—"The Curfew tolled the knell of parting day";
> Lieut. Ellis—"This world is but a fleeting show—"
> Myself—("Hic!) Berrer dog'n ole dog Tray!"
> (Twain and Harte 1991, 209)

Twain branched out to sketches, novels, comedy, essays, young adult literature, autobiography, satire, lectures, history, after-dinner speeches, and anecdotes. To this considerable list of genres he added travelogues on his visit to Panama, Nicaragua, the Azores, Gibraltar, Europe, Russia, Turkey, the Holy Land, and the Sandwich Islands, where in 1866 he interviewed and observed while on assignment for the Sacramento *Union*.

After a three-year courtship by letter, on February 2, 1870, Twain wed Olivia "Livy" Langdon, the refined, citified daughter of a wealthy coal merchant in Elmira, New York. The couple settled in Buffalo, where he edited his father-in-law's paper, the *Buffalo Express,* and watched over Livy. Despite frail health that stemmed from tuberculosis of the spine, she gave birth to son Langdon and survived typhoid fever. The loss of Langdon to diphtheria preceded the births of Susy in 1872, Clara in 1874, and Jean in 1880. After selling his share of the *Express,* Twain moved his family from New York into a gaudy, gingerbready riverboat mansion in Hartford, Connecticut, where he taught his children in a second-floor schoolroom.

Settled at last from his peripatetic adventures and newspaper career, Twain initiated a full-time writing career and produced *Innocents Abroad* (1869), *The Adventures of Tom Sawyer* (1876), *The Prince and the Pauper* (1882), and *Life on the Mississippi* (1883). On these and other projects, Livy served as editor and censor. He reached the height of his fame with *The Adventures of Huckleberry Finn* (1884), a classic of the young adult canon, and followed two years later with *A Connecticut Yankee in King Arthur's Court. A* chaotic masterwork, *A Connecticut Yankee* is a satiric historical novel that reflects the author's belief in freedom and human rights, endangered notions in both medieval England and the antebellum South and strong motivational forces during the settlement of the frontier.

Although Twain never struck it rich from his publications, he profited from his genial frontier wit and charm and became a popular after-dinner speaker. His later years brought world-famous visitors William Dean Howells, George Washington Cable, Helen Keller, Rudyard Kipling, and Harriet Beecher Stowe to hear a store of anecdotes and jokes. Dressed in a white linen suit, his face framed in silvery locks, he looked the picture of Old South contentment and thrilled English fans when he journeyed to Oxford to receive an honorary doctorate. In reality, lawsuits, poor financial planning, and, in 1885, ill-advised investments in the Paige compositor and Kaolatype machine depleted his savings, forcing him onto the lecture circuit to meet expenses. The deaths of daughter Susy in 1895 from meningitis and wife Olivia in 1904 and the severe epileptic seizures that killed daughter Jean in 1909 saddened and embittered him.

Some of Twain's most pointed satire, irony, and allegory attest to his unhappiness, in particular, "The Man Who Corrupted Hadleyburg" (1898), an allegory on hypocrisy and greed; *The Mysterious Stranger* (1916), a posthumous morality novella; and the caustic treatise on religion, "Letters from the Earth," published in 1963. To clarify public misconceptions about his life and blatantly atheistic philosophy, Twain, who claimed to use "a pen warmed up in hell," began his autobiography in 1906, which he dictated to stenographer A. B. Paine. Twain left it unfinished at his death from heart disease at Stormfield in Redding, Connecticut, on April 21, 1910. He was buried at Elmira. Paine, who became

Mark Twain, shipboard.

Twain's first literary editor, published the manuscript as *The Autobiography of Mark Twain* (1924).

Twain remains America's best-loved teller of tales and most frequently cited aphorist. Both Florida and Hannibal, Missouri, honor him with museums. On a knoll near Hannibal, a statue of Twain rises above the inscription: "His religion was humanity, and the whole world mourned for him when he died." His skill with humor, local color, and anecdote eased the disdainful message of his damning stories, which indicate a streak of doubt that foolish humanity is worth saving. Collections of his satiric aphorisms display shrewd observations and canny evaluations of weakness and sin, often his own. A master of control, Twain recounted droll memoirs of the West and rambling commentary on his journey to Hawaii to adoring audiences. A vehicle for Hal Holbrook and other imitators, one-man shows in the style of Twain continue to blend witty frontier humor with his decidedly dark view of the human condition. (Bloom 1986a; Boorstin 1965; Crystal 1987, 1995; Davis and Beidler 1984; Dobie 1996; Ehrlich and Carruth 1982; Emerson 1985; Findlay 1980; Hazard 1927; Hutchinson n.d.; Kaplan 1966; Lee 1966; Levine 1984; Lyttle 1994; McArthur 1992; O'Connor 1966; Rasmussen 1995; Shalit 1987; Thomas and Thomas 1943; Twain 1959, 1962a, 1962b, 1962c, 1962d, 1985, 1990, 1991, 1995, 1996a, 1996b; Twain and Harte 1991)

See also Bierce, Ambrose; "The Celebrated Jumping Frog of Calaveras County"; Harte, Bret; poetry of the frontier; prospecting; *Roughing It.*

WEST, JESSAMYN

The creator of some of literature's most beloved Western characters, Mary Jessamyn West knew the frontier and its people from girlhood. Born in 1907 to a Quaker mother and part-Indian father, she was a native of North Vernon, Indiana, and grew up in California, where she attended the original one-room school in the vicinity. After graduation from Fullerton Junior College and Whittier College, she taught in a one-room school in Hemet outside Los Angeles, then moved to England in 1929 to work on an advanced degree. She returned to the United States to study at the University of California, teach creative writing, and make a home for her family in Napa Valley. During a lengthy recuperation from bilateral tuberculosis, she lived with her mother and absorbed the lore of frontier Indiana. The material found its way into numerous academic articles and in short works for *Harper's, Ladies' Home Journal, New Yorker, Atlantic Monthly, Good Housekeeping, Reader's Digest,* and *McCall's.*

In West's memoir, *To See the Dream* (1957), she describes the filming of her witty domestic novel, *The Friendly Persuasion* (1945), for which she served as technical adviser. The story of Jess Birdwell, a jocular backwoods nurseryman who marries Eliza Cope, a straitlaced Quaker minister, conveys an endearing blend of love, mismatched wills, and domestic humor. The setting reaches into frontier history for realistic details of the Birdwell home on pleasant acreage along the banks of the Muscatatuck River:

> On a peg by the front door hung a starling in a wooden cage and at the back door stood a spring-house, the cold spring water running between crocks of yellow-skinned milk. At the front gate a mossrose said welcome and on a trellis over the parlor window a Prairie Queen nodded at the roses in the parlor carpet. (West 1945, 3)

The abundance of goldenrod, lilies, black bass, catfish, currant bushes, gooseberries, dewberries, cherries, pawpaws, persimmons, and serviceberries symbolizes the promise of the heartland. The movie version of *The Friendly Persuasion*, starring Gary Cooper, Dorothy McGuire, Anthony Perkins, and Marjorie Main, earned Allied Artists five nominations for Academy Awards—for best picture, screenplay, direction, male supporting actor, and Dimitri Tiomkin's theme song, "Thee I Love."

The sequel novel, *Except for Me and Thee* (1969), returns to the Birdwell family, whose westering spirit conveys the urgency of Easterners eager to try their luck on the frontier. West's re-creation of a family discussion pits a wily Eliza against an adamant Jess, who is serious about leaving Ohio to find room for expansion. On first view of the Indiana wilderness, he mentally sketches in apple trees, cornfields, a sawmill, a home:

> What he saw was beauty; but it was a homestead beauty, and in his mind's eye his children dabbled in that stream and Eliza's pesky geese muddied the clear water. He saw himself age there: a beard sprouted from his chin; the beard grew white and long like his father's. He died there, was buried under a tree he had himself planted. (West 1969, 60)

The land satisfies Jess's elemental longing for good pasturage, an unending sweep of horizon, and "grass so high the horse had to forge through it like an animal fording a stream at high water." The Birdwells move to a farm at the edge of the outback, where Jess raises berry bushes and pear and apple trees. Against the steady rhythm of his husbandry, Eliza conducts worship services and tries to keep peace between the peace lovers and warmongers, who fall on both sides of issues raised by the Fugitive Slave Law.

In 1975, West was haunted by an 1824 frontier confrontation between settlers and the Seneca. She researched the tragedy, which cost 12 lives and sent one man into self-imposed exile. Her historical novel, *The Massacre at Fall Creek* (1975), describes the struggle for justice when Native Americans accuse four whites of murdering nine Indians—two braves, three women, and four children. The historical upshot of the divisive incident was the hanging of three culprits, the first whites in the New World to be executed for killing Indians. In sympathy with both the Seneca and early settlers, West composed a valedictory that reminds the reader of "Midwestern winters against which they had insufficient protection, the loneliness, and the fierce retaliation of a proud people that resisted invasions of their land and destruction of their way of life." (West 1975, 371)

Central to *The Massacre at Fall Creek* is the influence of Handsome Lake, a pacifist Indian mystic known for rejecting alcohol, which was overpowering his people almost immediately upon fraternization with whites. In place of debauchery, he pressed for a utopian vision—a natural communion among all beings in nature, a concept paralleling Christ's Sermon on the Mount. West characterizes Handsome Lake as a forceful Native American orator addressing a preliterate people: "He preached the Old Long House religion, the old faith of the Senecas. The Senecas had no writing for their scriptures. Handsome Lake's teaching had to be memorized, word for word." (ibid., 7) In proof of Handsome Lake's charisma, West describes Folded Leaf, Red Cloud's preteen son, who memorizes the scriptures and trains to be one of Handsome Lake's Faithkeepers. The best-selling novel was a Literary Guild selection and a Reader's Digest Condensed Book. In addition to these three frontier novels, West is famous for her wry, compassionate stories of teen problems and for a recurrent protagonist, Cress Delahanty. West also wrote an opera, an operetta, science fiction, verse, and two screenplays, *The Big Country* and *The Friendly Persuasion,* which she coauthored with Robert Wyler. (Blain, Grundy and Clements 1990; Ehrlich and Carruth 1982; Waldman 1990; West 1945, 1969, 1975, 1986)

WILDER, LAURA INGALLS

Perhaps the most beloved and respected young adult author of Americana, Laura Elizabeth Ingalls Wilder's children's frontier books have been published around the world in English, Japanese, and 18 other languages, and the series has sold over 35 million volumes. Wilder immortalized Pepin, Wisconsin, her home town, in *Little House in the Big Woods* (1932), the initial work of her "Little House" series of eight reflective prairie stories that symbolize the westward movement. She cherished the experience of westering with her family and commented on frontier mores:

> The teachings of those early days have influenced me and the example set by my mother and father has been something I have tried to follow, with failures here and there, with rebellion at times, but always coming back to it as the compass needle to the star. (Zochert 1976, 210)

Wilder centered her writings on the themes of home, community, and mutual respect. The appeal of the television series, *Little House on the Prairie,* which ran from 1974 to 1983, echoes the family motif, which won Peoples' Choice awards in 1978 and 1979. The series, which remains a favorite rerun, earned recognition from parents' groups and educational organizations for stars Michael Landon, who played Pa, and Melissa Gilbert, who played Laura.

Wilder's success attests to the stalwart folk who settled the wilderness. Born to Charles Philip and Caroline Lake Quiner Ingalls, a teacher, on February 7, 1867, she was the descendant of courageous, patriotic frontier stock. Her uncles, Hiram and James Ingalls, fought for the Union during the Civil War. Influenced by the Homestead Act of 1862, which allowed settlers to live five years on a parcel of land, her father had worked a claim in Independence, Kansas, in 1868. Her French-Canadian grandmother was a carefree matriarch who could dance a jig in old age. Likewise sprightly, Laura, who was only five feet tall, admits in her writings to a lively curiosity, daring, stubbornness, and a wholesome joy.

Wilder's first book narrates the family's move to the Wisconsin woods on Walnut Creek near the Verdigris River, west of Springfield. Together in Osage territory, the family settled with Charles's parents, Lansford and Laura Ingalls (for whom Laura Ingalls Wilder was named), his sister and brother Henry, and Laura's cousins. From 1871 to 1872, the group lived in wagons and slept on the ground while they and helpful neighbors cut hardwoods and built cabins. Wilder recounts her relationship with two sisters—Mary Amelia, two years older than Laura, and baby Caroline "Carrie" Celestia—and describes the daily work of tending a garden, laying up winter stores, salting fish, making cheese, trapping, hunting, drying furs, and tending a homemade smokehouse built from a hollow log.

According to Wilder, frontier children enjoyed simple amusements: hand-made patterns on the frosted windowpane, a game called Mad Dog, dressing a rag doll named Charlotte, playing house under the trees, blowing up a pig's bladder to bat back and forth in a game of catch, collecting stones, sledding, picnicking, and listening to Pa's fireside yarns. Often, the girls had to abandon fun for churning, bed making, cooking pumpkins for pies, gathering berries for jam, and washing dishes. Supervised chores, like molding lead into bullets and cleaning the rifle, the girls shared with their parents. Holidays, birthdays, and relatives' visits were festive occasions marked by hearty country food; evenings concluded with readings from *The Wonders of the Animal World* or the Bible. Wilder's first novel recalls with special warmth the nut trees:

> Acorns were falling from the oaks, and Laura and Mary made little acorn cups and saucers for the playhouses. Walnuts and hickory nuts were dropping to the ground in the Big Woods, and squirrels were scampering busily every-where, gathering their winter's store of nuts and hiding them away in hollow trees. (Wilder 1971c, 215)

She recites favorite verses of "Nellie Gray," "Uncle Ned," "Pop Goes the Wea-sel," "The Arkansas Traveler," and "Captain Jenks of the Horse Marines," which the girls and their mother sang while Pa played his fiddle.

The women of the family managed alone while Charles went to Pepin to trade furs, hire out as a carpenter to provide necessary cash, or attend to legal matters. He valued lengthening daylight for cradling and harvesting oats with the aid of visiting threshers. On shorter trips, he robbed a bee tree and made sugar at Grandpa Ingalls's house. On rare occasions, the whole family perused bolts of calico, milled sugar and candy, tobacco, and new galluses at the dry-goods store. Less bucolic is Wilder's memory of the beauty of wild animals and her dismay that her father had to kill them to feed the family. Most impor-tant in early childhood was the security that her parents offered in the wilder-ness, where prowling bears and wolves frightened them, whooping cough and fever weakened them, and unnamed dangers worried the girls when their fa-ther was absent.

From Wisconsin, Wilder made the frontier trek that is described in seven of her works: *Little House on the Prairie* (1935), *On the Banks of Plum Creek* (1937), *By the Shores of Silver Lake* (1939), *The Long Winter* (1940), *Little Town on the Prai-rie* (1941), and *These Happy Golden Years* (1943). Wilder's second and third vol-umes, which cover the period from 1873 to 1876, describe a patriarchal family in which the father decrees the sale of the house in Pepin after the government redraws boundary lines. The Ingalls ventured west to Independence, Kansas, by covered wagon and then on to Plum Creek on the Cottonwood River, a few miles north of Walnut Grove, Minnesota. On the Kansas plains, life on the idyl-lic farm was marred by a towering prairie fire and by the drums and cries of Indians. Wilder writes that her father, after receiving a warning from a friendly Osage, stopped playing the fiddle and melted more lead for bullets. He reassured the girls that he, the dog Jack, and soldiers from Fort Gibson and Fort Dodge would protect the family. After the family endures more sleepless nights of fierce cries, two warring Indian tribes depart south and west and abandon their joint buffalo hunt. Wilder writes of seeing the stoic face of a chief, Soldat du Chêne, and native women with infants peering from baskets. Her father claims that Indians and wild animals are the reasons for their abandonment of the cabin.

As Wilder matured, she interpreted events from her life in a dugout with more realism than her beneficent memories of the home she had known in Kansas. Her father was no longer able to hunt and farm at will after he hired out as a miller, butcher, and farm laborer to supply the family with cash to buy a cow. In 1875, the Ingalls moved into the house that he built in Walnut Grove, Minnesota; that winter, brother Charles Frederick was born. Caroline's health declined. After a severe fever, she recovered, but baby Freddie died at age ten months.

From happier memories, Wilder describes the challenge of play on Plum Creek, where she nearly drowned while wading in a strong current against her father's orders. She reminisces about the natural setting and a plague of grasshoppers:

> All day the sun beat hot on the house. All day it was full of the crawling sound that went up the wall and over the roof and down. All day grasshoppers' heads with bulging eyes, and grasshoppers' legs clutching, were thick along the bottom edge of the shut windows; all day they tried to walk up the sleek glass and fell back, while thousands more pushed up and tried and fell. (Wilder 1971g, 265)

From a child's point of view, she adds that her father stops talking and his eyes cease twinkling. The reality of farming, where agricultural disaster and swarming insects deplete their crops, ends his romanticism of the pioneer life. *By the Shores of Silver Lake* follows the Ingalls family's train trip from Plum Creek in 1874. Defeated, Ingalls brought his family back to eastern Minnesota near his parents. For a few months, they roomed at Masters Hotel in Burr Oak, Iowa, until Caroline's strength returned. Before the birth of their fourth daughter, Grace Pearl, in 1877, they lived in a rented brick residence but disliked town life.

In 1879, the Ingalls contracted scarlet fever; Mary, the sickest, suffered a stroke and lost her vision. To work off debts, Ingalls kept accounts at his brother Hiram's general store. That summer, the family moved by wagon into the Dakota Territory. Wilder visualizes the feeling of crossing the prairie in a wagon:

> All morning Pa drove steadily along the dim wagon track, and nothing changed. The farther they went into the west, the smaller they seemed, and the less they seemed to be going anywhere. The wind blew the grass always with the same endless rippling, the horses' feet and the wheels going over the grass made always the same sound. The jiggling of the board seat was always the same jiggling . . . Only the sun moved. (Wilder 1971a, 59)

The family lived in a camp near Silver Lake on the Big Sioux River while Ingalls worked as paymaster and timekeeper for the Chicago and Northwestern Railroad. Wilder gives a detailed picture of the laborious job of rail-bed construction and its toll on men and animals.

That winter, Wilder's family moved temporarily to a surveyors' house in the new town of De Smet, South Dakota, where blizzards and wolves and a band of drunks disrupted the idyllic prairie scene. Ingalls registered for a government homestead and took a temporary job selling goods at the railroad's company stores near Brookings, South Dakota. They set out in the spring of 1880 for acreage east of the Big Slough, where he built a shanty in a grove of cottonwood saplings and dug a well. Wilder ends *By the Shores of Silver Lake* in 1880 with a blend of delight in the new house, annoyance at swarms of mosquitoes, and terror when Grace wanders away toward the Big Slough.

The fifth Little House book, *The Long Winter,* continues the frontier story with a move to town. Because an Indian predicted seven months of rough winter, the family lived in the Ingalls' store building in De Smet, South Dakota, so that Laura and Carrie could attend school. In Wilder's retelling, the arrival of treacherous weather startles even the teacher:

> Suddenly there was no sunshine. It went out, as if someone had blown out the sun like a lamp. The outdoors was gray, the windowpanes were gray, and at the same moment a wind crashed against the schoolhouse rattling windows and doors and shaking the walls. (Wilder 1971f, 84)

The fearful winter of 1880–1881 depleted stocks of kerosene, coal, meat, and tea because train deliveries were hampered by blizzards. Local men accidentally spooked a herd of antelope that might have provided them fresh meat. Caroline taught the children to twist hay to burn in the stove. To replace lantern light, she twisted calico around a button, set it in a dish of axle grease, and lit the ends of the calico for a wick.

After the last potato was eaten and the Ingalls were in the early stages of starvation, Almanzo James Wilder and a friend, Cap Garland, went south to buy 60 bushels of wheat. Almanzo's legs turned white; his feet ached, but he recovered without losing toes to frostbite. Ingalls accepted potatoes, flour, and pork fat stolen from a train car, rationalizing, "Let the railroad stand some damages! This isn't the only family in town that's got nothing to eat." (ibid., 321) The townspeople rejoiced in May over their postponed Christmas feast.

Wilder's *Little Town on the Prairie* picks up the story the next summer, when Ingalls rejected the idea of a girl clerking at the hotel but allowed Laura to work in town at Clancy's store sewing shirts for $1.50 a week. To the narrator, urban life lacks the clean smell of the grasslands:

> The town was like a sore on the beautiful, wild prairie. Old haystacks and manure piles were rotting around the stables, the backs of the stores' false fronts were rough and ugly. The grass was worn now . . . A dank smell came from the saloons and a musty sourness from the ground by the back doors where the dishwater was thrown out. (Wilder 1971e, 49)

Wilder preferred the freedom of life on the prairie, but, for several years, financial demands gave her father less choice in providing for the family, especially for his blind daughter.

In 1881, while Mary left by train to attend Barry Corner School in Vinton, Iowa, Wilder took charge of the younger girls. They thrived in the classroom of Eliza Jane Wilder. Wilder played with town children and developed a tenuous friendship with Nellie Oleson. On December 24, 1882, at the end of Wilder's eight years of schooling, she received certification in reading, spelling, writing, math, geography, grammar, and history to teach at "any common school in the country for the term of twelve months." (ibid., 106) Her best score was in history, her worst in reading.

Silver Lake was the site of Wilder's courtship. *Farmer Boy* (1933), Wilder's second publication, recounts the childhood of her husband, Almanzo, whom she met through her teacher. As described in *These Happy Golden Years,* which covers from 1883 to 1885, the couple exchanged the affectionate names of Bess and Manly. For three years, Wilder taught at the Wilkins School, held in an abandoned shanty south of De Smet, and boarded with the Bouchies. After Manly began ferrying her from work, she eased her homesickness by spending weekends at home and used her earnings of $40 to buy sheep and to pay for Mary's schooling. On August 25, 1885, Laura married Manly; a year and a half later, their daughter Rose was born in their small house north of De Smet.

The Wilder family met a series of misfortunes. Manly bought expensive machinery, which put them in debt. Their barn burned; hail destroyed crops. The Wilders fell ill with diphtheria, leaving Rose to the care of her grandparents. Wilder's marriage was hampered by Manly's paralysis following a stroke and by the death of their infant son Charles in 1889. Before Wilder recovered from the loss, their house burned; they moved in with his parents, James and Angeline Wilder, in Spring Valley, Minnesota. Wilder sold her sheep to pay for a move to Westville, Florida, but the sharp contrast in climate forced them back in 1892. Settled near the Ingalls' house in De Smet, Wilder worked as a dressmaker while her husband took small jobs.

Wilder kept a journal of these difficult years. The tone of her writings lifted in 1894, when she and Manly bought Rocky Ridge Farm in the Ozarks a mile east of Mansfield, Missouri, which Rose identified as "The Land of the Big Red Apple." Wilder's commentary on the move, printed in the *De Smet News,* was her first publication. She kept a daybook of the midsummer journey over the trail southeast from South Dakota to Lincoln, Nebraska; Fort Scott, Kansas; and Springfield, which lay east of Mansfield, Missouri. Along the way, they picked plums, grapes, black currants, and sweet clover and rejoiced at the first sight of oak groves. Some unexplained mishap caused them to lose $100, which Wilder kept in her writing desk.

In an addendum to *On the Way Home* (1962), Rose Wilder Lane recalls a starving man who sought work at the Wilder cabin. Against Wilder's protest, "Manly, *no! We've got Rose,"* her husband shared their meager supply of meal and pork fat for corn dodgers, the staple food in homesteaders' diets. (Wilder,

1962, 92) The man proved faithful to his debt and joined Manly in cutting wood, which they sold for 50 cents.

The Wilders enrolled Rose in a local school and made her a swing for afternoon entertainment. At night by the cabin fire, Laura read aloud from James Fenimore Cooper's *Leatherstocking Tales* and William Hickling Prescott's *Conquest of Mexico* and *Conquest of Peru*. The family dug a well and worked hard to make a living from an apple orchard and adjacent woodlot. The acreage increased from 40 to 200. After Rose left for Louisiana to live with her aunt, attend high school, and become a journalist, the Wilders built their last house.

Wilder's career grew from essays submitted to the *Christian Science Monitor, Missouri State Farmer, Missouri Ruralist*, and Saint Louis papers. From 1911 to 1927, she wrote two columns, "The Farm Home" and "As a Farm Woman Thinks." In addition to her chores, she organized local women for the Mansfield Farm Loan Association and served the Federal Loan Bank as a branch secretary-treasurer. During the Depression, Rose helped her mother begin writing her memories of pioneering under the title "Pioneer Girl," which her publisher later changed. Wilder summarized conservative frontier values: "They were courage, self-reliance, independence, integrity, and helpfulness. Cheerfulness and humor were handmaids to courage." (Zochert 1976, 239)

Wilder took less interest in publishing from her husband's death in 1949 until her own death on February 10, 1957. Her posthumous works include details of the move to Missouri in *The First Four Years* (1971) and her correspondence in *West from Home: Letters, San Francisco, 1915* (1974), the letters she wrote while visiting Rose and her husband Gillette Lane in San Francisco. Rose Lane complemented her mother's eight novels with *On the Way Home,* a recounting of her parents' move to Rocky Ridge, which Wilder had detailed in her journal. An adopted grandson, Roger Lea MacBride, used the original notes to publish additional works about the Wilders' marriage—*Little House on Rocky Ridge* (1993), *Little Farm in the Ozarks* (1994), and *In the Land of the Big Red Apple* (1995)— and to coauthor the *Little House on the Prairie* series for ABC-TV.

Laura Wilder's works have achieved an enviable position on most young adult reading lists, particularly *Little House on the Prairie,* which won a special Newbery-Caldecott award. Three years before her death, the American Library Association inaugurated the Laura Ingalls Wilder award, given every five years to outstanding contributors to children's literature. Other honors include the Spring Book Festival Prize from the *New York Herald*, the title of "living heroine" bestowed by *Horn Book*, libraries named for her, and the continued celebration of her birthday. Today, visitors follow the family's route over Highway 14, the Laura Ingalls Wilder Historic Highway.

In the 1990s, a furor among critics of children's literature resulted after William Holtz's *The Ghost in the Little House* (1993) cast doubt on Wilder's control of her publications. He claimed that Rose Lane was a ghostwriter for her mother. Other experts in children's literature categorized the two women's working relationship as a collaboration between writer and editor. The controversy made little impact on Wilder's reputation as an eyewitness to the settlement of the Midwest. (Blain, Grundy, and Clements 1990; Davidson and

Wagner-Martin 1995; Ehrlich and Carruth 1982; Greetham 1996; Holtz 1993; Huey 1994; Irby 1996; Lane and MacBride 1977; Lasky and Knight 1993; "Little Town on the Prairie" 1996; MacBride 1993, 1994, 1995; Marsh 1992; O'Neill 1992; Slegg 1996; Snodgrass 1992; Wilder 1962, 1971a, 1971b, 1971c, 1971d, 1971e, 1971f, 1971g; 1971h; Wilder and Lane 1988; Zochert 1976)

WINNEMUCCA, SARAH

The first female Native American to publish a major work on Indians, Sarah Winnemucca (Thocmetony, Toc-Me-To-Ne, or "Shell Flower"), daughter of Chief Winnemucca II, was born among northern Paiutes around 1844 on the Humboldt River at Humboldt Sink, Nevada. When she was four, she first saw whites after her mother moved her nine children across the Sierra Mountains to San Jose, California. Winnemucca recalls in her autobiography the terror of that day:

> My aunt overtook us, and she said to my mother: "Let us bury our girls, or we shall all be killed and eaten up." So they went to work and buried us, and told us if we heard any noise not to cry out, for if we did they would surely kill us and eat us. So our mothers buried me and my cousin, planted sage bushes over our faces to keep the sun from burning them, and there we were left all day. (Hopkins 1994, 11)

Winnemucca used her scholarly talents to acquaint herself with white settlers. Fluent in three native tongues, she studied English and Spanish at the home of Major William Ormsby in Genoa, Nevada, and, at her Grandfather Truckee's insistence, attended classes at the Sisters of Notre Dame Convent school when she was 16. Local bigots forced her out of the school after four weeks. On her own, she worked as a maid in Virginia City and sold needlework door-to-door to buy English books.

A recurrence of Paiute hostilities in 1866 caused the cavalry to force Winnemucca and her brother Naches to enter Fort McDermitt to determine how the government could best protect them. For the remainder of her life, she wrote letters to officials and served as a valued intermediary in the struggle to secure a permanent home for her tribe, who became political hostages and wandered the Pacific Northwest at the will of the military. Serving as interpreter, aide, and ombudsman for tribes of the Great Basin, she facilitated meetings in San Francisco and Gold Hill, Nevada, and followed the Paiutes to Malheur Reservation, Oregon, where she taught school. In 1878, she undertook a dangerous mission into hostile territory to rescue her father and assisted General Oliver Otis Howard during peace negotiations that ended the Bannock War.

Continued reshuffling of Paiutes, this time to Yakima, Washington, preceded Winnemucca's 1880 lecture before President Rutherford B. Hayes and Secretary of the Interior Carl Schurz in Washington, D.C., which her father attended. Speaking as "Princess Sarah," ambassador for her people, she blamed the corrupt and inefficient Indian Bureau for mismanaging funds and discounting the wishes and traditions of native peoples. The speech brought unfounded charges of low character against Winnemucca, but army officials insisted that her expertise in past sessions was invaluable. Government guarantees of settlement at Malheur Reservation and an annual allotment proved false. She continued her teaching career in 1881 at Vancouver, Washington, where she married a career soldier, Lieutenant Lambert H. Hopkins.

Dressed in shell-trimmed finery, Winnemucca, with the support of General Howard and educator Elizabeth Palmer Peabody, began a speaking campaign for Native American rights. She collected signatures on a petition and appeared before a congressional committee to demand food and medical attention to ease her people's plight. Using donated funds, she established the Peabody Indian School, a native language boarding academy near Lovelock, Nevada, on land donated by Senator Leland Stanford. Her first class consisted of 12 girls and 6 boys. Because of interference from Indian agents, the school closed four years later. Dispirited and grieving over her husband's death, she retired to her sister's home in Henry's Lake, Idaho; in 1891, Winnemucca died in Monida, Montana, of tuberculosis.

At age 39, Sarah Winnemucca Hopkins, with the assistance of Mary Peabody Mann, published *Life among the Piutes, Their Wrongs and Claims* (1883), an autobiography that covers the move of a West Coast tribe from autonomy to the control of government-paid whites serving as Indian agents. Written during an era when white women had no vote and Paiute women were discounted as ragged savages, the book lauded Paiute females, who took part in councils and in war. Winnemucca notes that her sister-in-law

> went out into the battle-field after her uncle was killed, and went into the front ranks and cheered the men on. Her uncle's horse was dressed in a splendid robe made of eagles' feathers and she snatched it off and swung it in the face of the enemy . . . and she staid and took her uncle's place, as brave as any of the men. (ibid., 53)

Ardent and patriotic, *Life among the Piutes* became an influential Paiute history. Because it preserves the author's intense labors in support of peace and coexistence with white settlers, the work drew criticism for what some tribe members described as Winnemucca's audacious self-promotion. Through frequent public appearances and private councils with her people, she extended support for the Dawes Act, which would allow Indians to make their own decisions. For being the first Native American woman to publish an autobiography, she was inducted into the Nevada Writers Hall of Fame.

In praise of Sarah Winnemucca's place in history, General Howard wrote a chapter about her father and one about her in *Famous Indian Chiefs I Have Known* (1907), a dated collection of sugary, patronizing biographies aimed at young adult readers. He summed up her aid to the government and added:

> if I could tell you but a tenth part of all she willingly did to help the white settlers and her own people to live peaceably together I am sure you would think, as I do, that the name of Toc-me-to-ne should have a place beside the name of Pocahontas in the history of our country. (Howard 1989, 237)

(Davidson and Wagner-Martin 1995; Hopkins 1994; Howard 1989; McHenry 1980; Milner et al. 1994; Morrison 1990; Patterson and Snodgrass 1994; Sherr and Kazickas 1994; Waldman 1990)
See also Howard, Oliver Otis.

WISTER, OWEN

Grouped with Jack Schaefer and Walter Van Tilburg Clark as a creator of mature frontier fiction, Owen Wister earned lasting fame as the author of *The Virginian: A Horseman of the Plains* (1902), the prototype of the literary Western. Wister shared with the era's prominent Western writers the traditions of the East. Born into affluence in Germantown, Pennsylvania, on July 14, 1860, he was the grandson of stage star Fanny Kemble and the son of intellectuals—physician Owen Jones and Sarah Butler Wister, a poet. He attended Germantown Academy and boarded at St. Paul's School in Concord, New Hampshire, and also studied in England and Switzerland. At Harvard, music, particularly French opera and piano classics, absorbed his academic energies and earned him a degree *summa cum laude* and membership in Phi Beta Kappa. While at Harvard, he made friends with Henry Cabot Lodge, Oliver Wendell Holmes, William Dean Howells, and Theodore Roosevelt, all Eastern notables who helped shape his values and outlook.

Wister was gifted in sight-singing, transposition, and orchestral scoring and intended to spend his life composing music; his father, however, forced him into finance. He took a job at the Union Safe Deposit Vaults in Boston but wearied of its lockstep tedium. He spent two years in Paris studying music and earned praise from composer Franz Liszt for one of his compositions. In 1885, Wister returned home ill and depleted. At his doctor's insistence on a change of scenery, he made a trip to the TTT, a cattle ranch in Kaycee, Wyoming, to recuperate from nervous exhaustion. He found the West more suited to his tastes and enjoyed riding a bronco, fishing for rainbow trout, and shooting grouse and elk.

Unsure of his career intentions, Wister returned to Harvard to earn a law degree, a solid investment in education, which his family approved. In private, his mind courted the West but to no known end. According to his daughter's introduction to *Owen Wister Out West* (1958), he filled 15 notebooks over a five-year period with glimpses of barkeeps, miners, army officers, Shoshones, squatters, lawmen, and tinhorns. Of these individuals, he commented:

> American! There are very few of them so far in our history. Every man, woman, and cowboy I see comes from the East. . . . I feel more certainly than ever that no matter how completely the East may be the headwaters from which the West has flown and is flowing, it won't be a century before the West is simply the true America, with thought, type, and life of its own kind. (Wister 1958, 32–33)

In the same vein as John Muir, Wister longed to nurture and protect Western grandeur and to ward off the moneygrubbing mining firms and developers who jeopardized the land. His protective attitude combined with a delight in all aspects of plains life, the opposite of Harvard law.

Like other newcomers to the West, Wister learned the lingo. For future reference, he recorded and defined terms such as a-comin' and a-goin', spot cash, puny, trifling, front name, pussyfoot, top-notch, cat's-claw cactus, gringo, doughboy, and necktie party, localisms that later energize the dialect conversations of his salty, true-to-the-bone characters. He admired the cowpuncher song "Git Along Little Dogies" and recorded it in his notes. In an original four-verse ode, he longed to "prison in my words and so hold by me all the year some portion of the Wilderness of freedom that I walk in here." (ibid., 92) His travels took him from British Columbia to Texas, but he felt most at home at the family camp in Jackson Hole, Wyoming.

After practicing law six years, first with the Philadelphia firm of Ralston and Rawle and then alone, Wister pondered the challenge of a friend, Walter Furness, to capture in stories the heroes of the Old West. Of this discussion, Wister wrote:

> Why wasn't some Kipling saving the sage-brush for American literature, before the sage-brush and all that it signified went the way of the California forty-niner, went the way of the Mississippi steam-boat, went the way of everything? Roosevelt had seen the sage-brush true, had felt its poetry; and also Remington, who illustrated his articles so well. But what was fiction doing, fiction, the only thing that has always outlived fact? Must it be perpetual tea-cups? (ibid., 11–12)

In reply to his rhetorical questions, Wister rebelled against the sterile prissi-ness of New England symbolized by the teacup and wrote "Hank's Woman" that same night. He published it along with "Balaam and Pedro," "Em'ly," and "How Lin McLean Went West" in *Harper's Magazine*. Critical recognition enabled him to abandon the legal profession, which he had come to detest, and to earn his living from freelance writing. In spring 1893, *Harper's* paid for his next fact-finding journey west. Three short story collections—*Red Men and White* (1896), *Lin McLean* (1897), and *The Jimmyjohn Boss* (1900)—preceded his masterwork, *The Virginian,* a solid best-seller illustrated by his contemporary, painter Frederic Remington.

Dedicated to Theodore Roosevelt, Wister's friend and critic, *The Virginian* is a paean to democracy and law and order. The hero serves as a human parallel of the settled frontier: his domestication replicates the taming of the West, a brutal, overtly racist, and opportunistic national phenomenon justified by the concept of manifest destiny. Told through the eyes of an uninitiated Eastern tenderfoot, the story is set in Medicine Bow, Wyoming, toward the end of the nineteenth century. Wister characterizes the town and its 29 buildings as typical of the West: "Scattered wide, they littered the frontier from the Columbia to the Rio Grande, from the Missouri to the Sierras." (Wister 1968, 7) Like a pack of well-palmed playing cards, the town sports discarded bottles and wind-blown garbage, yet enjoys a serenity unknown in the East.

At first glimpse, the unnamed Virginian embodies the insouciance of the cowboy with hat pushed back, handkerchief loose about his throat, and "one

Owen Wister wrote, "When you call me that, *smile!*" in his 1902 novel *The Virginian*. The novel gave the West a prototype hero, played here by Gary Cooper, wearing the white hat, against Walter Huston, in the black hat, in the 1929 movie.

casual thumb . . . hooked in the cartridge-belt that slanted across his hips." (ibid., 3) Soiled and wrinkled, his garments display the weathering that results from hard work and exposure to dry, dusty winds. To the observer, he is both shabby and splendid, the rumpled titan later imitated by Gary Cooper, John Wayne, Alan Ladd, Clint Eastwood, and other screen and television cowboys. In the opening chapters, Wister portrays his protagonist in the act of self-refinement. The hero begins his transformation from rowdy carouser, drinker, gambler, and skirt-chaser to responsible adult. After rescuing Molly Stark Wood, a stiffly refined young teacher from Bennington, Vermont, who is aboard a stagecoach stuck to its upper stokes in river mud, he courts her through letters and frequent rides to her Beard Creek home ostensibly to borrow books.

Wister portrays the Virginian as a callow but likable man modeled on a Philadelphia police officer he identifies in his journal as Corporal Skirdin. The Virginian gains the respect of his employer, Judge Henry, and of the cowboys who work Sunk Creek Ranch. The exception is a resentful churl, Trampas, who taunts and bullies the younger man and verbally abuses Molly. In one self-confident move, after Trampas has called him a "son-of-a———," the hero places his pistol on the card table and, gentle as a caress, drawls, "When you call me that, *smile!*," a fabled retort that has earned an honored place among Western one-liners. (ibid., 16) To the narrator, the voice sounds "the bell of death," a foreshadowing of Trampas's demise.

Critics connect Wister's ambivalence toward his Philadelphia law practice with the novel's conflict. The Virginian's developing love match with Molly founders after she discovers that he rides with a lynch party to capture and hang rustlers. Molly, the unconventional ingenue, departs from the East but carries it in her demeanor and heritage. As Wister characterizes her, "She could have been enrolled in the Boston Tea party, the Ethan Allen Ticonderogas, the Green Mountain Daughters, the Saratoga Sacred Circle, and the Confederated Colonial Chatelaines." (ibid., 49) The intervention of Judge Henry helps her—and the reader—to reconcile her Eastern values with the rough justice of the range. Wister exonerates the Virginian through Molly, who accepts him once more as her future husband, even though rumors spread in Bennington that "Miss Molly Wood was engaged to marry a *rustler!*" (ibid., 143). In a candid letter to Molly's great-aunt, he confesses, "I am not a boy now, and women are no new thing to me. A man like me who has travelled meets many of them as he goes and passes on but I stopped when I came to Miss Wood." With a touch of self-reproach, he predicts, "It is going to be hard for her to get used to a man like me." (ibid., 201)

Wister's denouement establishes the convention of the shoot-out, the West's traditional settler of dilemmas, which quells for good the hero's feisty high spirits and supplants his juvenile vision with a stoic maturity. Elements of tragedy cluster around the final conflict, which takes place the day before the hero's wedding. Once more, Molly questions her fiancé's morals in participating in a crude frontier duel. Begun with a challenge from the evil Trampas to leave town before sunset, the slow-motion clash pits the Virginian against an experienced gunman, who has already drawn on him. The Virginian gives Trampas good reason to wish that he had resorted to ambush rather than public duel. Their shoot-out leaves Trampas expiring on the ground. Wister concludes, "Two fingers twitched, and then ceased; for it was all." (ibid., 264) Molly again forgives the hero, whose reward is a long embrace, a wedding, and a monthlong honeymoon.

In a letter to his mother rebutting her criticism of *The Virginian*, Wister agrees that Molly is a vapid character and claims to have concentrated on the portrait of a man and the mores and ethics of the Western era. The text assures the reader that the Virginian is justly rewarded for making ethical choices. Speaking through the Judge, Wister insists, "Many an act that man does is right or wrong according to the time and place which form, so to speak, its context;

strip it of its particular circumstances, and you'll tear away its meaning." (ibid., 236) In the epilogue, Wister pictures a satisfying reciprocity: the union of a woman who longs for "a man's talk" and a man rescued from loneliness and potential self-destruction. Wister glosses over the birth of their first child, the hero's return to Sunk Creek, and his partnership with Judge Henry in the ranch. Because the two honest, responsible men are willing to drive out thieves, their investment flourishes and the Virginian becomes a solid citizen.

Critics label Wister's *The Virginian* the first modern Western novel and characterize the protagonist as a code hero, the model for the cowboy of conscience. Unlike the bloody, bombastic dime "horse opera," Wister's novel exalts the horseman as a restrained, pragmatic, and romantic figure—the West's true folk hero. Wister writes of him:

> Whatever he did, he did with his might. The bread that he earned was earned hard, the wages that he squandered were squandered hard . . . Well, he will be among us always, invisible, waiting his chance to live and play as he would like. His wild kind has been among us always, since the beginning, a young man with his temptations, a hero without wings. (ibid., 279)

Overall, the Virginian is a gentrified cowpuncher whose ethics and sensibilities remain intact among the brutish elements of the West. His family flourishes from the union of a prim schoolmarm from the East with the strong Westerner.

A huge success in the United States and Europe, the novel was the springboard for Kirk LaShell's 1903 stage adaptation, which debuted in Boston with Dustin Farnum in the lead role and Frank Campo playing Trampas. Wister contributed to the script and wrote for the villain the song "Ten Thousand Cattle," which flourished in sheet music and collections of cowboy tunes. The play toured the country for two decades; Henry Fonda once acted the part of the hero. The novel also fueled three movies, one of them a silent picture. Gary Cooper and Walter Huston starred in the 1929 Paramount black and white, which Victor Fleming directed. The last screen version, made by Paramount in 1946, was a color classic starring Joel McCrea, Brian Donlevy, and Barbara Britton.

Relieved of financial need, Wister, lauded as a Western expert and historian, lived at his estate in Bryn Mawr, Pennsylvania, and supplemented his writing career with numerous speaking engagements. He pursued multiple literary genres, including *Philosophy Four* (1903), a memoir of his Harvard days; *Lady Baltimore* (1906), a novel of manners; *The Pentecost of Calamity* (1915), a study of pre–World War I Europe; *A Straight Deal: or, the Ancient Grudge* (1920), an essay on Anglo-American relations; and the biographies *The Seven Ages of Washington* (1907) and *Roosevelt, the Story of a Friendship* (1930). Kudos to Wister's literary achievement include an honorary doctorate from the University of Pennsylvania and appointment as an overseer of Harvard.

Wister was a strong family man. Married to his second cousin, pianist and educator Mary Channing, he suffered a great loss at her death in 1913 while giving birth to their sixth child. Backed by a nanny and butler, he continued his trips West and taught his three sons and three daughters to love the frontier and to ride, hunt, and track with the skill of natives. He led his family on a tour of World War I battlefields so that they could appreciate Europe's sufferings. Near the end of his career, he spent most of his time in the East, writing music and relaxing with his family at Champs des Corbeaux, his summer home in Saunderstown, Rhode Island. He died of cerebral hemorrhage on July 21, 1938, in North Kingstown, Rhode Island, and was buried in Laurel Hill Cemetery in Philadelphia. His private papers are housed in the Library of Congress, but his children insisted that his diaries go to the University of Wyoming. In the epilogue to the journals, his daughter, Fanny Kemble Wister, makes a rueful declaration about her father's beloved West: "It is a vanished world. No journeys, save those which memory can take, will bring you to it now." (ibid., 259) (Calder 1975; *Contemporary Authors* 1994; Dobie 1996; Ehrlich and Carruth 1982; Folsom 1966; Herron 1939; Janke 1996; Kunitz 1942; Lomax 1947; Milner et al. 1994; Rainey 1996; Sarf 1983; Steckmesser 1965; Westbrook 1969; Wister 1958, 1968)

See also Clark, Walter Van Tilburg; law and order; Schaefer, Jack Warner.

WOMEN ON THE FRONTIER

Despite the predominence of males in the early history of Europe's exploration and dominance of the Western Hemisphere, the place of women in the later settlement of the Americas is crucial. No study of frontier literature can overlook the pragmatic mothers in Fred Gipson's *Old Yeller*, Marjorie Kinnan Rawlings's *The Yearling*, Bess Streeter Aldrich's *A Lantern in Her Hand*, or Laura Ingalls Wilder's Little House series. The wilderness canon has been enriched by the varied voices of the Chinese workers in Ruthanne Lum McCunn's *Thousand Pieces of Gold* (1981), domestic humor in Nannie T. Alderson and Helena Huntington Smith's *A Bride Goes West* (1942), adaptation to hardship in Sophie Trupin's *Dakota Diaspora: Memoirs of a Jewish Homesteader* (1984), and thwarted ideals in Carrie Young's account of the Dakota bride in *Nothing To Do but Stay* (1991) and her seven stories of domesticated plains life in *The Wedding Dress* (1992). The media thrive on depictions of Western women. Movies have pictured memorable frontier characters, notably Eliza Birdwell in Jessamyn West's *The Friendly Persuasion*, Cora Munro in James Fenimore Cooper's *The Last of the Mohicans*, and Evie Teale in Louis L'Amour's *Conagher*. Likewise, television has profited from strong Western women. A prime example is a duo of Hallmark Hall of Fame teleplays about prairie farm families, Patricia MacLachlan and Carol Sobieski's *Sara, Plain and Tall* and *The Skylark*.

The approach-avoidance syndrome forms the psychological basis of many stories that depict women who come from genteel backgrounds in more settled climes. With misgivings, they agree to resettle "out there," where law is as strained as relations between whites and Indians and where the niceties of home are replaced by the exigencies of the wilderness. As Nannie Tiffany Alderson phrases her reluctance in *A Bride Goes West*:

> I said Yes, of course I would. But when I did go out and sit down to table in the dirt-floored kitchen, with those grizzled coatless men in their grimy-looking flannel work shirts they had worn all day, a wave of homesickness came over me. (Alderson and Smith 1942)

For Nannie and her myriad westbound sisters, homesickness and the sight of unshaven men paled beside long-term retreats to forts during Indian attacks, rattlers in the corral, bouts of debilitating ague, lost livestock, and the perpetual sough of lonely prairie wind.

As featured in Dee Brown's *The Gentle Tamers* (1958), women were the seed of American riches and the force that insisted on peace in lawless communities. Whether cooks for the Butterfield Stage, farmers along the Pecos, teachers in Indian schools, or entertainers in Klondike dance halls, women balanced the macho elements of the frontier with an emphasis on gentility, education, cleanliness, and family concerns. They were more likely than men to demand a church and school for growing hamlets, to collect herbs for healing, to assist other women in childbirth, and to organize disaster relief in times of cholera, prairie fire, and cyclone. As letters and diaries imply, female settlers adapted well to the immense emptiness of the plains and found beauty and contentment in landscapes that dismayed men. Their handicrafts and writings echo the vigorous rhythms of the boomtown and growing cattle trails; their insights depict the frontier as a potential home.

The parallel strand of women writers in frontier literature is equally vital to a study of the themes and genres that express female and family experiences of pulling up roots and resettling in the wilderness. Two centuries after the explorer's role ended, female writers began recording their thoughts and aspirations in letters, journals, verse, song, and fiction. Traveling women such as Susan Magoffin, Mary Hunter Austin, and Isabella Bird produced the female perspective of the Oregon and Santa Fe Trails, New Mexico and Arizona deserts, Native American reservations, and the Sierras and Rocky Mountains; Francis Roe, Alice Grierson, Elizabeth Custer, Martha Summerhayes, and other military wives chronicled the hardships of forts, particularly those under siege during the pacification of Plains tribes. Sarah Winnemucca offered the Native American point of view with *Life among the Piutes: Their Wrongs and Claims* (1883); over a century later, Mary Crow Dog wrote a poignant native study in *Lakota Woman* (1990). With similar passion, Theodora Kroeber refused to let die the story of Ishi, and Caroline Gordon re-created the terror of abduction by Indians in "The Captive" (1952). One of the Midwest's most influential realists, Willa Cather, characterized the Scandinavian settlers of Nebraska in *O Pioneers!* (1913) and *My Ántonia* (1918). Rebecca Burlend chronicled the emigrant's experience in a log cabin in the wilderness; Lula Parker Betenson spoke for her brother, outlaw Butch Cassidy.

Gems worthy of inclusion in the frontier canon crop up in unlikely places. In 1990, Laurel Thatcher Ulrich reshaped the diary of Martha Ballard, a practical nurse from Kennebec, Maine, who kept a daybook of her experiences over a 27-year period. Entitled *A Midwife's Tale: The Life of Martha Ballard, Based on Her Diary, 1785–1812* (1990), the text presents a realistic look at the dangers faced by an itinerant healer in preindustrial America. Over rain-gorged rivers, through snow, and down dark country lanes, Ballard attends patients and safely delivers 768 babies to the 814 women she attends in labor. Usually on foot, she returns from her busy days to a walloping list of home chores—carding flax, distilling vinegar, bartering for supplies, and growing herbs, fruit, and vegetables in her garden. When weariness precipitated illness in spring 1778, she took to her bed and wrote:

> I Eat a little cold puding and Cold milk twice in the coars of the day and perform part of my washing. I Laid myself on the bed in the bedroom was not able to rise from ther . . . . How many times I have been necasatated to rest my self on the bed I am not able to say. God grant me patience to go thro the fatages of this life with fortitude looking forward to a more happy state. (Ulrich 1990, 226)

When called to a deathbed, Ballard nurses the patient with a sense of Christian duty. Of Parthenia Pitts's demise, the writes "She Expird in a very short space without a strugle Except distress for Breath. We have reason to hope our loss [is] her gain." (ibid., 253) The unsentimental study of Ballard on the edge of the wild ennobles a life dedicated to helping any neighbor in distress.

One of the most factual and readable frontier diaries was composed by a hardworking farm wife, Rebecca Burlend, who produced a first-rate account of her family's departure from Yorkshire, England, to Pike County, Illinois, in *A True Picture of Emigration* (1848), a memoir of 16 years in the American wilderness. A victim of England's high rents and low farm profits, the Burlends and their five children set out for America in 1831 and took passage up the Mississippi River from New Orleans to St. Louis. Her dismay at Phillip's Ferry, the meager dock where they disembark, is evident:

> we were utterly confounded: there was no appearance of a landing place, no luggage yard, nor even a building of any kind within sight; we, however, attended to our directions, and in a few minutes saw ourselves standing by the brink of the river, bordered by a dark wood, with no one near to notice us or tell us where we might procure accommodation or find harbour. (Burlend and Burlend 1987, 42–43)

Unable to reconcile her fantasies with reality, she asks herself, "Is this America?" Burlend's acquaintance with a more genteel society is evident in her tongue-in-cheek description of Illinois's everyday etiquette:

> No person, however slender his pretensions to knighthood, or how long soever the time since his small-clothes were new, is addressed without the courteous epithet of "Sir," and this practice is observed by the members of the same family in their intercourse with each other; of course the females are in like manner honoured with "Madam," *Ubi tu Caius, ego Caia.* (ibid., 46–47)

Her droll reference to the Roman marriage vow—*Where you are Caius, I am Caia*—equates wife with husband, a characteristic of frontier egalitarianism. Burlend's life models the importance of both mates to the success of a small farm that they scratch out for themselves and hang on to by guile and threat when squatters try to oust them.

The tone of the journal speaks amply of Burlend's dismay at the squalor and isolation of her new home in an outland crawling with snakes and echoing with the cries of wolves. With crisp disdain, she lists the rustic amenities of their log cabin, starting with squared timbers caulked with clay and mud and proceeding to windowless walls, a rickety dining table bearing the too-grand name of "sideboard," small pavers outlining the hearth, a candlestick made from an ear of corn, and a clutch of garden implements in one corner, which she sums up as "exhibiting specimens of workmanship rather homely." (ibid., 49) The author's tone grows more impersonal as the privations—cold, inclement weather, poverty, and epidemics of mange and ague—erode her enthusiasm. Moments of suppressed mirth poke through the text, for instance, her husband's victorious return with a dead bird "as if he had slain some champion hydra of the forest." (ibid., 74) Her dinner guest examines the discarded head and claws and proclaims the bird a buzzard. In exasperation, she shifts to formal address of her reader: "If thou hast any intentions of being an emigrant, I cordially wish thee success." (ibid., 79)

A vast contrast to Burlend's succinct word picture of frontier pragmatism is *Down the Santa Fe Trail & into Mexico* (1982), the daybook of Susan Shelby Magoffin, treasured darling wife of a merchant who, for no clear purpose, packed her along on a difficult journey to the Southwest. In 1846, Magoffin—probably the first white female to traverse the Santa Fe Trail—set out with a trading expedition from Independence, Missouri, over the trail and south from Bent's Fort through Apache country to Chihuahua. By way of departure, the group moved southeast through Durango to Brownsville, Texas. Published in 1926, Magoffin's journal describes the delights and terrors of her journey. She picks wildflowers and cultivates other homey touches in their tent; however, torrential rains sweep through the earth floor like a stream, obliging her to roll up the rug and retreat to her cot. On July 4, on leaving Pawnee Rock, she and her husband are slightly injured after their carriage topples over a cliff and lies crushed on the rocky expanse below. He rushes to her aid:

> *Mi alma* [my dear] forgetting himself and entirely enlisted for my safety carried me in his arms to a shade tree, almost entirely without my knowledge, and rubing [sic] my face and hands with whiskey soon brought me entire to myself. (Magoffin 1982, 42)

On examining their bruises, she realizes how close they came to disaster. One vehicle is in disarray and the trail scattered with guns, baskets, bottles, books, bags, and crates. In better humor on August 29, she describes the beauty of a native chapel at the Pecos Pueblo north of Albuquerque and admires a Hispanic woman's beauty. On departure from Mexico in September 1847, Magoffin describes the mute evidence of war: "the bones of murdered countrymen, remains of burned wagons, all destroyed by Mexicans." (ibid., 259) Overall, Magoffin's self-centered commentary supplies oddments of interest to the historian, but offers the feminist little evidence of womanly courage or strength.

A lighthearted account of frontier life in the Nebraska Territory comes from Mollie Sanford, author of *Mollie: The Journal of Mollie Dorsey Sanford in Nebraska and Colorado Territories, 1857–1866* (1959). Settled on Gold Hill in 1861, she describes her attempts to make a homely interior more livable. She stretches an oiled wagon cover over the dirt floor, nails white curtains above the only panes of glass, makes a rocker out of a barrel and a bedstead from slats taken from a discarded packing crate, and blends her own furniture polish from linseed oil and brick dust. Six weeks later, her entry for March 15 strays from the previous burst of optimism and contentment:

> O! dear me! There's no use in trying to see much romance in this wild life. My cabin is made of black logs. There is a doorway but no door, not even a *hole* for a window. All the light I have when it is cold is what comes in around the stovepipe where the hole is too large. A blanket is hung up to the door, a rock tied on the ends to keep it down. (Sanford 1959, 153)

In the prudish style of nineteenth-century female diarists, Sanford conceals her pregnancy until the birth of her son, whom "God took . . . to his fold, this one pet lamb." (ibid., 157) On her first view of him, he is lying in a coffin at a neighbor's house, "dressed in one of the sweetest of the robes I had made, into whose stitches I had woven dreams of my angel baby." She discloses that she bears her "first great grief" without the support of her husband, who is away from home.

From frontier experiences along the St. Lawrence and Lake Ontario come two notable, sophisticated, and opinionated writings: Susanna Moodie's *Roughing It in the Bush* (1850) and *Life in the Clearings* (1853). Both works sold well in the United States and Europe and influenced streams of pioneers. Typical of Moodie's attention to detail is a conversation with an old woman who explains how to make salt-rising bread:

> I put a double handful of bran into a small pot, or kettle, but a jug will do, and a teaspoonful of salt; but mind you don't kill it with salt, for if you do, it won't rise. I then add as much warm water, at blood-heat, as will mix it into a stiff batter. I then put the jug in to a pan of warm water, and set it on the hearth near the fire, and keep it at the same heat until it rises, which it generally will do, it you attend to it, in two or three hours' time. When the bran cracks at the top and you see white bubbles rising through it, you may strain it into your flour, and lay your bread. (Moodie 1966, 88)

In a less domestic mode, Moodie comments on the rise in crime from an influx of runaway slaves, whom she fears do not make good citizens because of "previous habits and education." (Moodie 1959, 157) She expands this commentary on crime and prison to the particular case of Grace Marks, a murderer who killed a housekeeper. At the end of this passage and at frequent intervals throughout the text, Moodie appends original verse as a summary or homily on various matters, including her homeland, herding, moral education, alcoholism, and the evanescence of female beauty.

Paralleling the experiences of Susan Magoffin, Susanna Moodie, and Mollie Sanford, the life of Susan Louisa Moir Allison, a native of Ceylon and author of *A Pioneer Gentlewoman in British Columbia* (1976), opens in 1860 on a 14-year-old wife who journeys from Hope, British Columbia, east to the Similkameen

Valley, which lies just north of the United States border. At a new log house and store, her husband, Englishman John Fall Allison, trades with Indian trappers; she assists with milking and corral work and impresses him with her toughness and frontier spirit:

> As it was getting near snow-fly when the Hope Mountain was closed and all travel stopped with horses or cattle, my husband could only spend two weeks at home, most of the time seeing to the horses and rounding up the cattle for another trip with beef for the Westminster market, so I was virtually alone. (Allison 1991, 23)

In anticipation of Christmas, she keeps busy with decorations and home improvements, attends to trade with local Chinook Indians, and later accompanies her husband onto the ice to poison predatory wolves, coyotes, and wolverines with pork fat wrapped around powdered strychnine.

A spunky, upbeat narrative, *A Pioneer Gentlewoman* moves matter-of-factly through Allison's mothering of 14 children and the family's move farther inland to Okanagan Lake in 1879. She takes an interest in the Indians and comments:

> Their civilization is very much retarded by their passion for strong drink for in spite of the stringent Canadian laws, the Indians in the interior of B.C. can get all the Whiskey they want—and they do get it, the settlers are all too indolent and apathetic to try to put an end to practices that may eventually bring ruin on themselves as well as demoralizing the unfortunate Savages. (ibid., xii)

In widowhood, Allison turned to the privations of the Similkameen Indians to compose *In-Cow-Mas-Ket*, a long narrative poem about Native American lives and customs. In retrospect of their sufferings, she comments, "Now they are nearly all gone, just a down-trodden remnant, whose land is coveted by some of their white neighbours. . . . The White man has much to be ashamed of in his treatment of the rightful owners of the land." Her interest in their welfare, beginning in 1860, predates the white community's concern by nearly a century.

Another stout, unshakable frontierswoman, Alice Kirk Grierson, wife of Major General Benjamin H. Grierson, produced letters from 1866 to 1888 chronicling the creation of the Buffalo Soldiers, the army's all-black Tenth Cavalry, and the hardships of military families during protracted war with the Plains Indians. Published as *The Colonel's Lady on the Western Frontier: The Correspondence of Alice Kirk Grierson* (1989), the work achieved stature for its first-person commentary on army wives on the frontier. Primary among her concerns is the frequency of conception, which brought her Charlie, Kirkie, Robert, Edie, Harry, and Georgie. In a letter to Ben dated December 20, 1871, and postmarked Chicago, she acknowledges postpartum depression and the anguish brought on by Edie's death. She ponders, "Whether I am again a Mother or not, I hope you will agree with me, both in theory, and practice, that quiet home joys entirely within our reach, are just the best, and most to be sought after, of all earth's good gifts." (Grierson 1989, 63) The dreary round of postsocial demands, child care, and home schooling depletes her energies, filling her letters with a querulousness born of fatigue and depression.

Along this same midwestern outback, Isabella Bird, an unmarried English-woman returning alone from Hawaii to England by way of Colorado, crossed the Rocky Mountains in 1873. Her dispatches to a British weekly, *Leisure Hour*, were the basis for *A Lady's Life in the Rocky Mountains* (1897), a popular personal narrative that went through eight editions by 1912 and was translated into French. An unconventional traveler in dress and expectation, Bird records her dependence on a worn umbrella, Hawaiian riding dress, and handkerchief over her face. To stave off sunburn, she ties her umbrella cover over her hat. Accompanying her is a gaunt and tattered guide wearing mismatched shoes and riding an equally lanky, unkempt mule. Her pack leaks; her bedroll is untidy, but the substance of her travels is in no way compromised. In spite of her untoward appearance, Bird studies the spectacular horizon of Estes Park with no thought toward making a fashion statement or adhering to an arbitrary Western dress code.

Although generally uncritical of people and morals, especially those of the outlaw "Mountain Jim," Bird does not stint on her criticism of the social stigma that demoralizes Native Americans. On her way to Denver, she travels through a Ute encampment sullied by "a disorderly and dirty huddle of lodges, ponies, men, squaws, children, skins, bones, and raw meat." (Bird 1960, 183) Like a peeved schoolmarm, she verbally chastises Americans for degrading the native to "pauperism, devoid of the very first elements of civilization," for allowing fraud and corruption to overrun the Indian Agency, and for introducing Indians to "vitriolated whisky." (ibid., 184) Bristling with disapproval and marked pomposity, she declares, "Americans specially love superlatives. The phrases 'biggest in the world,' 'finest in the world,' are on all lips." (ibid.) She concludes that President Rutherford B. Hayes must take action to reverse the situation lest he administer a government "composed of the 'biggest scoundrels' in the world." (ibid., 185)

A realistic experience similar to those of Alice Grierson and Isabella Bird marks the writing of Agnes Morley Cleaveland, author of a good-natured, informative memoir, *No Life for a Lady*. Published in 1941, the work describes growing up in New Mexico in the mid-1880s. Her father, manager of the Maxwell Land Grant and editor of the *Cimarron News and Press*, tramples on local interests with a series of crusading articles about opportunism on the frontier. As a result, his partner, F. J. Tolby, is assassinated. Lawlessness in many forms rattles the citizenry: a local villain dumps the printing press into the river, deliberate stampeding of livestock destroys a life's savings, and run-of-the-mill shootings are a ritual of cattle country. Of outlaws, she comments on the swift arrival of an unidentified stranger who needed a meal, fresh horse, and change of hats. In payment, the man leaves the author his horse. She recalls that his departure prefaced many such in-and-out encounters with the lawless of western Socorro Country, which "because of its wildness, was sanctuary to many a man 'on the dodge.'" (Cleaveland 1941, 38)

From the perspective of adulthood in the twentieth century, Cleaveland summarizes the changes that sweep over the country. The first change affects the land itself:

> It was the barbed wire that dealt the first blow to the open range. Even before the war produced its shortage of cowhands, barbed wire began to supplant horseflesh in the business of keeping cattle within bounds. Everybody fenced in as much territory as he could afford barbed wire to stretch around. (ibid., 320)

She concludes that the coming of civilization sets off a new type of lawlessness that supplants the rustlers and bushwhackers of wilder times. The new brigand is the fence cutter. The victim, she adds, has no choice but "to resort to Colt's law." Another jolt to the cattle rancher is the establishment of National Forests, land formerly taken for granted, which, under the control of Uncle Sam, could be used only by permit.

An autobiography set on the Canadian outback in the last quarter of the nineteenth century comes from Nellie Letitia Mooney McClung, author of *Clearing in the West* (1935). A feminist from Chatsworth, Ontario, she wrote numerous works about prairie life in Manitoba, where she taught school. Recalling how her family set out for the wild, she exults:

> Never had I experienced as great a moment as came to me, when the oxen's heads were turned west on Portage Avenue and the long trail received us unto itself. I felt that life was leading me by the hand and I followed on light feet. We would travel with the sun, until we came to that flower starred prairie where no stone would impede the plow; where strawberries would redden the oxen's fetlocks; where eight-hundred acres of rich black soil was waiting for us. (McClung 1965, 56)

Prior to her marriage to Wes McClung, her roseate dreams of a lush prairie home carry her on the long journey, which halts at the Hudson's Bay store for supplies. An episodic, often sentimental narrative similar to the writings of Laura Ingalls Wilder, *Clearing in the West* offers candid glimpses of girlhood on the prairie.

A contemporary of McClung, Dr. Mary Canaga Rowland wrote *As Long as Life: The Memoirs of a Frontier Woman Doctor* (1995), which opens during her childhood and schooling in Indianola, Nebraska, and follows her in early marriage to Herndon, Kansas, where her husband, Dr. J. Walter Rowland, had a small medical practice. She graduated in 1901 from the Woman's Medical College of Kansas City, Missouri, and returned to Herndon to practice. In the first weeks of her daughter Nellie's life, Walter was murdered in the local store. Rowland moves briskly over the details, explaining that she reopened her practice when her child was a month old. The lengthy court case, appeals, pardon, and climate of gossip concerning the killing consume much of Rowland's attention. In the final two decades of her career, she serves the Chemawa Indian school at Forest Grove, Oregon. In the final chapters, she outlines some of the frontier's crude methods of treatment for broken bones, cholera, convulsions, influenza, and childbirth. The forthright justification of her methods and her outspoken support of threatened, battered, abused, and suffering women prefigures the feminist writings nearly a century after her frontier experiences.

A contemporary of Dr. Rowland, Sophie Trupin, narrates her own tale of womanhood in a volume of distinct essays—*Dakota Diaspora: Memoirs of a Jewish*

Homesteader (1988), the story of a family of Russian Jews who emigrate in 1908 to "Nordokota," where

> Each was a Moses in his own right leading his people out of the land of bondage—out of czarist Russia, out of anti-Semitic Poland, out of Romania and Galicia. Each was leading his family to a promised land; only this was no land flowing with milk and honey—no land of olive trees and vineyards. (Trupin 1988, cover)

In hills and valleys that roll endlessly with undulations of steel gray grass, Trupin ponders her father's vision of land free to any purchaser, even a Jew. In dignity and peace, he meets the challenge of physical toil and comforts his wife, who had expected more than a humble sod hut and barn, rough-hewn furnishings, and endless chores. Trupin captures the paradox of her father's hope and her mother's despair, "How can one bring the close, intimate life of the Russian *shtetl* to the vast open wilderness of the prairie?" (ibid., 39) In the epilogue to her lyrical memoir, she recalls the misery of adjusting to the plains. After weighing "the bad and the good, the weak and the strong," she concludes that she would not change her parents. "They had integrity, honesty, fidelity, character, compassion." She looks from adult eyes and remembers, "I wanted them to be perfect, but they were only human." (ibid., 149) (Alderson and Smith 1942; Allison 1991; Backhouse 1995; Bird 1960; Burlend and Burlend 1987; de Baca 1989; Cather 1977, 1991; Cleaveland 1941; Davidson and Wagner-Martin 1995; Gipson 1956; Grierson 1989; Levenson 1973; Magoffin 1982; McClung 1965; Miller 1995; Moodie 1959, 1966; Morris 1994; Piekarski 1988; Rowland 1995; Sanford 1959; Schlissel, Ruiz, and Munk 1988; Story 1967; Trupin 1988; Ulrich 1990; Wallace 1963; Wilder 1971a–h; Young 1991, 1992)

See also Asian Americans on the frontier; Austin, Mary Hunter; captivity motif; Cather, Willa; Gipson, Fred; L'Amour, Louis; *My Ántonia; O Pioneers!;* Rawlings, Marjorie Kinnan; West, Jessamyn; Wilder, Laura Ingalls; Winnemucca, Sarah.

WRIGHT, HAROLD BELL

A vivid local colorist and Christian apologist, Harold Bell Wright is best known for inspirational novels and romances reflecting the demise of the wilderness and the rise of an industrialized society. Central to his work is an emphasis on the pioneer stereotype of self-sufficient woodsman, settler, or adventurer, a thematic outgrowth of his family's pride in their pioneer forebears. Born in Rome, New York, he attended Hiram College in Hiram, Ohio, but ended his studies in his junior year because of eye strain and pneumonia. He settled in Pierce City, Missouri, and, without theological training, initiated a ten-year ministry to isolated people.

While working at a pastorate at a Disciples of Christ church in Pittsburg, Kansas, Wright discovered that he had contracted tuberculosis. While his strength held out, he preached at churches in Kansas City and Lebanon, Missouri, and in Redlands, California. In 1896, when diseased lungs impeded continued denominational service, he took the train to the end of the line at Marionville in southwestern Missouri, rode horseback into the hills, and stopped at the flooded banks of the White River. That summer, he boarded with homesteaders John and Anna Ross near Mutton Hollow, indulged in the relaxing hobby of landscape painting, and conducted an informal ministry among hill people. The location and relationships were so beneficial to his health, vigor, and outlook that he returned annually for eight years for summer respites.

Wright's interest in Ozarkans precipitated his first major novel, *The Shepherd of the Hills* (1907), in which the Rosses appear as the characters Old Matt and Aunt Mollie. Living close to valley people placed Wright in a sanctuary—a sharing community where he could refine methods of problem solving and seek solace and fresh air. Local sufferings during the drought of 1902 and resultant famine gave him material for the novel, which he intended to read serially to his congregation. The work became the turning point of his successful career change to inspirational fiction. He wrote plays and 19 sentimental novels, which appealed to rural and small-town readers for their predictable plots, clearcut Christian ethics, and understated examples of faith in action. In 1920, he and his second wife settled at Quiet Hills Farm in Escondido outside San Diego, California, where he lived until a month before his death in 1944 in a La Jolla hospital.

Wright's most popular works include *The Call of Dan Matthews* (1909), *When a Man's a Man* (1916), *The Uncrowned King* (1910), and the best-selling *The Winning of Barbara Worth* (1911), source of the 1926 Samuel Goldwyn movie, which starred Ronald Colman, Velma Banks, and Gary Cooper. *The Shepherd of the Hills*, which sold 2.5 million copies in Wright's lifetime, is a reflective framework narrative dependent on a pervasive motif in frontier literature—flight from the ruined relationships, stifling cities, or polluted surroundings of the East. His characters thrive from a simple pioneer lifestyle in a cohesive community in an untainted woodland setting. To achieve maximum separation from urban behaviors and values, the novelist employs an uncluttered style and mountain dialect and folkways. With straightforward, moralistic plot, the story details the escape of Daniel Howitt, a scholar and man of God, to the Mutton Hollow community. Wright's vignettes depict uncomplicated gatherings such as the clientele of the Matthews gristmill, where mountaineers travel by horseback with sacks of grain and wait their turn at the mill while sharing news with distant folk or pitching horseshoes or competing in shooting or wrestling matches.

At the mill and other common meeting places, Howitt, a newcomer to the Ozarks, assesses the needs and emotional trials of local people and offers encouragement and spiritual advice. When Parson Bigelow fails to make the circuit ride to the Forks church, Howatt speaks to the congregation and undertakes the role of unofficial doctor, consultant, and religious leader. After he is accepted as friend and spiritual shepherd, the people call him Dad or Father Howitt. When he feels secure in local folks' trust, he admits that he settled among them to elude a troubled past—the suicide attempt of his son, an artist. In his confession, he proclaims that the spirit of the Ozarks rekindled his faith. A reunion with his son, who survived and moved to a mountainside cave, precedes the son's death. According to the narrator, both the son and Howitt are buried among the mountaineers, who loved them for human strengths and in spite of their frailties. Paramount filmed the novel in 1941, starring John Wayne, Beulah Bondi, and Ward Bond. Designed to appeal to rural audiences, the movie was a perennial favorite.

An outdoor drama drawn from *The Shepherd of the Hills* attracts 200,000 tourists annually to Branson, Missouri, where readers hike into the hills to see Matthew's cabin and Inspiration Point. Residents discovered that visitors identified with Dad Howatt's personal quandary and his involvement with the homesteader's crises. In 1909, reader curiosity about Old Matt's Cabin led to the creation of a resort, complete with museum and park—all mirroring the reassuring country values of love, labor, candor, and spirituality. At the amphitheater, built in 1957 on the legend's site, the play has run since 1960, requiring 100 players, most of whom are natives of the Ozarks. ("Arcadian" 1996; Charles 1996; Ehrlich and Carruth 1982; Hart 1983; Kunitz 1942; "Outdoor Drama" 1996; Rainey 1996; "Shepherd" 1907; Trent et al. 1946; "Welcome" 1995; Wright 1907)

See also theater of the frontier.

A TIMELINE OF FRONTIER LITERATURE

Note: The date to the left of each title is the first date of publication of the work, not the date of its completion. In some cases, a century or more may separate the manuscript from its appearance in print.

1532 Bartolomé de Las Casas, *A History of the Indies*

1566 Bartolomé de Las Casas, *A Short Account of the Destruction of the Indies*
Diego de Landa, *Yucatan before and after the Conquest*

1582 Richard Hakluyt, *The Principal Navigations, Voyages, and Discoveries of the English Nation*

1586 Thomas Harriot, *A Briefe and True Report of the New Found Land of Virginia*

1601 Antonio Galvano, *Discoveries of the World*

1608 Captain John Smith, *A True Relation of such occurrences and accidents of noate as hath hapned in Virginia since the first planting of that Collony*

1609 Hernando de Soto, *Virginia Richly Valued by the Description of Florida*

1624 Captain John Smith, *Generall Historie of Virginia, New England and the Summer Isles*

1658 anonymous, *May-Day*

1665 anonymous, *Ye Beare and Ye Cubb*

1682 Mary White Rowlandson, *The Narrative of the Captivity and Restoration of Mrs. Mary White Rowlandson*

1707 John Williams, *The Redeemed Captive Returning to Zion*

1764 anonymous, "The Paxtoniade"

1766 George Cockings, *The Conquest of Canada*
Robert Rogers, *Ponteach*

1767 Andrew Barton, *The Disappointment, or The Force of Credulity*
Thomas Godfrey, *The Prince of Parthia*

1771 Hugh Henry Brackenridge and Philip Freneau, *The Rising Glory of America*

1778 Jonathan Carver, *Travels through the Interior Parts of North America*

1779 Captain James Cook, *The Explorations of Captain James Cook in the Pacific as Told by Selections of His Own Journals, 1768–1779*

1784 John Filson, *The Adventures of Col. Daniel Boon [sic], Containing Narrative of the Wars of Kentucke*
Philip Freneau, "The Dying Indian"

1787 Joel Barlow, *The Vision of Columbus*
Royall Tyler, *The Contrast*

1788 Philip Freneau, "The Indian Burying Ground"
David Humphrey, *Essay on the Life of the Honorable Major-General Israel Putnam*

1791 William Bartram, *Travels*

1802 Joseph Croswell, *A New World Planted*

1807 Joel Barlow, *Columbiad*

1808 James N. Barker, *The Indian Princess or La Belle Sauvage*

1809 Everard Hall, *Nolens Volens; or The Biter Bit*
Washington Irving, *A History of New York, from the Beginning of the World to the End of the Dutch Dynasty*

1810 William Cooper, *A Guide in the Wilderness or the History of the First Settlements in the Western Counties of New York*

1813 Daniel Bryan, *The Mountain Muse: Comprising the Adventures of Daniel Boone; and the Power of Virtuous and Refined Beauty*

1819 John Heckewelder, *Account of the History, Manners, and Customs of the Indian Nations Who Once Inhabited Pennsylvania and the Neighboring States*

1820 Samuel L. Metcalfe, *A Collection of Some of the Most Interesting Narratives of Indian Warfare in the West, Containing an Account of the Adventures of Daniel Boone, One of the First Settlers of Kentucky*

1822 Washington Irving, "Rip Van Winkle," "The Legend of Sleepy Hollow," and "The Spectre Bridegroom, A Traveller's Tale"

1823 James Fenimore Cooper, *The Pioneers or, The Sources of the Susquehanna*
Joseph Hutton, *The Falls of Niagara*
Stephen Harriman Long, *From Pittsburgh to the Rocky Mountains*

1824 James N. Barker, *Superstition*
Washington Irving, "The Devil and Tom Walker"
———, *Tales of a Traveller*
Lemuel Sawyer, *Blackbeard*

1825 Samuel Woodworth and John Davies, *The Forest Rose, or American Farmers*

1826 James Fenimore Cooper, *The Last of the Mohicans*

1827 James Fenimore Cooper, *The Prairie*

1828 William Dunlop, *A Trip to Niagara or Travellers in America*
Thomas Flynn, *Rip Van Winkle, or The Demons of the Catskill Mountains! A National Drama*

Washington Irving, *The Life and Voyages of Christopher Columbus*
John Augustus Stone, *Metamora, or the Last of the Wampanoags*

1830   George Washington Parke Custis, *Pocahontas, or The Settlers of Virginia*
Adam Kidd, *The Huron Chief*
Joseph Smith, *Book of Mormon*

1831   Washington Irving, *Voyages and Discoveries of the Companions of Columbus*
James Kirke Paulding, *The Lion of the West*

1833   *The Autobiography of Black Hawk*
Mathew St. Clair Clarke, *The Life and Adventures of Colonel David Crockett of West Tennessee*

1834   Thomas Chilton, *Narrative of the Life of David Crockett of the State of Tennessee*
Davy Crockett, *Narrative of the Life of David Crockett of the State of Tennessee*
Samuel G. Drake, *Biography and History of the Indians of North America*

1835   Robert Bird, *The Infidel*
Davy Crockett, *An Account of Colonel Crockett's Tour to the North and Down East*
——, *Crockett Almanack*
Washington Irving, *A Tour of the Prairies*
William Gilmore Simms, *The Yemassee: A Romance of Carolina*

1836   Washington Irving, *Astoria*
Richard Penn Smith, *Colonel Crockett's Exploits and Adventures in Texas*
Narcissa Prentiss Whitman, *My Journal, 1836*

1837   Robert Bird, *Nick of the Woods*
Washington Irving, *The Adventures of Captain Bonneville, U. S. A.*
Robert Dale Owen, *Pocahontas*

1838   John James Audubon, *The Birds of America*
——. *Synopsis of the Birds of America*

1839   Charles Darwin, *Voyage of the Beagle*
Thomas Farnham, *Travels in the Great Western Prairies*

1840   James Clyman, *Journal of a Mountain Man*

1841   John James Audubon, *American Ornithological Biography*
George Catlin, *Letters and Notes on the Manners, Customs and Condition of the North American Indians during Eight Years' Travel amongst the Wildest Tribes of Indians of North America*
James Fenimore Cooper, *The Deerslayer*
——, *The Pathfinder: or The Inland Sea*
Thomas Jefferson Farnham, *Travels in the Great Western Prairies*
J. B. Jones, *Wild Western Scenes; A Narrative of Adventures in the Western Wilderness, Forty Years Ago; Wherein the Conduct of Daniel Boone, the Great American Pioneer, Is Particularly Described*

1843   James Fenimore Cooper, *Wyandotte*

1844   George Catlin, *North American Indian Portfolio: Hunting Scenes and Amusements of the Rocky Mountains and Prairies of America*

1845   John James Audubon, *The Viviparous Quadrupeds of North America*
       John C. Fremont, *Report of the Exploring Expeditions of 1842 and 1843–44*
       Lansford W. Hastings, *The Emigrants' Guide to Oregon and California*

1846   Eliza Farnham, *Life in Prairie Land*
       James Fenimore Cooper, *The Redskins*
       Thomas Jefferson Farnham, *Life and Adventures in California*
       Francis Parkman, *The Oregon Trail: Sketches of Prairie and Rocky Mountain Life*
       William Henry Rhodes, *Theodosia, The Pirate's Prisoner*
       J. M. Shively, *Route and Distances to Oregon and California*

1847   David H. Coyner, *The Lost Trappers*
       Henry Wadsworth Longfellow, *Evangeline, a Tale of Arcadie*
       Benjamin Webster, *The Golden Farmer*

1848   Rebecca Burlend and Edward Burlend, *A True Picture of Emigration*
       Charlotte Barnes Conner, *Forest Princess*

1849   Mary H. Eastman, *Dacotah, or Life and Legends of the Sioux around Fort Snelling*
       Edgar Allan Poe, "Eldorado"

1850   John Woodhouse Audubon, *Audubon's Western Journal, 1849–1850*
       Charles Burke, *Rip Van Winkle, a Legend of the Catskills*
       Susanna Moodie, *Roughing It in the Bush*
       Anna Cora Mowatt, *Fashion*

1851   Lewis Henry Morgan, *League of the Ho-de-no-sau-nee or Iroquois*
       Francis Parkman, *The History of the Conspiracy of Pontiac*

1853   Joseph Glover Baldwin, *The Flush Times of California*
       Susanna Moodie, *Life in the Clearings*

1854   Timothy Flint, *The First White Man of the West, or the Life and Exploits of Col. Dan'l. Boone, the First Settler of Kentucky; Interspersed with Incidents in the Early Annals of the Country*
       John P. Sherburne, *Through Indian Country to California*

1855   John Brougham, *Po-Ca-Hon-Tas, or The Gentle Savage*
       Cabeza de Vaca, *The Castaways*
       Washington Irving, *Wolfert's Roost and Miscellanies*
       Henry Wadsworth Longfellow, *The Courtship of Miles Standish*

1856   Thomas D. Bonner, *The Life of James Pierson Beckwourth, Mountaineer, Scout, Pioneer and Chief of the Crow Nation*
       William H. Prescott, *History of the Conquest of Mexico*

1857   W. H. Bogart, *Daniel Boone and the Hunters of Kentucky*
       Henry Rowe Schoolcraft, *Historical and Statistical Information Respecting the History, Condition and Prospects of the Indian Tribes of the United States*

A TIMELINE OF FRONTIER LITERATURE

1858   Tom Taylor, *Our American Cousin*

1859   Dion Boucicault, *The Octoroon*
        Rev. R. B. Stratton, *Captivity of the Oatman Girls: Being an Interesting Narrative of Life among the Apache and Mohave Indians*

1861   Alexander McLachlan, "The Emigrant"

1862   Ambrose Bierce, *The Birth of the Rail*
        James Fenimore Cooper, *The Last of the Mohicans*

1864   Joseph Glover Baldwin, *Ebb Tide*
        Mark Twain, "The Killing of Julius Caesar 'Localized'"

1865   Francis Parkman, *Pioneers of France in the New World*
        Mark Twain, "The Celebrated Jumping Frog of Calaveras County"

1866   Mordecai M. Noah, *She Would Be a Soldier, or The Plains of Chippewa*

1867   George Catlin, *Catlin's Notes of Eight Years' Travels and Residence in Europe*
        ——, *My Life among the Indians*
        ——, *Okeepa, a Religious Ceremony, and Other Customs of the Mandans*
        Francis Parkman, *The Jesuits in North America in the Seventeenth Century*

1868   George Catlin, *Last Rambles amongst the Indians of the Rocky Mountains and the Andes*
        Bret Harte, "The Luck of Roaring Camp"
        Joaquin Miller, *Specimens*

1869   Bret Harte, "The Outcasts of Poker Flat"
        Joaquin Miller, *Joaquin et al.*
        Francis Parkman, *La Salle and the Discovery of the Great West*

1870   Mark Twain, "The Noble Red Man"

1871   Edward Eggleston, *The Hoosier Schoolmaster*
        Joaquin Miller, *Song of the Sierras*
        Catherine Parr Traill, *The Backwoods of Canada*

1872   Ambrose Bierce, *The Fiend's Delight*
        ——, *Nuggets and Dust Panned Out in California*
        Frank H. Murdoch, *Davy Crockett*
        Mark Twain, *Roughing It*

1873   Joaquin Miller, *Unwritten History: Life among the Modocs*

1874   Ambrose Bierce, *Cobwebs from an Empty Skull*
        George Armstrong Custer, *My Life on the Plains*
        Francis Parkman, *The Old Régime in Canada*

1875   Thomas C. Battey, *The Life and Adventures of a Quaker among the Indians*

1876   Bret Harte, *The Two Men of Sandy Bar*
        Bret Harte and Mark Twain, *Ah Sin, the Heathen Chinee*

1877 Bret Harte, "At the Mission of San Carmel"
——, *The Story of a Mine and Other Tales*
Joaquin Miller, *The Danites in the Sierras*
Francis Parkman, *Count Frontenac and New France under Louis XIV*

1881 Bronson Crocker Howard, *Shenandoah*
Oliver Otis Howard, *Nez Perce Joseph*
Helen Hunt Jackson, *A Century of Dishonor*
Joaquin Miller, *Forty-Nine*
——, *An Oregon Idyll*
——, *Tally Ho!*

1882 Richard Irving Dodge, *Our Wild Indians: Thirty-Three Years' Personal Experience among the Red Men of the Great West*

1883 Mark Twain, *Life on the Mississippi*
Sarah Winnemucca, *Life among the Piutes, Their Wrongs and Claims*

1884 Henry B. Carrington, *The Indian Question, an Address*
Edward S. Ellis, *The Life and Time of Col. Daniel Boone, Hunter, Soldier, and Pioneer*
Helen Hunt Jackson, *Ramona*
Francis Parkman, *Montcalm and Wolfe*

1885 Elizabeth Bacon Custer, *Boots and Saddles: Life in Dakota with General Custer*
Charles A. Siringo, *A Texas Cowboy, or, Fifteen Years on the Hurricane Deck of a Spanish Cow Pony*

1887 Elizabeth Bacon Custer, *Tenting on the Plains*

1888 King David Kalakaua, *The Legends and Myths of Hawaii*
Theodore Roosevelt, *Ranch Life and the Hunting Trail*

1889 George Bird Grinnell, *Pawnee Hero Stories and Folk Tales*
H. H. McConnell, *Five Years a Cavalryman or, Sketches of Regular Army Life on the Texas Frontier, 1866–1871*
Theodore Roosevelt, *The Winning of the West*

1890 *The Autobiography of Joseph Jefferson*
Elizabeth Bacon Custer, *Following the Guidon*

1891 Ambrose Bierce, *Tales of Soldiers and Civilians*
Hamlin Garland, *Main-Travelled Roads*
Charles Hoyt, *A Trip to Chinatown*
Joaquin Miller, *Shadows of Shasta*

1892 Ambrose Bierce, *Black Beetles in Amber*
——, *The Monk and the Hangman's Daughter*
C. Falkenhorst, *With Cortéz in Mexico*
George Bird Grinnell, *Blackfoot Lodge Tales*
Robert Louis Stevenson, *Across the Plains*

1893 Ambrose Bierce, *Can Such Things Be?*
Augustus Thomas, *In Mizzoura*

1894   Gertrude Atherton, "The Wash-Tub Mail"
Bret Harte, *A Protégée of Jack Hamlin's and Other Stories*
Joaquin Miller, *The Illustrated History of Montana*
John Muir, *The Mountains of California*
Francis Parkman, *Half-Century of Conflict*

1895   Mark Twain, "Fenimore Cooper's Literary Offenses"

1896   *The Life of John Wesley Hardin as Written by Himself*
Owen Wister, *Red Men and White*

1897   Isabella Bird, *A Lady's Life in the Rocky Mountains*

1898   Stephen Crane, "The Bride Comes to Yellow Sky"

1899   Ambrose Bierce, *Fantastic Fables*
Augustus Thomas, *Arizona*

1900   William F. Drannan, *Thirty-One Years on the Plains and in the Mountains*
       or, The Last Voice from the Plains
Jack London, *Daughter of the Snows*
——, *The Son of the Wolf: Tales of the Far North*

1901   John Muir, *Our National Parks*

1902   Charles Alexander Eastman, *Indian Boyhood*
Hamlin Garland, *The Captain of the Gray Horse Troop*
Bret Harte, *Condensed Novels*
——, *The Poetical Works of Bret Harte*
Jim McIntire, *Early Days in Texas, A Trip to Hell and Heaven*
Theodore Roosevelt, *Rough Riders*
Owen Wister, *The Virginian: A Horseman of the Plains*

1903   Andy Adams, *The Log of a Cowboy: A Narrative of the Old Trail Days*
Mary Hunter Austin, *The Land of Little Rain*
Ambrose Bierce, *Shapes of Clay*
Zane Grey, *Betty Zane*
Jack London, *The Call of the Wild*
Robert Service, "The Shooting of Dan McGrew"
Frank E. Stevens, *The Black Hawk War*
Walter Woods, *Billy the Kid*

1904   Mary Hunter Austin, *The Basket Woman*
William F. Cody, *The Adventures of Buffalo Bill*
Life of Tom Horn
Jack London, *White Fang*
Thomas Henry Tibbles, *Buckskin and Blanket Days*

1905   Mary Hunter Austin, *Isidro*
David Belasco, *The Girl of the Golden West*
Robert Service, "The Cremation of Sam McGee"

1906   David Belasco, *The Rose of the Rancho*
Ambrose Bierce, *The Devil's Dictionary*
——, *Shadow on the Dial*

1906 *continued*
Geronimo's Story of His Life
Zane Grey, *Spirit of the Border*
Dan Marble, *Sam Patch, the Jumper of Niagara Falls*
William Vaughn Moody, *The Great Divide*

1907 *The Life and Adventures of Nat Love, Better Known in the Cattle Country*
as Deadwood Dick
O. Henry, *Heart of the West*
Oliver Otis Howard, *My Life and Experiences among Our Hostile Indians*
Robert Service, *Songs of a Sourdough*
Harold Bell Wright, *The Shepherd of the Hills*

1908 Mary Hunter Austin, *Santa Lucia*
Zane Grey, *The Last of the Plainsmen*
Oliver Otis Howard, *Famous Indian Chiefs I Have Known*
Jack London, "To Build a Fire"
William Lightfoot Visscher, *The Pony Express: A Thrilling and Truthful*
History

1909 Mary Hunter Austin, *Lost Borders*
Zane Grey, *The Last Trail*
John Muir, "Stickeen"

1910 Mary Hunter Austin, *The Arrow-Maker*
Hamlin Garland, *Cavanagh, Forest Ranger: A Romance of the Mountain West*
Zane Grey, *The Heritage of the Desert*
John Lomax, *Cowboy Songs and Other Frontier Ballads*

1911 Charles Alexander Eastman, *The Soul of the Indian: An Interpretation*
John Muir, *My First Summer in the Sierra*
Robert Service, *The Trail of '98: A Northland Romance*

1912 Ambrose Bierce, *Collected Works*
Zane Grey, *Riders of the Purple Sage*
John Muir, *Yosemite*
O. E. Rölvaag, *Letters from America*
Charles A. Siringo, *The Cowboy Detective*

1913 Willa Cather, *O Pioneers!*
Zane Grey, *Desert Gold*
Oscar Michaux, *The Conquest: The Story of a Negro Pioneer*
John Muir, *The Story of My Boyhood and Youth*

1914 Charles Alexander Eastman, *Indian Scout Craft and Lore*
John Reed, *Insurgent Mexico*
O. E. Rölvaag, *On Forgotten Paths*
Osborne Russell, *Journal of a Trapper*
Elinore Pruitt Stewart, *Letters of a Woman Homesteader*

1915 Mariano Azuela, *The Underdogs: A Novel of the Mexican Revolution*
George Bird Grinnell, *The Fighting Cheyenne*
Constance D'Arcy Mackay, *Plays of the Pioneers*
John Muir, *Travels in Alaska*

——, *Letters to a Friend*
John G. Neihardt, *The Song of Hugh Glass*
Charles A. Siringo, *Two Evil Isms: Pinkertonism and Anarchism*
Elinore Pruitt Stewart, *Letters on an Elk Hunt*

1916   Charles Alexander Eastman, *From the Deep Woods to Civilization*
John Muir, *A Thousand Mile Walk to the Gulf*
Paul Radin, *The Winnebago Tribe*

1917   Zane Grey, *Wildfire*
John Lomax, *Songs of the Cattle Trail and Cow Camp*

1918   Mary Hunter Austin, *The Trail Book*
Willa Cather, *My Ántonia*
Philip Moeller, *Pokey, or The Beautiful Legend of the Amorous Indian*
John Muir, *Steep Trails*

1919   Percy MacKaye, *Rip Van Winkle, a Folk Opera*
John G. Neihardt, *The Song of Three Friends*
Paul Radin, *The Genetic Relationship of the North American Indian Languages*
Charles A. Siringo, *A Lone Star Cowboy*
——, *A Song Companion of a Lone Star Cowboy*

1920   Paul Green, *The Last of the Lowries: A Play of the Croatan Outlaws of Robeson County*
Paul Radin, *The Autobiography of a Winnebago Indian*
O. E. Rölvaag, *Two Fools*
Charles A. Siringo, *A History of Billy the Kid*

1921   Hamlin Garland, *Daughter of the Middle Border*
James B. Gillett, *Six Years with the Texas Rangers, 1875–1881*
Zane Grey, *To the Last Man*
Ted Paramore, "The Ballad of Yukon Jake"

1922   Zane Grey, *The Vanishing American*
Katherine Anne Porter, "María Concepción"
O. E. Rölvaag, *Concerning Our Heritage*
——, *The Ship of Longing*
Stewart Edward White, *Daniel Boone: Wilderness Scout*

1923   Willa Cather, *A Lost Lady*
Zane Grey, *The Thundering Herd*
George Bird Grinnell, *The Cheyenne Indians*
D. H. Lawrence, *Birds, Beasts and Flowers*
——, "The Spirit of Place"
——, *Studies in Classic American Literature*
Lula Vollmer, *Sun-Up*

1924   *The Autobiography of Mark Twain*
Johan Bojer, *The Emigrants*
William Norment Cox, *The Scuffletown Outlaws: A Tragedy of the Lowrie Gang*
Edna Ferber, *So Big*
Zane Grey, *Call of the Canyon*

1925   Paul Green, *The No'Count Boy*
       ——, *Quare Medicine*
       John G. Neihardt, *The Song of the Indian Wars*
       Hector St. John de Crèvecoeur, *American Landscapes*

1926   Walter Noble Burns, *The Saga of Billy the Kid*
       Edna Ferber, *Show Boat*
       George Bird Grinnell, *By Cheyenne Campfires*
       Kit Carson's Autobiography
       D. H. Lawrence, *The Plumed Serpent*
       Annie Oakley, *The Story of My Life*

1927   Willa Cather, *Death Comes for the Archbishop*
       Courtney Ryley Cooper, *Annie Oakley, Woman at Arms*
       Paul Green, *In Abraham's Bosom*
       Stuart N. Lake, *Wyatt Earp, Frontier Marshall*
       D. H. Lawrence, *Mornings in Mexico*
       Paul Radin, *The Genetic Relationship of the North American Indian Languages*
       ——, *Primitive Man as Philosopher*
       O. E. Rölvaag, *Giants in the Earth: A Saga of the Prairie*
       Charles A. Siringo, *Riata and Spurs*

1928   Mary Hunter Austin, *Children Sing in the Far West*
       Frank Dobie, *Apache Gold and Yaqui Silver*
       George Bird Grinnell, *Two Great Scouts and Their Pawnee Battalion*

1929   Britton Davis, *The Truth about Geronimo*
       Edna Ferber, *Cimarron*
       Marquis James, *The Raven*
       Oliver La Farge, *Laughing Boy*
       O. E. Rölvaag, *Peder Victorious*

1930   Frank Dobie, *Coronado's Children*
       ——, *A Vaquero of the Brush Country*
       Ethan Allan Hitchcock, *A Traveller in Indian Territory*

1931   Mary Hunter Austin, *Starry Adventure*
       Grey Owl, *The Men of the Last Frontier*
       O. E. Rölvaag, *Their Fathers' God*
       Luther Standing Bear, *My Indian Boyhood*

1932   Paul Green, *The Laughing Pioneer*
       Zane Grey, *Robber's Roost*
       Bernice Kelly Harris, *Ca'line*
       Frank B. Linderman, *Pretty-Shield, Medicine Woman of the Crows*
       John G. Neihardt, *Black Elk Speaks: The Life Story of a Holy Man of the Oglala Sioux*
       Sarah Eleanor Bayliss Royce, *A Frontier Lady: Recollections of the Gold Rush and Early California*
       Carl Sandburg, "Buffalo Bill"
       Laura Ingalls Wilder, *Little House in the Big Woods*

1933   Mary Hunter Austin, *Earth Horizon*
William Rose Benét, *Golden Fleece*
Rosemary and Stephen Vincent Benét, *A Book of Americans*
Paul Radin, *Method and Theory of Ethnology*
Laura Ingalls Wilder, *Farmer Boy*

1934   Mary Hunter Austin, *One-Smoke Stories*
Frank Dobie, *The Mustang*
Zane Grey, *Blue Feather*
Alan Lomax and John Lomax, *American Ballads and Folk Songs*
Scott O'Dell, *Woman of Spain: A Story of Old California*
Paul Radin, *The Story of the American Indian*
Luther Standing Bear, *Stories of the Sioux*

1935   H. L. Davis, *Honey in the Horn*
Edna Ferber, *Come and Get It*
Fred Koch, Jr., *Wash Carver's Mouse Trap*
Nellie Letitia Mooney McClung, *Clearing in the West*
John Muir, *The Cruise of the Corwin*
John G. Neihardt, *The Song of the Messiah*
Grey Owl, *Sajo and the Beaver People*
——, *Pilgrims of the Wild*
Laura Ingalls Wilder, *Little House on the Prairie*

1936   Walter Dumaux Edmonds, *Drums along the Mohawk*
Conrad Richter, *Early Americana and Other Stories*

1937   Paul Green, *The Lost Colony*
John Steinbeck, "The Leader of the People"
Laura Ingalls Wilder, *On the Banks of Plum Creek*

1938   John Muir, *John of the Mountains*
Paul Radin, *Primitive Religion*
Marjorie Kinnan Rawlings, *The Yearling*

1939   Laura Ingalls Wilder, *By the Shores of Silver Lake*
Thomas Wolfe, *A Western Journal*

1940   Walter Van Tilburg Clark, *The Ox-Bow Incident*
Lovat Dickson, *My Life with Grey Owl*
Herbert and Dorothy Fields, *Annie Get Your Gun*
Jessamyn West, *The Friendly Persuasion*
Laura Ingalls Wilder, *The Long Winter*

1941   Agnes Morley Cleaveland, *No Life for a Lady*
Frank Dobie, *The Longhorns*
Howard Fast, *The Last Frontier*
Edna Ferber, *Saratoga Trunk*
John Lomax, *Negro Folk Songs as Sung by Lead Belly*
——, *Our Singing Country*
John G. Neihardt, *The Song of Jed Smith*
Laura Ingalls Wilder, *Little Town on the Prairie*

1942   Nannie T. Alderson and Helena Huntington Smith, *A Bride Goes West*
Dee Brown, *Wave High the Banner*
William Faulkner, "The Bear"
Robert E. Holland, *The Song of Tekakwitha*
Conrad Richter, *Tacey Cromwell*
Mari Sandoz, *Crazy Horse: The Strange Man of the Oglalas*
Luke Short, *Hardcase*
———, *Ride the Man Down*

1943   Frank Dobie, *Guide to Life and Literature of the Southwest*
Conrad Richter, *The Free Man*
Laura Ingalls Wilder, *These Happy Golden Years*

1944   Ella Deloria, *Waterlily*

1945   Walter Van Tilburg Clark, *The City of Trembling Leaves*
Edna Ferber, *Great Son*
Caroline Gordon, *The Forest of the South*
Marquis James, *Cherokee Strip*
Paul Radin, *The Road of Life and Death*
Howard Richardson, *Dark of the Moon*

1946   Richard Rodgers and Oscar Hammerstein, *Annie Get Your Gun*

1947   A. B. Guthrie, *The Big Sky*
Hilda Mary Hooke, *Brown Lady Johnson*
John Lomax, *Adventures of a Ballad Hunter*
———, *Folk Song U.S.A.*
Charles Windolph, *I Fought with Custer: The Story of Sergeant Windolph, Last Survivor of the Battle of the Little Big Horn*

1948   Fred Gipson, *Cowhand: The Story of a Working Cowboy*

1949   A. B. Guthrie, *The Way West*
Dorothy Marie Johnson, *Indian Country*
Paul Radin, *The Culture of the Winnebago: As Described by Themselves*
Jack Schaefer, *Shane*
Jessamyn West, *Except for Me and Thee*

1950   Mary Hunter Austin, *Mother Felipe and Other Early Stories*
Frank Dobie, *The Ben Lilly Legend*
George E. Hyde, *The Pawnee Indians*
Louis L'Amour, *Westward the Tide*

1952   Dee Brown and Martin Schmitt, *Fighting Indians of the West*
———, *Trail Driving Days*
Edna Ferber, *Giant*
Jan Hartman, *The Legend of Daniel Boone*
Kermit Hunter, *Horn in the West*
J. O. Langford and Fred Gipson, *Big Bend: A Homesteader's Story*
John Steinbeck, *East of Eden*

1953   Joseph Epes Brown, *The Sacred Pipe*
Louis L'Amour, *Hondo*

Conrad Richter, *The Light in the Forest*
Mari Sandoz, *Cheyenne Autumn*
Jack Schaefer, *The Big Range*
——, *The Canyon*
——, *First Blood*

1954   Mari Sandoz, *The Buffalo Hunters*
Jack Schaefer, *The Pioneers*

1955   Dee Brown and Martin Schmitt, *The Settlers West*
Frank Dobie, *Tales of Old-Time Texas*
Fred Gipson, *The Trail-Driving Rooster*
Paul Green, *Wilderness Road*
Louis L'Amour, *Guns of the Timberland*
Jack Schaefer, *Out West*

1956   Hal Borland, *High, Wide, and Lonesome*
Austin and Alta Fife, *Saints of Sage and Saddle*
Janice Holt Giles, *Hannah Fowler*
Fred Gipson, *Old Yeller*
A. B. Guthrie, *These Thousand Hills*
George E. Hyde, *A Sioux Chronicle*
Louis L'Amour, *The Burning Hills*
——, *Silver Canyon*
Paul Radin, *The Trickster: A Study in American Indian Mythology*

1957   Dee Brown, *Yellowhorse*
Louis L'Amour, *Sitka*
Jack Schaefer, *Company of Cowards*

1958   Dee Brown, *The Gentle Tamers: Women of the Old Wild West*
Edna Ferber, *Ice Palace*
Owen Wister Out West: His Journals and Letters
Mari Sandoz, *The Cattlemen: From the Rio Grande across the Far Marias*

1959   Jason Betzinez, *I Fought with Geronimo*
George E. Hyde, *Indians of the High Plains*
James Michener, *Hawaii*
Mollie: The Journal of Mollie Dorsey Sanford in Nebraska and Colorado Territories, 1857–1866
Henry Lewis Morgan, *The Indian Journals, 1859–1862*
Jack Schaefer, *The Kean Land and Other Stories*

1960   Mariano Azuela, *Madero*
Frederic Remington's Own West
Scott O'Dell, *Island of the Blue Dolphins*
Jack Schaefer, *Old Ramon*

1961   George E. Hyde, *Spotted Tail's Folk*

1962   Dee Brown, *The Fetterman Massacre*
Fred Gipson, *Savage Sam*
George E. Hyde, *Indians of the Woodlands*

1962 *continued*
Louis L'Amour, *Shalako*
Rose Wilder Lane, *On the Way Home*

1963 Hal Borland, *When the Legends Die*
Dee Brown, *Galvanized Yankees*
Jack Schaefer, *The Great Endurance Horse Race*
———, *Monte Walsh*
———, *The Plainsman*

1964 Tom Berger, *Little Big Man*
Frank Dobie, *Cow People*
Theodora Kroeber, *Ishi, Last of His Tribe*
Louis L'Amour, *Conagher*
Mari Sandoz, *The Beaver Men: Spearheads of Empire*
Jack Schaefer, *Heroes without Glory*
———, *Stubby Pringle's Christmas*

1966 Scott O'Dell, *The King's Fifth*
Conrad Richter, *The Awakening Land*
———, *A Country of Strangers*
Mari Sandoz, *The Battle of the Little Bighorn*
J. W. Vaughn, *Indian Fights: New Facts on Seven Encounters*

1967 Frank Dobie, *Some Part of Myself*
Scott O'Dell, *The Black Pearl*
Jack Schaefer, *Mavericks*
———, *New Mexico*

1968 George E. Hyde, *The Life of George Bent*
N. Scott Momaday, *House Made of Dawn*
Charles Portis, *True Grit*

1969 Charles S. Brant, *The Autobiography of a Kiowa Apache Indian*
N. Scott Momaday, *The Way to Rainy Mountain*
Wallace Stegner, *The Sound of Mountain Water*

1970 Dee Brown, *Bury My Heart at Wounded Knee: An Indian History of the American West* (1970)
Scott O'Dell, *Sing Down the Moon*

1971 Laura Ingalls Wilder, *The First Four Years*

1972 Lovat Dickson, *Devil in Deerskins*
Richard Erdoes and John Lame Deer, *Lame Deer, Seeker of Visions*
Jean Craighead George, *Julie of the Wolves*

1973 Rudolfo Anaya, *Bless Me, Ultima*
Margaret Craven, *I Heard the Owl Call My Name*

1974 James Michener, *Centennial*
Laura Ingalls Wilder, *West from Home: Letters, San Francisco, 1915*

1975 Lula Parker Betenson, *Butch Cassidy, My Brother*
Jessamyn West, *The Massacre at Fall Creek*

Laurence Yep, *Dragonwings*
Ann Zwinger, *Run, River, Run*

1976   Susan Louisa Moir Allison, *A Pioneer Gentlewoman in British Columbia*
Rudolfo Anaya, *Heart of Aztlán*

1977   Edward Abbey, *The Journey Home: Some Words in Defense of the American West*
Dee Brown, *Hear That Lonesome Whistle Blow: Railroads in the West*
Bailey C. Hanes, *Bill Pickett, Bulldogger*

1978   Fred Gipson, *Little Arliss*
Barry Lopez, *Of Wolves and Men*
Conrad Richter, *The Rawhide Knot*
Alida Young, *Land of the Iron Dragon*

1979   Rudolfo Anaya, *Tortuga*

1980   Dee Brown, *Creek Mary's Blood*
Scott O'Dell, *Sarah Bishop*

1981   Louis L'Amour, *The Comstock Lode*
Ruthanne Lum McCunn, *Thousand Pieces of Gold*

1982   Susan Shelby Magoffin, *Down the Santa Fe Trail & into Mexico*
Glenn Shirley, *Belle Starr and Her Times: The Literature, the Facts, and the Legends*

1983   Elizabeth Speare, *The Sign of the Beaver*

1984   Ed Sager and Mike Frye, *The Bootlegger's Lady*
Sophie Trupin, *Dakota Diaspora: Memoirs of a Jewish Homesteader*

1985   Carlos Fuentes, *The Old Gringo*
Larry McMurtry, *Lonesome Dove*
James Michener, *Texas*

1986   Scott O'Dell, *Streams to the River, River to the Sea*

1987   William Kittredge, *Owing It All*

1988   Michael Blake, *Dances with Wolves*
John Ehle, *Trail of Tears: The Rise and Fall of the Cherokee Nation*
Louis L'Amour, *The Education of a Wandering Man*
——, *The Sackett Companion: A Personal Guide to the Sackett Novels*
——, *A Trail of Memories: The Quotations of Louis L'Amour*
James Michener, *Alaska*
Jasper Wyman, *Journey to the Koyukuk*

1989   *The Colonel's Lady on the Western Frontier: The Correspondence of Alice Kirk Grierson*
Guests Never Leave Hungry: The Autobiography of James Sewid, a Kwakiutl Indian
Basil H. Johnston, *Indian School Days*

1990   Mary Crow Dog, *Lakota Woman*
Laurel Thatcher Ulrich, *A Midwife's Tale: The Life of Martha Ballard, Based on Her Diary, 1785–1812*

1991   Laura Esquivel, *Like Water for Chocolate*
Barbara Kingsolver, *Animal Dreams*
Francis Parkman, *The Parkman Reader*
Carrie Young, *Nothing To Do but Stay*

1992   Catherine Haun, *A Woman's Trip across the Plains in 1849*
Sylvia Lopez-Medina, *Cantora*
Scott O'Dell, *Thunder Rolling in the Mountains*
Samuel Washington Woodhouse, *A Naturalist in Indian Territory*
Laurence Yep, *Dragon's Gate*
Carrie Young, *The Wedding Dress*

1993   Dee Brown, *When the Century Was Young*
Lauren Kessler, *Stubborn Twig: Three Generations in the Life of a Japanese American Family*
Larry McMurtry, *The Streets of Laredo*
Velma Wallis, *Two Old Women: An Alaska Legend of Betrayal, Courage and Survival*

1994   Roger Lea MacBride, *Little Farm in the Ozarks*
——, *Little House on Rocky Ridge*
Mary Canaga Rowland, *As Long as Life: The Memoirs of a Frontier Woman Doctor*

1995   James Carlos Blake, *The Pistoleer*
Roger Lea MacBride, *In the Land of the Big Red Apple*
O. M. Spencer, *The Indian Captivity of O. M. Spencer*

1996   Rudolfo Anaya, *Rio Grande Fall*
William Rodney, *Kootenai Brown, Canada's Unknown Frontiersman*
Winter Quarters, *The 1846–1848 Life Writings of Mary Haskin Parker Richards*

 MAJOR WORKS OF FRONTIER LITERATURE

An Account of Colonel Crockett's Tour to the North and Down East, Davy
    Crockett
*Account of the History, Manners, and Customs of the Indian Nations Who Once
    Inhabited Pennsylvania and the Neighboring States,* John Heckewelder
Across the Plains, Robert Louis Stevenson
Adventures of a Ballad Hunter, John Lomax
The Adventures of Buffalo Bill, William F. Cody
The Adventures of Captain Bonneville, U. S. A., Washington Irving
*The Adventures of Col. Daniel Boon [sic], Containing Narrative of the Wars of
    Kentucke,* John Filson
Ah Sin, the Heathen Chinee, Bret Harte and Mark Twain
Alaska, James Michener
American Ballads and Folk Songs, John Lomax and Alan Lomax
American Landscapes, Hector St. John de Crèvecoeur
American Ornithological Biography, John James Audubon
Animal Dreams, Barbara Kingsolver
Annie Get Your Gun, Herbert Fields and Dorothy Fields
Annie Get Your Gun, Richard Rodgers and Oscar Hammerstein
Annie Oakley, Woman at Arms, Courtney Ryley Cooper
Apache Gold and Yaqui Silver, Frank Dobie
Arizona, Augustus Thomas
The Arrow-Maker, Mary Hunter Austin
As Long as Life: The Memoirs of a Frontier Woman Doctor, Mary Canaga
    Rowland
Astoria, Washington Irving
"At the Mission of San Carmel," Bret Harte
Audubon's Western Journal 1849–1850, John Woodhouse Audubon
The Autobiography of a Kiowa Apache Indian, Charles S. Brant
The Autobiography of a Winnebago Indian, Paul Radin
The Autobiography of Black Hawk
The Autobiography of Joseph Jefferson

The Autobiography of Mark Twain
The Awakening Land, Conrad Richter

The Backwoods of Canada, Catherine Parr Traill
"The Ballad of Yukon Jake," Ted Paramore
The Basket Woman, Mary Hunter Austin
The Battle of the Little Bighorn, Mari Sandoz
"The Bear," William Faulkner
The Beaver Men: Spearheads of Empire, Mari Sandoz
Belle Starr and Her Times: The Literature, the Facts, and the Legends, Glenn
    Shirley
The Ben Lilly Legend, Frank Dobie
Betty Zane, Zane Grey
Big Bend: A Homesteader's Story, J. O. Langford and Fred Gipson
The Big Range, Jack Schaefer
The Big Sky, A. B. Guthrie
Bill Pickett, Bulldogger, Bailey C. Hanes
Billy the Kid, Walter Woods
Biography and History of the Indians of North America, Samuel G. Drake
Birds, Beasts and Flowers, D. H. Lawrence
The Birds of America, John James Audubon
Birth of the Rail, Ambrose Bierce
Black Beetles in Amber, Ambrose Bierce
Black Elk Speaks: The Life Story of a Holy Man of the Oglala Sioux, John G.
    Neihardt
The Black Hawk War, Frank E. Stevens
The Black Pearl, Scott O'Dell
Blackbeard, Lemuel Sawyer
Blackfoot Lodge Tales, George Bird Grinnell
Bless Me, Ultima, Rudolfo Anaya
Blue Feather, Zane Grey
A Book of Americans, Rosemary and Stephen Vincent Benét
Book of Mormon, Joseph Smith
The Bootlegger's Lady, Ed Sager and Mike Frye
Boots and Saddles: Life in Dakota with General Custer, Elizabeth Bacon Custer
"The Bride Comes to Yellow Sky," Stephen Crane
A Bride Goes West, Nannie T. Alderson and Helena Huntington Smith
A Briefe and True Report of the New Found Land of Virginia, Thomas Harriot
Brown Lady Johnson, Hilda Mary Hooke
Buckskin and Blanket Days, Thomas Henry Tibbles
"Buffalo Bill," Carl Sandburg
The Buffalo Hunters, Mari Sandoz
The Burning Hills, Louis L'Amour
Bury My Heart at Wounded Knee: An Indian History of the American West, Dee
    Brown
Butch Cassidy, My Brother, Lula Parker Betenson

By Cheyenne Campfires, George Bird Grinnell
By the Shores of Silver Lake, Laura Ingalls Wilder

Ca'line, Bernice Kelly Harris
Call of the Canyon, Zane Grey
The Call of the Wild, Jack London
Can Such Things Be?, Ambrose Bierce
Cantora, Sylvia Lopez-Medina
The Canyon, Jack Schaefer
The Captain of the Gray Horse Troop, Hamlin Garland
*Captivity of the Oatman Girls: Being an Interesting Narrative of Life among the
    Apache and Mohave Indians*, Reverend R. B. Stratton
The Castaways, Cabeza de Vaca
Catlin's Notes of Eight Years' Travels and Residence in Europe, George Catlin
The Cattlemen: From the Rio Grande across the Far Marias, Mari Sandoz
Cavanagh, Forest Ranger: A Romance of the Mountain West, Hamlin Garland
"The Celebrated Jumping Frog of Calaveras County," Mark Twain
Centennial, James Michener
A Century of Dishonor, Helen Hunt Jackson
Cherokee Strip, Marquis James
Cheyenne Autumn, Mari Sandoz
The Cheyenne Indians, George Bird Grinnell
Children Sing in the Far West, Mary Hunter Austin
Cimarron, Edna Ferber
The City of Trembling Leaves, Walter Van Tilburg Clark
Clearing in the West, Nellie Letitia Mooney McClung
Cobwebs from an Empty Skull, Ambrose Bierce
Collected Works, Ambrose Bierce
*A Collection of Some of the Most Interesting Narratives of Indian Warfare in the
    West, Containing an Account of the Adventures of Daniel Boone, One of the
    First Settlers of Kentucky*, Samuel L. Metcalfe
Colonel Crockett's Exploits and Adventures in Texas, Richard Penn Smith
*The Colonel's Lady on the Western Frontier: The Correspondence of Alice Kirk
    Grierson*
Columbiad, Joel Barlow
Come and Get It, Edna Ferber
Company of Cowards, Jack Schaefer
The Comstock Lode, Louis L'Amour
Conagher, Louis L'Amour
Concerning Our Heritage, O. E. Rölvaag
Condensed Novels, Bret Harte
The Conquest of Canada, George Cockings
The Conquest: The Story of a Negro Pioneer, Oscar Micheaux
The Contrast, Royall Tyler
Coronado's Children, Frank Dobie
Count Frontenac and New France under Louis XIV, Francis Parkman

A Country of Strangers, Conrad Richter
The Courtship of Miles Standish, Henry Wadsworth Longfellow
Cow People, Frank Dobie
The Cowboy Detective, Charles A. Siringo
Cowboy Songs and Other Frontier Ballads, John Lomax
Cowhand: The Story of a Working Cowboy, Fred Gipson
Crazy Horse: The Strange Man of the Oglalas, Mari Sandoz
Creek Mary's Blood, Dee Brown
"The Cremation of Sam McGee," Robert Service
Crockett Almanack, Davy Crockett
The Cruise of the Corwin, John Muir
The Culture of the Winnebago: As Described by Themselves, Paul Radin

Dacotah, or Life and Legends of the Sioux around Fort Snelling, Mary H. Eastman
Dakota Diaspora: Memoirs of a Jewish Homesteader, Sophie Trupin
Dances with Wolves, Michael Blake
Daniel Boone and the Hunters of Kentucky, W. H. Bogart
Daniel Boone: Wilderness Scout, Stewart Edward White
The Danites in the Sierras, Joaquin Miller
Dark of the Moon, Howard Richardson
Daughter of the Middle Border, Hamlin Garland
Daughter of the Snows, Jack London
Davy Crockett, Frank H. Murdoch
Death Comes for the Archbishop, Willa Cather
The Deerslayer, James Fenimore Cooper
Desert Gold, Zane Grey
"The Devil and Tom Walker," Washington Irving
Devil in Deerskins, Lovat Dickson
The Devil's Dictionary, Ambrose Bierce
The Disappointment, or The Force of Credulity, Andrew Barton
Discoveries of the World, Antonio Galvano
Down the Santa Fe Trail & into Mexico, Susan Shelby Magoffin
Dragon's Gate, Laurence Yep
Dragonwings, Laurence Yep
Drums along the Mohawk, Walter Dumaux Edmonds
"The Dying Indian," Philip Freneau

Early Americana and Other Stories, Conrad Richter
Early Days in Texas, A Trip to Hell and Heaven, Jim McIntire
Earth Horizon, Mary Hunter Austin
East of Eden, John Steinbeck
Ebb Tide, Joseph Glover Baldwin
The Education of a Wandering Man, Louis L'Amour
"Eldorado," Edgar Allan Poe
"The Emigrant," Alexander McLachlan
The Emigrants, Johan Bojer

The Emigrants' Guide to Oregon and California, Lansford W. Hastings
Essay on the Life of the Honorable Major-General Israel Putnam, David
    Humphrey
Evangeline, a Tale of Arcadie, Henry Wadsworth Longfellow
Except for Me and Thee, Jessamyn West
The Explorations of Captain James Cook in the Pacific as Told by Selections of His
    Own Journals, 1768–1779, Captain James Cook

The Falls of Niagara, Joseph Hutton
Famous Indian Chiefs I Have Known, Oliver Otis Howard
Fantastic Fables, Ambrose Bierce
Farmer Boy, Laura Ingalls Wilder
Fashion, Anna Cora Mowatt
"Fenimore Cooper's Literary Offenses," Mark Twain
The Fetterman Massacre, Dee Brown
The Fiend's Delight, Ambrose Bierce
The Fighting Cheyenne, George Bird Grinnell
Fighting Indians of the West, Dee Brown and Martin Schmitt
First Blood, Jack Schaefer
The First Four Years, Laura Ingalls Wilder
The First White Man of the West, or the Life and Exploits of Col. Dan'l. Boone, the
    First Settler of Kentucky; Interspersed with Incidents in the Early Annals of the
    Country, Timothy Flint
Five Years a Cavalryman or, Sketches of Regular Army Life on the Texas Frontier,
    1866–1871, H. H. McConnell
The Flush Times of California, Joseph Glover Baldwin
Folk Song U.S.A., John Lomax
Following the Guidon, Elizabeth Bacon Custer
The Forest of the South, Caroline Gordon
Forest Princess, Charlotte Barnes Conner
The Forest Rose, or American Farmers, Samuel Woodworth and John Davies
Forty-Nine, Joaquin Miller
Frederic Remington's Own West
The Free Man, Conrad Richter
The Friendly Persuasion, Jessamyn West
From Pittsburgh to the Rocky Mountains, Stephen Harriman Long
From the Deep Woods to Civilization, Charles Alexander Eastman
A Frontier Lady: Recollections of the Gold Rush and Early California, Sarah
    Eleanor Bayliss Royce

Galvanized Yankees, Dee Brown
Generall Historie of Virginia, New England and the Summer Isles, Captain John
    Smith
The Genetic Relationship of the North American Indian Languages, Paul Radin
The Gentle Tamers: Women of the Old Wild West, Dee Brown
Geronimo's Story of His Life

Giant, Edna Ferber
Giants in the Earth: A Saga of the Prairie, O. E. Rölvaag
The Girl of the Golden West, David Belasco
The Golden Farmer, Benjamin Webster
Golden Fleece, William Rose Benét
The Great Divide, William Vaughn Moody
The Great Endurance Horse Race, Jack Schaefer
Great Son, Edna Ferber
Guests Never Leave Hungry: The Autobiography of James Sewid, a Kwakiutl Indian
*A Guide in the Wilderness or the History of the First Settlements in the Western
 Counties of New York*, William Cooper
Guide to Life and Literature of the Southwest, Frank Dobie
Guns of the Timberland, Louis L'Amour

Half-Century of Conflict, Francis Parkman
Hannah Fowler, Janice Holt Giles
Hardcase, Luke Short
Hawaii, James Michener
Hear That Lonesome Whistle Blow: Railroads in the West, Dee Brown
Heart of Aztlán, Rudolfo Anaya
Heart of the West, O. Henry
The Heritage of the Desert, Zane Grey
Heroes without Glory, Jack Schaefer
High, Wide, and Lonesome, Hal Borland
*Historical and Statistical Information Respecting the History, Condition and
 Prospects of the Indian Tribes of the United States*, Henry Rowe Schoolcraft
A History of Billy the Kid, Charles A. Siringo
*A History of New York, from the Beginning of the World to the End of the Dutch
 Dynasty*, Washington Irving
History of the Conquest of Mexico, William H. Prescott
The History of the Conspiracy of Pontiac, Francis Parkman
A History of the Indies, Bartolomé de Las Casas
Hondo, Louis L'Amour
Honey in the Horn, H. L. Davis
The Hoosier Schoomaster, Edward Eggleston
Horn in the West, Kermit Hunter
House Made of Dawn, N. Scott Momaday
The Huron Chief, Adam Kidd

*I Fought with Custer: The Story of Sergeant Windolph, Last Survivor of the Battle
 of the Little Big Horn*, Charles Windolph
I Fought with Geronimo, Jason Betzinez
I Heard the Owl Call My Name, Margaret Craven
Ice Palace, Edna Ferber
The Illustrated History of Montana, Joaquin Miller

In Abraham's Bosom, Paul Green
In Mizzoura, Augustus Thomas
In the Land of the Big Red Apple, Roger Lea MacBride
Indian Boyhood, Charles Alexander Eastman
"The Indian Burying Ground," Philip Freneau
The Indian Captivity of O. M. Spencer, O. M. Spencer
Indian Country, Dorothy Marie Johnson
Indian Fights: New Facts on Seven Encounters, J. W. Vaughn
The Indian Journals, 1859–1862, Henry Lewis Morgan
The Indian Princess or La Belle Sauvage, James N. Barker
The Indian Question, an Address, Henry B. Carrington
Indian School Days, Basil H. Johnston
Indian Scout Craft and Lore, Charles Alexander Eastman
Indians of the High Plains, George E. Hyde
Indians of the Woodlands, George E. Hyde
The Infidel, Robert Bird
Insurgent Mexico, John Reed
Ishi, Last of His Tribe, Theodora Kroeber
Isidro, Mary Hunter Austin
Island of the Blue Dolphins, Scott O'Dell

The Jesuits in North America in the Seventeenth Century, Francis Parkman
Joaquin et al., Joaquin Miller
John of the Mountains, John Muir
Journal of a Mountain Man, James Clyman
Journal of a Trapper, Osborne Russell
The Journey Home: Some Words in Defense of the American West, Edward Abbey
Journey to the Koyukuk, Jasper Wyman
Julie of the Wolves, Jean Craighead George

The Kean Land and Other Stories, Jack Schaefer
"The Killing of Julius Caesar 'Localized,' " Mark Twain
The King's Fifth, Scott O'Dell
Kit Carson's Autobiography
Kootenai Brown, Canada's Unknown Frontiersman, William Rodney

La Salle and the Discovery of the Great West, Francis Parkman
A Lady's Life in the Rocky Mountains, Isabella Bird
Lakota Woman, Mary Crow Dog
Lame Deer, Seeker of Visions, Richard Erdoes and John Lame Deer
The Land of Little Rain, Mary Hunter Austin
Land of the Iron Dragon, Alida Young
The Last Frontier, Howard Fast
The Last of the Lowries: A Play of the Croatan Outlaws of Robeson County, Paul Green
The Last of the Mohicans, James Fenimore Cooper

The Last of the Plainsmen, Zane Grey
Last Rambles amongst the Indians of the Rocky Mountains and the Andes, George
    Catlin
The Last Trail, Zane Grey
Laughing Boy, Oliver La Farge
The Laughing Pioneer, Paul Green
"The Leader of the People," John Steinbeck
League of the Ho-de-no-sau-nee or Iroquois, Lewis Henry Morgan
The Legend of Daniel Boone, Jan Hartman
"The Legend of Sleepy Hollow," Washington Irving
The Legends and Myths of Hawaii, King David Kalakaua
*Letters and Notes on the Manners, Customs and Condition of the North American
    Indians during Eight Years' Travel amongst the Wildest Tribes of Indians of
    North America*, George Catlin
Letters from America, O. E. Rölvaag
Letters of a Woman Homesteader, Elinore Pruitt Stewart
Letters on an Elk Hunt, Elinore Pruitt Stewart
Letters to a Friend, John Muir
Life among the Piutes, Their Wrongs and Claims, Sarah Winnemucca
Life and Adventures in California, Thomas Jefferson Farnham
The Life and Adventures of a Quaker among the Indians, Thomas C. Battey
The Life and Adventures of Colonel David Crockett of West Tennessee, Mathew St.
    Clair Clarke
*The Life and Adventures of Nat Love, Better Known in the Cattle Country as
    Deadwood Dick*
The Life and Time of Col. Daniel Boone, Hunter, Soldier, and Pioneer, Edward S. Ellis
The Life and Voyages of Christopher Columbus, Washington Irving
Life in Prairie Land, Eliza Farnham
Life in the Clearings, Susanna Moodie
The Life of George Bent, George E. Hyde
*The Life of James Pierson Beckwourth, Mountaineer, Scout, Pioneer and Chief of the
    Crow Nation*, Thomas D. Bonner
The Life of John Wesley Hardin as Written by Himself
Life of Tom Horn, Government Scout and Interpreter
Life on the Mississippi, Mark Twain
The Light in the Forest, Conrad Richter
Like Water for Chocolate, Laura Esquivel
The Lion of the West, James Kirke Paulding
Little Arliss, Fred Gipson
Little Big Man, Thomas Berger
Little Farm in the Ozarks, Roger Lea MacBride
Little House in the Big Woods, Laura Ingalls Wilder
Little House on Rocky Ridge, Roger Lea MacBride
Little House on the Prairie, Laura Ingalls Wilder
Little Town on the Prairie, Laura Ingalls Wilder
The Log of a Cowboy: A Narrative of the Old Trail Days, Andy Adams

A Lone Star Cowboy, Charles A. Siringo
Lonesome Dove, Larry McMurtry
The Long Winter, Laura Ingalls Wilder
The Longhorns, Frank Dobie
Lost Borders, Mary Hunter Austin
The Lost Colony: A Symphonic Drama in Two Acts, Paul Green
A Lost Lady, Willa Cather
The Lost Trappers, David H. Coyner
"The Luck of Roaring Camp," Bret Harte

Madero, Mariano Azuela
Main-Travelled Roads, Hamlin Garland
"María Concepción," Katherine Anne Porter
The Massacre at Fall Creek, Jessamyn West
Mavericks, Jack Schaefer
May-Day, anonymous
The Men of the Last Frontier, Grey Owl
Metamora, or the Last of the Wampanoags, John Augustus Stone
Method and Theory of Ethnology, Paul Radin
A Midwife's Tale: The Life of Martha Ballard, Based on Her Diary, 1785–1812,
    Laurel Thatcher Ulrich
*Mollie: The Journal of Mollie Dorsey Sanford in Nebraska and Colorado Territories,
    1857–1866*
The Monk and the Hangman's Daughter, Ambrose Bierce
Montcalm and Wolfe, Francis Parkman
Monte Walsh, Jack Schaefer
Mornings in Mexico, D. H. Lawrence
Mother Felipe and Other Early Stories, Mary Hunter Austin
*The Mountain Muse: Comprising the Adventures of Daniel Boone; and the Power of
    Virtuous and Refined Beauty*, Daniel Bryan
The Mountains of California, John Muir
The Mustang, Frank Dobie
My Ántonia, Willa Cather
My First Summer in the Sierra, John Muir
My Indian Boyhood, Luther Standing Bear
My Journal, 1836, Narcissa Prentiss Whitman
My Life among the Indians, George Catlin
My Life and Experiences among Our Hostile Indians, Oliver Otis Howard
My Life on the Plains, George Armstrong Custer
My Life with Grey Owl, Lovat Dickson

A Narrative of the Captivity, Sufferings and Removes of Mrs. Mary Rowlandson,
    Mary White Rowlandson
Narrative of the Life of David Crockett of the State of Tennessee, Davy Crockett
Narrative of the Life of David Crockett of the State of Tennessee, Thomas Chilton
A Naturalist in Indian Territory, Samuel Washington Woodhouse

Negro Folk Songs as Sung by Lead Belly, John Lomax
New Mexico, Jack Schaefer
A New World Planted, Joseph Croswell
Nez Perce Joseph, Oliver Otis Howard
Nick of the Woods, Robert Bird
No Life for a Lady, Agnes Morley Cleaveland
"The Noble Red Man," Mark Twain
The No'Count Boy, Paul Green
Nolens Volens; or The Biter Bit, Everard Hall
North American Indian Portfolio: Hunting Scenes and Amusements of the Rocky Mountains and Prairies of America, George Catlin
Nothing To Do but Stay, Carrie Young
Nuggets and Dust Panned Out in California, Ambrose Bierce

O Pioneers!, Willa Cather
The Octoroon, Dion Boucicault
Of Wolves and Men, Barry Lopez
Okeepa, a Religious Ceremony, and Other Customs of the Mandans, George Catlin
The Old Gringo, Carlos Fuentes
Old Ramon, Jack Schaefer
The Old Régime in Canada, Francis Parkman
Old Yeller, Fred Gipson
On Forgotten Paths, O. E. Rölvaag
On the Banks of Plum Creek, Laura Ingalls Wilder
On the Way Home, Rose Wilder Lane
One-Smoke Stories, Mary Hunter Austin
An Oregon Idyll, Joaquin Miller
The Oregon Trail: Sketches of Prairie and Rocky Mountain Life, Francis Parkman
Our American Cousin, Tom Taylor
Our National Parks, John Muir
Our Singing Country, John Lomax
Our Wild Indians: Thirty-Three Years' Personal Experience among the Red Men of the Great West, Richard Irving Dodge
Out West, Jack Schaefer
"The Outcasts of Poker Flat," Bret Harte
Owen Wister Out West: His Journals and Letters
Owing It All, William Kittredge
The Ox-Bow Incident, Walter Van Tilburg Clark

The Parkman Reader, Francis Parkman
The Pathfinder: or The Inland Sea, James Fenimore Cooper
Pawnee Hero Stories and Folk Tales, George Bird Grinnell
The Pawnee Indians, George E. Hyde
"The Paxtoniade," anonymous
Peder Victorious, O. E. Rölvaag
Pilgrims of the Wild, Grey Owl

A Pioneer Gentlewoman in British Columbia, Susan Louisa Moir Allison
The Pioneers, Jack Schaefer
Pioneers of France in the New World, Francis Parkman
The Pioneers or, The Sources of the Susquehanna, James Fenimore Cooper
The Pistoleer, James Carlos Blake
The Plainsman, Jack Schaefer
Plays of the Pioneers, Constance D'Arcy Mackay
The Plumed Serpent, D. H. Lawrence
Pocahontas, Robert Dale Owen
Po-Ca-Hon-Tas, or The Gentle Savage, John Brougham
Pocahontas, or The Settlers of Virginia, George Washington Parke Custis
The Poetical Works of Bret Harte, Bret Harte
Pokey, or The Beautiful Legend of the Amorous Indian, Philip Moeller
Ponteach, Robert Rogers
The Pony Express: A Thrilling and Truthful History, William Lightfoot Visscher
The Prairie, James Fenimore Cooper
Pretty-Shield, Medicine Woman of the Crows, Frank B. Linderman
Primitive Man as Philosopher, Paul Radin
Primitive Religion, Paul Radin
The Prince of Parthia, Thomas Godfrey
The Principal Navigations, Voyages, and Discoveries of the English Nation, Richard Hakluyt
A Protégée of Jack Hamlin's and Other Stories, Bret Harte

Quare Medicine, Paul Green

Ramona, Helen Hunt Jackson
Ranch Life and the Hunting Trail, Theodore Roosevelt
The Raven, Marquis James
The Rawhide Knot, Conrad Richter
Red Men and White, Owen Wister
The Redeemed Captive Returning to Zion, John Williams
The Redskins, James Fenimore Cooper
Report of the Exploring Expeditions of 1842 and 1843–44, John C. Fremont
Riata and Spurs, Charles A. Siringo
Ride the Man Down, Luke Short
Riders of the Purple Sage, Zane Grey
Rio Grande Fall, Rudolfo Anaya
"Rip Van Winkle," Washington Irving
Rip Van Winkle, a Folk Opera, Percy MacKaye
Rip Van Winkle, a Legend of the Catskills, Charles Burke
Rip Van Winkle, or The Demons of the Catskill Mountains! A National Drama, Thomas Flynn
The Rising Glory of America, Hugh Henry Brackenridge and Philip Freneau
The Road of Life and Death, Paul Radin
Robber's Roost, Zane Grey

The Rose of the Rancho, David Belasco
Rough Riders, Theodore Roosevelt
Roughing It, Mark Twain
Roughing It in the Bush, Susanna Moodie
Route and Distances to Oregon and California, J. M. Shively
Run, River, Run, Ann Zwinger

The Sackett Companion: A Personal Guide to the Sackett Novels, Louis L'Amour
The Sacred Pipe, Joseph Epes Brown
The Saga of Billy the Kid, Walter Noble Burns
Saints of Sage and Saddle, Austin Fife and Alta Fife
Sajo and the Beaver People, Grey Owl
Sam Patch, the Jumper of Niagara Falls, Dan Marble
Santa Lucia, Mary Hunter Austin
Sarah Bishop, Scott O'Dell
Saratoga Trunk, Edna Ferber
Savage Sam, Fred Gipson
The Scuffletown Outlaws: A Tragedy of the Lowrie Gang, William Norment Cox
The Settlers West, Dee Brown and Martin Schmitt
Shadow on the Dial, Ambrose Bierce
Shadows of Shasta, Joaquin Miller
Shalako, Louis L'Amour
Shane, Jack Schaefer
Shapes of Clay, Ambrose Bierce
She Would Be a Soldier, or The Plains of Chippewa, Mordecai M. Noah
Shenandoah, Bronson Crocker Howard
The Shepherd of the Hills, Harold Bell Wright
The Ship of Longing, O. E. Rölvaag
"The Shooting of Dan McGrew," Robert Service
A Short Account of the Destruction of the Indies, Bartolomé de Las Casas
Show Boat, Edna Ferber
The Sign of the Beaver, Elizabeth Speare
Silver Canyon, Louis L'Amour
Sing Down the Moon, Scott O'Dell
A Sioux Chronicle, George E. Hyde
Sitka, Louis L'Amour
Six Years with the Texas Rangers, 1875–1881, James B. Gillett
So Big, Edna Ferber
Some Part of Myself, Frank Dobie
The Son of the Wolf: Tales of the Far North, Jack London
A Song Companion of a Lone Star Cowboy, Charles A. Siringo
The Song of Hugh Glass, John G. Neihardt
The Song of Jed Smith, John G. Neihardt
The Song of Tekakwitha, Robert E. Holland
The Song of the Indian Wars, John G. Neihardt
The Song of the Messiah, John G. Neihardt

Song of the Sierras, Joaquin Miller
The Song of Three Friends, John G. Neihardt
Songs of a Sourdough, Robert Service
Songs of the Cattle Trail and Cow Camp, John Lomax
The Soul of the Indian: An Interpretation, Charles Alexander Eastman
The Sound of Mountain Water, Wallace Stegner
Specimens, Joaquin Miller
"The Spectre Bridegroom, A Traveller's Tale," Washington Irving
"The Spirit of Place," D. H. Lawrence
Spirit of the Border, Zane Grey
Spotted Tail's Folk, George E. Hyde
Starry Adventure, Mary Hunter Austin
Steep Trails, John Muir
"Stickeen," John Muir
Stories of the Sioux, Luther Standing Bear
The Story of a Mine and Other Tales, Bret Harte
The Story of My Boyhood and Youth, John Muir
The Story of My Life, Annie Oakley
The Story of the American Indian, Paul Radin
Streams to the River, River to the Sea, Scott O'Dell
The Streets of Laredo, Larry McMurtry
Stubborn Twig: Three Generations in the Life of a Japanese American Family,
    Lauren Kessler
Stubby Pringle's Christmas, Jack Schaefer
Studies in Classic American Literature, D. H. Lawrence
Sun-Up, Lula Vollmer
Superstition, James N. Barker
Synopsis of the Birds of America, John James Audubon

Tacey Cromwell, Conrad Richter
Tales of a Traveller, Washington Irving
Tales of Old-Time Texas, Frank Dobie
Tales of Soldiers and Civilians, Ambrose Bierce
Tally Ho!, Joaquin Miller
Tenting on the Plains, Elizabeth Bacon Custer
Texas, James Michener
A Texas Cowboy, or, Fifteen Years on the Hurricane Deck of a Spanish Cow Pony,
    Charles A. Siringo
Their Fathers' God, O. E. Rölvaag
Theodosia, The Pirate's Prisoner, William Henry Rhodes
These Happy Golden Years, Laura Ingalls Wilder
These Thousand Hills, A. B. Guthrie
*Thirty-One Years on the Plains and in the Mountains or, The Last Voice from the
    Plains*, William F. Drannan
A Thousand Mile Walk to the Gulf, John Muir
Thousand Pieces of Gold, Ruthanne Lum McCunn

Through Indian Country to California, John P. Sherburne
Thunder Rolling in the Mountains, Scott O'Dell
The Thundering Herd, Zane Grey
"To Build a Fire," Jack London
To the Last Man, Zane Grey
Tortuga, Rudolfo Anaya
A Tour of the Prairies, Washington Irving
The Trail Book, Mary Hunter Austin
Trail Driving Days, Dee Brown and Martin Schmitt
A Trail of Memories: The Quotations of Louis L'Amour, Louis L'Amour
The Trail of '98: A Northland Romance, Robert Service
Trail of Tears: The Rise and Fall of the Cherokee Nation, John Ehle
The Trail-Driving Rooster, Fred Gipson
A Traveller in Indian Territory, Ethan Allan Hitchcock
Travels, William Bartram
Travels in Alaska, John Muir
Travels in the Great Western Prairies, Thomas Farnham
Travels in the Great Western Prairies, Thomas Jefferson Farnham
Travels through the Interior Parts of North America, Jonathan Carver
The Trickster: A Study in American Indian Mythology, Paul Radin
A Trip to Chinatown, Charles Hoyt
A Trip to Niagara or Travellers in America, William Dunlop
True Grit, Charles Portis
A True Picture of Emigration, Rebecca Burlend and Edward Burlend
A True Relation of such occurrences and accidents of noate as hath hapned in
     Virginia since the first planting of that Collony, Captain John Smith
The Truth about Geronimo, Britton Davis
Two Evil Isms: Pinkertonism and Anarchism, Charles A. Siringo
Two Fools, O. E. Rölvaag
Two Great Scouts and Their Pawnee Battalion, George Bird Grinnell
The Two Men of Sandy Bar, Bret Harte
Two Old Women: An Alaska Legend of Betrayal, Courage and Survival, Velma Wallis

The Underdogs: A Novel of the Mexican Revolution, Mariano Azuela
Unwritten History: Life among the Modocs, Joaquin Miller

The Vanishing American, Zane Grey
A Vaquero of the Brush Country, Frank Dobie
Virginia Richly Valued by the Description of Florida, Hernando de Soto
The Virginian: A Horseman of the Plains, Owen Wister
The Vision of Columbus, Joel Barlow
The Viviparous Quadrupeds of North America, John James Audubon
Voyage of the Beagle, Charles Darwin
Voyages and Discoveries of the Companions of Columbus, Washington Irving

Wash Carver's Mouse Trap, Fred Koch, Jr.
"The Wash-Tub Mail," Gertrude Atherton

Waterlily, Ella Deloria
Wave High the Banner, Dee Brown
The Way to Rainy Mountain, N. Scott Momaday
The Way West, A. B. Guthrie
The Wedding Dress, Carrie Young
West from Home: Letters, San Francisco, 1915, Laura Ingalls Wilder
A Western Journal, Thomas Wolfe
Westward the Tide, Louis L'Amour
When the Century Was Young, Dee Brown
When the Legends Die, Hal Borland
White Fang, Jack London
Wild Western Scenes; A Narrative of Adventures in the Western Wilderness, Forty Years Ago; Wherein the Conduct of Daniel Boone, the Great American Pioneer, Is Particularly Described, J. B. Jones
Wilderness Road, Paul Green
Wildfire, Zane Grey
The Winnebago Tribe, Paul Radin
The Winning of the West, Theodore Roosevelt
Winter Quarters, The 1846–1848 Life Writings of Mary Haskin Parker Richards
With Cortéz in Mexico, C. Falkenhorst
Wolfert's Roost and Miscellanies, Washington Irving
Woman of Spain: A Story of Old California, Scott O'Dell
A Woman's Trip across the Plains in 1849, Catherine Haun
Wyandotte, James Fenimore Cooper
Wyatt Earp, Frontier Marshall, Stuart N. Lake

Ye Beare and Ye Cubb, anonymous
The Yearling, Marjorie Kinnan Rawlings
Yellowhorse, Dee Brown
The Yemassee: A Romance of Carolina, William Gilmore Simms
Yosemite, John Muir
Yucatan before and after the Conquest, Diego de Landa

MAJOR AUTHORS OF FRONTIER
LITERATURE AND THEIR WORKS

Abbey, Edward
  The Journey Home: Some Words in Defense of the American West
Adams, Andy
  The Log of a Cowboy: A Narrative of the Old Trail Days
Alderson, Nannie T.
  A Bride Goes West
Allison, Susan Louisa Moir
  A Pioneer Gentlewoman in British Columbia
Anaya, Rudolfo
  Bless Me, Ultima
  Heart of Aztlán
  Rio Grande Fall
  Tortuga
anonymous
  May-Day
  "The Paxtoniade"
  Ye Beare and Ye Cubb
Atherton, Gertrude
  "The Wash-Tub Mail"
Audubon, John James
  American Ornithological Biography
  The Birds of America
  Synopsis of the Birds of America
  The Viviparous Quadrupeds of North America
Audubon, John Woodhouse
  Audubon's Western Journal, 1849–1850

Austin, Mary Hunter
 The Arrow-Maker
 The Basket Woman
 Children Sing in the Far West
 Earth Horizon
 Isidro
 The Land of Little Rain
 Lost Borders
 Mother Felipe and Other Early Stories
 One-Smoke Stories
 Santa Lucia
 Starry Adventure
 The Trail Book

Azuela, Mariano
 Madero
 The Underdogs: A Novel of the Mexican Revolution

Baldwin, Joseph Glover
 Ebb Tide
 The Flush Times of California

Barker, James N.
 The Indian Princess or La Belle Sauvage
 Superstition

Barlow, Joel
 Columbiad
 The Vision of Columbus

Barton, Andrew
 The Disappointment, or The Force of Credulity

Bartram, William
 Travels

Battey, Thomas C.
 The Life and Adventures of a Quaker among the Indians

Belasco, David
 The Girl of the Golden West
 The Rose of the Rancho

Benét, Rosemary
 A Book of Americans

Benét, Stephen Vincent
 A Book of Americans

Benét, William Rose
 Golden Fleece

Berger, Thomas
 Little Big Man

Betenson, Lula Parker
Butch Cassidy, My Brother

Betzinez, Jason
I Fought with Geronimo

Bierce, Ambrose
Birth of the Rail
Black Beetles in Amber
Can Such Things Be?
Cobwebs from an Empty Skull
Collected Works
The Devil's Dictionary
Fantastic Fables
The Fiend's Delight
The Monk and the Hangman's Daughter
Nuggets and Dust Panned Out in California
Shadow on the Dial
Shapes of Clay
Tales of Soldiers and Civilians

Bird, Isabella
A Lady's Life in the Rocky Mountains

Bird, Robert
The Infidel
Nick of the Woods

Black Hawk
The Autobiography of Black Hawk

Blake, James Carlos
The Pistoleer

Blake, Michael
Dances with Wolves

Bogart, W. H.
Daniel Boone and the Hunters of Kentucky

Bojer, Johan
The Emigrants

Bonner, Thomas D.
The Life of James Pierson Beckwourth, Mountaineer, Scout, Pioneer and Chief of the Crow Nation

Borland, Hal
High, Wide, and Lonesome
When the Legends Die

Boucicault, Dion
The Octoroon
Rip Van Winkle

Brackenridge, Hugh Henry
The Rising Glory of America

Brant, Charles S.
The Autobiography of a Kiowa Apache Indian

Brougham, John
Po-Ca-Hon-Tas, or The Gentle Savage

Brown, Dee
Bury My Heart at Wounded Knee: An Indian History of the American West
Creek Mary's Blood
The Fetterman Massacre
Fighting Indians of the West
Galvanized Yankees
The Gentle Tamers: Women of the Old Wild West
Hear That Lonesome Whistle Blow: Railroads in the West
The Settlers West
Trail Driving Days
Wave High the Banner
When the Century Was Young
Yellowhorse

Brown, Joseph Epes
The Sacred Pipe

Bryan, Daniel
The Mountain Muse: Comprising the Adventures of Daniel Boone; and the Power of Virtuous and Refined Beauty

Burke, Charles
Rip Van Winkle, a Legend of the Catskills

Burlend, Rebecca and Edward Burlend
A True Picture of Emigration

Burns, Walter Noble
The Saga of Billy the Kid

Cabeza de Vaca, Alvar Núñez
The Castaways

Carrington, Henry B.
The Indian Question, an Address

Carson, Kit
Kit Carson's Autobiography

Carver, Jonathan
Travels through the Interior Parts of North America

Cather, Willa
Death Comes for the Archbishop
A Lost Lady
My Ántonia
O Pioneers!

Catlin, George
  Catlin's Notes of Eight Years' Travels and Residence in Europe
  Last Rambles amongst the Indians of the Rocky Mountains and the Andes
  *Letters and Notes on the Manners, Customs and Condition of the North Ameri-
    can Indians during Eight Years' Travel amongst the Wildest Tribes of
    Indians of North America*
  My Life among the Indians
  *North American Indian Portfolio: Hunting Scenes and Amusements of the
    Rocky Mountains and Prairies of America*
  Okeepa, a Religious Ceremony, and Other Customs of the Mandans

Chilton, Thomas
  Narrative of the Life of David Crockett of the State of Tennessee

Clark, Walter Van Tilburg
  The City of Trembling Leaves
  The Ox-Bow Incident

Clarke, Mathew St. Clair
  The Life and Adventures of Colonel David Crockett of West Tennessee

Cleaveland, Agnes Morley
  No Life for a Lady

Clyman, James
  Journal of a Mountain Man

Cockings, George
  The Conquest of Canada

Cody, William F.
  The Adventures of Buffalo Bill

Conner, Charlotte Barnes
  Forest Princess

Cook, Captain James
  *The Explorations of Captain James Cook in the Pacific as Told by Selections of
    His Own Journals, 1768–1779*

Cooper, Courtney Ryley
  Annie Oakley, Woman at Arms

Cooper, James Fenimore
  The Deerslayer
  The Last of the Mohicans
  The Pathfinder: or The Inland Sea
  The Pioneers or, The Sources of the Susquehanna
  The Prairie
  The Redskins
  Wyandotte

Cooper, Williamm
  *A Guide in the Wilderness or the History of the First Settlements in the Western
    Counties of New York*

Cox, William Norment
The Scuffletown Outlaws: A Tragedy of the Lowrie Gang

Coyner, David H.
The Lost Trappers

Crane, Stephen
"The Bride Comes to Yellow Sky"

Craven, Margaret
I Heard the Owl Call My Name

Crèvecoeur, Hector St. John de
American Landscapes

Crockett, Davy
An Account of Colonel Crockett's Tour to the North and Down East
Crockett Almanack
Narrative of the Life of David Crockett of the State of Tennessee

Croswell, Joseph
A New World Planted

Crow Dog, Mary
Lakota Woman

Custer, Elizabeth Bacon
Boots and Saddles: Life in Dakota with General Custer
Following the Guidon
Tenting on the Plains

Custer, George Armstrong
My Life on the Plains

Custis, George Washington Parke
Pocahontas, or The Settlers of Virginia

Darwin, Charles
Voyage of the Beagle

Davies, John
The Forest Rose, or American Farmers

Davis, Britton
The Truth about Geronimo

Davis, H. L.
Honey in the Horn

de Soto, Hernando
Virginia Richly Valued by the Description of Florida

Deloria, Ella
Waterlily

Dickson, Lovat
Devil in Deerskins
My Life with Grey Owl

Dobie, Frank
  Apache Gold and Yaqui Silver
  The Ben Lilly Legend
  Coronado's Children
  Cow People
  Guide to Life and Literature of the Southwest
  The Longhorns
  The Mustang
  Some Part of Myself
  Tales of Old-Time Texas
  A Vaquero of the Brush Country
Dodge, Richard Irving
  *Our Wild Indians: Thirty-Three Years' Personal Experience among the Red Men
    of the Great West*
Drake, Samuel G.
  Biography and History of the Indians of North America
Drannan, William F.
  *Thirty-One Years on the Plains and in the Mountains or, The Last Voice from
    the Plains*
Dunlop, William
  A Trip to Niagara or Travellers in America
Eastman, Charles Alexander
  From the Deep Woods to Civilization
  Indian Boyhood
  Indian Scout Craft and Lore
  The Soul of the Indian: An Interpretation
Eastman, Mary H.
  Dacotah, or Life and Legends of the Sioux around Fort Snelling
Edmonds, Walter Dumaux
  Drums along the Mohawk
Eggleston, Edward
  The Hoosier Schoomaster
Ehle, John
  Trail of Tears: The Rise and Fall of the Cherokee Nation
Ellis, Edward S.
  The Life and Time of Col. Daniel Boone, Hunter, Soldier, and Pioneer
Erdoes, Richard
  Lame Deer, Seeker of Visions
Esquivel, Laura
  Like Water for Chocolate
Falkenhorst, C.
  With Cortéz in Mexico

Farnham, Eliza
  Life in Prairie Land
Farnham, Thomas Jefferson
  Life and Adventures in California
  Travels in the Great Western Prairies
Fast, Howard
  The Last Frontier
Faulkner, William
  "The Bear"
Ferber, Edna
  Cimarron
  Come and Get It
  Giant
  Great Son
  Ice Palace
  Saratoga Trunk
  Show Boat
  So Big
Fields, Dorothy
  Annie Get Your Gun
Fields, Herbert
  Annie Get Your Gun

Fife, Alta
  Saints of Sage and Saddle
Fife, Austin
  Saints of Sage and Saddle
Filson, John
  The Adventures of Col. Daniel Boon [sic], Containing Narrative of the Wars of Kentucke

Flint, Timothy
  The First White Man of the West, or the Life and Exploits of Col. Dan'l. Boone, the First Settler of Kentucky; Interspersed with Incidents in the Early Annals of the Country

Flynn, Thomas
  Rip Van Winkle, or The Demons of the Catskill Mountains! A National Drama
Fremont, John C.
  Report of the Exploring Expeditions of 1842 and 1843–44
Freneau, Philip
  "The Dying Indian"
  "The Indian Burying Ground"
  The Rising Glory of America

Fuentes, Carlos
The Old Gringo

Galvano, Antonio
Discoveries of the World

Garland, Hamlin
The Captain of the Gray Horse Troop
Cavanagh, Forest Ranger: A Romance of the Mountain West
Daughter of the Middle Border
Main-Travelled Roads

George, Jean Craighead
Julie of the Wolves

Geronimo
Geronimo's Story of His Life

Giles, Janice Holt
Hannah Fowler

Gillett, James B.
Six Years with the Texas Rangers, 1875–1881

Gipson, Fred
Cowhand: The Story of a Working Cowboy
Little Arliss
Old Yeller
Savage Sam
The Trail-Driving Rooster

Godfrey, Thomas
The Prince of Parthia

Gordon, Caroline
The Forest of the South

Green, Paul
In Abraham's Bosom
The Last of the Lowries: A Play of the Croatan Outlaws of Robeson County
The Laughing Pioneer
The Lost Colony: A Symphonic Drama in Two Acts
The No'Count Boy
Quare Medicine
Wilderness Road

Grey, Zane
Betty Zane
Blue Feather
Call of the Canyon
Desert Gold
The Heritage of the Desert

Grey, Zane, *continued*
 The Last of the Plainsmen
 The Last Trail
 Riders of the Purple Sage
 Robber's Roost
 Spirit of the Border
 The Thundering Herd
 To the Last Man
 The Vanishing American
 Wildfire

Grey Owl
 The Men of the Last Frontier
 Pilgrims of the Wild
 Sajo and the Beaver People

Grierson, Alice Kirk
 The Colonel's Lady on the Western Frontier: The Correspondence of Alice Kirk Grierson

Grinnell, George Bird
 Blackfoot Lodge Tales
 By Cheyenne Campfires
 The Cheyenne Indians
 The Fighting Cheyenne
 Pawnee Hero Stories and Folk Tales
 Two Great Scouts and Their Pawnee Battalion

Guthrie, A. B.
 The Big Sky
 These Thousand Hills
 The Way West

Hakluyt, Richard
 The Principal Navigations, Voyages, and Discoveries of the English Nation

Hall, Everard
 Nolens Volens; or The Biter Bit

Hammerstein, Oscar
 Annie Get Your Gun

Hanes, Bailey C.
 Bill Pickett, Bulldogger

Hardin, John Wesley
 The Life of John Wesley Hardin as Written by Himself

Harriot, Thomas
 A Briefe and True Report of the New Found Land of Virginia

Harris, Bernice Kelly
 Ca'line

Harte, Bret
Ah Sin, the Heathen Chinee
"At the Mission of San Carmel"
Condensed Novels
"The Luck of Roaring Camp"
"The Outcasts of Poker Flat"
The Poetical Works of Bret Harte
A Protégée of Jack Hamlin's and Other Stories
The Story of a Mine and Other Tales
The Two Men of Sandy Bar

Hartman, Jan
The Legend of Daniel Boone

Hastings, Lansford W.
The Emigrants' Guide to Oregon and California

Haun, Catherine
A Woman's Trip across the Plains in 1849

Heckewelder, John
Account of the History, Manners, and Customs of the Indian Nations Who Once Inhabited Pennsylvania and the Neighboring States

Henry, O.
Heart of the West

Hitchcock, Ethan Allan
A Traveller in Indian Territory

Holland, Robert E.
The Song of Tekakwitha

Hooke, Hilda Mary
Brown Lady Johnson

Horn, Tom
Life of Tom Horn, Government Scout and Interpreter

Howard, Bronson Crocker
Shenandoah

Howard, Oliver Otis
Famous Indian Chiefs I Have Known
My Life and Experiences among Our Hostile Indians
Nez Perce Joseph

Hoyt, Charles
A Trip to Chinatown

Humphrey, David
Essay on the Life of the Honorable Major-General Israel Putnam

Hunter, Kermit
Horn in the West

Hutton, Joseph
The Falls of Niagara

Hyde, George E.
Indians of the High Plains
Indians of the Woodlands
The Life of George Bent
The Pawnee Indians
A Sioux Chronicle
Spotted Tail's Folk

Irving, Washington
The Adventures of Captain Bonneville, U. S. A.
Astoria
"The Devil and Tom Walker"
A History of New York, from the Beginning of the World to the End of the
    Dutch Dynasty
"The Legend of Sleepy Hollow"
The Life and Voyages of Christopher Columbus
"Rip Van Winkle"
"The Spectre Bridegroom, A Traveller's Tale"
Tales of a Traveller
A Tour of the Prairies
Voyages and Discoveries of the Companions of Columbus
Wolfert's Roost and Miscellanies

Jackson, Helen Hunt
A Century of Dishonor
Ramona

James, Marquis
Cherokee Strip
The Raven

Jefferson, Joseph, III
The Autobiography of Joseph Jefferson

Johnson, Dorothy Marie
Indian Country

Johnston, Basil H.
Indian School Days

Jones, J. B.
Wild Western Scenes; A Narrative of Adventures in the Western Wilderness,
    Forty Years Ago; Wherein the Conduct of Daniel Boone, the Great American
    Pioneer, Is Particularly Described

Kalakaua, King David
The Legends and Myths of Hawaii

Kessler, Lauren
Stubborn Twig: Three Generations in the Life of a Japanese American Family

Kidd, Adam
The Huron Chief

Kingsolver, Barbara
Animal Dreams

Kittredge, William
Owing It All

Koch, Fred, Jr.
Wash Carver's Mouse Trap

Kroeber, Theodora
Ishi in Two Worlds
Ishi, Last of His Tribe

La Farge, Oliver
Laughing Boy

Lake, Stuart N.
Wyatt Earp, Frontier Marshall

Lame Deer, John
Lame Deer, Seeker of Visions

L'Amour, Louis
The Burning Hills
The Comstock Lode
Conagher
The Education of a Wandering Man
Guns of the Timberland
Hondo
The Sackett Companion: A Personal Guide to the Sackett Novels
Shalako
Silver Canyon
Sitka
A Trail of Memories: The Quotations of Louis L'Amour
Westward the Tide

Landa, Diego de
Yucatan before and after the Conquest

Lane, Rose Wilder
On the Way Home

Langford, J. O., and Fred Gipson
Big Bend: A Homesteader's Story

Las Casas, Bartolomé de
A History of the Indies
A Short Account of the Destruction of the Indies

Lawrence, D. H.
Birds, Beasts and Flowers
Mornings in Mexico

Lawrence, D. H., *continued*
  The Plumed Serpent
  "The Spirit of Place"
  Studies in Classic American Literature

Linderman, Frank B.
  Pretty-Shield, Medicine Woman of the Crows

Lomax, John
  Adventures of a Ballad Hunter
  Cowboy Songs and Other Frontier Ballads
  Folk Song U.S.A.
  Negro Folk Songs as Sung by Lead Belly
  Our Singing Country
  Songs of the Cattle Trail and Cow Camp

Lomax, John, and Alan Lomax
  American Ballads and Folk Songs

London, Jack
  The Call of the Wild
  Daughter of the Snows
  The Son of the Wolf: Tales of the Far North
  "To Build a Fire"
  White Fang

Long, Stephen Harriman
  From Pittsburgh to the Rocky Mountains

Longfellow, Henry Wadsworth
  The Courtship of Miles Standish
  Evangeline, a Tale of Arcadie

Lopez, Barry
  Of Wolves and Men

Lopez-Medina, Sylvia
  Cantora

Love, Nat
  The Life and Adventures of Nat Love, Better Known in the Cattle Country as Deadwood Dick

MacBride, Roger Lea
  In the Land of the Big Red Apple
  Little Farm in the Ozarks
  Little House on Rocky Ridge

Mackay, Constance D'Arcy
  Plays of the Pioneers

MacKaye, Percy
  Rip Van Winkle, a Folk Opera

Magoffin, Susan Shelby
  Down the Santa Fe Trail & into Mexico

Marble, Dan
Sam Patch, the Jumper of Niagara Falls

McClung, Nellie Letitia Mooney
Clearing in the West

McConnell, H. H.
Five Years a Cavalryman or, Sketches of Regular Army Life on the Texas Frontier, 1866–1871

McCunn, Ruthanne Lum
Thousand Pieces of Gold

McIntire, Jim
Early Days in Texas, A Trip to Hell and Heaven

McLachlan, Alexander
"The Emigrant"

McMurtry, Larry
Lonesome Dove
The Streets of Laredo

Metcalfe, Samuel L.
A Collection of Some of the Most Interesting Narratives of Indian Warfare in the West, Containing an Account of the Adventures of Daniel Boone, One of the First Settlers of Kentucky

Micheaux, Oscar
The Conquest: The Story of a Negro Pioneer

Michener, James
Alaska
Centennial
Hawaii
Texas

Miller, Joaquin
The Danites in the Sierras
Forty-Nine
The Illustrated History of Montana
Joaquin et al.
An Oregon Idyll
Shadows of Shasta
Song of the Sierras
Specimens
Tally Ho!
Unwritten History: Life among the Modocs

Moeller, Philip
Pokey, or The Beautiful Legend of the Amorous Indian

Momaday, N. Scott
House Made of Dawn
The Way to Rainy Mountain

Moodie, Susanna
Life in the Clearings
Roughing It in the Bush

Moody, William Vaughn
The Great Divide

Morgan, Lewis Henry
The Indian Journals, 1859–1862
League of the Ho-de-no-sau-nee or Iroquois

Mowatt, Anna Cora
Fashion

Muir, John
The Cruise of the Corwin
John of the Mountains
Letters to a Friend
The Mountains of California
My First Summer in the Sierra
Our National Parks
Steep Trails
"Stickeen"
The Story of My Boyhood and Youth
A Thousand Mile Walk to the Gulf
Travels in Alaska
Yosemite

Murdoch, Frank H.
Davy Crockett

Neihardt, John G.
Black Elk Speaks: The Life Story of a Holy Man of the Oglala Sioux
The Song of Hugh Glass
The Song of Jed Smith
The Song of the Indian Wars
The Song of the Messiah
The Song of Three Friends

Noah, Mordecai M.
She Would Be a Soldier, or The Plains of Chippewa

Oakley, Annie
The Story of My Life

O'Dell, Scott
The Black Pearl
Island of the Blue Dolphins
The King's Fifth
Sarah Bishop
Sing Down the Moon
Streams to the River, River to the Sea

Thunder Rolling in the Mountains
Woman of Spain: A Story of Old California

Owen, Robert Dale
Pocahontas

Paramore, Ted
"The Ballad of Yukon Jake"

Parkman, Francis
Count Frontenac and New France under Louis XIV
Half-Century of Conflict
The History of the Conspiracy of Pontiac
The Jesuits in North America in the Seventeenth Century
La Salle and the Discovery of the Great West
Montcalm and Wolfe
The Old Régime in Canada
The Oregon Trail: Sketches of Prairie and Rocky Mountain Life
The Parkman Reader
Pioneers of France in the New World

Paulding, James Kirke
The Lion of the West

Poe, Edgar Allan
"Eldorado"

Porter, Katherine Anne
"María Concepción"

Portis, Charles
True Grit

Prescott, William H.
History of the Conquest of Mexico

Radin, Paul
The Autobiography of a Winnebago Indian
The Culture of the Winnebago: As Described by Themselves
The Genetic Relationship of the North American Indian Languages
Method and Theory of Ethnology
Primitive Man as Philosopher
Primitive Religion
The Road of Life and Death
The Story of the American Indian
The Trickster: A Study in American Indian Mythology
The Winnebago Tribe

Rawlings, Marjorie Kinnan
The Yearling

Reed, John
Insurgent Mexico

Remington, Frederic
Frederic Remington's Own West

Rhodes, William Henry
Theodosia, The Pirate's Prisoner

Richards, Mary Haskin Parker
Winter Quarters, The 1846–1848 Life Writings of Mary Haskin Parker Richards

Richardson, Howard
Dark of the Moon

Richter, Conrad
The Awakening Land
A Country of Strangers
Early Americana and Other Stories
The Free Man
The Light in the Forest
The Rawhide Knot
Tacey Cromwell

Rodgers, Richard
Annie Get Your Gun

Rodney, William
Kootenai Brown, Canada's Unknown Frontiersman

Rogers, Robert
Ponteach

Rölvaag, O. E.
Concerning Our Heritage
Giants in the Earth: A Saga of the Prairie
Letters from America
On Forgotten Paths
Peder Victorious
The Ship of Longing
Their Fathers' God
Two Fools

Roosevelt, Theodore
Ranch Life and the Hunting Trail
Rough Riders
The Winning of the West

Rowland, Mary Canaga
As Long as Life: The Memoirs of a Frontier Woman Doctor

Rowlandson, Mary White
A Narrative of the Captivity, Sufferings and Removes of Mrs. Mary Rowlandson

Royce, Sarah Eleanor Bayliss
A Frontier Lady: Recollections of the Gold Rush and Early California

Russell, Osborne
Journal of a Trapper

Sager, Ed, and Mike Frye
The Bootlegger's Lady

Sandburg, Carl
"Buffalo Bill"

Sandoz, Mari
The Battle of the Little Bighorn
The Beaver Men: Spearheads of Empire
The Buffalo Hunters
The Cattlemen: From the Rio Grande across the Far Marias
Cheyenne Autumn
Crazy Horse: The Strange Man of the Oglalas

Sanford, Mollie
Mollie: The Journal of Mollie Dorsey Sanford in Nebraska and Colorado Territories, 1857–1866

Sawyer, Lemuel
Blackbeard

Schaefer, Jack
The Big Range
The Canyon
Company of Cowards
First Blood
The Great Endurance Horse Race
Heroes without Glory
The Kean Land and Other Stories
Mavericks
Monte Walsh
New Mexico
Old Ramon
Out West
The Pioneers
The Plainsman
Shane
Stubby Pringle's Christmas

Schmitt, Martin
Fighting Indians of the West
The Settlers West
Trail Driving Days

Schoolcraft, Henry Rowe
Historical and Statistical Information Respecting the History, Condition and Prospects of the Indian Tribes of the United States

Service, Robert
"The Cremation of Sam McGee"
"The Shooting of Dan McGrew"
Songs of a Sourdough
The Trail of '98: A Northland Romance

Sewid, James
Guests Never Leave Hungry: The Autobiography of James Sewid, a Kwakiutl Indian

Sherburne, John P.
Through Indian Country to California

Shirley, Glenn
Belle Starr and Her Times: The Literature, the Facts, and the Legends

Shively, J. M.
Route and Distances to Oregon and California

Short, Luke
Hardcase
Ride the Man Down

Simms, William Gilmore
The Yemassee: A Romance of Carolina

Siringo, Charles A.
The Cowboy Detective
A History of Billy the Kid
A Lone Star Cowboy
Riata and Spurs
A Song Companion of a Lone Star Cowboy
A Texas Cowboy, or, Fifteen Years on the Hurricane Deck of a Spanish Cow Pony
Two Evil Isms: Pinkertonism and Anarchism

Smith, Captain John
Generall Historie of Virginia, New England and the Summer Isles
A True Relation of such occurrences and accidents of noate as hath hapned in Virginia since the first planting of that Collony

Smith, Helena Huntington
A Bride Goes West

Smith, Joseph
Book of Mormon

Smith, Richard Penn
Colonel Crockett's Exploits and Adventures in Texas

Speare, Elizabeth
The Sign of the Beaver

Spencer, O. M.
The Indian Captivity of O. M. Spencer

Standing Bear, Luther
My Indian Boyhood
Stories of the Sioux

Stegner, Wallace
The Sound of Mountain Water

Steinbeck, John
East of Eden
"The Leader of the People"

Stevens, Frank E.
The Black Hawk War

Stevenson, Robert Louis
Across the Plains

Stewart, Elinore Pruitt
Letters of a Woman Homesteader
Letters on an Elk Hunt

Stone, John Augustus
Metamora, or the Last of the Wampanoags

Stratton, Reverend R. B.
Captivity of the Oatman Girls: Being an Interesting Narrative of Life among the Apache and Mohave Indians

Taylor, Tom
Our American Cousin

Thomas, Augustus
Arizona
In Mizzoura

Tibbles, Thomas Henry
Buckskin and Blanket Days

Traill, Catherine Parr
The Backwoods of Canada

Trupin, Sophie
Dakota Diaspora: Memoirs of a Jewish Homesteader

Twain, Mark
Ah Sin, the Heathen Chinee
The Autobiography of Mark Twain
"The Celebrated Jumping Frog of Calaveras County"
"Fenimore Cooper's Literary Offenses"
"The Killing of Julius Caesar 'Localized'"
Life on the Mississippi
"The Noble Red Man"
Roughing It

Tyler, Royall
The Contrast

Ulrich, Laurel Thatcher
A Midwife's Tale: The Life of Martha Ballard, Based on Her Diary, 1785–1812

Vaughn, J. W.
Indian Fights: New Facts on Seven Encounters

Visscher, William Lightfoot
The Pony Express: A Thrilling and Truthful History

Vollmer, Lula
Sun-Up

Wallis, Velma
Two Old Women: An Alaska Legend of Betrayal, Courage and Survival

Webster, Benjamin
The Golden Farmer

West, Jessamyn
Except for Me and Thee
The Friendly Persuasion
The Massacre at Fall Creek

White, Stewart Edward
Daniel Boone: Wilderness Scout

Whitman, Narcissa Prentiss
My Journal, 1836

Wilder, Laura Ingalls
By the Shores of Silver Lake
Farmer Boy
The First Four Years
Little House in the Big Woods
Little House on the Prairie
Little Town on the Prairie
The Long Winter
On the Banks of Plum Creek
These Happy Golden Years
West from Home: Letters, San Francisco, 1915

Williams, John
The Redeemed Captive Returning to Zion

Windolph, Charles
I Fought with Custer: The Story of Sergeant Windolph, Last Survivor of the Battle of the Little Big Horn

Winnemucca, Sarah
Life among the Piutes, Their Wrongs and Claims

Wister, Owen
Owen Wister Out West: His Journals and Letters
Red Men and White
The Virginian: A Horseman of the Plains

Wolfe, Thomas
A Western Journal

Woodhouse, Samuel Washington
A Naturalist in Indian Territory

Woods, Walter
Billy the Kid

Woodworth, Samuel
The Forest Rose, or American Farmers

Wright, Harold Bell
The Shepherd of the Hills

Wyman, Jasper
Journey to the Koyukuk

Yep, Laurence
Dragon's Gate
Dragonwings

Young, Alida
Land of the Iron Dragon

Young, Carrie
Nothing To Do but Stay
The Wedding Dress

Zwinger, Ann
Run, River, Run

A TIMELINE OF FILMS OF MAJOR
WORKS OF FRONTIER LITERATURE

1929 *The Virginian* (Paramount)

1931 *Riders of the Purple Sage* (Universal-International)

1934 *A Lost Lady* (Warner)

1936 *Come and Get It* (Samuel Goldwyn)
The Last of the Mohicans (Edward Small)
The Sea of Grass (MGM)

1937 *The Outcasts of Poker Flat* (RKO)

1939 *Drums along the Mohawk* (Twentieth Century Fox)

1941 *The Shepherd of the Hills* (Paramount)

1942 *One Desire* (Universal)

1943 *The Ox-Bow Incident* (Twentieth Century Fox)
Saratoga Trunk (Warner)

1946 *The Virginian* (Paramount)
The Yearling (MGM)

1949 *The Red Pony* (Republic)

1950 *Annie Get Your Gun* (MGM)

1951 *Showboat* (MGM)

1952 *The Big Sky* (RKO/Winchester)
The Outcasts of Poker Flat (Twentieth Century Fox)

1953 *Hondo* (Wayne-Fellows)
Shane (Paramount)
So Big (Warner)

1954 *Davy Crockett, King of the Wild Frontier* (Walt Disney)
Cheyenne Autumn (Warner)

1955 *East of Eden* (Warner)
Robber's Roost (United Artists)

1956 *The Burning Hills* (Warner)
       The Friendly Persuasion (Allied Artists)
       Giant (Warner)

1958 *The Light in the Forest* (Walt Disney)
       These Thousand Hills (Twentieth Century Fox)

1960 *Cimarron* (MGM)
       Guns of the Timberland (Jaguar)
       Ice Palace (MGM-UA)

1962 *Savage Sam* (Walt Disney)

1963 *Old Yeller* (Walt Disney)

1964 *The Island of the Blue Dolphins* (Universal)

1966 *Hawaii* (United Artists/Mirisch)

1967 *The Way West* (United Artists)

1968 *Shalako* (Kingston/Dimitri de Grunwald)

1969 *True Grit* (Paramount)

1970 *Little Big Man* (Stockbridge/HIller/Cinema Center)
       Monte Walsh (Cinema Center)

1972 *When the Legends Die* (Twentieth Century Fox)

1976 *The Black Pearl* (Diamond Films)

1979 *Tom Horn* (Warner/Solar/First Artists)

1989 *Old Gringo* (Columbia TriStar)

1990 *Dances with Wolves* (Guild/Tig)
       White Fang (Warner)

1991 *Like Water for Chocolate* (Electric/Cinevista)

1992 *The Last of the Mohicans* (WarnerMorgan)

1994 *Pocahontas* (Walt Disney)

PRIMARY SOURCES
Books

Adams, Andy. 1975. *The Log of a Cowboy: A Narrative of the Old Trail Days.* Williamston, Mass.: Corner House.

Aimard, Gustave. 1991. *The Trappers of Arkansas.* In *American Pioneer Writers.* New York: Gallery.

Alderson, Nannie, and Helena Huntington Smith. 1942. *A Bride Goes West.* Lincoln: University of Nebraska Press.

Allison, Susan. 1991. *A Pioneer Gentlewoman in British Columbia.* Vancouver: University of British Columbia Press.

Anaya, Rudolfo A. 1972. *Bless Me, Ultima.* Berkeley, Calif.: TOS Publications.

Anderson, Eva G. 1951. *Chief Seattle.* Caldwell, Idaho: Caxton Printers.

Atherton, Gertrude. 1991. *Before the Gringo Came.* In *American Pioneer Writers.* New York: Gallery.

Audubon, John James. 1940. *Audubon's America.* Boston: Houghton Mifflin.

Audubon, John Woodhouse. 1984. *Audubon's Western Journal 1849–1850.* Tucson: University of Arizona Press.

Austin, Mary. 1903. *The Land of Little Rain.* Boston: Houghton Mifflin.

———. 1928. *Children Sing in the Far West.* Boston: Houghton Mifflin.

———. 1932. *Earth Horizon.* Albuquerque: University of New Mexico Press.

———. 1987. *Western Trails.* Reno: University of Nevada Press.

Azuela, Mariano. 1962. *The Underdogs: A Novel of the Mexican Revolution.* New York: Signet.

Baldwin, Joseph Glover. 1966. *The Flush Times of California.* Athens: University of Georgia Press.

Barlow, Joel. 1970. *The Works of Joel Barlow, Vols. 1 & 2*. Gainesville, Fla.: Scholars' Facsmiles & Reprints.

Battey, Thomas C. 1972. *The Life and Adventures of a Quaker among the Indians*. Williamstown, Mass.: Corner House.

Beal, Allen. 1963. *I Will Fight No More Forever*. Seattle: University of Washington Press.

Beecher, Catherine E., and Harriet Beecher Stowe. 1994. *American Woman's Home*. Hartford, Conn.: Stowe-Day Foundation.

Benét, Rosemary, and Stephen Vincent Benét. 1933. *A Book of Americans*. New York: Farrar and Rinehart.

Benét, Stephen Vincent. 1943. *Western Star*. New York: Holt, Rinehart, and Winston.

Benét, William Rose. 1965. "Jesse James." In *Accent: U. S. A.* Chicago: Scott, Foresman.

Berger, Thomas. 1964. *Little Big Man*. Greenwich, Conn.: Fawcett.

Betenson, Lula Parker. 1975. *Butch Cassidy, My Brother*. Provo, Utah: Brigham Young University Press.

Betzinez, Jason. 1959. *I Fought with Geronimo*. Lincoln: University of Nebraska Press.

Bierce, Ambrose. 1963. *The Sardonic Humor of Ambrose Bierce*. New York: Dover.

———. 1964. *Ghost and Horror Stories of Ambrose Bierce*. New York: Dover.

———. 1977. *The Stories and Fables of Ambrose Bierce*. Owings Mills, Md.: Stemmer House.

———. 1984. *The Complete Short Stories of Ambrose Bierce*. Lincoln: University of Nebraska Press.

———. 1994. *Civil War Songs*. New York: Dover.

Bird, Isabella L. 1960. *A Lady's Life in the Rocky Mountains*. Norman: University of Oklahoma Press.

Black Hawk. 1955. *An Autobiography*. Urbana: University of Illinois Press.

———. 1994. *Life of Black Hawk*. New York: Dover.

Blacker, Irwin R., ed. 1961. *The Old West in Fiction*. New York: Ivan Obolensky.

Blake, James Carlos. 1995. *The Pistoleer*. New York: Berkley Books.

———. 1996. *The Friends of Pancho Villa*. New York: Berkley Books.

Blake, Michael. 1988. *Dances with Wolves*. New York: Ballantine Books.

Bojer, Johan. 1974. *The Emigrants*. Westport, Conn.: Greenwood.

———. 1991. *The Emigrants*. St. Paul: Minnesota Historical Society.

Bonner, Thomas. 1972. *The Life and Adventures of Beckwourth*. Lincoln: University of Nebraska Press.

Bontemps, Arna, ed. 1969. *Great Slave Narratives*. Boston: Beacon Press.

Borland, Hal. 1956. *High, Wide, and Lonesome*. New York: Lippincott.

———. 1963. *This Hill, This Valley*. New York: Lippincott.

———. 1989. *When the Legends Die*. New York: Bantam.

Bradford, William. 1966. *Of Plymouth Plantation*. New York: Alfred A. Knopf.

Brant, Charles S., ed. 1969. *The Autobiography of a Kiowa Apache Indian*. New York: Dover.

Brougham, John. 1966. *Po-Ca-Hon-Tas, or The Gentle Savage*. In *Dramas from American Theatre 1762–1909*. Cleveland: World Publishing.

Brown, Dee. 1945. *Wave High the Banner*. Philadelphia: Macrae-Smith.

———. 1958. *The Gentle Tamers: Women of the Old Wild West*. Lincoln: University of Nebraska Press.

———. 1962. *The Fetterman Massacre*. Lincoln: University of Nebraska Press.

———. 1970. *Bury My Heart at Wounded Knee: An Indian History of the American West*. New York: Henry Holt.

———. 1977. *Hear That Lonesome Whistle Blow: Railroads in the West*. New York: Touchstone.

———. 1993. *When the Century Was Young*. Little Rock, Ark.: August House.

Brown, Joseph Epes, ed. 1989. *The Sacred Pipe: Black Elk's Account of the Seven Rites of the Oglala Sioux*. Norman: University of Oklahoma Press.

Burlend, Rebecca, and Edward Burlend. 1987. *A True Picture of Emigration*. Lincoln: University of Nebraska Press.

Burns, Walter Noble. 1926. *The Saga of Billy the Kid*. Garden City, N.Y.: Doubleday, Page & Co.

Cabeza de Vaca, Alvar Núñez. 1993a. *Castaways*. Berkeley: University of California Press.

———. 1993. *Relation*. Houston: Arte Publico.

Canadian Poetry: From the Beginnings through the First World War. 1994. Toronto: McClelland & Stewart.

Carmony, Neil B., ed. 1992. *Afield with J. Frank Dobie: Tales of Critters, Campfires, and the Hunting Trail*. Silver City, N.M.: High-Lonesome Books.

Carrington, Henry B. 1909. *The Indian Question*. Mattituck, N.Y.: J. M. Carroll.

Carson, Kit. 1966. *Kit Carson's Autobiography*. Lincoln: University of Nebraska Press.

Carter, Forrest. 1976. *The Education of Little Tree*. Albuquerque: University of New Mexico Press.

Castañeda, Pedro de. 1990. *The Journey of Coronado*. New York: Dover.

Cather, Willa. 1931. *Shadows on the Rock*. New York: Alfred A. Knopf.

———. 1947. *Death Comes for the Archbishop*. New York: Alfred A. Knopf.

———. 1972. *A Lost Lady*. New York: Random House.

———. 1977. *My Ántonia*. Boston: Houghton Mifflin.

———. 1991. *O Pioneers!* In *American Pioneer Writers*. New York: Gallery.

Catlin, George. 1965. *Letters and Notes on the Manners, Customs and Condition of the North American Indians during Eight Years' Travel amongst the Wildest Tribes of Indians of North America*. Minneapolis, Minn.: Ross & Haines.

———. 1989. *North American Indians*. New York: Penguin.

Champlain, Samuel de. 1923. *Works*. Toronto: Champlain Society.

Cieza de Leon, Piedro. 1883. *The Second Part of the Chronicle of Peru*. London: Hakluyt Society.

Clark, Barrett, gen. ed. 1963. *America's Lost Plays*. Bloomington: Indiana University Press.

Clark, Walter Van Tilburg. 1968. *The Ox-Bow Incident*. New York: New American Library.

Cleaveland, Agnes. 1941. *No Life for a Lady*. Lincoln: University of Nebraska Press.

Clyman, James. 1984. *Journal of a Mountain Man*. Missoula, Mont.: Mountain Press.

Cody, William F. 1904. *The Adventures of Buffalo Bill*. New York: Harper & Brothers.

Coleman, Rufus A., ed. 1932. *The Golden West in Story and Verse*. New York: Harper & Brothers.

Columbus, Christopher. 1924. *Journal of the First Voyage to America*. New York: Boni.

———. 1969. *The Four Voyages*. London: Penguin.

———. 1988. *The Four Voyages of Columbus*. London: Hakluyt Society.

———. 1992. *The Voyage of Christopher Columbus*. New York: St. Martin's.

Cook, James. 1971. *The Explorations of Captain James Cook in the Pacific as Told by Selections of His Own Journals, 1768–1779*. New York: Dover.

Cooper, Courtney Riley. 1927. *Annie Oakley, Woman at Arms*. New York: Duffield and Co.

Cooper, James Fenimore. n.d. *The Spy*. New York: Grosset & Dunlap.

———. 1958. *The Prairie*. New York: Rinehart.

———. 1963. *The Bravo*. New Haven, Conn.: College & University Press.

———. 1964. *The Pathfinder: or The Inland Sea*. New York: Airmont.

———. 1968. *The Pioneers*. New York: Magnum.

———. 1980. *The Deerslayer*. New York: New American Library.

———. 1989. *The Last of the Mohicans*. New York: New American Library.

Cooper, William. 1970. *A Guide in the Wilderness or the History of the First Settlements in the Western Counties of New York*. Freeport, N.Y.: Books for Libraries Press.

Coyner, David H. 1995. *The Lost Trappers*. Norman: University of Oklahoma Press.

Craven, Margaret. 1973. *I Heard the Owl Call My Name*. New York: Dell.

Crockett, David. 1834. *Narrative of the Life of David Crockett of the State of Tennessee*. Cincinnati: U. P. James.

———. 1987. *The Tall Tales of Davy Crockett*. Knoxville: University of Tennessee Press.

Crow Dog, Mary. 1990. *Lakota Woman*. New York: HarperCollins.

Custer, Elizabeth. 1961. *Boots and Saddles*. Norman: University of Oklahoma Press.

Custer, George A. 1962. *My Life on the Plains*. New York: Citadel.

Custis, George Washington Parke. 1938. *Pocahontas, or The Settlers of Virginia*. In *Representative American Plays from 1767 to the Present Day*. New York: D. Appleton-Century.

Darwin, Charles. 1989. *Voyage of the Beagle*. London: Penguin.

Davis, Britton. 1929. *The Truth about Geronimo*. New Haven: Yale University Press.

Davis, H. L. 1992. *Honey in the Horn*. Moscow: University of Idaho Press.

de Gaspé, Philippe-Joseph Aubert. 1990. *Yellow-Wolf and Other Tales of the Saint Lawrence*. Montreal: Vehicule.

De Soto, Hernando. 1968. *Narratives of the Career of Hernando De Soto in the Conquest of Florida*. Gainesville, Fla.: Palmetto Books.

Deloria, Ella. 1988. *Waterlily*. Lincoln: University of Nebraska Press.

Deloria, Vine. 1969. *Custer Died for Your Sins.* New York: Macmillan.

———. 1973. *God Is Red.* New York: Delta.

Dobie, J. Frank. 1952. *The Mustang.* Boston: Little, Brown.

———. 1978. *The Ben Lilly Legend.* Austin: University of Texas Press.

———. 1990. *Apache Gold and Yaqui Silver.* Austin: University of Texas Press.

Dodge, Richard Irving. 1978. *Our Wild Indians: Thirty-Three Years' Personal Experience among the Red Men of the Great West.* Williamstown, Mass.: Corner House.

Drake, Samuel G. 1834. *Biography and History of the Indians of North America.* Boston: O. L. Perkins.

Drannan, William F. 1900. *Thirty-One Years on the Plains and in the Mountains or, The Last Voice from the Plains.* Chicago: Rhodes & McClure.

Driggs, Howard R. 1935. *The Pony Express Goes Through.* New York: Lippincott.

Eastman, Charles A. 1974. *Indian Scout Craft and Lore.* New York: Dover.

———. 1975. *Indian Boyhood.* Williamstown, Mass.: Corner House.

———. 1980. *The Soul of the Indian: An Interpretation.* Lincoln: University of Nebraska Press.

Edmonds, Walter D. 1936. *Drums along the Mohawk.* Boston: Little, Brown.

Eggleston, Edward. 1903. *The Hoosier Schoolmaster.* New York: Orange Judd.

Eggleston, Wilfrid. 1977. *The Frontier and Canadian Letters.* Toronto: McClelland & Stewart.

Esquivel, Laura. 1991. *Like Water for Chocolate.* New York: Anchor Books.

Falkenhorst, C. 1892. *With Cortéz in Mexico.* New York: Hurst.

Farnham, Thomas. 1983. *An 1839 Wagon Train Journal.* New York: Greenley & McElrath.

Faulkner, William, 1967. *The Portable Faulkner.* New York: Penguin.

———. 1977. *Collected Stories.* New York: Vintage.

Ferber, Edna. 1945. *Great Son.* New York: Avon.

———. 1981. *Five Complete Novels.* New York: Avenel.

Fields, Herbert, and Dorothy Fields. 1946. *Annie Get Your Gun.* (stage play) Chicago: Dramatic Publishing.

———. 1952. *Annie Get Your Gun.* (musical) London: Chappell & Co.

Fisher, Leonard Everett. 1992. *Tracks across America.* New York: Holiday House.

Fowke, Edith. 1976. *Folklore of Canada*. Toronto: McClelland & Stewart.

Franklin, Benjamin. 1982. *The Autobiography and Other Writings*. New York: Bantam.

Fuentes, Carlos. 1985. *The Old Gringo*. New York: Farrar, Straus & Giroux.

Gardner, Martin, ed. 1995. *Famous Poems from Bygone Days*. New York: Dover.

Garland, Hamlin. 1928. *A Son of the Middle Border*. New York: Macmillan.

———. 1970. *Main-Travelled Roads*. Columbus, Ohio: Charles E. Merrill.

———. 1995. *Main-Travelled Roads*. Lincoln: University of Nebraska Press.

Garrett, Pat F. 1954. *The Authentic Life of Billy, the Kid*. Norman: University of Oklahoma Press.

Gassner, John, ed. 1967. *Best Plays of the American Theatre*. New York: Crown.

George, Jean Craighead. 1972. *Julie of the Wolves*. New York: Harper & Row.

Geronimo. 1989. *Geronimo's Story of His Life*. Williamstown, Mass.: Corner House.

Giles, Janice Holt. 1956. *Hannah Fowler*. Boston: Houghton Mifflin.

Gillett, James. 1976. *Six Years with the Texas Rangers, 1875–1881*. Lincoln: University of Nebraska Press.

Gipson, Fred. 1953. *Cowhand: The Story of a Working Cowboy*. New York: Harper & Brothers.

———. 1956. *Old Yeller*. New York: Harper & Row.

Gloss, Molly. 1989. *The Jump Off Creek*. Boston: Houghton Mifflin.

Gorgas, Marie D., and Burton J. Hendrick. 1924. *William Crawford Gorgas: His Life and Work*. Garden City, N.Y.: Garden City Publishing.

Green, Paul. 1937. *The Lost Colony: A Symphonic Drama in Two Acts*. Chapel Hill: University of North Carolina Press.

———. 1956. *Quare Medicine*. In *North Carolina Drama*. Richmond, Va.: Garret & Massie.

Gregg, John J, and Barbara T. Gregg. 1980. *Best Loved Poems of the American West*. Garden City, N.Y.: Doubleday.

Grey, Zane. 1918. *The U. P. Trail*. New York: Grosset & Dunlap.

———. 1940. *Riders of the Purple Sage*. Roslyn, N.Y.: Walter J. Black.

———. 1978. *The Last of the Plainsmen*. Mattituck, N.Y.: American Reprint.

———. 1988. *Blue Feather and Other Stories*. Boston: G. K. Hall.

Grey Owl. 1972. *The Men of the Last Frontier*. Toronto: Stoddart.

———. 1990. *Pilgrims of the Wild*. Toronto: Macmillan.

———. 1991. *Sajo and the Beaver People*. Toronto: Stoddart.

———. 1992. *Tales of an Empty Cabin*. Toronto: Stoddart.

Grierson, Alice. 1989. *The Colonel's Lady on the Western Frontier: The Correspondence of Alice Kirk Grierson*. Lincoln: University of Nebraska Press.

Grinnell, George Bird. 1972. *Blackfoot Lodge Tales*. Williamstown, Conn.: Corner House.

Grove, Frederick Philip. 1982. *A Search for America*. Toronto: McClelland & Stewart.

———. 1989. *Settlers of the Marsh*. Toronto: McClelland & Stewart.

———. 1992. *Fruits of the Earth.* Toronto: McClelland & Stewart.

Guthrie, A. B. 1960. *The Way West*. New York: Pocket Books.

Hakluyt, Richard. 1826. *The Principal Navigations, Voyages, and Discoveries of the English Nation*. New York: Brown.

———. 1958. *Voyages and Documents*. London: Oxford Press.

———. 1962. *Voyages*. Vols. 1–8. New York: Everyman's Library.

Hanners, LaVerne. 1994. *Girl on a Pony*. Norman: University of Oklahoma Press.

Hardin, John Wesley. 1961. *The Life of John Wesley Hardin as Written by Himself*. Norman: University of Oklahoma Press.

Harriot, Thomas. 1972. *A Briefe and True Report of the New Found Land of Virginia*. New York: Dover.

Harte, Bret. 1883. *In the Carquinez Woods and Other Tales*. Boston: Houghton Mifflin.

———. 1896. *The Story of a Mine and Other Tales*. Boston: Houghton Mifflin.

———. 1902. *The Complete Poetical Works*. New York: P. F. Collier.

———. 1992. *The Luck of Roaring Camp and Other Short Stories*. New York: Dover.

Hastings, Lansford W. 1845. *The Emigrants' Guide to Oregon and California*. Bedford, Mass.: Applewood.

Henry, O. 1993. *Heart of the West*. Pleasantville, N.Y.: Reader's Digest.

Hitchcock, Ethan Allen. 1996. *A Traveler in Indian Territory*. Norman: University of Oklahoma Press.

Holland, Robert E. 1942. *The Song of Tekakwitha: The Lily of the Mohawks*. New York: Fordham University Press.

Hooke, Hilda Mary. 1942. *One-Act Plays from Canadian History*. Toronto: Longmans, Green.

Hopkins, Sarah Winnemucca. 1994. *Life among the Piutes, Their Wrongs and Claims*. Reno: University of Nevada Press.

Horn, Tom. 1964. *Life of Tom Horn, Government Scout and Interpreter*. Norman: University of Oklahoma Press.

Howard, O. O. 1972. *Nez Perce Joseph: An Account of His Ancestors, His Lands, His Confederates, His Enemies, His Murders, His War, His Pursuit and Capture*. New York: Da Capo.

———. 1989. *Famous Indian Chiefs I Have Known*. Lincoln: University of Nebraska Press.

Hyde, George E. 1951. *The Pawnee Indians*. Norman: University of Oklahoma Press.

Irving, Washington. n.d. *The Best Known Works of Washington Irving*. Garden City, N.Y.: Book Club Associates.

———. 1851. *The Life and Voyages of Christopher Columbus*. New York: Putnam.

———. 1855. *Wolfert's Roost and Miscellanies*. New York: G. P. Putnam.

———. 1944. *The Western Journals*. Norman: University of Oklahoma Press.

———. 1983. *Bracebridge Hall; Tales of a Traveller; The Alhambra*. New York: Library of America.

Jackson, Helen Hunt. 1931. *Ramona*. Boston: Little, Brown.

———. 1979. *A Century of Dishonor*. Williamstown, Mass.: Corner House.

Jacobs, Harriet. 1988. *Incidents in the Life of a Slave Girl*. New York: Oxford University Press.

James, Marquis. 1929. *The Raven*. Indianapolis, Ind.: Bobbs-Merrill.

———. 1993. *Cherokee Strip*. Norman: University of Oklahoma Press.

Jefferson, Joseph. 1964. *The Autobiography of Joseph Jefferson*. Cambridge, Mass.: Harvard University Press.

Johnson, Dorothy M. 1953. *Indian Country*. New York: Ballantine.

Johnston, Basil H. 1989. *Indian School Days*. Norman: University of Oklahoma Press.

Jones, Nard. 1964. *Swift Flows the River*. Portland, Ore.: Binfords & Mort.

Kalakaua, King David. 1972. *The Legends and Myths of Hawaii: The Fables and Folk-Lore of a Strange People*. Rutland, Ver.: Charles E. Tuttle.

Kessler, Lauren. 1993. *Stubborn Twig: Three Generations in the Life of a Japanese American Family*. New York: Random House.

Kidd, Adam. 1830. *The Huron Chief and Other Poems*. Montreal: Herald & New Gazette.

Kroeber, A. L., and G. B. Kroeber. 1973. *A Mohave War Reminiscence, 1854–1880*. New York: Dover.

Kroeber, Theodora. 1962. *Ishi in Two Worlds: A Biography of the Last Wild Indian in North America*. Berkeley: University of California Press.

———. 1987. *Ishi, Last of His Tribe*. New York: Bantam.

La Farge, Oliver. 1929. *Laughing Boy*. Cambridge, Mass.: Houghton Mifflin.

La Salle, René Robert. 1922. *The Journeys of René Robert Cavelier Sieur de La Salle*. New York: Allerton Book Co.

Lake, Stuart N. 1994. *Wyatt Earp: Frontier Marshall*. New York: Pocket Books.

Lame Deer, John Fire, and Richard Erdoes. 1972. *Lame Deer, Seeker of Visions*. New York: Washington Square.

L'Amour, Louis. 1953. *Hondo*. Greenwich, Conn.: Fawcett.

———. 1961. *Sackett*. New York: Bantam.

———. 1978. *Fair Blows the Wind*. New York: E. P. Dutton.

———. 1979. *Conagher*. Leicester, Eng.: Ulverscroft.

———. 1981. *The Comstock Lode*. New York: Bantam.

———. 1983. *Sitka*. New York: Bantam.

———. 1985. *Jubal Sackett*. New York: Bantam.

———. 1989. *The Education of a Wandering Man*. New York: Bantam.

Landa, Diego de. 1978. *Yucatan before and after the Conquest*. New York: Dover.

Lane, Rose. 1963. *Old Home Town*. Lincoln: University of Nebraska Press.

Lane, Rose Wilder, and Roger Lea MacBride. 1977. *Rose Wilder Lane: Her Story*. New York: Stein and Day.

Las Casas, Bartolomé de. 1992. *A Short Account of the Destruction of the Indies*. London: Penguin.

Lawrence, D. H. 1974. *Birds, Beasts and Flowers*. New York: Haskell House.

———. 1976. *The Complete Short Stories, Vol. II*. New York: Penguin.

———. 1992. *The Plumed Serpent*. New York: Vintage Books.

Lewis, Meriwether, and William Clark. 1922. *Lewis and Clark Journals*. New York: Atherton.

———. 1953. *The Journals of Lewis and Clark*. Cambridge, Mass.: Riverside.

Linderman, Frank. 1972. *Pretty-Shield, Medicine Woman of the Crows*. Lincoln: University of Nebraska Press.

Lochhead, Douglas, and Raymond Souster. 1974. *100 Poems of Nineteenth Century Canada*. Toronto: Macmillan.

Lomax, John. 1947. *Adventures of a Ballad Hunter*. New York: Macmillan.

Lomax, John and Alan Lomax. 1968. *American Ballads and Folk Songs*. New York: Macmillan.

London, Jack. 1964. *The Call of the Wild*. New York: Airmont.

———. 1965. *Jack London's Stories of the North*. New York: Scholastic.

———. 1980. *White Fang*. Mahwah, N.J.: Watermill Press.

———. 1982. *The Iron Heel*. In *Novels and Social Writings*. New York: Library of America.

———. 1991. *Sea Wolf*. New York: Bantam.

———. 1992. *Five Great Short Stories*. New York: Dover.

Long, Stephen. 1988. *From Pittsburgh to the Rocky Mountains*. Golden, Colo.: Fulcrum.

Longfellow, Henry Wordsworth. 1951. *Evangeline, a Tale of Arcadie*. Halifax, Nova Scotia: Nimbus.

———. 1993. *The Song of Hiawatha*. London: J. M. Dent.

Lopez-Medina, Sylvia. 1992. *Cantora*. New York: Ballantine.

Love, Nat. 1988. *The Life and Adventures of Nat Love, Better Known in the Cattle Country as Deadwood Dick*. Baltimore, Md.: Black Classic Press.

Mackay, James. 1995. *Vagabond of Verse*. London: Mainstream.

Magoffin, Susan. 1982. *Down the Santa Fe Trail & into Mexico*. Lincoln: University of Nebraska Press.

McClung, Nellie L. 1965. *Clearing in the West*. Toronto: Thomas Allen & Son.

McConnell, H. 1996. *Five Years a Cavalryman or, Sketches of Regular Army Life on the Texas Frontier, 1866–1871*. Norman: University of Oklahoma Press.

McCunn, Ruthanne Lum. 1981. *Thousand Pieces of Gold*. San Francisco: Design Enterprises of San Francisco.

McIntire, Jim. 1992. *Early Days in Texas: A Trip to Hell and Heaven*. Norman: University of Oklahoma Press.

McIntosh, John. 1844. *Origin of the North American Indians*. New York: Nafis & Cornish.

McMurtry, Larry. 1985. *Lonesome Dove*. New York: Simon & Schuster.

———. 1991. *Buffalo Girls*. Boston: G. K. Hall.

Micheaux, Oscar. 1994. *The Conquest: The Story of a Negro Pioneer*. Lincoln: University of Nebraska Press.

Michener, James. 1959. *Hawaii*. New York: Random House.

———. 1974. *Centennial*. New York: Random House.

———. 1985. *Texas*. New York: Random House.

———. 1988. *Alaska*. New York: Random House.

Miller, James E., Jr. 1970. *From Spain and the Americas*. Glenview, Ill: Scott, Foresman.

Miller, Joaquin. 1922. *Danites of the Sierras*. Oakland, Calif.: privately printed.

Momaday, N. Scott. 1968. *House Made of Dawn*. New York: New American Library.

———. 1969. *The Way to Rainy Mountain*. Albuquerque: University of New Mexico Press.

Montesinos, Fernando. 1991. *Memorias Antiguas Historiales del Peru*. USA: Hakluyt Society.

Moodie, Susanna. 1959. *Life in the Clearings*. Toronto: Macmillan.

———. 1966. *Roughing It in the Bush*. Aylesbury, Eng.: Hazell, Watson & Viney.

Moody, William Vaughn. 1966. *The Great Divide*. In *Dramas from American Theatre 1762–1909*. Cleveland: World Publishing.

Morey, Walt. 1965. *Gentle Ben*. New York: E. P. Dutton.

Morgan, Lewis Henry. 1959. *The Indian Journals, 1859–1862*. New York: Dover.

Moses, Daniel David, and Terry Goldie, eds. 1992. *An Anthology of Canadian Native Literature in English*. Ontario: Oxford Press.

Mowat, Farley. 1975. *The Snow Walker*. Toronto: Seal.

———. 1989. *The Polar Passion*. Toronto: McClelland & Stewart.

Mowatt, Anna Cora. 1966. *Fashion*. In *Dramas from American Theatre 1762–1909*. Cleveland: World Publishing.

Muir, John. 1988. *My First Summer in the Sierra*. Surrey, Eng.: Cannongate Classics.

———. 1992. *A Thousand Mile Walk to the Gulf*. New York: Penguin.

———. 1993. *The Mountains of California*. New York: Penguin.

———. 1993. *Travels in Alaska*. New York: Penguin.

Neihardt, John G. 1953. *The Mountain Men*. Lincoln: University of Nebraska Press.

———. 1993. *Black Elk Speaks: The Life Story of a Holy Man of the Oglala Sioux*. Lincoln: University of Nebraska Press.

O'Dell, Scott. 1967. *The Black Pearl*. New York: Dell.

————. 1970. *Sing Down the Moon*. New York: Dell.

————. 1980. *Sarah Bishop*. New York: Dell.

————. 1986. *Streams to the River, River to the Sea*. New York: Fawcett Juniper.

O'Dell, Scott, and Elizabeth Hall. 1992. *Thunder Rolling in the Mountains*. Boston: Houghton Mifflin.

Parkman, Francis. 1955. *The Parkman Reader*. Boston: Little, Brown.

————. 1962. *The Conspiracy of Pontiac*. New York: Collier.

————. 1973. *The Oregon Trail: Sketches of Prarie and Rocky Mountain Life*. London: Folio Society.

————. 1991. *The Oregon Trail, The Conspiracy of Pontiac*. New York: Library of America.

Perdue, Theda. 1993. *Nations Remembered*. Norman: University of Oklahoma Press.

Piekarski, Vicki, ed. 1988. *Westward the Women: An Anthology of Western Stories by Women*. Albuquerque: University of New Mexico Press.

Poe, Edgar Allan. 1962. *Selected Stories and Poems*. New York: Airmont.

Porter, Katherine Anne. 1965. *The Collected Stories of Katherine Anne Porter*. New York: Harcourt, Brace and World.

Portis, Charles. 1968. *True Grit*. New York: New American Library.

Prescott, William H. n.d. *History of the Conquest of Mexico* and *History of the Conquest of Peru*. New York: Modern Library.

Radin, Paul. 1934. *The Story of the American Indian*. Garden City, N.Y.: Garden City Publishing.

————. 1963. *The Autobiography of a Winnebago Indian*. New York: Dover.

————. 1972. *The Trickster: A Study in American Indian Mythology*. New York: Schocken.

Rawlings, Marjorie Kinnan. 1970. *The Yearling*. New York: Charles Scribner's Sons.

Reed, John. 1969. *Insurgent Mexico*. New York: Greenwood Press.

Remington, Frederic. 1994. *Frederic Remington's Own West*. New York: Promontory Press.

Richards, Mary. 1996. *Winter Quarters: The 1846–1848 Life Writings of Mary Haskin Parker Richards*. Logan: Utah State University.

Richardson, John. 1991. *Wacousta*. Toronto: McClelland & Stewart.

Richter, Conrad. 1940. *The Trees*. New York: Alfred A. Knopf.

————. 1947. *Always Young and Fair*. New York: Alfred A. Knopf.

———. 1950. *The Town*. New York: Bantam.

———. 1953. *The Light in the Forest*. New York: Bantam.

———. 1960. *The Waters of Kronos*. New York: Alfred A. Knopf.

———. 1965. *The Sea of Grass*. New York: Time.

———. 1966. *A Country of Strangers*. New York: Alfred A. Knopf.

———. 1978. *The Rawhide Knot and Other Stories*. New York: Alfred A. Knopf.

Richter, Harvena. 1988. *Writing To Survive: The Private Notebooks of Conrad Richter*. Albuquerque: University of New Mexico Press.

Rip Van Winkle. 1938. In *Representative American Plays from 1767 to the Present Day*. New York: D. Appleton-Century.

Rodney, William. 1996. *Kootenai Brown, Canada's Unknown Frontiersman*. Surrey, B.C.: Heritage House.

Rölvaag, O. E. 1927. *Giants in the Earth: A Saga of the Prairie*. New York: Harper & Brothers.

———. 1955. *Giants in the Earth*. New York: Harper & Row.

———. 1971. *The Third Life of Per Smevik*. New York: Harper & Row.

Roosevelt, Theodore. 1983. *Ranch Life and the Hunting Trail*. Lincoln: University of Nebraska Press.

———. 1990. *The Rough Riders*. New York: Da Capo.

Rose, Cynthia. 1994. *Native North American Almanac*. Detroit: Gale Research.

Rowland, Mary Canaga. 1995. *As Long as Life: The Memoirs of a Frontier Woman Doctor*. New York: Fawcett Crest.

Royce, Sarah. 1977. *A Frontier Lady: Recollections of the Gold Rush and Early California*. Lincoln: University of Nebraska Press.

Russell, Osborne. 1965. *Journal of a Trapper*. Lincoln: University of Nebraska Press.

Sager, Ed, and Mike Frye. 1993. *The Bootlegger's Lady*. Surrey, B.C.: Hancock House.

Sandoz, Mari. 1942. *Crazy Horse: The Strange Man of the Oglalas*. New York: Alfred A. Knopf.

———. 1954. *The Buffalo Hunters*. Lincoln: University of Nebraska Press.

———. 1958. *The Cattleman*. Lincoln: University of Nebraska Press.

———. 1963. *Old Jules*. Lincoln: University of Nebraska Press.

———. 1964. *The Beaver Men*. Lincoln: University of Nebraska Press.

———. 1966. *The Battle of the Little Bighorn*. Lincoln: University of Nebraska Press.

Sanford, Mollie. 1959. *Mollie: The Journal of Mollie Dorsey Sanford in Nebraska and Colorado Territories, 1857–1866.* Lincoln: University of Nebraska Press.

Schaefer, Jack. 1949. *Shane.* New York: Bantam.

———. 1967. *The Short Novels of Jack Schaefer.* Boston: Houghton Mifflin.

Scott, Duncan Campbell. 1974. *Selected Poetry of Duncan Campbell Scott.* Ottawa: Tecumseh.

Scott, F. R., and A. J. M. Smith, eds. 1976. *The Blasted Pine: An Anthology of Satire, Invective and Disrespectful Verse.* Toronto: Macmillan.

Sewid, James. 1989. *Guests Never Leave Hungry: The Autobiography of James Sewid, a Kwakiutl Indian.* Montreal: McGill-Queen's University Press.

Sherburne, John P., ed. 1988. *Through Indian Country to California.* Stanford, Calif.: Stanford University Press.

Short, Luke. 1942. *Hardcase.* Garden City, N.Y.: Doubleday.

———. 1942. *Ride the Man Down.* Garden City, N.Y.: Doubleday.

Silko, Leslie Marmon. 1993. *Yellow Woman.* New Brunswick, N.J.: Rutgers University Press.

Simms, William Gilmore. 1964. *The Yemassee: A Romance of Carolina.* New Haven, Conn.: College & University Press.

Sinclair, David, ed. 1972. *Nineteenth-Century Narrative Poems.* Toronto: McClelland & Stewart.

Siringo, Charles. 1950. *A Texas Cowboy.* Lincoln: University of Nebraska Press.

Smith, John. 1967. *Captain John Smith's America: Selections from His Writings.* New York: Harper & Row.

Speare, Elizabeth. 1983. *The Sign of the Beaver.* New York: Dell.

Spencer, O. M. 1917. *The Indian Captivity of O. M. Spencer.* New York: Dover.

Standing Bear, Luther. 1988. *My Indian Boyhood.* Lincoln: University of Nebraska Press.

———. 1988. *Stories of the Sioux.* Lincoln: University of Nebraska Press.

Steinbeck, John. 1952. *East of Eden.* New York: Bantam.

———. 1970. *The Red Pony.* New York: Bantam.

Stewart, Elinore Pruitt. 1979. *Letters on an Elk Hunt.* Boston: Houghton Mifflin.

———. 1988. *Letters of a Woman Homesteader.* Boston: Houghton Mifflin.

Stone, John Augustus. 1966. *Metamora, or The Last of the Wampanoags.* In *Dramas from American Theatre 1762–1909.* Cleveland: World Publishing.

Stratton, R. B. 1983. *Captivity of the Oatman Girls*. Lincoln: University of Nebraska Press.

Tibbles, Thomas Henry. 1957. *Buckskin and Blanket Days*. Garden City, N.Y.: Doubleday.

Traill, Catharine Parr. 1966. *The Backwoods of Canada*. Toronto: McClelland & Stewart.

Trupin, Sophie. 1988. *Dakota Diaspora: Memoirs of a Jewish Homesteader*. Lincoln: University of Nebraska Press.

Twain, Mark. 1959. *The Autobiography of Mark Twain*. New York: HarperPerennial.

———. 1962. *The Adventures of Huckleberry Finn*. New York: Airmont.

———. 1962. *The Adventures of Tom Sawyer*. New York: Airmont.

———. 1962. *Letters from the Earth*. New York: Harper & Row.

———. 1962. *Roughing It*. New York: New American Library.

———. 1990. *Life on the Mississippi*. New York: Oxford University Press.

———. 1991. *A Pen Warmed Up in Hell: Mark Twain in Protest*. San Bernardino, Calif.: Borgo Press.

———. 1996. *The Adventures of Huckleberry Finn*. New York: Random House.

Twain, Mark, and Bret Harte. 1991. *California Sketches*. New York: Dover.

Ulrich, Laurel Thatcher. 1990. *A Midwife's Tale: The Life of Martha Ballard, Based on Her Diary, 1785–1812*. New York: Alfred A. Knopf.

Visscher, William Lightfoot. 1980. *The Pony Express: A Thrilling and Truthful History*. Golden, Colo.: Outbooks.

Vollmer, Lula. 1938. *Sun-Up*. In *Representative American Plays from 1767 to the Present Day*. New York: D. Appleton-Century.

Wallis, Velma. 1993. *Two Old Women: An Alaska Legend of Betrayal, Courage and Survival*. Fairbanks, Alaska: Epicenter.

West, Jessamyn. 1945. *The Friendly Persuasion*. New York: Harcourt, Brace & World.

———. 1969. *Except for Me and Thee*. New York: Avon.

———. 1975. *The Massacre at Fall Creek*. New York: Harcourt Brace Jovanovich.

———. 1986. *Collected Stories of Jessamyn West*. San Diego, Calif.: Harcourt Brace Jovanovich.

Wetherill, Merietta. 1992. *Marietta Wetherill: Reflections on Life with the Navajos in Chaco Canyon*. Boulder, Colo.: Johnson Books.

Wilder, Laura Ingalls. 1962. *On The Way Home*. New York: Harper & Row.

———. 1971. *By the Shores of Silver Lake*. New York: HarperCollins.

———. 1971. *Farmer Boy*. New York: HarperCollins.

———. 1971. *Little House in the Big Woods*. New York: Harper & Row.

———. 1971. *Little House on the Prairie*. New York: HarperCollins.

———. 1971. *Little Town on the Prairie*. New York: HarperCollins.

———. 1971. *The Long Winter*. New York: HarperCollins.

———. 1971. *On the Banks of Plum Creek*. New York: HarperCollins.

———. 1971. *These Happy Golden Years*. New York: HarperCollins.

Wilder, Laura Ingalls, and Rose Wilder Lane. 1988. *A Little House Sampler*. Lincoln: University of Nebraska Press.

Williams, R. H. 1982. *With the Border Ruffians: Memories of the Far West, 1852–1868*. Lincoln: University of Nebraska Press.

Windolph, Charles. 1947. *I Fought with Custer: The Story of Sergeant Windolph, Last Survivor of the Battle of the Little Big Horn*. Lincoln: University of Nebraska Press.

Wister, Owen. 1958. *Owen Wister Out West: His Journals and Letters*. Chicago: University of Chicago Press.

———. 1968. *The Virginian: A Horseman of the Plains*. Chicago: Children's Press.

Wolfe, Thomas. 1967. *A Western Journal*. Pittsburgh, Penn.: University of Pittsburgh.

Woodhouse, S. W. 1996. *A Naturalist in Indian Territory*. Norman: University of Oklahoma Press.

Work, James C., ed. 1996. *Gunfight! Thirteen Western Stories*. Lincoln: University of Nebraska Press.

Wright, Harold Bell. 1907. *The Shepherd of the Hills*. New York: Grosset & Dunlap.

Wyman, J. N. 1988. *Journey to the Koyukuk*. Missoula, Mont.: Pictorial HIstories Publishing.

Yep, Laurence. 1975. *Dragonwings*. New York: Harper & Row.

———. 1992. *Dragon's Gate*. New York: HarperCollins.

Young, Alida E. 1978. *Land of the Iron Dragon*. Garden City, N.Y.: Doubleday.

Young, Carrie. 1991. *Nothing To Do but Stay*. New York: Dell.

———. 1992. *The Wedding Dress: Stories from the Dakota Plains*. New York: Dell.

Articles and Short Works

Brown, Dee. 1988. "Process and Plot in the Historical Novel." *The Writer* (January 21), 23.

Cabeza de Baca, Fabiola. 1989. "The Pioneer Women." In *Adventures for Readers*. San Diego, Calif.: Harcourt Brace.

Cather, Willa. 1978. "The Sentimentality of William Tavener." In *Focus on Literature: America*. Boston: Houghton Mifflin.

———. 1979. "The Sculptor's Funeral." In *American Literature: Themes and Writers*. New York: McGraw-Hill.

———. 1987. "A Wagner Matinee." In *The United States in Literature*. Glenview, Ill.: Scott, Foresman.

———. 1992. "Old Mrs. Harris." In *American Women Regionalists*. New York: W. W. Norton.

Crane, Stephen. 1985. "The Bride Comes to Yellow Sky." In *The United States in Literature*. Glenview, Ill.: Scott, Foresman.

Gordon, Caroline. 1952. "The Captive." In *The Forest of the South*. Chicago: Scott, Foresman.

Grey, Zane. 1970. "Oak Creek Canyon." In *Arizona in Literature*. New York: Haskell House.

Hakluyt, Richard. 1954. "Divers Voyages Touching the Discovery of America, and the Ilands Adjacent unto the Same." In *The Renaissance in England*. Boston: D. C. Heath.

"Hal Borland, Naturalist, Dies in Connecticut." 1978. *Nebraska Star* (February 24), n.p.

Harris, Joel Chandler. 1952. "Uncle Remus Stories." In *The Literature of the South*. Chicago: Scott, Foresman.

Haun, Catherine. 1992. *A Woman's Trip across the Plains in 1849*. In *Women's Diaries of the Westward Journey*. New York: Schocken.

Hunter, Kermit. 1967. "Out of History . . . A Lesson." *Unto These Hills* program, 24–27.

Irving, Washington. 1978. "Rip Van Winkle." In *Focus on Literature: America*. Boston: Houghton Mifflin.

———. 1987. "The Devil and Tom Walker." In *The United States in Literature*. Glenview, Ill.: Scott, Foresman.

Joseph, Chief. 1979. "An Indian's View of Indian Affairs." *North American Review* (April), 415–433.

———. 1987. "I Will Fight No More Forever." In *The United States in Literature*. Glenview, Ill.: Scott, Foresman.

Lawrence, D. H. 1969. "The Spirit of Place." In *The Norton Reader: An Anthology of Expository Prose*. New York: W. W. Norton.

Lomax, John. 1965. "Starving to Death on a Government Claim." In *Accent: U.S.A.* Chicago: Scott, Foresman.

McLachlan, Alexander. 1972. "The Emigrant." In *Nineteenth-Century Narrative Poems*. Toronto: McClelland & Stewart.

"Mike Fink and Davy Crockett." 1968. In *Annals of America: 1840*, 574–575. Chicago: Encyclopaedia Britannica.

"Old Man Coyote and Buffalo Power." 1975. In *Plains Indian Mythology*. New York: Meridian Books.

Portis, Charles. 1968. "True Grit." *Saturday Evening Post* (May 18).

Reed, John. 1936. "Almost Thirty." *New Republic* (April 29), 332–336.

Richter, Conrad. 1965. "The Free Man." In *Accent U.S.A.* Chicago: Scott, Foresman.

———. 1965. "Smoke over the Prairie." In *Accent U.S.A.* Chicago: Scott, Foresman.

Rowlandson, Mary White. 1985. "A Narative of the Captivity and Restoration of Mrs. Mary White Rowlandson." In *The Norton Anthology of Literature by Women*. New York: W. W. Norton.

Satanta. 1987. "My Heart Feels Like Bursting." In *The United States in Literature*. Glenview, Ill.: Scott, Foresman.

Seattle. 1987. "This Sacred Soil." In *The United States in Literature*. Glenview, Ill.: Scott, Foresman.

Steinbeck, John. 1985. "The Leader of the People." In *The United States in Literature*. Glenview, Ill.: Scott, Foresman.

Twain, Mark. 1985. "The Jumping Frog." Wakefield, R.I.: Moyer Bell.

Ward, Artemus. 1939. "A Humorist Exploits the Mormons" In *The Literature of the Rocky Mountain West*. Caldwell, Idaho: Caxton Printers.

White, Lillian Zellhoefer. 1965. "Hangman's Tree." In *Accent: U.S.A.* Chicago: Scott, Foresman.

Woods, Walter. 1940. "Billy the Kid." In *The Great Diamond Robbery and Other Recent Melodramas*. Princeton, N.J.: Princeton University Press.

Audiocassettes, Videos, and CD-ROM

———. 1957. *Old Yeller* (video). Hollywood: Walt Disney.

Gipson, Fred. 1993. *Old Yeller* (audiocassette). Prince Fredrick, Md.: Recorded Books.

Ishi. 1992. *Ishi the Last Yahi* (audiocassette). San Francisco: Wild Sanctuary Communications.

MacLachlan, Patricia, and Carol Sobieski. 1991. *Sara, Plain and Tall* (video). Los Angeles: Republic Pictures.

———. 1993. *The Skylark* (video). Los Angeles: Republic Pictures.

Old Gringo (video). 1989. Hollywood: Columbia Pictures.

Parlour Poetry (audiocassette). n.d. Cheltenham, Eng.: This England.

Service, Robert. 1992. "Jean Shepherd Reads Poems of Robert Service" (audiocassette). Washington, D.C.: Smithsonian Folkways.

Sewid, James. 1989. *Guests Never Leave Hungry: The Autobiography of James Sewid, a Kwakiutl Indian.* Montreal: McGill-Queen's University.

True Grit (video). 1969. Hollywood: Paramount Studios.

Twain, Mark. 1995. "The Celebrated Jumping Frog of Calaveras County" (audiocassette and guide). Prince Frederick, Md.: Recorded Books.

Whitman, Walt. 1992. "Pioneers, O Pioneers!" *Great Literature Personal Library Series* (CD-ROM). Parsippany, N.J.: Bureau Development.

Internet

Audubon, John James. 1995. *The Birds of America.* http://quality.cqs.ch/~rrb/Audubon.html.

Bierce, Ambrose. 1996. *Can Such Things Be?* ftp://wiretap.spies.com/Library/Classic/cansuch.txt (June 25).

———. 1996. *The Devil's Dictionary.* gopher://wiretap.spies.com/00/Library/Classic/devils.txt (June 25).

———. 1996. *Fantastic Fables.* ftp://uiarchive.cso.uiuc.edu/pub/etext/gutenberg/etext95/fanfb10.txt (June 25).

———. 1996. *My Favorite Murder.* http://etext.lib.virginia.edu/cgibin/browse-mixed?id=BieFavo&tag=public&images=images/modeng&data=/lv1/Archive/eng-parsed (June 25).

———. 1996. *Occurrence at Owl Creek Bridge.* ftp://uiarchive.cso.uiuc.edu/pub/etext/gutenberg/etext95/owlcr10.txt (June 25).

Borland, Hal. 1996. "Creed." http://www.icss.com/usflag/essays.html#CRE (October 1).

Crockett, David. 1996. "Colonel Davy Crockett Delivering His Celebrated Speech to Congress on the State of Finances, State Officers, and State Affairs in General." http://www.towson.edu/~duncan/crockett.html (July 30).

de Tocqueville, Alexis. 1996. *Democracy in America.* http://xroads.virginia.edu/~HYPER/DETOC/home.html (October 8).

London, Jack. 1996. "Wit of Porportuk." http://www.gopher.cc.columbia.edu:71/11/miscellaneous/cubooks/offbooks/london (July 22).

———. 1996. "Batard." http://www.gopher.cc.columbia.edu:71/11/miscellaneous/cubooks/offbooks/london (July 22).

Muir, John. 1996. "Stickeen: The Story of a Dog." http://www.sierraclub.org/john_muir_exhibit/writings/stickeen/ (June 3).

Service, Robert. 1996. "Robert W. Service Page." http://www.inch.com/~kdka/public_html/r~service.html (September 23).

———. 1996. *The Spell of the Yukon and Other Verses.* http://www.teachersoft.com/Library/poetry/service/spell/contents.htm (September 23).

Twain, Mark. 1996. "The Noble Red Man." http://www.amren.com/indians.htm (June 7).

BIBLIOGRAPHY

Adams, Agatha Boyd. 1951. *Paul Green of Chapel Hill*. Chapel Hill: University of North Carolina Library Press.

Adams, Andy. 1975. *The Log of a Cowboy: A Narrative of the Old Trail Days*. Williamston, Mass.: Corner House.

Adamson, Lynda G. 1994. *Recreating the Past: A Guide to American and World Historical Fiction for Children and Young Adults*. Westport, Conn.: Greenwood Press.

Adkins, Carl A. 1968. "A Novel for High School Seniors: Hal Borland's *When the Legends Die*." *English Journal* (January), 30–31.

Aimard, Gustave. 1991. *The Trappers of Arkansas*. In *American Pioneer Writers*. New York: Gallery.

Alderson, Nannie, and Helena Huntington Smith. 1942. *A Bride Goes West*. Lincoln: University of Nebraska Press.

Allison, Susan. 1991. *A Pioneer Gentlewoman in British Columbia*. Vancouver: University of British Columbia Press.

Ambrose, Stephen E. 1996. *Undaunted Courage: Meriwether Lewis, Thomas Jefferson, and the Opening of the American West*. New York: Simon & Schuster.

American Pioneer Writers. 1991. New York: Gallery.

Anaya, Rudolfo A. 1972. *Bless Me, Ultima*. Berkeley, Calif.: TOS Publications.

———. 1996. *Rio Grande Fall*. New York: Warner.

Anderson, Eva G. 1951. *Chief Seattle*. Caldwell, Idaho: Caxton Printers.

"The Arcadian Story." 1996. http://www.branson.net/hist/Arcad.html (May 27).

Armstrong, M. J. 1996. "John James Audubon." http://rmc-library.cornell.edu/HFJ/Aud.Folio.html (August 22).

Arner, Robert D. 1985. *The Lost Colony in Literature*. Raleigh, N.C.: Department of Cultural Resources.

Arrington, Leonard, and Jon Haupt. 1973. "Community and Isolation: Some Aspects of 'Mormon Westerns.'" *Western American Literature* (Spring and Summer) 15–31.

Atherton, Gertrude. 1991. *Before the Gringo Came*. In *American Pioneer Writers*. New York: Gallery.

Audubon, John James. 1940. *Audubon's America*. Boston: Houghton Mifflin.

———. 1995. *The Birds of America*. http://quality.cqs.ch/~rrb/Audubon.html.

Audubon, John Woodhouse. 1984. *Audubon's Western Journal 1849–1850*. Tucson: University of Arizona Press.

Austin, Mary. 1903. *The Land of Little Rain*. Boston: Houghton Mifflin.

———. 1928. *Children Sing in the Far West*. Boston: Houghton Mifflin.

———. 1932. *Earth Horizon*. Albuquerque: University of New Mexico Press.

———. 1987. *Western Trails*. Reno: University of Nevada Press.

"Author Hal Borland Dies; Was Native of Nebraska." 1978. *Omaha World Herald* (February 24), n.p.

Azuela, Mariano. 1962. *The Underdogs: A Novel of the Mexican Revolution*. New York: Signet.

Backhouse, Frances. 1995. *Women of the Klondike*. Vancouver: White Cap.

Baldwin, Joseph Glover. 1966. *The Flush Times of California*. Athens: University of Georgia Press.

"The Ballad of Davy Crockett." 1996. http://www.cs.monash.edu.au/~tbp/disney/lyrics/tv/davy (July 30).

Barlow, Joel. 1970. *The Works of Joel Barlow, Vols. 1 & 2*. Gainesville, Fla.: Scholars' Facsmiles & Reprints.

Barnes, Robert J. 1968. *Conrad Richter*. New York: Steck-Vaughn.

Bartlett, John. *Bartlett's Familiar Quotations*, 7th ed. Boston: Little, Brown, 1992.

Battey, Thomas C. 1972. *The Life and Adventures of a Quaker among the Indians*. Williamstown, Mass.: Corner House.

Bauer, Erwin A. 1988. "Zane Grey: Ohio's Writer of the Purple Sage." In Zane Grey's *Blue Feather and Other Stories*. Boston: G. K. Hall.

Bayly, Dr. Christopher, gen. ed. 1989. *Atlas of the British Empire*. New York: Facts on File.

Beal, Allen. 1963. *I Will Fight No More Forever*. Seattle: University of Washington Press.

Beatty, Richmond Croom, et al., eds. 1952. *The Literature of the South*. Chicago: Scott, Foresman.

Beauchamp, Gorman. 1984. *Jack London*. San Bernardino, Calif.: Borgo Press.

Beecher, Catherine E., and Harriet Beecher Stowe. 1994. *American Woman's Home*. Hartford, Conn.: Stowe-Day Foundation.

"Before Jamestown and Plymouth Rock." 1990. In *The Lost Colony 1990 Souvenir Program*. Roanoke Island, N.C.: Roanoke Island Historical Association.

Bell, Loren C. 1984. "The Onion and *When the Legends Die*." *English Journal* (November), 56–57.

"Beloved Books Focus of Dispute." 1992. *Hickory Daily Record* (November 3), 4B.

Bemister, Margaret. 1973. *Thirty Indian Legends of Canada*. Vancouver: Douglas & McIntyre.

Benét, Rosemary, and Stephen Vincent Benét. 1933. *A Book of Americans*. New York: Farrar and Rinehart.

Benét, Stephen Vincent. 1943. *Western Star*. New York: Holt, Rinehart, and Winston.

Benét, William Rose. 1965. "Jesse James." In *Accent: U. S. A*. Chicago: Scott, Foresman.

Bennett, Ross, ed. 1975. *The New America's Wonderlands: Our National Parks*. Washington, D.C.: National Geographic Society.

Berger, Thomas. 1964. *Little Big Man*. Greenwich, Conn.: Fawcett.

Bernard, André. 1955. *Now All We Need Is a Title: Famous Book Titles and How They Got That Way*. New York: W. W. Norton.

Betenson, Lula Parker. 1975. *Butch Cassidy, My Brother*. Provo, Utah: Brigham Young University Press.

Betzinez, Jason. 1959. *I Fought with Geronimo*. Lincoln: University of Nebraska Press.

Bevilacqua, Winifred Farrant. 1981. "Dee Brown." In *Dictionary of Literary Biography*. Detroit: Gale Research.

Bierce, Ambrose. 1963. *The Sardonic Humor of Ambrose Bierce*. New York: Dover.

———. 1964. *Ghost and Horror Stories of Ambrose Bierce*. New York: Dover.

———. 1977. *The Stories and Fables of Ambrose Bierce*. Owings Mills, Md.: Stemmer House.

———. 1982. *In the Midst of Life: Tales of Soldiers*. Mattituck, N.Y.: Amereon House.

———. 1984. *The Complete Short Stories of Ambrose Bierce*. Lincoln: University of Nebraska Press.

———. 1994. *Civil War Songs*. New York: Dover.

————. 1996a. *Can Such Things Be?* ftp://wiretap.spies.com/Library/Classic/cansuch.txt (June 25).

————. 1996b. *The Devil's Dictionary.* gopher://wiretap.spies.com/00/Library/Classic/devils.txt (June 25).

————. 1996c. *Fantastic Fables.* ftp://uiarchive.cso.uiuc.edu/pub/etext/gutenberg/etext95/fanfb10.txt (June 25).

————. 1996d. *My Favorite Murder.* http://etext.lib.virginia.edu/cgibin/browse-mixed?id=BieFavo&tag=public&images=images/modeng&data=/lv1/Archive/eng-parsed (June 25).

————. 1996e. *Occurrence at Owl Creek Bridge.* ftp://uiarchive.cso.uiuc.edu/pub/etext/gutenberg/etext95/owlcr10.txt (June 25).

"Bierce Papers." 1996. http://sunsite.berkeley.edu:8008/findaids/berkeley/bierce/1.toc (June 24).

Bigelow, Gordon E. 1966. *Frontier Eden: The Literary Career of Marjorie Kinnan Rawlings.* Gainesville, Fla.: University of Florida Press.

Bird, Isabella L. 1960. *A Lady's Life in the Rocky Mountains.* Norman: University of Oklahoma Press.

"A Bit of Thoreau." 1964. *Newsweek* (April 6), 82.

Black Hawk. 1955. *An Autobiography.* Urbana: University of Illinois Press.

————. 1994. *Life of Black Hawk.* New York: Dover.

Blacker, Irwin R., ed. 1961. *The Old West in Fiction.* New York: Ivan Obolensky.

Blain, Virginia, Isobel Grundy, and Patricia Clements. 1990. *The Feminist Companion to Literature in English.* New Haven, Conn.: Yale University Press.

Blair, Linda. 1991. "Alienation, Assimilation, and Acculturation—*Bless Me, Ultima* by Rudolfo Anaya." *English Journal* (December 26).

Blair, Walter. 1937. *Native American Humor.* New York: American Book.

————. 1944. *Tall Tale America.* New York: Coward-McCann.

Blake, James Carlos. 1995. *The Pistoleer.* New York: Berkley Books.

————. 1996. *The Friends of Pancho Villa.* New York: Berkley Books.

Blake, Michael. 1988. *Dances with Wolves.* New York: Ballantine Books.

Blankenship, Russell. 1931. *American Literature as an Expression of the National Mind.* New York: Henry Holt.

Bloom, Edward, and Lillian D. Bloom. 1962. *Willa Cather's Gift of Sympathy.* Carbondale: Southern Illinois University Press.

Bloom, Harold. 1986a. *Mark Twain.* New York: Chelsea House.

———. 1986b. *Willa Cather*. New York: Twayne.

Blum, Daniel. 1951. *A Pictorial History of the American Theatre, 1900–1951*. New York: Greenberg.

Bode, Barbara. 1993. "Imagination Man." *New York Times*, March 14.

Boger, Mary. 1970. "O. Henry: Sad But Charming." *Charlotte Observer* (July 19), n.p.

Bohlke, L. Brent, ed. 1986. *Willa Cather in Person*. Lincoln: University of Nebraska Press.

Bojer, Johan. 1974. *The Emigrants*. Westport, Conn.: Greenwood Press.

———. 1991. *The Emigrants*. St. Paul: Minnesota Historical Society.

Bolton, Herbert E. 1921. *The Spanish Borderlands*. New Haven, Conn.: Yale University Press.

Bonner, Thomas. 1972. *The Life and Adventures of Beckwourth*. Lincoln: University of Nebraska Press.

Bontemps, Arna, ed. 1969. *Great Slave Narratives*. Boston: Beacon Press.

———. 1974. *American Negro Poetry*. New York: Hill and Wang.

Books for Children: 1960–1965. 1966. Chicago: American Library Association.

Boorstin, Daniel J. 1958. *The Americans: The National Experience*. New York: Vintage.

———. 1965. *The Americans: The Colonial Experience*. New York: Vintage.

———. 1974. *The Americans: The Democratic Experience*. New York: Vintage.

———. 1992. *The Creators: A History of Heroes of the Imagination*. New York: Vintage.

Borland, Hal. 1956. *High, Wide, and Lonesome*. New York: Lippincott.

———. 1963. *This Hill, This Valley*. New York: Lippincott.

———. 1989. *When the Legends Die*. New York: Bantam.

———. 1996. "Creed." http://www.icss.com/usflag/essays.html#CRE (October 1).

Botkin, B. A., ed. 1944. *A Treasury of American Folklore*. New York: Crown.

Bowden, Mary. 1981. *Washington Irving*. Boston: Twayne.

Boyle, Thomas E. 1970. "Frederick Jackson Turner and Thomas Wolfe: The Frontier as History and as Literature." *Western American Literature* (Winter), 276.

Bradford, William. 1966. *Of Plymouth Plantation*. New York: Alfred A. Knopf.

Brant, Charles S., ed. 1969. *The Autobiography of a Kiowa Apache Indian*. New York: Dover.

Brebner, John B. 1955. *The Explorers of North America*. New York: Meridian.

Breeden, Robert L., ed. 1979. *Trails West*. Washington, D.C.: National Geographic Society.

Brockett, Oscar G. 1968. *History of the Theatre*. Boston: Allyn & Bacon.

Brooke, Barbara. 1989. *The Sioux*. Vero Beach, Fla.: Rourke.

Brooks, Van Wyck. 1940. *New England: Indian Summer, 1865–1915*. Cleveland: World Publishing.

———. 1944. *The World of Washington Irving*. Cleveland: World Publishing.

Brougham, John. 1966. *Po-Ca-Hon-Tas, or The Gentle Savage*. In *Dramas from American Theatre 1762–1909*. Cleveland: World Publishing.

Brower, Kenneth. 1990. *Yosemite: An American Treasure*. Washington, D.C.: National Geographic Society.

Brown, Carolyn S. 1987. *The Tall Tale in American Folklore and Literature*. Knoxville: University of Tennessee Press.

Brown, Dee. 1945. *Wave High the Banner*. Philadelphia: Macrae-Smith.

———. 1958. *The Gentle Tamers: Women of the Old Wild West*. Lincoln: University of Nebraska Press.

———. 1962. *The Fetterman Massacre*. Lincoln: University of Nebraska Press.

———. 1970. *Bury My Heart at Wounded Knee: An Indian History of the American West*. New York: Henry Holt.

———. 1974. *Wounded Knee: An American History of the Indian West*. New York: Dell.

———. 1977. *Hear That Lonesome Whistle Blow: Railroads in the West*. New York: Touchstone.

———. 1988. "Process and Plot in the Historical Novel." *The Writer* (January 21), 23.

———. 1993. *When the Century Was Young*. Little Rock, Ark.: August House.

Brown, Dee, and Martin F. Schmitt. 1948. *Fighting Indians of the West*. New York: Ballantine.

Brown, E. K. 1987. *Willa Cather: A Critical Biography*. Lincoln: University of Nebraska Press.

Brown, John. 1971. *Old Frontiers*. New York: Arno.

Brown, Joseph Epes, ed. 1989. *The Sacred Pipe: Black Elk's Account of the Seven Rites of the Oglala Sioux*. Norman: University of Oklahoma Press.

Bruce-Novoa, Juan. 1980. *Chicano Authors: Inquiry by Interview*. Austin: University of Texas Press.

Brunvand, Jan Harold, ed. 1996. *American Folklore: An Encyclopedia*. New York: Garland.

Buck, Claire, ed. 1992. *The Bloomsbury Guide to Women's Literature*. New York: Prentice Hall.

Budd, Louis J. 1983. *Critical Essays on Mark Twain*. Boston: G. K. Hall.

Burdick, Jacques. 1974. *Theater*. New York: Newsweek Books.

Burgess, Anthony. 1985. *Flame into Being: The Life and Work of D. H. Lawrence*. New York: Arbor House.

Burlend, Rebecca, and Edward Burlend. 1987. *A True Picture of Emigration*. Lincoln: University of Nebraska Press.

Burns, Ken, and Stephen Ives. 1996a. "The West." http://www3.pbs.org/weta/thewest/ (September 17).

———. 1996b. *The West* (television series). PBS-TV (September 15–19).

Burns, Walter Noble. 1926. *The Saga of Billy the Kid*. Garden City, N.Y.: Doubleday, Page & Co.

Byrne, Kathleen D., and Richard C. Snyder. 1980. *Chrysalis: Willa Cather in Pittsburgh, 1896–1906*. Pittsburgh: Historical Society of West Pennsylvania.

Cabeza de Baca, Fabiola. 1989. "The Pioneer Women." In *Adventures for Readers*. San Diego, Calif.: Harcourt Brace.

Cabeza de Vaca, Alvar Núñez. 1993a. *Castaways*. Berkeley: University of California Press.

———. 1993b. *Relation*. Houston: Arte Publico.

Cady, Edwin H. 1967. *Literature of the Early Republic*. San Francisco: Rinehart.

Calder, Jenni. 1975. *There Must Be a Long Ranger*. New York: Taplinger.

Calderon, Hector. 1986. "Rudolfo Anaya's *Bless Me, Ultima*: A Chicano Romance of the Southwest." *Critica* (Fall), 21–47.

Canadian Poetry: From the Beginnings through the First World War. 1994. Toronto: McClelland & Stewart.

Canadian Writers before 1890. 1990. Detroit: Gale Research.

Candelaria, Cordelia. 1985. *Chicano Literature: A Reference Guide*. Westport, Conn.: Greenwood Press.

Carlsen, G. Robert. 1967. *Books and the Teen-Age Reader*. New York: Harper & Row.

———, ed. 1979. "Washington Irving." In *American Literature*. New York: McGraw-Hill.

Carmony, Neil B., ed. 1992. *Afield with J. Frank Dobie: Tales of Critters, Campfires, and the Hunting Trail*. Silver City, N.M.: High-Lonesome Books.

Carrington, Henry B. 1909. *The Indian Question*. Mattituck, N.Y.: J. M. Carroll.

Carson, Kit. 1966. *Kit Carson's Autobiography*. Lincoln: University of Nebraska Press.

BIBLIOGRAPHY

Carter, Forrest. 1976. *The Education of Little Tree*. Albuquerque: University of New Mexico Press.

Castañeda, Pedro de. 1990. *The Journey of Coronado*. New York: Dover.

Cather, Willa. 1931. *Shadows on the Rock*. New York: Alfred A. Knopf.

———. 1947. *Death Comes for the Archbishop*. New York: Alfred A. Knopf.

———. 1972. *A Lost Lady*. New York: Random House.

———. 1977. *My Ántonia*. Boston: Houghton Mifflin.

———. 1978. "The Sentimentality of William Tavener." In *Focus on Literature: America*. Boston: Houghton Mifflin.

———. 1979. "The Sculptor's Funeral." In *American Literature: Themes and Writers*. New York: McGraw-Hill.

———. 1987. "A Wagner Matinee." In *The United States in Literature*. Glenview, Ill.: Scott, Foresman.

———. 1991. *O Pioneers!* In *American Pioneer Writers*. New York: Gallery.

———. 1992. "Old Mrs. Harris." In *American Women Regionalists*. New York: W. W. Norton.

Catlin, George. 1965. *Letters and Notes on the Manners, Customs and Condition of the North American Indians during Eight Years' Travel amongst the Wildest Tribes of Indians of North America*. Minneapolis, Minn.: Ross & Haines.

———. 1989. *North American Indians*. New York: Penguin.

Cavendish, Marshall. 1970. *Man, Myth and Magic*. New York: Marshall Cavendish Corp.

Cawelti, John G. 1970. *The Six-Gun Mystique*. Bowling Green, Ky.: Bowling Green State University Popular Press.

Champagne, Duane. 1995. *Native North American Chronology*. Detroit: Gale Research.

Champion, Neil. 1989. *D. H. Lawrence: Life and Works*. East Sussex, Eng.: Wayland.

Champlain, Samuel de. 1923. *Works*. Toronto: Champlain Society.

Chant, Christopher. 1995. *The New Encyclopedia of Handguns and Small Arms*. London: Multimedia.

Chapman, Abraham, ed. 1968. *Black Voices*. New York: New American Library.

Charles, Jill, ed. 1996. *Summer Theatre Directory 1996*. Dorset, Vt.: American Theatre Works.

Chavez, John R. 1984. *The Lost Land: The Chicano Image of the Southwest*. Albuquerque: University of New Mexico Press.

Chepsiuk, Ron. 1991."In Pursuit of the Muse: Librarians Who Write." *American Library* (November 19, 1991), 998.

Chronicles of American Indian Protest. 1971. Greenwich, Conn.: Fawcett.

Cieza de Leon, Piedro. 1883. *The Second Part of the Chronicle of Peru.* London: Hakluyt Society.

Clark, Barrett, gen. ed. 1963. *America's Lost Plays.* Bloomington: Indiana University Press.

Clark, Walter Van Tilburg. 1968. *The Ox-Bow Incident.* New York: New American Library.

Cleaveland, Agnes. 1941. *No Life for a Lady.* Lincoln: University of Nebraska Press.

Clyman, James. 1984. *Journal of a Mountain Man.* Missoula, Mont.: Mountain Press.

Clymer, William B. 1969. *James Fenimore Cooper.* Brooklyn, N.Y.: Haskell.

Coad, Oral Sumner, and Edwin Mims, Jr. 1929. *The American Stage.* New Haven, Conn.: Yale University Press.

Cody, William F. 1904. *The Adventures of Buffalo Bill.* New York: Harper & Brothers.

Coleman, Rufus A., ed. 1932. *The Golden West in Story and Verse.* New York: Harper & Brothers.

Collier, John. 1947. *Indians of the Americas.* New York: New American Library.

Colliss, Maurice. 1954. *Cortes and Montezuma.* New York: Avon.

Columbus, Christopher. 1924. *Journal of the First Voyage to America.* New York: Boni.

———. 1969. *The Four Voyages.* London: Penguin.

———. 1988. *The Four Voyages of Columbus.* London: Hakluyt Society.

———. 1992. *The Voyage of Christopher Columbus.* New York: St. Martin's.

Combs, Barry. 1969. *Westward to Promontory.* Palo Alto, Calif.: American West.

Contemporary Authors (CD-ROM). 1994. Detroit: Gale Research.

Cook, James. 1971. *The Explorations of Captain James Cook in the Pacific as Told by Selections of His Own Journals, 1768–1779.* New York: Dover.

Cooper, Courtney Riley. 1927. *Annie Oakley, Woman at Arms.* New York: Duffield and Co.

Cooper, James Fenimore. n.d. *The Spy.* New York: Grosset & Dunlap.

———. 1958. *The Prairie.* New York: Rinehart.

———. 1963. *The Bravo*. New Haven, Conn.: College & University Press.

———. 1964. *The Pathfinder: or The Inland Sea*. New York: Airmont.

———. 1968. *The Pioneers*. New York: Magnum.

———. 1980. *The Deerslayer*. New York: New American Library.

———. 1989. *The Last of the Mohicans*. New York: New American Library.

Cooper, William. 1970. *A Guide in the Wilderness or the History of the First Settlements in the Western Counties of New York*. Freeport, N.Y.: Books for Libraries Press.

Correll, John T. 1961. "'Horn in West' Debut Finds Many Hickoryites Taking Part in Historic Pageant.'" *Hickory (N.C.) Daily Record* (July 4).

Costo, Rupert, and Jeannette Henry. 1977. *Indian Treaties: Two Centuries of Dishonor*. San Francisco: Indian Historian Press.

Courtmanche-Ellis, Anne. 1978. "Meet Dee Brown: Author, Teacher, Librarian." *Wilson Library Journal* (March), 553–561.

Cowie, Alexander. 1951. *The Rise of the American Novel*. New York: American Book.

Coyner, David H. 1995. *The Lost Trappers*. Norman: University of Oklahoma Press.

Crane, Stephen. 1985. "The Bride Comes to Yellow Sky." In *The United States in Literature*. Glenview, Ill.: Scott, Foresman.

Craven, Margaret. 1973. *I Heard the Owl Call My Name*. New York: Dell.

Crockett, David. 1834. *Narrative of the Life of David Crockett of the State of Tennessee*. Cincinnati: U. P. James.

———. 1987. *The Tall Tales of Davy Crockett*. Knoxville: University of Tennessee Press.

———. 1996. "Colonel Davy Crockett Delivering His Celebrated Speech to Congress on the State of Finances, State Officers, and State Affairs in General." http://www.towson.edu/~duncan/crockett.html (July 30).

Crow Dog, Mary. 1990. *Lakota Woman*. New York: HarperCollins.

Crystal, David. 1987. *The Cambridge Encyclopedia of Language*. New York: Cambridge University Press.

———. 1995. *The Cambridge Encyclopedia of the English Language*. New York: Cambridge University Press.

Cuevas, Lou. 1991. *Apache Legends*. Happy Camp, Calif.: Naturegraph Publishers.

Custer, Elizabeth. 1961. *Boots and Saddles*. Norman: University of Oklahoma Press.

Custer, George A. 1962. *My Life on the Plains*. New York: Citadel.

Custis, George Washington Parke. 1938. *Pocahontas, or The Settlers of Virginia*. In *Representative American Plays from 1767 to the Present Day*. New York: D. Appleton-Century.

Dahlin, Robert. 1980. "PW Interviews Dee Brown." *Publishers Weekly* (March 21), 14–15.

"Daniel Boone." 1996. http://www.berksweb.com/boonetext.html (September 27).

"Daniel Boone: American Pioneer and Trailblazer." 1996. http://www2.lucidcafe.com/lucidcafe/library/95nov/boone.html (September 27).

Darwin, Charles. 1989. *Voyage of the Beagle*. London: Penguin.

"David 'Davy' Crockett." 1996. http://www.numedia.tddc.net/sa/alamo/crockett.html (July 30).

Davidson, Cathy N., and Linda Wagner-Martin. 1995. *The Oxford Companion to Women's Writing*. New York: Oxford University Press.

Davidson, Levette Jay, and Prudence Bostwick. 1939. *The Literature of the Rocky Mountain West*. Caldwell, Idaho: Caxton Printers.

Davis, Britton. 1929. *The Truth about Geronimo*. New Haven: Yale University Press.

Davis, H. L. 1992. *Honey in the Horn*. Moscow: University of Idaho Press.

Davis, Sara de Saussure, and Philip F. Beidler, eds. 1984. *The Mythologizing of Mark Twain*. Tuscaloosa: University of Alabama Press.

de Gaspé, Philippe-Joseph Aubert. 1990. *Yellow-Wolf and Other Tales of the Saint Lawrence*. Montreal: Vehicule.

De Soto, Hernando. 1968. *Narratives of the Career of Hernando De Soto in the Conquest of Florida*. Gainesville, Fla.: Palmetto Books.

de Tocqueville, Alexis. 1996. *Democracy in America*. http://xroads.virginia.edu/~HYPER/DETOC/home.html (October 8).

Dekker, George, and John P. McWilliams, eds. 1973. *Fenimore Cooper: The Critical Heritage*. New York: Routledge, Chapman and Hall.

Deloria, Ella. 1988. *Waterlily*. Lincoln: University of Nebraska Press.

Deloria, Vine. 1969. *Custer Died for Your Sins*. New York: Macmillan.

———. 1973. *God Is Red*. New York: Delta.

Derr, Mark. 1993. *The Frontiersman: The Real Life and the Many Legends of Davy Crockett*. New York: William Morrow.

Deur, Lynne. 1972. *Indian Chiefs*. Minneapolis, Minn.: Lerner.

Devlin, John C. 1964. "Hal Borland and the Voice of Nature." *Audubon* (May–June), 175–177.

Dexter, D. Gilbert. 1972. *Life and Works of Henry Wadsworth Longfellow*. New York: Gordon Press.

Diaz del Castillo, Bernal. 1956. *Discovery and Conquest of Mexico*. New York: Farrar, Staus & Cudahy.

Dickson, Lovat. 1975. *Wilderness Man: The Strange Story of Grey Owl*. New York: New American Library.

Dictionary of Literary Biography, Vol. 30. 1984. Detroit: Gale Research.

DISCovering Authors (CD-ROM). 1993. Detroit: Gale Research.

Dobie, J. Frank. 1952a. *Guide to Life and Literature of the Southwest*. Dallas: SMU Press.

———. 1952b. *The Mustang*. Boston: Little, Brown.

———. 1978. *The Ben Lilly Legend*. Austin: Texas Press.

———. 1990. *Apache Gold and Yaqui Silver*. Austin: Texas Press.

———. 1996. *Guide to Life and Literature of the Southwest*. http://www.islandmm.com/llsw/llswp.htm (August 16).

Dodge, Richard Irving. 1978. *Our Wild Indians: Thirty-Three Years' Personal Experience among the Red Men of the Great West*. Williamstown, Mass.: Corner House.

Donahue, Deirdre. 1996. "On the Trail of History." *USA Today* (March 21), D1–2.

Dorson, Richard M. 1959. *American Folklore*. Chicago: University of Chicago Press.

Downes, Brian. 1996. "Legendary Cowboy's Getting Top Bill-ing." *Charlotte Observer* (June 9), 5F, 10F.

Drabble, Margaret, ed. 1985. *The Oxford Companion to English Literature*. New York: Oxford University Press.

Drake, Benjamin. 1851. *The Life and Adventures of Black Hawk*. Cincinnati, Ohio: Applegate.

Drake, Samuel G. 1834. *Biography and History of the Indians of North America*. Boston: O. L. Perkins.

Drannan, William F. 1900. *Thirty-One Years on the Plains and in the Mountains, or The Last Voice from the Plains*. Chicago: Rhodes & McClure.

Driggs, Howard R. 1935. *The Pony Express Goes Through*. New York: Lippincott.

Duffy, Martha. 1973. "The Old Sod." *Time* (August 13), 80.

Dunham, Montrew. 1975. *John Muir: Young Naturalist*. Indianapolis, Ind.: Bobbs-Merrill.

Eagle, Dorothy, and Meic Stephens, eds. 1992. *The Oxford Illustrated Literary Guide to Great Britain and Ireland*. New York: Oxford University Press.

Eastman, Charles A. 1974. *Indian Scout Craft and Lore*. New York: Dover.

———. 1975. *Indian Boyhood*. Williamstown, Mass.: Corner House.

———. 1980. *The Soul of the Indian: An Interpretation*. Lincoln: University of Nebraska Press.

Ecchevarria, Evelio. 1993. "Mariano Azuela: The Underdogs." *Studies in Short Fiction* (Fall), 616.

Eckert, Allan W. 1967. *The Frontiersman*. Boston: Little, Brown.

Edmonds, Walter D. 1936. *Drums along the Mohawk*. Boston: Little, Brown.

Edwards, Clifford Duane. 1971. *Conrad Richter's Ohio Trilogy: Its Ideas, Themes, and Relationship to Literary Tradition*. Hawthorne, N.Y.: Mouton.

Eggleston, Edward. 1903. *The Hoosier Schoolmaster*. New York: Orange Judd.

Eggleston, Wilfrid. 1977. *The Frontier and Canadian Letters*. Toronto: McClelland & Stewart.

Ehle, John. 1988. *Trail of Tears: The Rise and Fall of the Cherokee Nation*. New York: Anchor.

Ehrlich, Eugene, and Gorton Carruth. 1982. *The Oxford Illustrated Literary Guide to the United States*. New York: Oxford University Press.

Eliade, Mircea, ed. 1987. *The Encyclopedia of Religion*. New York: Macmillan.

Emerson, Everett. 1985. *The Authentic Mark Twain: A Literary Biography of Samuel L. Clemens*. Philadelphia: University of Pennsylvania Press.

Esquivel, Laura. 1991. *Like Water for Chocolate*. New York: Anchor Books.

Estell, Kenneth, ed. 1993. *The African-American Almanac*. Detroit: Gale Research.

Estrada, Richard. 1979. "The Mexican Revolution." *Password*, 55–69.

Evans, Chad. 1983. *Frontier Theatre*. Victoria, B.C.: Sono Nis Press.

Falkenhorst, C. 1892. *With Cortéz in Mexico*. New York: Hurst.

Faragher, John Mack. 1995. "Chronology" from *Daniel Boone: The Life and Legend of an American Pioneer*. http://xroads.virginia.edu/~hyper/CONTEXTS/Boone/chronolo.html (November 10).

"Farewell to Two Artists." 1978. *Nebraska Journal* (February 24), n.p.

Farnham, Charles. 1968. *A Life of Francis Parkman*. New York: Haskell House.

Farnham, Thomas. 1983. *An 1839 Wagon Train Journal*. New York: Greenley & McElrath.

Faulkner, William, 1967. *The Portable Faulkner*. New York: Penguin.

———. 1977. *Collected Stories*. New York: Vintage.

———. 1985. "The Bear." In *The United States in Literature*. Glenview, Ill.: Scott, Foresman.

Fay, Eliot. 1953. *Lorenzo in Search of the Sun*. New York: Bookman Associates.

Feldman, Susan, ed. 1965. *The Story-Telling Stone*. New York: Laurel.

Ferber, Edna. 1945. *Great Son*. New York: Avon.

———. 1981. *Five Complete Novels*. New York: Avenel.

Ferdinand. 1992. *The Life of the Admiral Christopher Columbus*. New Brunswick, N.J.: Rutgers University Press.

Fields, Herbert, and Dorothy Fields. 1946. *Annie Get Your Gun* (stage play). Chicago: Dramatic Publishing.

———. 1952. *Annie Get Your Gun* (musical). London: Chappell & Co.

Fife, Austin, and Alta Fife. 1956. *Saints of Sage and Saddle*. Bloomington: Indiana University Press.

Findlay, Rowe. 1980. "The Pony Express." *National Geographic* (July), 45–71.

Fisher, Leonard Everett. 1992. *Tracks across America*. New York: Holiday House.

Folsom, James K. 1966. *The American Western Novel*. New Haven: College & University Press.

Fowke, Edith. 1976. *Folklore of Canada*. Toronto: McClelland & Stewart.

Franchere, Ruth. 1962. *Jack London: The Pursuit of a Dream*. New York: Thomas Y. Crowell.

Franklin, Benjamin. 1982. *The Autobiography and Other Writings*. New York: Bantam.

Franklin, Wayne. 1982. *The New World of James Fenimore Cooper*. Chicago: University of Chicago Press.

Fraser, Frances. 1968. *The Bear Who Stole the Chinook*. Vancouver: Douglas & McIntyre.

Frost, O. W. 1967. *Joaquin Miller*. New York: Twayne.

Fuentes, Carlos. 1985. *The Old Gringo*. New York: Farrar, Straus & Giroux.

Fuller, Edmond. 1968. "Two on Lighter Side." *Wall Street Journal* (July 2).

Fuller, Muriel, ed. 1961. *More Junior Authors*. New York: H. W. Wilson.

Gabriel, Kathryn. 1992. *Marietta Wetherill*. Boulder, Colo.: Johnson Books.

Gad, Carl. 1974. *Johan Bojer: The Man and His Works*. Westport, Conn.: Greenwood Press.

Gallo, Donald R., ed. 1990. *Speaking for Ourselves*. Urbana, Ill.: National Council of Teachers of English.

Gardner, Martin, ed. 1995. *Famous Poems from Bygone Days*. New York: Dover.

Garland, Hamlin. 1928. *A Son of the Middle Border*. New York: Macmillan.

———. 1970. *Main-Travelled Roads*. Columbus, Ohio: Charles E. Merrill.

———. 1995. *Main-Travelled Roads*. Lincoln: University of Nebraska Press.

Garnett, Stephen. 1996. "Robert Service." *This England* (Spring), 12–17.

Garrett, Pat F. 1954. *The Authentic Life of Billy, the Kid*. Norman: University of Oklahoma Press.

Gassner, John, ed. 1967. *Best Plays of the American Theatre*. New York: Crown.

Gassner, John, and Edward Quinn, eds. 1969. *The Reader's Encyclopedia of World Drama*. New York: Thomas Y. Crowell.

Gaston, Edwin. 1965. *Conrad Richter*. New York: Twayne.

George, Jean Craighead. 1972. *Julie of the Wolves*. New York: Harper & Row.

Georgiou, Constantine. 1969. *Children and Their Literature*. New York: Prentice Hall.

Geronimo. 1989. *Geronimo's Story of His Life*. Williamstown, Mass.: Corner House.

Gilbert, Julie Goldsmith. 1978. *Ferber: A Biography of Edna Ferber and Her Circle*. Garden City, N.Y.: Doubleday.

Giles, Janice Holt. 1956. *Hannah Fowler*. Boston: Houghton Mifflin.

Gillespie, John, and Diana Lembo. 1967. *Junior Plots: A Book Talk Manual for Teachers and Librarians*. New York: R. R. Bowker.

Gillett, James. 1976. *Six Years with the Texas Rangers, 1875–1881*. Lincoln: University of Nebraska Press.

Gillett, Rupert. 1952. " 'Horn in the West,' Youngest N.C. Historical Drama, Opens." *Charlotte Observer* (June 29), 6D.

Gipson, Fred. 1953. *Cowhand: The Story of a Working Cowboy*. New York: Harper & Brothers.

————. 1956. *Old Yeller*. New York: Harper & Row.

————. 1957. *Old Yeller* (video). Hollywood: Walt Disney.

————. 1993. *Old Yeller* (audiocassette). Prince Frederick, Md.: Recorded Books.

Gislason, Eric J. 1996a. "Edna Ferber's *Ice Palace:* The *Uncle Tom's Cabin* of Alaska Statehood." http://xroads.virginia.edu/~CAP/BARTLETT/palace.html (August 21).

————. 1996b. *Virgin Land: The American West as Symbol and Myth*. http://xroads.virginia.edu/~HYPER/HNS2/synoptic.html (September 27).

Gloss, Molly. 1989. *The Jump Off Creek*. Boston: Houghton Mifflin.

Goetzmann, William H. 1986. *New Lands, New Men*. New York: Penguin.

Goldfarb, David A. 1995. "The Soviet Novel and the Western." http://www.echonyc.com/~goldfarb/sovwest.htm (September 10).

Gonzáles-Trujillo, César A., ed. 1989. *Rudolfo A. Anaya: Focus on Criticism*. Wellesley Hills: Massachusetts Bay Press.

Gordon, Caroline. 1952. "The Captive." In *The Forest of the South*. Chicago: Scott, Foresman.

Gorgas, Marie D., and Burton J. Hendrick. 1924. *William Crawford Gorgas: His Life and Work*. Garden City, N.Y.: Garden City Publishing.

Goring, Rosemary, ed. 1994. *Larousse Dictionary of Writers*. New York: Larousse Kingfisher Chambers.

Graff, Henry F., ed. 1996. *The Presidents: A Reference History*. New York: Charles Scribner's Sons.

Grafton, John. 1992. *The American West*. New York: Dover Publications.

Gray, William R. 1975. *The Pacific Crest Trail*. Washington, D.C.: National Geographic Society.

Graymont, Barbara. 1972. *The Iroquois in the American Revolution*. Syracuse, N.Y.: Syracuse University Press.

Green, Paul. 1937. *The Lost Colony: A Symphonic Drama in Two Acts*. Chapel Hill: University of North Carolina Press.

————. 1956. *Quare Medicine*. In *North Carolina Drama*. Richmond, Va.: Garret & Massie.

Greene, A. C. 1968. "Female with a Head on Her." Austin (Tex.) *American-Statesman* (July 8).

Greene, John C. 1963. *Darwin and the Modern World View*. New York: Mentor.

Greetham, Phil. 1996. "Laura Ingalls Wilder." http://www.ourworld.compuserve.com/homepages/p-greetham/ingalls.htm (May 24).

Gregg, John J., and Barbara T. Gregg. 1980. *Best Loved Poems of the American West*. Garden City, N.Y.: Doubleday.

Gremstead, David. 1968. *Melodrama Unveiled: American Theater and Culture 1800–1850*. Berkeley: University of California Press.

Grenander, M. E. 1971. *Ambrose Bierce*. New York: Twayne.

Grey, Zane. 1918. *The U. P. Trail*. New York: Grosset & Dunlap.

———. 1940. *Riders of the Purple Sage*. Roslyn, N.Y.: Walter J. Black.

———. 1970. "Oak Creek Canyon." In *Arizona in Literature*. New York: Haskell House.

———. 1978. *The Last of the Plainsmen*. Mattituck, N.Y.: American Reprint.

———. 1988. *Blue Feather and Other Stories*. Boston: G. K. Hall.

Grey Owl. 1972. *The Men of the Last Frontier*. Toronto: Stoddart.

———. 1990. *Pilgrims of the Wild*. Toronto: Macmillan.

———. 1991. *Sajo and the Beaver People*. Toronto: Stoddart.

———. 1992. *Tales of an Empty Cabin*. Toronto: Stoddart.

Grierson, Alice. 1989. *The Colonel's Lady on the Western Frontier: The Correspondence of Alice Kirk Grierson*. Lincoln: University of Nebraska Press.

Griner, David. 1995. "Missouri Review Coup: Zane Grey." http://www.cclabs.missouri.edu/~maneater/100395/grey011.html (September 3).

Grinnell, George Bird. 1972. *Blackfoot Lodge Tales*. Williamstown, Conn.: Corner House.

Gross, Theodore L. 1971. *The Heroic Ideal in American Literature*. New York: Free Press.

Grossman, James. 1949. *James Fenimore Cooper*. Toronto: William Sloane.

Grove, Frederick Philip. 1982. *A Search for America*. Toronto: McClelland & Stewart.

———. 1989. *Settlers of the Marsh*. Toronto: McClelland & Stewart.

———. 1992. *Fruits of the Earth*. Toronto: McClelland & Stewart.

Gruber, Frank. 1970. *Zane Grey*. New York: World Publishing.

Gullette, Alan. 1996. "Ambrose Bierce, Master of the Macabre." http://www.creative.net/~alang/lit/horror/bierce.sht (June 24).

Gurko, Miriam. 1970. *Indian America: The Black Hawk War*. New York: Crowell.

Guthrie, A. B. 1960. *The Way West*. New York: Pocket Books.

Hakluyt, Richard. 1826. *The Principal Navigations, Voyages, and Discoveries of the English Nations*. New York: Brown.

———. 1954. "Divers Voyages Touching the Discovery of America and the Ilands Adjacent unto the Same." In *The Renaissance in England*. Boston: D. C. Heath.

———. 1958. *Voyages and Documents*. London: Oxford Press.

———. 1962. *Voyages*. Vols. 1–8. New York: Everyman's Library.

"Hal Borland, Naturalist, Dies in Connecticut." 1978. *Nebraska Star* (February 24), n.p.

Halliwell, Leslie. 1995. *Halliwell's Film Guide*. New York: HarperPerennnial.

Hamilton, Allan McLane. 1916. *Recollections of an Alienist*. New York: George H. Doran.

Hanes, Colonel. 1989. *Bill Pickett*. Norman: University of Oklahoma Press.

Hanners, LaVerne. 1994. *Girl on a Pony*. Norman: University of Oklahoma Press.

Hardacre, Emma. 1961. "The Lone Woman of San Nicolas Island." In *The California Indians*, ed. by Robert Heizer and M. A. Whipple. Berkeley: University of California Press.

Hardin, John Wesley. 1961. *The Life of John Wesley Hardin as Written by Himself*. Norman: University of Oklahoma Press.

Harriot, Thomas. 1972. *A Briefe and True Report of the New Found Land of Virginia*. New York: Dover.

Harris, Joel Chandler. 1952. Uncle Remus Stories. In *The Literature of the South*. Chicago: Scott, Foresman.

Harris, Leon A. 1964. *The Fine Art of Political Wit*. New York: E. P. Dutton.

Hart, James D. 1983. *The Oxford Companion to American Literature*. New York: Oxford University Press.

Harte, Bret. 1883. *In the Carquinez Woods and Other Tales*. Boston: Houghton Mifflin.

———. 1896. *The Story of a Mine and Other Tales*. Boston: Houghton Mifflin.

———. 1902. *The Complete Poetical Works*. New York: P. F. Collier.

———. 1991. "The Luck of Roaring Camp." In *American Pioneer Writers*. New York: Gallery.

———. 1992. *The Luck of Roaring Camp and Other Short Stories*. New York: Dover.

Hartnoll, Phyllis, ed. 1983. *The Oxford Companion to the Theater*. New York: Oxford University Press.

Hastings, Lansford W. 1845. *The Emigrants' Guide to Oregon and California*. Bedford, Mass.: Applewood.

Haun, Catherine. 1992. *A Woman's Trip across the Plains in 1849*. In *Women's Diaries of the Westward Journey*. New York: Schocken.

Haverstock, Mary. 1973. *Indian Gallery: The Story of George Catlin*. New York: Four Winds Press.

Hazard, Lucy Lockwood. 1927. *The Frontier in American Literature*. New York: Thomas Y. Crowell.

Hebard, Grace Raymond, and A. E. Brininstool. 1990. *The Bozeman Trail* (Vol. 1). Lincoln: University of Nebraska Press.

————. 1992. *The Bozeman Trail* (Vol. 2). Lincoln: University of Nebraska Press.

Hedrick, Joan D. 1982. *Solitary Comrade: Jack London and His Work*. Chapel Hill: University of North Carolina Press.

Hendrick, George. 1965. *Katherine Anne Porter*. New York: Twayne.

Henry, O. 1993. *Heart of the West*. Pleasantville, N.Y.: Reader's Digest.

Herron, Ima Honaker. 1939. *The Small Town in American Literature*. Durham, N. C.: Duke University Press.

Hewitt, Barnard. 1959. *Theatre U. S. A.: 1665–1957*. New York: McGraw-Hill.

Heyne, Eric, ed. 1992. *Desert, Garden, Margin, Range: Literature on the American Frontier*. New York: Twayne.

Hispanic Literature Criticism, Vol. 1. 1989. Detroit: Gale Research.

"The History of the Oregon Trail." 1996. http://www.mecc.com/MECC-HOME/OT11.Files/OT11.History.html (June 4).

Hitchcock, Ethan Allen. 1996. *A Traveller in Indian Territory*. Norman: University of Oklahoma Press.

Hitchcock, H. Wiley, and Stanley Sadie, eds. 1980. *The New Grove Dictionary of American Music*. New York: Macmillan.

Hodge, Francis. 1964. *Yankee Theatre*. Austin: University of Texas Press.

Hoffman, A. J. 1988. *Twain's Heroes, Twain's Worlds*. Philadelphia: University of Pennsylvania Press.

Hoffman, Miriam, and Eva Samuels. 1972. *Authors and Illustrators of Children's Books*. New York: Bowker.

Hogg, Peter. 1979. *Slavery: The Afro-American Experience*. London: British Library.

Holland, Robert E. 1942. *The Song of Tekakwitha: The Lily of the Mohawks*. New York: Fordham University Press.

Holtz, William. 1993. *The Ghost in the Little House*. Columbia: University of Missouri Press.

Hooke, Hilda Mary. 1942. *One-Act Plays from Canadian History*. Toronto: Longmans, Green.

Hopkins, Robert S. 1969. *Darwin's South America*. New York: John Day.

Hopkins, Sarah Winnemucca. 1994. *Life among the Piutes, Their Wrongs and Claims*. Reno: University of Nevada Press.

Horgan, Paul. 1984. *Of America East & West*. New York: HarperCollins.

———. 1991. *Great River: The Rio Grande in North American History*. Hanover, N.H.: Wesleyan University Press.

Horn, Tom. 1964. *Life of Tom Horn, Government Scout and Interpreter.* Norman: University of Oklahoma Press.

" 'Horn in the West' to Hold Catawba County Night." 1990. (Newton, N.C.) *Observer-News-Enterprise* (July 27), 9.

Hornsby, Alton. 1994. *African American Chronology.* Detroit: Gale Research.

Hornstein, Lillian Herlands, ed. 1973. *The Reader's Companion to World Literature*. New York: New American Library.

Howard, O. O. 1972. *Nez Perce Joseph: An Acccount of His Ancestors, His Lands, His Confederates, His Enemies, His Murders, His War, His Pursuit and Capture.* New York: Da Capo.

———. 1989. *Famous Indian Chiefs I Have Known*. Lincoln: University of Nebraska Press.

Hoyle, Bernadette. 1956. *Tar Heel Writers I Know*. Winston-Salem, N.C.: John F. Blair.

Hoyt, Harlowe R. 1955. *Town Hall Tonight: Intimate Memories of the Grassroots Days of the American Theatre*. Englewood Cliffs, N.J.: Prentice-Hall.

Huey, Pamela. 1994. "Children's Book Basis for New Historic Highway." *Hickory Daily Record* (November 13), 1B.

Hughes, Glenn. 1938. *The Story of the Theatre*. New York: Samuel French.

———. 1951. *A History of American Theatre 1700–1750*. New York: Samuel French.

Hunter, Kermit. 1967. "Out of History . . . A Lesson." *Unto These Hills* program, 24–27.

Hutchinson, Stuart, ed. n.d. "Mark Twain: Critical Assessments" (brochure). East Sussex, Eng.: Helm Information.

Hutchinson, W. H. 1963. "The Caesarean Delivery of Paul Bunyan." *Western Folklore* (January), 1–15.

Hyde, George E. 1951. *The Pawnee Indians*. Norman: University of Oklahoma Press.

Irby, Rebecca LeeAnne. 1996. "Laura Ingalls Wilder." http:// webpages.marshall.edu/~irby1/laura.htmlx (May 24).

Irving, Washington. n.d. *The Best Known Works of Washington Irving*. Garden City, N.Y.: Book Club Associates.

———. 1851. *The Life and Voyages of Christopher Columbus*. New York: Putnam.

———. 1855. *Wolfert's Roost and Miscellanies*. New York: Putnam.

———. 1944. *The Western Journals*. Norman: University of Oklahoma Press.

———. 1978. "Rip Van Winkle." In *Focus on Literature: America*. Boston: Houghton Mifflin.

———. 1983. *Bracebridge Hall; Tales of a Traveller; The Alhambra*. New York: Library of America.

———. 1987. "The Devil and Tom Walker." In *The United States in Literature*. Glenview, Ill.: Scott, Foresman.

Ishi. 1992. *Ishi the Last Yahi* (audiocassette). San Francisco: Wild Sanctuary Communications.

"Jack London State Historic Park." 1996. http://www.parks.sonoma.net/ JLPark.html (July 22).

Jackson, Helen Hunt. 1931. *Ramona*. Boston: Little, Brown.

———. 1979. *A Century of Dishonor*. Williamstown, Mass.: Corner House.

Jacobs, Harriet. 1988. *Incidents in the Life of a Slave Girl*. New York: Oxford University Press.

Jacobs, Wilbur. 1991. *Francis Parkman, Historian as Hero*. Austin: University of Texas Press.

James, Marquis. 1929. *The Raven*. Indianapolis, Ind.: Bobbs-Merrill.

———. 1993. *Cherokee Strip*. Norman: University of Oklahoma Press.

Janke, Jim. 1996. "Western Novels and Novelists." http://www.dsu.edu/ ~jankej/oldwest/novels.html (April 1).

Jefferson, Joseph. 1964. *The Autobiography of Joseph Jefferson*. Cambridge, Mass.: Harvard University Press.

Johnson, Allen, and Dumas Malone, eds. 1930. *Dictionary of American Biography*. New York: Charles Scribner's Sons.

Johnson, Broderick H. 1975. *Navajo Stories of the Long Walk Period*. Tsaile, Ariz.: Navajo Community College Press.

Johnson, Dorothy M. 1953. *Indian Country*. New York: Ballantine.

Johnson, Linck C. 1986. *Thoreau's Complex Weave: The Writing of* A Week on the Concord and Merrimack Rivers. Charlottesville: University of Virginia Press.

Johnston, Basil H. 1989. *Indian School Days*. Norman: University of Oklahoma Press.

Jones, Margaret. 1990. "Bless This Book." *Publishers Weekly* (October 12), 30.

Jones, Nard. 1964. *Swift Flows the River*. Portland, Ore.: Binfords & Mort.

Joseph, Chief. 1979. "An Indian's View of Indian Affairs." *North American Review* (April), 415–433.

————. 1987. "I Will Fight No More Forever." In *The United States in Literature*. Glenview, Ill.: Scott, Foresman.

Kalakaua, King David. 1972. *The Legends and Myths of Hawaii: The Fables and Folk-Lore of a Strange People*. Rutland, Vt.: Charles E. Tuttle.

Kaplan, Justin, gen. ed. 1966. *Mister Clemens and Mark Twain: A Biography*. New York: Simon & Schuster.

Kasper, Shirl. 1992. *Annie Oakley*. Norman: University of Oklahoma Press.

Katz, Ephraim. 1982. *The Film Encyclopedia*. New York: Perigee Books.

Kelly, William P. 1984. *Plotting America's Past: Fenimore Cooper and the Leatherstocking Tales*. Edwardsville: Southern Illinois University Press.

Kennedy, W. Sloane. 1972. *Henry W. Longfellow: Biography, Anecdote, Letters, Criticism*. Brooklyn, N.Y.: Haskell.

Kessler, Lauren. 1993. *Stubborn Twig: Three Generations in the Life of a Japanese American Family*. New York: Random House.

Kesterson, David B., ed. 1979. *Critics on Mark Twain*. Baltimore, Md.: University of Miami Press.

Kidd, Adam. 1830. *The Huron Chief and Other Poems*. Montreal: Herald & New Gazette.

————. 1997. "The Huron Chief." http://bosshog.arts.wwo.ca/eng/poetry/huron.html (February 2).

Kingston, Carolyn T. 1974. *The Tragic Mode in Children's Literature*. New York: Columbia University Teachers College Press.

Kirkpatrick, D. L., ed. 1983. *Twentieth-Century Children's Writers*. New York: St. Martin's.

Kirsch, Robert, and William S. Murphy. 1967. *West of the West*. New York: E. P. Dutton.

Klein, Dianne. 1992. "Coming of Age in Novels by Rudolfo Anaya and Sandra Cisneros." *English Journal* (September), 21–26.

Klein, Leonard S., ed. 1981. *Encyclopedia of World Literature in the Twentieth Century*. New York: Ungar.

Koch, Frederick, H. 1922. *Carolina Folk-Plays*. New York: Henry Holt.

Krasnowsky, Marc. 1989. "Missing Willa Cather Plaque Has Returned." *Lincoln Star* (February 21), 2.

Kroeber, A. L., and G. B. Kroeber. 1973. *A Mohave War Reminiscence, 1854–1880*. New York: Dover.

Kroeber, Theodora. 1962. *Ishi in Two Worlds: A Biography of the Last Wild Indian in North America*. Berkeley: University of California Press.

———. 1987. *Ishi, Last of His Tribe*. New York: Bantam.

Kunitz, Stanley J. 1942. *Twentieth Century Authors*. New York: H. W. Wilson.

Kunitz, Stanley J., and Howard Haycraft. 1938. *American Authors: 1600–1900*. New York: H. W. Wilson.

La Farge, Oliver. 1929. *Laughing Boy*. Cambridge, Mass.: Houghton Mifflin.

La Salle, René Robert. 1922. *The Journeys of René Robert Cavelier Sieur de La Salle*. New York: Allerton Book Co.

Labor, Earle. 1974. *Jack London*. Boston: Twayne.

Labor, Earle, and Jeanne Campbell Reesman. 1994. *Jack London*. New York: Macmillan.

Ladd, Maria de Armas. 1996. "James Fenimore Cooper." http://www.en.utexas.edu/~maria/cooper/jfe_home.htm (July 3).

Lagarde, André, and Laurent Michard. 1985. *Dix-Neuvieme Siecle: Les Grands Auteurs Français du Programme*. Paris: Bordas.

LaHood, Marvin J. 1975. *Conrad Richter's America*. Hawthorne, N.Y.: Mouton.

Lake, Stuart N. 1994. *Wyatt Earp: Frontier Marshall*. New York: Pocket Books.

Lamar, Howard R., ed. 1977. *The Reader's Encyclopedia of the American West*. New York: Harper & Row.

Lame Deer, John Fire, and Richard Erdoes. 1972. *Lame Deer, Seeker of Visions*. New York: Washington Square.

L'Amour, Louis. 1953. *Hondo*. Greenwich, Conn.: Fawcett.

———. 1961. *Sackett*. New York: Bantam.

———. 1978. *Fair Blows the Wind*. New York: E. P. Dutton.

———. 1979. *Conagher*. Leicester, Eng.: Ulverscroft.

———. 1981. *The Comstock Lode*. New York: Bantam.

———. 1983. *Sitka*. New York: Bantam.

———. 1985. *Jubal Sackett*. New York: Bantam.

———. 1988. *The Sackett Companion: A Personal Guide to the Sackett Novels*. New York: Bantam.

———. 1989. *The Education of a Wandering Man*. New York: Bantam.

Landa, Diego de. 1978. *Yucatan before and after the Conquest*. New York: Dover.

Lane, Rose. 1963. *Old Home Town*. Lincoln: University of Nebraska Press.

Lane, Rose Wilder, and Roger Lea MacBride. 1977. *Rose Wilder Lane: Her Story*. New York: Stein and Day.

Langford, J. O., and Fred Gipson. 1973. *Big Bend: A Homesteader's Story*. Austin: University of Texas Press.

Langford, Walter M. 1971. *The Mexican Novel Comes of Age*. South Bend, Ind.: University of Notre Dame Press.

Larson, Charles R. 1979. "Books in English from the Third World." *World Literature Today* (Spring) 245–247.

Las Casas, Bartolomé de. 1992. *A Short Account of the Destruction of the Indies*. London: Penguin.

Lasky, Kathryn, and Meribah Knight. 1993. *Searching for Laura Ingalls: A Reader's Journey*. New York: Macmillan.

The Last of His Tribe (video). New York: ABC-TV, 1995.

Lattin, Vernon E. 1986. *Contemporary Chicano Fiction: A Critical Survey*. Binghamton, N.Y.: Bilingual/Editorial Bilingue.

Lavender, David. 1988. *The Way to the Western Sea*. New York: Harper & Row.

Lawrence, D. H. 1969. "The Spirit of Place." In *The Norton Reader: An Anthology of Expository Prose*. New York: W. W. Norton.

———. 1974. *Birds, Beasts and Flowers*. New York: Haskell House.

———. 1976. *The Complete Short Stories, Vol. II*. New York: Penguin.

———. 1992. *The Plumed Serpent*. New York: Vintage Books.

Leal, Luis. 1971. *Mariano Azuela*. Boston: Twayne.

Lee, Hector. 1949. *The Three Nephites: The Substance and Significance of the Legend in Folklore*. Albuquerque: University of New Mexico Press.

———. 1975. "Tales and Legends in Western American Literature." *Western American Literature* (Winter).

Lee, Robert Edson. 1966. *From West to East: Studies in the Literature of the American West*. Urbana: University of Illinois Press.

Leeming, David Adams. 1990. *The World of Myth*. New York: Oxford University Press.

"The Legend and Facts of Daniel Boone." 1972. *Horn in the West* Souvenir Program, 8–9.

Leisy, Ernest E. 1950. *The American Historical Novel*. Norman: University of Oklahoma Press.

Levenson, Dorothy. 1973. *Women of the West*. New York: Franklin Watts.

Levine, Miriam. 1984. *A Guide to Writers' Homes in New England*. Cambridge, Mass.: Apple-Wood Books.

Levine, Robert. 1989. *Conspiracy and Romance: Studies in Brockden Brown, Cooper, Hawthorne, and Melville*. London: Cambridge University Press.

Lewis, Kate Porter. 1943. *Alabama Folk Plays*. Chapel Hill: University of North Carolina Press.

Lewis, Meriwether, and William Clark. 1922. *Lewis and Clark Journals*. New York: Atherton.

———. 1953. *The Journals of Lewis and Clark*. Cambridge, Mass.: Riverside.

Linderman, Frank. 1972. *Pretty-Shield, Medicine Woman of the Crows*. Lincoln: University of Nebraska Press.

"Little House on the Prairie." 1996. http://www.members.aol.com/biblioholc/Laura.html (May 27).

"Little Town on the Prairie," 1996. http://www.state.sd.us/state/executive/tourism/20reason/town.htm (May 24).

Lochhead, Douglas, and Raymond Souster. 1974. *100 Poems of Nineteenth Century Canada*. Toronto: Macmillan.

Lomax, John. 1947. *Adventures of a Ballad Hunter*. New York: Macmillan.

———. 1965. "Starving to Death on a Government Claim." In *Accent: U.S.A.* Chicago: Scott, Foresman.

Lomax, John, and Alan Lomax. 1968. *American Ballads and Folk Songs*. New York: Macmillan.

London, Jack. 1964. *The Call of the Wild*. New York: Airmont.

———. 1965. *Jack London's Stories of the North*. New York: Scholastic.

———. 1980. *White Fang*. Mahwah, N.J.: Watermill Press.

———. 1982. *The Iron Heel*. In *Novels and Social Writings*. New York: Libraries of America.

———. 1991. *The Sea-Wolf*. New York: Bantam.

———. 1992. *Five Great Short Stories*. New York: Dover.

———. 1996a. "Wit of Porportuk." http://www.gopher.cc.columbia.edu:71/11/miscellaneous/cubooks/offbooks/london (July 22).

———. 1996b. "Batard." http://www.gopher.cc.columbia.edu:71/11/miscellaneous/cubooks/offbooks/london (July 22).

London, Joan. 1990. *Jack London and His Daughters*. Berkeley, Calif.: Heyday Books.

Long, Robert Emmet. 1990. *James Fenimore Cooper*. New York: Frederick Ungar Books.

Long, Stephen. 1988. *From Pittsburgh to the Rocky Mountains*. Golden, Colo.: Fulcrum.

Longfellow, Henry Wordsworth. 1951. *Evangeline, a Tale of Arcadie*. Halifax, Nova Scotia: Nimbus.

———. 1993. *The Song of Hiawatha*. London: J. M. Dent.

Lopez-Medina, Sylvia. 1992. *Cantora*. New York: Ballantine.

"The Lost Colony." 1996. http://204.107.79.7/lost.html (May 18).

"The Lost Colony" Playbill. 1990. Roanoke, Va.: Roanoke Island Historical Association.

"The Lost Colony: America's Beginning." 1996. http://www.outerbanks-nc.com/lostcolony/ (May 18).

Love, Nat. 1988. *The Life and Adventures of Nat Love, Better Known in the Cattle Country as Deadwood Dick*. Baltimore, Md.: Black Classic Press.

Low, W. Augustus, and Virgil A. Clift, eds. 1981. *Encyclopedia of Black America*. New York: Da Capo.

Lummis, Charles F. 1992. *Pueblo Indian Folk-Stories*. Lincoln: University of Nebraska Press.

Lundquist, James. 1987. *Jack London: Adventures, Ideas and Fiction*. New York: Ungar Press.

Lyttle, Richard B. 1994. *Mark Twain: The Man and His Adventures*. New York: Atheneum.

MacBride, Roger Lea. 1993. *Little House on Rocky Ridge*. New York: HarperCollins.

———. 1994. *Little Farm in the Ozarks*. New York: HarperCollins.

———. 1995. *In the Land of the Big Red Apple*. New York: HarperCollins.

Machado, Manuel A., Jr. 1988. *Centaur of the North*. Austin, Tex.: Eakin Press.

Mackay, Constance D'Arcy. 1976. *Plays of the Pioneers: A Book of Historical Pageant-Plays*. Great Neck, N.Y.: Core Collection.

Mackay, James. 1995. *Vagabond of Verse*. London: Mainstream.

MacLachlan, Patricia, and Carol Sobieski. 1991. *Sara, Plain and Tall* (video). Los Angeles: Republic Pictures.

———. 1993. *The Skylark* (video). Los Angeles: Republic Pictures.

Maggio, Rosalie, comp. 1992. *The Beacon Book of Quotations by Women*. Boston: Beacon Press.

Magill, Frank N., ed. 1958. *Cyclopedia of World Authors*. New York: Harper & Brothers.

Magnusson, Magnus, gen. ed. 1990. *Cambridge Biographical Dictionary*. New York: Cambridge University Press.

Magoffin, Susan. 1982. *Down the Santa Fe Trail & into Mexico*. Lincoln: University of Nebraska Press.

Malia, Peter. 1983. "Washington Irving." *American History Illustrated* (May), 17–25.

Malone, Dumas, ed. 1933. *Dictionary of American Biography*. New York: Charles Scribner's Sons.

"Mariano Azuela." 1996. http://www.mexplaza.udg.mx/fce/ingles/autores/inautor9.html (July 16).

Marriott, Alice, and Carol K. Rachlin. 1975. *Plains Indian Mythology*. New York: Meridian Books.

Marsh, Earle. 1992. *The Complete Directory to Prime Time Network TV Shows, 1946–Present*. New York: Ballantine.

Martinez, Eliud. 1980. *The Art of Mariano Azuela*. Pittsburgh: Latin American Literary Review Press.

McArthur, Tom, ed. 1992. *The Oxford Companion to the English Language*. New York: Oxford University Press.

McCall, Edith S. 1963. *Pioneer Show Folk*. Chicago: Children's Press.

McClung, Nellie L. 1965. *Clearing in the West*. Toronto: Thomas Allen & Son.

McConnell, H. 1996. *Five Years a Cavalryman, Sketches of Regular Army Life on the Texas Frontier, 1866–1871*. Norman: University of Oklahoma Press.

McCracken, Harold. 1959. *George Catlin and the Old Frontier*. New York: Dial Press.

McCunn, Ruthanne Lum. 1981. *Thousand Pieces of Gold*. San Francisco: Design Enterprises of San Francisco.

McHenry, Robert. 1980. *Liberty's Women*. Springfield, Mass.: G. & C. Merriam.

McIntire, Jim. 1992. *Early Days in Texas: A Trip to Hell and Heaven*. Norman: University of Oklahoma Press.

McIntosh, John. 1844. *Origin of the North American Indians*. New York: Nafis & Cornish.

McLachlan, Alexander. 1972. "The Emigrant." In *Nineteenth-Century Narrative Poems*. Toronto: McClelland & Stewart.

McMurtry, Larry. 1985. *Lonesome Dove*. New York: Simon & Schuster.

———. 1991. *Buffalo Girls*. Boston: G. K. Hall.

McVoy, Lizzie Carter, ed. 1940. *Louisiana in the Short Story*. Baton Rouge: Louisiana State University.

McWilliams, Carey. 1939. *Factories in the Field: The Story of Migratory Farm Labor in California*. Boston: Little, Brown.

Meigs, Cornelia, ed. 1969. *A Critical History of Children's Literature*. New York: Macmillan.

Melham, Tom. 1976. *John Muir's Wild America*. Washington, D.C.: National Geographic Society.

Micheaux, Oscar. 1994. *The Conquest: The Story of a Negro Pioneer*. Lincoln: University of Nebraska Press.

Michener, James. 1959. *Hawaii*. New York: Random House.

———. 1974. *Centennial*. New York: Random House.

———. 1985. *Texas*. New York: Random House.

———. 1988. *Alaska*. New York: Random House.

Miguel, Maribeth. 1996. "Captivity Theme: A Thing of the Past." http://www.en.utexas.edu/~maria/cooper/captivit.htm (August 14).

"Mike Fink and Davy Crockett." 1968. In *Annals of America: 1840*, 574–575. Chicago: Encyclopaedia Britannica.

Miller, Brandon Marie. 1995. *Buffalo Gals*. Minneapolis: Lerner Publications.

Miller, James E., Jr. 1970. *From Spain and the Americas*. Glenview, Ill: Scott, Foresman.

Miller, Joaquin. 1922. *Danites of the Sierras*. Oakland, Calif.: privately printed.

Miller, Luree. 1989. *Literary Villages of London*. Washington, D.C.: Starrhill Press.

Milner, Clyde A., et al., eds. 1994. *The Oxford History of the American West*. New York: Oxford University Press.

Mogen, David, et al., eds. 1989. *The Frontier Experience and the American Dream*. College Station: Texas A & M Press.

Momaday, N. Scott. 1968. *House Made of Dawn*. New York: New American Library.

———. 1969. *The Way to Rainy Mountain*. Albuquerque: University of New Mexico Press.

———. 1992. *In the Presence of the Sun: Stories and Poems 1961–1991*. New York: St. Martin's.

Monaco, James, ed. 1991. *The Encyclopedia of Film*. New York: Perigee.

Montesinos, Fernando. 1991. *Memorias Antiguas Historiales del Peru*. USA: Hakluyt Society.

Moodie, Susanna. 1959. *Life in the Clearings*. Toronto: Macmillan.

———. 1966. *Roughing It in the Bush*. Aylesbury, Eng.: Hazell, Watson & Viney.

Moody, Richard. 1966. *Dramas from American Theatre 1762–1909*. Cleveland: World Publishing.

Moody, William Vaughn. 1966. *The Great Divide*. In *Dramas from American Theatre 1762–1909*. Cleveland: World Publishing.

Moore, Pamela. 1996. "London, Jack: The Law of Life." http://www.mchip00.med.nyu.edu/lit-med-lit-med-db/webdocs/webdescrips/london292-des-.html (July 22).

Morey, Walt. 1965. *Gentle Ben*. New York: E. P. Dutton.

Morgan, Lewis Henry. 1959. *The Indian Journals, 1859–1862*. New York: Dover.

Morris, Edmund. 1979. *The Rise of Theodore Roosevelt*. New York: Coward, McCann & Geoghegan.

Morris, Juddi. 1994. *The Harvey Girls: The Women Who Civilized the West*. New York: Walker.

Morris, Roy, Jr. 1995. *Ambrose Bierce: Alone in Bad Company*. New York: Crown.

Morrison, Dorothy Nafus. 1990. *Chief Sarah: Sarah Winnemucca's Fight for Indian Rights*. Portland: Oregon Historical Society.

Morrison, Samuel Eliot. 1971. *The European Discovery of America: Northern Voyages*. New York: Oxford University Press.

———. 1973. "Francis Parkman" (brochure). Boston: Massachusetts Historical Society.

———. 1974. *The European Discovery of America: Southern Voyages*. New York: Oxford University Press.

Morton, Desmond. 1994. *A Short History of Canada*. Toronto: McClelland & Stewart.

Moses, Daniel David, and Terry Goldie, eds. 1992. *An Anthology of Canadian Native Literature in English*. Ontario: Oxford University Press.

Motley, Warren. 1988. *The American Abraham: James Fenimore Cooper and the Frontier Patriarch*. London: Cambridge University Press.

Mowat, Farley. 1975. *The Snow Walker*. Toronto: Seal.

———. 1989. *The Polar Passion*. Toronto: McClelland & Stewart.

Mowatt, Anna Cora. 1966. *Fashion*. In *Dramas from American Theatre 1762–1909*. Cleveland: World Publishing.

Muir, John. 1988. *My First Summer in the Sierra*. Surrey, Eng.: Cannongate Classics.

——. 1992. *A Thousand Mile Walk to the Gulf*. New York: Penguin.

——. 1993a. *The Mountains of California*. New York: Penguin.

——. 1993b. *Travels in Alaska*. New York: Penguin.

——. 1996. "Stickeen: The Story of a Dog." http://www.sierraclub.org/ john_muir_exhibit/writings/stickeen/ (June 3).

Musick, John R. 1996. "Pocahontas: A Story of Virginia, 1890." http:// www.darwin.clas.virginia.edu/~jab3w/pocanew5.html (May 18).

Myres, Sandra, ed. 1991. *Ho for California!* San Marino, Calif.: Huntington Library.

Naden, Corinne J., and Rose Blue. 1992. *John Muir*. Brookfield, Conn.: Millbrook Press.

Nagel, Rob. 1995. *Hispanic American Biography*. Detroit: Gale Research.

The National Cyclopedia of American Biography. 1967. Ann Arbor, Mich.: University Microfilms.

Negley, Glenn, and J. Max Patrick. 1952. *The Quest for Utopia*. New York: Henry Schumann.

Neihardt, Hilda. 1995. *Black Elk and Flaming Rainbow*. Lincoln: University of Nebraska Press.

Neihardt, John G. 1953. *The Mountain Men*. Lincoln: University of Nebraska Press.

——. 1993. *Black Elk Speaks: The Life Story of a Holy Man of the Oglala Sioux*. Lincoln: University of Nebraska Press.

Neuendorf, David W. 1995. "Davy Crockett on Social Spending." http:// www.seidata.com/~neusys/colm0009.html.

Nevins, Allan. 1955. *The Emergence of Modern America*. Chicago: Quadrangle.

Nicoll, Allardyce. 1937. *The Development of the Theatre*. New York: Harcourt, Brace.

Noble, Mike. 1995. "A Biography of Alexis de Tocqueville." http:// oasis.bellevue.k12.wa.us/sammamish/sstudies.dir/hist_docs.dir/ tocqueville.mn.html.

North Carolina Authors: A Selective Handbook. 1952. Chapel Hill: The University of North Carolina Library Extension Publication (October).

"North Side: Willa Cather." 1996. http://www.hamlet.phyast.pitt.edu/ exhibit/neighborhoods/northside/nor_n111.html (June 10).

O'Brien, Sharon. 1986. *Willa Cather: The Emerging Voice*. New York: Oxford University Press.

O'Connor, Richard. 1964. *Jack London, A Biography*. Boston: Little, Brown.

———. 1966. *Bret Harte: A Biography*. Boston: Little, Brown.

O'Dell, Scott. 1943. "An Embarrassing Plenty." *Saturday Review* (October 30).

———. 1961. "Newbery Award Acceptance Speech." *Horn Book* (August).

———. 1967. *The Black Pearl*. New York: Dell.

———. 1970. *Sing Down the Moon*. New York: Dell.

———. 1972. "Acceptance Speech: Hans Christian Andersen Award." *Horn Book* (October).

———. 1980. *Sarah Bishop*. New York: Dell.

———. 1982. "The Tribulations of a Trilogy." *Horn Book* (April), 137–144.

———. 1986. *Streams to the River, River to the Sea*. New York: Fawcett Juniper.

O'Dell, Scott, and Elizabeth Hall. 1992. *Thunder Rolling in the Mountains*. Boston: Houghton Mifflin.

Oglesby, Richard. 1963. *Manual Lisa and the Opening of the Missouri Fur Trade*. Norman: University of Oklahoma Press.

Old Gringo (video). 1989. Hollywood: Columbia Pictures.

"Old Man Coyote and Buffalo Power." 1975. In *Plains Indian Mythology*. New York: Meridian Books.

"The Old West." 1996. http://www.nmt.edu/~joy/west.html (June 14).

Olson, Steven. 1994. *The Prairie in Nineteenth-Century American Poetry*. Norman: University of Oklahoma Press.

O'Neil, Paul. 1979. *The Old West: The End and the Myth*. Alexandra, Va.: Time-Life Books.

O'Neill, Thomas. 1992. *The Emmys*. New York: Penguin.

"Outdoor Drama." 1996. http://www.unc.edu/depts/outdoor/index.html (May 19).

Oviedo y Valdés, Gonzalo Fernandez de. 1959. *Natural History of the West Indies*. Chapel Hill: University of North Carolina Press.

"Pardon Asked for O. Henry in Theft." 1958. *Charlotte Observer* (December 3), n.p.

Parkman, Francis. 1955. *The Parkman Reader*. Boston: Little, Brown.

———. 1962. *The Conspiracy of Pontiac*. New York: Collier.

———. 1973. *The Oregon Trail: Sketches of Prairie and Rocky Mountain Life*. London: Folio Society.

———. 1991. *The Oregon Trail, The Conspiracy of Pontiac*. New York: Library of America.

Parlour Poetry (audiocassette). n.d. Cheltenham, Eng.: This England.

Parsons, Elsie. 1992. *North Amerian Indian Life*. New York: Dover.

Patterson, Lotsee, and Mary Ellen Snodgrass. 1994. *Indian Terms*. Englewood, Colo.: Libraries Unlimited.

Pederson, Jay. 1994. *African American Almanac*. Detroit: Gale Research.

Perdue, Theda. 1993. *Nations Remembered*. Norman: University of Oklahoma Press.

Perkins, George, et al., eds. 1991. *Benét's Reader's Encyclopedia of American Literature*. New York: HarperCollins.

Perry, John. 1981. *Jack London: An American Myth*. Chicago: Nelson-Hall.

Piekarski, Vicki, ed. 1988. *Westward the Women: An Anthology of Western Stories by Women*. Albuquerque: University of New Mexico Press.

Pierce, T. M. 1965. *Mary Hunter Austin*. New York: Twayne.

Ploski, Harry A., and James Williams, eds. 1989. *The Negro Almanac*. Detroit: Gale Research.

Poe, Edgar Allan. 1962. *Selected Stories and Poems*. New York: Airmont.

"The Poetry of Bret Harte." 1996. http://www.solopublications.com/jurn6103.htm (June 10).

"The Poetry of Joaquin Miller." 1996. http://www.solopublications.com/jurn6101.htm (June 10).

Porter, Dorothy. 1995. *Early Negro Writing: 1760–1837*. Baltimore: Black Classic Press.

Porter, Katherine Anne. 1965. *The Collected Stories of Katherine Anne Porter*. New York: Harcourt, Brace & World.

Portis, Charles. 1968a. "True Grit." *Saturday Evening Post* (May 18).

———. 1968b. *True Grit*. New York: New American Library.

Powell, Brenda. 1994. *African American Biography*. Detroit: Gale Research.

Prescott, William H. n.d. *History of the Conquest of Mexico* and *History of the Conquest of Peru*. New York: Modern Library.

Quinn, Arthur Hobson. 1936. *American Fiction: An Historical and Critical Survey*. New York: D. Appleton-Century.

———. 1938. *Representative American Plays from 1767 to the Present Day*. New York: D. Appleton-Century.

Rabe, Roberto. 1996. "Henry Wadsworth Longfellow." http://www.duc.auburn.edu/~vestmon/longfellow_bio.html (June 28).

Radin, Paul. 1934. *The Story of the American Indian*. Garden City, N.Y.: Garden City Publishing.

———. 1963. *The Autobiography of a Winnebago Indian*. New York: Dover.

———. 1972. *The Trickster: A Study in American Indian Mythology*. New York: Schocken.

Rainey, Buck. 1996. *The Reel Cowboy: Essays on the Myth in Movies and Literature*. Jefferson, N.C.: McFarland.

Ramos, Manuel. 1996. "New Mexico in Autumn Setting for Anaya Thriller." *Denver Post* (September 1), 8D.

Rankin, Hugh F. 1965. *The Theater in Colonial America*. Chapel Hill: University of North Carolina Press.

Rasmussen, R. Kent. 1995. *Mark Twain A to Z: The Essential Reference to His Life and Writings*. New York: Facts on File.

Ravitch, Diane, ed. 1990. *The American Reader: Words That Moved a Nation*. New York: HarperCollins.

Rawlings, Marjorie Kinnan. 1970. *The Yearling*. New York: Charles Scribner's Sons.

Rawson, Hugh, and Margaret Miner, comps. 1986. *The New International Dictionary of Quotations*. New York: Mentor.

Reed, John. 1936. "Almost Thirty." *New Republic* (April 29), 332–336.

———. 1969. *Insurgent Mexico*. New York: Greenwood Press.

Reigstad, Paul. 1972. *Rölvaag: His Life and Art*. Lincoln: University of Nebraska Press.

Remington, Frederic. 1994. *Frederic Remington's Own West*. New York: Promontory Press.

"Review: *Old Yeller*." 1956. *Saturday Review of Literature* (November 17), 70.

Rhodes, Richard. 1968. "Mattie Ross's True Account." *New York Times Book Review* (July 7).

Rice, Julian. 1992. *Deer Women and Elk Men: The Lakota Narratives of Ella Deloria*. Albuquerque: University of New Mexico Press.

Richards, Mary. 1996. *Winter Quarters: The 1846–1848 Life Writings of Mary Haskin Parker Richards*. Logan: Utah State University.

Richardson, John. 1991. *Wacousta*. Toronto: McClelland & Stewart.

Richter, Conrad. 1940. *The Trees*. New York: Alfred A. Knopf.

———. 1947. *Always Young and Fair*. New York: Alfred A. Knopf.

———. 1950. *The Town*. New York: Bantam.

———. 1953. *The Light in the Forest*. New York: Bantam.

———. 1960. *The Waters of Kronos*. New York: Alfred A. Knopf.

———. 1965a. "The Free Man." In *Accent U.S.A.* Chicago: Scott, Foresman.

———. 1965b. *The Sea of Grass*. New York: Time.

———. 1965c. "Smoke over the Prairie." In *Accent U.S.A.* Chicago: Scott, Foresman.

———. 1966. *A Country of Strangers*. New York: Alfred A. Knopf.

———. 1978. *The Rawhide Knot and Other Stories*. New York: Alfred A. Knopf.

Richter, Harvena. 1988. *Writing To Survive: The Private Notebooks of Conrad Richter*. Albuquerque: University of New Mexico Press.

Ricks, Christopher, and William L. Vance. 1992. *The Faber Book of America*. London: Faber and Faber.

"Riders of the Purple Sage." 1996. http://unp.unl.edu/UP/grerix.htm (August 6).

Ridge, Martin. 1993. *Atlas of American Frontiers*. Chicago: Rand McNally.

Rigg, Howard V. 1977. "The Invention of *Los de Abajo:* Four Perspectives" (master's thesis). El Paso: University of Texas Press.

Ringe, Donald A. 1988. *James Fenimore Cooper*. Boston: G. K. Hall.

Rip Van Winkle. 1938. In *Representative American Plays from 1767 to the Present Day*. New York: D. Appleton-Century.

Robbins, Jim. 1996. "Into the Storm." *Traveler* (September) 142–149, 160–168.

Robe, Stanley Linn. 1979. *Azuela and the Mexican Underdogs*. Berkeley: University of California Press.

Roberts, Vera Mowry. 1962. *On Stage: A History of Theatre*. New York: Harper & Row.

Robinson, Forrest G. 1996. "An 'Unconscious and Profitable Cerebration': Mark Twain and Literary Intentionality." http://sunsite.berkeley.edu:8080/scan/ncl-e/503/articles/robinson.art503.html (June 7).

Robinson, Phyllis C. 1983. *Willa: The Life of Willa Cather*. Garden City, N.Y.: Doubleday.

Rodney, William. 1996. *Kootenai Brown, Canada's Unknown Frontiersman*. Surrey, B.C.: Heritage House.

Roemer, Kenneth M., ed. 1988. *Approaches to Teaching Momaday's* The Way to Rainy Mountain. New York: Modern Language Association.

Roginski, Jim. 1985. *Behind the Covers: Interviews with Authors and Illustrators of Books for Children and Young Adults*. Englewood, Colo.: Libraries Unlimited.

Rohill, Frank. 1967. *The World of Melodrama*. University Park: Pennsylvania State University Press.

Rölvaag, O. E. 1927. *Giants in the Earth: A Saga of the Prarie.* New York: Harper & Brothers.

———. 1955. *Giants in the Earth.* New York: Harper & Row.

———. 1971. *The Third Life of Per Smevik.* New York: Harper & Row.

Roop, Peter. 1984. "Profile: Scott O'Dell." *Language Arts* (November).

Roosevelt, Theodore. 1983. *Ranch Life and the Hunting Trail.* Lincoln: University of Nebraska Press.

———. 1990. *Rough Riders.* New York: Da Capo.

Rose, Cynthia. 1994. *Native North American Almanac.* Detroit: Gale Research.

Rose, Julie K. 1995. "Daniel Boone: Myth and Reality in American Consciousness." http://xroads.virginia.edu/~HYPER/HNS/Boone/smithhome.html (November 10).

Rosenstiel, Annette. 1983. *Red and White: Indian Views of the White Man, 1492–1982.* New York: University Books.

Rottenberg, Dan. 1996. "The Forgotten Gunfighter." *Civilization* (March/April), 56–61.

Rowland, Mary Canaga. 1995. *As Long as Life: The Memoirs of a Frontier Woman Doctor.* New York: Fawcett Crest.

Rowlandson, Mary White. 1985. "A Narrative of the Captivity and Restoration of Mrs. Mary White Rowlandson." In *The Norton Anthology of Literature by Women.* New York: W. W. Norton.

Royce, Sarah. 1977. *A Frontier Lady: Recollections of the Gold Rush and Early California.* Lincoln: University of Nebraska Press.

Ruland, Richard, and Malcolm Bradbury. 1991. *From Puritanism to Postmodernism: A History of American Literature.* New York: Penguin.

Russell, Don, ed. 1975. *Trails of the Iron Horse: An Informal History by the Western Writers of America.* Garden City, N.Y.: Doubleday.

Russell, Osborne. 1965. *Journal of a Trapper.* Lincoln: University of Nebraska Press.

Ryan, Bryan. 1995. *Hispanic American Almanac.* Detroit: Gale Research.

Saari, Peggy, and Daniel B. Baker. 1995. *Explorers and Discoverers: From Alexander the Great to Sally Ride.* Detroit: Gale Research.

Sackett, Susan. 1996. *The Hollywood Reporter Book of Box Office Hits.* New York: Billboard Books.

Sager, Ed, and Mike Frye. 1993. *The Bootlegger's Lady.* Surrey, B.C.: Hancock House.

Sandoz, Mari. 1942. *Crazy Horse: The Strange Man of the Oglalas.* New York: Alfred A. Knopf.

————. 1954. *The Buffalo Hunters*. Lincoln: University of Nebraska Press.

————. 1958. *The Cattleman*. Lincoln: University of Nebraska Press.

————. 1963. *Old Jules*. Lincoln: University of Nebraska Press.

————. 1964. *The Beaver Men*. Lincoln: University of Nebraska Press.

————. 1966. *The Battle of the Little Bighorn*. Lincoln: University of Nebraska Press.

Sanford, Mollie. 1959. *Mollie: The Journal of Mollie Dorsey Sanford in Nebraska and Colorado Territories, 1857–1866*. Lincoln: University of Nebraska Press.

Sarf, Wayne Michael. 1983. *God Bless You, Buffalo Bill*. East Brunswick, N.J.: Associated University Press.

Satanta. 1987. "My Heart Feels Like Bursting." In *The United States in Literature*. Glenview, Ill.: Scott, Foresman.

Sayers, Isabelle. 1981. *Annie Oakley*. New York: Dover.

Schaefer, Jack. 1949. *Shane*. New York: Bantam.

————. 1967. *The Short Novels of Jack Schaefer*. Boston: Houghton Mifflin.

Schlesinger, Arthur Meier. 1971. *The Rise of the City*. New York: Macmillan.

————. 1988. *Western Woman*. Albuquerque: University of New Mexico Press.

Schlissel, Lillian, Vicki L. Ruiz, and Janice Munk, eds. 1988. *Western Women, Their Land, Their Lives*. Albuquerque: University of New Mexico Press.

Schon, Isabel. 1986. "A Master Storyteller and His Distortions of Pre-Columbian and Hispanic Cultures." *Journal of Reading*, (January) 322–325.

Scott, Duncan Campbell. 1974. *Selected Poetry of Duncan Campbell Scott*. Ottawa: Tecumseh.

Scott, F. R., and A. J. M. Smith, eds. 1976. *The Blasted Pine: An Anthology of Satire, Invective and Disrespectful Verse*. Toronto: Macmillan.

Seattle. 1987. "This Sacred Soil." In *The United States in Literature*. Glenview, Ill.: Scott, Foresman.

Service, Robert. 1948. *Harper of Heaven*. New York: Dodd, Mead.

————. 1992. "Jean Shepherd Reads Poems of Robert Service" (audiocassette). Washington, D.C.: Smithsonian Folkways.

————. 1996a. "Robert W. Service Page." http://www.inch.com/~kdka/public_html/r~service.html (September 23).

————. 1996b. *The Spell of the Yukon and Other Verses*. http://www.teachersoft.com/Library/poetry/service/spell/contents.htm (September 23).

Sewid, James. 1989. *Guests Never Leave Hungry: The Autobiography of James Sewid, a Kwakiutl Indian*. Montreal: McGill-Queen's University Press.

Shalit, Gene, ed. 1987. *Laughing Matters: A Celebration of American Humor.* Garden City, N.Y.: Doubleday.

"The Shepherd of the Hills." 1907. *New York Times* (October 26), 684.

Sherburne, John P., ed. 1988. *Through Indian Country to California.* Stanford, Calif.: Stanford University Press.

Sherr, Lynn, and Jurate Kazickas. 1994. *Susan B. Anthony Slept Here: A Guide to American Women's Landmarks.* New York: Random House.

Shirley, Glenn. 1990. *Belle Starr and Her Times: The Literature, the Facts, and the Legends.* Norman: University of Oklahoma Press.

Short, Luke. 1942a. *Hardcase.* Garden City, N.Y.: Doubleday.

————. 1942b. *Ride the Man Down.* Garden City, N.Y.: Doubleday.

Shrader, Dorothy. 1993. *Steamboat Legacy.* Hermann, Mo.: Wein Press.

Silko, Leslie Marmon. 1993. *Yellow Woman.* New Brunswick, N.J.: Rutgers University Press.

Sills, David L., ed. 1968. *International Encyclopedia of the Social Sciences.* New York: Macmillan Company & The Free Press.

Simms, William Gilmore. 1964. *The Yemassee: A Romance of Carolina.* New Haven, Conn.: College & University Press.

Sinclair, Andrew. 1983. *Jack: Biography of Jack London.* New York: Washington Square Press.

Sinclair, David, ed. 1972. *Nineteenth-Century Narrative Poems.* Toronto: McClelland and Stewart.

Siringo, Charles. 1950. *A Texas Cowboy, or, Fifteen Years on the Hurricane Deck of a Spanish Cow Pony.* Lincoln: University of Nebraska Press.

Slatta, Richard W. 1994. *The Cowboy Encyclopedia.* Santa Barbara, Calif.: ABC-CLIO.

Slegg, Jennifer. 1996. "My Little House on the Prairie Home Page." http://vvv.com/~jenslegg/ (May 24).

Slotkin, Richard. 1985. *The Fatal Environment: The Myth of the Frontier in the Age of Industrialization, 1800–1890.* New York: HarperPerennial.

Smith, Herbert F. 1965. *John Muir.* New York: Twayne.

Smith, Horatio, ed. 1947. *Columbia Dictionary of Modern European Literature.* New York: Columbia University Press.

Smith, John. 1967. *Captain John Smith's America: Selections from His Writings.* New York: Harper & Row.

Snodgrass, Mary Ellen. 1991. *Characters from Young Adult Literature.* Englewood, Colo.: Libraries Unlimited.

———. 1992. *Late Achievers: Famous People Who Succeeded Late in Life.* Englewood, Colo.: Libraries Unlimited.

———. 1995a. *Encyclopedia of Utopian Literature.* Santa Barbara, Calif.: ABC-CLIO.

———. 1995b. *Literary Maps from Young Adult Literature.* Englewood, Colo.: Libraries Unlimited.

———. 1996. *The Encyclopedia of Satirical Literature.* Santa Barbara, Calif.: ABC-CLIO.

Snyder, Gerald S. 1970. *In the Footsteps of Lewis and Clark.* Washington, D.C.: National Geographic Society.

Solomon, Barbara H., ed. 1992. *Other Voices, Other Vistas: Short Stories from Africa, China, India, Japan, and Latin America.* New York: Mentor.

Something about the Author. 1972. Vol. 3. Detroit: Gale Research.

Speare, Elizabeth. 1983. *The Sign of the Beaver.* New York: Dell.

Spearman, Walter. 1953. *North Carolina Writers.* Chapel Hill: University of North Carolina Press.

Spell, Jefferson Rea. 1968. *Contemporary Spanish-American Fiction.* Cheshire, Conn.: Biblo & Tannen.

Spencer, O. M. 1917. *The Indian Captivity of O. M. Spencer.* New York: Dover.

Spiller, Robert E. 1991. *James Fenimore Cooper.* Ann Arbor: Books Demand UMI.

Spiller, Robert E., and Harold Blodgett, eds. 1949. *The Roots of National Culture.* New York: Macmillan.

Sprague, Marshall. 1966. *A Gallery of Dudes.* Boston: Little, Brown.

Standing Bear, Luther. 1988a. *My Indian Boyhood.* Lincoln: University of Nebraska Press.

———. 1988b. *Stories of the Sioux.* Lincoln: University of Nebraska Press.

Stauffer, Helen Winter. 1982. *Mari Sandoz: Story Catcher of the Plains.* Lincoln: University of Nebraska Press.

Steckmesser, Kent Ladd. 1965. *The Western Hero in History and Legend.* Norman: University of Oklahoma Press.

Steinbeck, John. 1952. *East of Eden.* New York: Bantam.

———. 1970. *The Red Pony.* New York: Bantam.

———. 1985. "The Leader of the People." In *The United States in Literature.* Glenview, Ill.: Scott, Foresman.

Steltenkamp, Michael. 1993. *Black Elk.* Norman: University of Oklahoma Press.

Stewart, Elinore Pruitt. 1979. *Letters on an Elk Hunt.* Boston: Houghton Mifflin.

————. 1988. *Letters of a Woman Homesteader*. Boston: Houghton Mifflin.

Stewart, Paul W., and Wallace Y. Ponce. 1986. *Black Cowboys*. Broomfield, Colo.: Phillips Publishing.

Stick, David. 1983. *Roanoke Island: The Beginnings of English America*. Chapel Hill: University of North Carolina Press.

Stockel, H. Henriette. 1996. "Geronimo." http://www.maxwell.syr.edu/nativeweb/subject/music/geronimo.html (June 25).

Stone, Irving. 1978. *Jack London: Sailor on Horseback*. New York: Doubleday.

Stone, John Augustus. 1966. *Metamora, or The Last of the Wampanoags*. In *Dramas from American Theatre 1762–1909*. Cleveland: World Publishing.

Story, Norah. 1967. *The Oxford Companion to Canadian History and Literature*. Toronto: Oxford University Press.

Stratton, R. B. 1983. *Captivity of the Oatman Girls: Being an Interesting Narrative of Life among the Apache and Mohave Indians*. Lincoln: University of Nebraska Press.

Straub, Deborah Gillan, ed. 1996. *Voices of Multicultural America: Notable Speeches Delivered by African, Asian, Hispanic, and Native Americans, 1790–1995*. Detroit: Gale Research.

Stuckey, W. J. 1966. *The Pulitzer Prize Novels: A Critical Backwood Look*. Norman: University of Oklahoma Press.

Sullivan, Jack. 1986. *Horror and the Supernatural*. New York: Viking Penguin.

Swift, James V. n.d. "Steamboating: Transshipment on the Missouri River." In *Gone West*. St. Louis, Mo.: Jefferson National Expansion Memorial.

Tatum, Stephen. 1982. *Inventing Billy the Kid: Visions of the Outlaw in America, 1881–1981*. Albuquerque: University of New Mexico Press.

Tavernier-Courbin, Jacqueline. 1994. *The Call of the Wild: A Naturalistic Romance*. New York: Twayne.

Thomas, Brook. 1987. *Cross-Examination of Law and Literature: Cooper, Hawthorne, Stowe, and Melville*. London: Cambridge University Press.

"Thomas Harriot." 1996. http://es.rice.edu/ES/humsoc/Galileo/People/harriot.html (June 14).

Thomas, Henry, and Dana Lee Thomas. 1943. *Living Biographies of Famous Novelists*. Garden City, N.Y.: Blue Ribbon Books.

Tibbles, Thomas Henry. 1957. *Buckskin and Blanket Days*. Garden City, N.Y.: Doubleday.

Tilton, Robert S. 1994. *Pocahontas: The Evolution of an American Narrative*. New York: Cambridge University Press.

———. 1996. "Pocahontas: The Evolution of an American Narrative." http://www.cup.cam.ac.uk/titles/3/0521469597.html (May 18).

Tindall, William York. 1939. *D. H. Lawrence and Susan His Cow*. New York: Columbia University Press.

Tolan, Sally. 1990. *John Muir*. Milwaukee, Wisc.: Gareth Stevens.

Toppman, Lawrence. 1996. "How the West Was Gone." *Charlotte Observer* (June 16), F1–F2.

Townsend, John Rowe. 1965. *Written for Children: An Outline of English Language Children's Literature*. New York: Lippincott.

———. 1971. *A Sense of Story: Essays on Contemporary Writing for Children*. New York: Lippincott.

Traill, Catharine Parr. 1966. *The Backwoods of Canada*. Toronto: McClelland & Stewart.

Trent, William Peterfield, et al., eds. 1946. *The Cambridge History of American Literature*. New York: Macmillan.

Trimble, Martha Scott. 1973. *N. Scott Momaday*. Boise, Idaho: Boise State College Press.

True Grit (video). 1969. Hollywood: Paramount Studios.

Trupin, Sophie. 1988. *Dakota Diaspora: Memoirs of a Jewish Homesteader*. Lincoln: University of Nebraska Press.

Turcotte, Jean-Claude. 1996. "Kateri: Notre Soeur Dans la Foi." *Le Journal de Montreal* (April 14), 8.

Turner, Frederick, ed. 1974. *The Portable North American Indian Reader*. New York: Penguin.

Tuska, Jan, and Vicki Piekarski, eds. 1983. *The Encyclopedia of Frontier and Western Fiction*. New York: McGraw-Hill.

Twain, Mark. 1959. *The Autobiography of Mark Twain*. New York: HarperPerennial.

———. 1962a. *The Adventures of Huckleberry Finn*. New York: Airmont.

———. 1962b. *The Adventures of Tom Sawyer*. New York: Airmont.

———. 1962c. *Letters from the Earth*. New York: Harper & Row.

———. 1962d. *Roughing It*. New York: New American Library.

———. 1985. "The Jumping Frog." Wakefield, R.I.: Moyer Bell.

———. 1990. *Life on the Mississippi*. New York: Oxford University Press.

———. 1991. *A Pen Warmed Up in Hell: Mark Twain in Protest*. San Bernardino, Calif.: Borgo Press.

———. 1995. "The Celebrated Jumping Frog of Calaveras County" (audio-cassette and guide). Prince Frederick, Md.: Recorded Books.

———. 1996a. *The Adventures of Huckleberry Finn*. New York: Random House.

———. 1996b. "The Noble Red Man." http://www.amren.com/indians.htm (June 7).

Twain, Mark, and Bret Harte. 1991. *California Sketches*. New York: Dover.

Twentieth-Century Children's Writers. 1983. New York: St. Martin's.

Tysver, Robynn. 1991. "Willa Cather Faithfuls Gather in Red Cloud." *Lincoln Journal-Star* (May 5).

Ulrich, Laurel Thatcher. 1990. *A Midwife's Tale: The Life of Martha Ballard, Based on Her Diary, 1785–1812*. New York: Alfred A. Knopf.

Unruh, John D., Jr. 1993. *The Plains Across: The Overland Emigrants and the Trans-Mississippi West, 1840–1860*. Urbana: University of Illinois Press.

Van Deventer, Betty. 1992. "Momaday Tells Enchanting Tales." *Lincoln* (Neb.) *Star* (October 1).

Van Doren, Mark, ed. 1936. *An Anthology of World Poetry*. New York: Harcourt, Brace.

Vasallo, Paul, ed. 1982. *The Magic of Words: Rudolfo A. Anaya and His Writings*. Albuquerque: University of New Mexico Press.

Velie, Alan R. 1982. *Four Americans: Literary Masters*. Norman: University of Oklahoma Press.

Villiers, Alan. 1967. *Captain James Cook*. New York: Charles Scribner's Sons.

Visscher, William Lightfoot. 1980. *The Pony Express: A Thrilling and Truthful History*. Golden, Colo.: Outbooks.

Vollmer, Lula. 1938. *Sun-Up*. In *Representative American Plays from 1767 to the Present Day*. New York: D. Appleton-Century.

Wagenknecht, Edward. 1952. *Cavalcade of the American Novel*. New York: Holt, Rinehart and Winston.

———. 1986. *Henry Wadsworth Longfellow: His Poetry and Prose*. New York: Continuum.

Waldman, Carl. 1990. *Who Was Who in Native American History*. New York: Facts on File.

Walker, John, ed. 1994. *Halliwell's Film Guide*. New York: HarperPerennial.

Walker, S. Warren. 1962. *James Fenimore Cooper*. New York: Barnes & Noble.

Wallace, James D. 1986. *Early Cooper and His Audience*. New York: Columbia University Press.

Wallace, W. Stewart. 1963. *The Macmillan Dictionary of Canadian Biography.* London: Macmillan.

Wallis, Velma. 1993. *Two Old Women: An Alaska Legend of Betrayal, Courage and Survival.* Fairbanks, Alaska: Epicenter.

Walser, Richard. 1955. "Bernice Kelly Harris, Storyteller of Eastern Carolina." Pamphlet. Chapel Hill: University of North Carolina Press.

————, ed. 1956. *North Carolina Drama.* Richmond, Va.: Garrett & Massie.

Wann, Louis, ed. 1933. *The Rise of Realism.* New York: Macmillan.

Ward, Artemus. 1939. "A Humorist Exploits the Mormons." In *The Literature of the Rocky Mountain West.* Caldwell, Idaho: Caxton Printers.

Ward, Martha E., and Dorothy A. Marquardt. 1979. *Authors of Books for Young People.* Metuchen, N.J.: Scarecrow.

Ward, Philip, ed. 1978. *The Oxford Companion to Spanish Literature.* Oxford: Clarendon Press.

Warfel, Harry. 1951. *American Novelists of Today.* New York: American Book.

"Washington Irving." 1979. In *American Literature.* New York: McGraw-Hill.

Watts, Peter. 1977. *A Dictionary of the Old West, 1850–1900.* New York: Wings.

Weatherford, Doris. 1994. *American Women's History.* New York: Prentice Hall.

"Welcome to the Shepherd of the Hills." 1995. http://www.usa.net/branson/shepherd/shepherd.htm (May 27).

Werner, Emmy. 1995. *Pioneer Children on the Journey West.* Boulder, Colo.: HarperCollins.

Weslager, C. A. 1968. *Delaware's Buried Past: A Story of Archeological Adventure.* New Brunswick, N.J.: Rutgers University Press.

Wesselhoeft, Conrad. 1984. "Blue Dolphins Author Tells Why He Writes for Children." *New York Times* (April 15).

West, Jessamyn. 1945. *The Friendly Persuasion.* New York: Harcourt, Brace & World.

————. 1969. *Except for Me and Thee.* New York: Avon.

————. 1975. *The Massacre at Fall Creek.* New York: Harcourt Brace Jovanovich.

————. 1986. *Collected Stories of Jessamyn West.* San Diego, Calif.: Harcourt Brace Jovanovich.

Westbrook, Max. 1969. *Walter Van Tilburg Clark.* New York: Twayne.

Westbrook, Perry D. 1988. *A Literary History of New England.* London: Associated University Press.

Wetherill, Merietta. 1992. *Marietta Wetherill: Reflections on Life with the Navajos in Chaco Canyon.* Boulder, Colo.: Johnson Books.

Wexler, Alan. 1995. *Atlas of Westward Expansion.* New York: Facts on File.

White, Lillian Zellhoefer. 1965. "Hangman's Tree." In *Accent: U.S.A.* Chicago: Scott, Foresman.

Whitman, Walt. 1992. "Pioneers, O Pioneers!" *Great Literature Personal Library Series* (CD-ROM). Parsippany, N.J.: Bureau Development.

Wiggins, Robert A. 1964. *Ambrose Bierce.* Minneapolis: University of Minnesota Press.

Wiggins, Rosalind, ed. 1996. *Captain Paul Cuffe's Logs and Letters, 1808–1817.* Washington, D.C.: Howard University Press.

Wild Women of the Old West (video). 1994. Plymouth, Minn.: Simitar Entertainment.

Wilder, Laura Ingalls. 1962. *On The Way Home.* New York: Harper & Row.

———. 1971a. *By the Shores of Silver Lake.* New York: HarperCollins.

———. 1971b. *Farmer Boy.* New York: HarperCollins.

———. 1971c. *Little House in the Big Woods.* New York: Harper & Row.

———. 1971d. *Little House on the Prairie.* New York: HarperCollins.

———. 1971e. *Little Town on the Prairie.* New York: HarperCollins.

———. 1971f. *The Long Winter.* New York: HarperCollins.

———. 1971g. *On the Banks of Plum Creek.* New York: HarperCollins.

———. 1971h. *These Happy Golden Years.* New York: HarperCollins.

Wilder, Laura Ingalls, and Rose Wilder Lane. 1988. *A Little House Sampler.* Lincoln: University of Nebraska Press.

Williams, Cecil B. 1964. *Henry Wadsworth Longfellow.* New York: Macmillan.

Williams, R. H. 1982. *With the Border Ruffians: Memories of the Far West, 1852–1868.* Lincoln: University of Nebraska Press.

Wilson, Charles Reagan, and William Ferris, eds. 1989. *Encyclopedia of Southern Culture.* Chapel Hill: University of North Carolina Press.

Windolph, Charles. 1947. *I Fought with Custer: The Story of Sergeant Windolph, Last Survivor of the Battle of the Little Big Horn.* Lincoln: University of Nebraska Press.

Winther, Oscar Osburn. 1964. *The Transportation Frontier: Trans-Mississippi West, 1865–1890*. New York: Holt, Rinehart and Winston.

Wintle, Justin, and Emma Fisher. 1974. *The Pied Pipers: Interviews with the Influential Creators of Children's Literature*. London: Paddington Press.

Wister, Owen. 1958. *Owen Wister Out West: His Journals and Letters*. Chicago: University of Chicago Press.

———. 1968. *The Virginian: A Horseman of the Plains*. Chicago: Children's Press.

Wolfe, Thomas. 1967. *A Western Journal*. Pittsburgh, Penn.: University of Pittsburgh.

Wolff, Geoffrey. 1968. "Daddy's Little Avenger." *Washington Post* (July 6).

"Women in Rodeo." 1996. http://www.mother.com/~asw/skywomen/rodeo.htm (June 14).

Wood, Harold, and Harvey Chinn. 1996. "The John Muir Exhibit." http://www.sierraclub.org/john_muir_exhibit/ (June 3).

Wood, Scott. 1973. "Bless Me, Ultima." *America* (January 27), 72–74.

Woodard, Charles L. 1989. *Ancestral Voice: Conversations with N. Scott Momaday*. Lincoln: University of Nebraska Press.

Woodhouse, S. W. 1996. *A Naturalist in Indian Territory*. Norman: University of Oklahoma Press.

Woodress, James. 1982. *Willa Cather: Her Life and Art*. Lincoln: University of Nebraska Press.

Woods, Walter. 1940. "Billy the Kid." In *The Great Diamond Robbery and Other Recent Melodramas*. Princeton, N.J.: Princeton University Press.

Woodward, Grace Steele. 1969. *Pocahontas*. Norman: University of Oklahoma Press.

Work, James C., ed. 1996. *Gunfight! Thirteen Western Stories*. Lincoln: University of Nebraska Press.

Wright, Harold Bell. 1907. *The Shepherd of the Hills*. New York: Grosset & Dunlap.

The Writer's Directory. 1983. New York: St. James Press.

Wyman, J. N. 1988. *Journey to the Koyukuk*. Missoula, Mont.: Pictorial Histories Publishing.

Wynn, Rhoda. 1990. "Paul Green: Deep Roots of Artistic Expression from a Native Son." In *The Lost Colony 1990 Souvenir Program*. Roanoke Island, N.C.: Roanoke Island Historical Association.

Yep, Laurence. 1975. *Dragonwings*. New York: Harper & Row.

———. 1992. *Dragon's Gate*. New York: HarperCollins.

Young, Alida E. 1978. *Land of the Iron Dragon*. Garden City, N.Y.: Doubleday.

Young, Carrie. 1991. *Nothing To Do but Stay*. New York: Dell.

———. 1992. *The Wedding Dress: Stories from the Dakota Plains*. New York: Dell.

Zitkala-Sa. 1985. *Old Indian Legends*. Lincoln: University of Nebraska Press.

Zochert, Donald. 1976. *Laura: The Life of Laura Ingalls Wilder*. Chicago: Henry Regnery.

ILLUSTRATION CREDITS

ILLUSTRATION CREDITS

152 Photograph by Walter H. Horne. Western History Collection F25058, Denver Public Library.

167 Archive Photos

173 Courtesy Library of Congress, Prints and Photographs Division LC-BH83-1837

178 UPI/Corbis-Bettman

183 Archive Photos

194 Archive Photos

214 Denver Public LIbrary Western History/Genealogy Department

218 Courtesy Library of Congress, Prints and Photographs Division LC-USZ62-119515

248 Colorado Historical Society 1355-WPA

253 Library of Congress

262 Archive Photos

269 Nebraska State Historical Society; AS47-45

291 Archive Photos

301 Photofest

305 Photograph by Alex Martin. Colorado Historical Society F12,389.

315 Courtesy Library of Congress, Prints and Photographs Division LC-USZ62-78094

335 Photograph by Hans Knopf. Nebraska State Historical Society.

338 Photofest

365 Archive Photos

379 Photofest

INDEX

Note: Page numbers in **boldface** denote major entry headings. Numbers in parentheses indicate illustrations.

INDEX

INDEX

INDEX